ARTHURSDALE BOY
NIDDERDALE GIRL

ARTHURSDALE BOY NIDDERDALE GIRL

memoirs

FRANK PEDLEY

Matador
Unit E2 Airfield Business Park,
Harrison Road, Market Harborough,
Leicestershire. LE16 7UL
Tel: 0116 2792299
Email: books@troubador.co.uk
Web: www.troubador.co.uk/matador
Twitter: @matadorbooks

ISBN 978 1803135 069

British Library Cataloguing in Publication Data.
A catalogue record for this book is available from the British Library.

Printed and bound by CPI Group (UK) Ltd, Croydon, CR0 4YY
Typeset in 12pt Adobe Garamond Pro by Troubador Publishing Ltd, Leicester, UK

Matador is an imprint of Troubador Publishing Ltd

For my family

CONTENTS

FOREWORD

This book is a unique biography; a time capsule of the lives of two people without fame in a bygone age that spans a 75 year period of worldwide turmoil, catastrophe, bloodshed and sacrifice, with rapid changes of lifestyle, communication and expectation. It incorporates levels of candidness, honesty, detail and integrity never found in celebrity biographies. Beginning during the Great Depression in the 1930s, it ends when death did part Arthursdale Boy from his beloved Nidderdale Girl in 2007. We were planning our Golden celebrations at the time.

However, it is a book of joy, containing a stream of unexpected situations, events and challenges; of family resolve and achievement. It blends personal recollections with historical research into the lives of lead mining and farming ancestors, some as distant as the 17th Century. It also reveals the name of Arthursdale Boy's hitherto unknown father (discovered in the 1921 census, published in January 2022).

I have always been attracted to reading the biographies of famous people; eagerly turning to the first chapters to find out how it all began. So often I discovered a privileged family background, education, level of security and long term dedicated support that is denied to the vast majority of people. Ruth and I were at the other end of the spectrum; humble Yorkshire children of the 1930s who met in the same form at

Tadcaster Grammar School shortly before the end of the Second World War. It was not long before I became more than enchanted with this attractive brunette with her short pigtails and large hockey stick.

This final edition is inspired by my wonderful family and their achievements. It is written primarily for them and those not yet born ... and their descendants . It includes some DNA results and a plethora of additional personal recollections.

Arthursdale Boy, Nidderdale Girl is fast becoming a time capsule of a bygone age, containing glimpses of Yorkshire childhood and education; military and social life in different parts of the world; of the Cold War; the Royal Tournament; Wensleydale sheep; the Foot & Mouth disease epidemic; cricket; politics; exotic cruises and so much more ...

It is a biography which could be a blueprint inspiration to others without fame to write their memoirs; for the benefit of their families and descendants.

MY PEDIGREE AND NEW REVELATIONS

I was born on 6 February 1934 at 'Wycoller', Nook Road, Arthursdale, Scholes, Barwick in Elmet, in the sub-district of Aberford in the county of Yorkshire (West Riding), the illegitimate son of Doris Pedley, who lived at this address with her father and mother; Francis George Pedley and Elizabeth Pedley (née Christelow). I never sought to learn the name of my father, but when I was about 15 years old my mother asked me if I wished to know about him. She told me that his name was Wood (it might have been Woods) and that he lived at Thorner. I did not wish to hear more, for I had already experienced the strong stigma against illegitimacy that existed at that time on numerous occasions, and I felt both embarrassed and annoyed at my status. My illegitimacy remained a shadow over the greater part of my life; I was bonded to my wonderful grandparents and never sought or received any additional information about my father, except the news of his death many years later. *However, in January 2022 the 1921 census was published, revealing his identity – see page 576.* I was baptised at Barwick-in-Elmet Church on 1st April 1934 (Easter Day); the sponsors were a Margery Riley, a Jane H Kaye and my grandfather (Francis George Pedley).

My grandfather was known as Frank. He was born on 27th April 1879 in Haworth, Yorkshire. When I was about ten he took me to Haworth and when we were in Main Street pointed out the property that is on page

30 of Mrs Gaskell's *The Life of Charlotte Brontë*, which he told me was his birthplace – in the room on the right, first floor. I visited Haworth in 2011 and found both the building and the street virtually unchanged. In July 2014 I watched with pleasure on television the Tour de France cycle race riders virtually brush its walls as they climbed the narrow, cobbled street.

He told me that he was the son of John Pedley, who became a master auctioneer, and Harriet Emma [née Hillary], born in Haworth. I don't have the precise date of her marriage to John Pedley, but it was in the last quarter of 1878, when she was aged 22. My grandfather took me to see his mother at 11a, St. Ann's Avenue, Leeds (close to Haddon Hall) shortly before her death on 8th December 1951 (aged 95). Look at a street map and the junction of Burley Road and St. Michael's Lane; just to the right is Knowle Terrace, with St. Ann's Avenue below. She was being looked after by her granddaughter, Nora Sykes. He also told me that his ancestors were lead miners in Swaledale. My grandmother was born on 3rd August 1880 in the Morrison's Buildings, West Cornforth, County Durham, a mining village two miles north of Ferryhill. Her father was John Christelow, a clerk at the ironworks, and her mother was Rebekah Christelow, formerly McKenzie. They were married on Boxing Day 1905 at the Church Field Chapel, Hartlepool. Elizabeth's name is recorded as Lizzie on the marriage certificate, and this was the name that was generally used within the family. My mother was their only child. My grandparents maintained a close family relationship with my grandmother's Christelow and McKenzie relatives, particularly with my maternal great aunts Rebekah (Peppie), Ada and Nell. They had left Hartlepool in a hurry following the German bombardment of the town on 16 December 1914 and were now living in Harrogate.

Before I launch into recollections of my childhood and teenage years, I will now describe some surprising family information, movements and activities between 1870 and 1910, unknown to me when the first edition of my memoirs was published in 2015.

Genealogical research has revealed that John Pedley (born 1858) was a lead ore miner, born in the hamlet of Healaugh, three miles to the west of Reeth in upper Swaledale. He worked from boyhood in the mines on Reeth High Moor, one of a multitude of PEDLEY lead miners and smelters whose history I have now traced to the early 18th Century and recorded as an appendix. The industry began to collapse from about 1875 and John Pedley had the foresight and enterprise to leave, without procrastination. He sought his fortune in Haworth, where he met and married local girl Harriet Emma Hillary, progressing over the years from local book seller to master auctioneer. My grandfather was their first child, followed by Mary Anna (22 May 1880) and Elsie (Jan 1889).

At the turn of the Century [1900], Britain was the master of the world: the leading nation on our planet in terms of engineering, exploration, science, literature, invention and conquest – but its once thriving lead mining industry had collapsed.

The 1901 census records the family as still being in Haworth, but at a different address; 20, Mytholme Lane:

Harriet Emma Pedley	Head	aged 44	
Francis George Pedley	son	aged 21	auctioneer
Mary Anna Pedley	daughter	aged 20	draper's assistant
Elsie Pedley	daughter	aged 12	

The absence of my gt.grandfather (John Pedley) may have been attributable to employment commitments as a master auctioneer. However, the family was soon to move from Haworth to Wensleydale, except for my grandfather who changed from auctioneer to the hosiery business, employed by Holt & Co. (Leeds) Ltd [hosiery manufacturers and wholesale warehousemen] in September 1902. I am unsure of the year that they moved to Wensleydale, but a clue might be the inscription on a silver snuff box that was passed down to me: *JP* 28 Sep 1903. Perhaps it was a farewell gift from his Leeds auction house employers? 1904 seems to be a likely removal year, for in April 1905 my gt. aunt Mary Anna married George Scarr Foster Sykes (a draper's assistant from Askrigg) in Aysgarth church [Wensleydale].

I believe that my gt. grandfather John Pedley (aged 46 years in 1904) wished to return to the area of his ancestral lead mining roots and that he had obtained employment with Thomas Watson Auctioneers of Darlington (established 1840), a major northern auction house, continuing as such to-day. He would have selected Wensleydale rather than Swaledale because Wensleydale had a railway branch line from the main line Edinburgh-London (Kings X) route at Northallerton, whilst Darlington was the next northern stop. John and Harriet chose the hamlet of Worton (40-50 inhabitants) for their new home – a mile from Askrigg station and only 7 miles south of Healaugh and the lead mines where John and his ancestors had toiled for at least a century. The western terminus of the Wensleydale railway was at Hawes with stops at 14 villages along the dale, including Bedale, Leyburn and Aysgarth. John may not have travelled daily to Darlington. This supposition is confirmed in the 1911 census which lists him as a boarder on the census record day at 8 Burleigh Place, Darlington. This census also reveals that my gt. aunt Mary Anna and her husband now had their own home in Worton and a month-old baby daughter (Nora Sykes), whilst gt. aunt Elsie (now aged 22 years and single) had a four years old son, named John James Tennant Pedley. Living nearby (in Worton Hall) was a farmer's son named James Tennant!

I have no record of John Pedley's death. On 16th May 2019 Mark drove me to Askrigg and we walked down to the site of the old railway station, across the Askrigg Bottoms (the original stone stepping stones still intact) and over the river bridge into Worton. Afterwards, I studied the 1904 railway timetable again and concluded that John Pedley would not have travelled daily to Darlington.

ARTHURSDALE

My birthplace was a semi-detached house in Arthursdale, a quarter of a mile from the village of Scholes and five miles north-east of central Leeds. Arthursdale was a small residential development created by a builder, farmer and businessman called Arthur Chippindale. Building began in 1901 with a house for himself and his wife on the north bank of Rake Beck, which subsequently flowed east through Barwick in Elmet to join Cock Beck. The approach to his home was called 'The Avenue'.

A few more houses of similar fine quality followed, but it was not until the early 1930s, when several semi-detached properties were built along Nook Road, adjacent to the Leeds–Wetherby railway, that the development of Arthursdale really began. It was at this time that my grandparents, who were now living in a quite large but semi-detached house called 'Claremont' in Thorner (the next station up the line from Scholes station) decided to move to Arthursdale. I wondered in later life if the move was prompted by the pending stigma of my illegitimate birth, but examination of my grandfather's mortgage arrangement with the Halifax Building Society on 5 April 1933 indicates that this was not the case. More likely, my grandfather appreciated the attractiveness of Arthursdale as he passed it twice a day on his rail journeys to and from his place of work in central Leeds, as well as the slightly reduced travel time and fare and the sizeable garden space. It was only in January

2022 that I learnt that Claremont was not only a *semi-detached* property built circa 1901, but also that it was on the northern side of the village; just into the Bramham Road from its junction with Church Hill, quite close to the old Thorner railway station. Neither of my grandparents could drive; with such a comprehensive and reliable railway system in the country a car was unnecessary, arguably a hindrance. In Arthursdale they chose a house halfway up Nook Road, adjacent to the railway line, and named it 'Wycoller', later numbered 23. My grandfather selected the name 'Wycoller' because he was an avid fan of the Brontë sisters and it is generally accepted that Ferndean Manor in Charlotte Brontë's classic novel *Jane Eyre* was Wycoller Hall, with Wuthering Heights above. My grandparents would almost certainly have visited Wycoller Hall together, perhaps treasuring happy courtship memories. My grandfather arranged the purchase of Wycoller in the spring of 1933.

My earliest recollections of Wycoller are of an immaculate and quite lengthy back garden with symmetrical cinder paths, mostly featuring enormous chrysanthemums, carnations, nasturtiums, marigolds and fruit trees, terminated by the post and rail fence and low embankment of the railway. My bedroom overlooked the back garden and the railway. Beyond the railway was mixed farming land and the A64 Leeds to Tadcaster road. The front garden was a much smaller rose garden – my grandfather's pride and joy. When the roses were in bloom he would routinely select a choice flower for his silver buttonhole insert each day, before walking the quarter mile to Scholes railway station, where he would take the eight o'clock train to Leeds. The front and back gardens were divided by a 6 foot high wooden partition with doorway which ran from a greenhouse cum porch at the back door to a garden shed (almost the size of a garage) with a window, small folding workbench and shelving. Here, my grandfather kept his garden tools and associated paraphernalia. Eventually, it gave up space for some items of my paraphernalia; tiered hutches for pet Dutch rabbits; kites; self-made bows/arrows/catapults; football; sledge …

Because of very troublesome varicose veins in her leg my grandmother rarely walked any distance from the house. She was a very loving gran and a very good cook. Sadly, she smoked; *'Passing Clouds'* cigarettes her favourites. My grandfather smoked a pipe. I do not recall them ever quarrelling. They had one child – my mother, Doris. I do not remember my mother living in the house for any length of time, though she may have done when I was a baby. My father was never mentioned.

Other very early recollections are of playing on the sands with a bucket and spade, probably at Filey, and having to sit on a potty for an excessively long time, with my grandmother repeatedly coercing me with the words, 'Try, try and try again', which I have often thought would make a good family motto – *Tendo, tendo quod tendo iterum.*

Arthursdale was an attractive, tranquil and safe place for a young child in that pre–World War II period, with both Nook Road and The Avenue bordered by a variety of attractive trees. One rarely saw any vehicles apart from a few private cars, the occasional taxi and the doctor's car. They were always driven at a slow speed, if only because Mr Arthur Chippindale had become bankrupt and the road had many potholes, having never been properly surfaced. My grandmother ordered groceries by telephone each week from the Co-op in Crossgates. They were delivered on a Friday by a pair of shire horses drawing a large cart. Milk was delivered early each morning by horse-drawn float, together with fresh free-range eggs, if required. The Scholes village shop cum bakery above the railway station also provided most essential items, whilst in the centre of the village there was a post office next to the doctor's surgery, as well as a primary school, a church, a Methodist chapel, and the Barley Corn public house. Mail (two deliveries on full working days), newspapers and telegrams were delivered by bicycle. Any crime was dealt with by a middle aged village constable, who lived a rather quiet life about a hundred yards from the school.

A far more detailed history and description of Arthursdale is given in "The Development of Arthursdale [from The Barwicker No.82 June 2006]", whilst a splendid history of Scholes from the 13th century is provided in the book "SCHOLES IS OUR VILLAGE", compiled by

S.A. Talaga and the villagers of Scholes, published circa 1982.

I have early (3-4 years age) recollections of rushing to the end of our back garden whenever I heard a southbound train approaching, climbing the fence that bordered the low embankment and waving to the drivers and passengers. Passenger-trains that were to stop at the Scholes station would pass very slowly as they approached the station and such trains were, of course, on the track nearest to me, only about 20 feet away, sometimes with carriage door windows open and passengers leaning out in the summer. I always received friendly waves from drivers and passengers alike and by the time that I started school I was intent on being an engine driver.

It was usually an 18 minutes journey between Scholes and the Leeds "New Station", with stops at Cross Gates and Marsh Lane; no hassle and no parking, and with refreshing conversation and banter between passengers. Interestingly, the LNER 1932 timetable records an express train that left the Leeds "New Station" at 5.20pm with Scholes as first stop at 5.32pm, followed by Collingham Bridge at 5.43pm and Wetherby at 5.46pm. Passenger-trains were mostly pulled by tank engines, of the G5 (0-4-4) class. Sadly, none of them survived into preservation, but original construction drawings and other detail were preserved and a thriving "G5 Locomotive Company Limited" is flourishing [see www.g5locomotiveltd.co.uk]. These G5 tank engines were also the 'workhorses' of the Wensleydale Railway at the time that my maternal ancestors lived in Worton, close to Askrigg station. There are several splendid photographs of them (and Askrigg station) in the third edition of THE WENSLEYDALE RAILWAY by Christine Hallas. My first rail travel experiences, in the late 1930s, were of comfortable, spacious carriages which were rarely crowded, journeys on time and without hassle; and very exciting for a young boy.

The railway, in which I became increasingly interested, was built by the North Eastern Railway, to provide a link between Cross Gates and Wetherby, with Scholes station opening on 1st May 1876. It was single track at that time, though the Scholes station soon had a siding, provided to facilitate the loading of light freight and livestock. It became double track circa 1901, with an upgrading to the station that not only incorporated a second platform but also two more sidings and a controlling signal box, located just to the north of the western platform.

One of the sidings provided the facility for coal drops, whilst another served as a cattle dock. When I was older I regularly watched the shunting activity in the goods yard, fascinated by the economic and time saving use of the gradient to run loose trucks into position at precisely the desired "hook-on" speed.

When I was perhaps four years old I recollect being woken late one evening by my grandmother and taken downstairs. My mother was there, with a man named Herbert, to whom I was introduced. They had met in Leeds, where my mother worked in a music shop in Boar Lane. I do not recollect their marriage, nor do I have a record of its date or location, or of where they lived. It must have been about the same time that I began my education, in the infants' class of Scholes Primary School, with a rather elderly Miss Ayliffe as my teacher. A ginger-haired son was born to my mother and Herbert about a year later, and he was named Francis Herbert McKenzie Shipman (FHMS). I sometimes wondered how I came to have the Scottish name of Hamish, concluding that it is probably because my mother's maternal grandmother was of Scottish descent; Rebekah McKenzie, born in Newcastle in 1853, who married John Christelow circa 1872. John and Rebekah were residing in Knaresborough when they died (1927 and 1925), so it is likely that my mother knew them quite well as a young girl.

THE INFANTS' CLASS

It was not necessary for parents to escort their children to the Scholes Primary School as there were very few vehicles and no predators. The custom was for the elder children to look after the infants, with arrangements made by parents. The school was only a half mile from my home and for the first few weeks I was escorted by two elder girls who lived in Arthursdale. They were always interesting walks; a continuous chatter. Miss Ayliffe was a good teacher, of the 'old school'. She was kindly, but strict. There were about 15–20 of us in the class and she ensured that her pupils progressed at a good pace in the three Rs. Multiplication tables were chanted repetitively, while reading was based on the traditional 'the cat sat on the mat' system. Most of us had learned the basics of reading well before starting school; inspired by comics and cornflakes packets. At precisely 10.30 a.m. there was a 'milk break'. When World War II began (at the start of my second term) every pupil was given a free half pint bottle of milk with a cardboard top which had a circular perforation to press and insert your straw. I believe that this free milk was the custom throughout the country during the war; typical of the help that was given to the young in those difficult times. We collected the different bottle tops and also cigarette cards. Sometimes the birds pecked through the cardboard tops, stealing a quick drink from bottles at the top of the crate before they were brought inside. We were soon issued with gas masks and given thorough training in their use, including tests in a gas filled tent and sometimes in the boiler room. It became an offence not to be in possession of a gas mask for gas had been regularly used as a weapon in World War I, with catastrophic results.

I still remember the smell of the plasticine, the sand trays and small shells for counting, and the song that was sung in assembly on my first day – 'All Things Bright and Beautiful'. I also remember that on that first day I was sitting on the front row and the girl who was sitting next to me (Shirley Pattinson) put her hand up my trouser leg. I pushed her hand away. I suspect that Miss Ayliffe noticed the manoeuvre, but Shirley never repeated it and there was no response or change in our seating positions. I wonder what actions a teacher observing such a 'sexual assault' is required to take today? It might have been only intended as a tickle, but it has stubbornly remained in my memory for more than four score years. It is a quirk of advancing age that one can remember names and events of one's childhood and yet forget the name of someone to whom one was introduced the previous day.

We were taught manners, courtesy and good behaviour. Severe scoldings and punishments, such as sitting for long periods with hands on your head, or not getting a playtime break, were routine. After all, when one moved to the next class and misbehaved, the punishment was a heavy application of a wooden ruler to the hand by Miss Spensley, so one needed to be prepared for such future discipline. As 'home time' approached we were given mental arithmetic questions, with those giving correct answers being allowed to leave early. A north-bound express train, pulled by a strong engine, passed through Scholes station shortly before 4 p.m., and I was usually one of a group of Arthursdale boys who ran out of school to the station bridge to see it 'thunder– through', in a cloud of smoke. When they saw us, some of the engine drivers would add to the drama by sounding the whistle as it passed beneath the bridge.

I enjoyed two summer holidays with my grandparents at Filey at this time, probably 1939 and 1940, staying in a modest but very pleasant guest house. I particularly remember some thrilling donkey rides, building brilliant sand castles, and a scorching sun that blistered my feet. I also recollect my grandparents being very keen to see what is still regarded as one of the greatest films of all time; *Gone with the Wind* starring Clark Gable and Vivien Leigh. We attended a late screening, which would end well past my bedtime – I fell asleep within a few minutes. 1940 was probably the pinnacle of Hollywood's Golden Age, with Academy award best picture nominees also including *The Wizard of Oz*, *Goodbye Mr Chips*, *Mr Smith goes to Washington*, *Of Mice and Men*, *Wuthering Heights* and *Stagecoach*.

Another personal recollection of this period was having my tonsils removed. The operation was performed on our dining room table by the village doctor and I remember being given a large silver coin when I regained consciousness. I think it was Dr. Bean who performed the operation, but it could have been his new junior partner, Dr. Shires. They were both excellent family doctors. Dr. Shires served the local community for 31 years, retiring in 1970.

I wrote with my left hand, but with the wrist away from me. Miss Ayliffe tried to correct my wrist position, but it gradually slipped back again. I remember her discussing the matter with a school inspector when she called. They decided that it was best to let me continue to write in my very unorthodox manner. I have only come across a handful of people in my life who have written in this unusual left-handed style. My right arm and hand were always my stronger and I naturally threw a ball or held a racket using my right hand. I shot with a bow and arrow, or a rifle, in the conventional manner, yet I was a left-hand bat at cricket. The only disadvantage of this unorthodoxy that I found in life was that I could not write as quickly as my peers and this was rather a handicap during written examinations. I also got an uncomfortable pain in the palm of my hand during long periods of writing.

PRIMARY SCHOOL YEARS

I was very fortunate to live in an area of attractive countryside. It was not spectacular like the Yorkshire Dales or Yorkshire Moors, but at that time it was unspoilt and tranquil. The most interesting feature to me was Rake Beck with its adjacent copses, scrub and grassland, which contained an abundance of wildlife. The beck was not particularly deep, but it had steep sides and could become quite a torrent at times. It entered Arthursdale through a narrow four-foot-high stone channel beneath the railway, some 250 yards from my home, and continued eastwards to Barwick in Elmet, eventually joining Cock Beck above Aberford. The steep railway embankment contributed an additional area of safe habitat for the fauna, insects, birds and small mammals that I was to discover.

The beck contained sticklebacks and minnows, while moorhens and coots nested at the water edge. In addition to the common garden birds, there were many species of finches and warblers, together with swallows, house martins, plovers and larks. Cuckoos were heard and observed on almost a daily basis in May and June, while there must have been at least twenty species of butterfly, with an abundance of crickets and grasshoppers chirping throughout the day in warm weather. I spent many happy hours exploring this exciting world as a young boy, without any supervision. Initially, my exploration was restricted to places that were within shouting distance from Wycoller, but this gradually increased as

I grew older. I loved to lie on my back in this countryside, just listening to the orchestra of country noises and watching whatever might appear. Overhead, this would be birds and insects passing by, with skylarks soaring up above and sometimes a glimpse of aeroplanes. On the ground there would be the occasional sighting of a vole, hedgehog, stoat or weasel. I was able to follow the time of the day by the trains that came past. I experienced the excitement of catching the small fish and umpteen other creatures of the beck in a jar and running home to show them to my grandparents. I had several 'hide' locations. My favourite was beneath a thicket covering a fallen wind pump which lay in a plantation of trees and bushes at the bottom of Nook Road. It was an ideal lair from which to observe birdlife, trying to identify the birds not only by sight but also from their calls and song. The calls of the male yellow buntings were particularly distinctive; 'a little bit of bread and no cheese' in high-pitched chinking notes, followed by a long wheezing note (the 'cheese'). House sparrows were by far the most common bird in Arthursdale, and the eaves of our house were a favourite nesting and roosting location. It was difficult to oversleep because of their constant chirping and squabbling; much to the displeasure of my grandparents on Sunday mornings. Sadly, these likeable, cheeky birds have now reduced in numbers to such an extent that they appear in the UK Red List of Birds of Conservation Concern. The wind pump location is shown on old maps.

One day the water level of the beck was particularly low, enabling me to explore the undiscovered land on the other side of the railway. I took off my shoes and socks and entered the channel beneath the railway, slowly paddling to the other side. It was idyllic, undisturbed countryside with more birds' nests, wild strawberries and blackberries. I found some newts and frogs in a small pond beside the beck, which soon became lost in an overgrown thicket. I was thrilled to find the nest of a pair of yellow buntings and watched the young being fed, their discarded scribble-pattern egg shells lying on the ground beneath the nest, and a lapwing lured me away from its nest by pretending to have a broken wing. This became my secret world. Perhaps the most popular school playground activity was skipping. For the older and more proficient pupils this consisted of skipping inside a long rope, usually wielded by two teachers, for it was quite heavy. It began with one or two *skippers*; then others ran-in. The aim was to to gather as many *skippers* as possible and then 'run-out', without fouling the rope. It required good timing and stamina – there were no fat children [or teachers]! Other popular playground activities [according to age] were 'pig in the middle', 'French cricket', 'Simon says [do this/ that]', marbles, and (in the autumn) 'conkers'. We would harden our conkers by insertion in vinegar and/or in hot ashes of a fire – it was serious technical competition.

I made friends with four other boys of a similar age to myself who lived in Arthursdale and went to the same school. We had a common interest in exploring the countryside, and their parents and my grandparents did not seem to mind if we went further afield – provided we stated where we were going, kept together, and returned home together by a stated time. Watches were an expensive luxury, even for adults, so we had to rely on sensible guesswork and the trains, which we didn't need to see – our hearing and our knowledge of them was sufficiently acute for us to identify them, eliminating freight trains.

Popular activities were playing at Stockheld Grange Farm, where we also helped at harvest time, climbing trees, messing about on the Chippindales' abandoned old cars in the corner of a field near the Chippindale home, and acquiring very basic cricket and football skills on the Arthursdale cricket club field. Sadly, there were no cricket net facilities, nor was there anyone to coach us. We also spent much time making bows and arrows, slings and catapults, and became quite proficient in their use.

These were very happy times for a young boy, but I was well-aware of the events of World War II and experienced food shortage, an air raid and the threat of enemy invasion. Most evenings I would sit with my grandparents and listen to the BBC radio news (usually read by Bruce Belfrage or Frank Phillips) and their concerned discussions and speculations. Occasionally, we would listen to and laugh at William Joyce [Lord Haw-Haw], a fascist of Irish/American ancestry who became a German citizen in 1940. His propaganda broadcasts always began with the chilling words,

"Germany Calling – Germany Calling". He was hanged for high treason at Wandsworth on 3rd January 1946. In addition to news broadcasts, I recollect listening to a lady with a lovely voice singing: *"There'll Always Be an England"; "Wish Me Luck as You Wave Me Goodbye"; "We'll meet again, don't know where, don't know when – but I know we'll meet again some sunny day"* – and many others. My grandparents' eyes moistened as they listened, as did mine, many years later, as I watched the funeral of Dame Vera Lynn (aged 103 years) on 10th July 2020.

My grandfather was familiar with warfare, having experienced active service in Flanders and at the Somme with the Royal Garrison Artillery during World War I. The Christelow family had also experienced German aggression during that war. The 1901 census records the family, including my grandmother, as living at Battle House, Battle Terrace, Hartlepool, but by the outbreak of war in 1914 they were living at 2 Bath Terrace on the Headland. This was only 200 yards from the Heugh Battery that attracted much of the bombardment from two German cruisers on 16 December 1914 as they moved up the east coast, shelling Whitby, Scarborough and Hartlepool, causing 137 deaths and 600 casualties. The first British military death of World War I was that of a soldier of the Heugh Battery during this engagement, only a few yards from the Christelow family home. There was a large drawing on the wall of our sitting room depicting this enemy action, with a dog barking in defiance at the German ships at the end of the pier. I remember the bombardment being described to me by my great-aunts, who emphasised the terror that it caused to the civilian population of these three towns.

I later learned that my grandparents were living in Leeds at the time of this bombardment. On their wedding day (26 December 1905) my grandfather (FGP) was living at 10 Beamsley Mount, Headingley, Leeds (just off Cardigan Road), only a ½ mile from the famous cricket ground. The 1911 Census records them residing at nearby 26, Walmsley Road (even closer to the cricket ground), together with their recently born daughter (my mother Doris) and one of Lizzie's sisters (Rebekah Christelow), who would have been giving a hand. My grandfather told me that he was a regular spectator at Headingley, encompassing the golden years of Yorkshire cricket (1900 – start of WW1) when they were either champions or runners-up in all but five years, every player born in the county. He described the achievements of Wilfred Rhodes and George Hirst to me with great pride.

I don't know when my grandparents and daughter Doris moved to Thorner. However, the 1914 electoral roll records my grandfather residing at Avondale Villas in the Sandhills area [no franchise for women at that time] and I suspect that my grandmother and Doris would have continued living there whilst my grandfather served his country during World War I. The family then moved to Claremont, but I do not have the date. My grandfather's significant community involvement in the village is confirmed in some photographs that I hold; the Thorner football team photograph of 1921/22 in which he appears to be the manager, and playing bowls on the Thorner Mexborough green [he was President of the Barkston Ash Bowling Association and Thorner was his home club]. I have never visited Claremont. I thought it was in the Sandhills area, not realising that is the Avondale Villas location, whilst Claremont is above the church, near the old railway station.

I well remember the despondency following Dunkirk. Hospital trains began to pass by and people would talk in whispers about someone who was 'missing'. Everyone feared the sight of the telegram delivery lady on her bicycle and prayed that she would not stop at their home. We did not see any of the Battle of Britain actions as we were too far north, but Spitfires and Hurricanes in training and formations of Wellington and Lancaster Bombers en route to their targets became a regular sight. I was thrilled when a Spitfire skimmed the rooftop of a nearby house in Arthursdale on one occasion, perhaps a pilot showing-off to a member of his family.

Following the heavy bombing of Coventry it was clear that Leeds might become a target and my grandmother prepared a bed beneath the stairs for me, with my gas mask nearby. Some people had shelters in their garden, but I think it would have broken my grandfather's heart for his to contain one of these monstrosities. There were a few minor raids on Leeds that were of no real consequence, but on 14 March 1941, shortly after my seventh birthday, I was awakened by Gran and taken to my bed beneath the stairs. Some 40 enemy planes were dropping their bombs on Leeds; the Leeds blitz. It was a frightening experience because of the cumulative noise of bombs exploding, anti-aircraft fire and the aircraft, and one was not to know where stray bombs might land. My grandmother sat at my side – Grandpa had reported for his duties as a special constable. I remember him returning home several hours later when the noise had subsided and describing what he had seen of the blitz. The following morning was one of excitement for me and my friends and we were full of bravado. There were several subsequent alerts, and for a time my bed beneath the stairs was routinely used, so as not to disturb my sleep.

It was shortly after this bombing that Arthursdale received eight evacuees of about my age from London. We had been told by teachers and parents of the reason for their evacuation and were instructed to be kind and make them very welcome. My friends and I were alarmed when we learned that they were to live in a large, uninhabited property with an overgrown garden in Nook Road, which we believed to be haunted. We discussed the matter very seriously between ourselves and eventually decided that it was best not to say anything. The evacuees survived the ghosts and witches and we had much enjoyment showing them our countryside and way of life. It was a different world to them. I don't think we ever talked about their experiences in the London blitz and we never mentioned the relatively modest Leeds blitz. I learned later that the haunted, unoccupied property was in fact two homes; numbers 6 and 8, built circa 1911 for Arthur Chippindale's sisters. Miranda is recorded as living at 6 (Plumfield) and Kate at 8 (Cherryfield), with the names matching very attractive plum and cherry trees that were planted in their front garden, facing Nook Road. In 1941 the trees had reached bedroom height, their blossom providing a spectacular cascade. The refugees were good company. My friends and I introduced them to our country activities; climbing trees, bird nesting, kite flying, making bows and arrows, 'helping' at the Stockheld Grange farm – particularly enjoying threshing time (trying to hit the rats as they ran out of the barn, but the dogs got them first). My reference book for making bows and arrows and other Indian and backwoodsman activities was a used Canadian book of c1900 that I had been given as a

Christmas present. Balanced walking along the top rail of the fence at the side of the railway was a popular activity, with competition to see who could walk the farthest up the slope towards the station without falling off. The fence was rather wobbly in places and there were some quite nasty falls, particularly painful when legs fell astride the top rail. The evacuation of young children from London to rural areas has been well documented, with most headline pictures taken on the northbound platform of Kings Cross station. However, there were many other evacuations, not least from Tyneside to the North Riding of Yorkshire and South West Durham. For example, as early as 1st and 2nd September 1939, some 7,500 evacuees travelled by trains from Gateshead to North Riding locations, and more later in the month. This was during the period of what was known as the 'phoney war' and many refugees returned home by the end of the year. A second phase of evacuation then became necessary in early 1940 following the German invasion of the Low Countries and France, and the ensuing blitz on London and other cities. We received a talk at school one day from our village policeman, telling us to be vigilant and report to him if we saw any strangers or unusual occurrences. One of my friends and I remembered this talk when we saw a dishevelled man moving slowly and carefully along the beck one day. We stalked him, Red Indian style, almost as far as Barwick, before running to the police house and reporting our sighting. The policeman was very appreciative, but we never learnt whether the man was an escaped POW, a deserter, a tramp or a spy.

I remember a visit to our Arthursdale home at about this time by my great-aunts Ada Mary (Ada) and Rebekah (Peppie) Christelow from Harrogate. They travelled, of course, by train, and I went to meet them. My hearing was very acute and I set off when I could hear their train departing from Thorner station. Impulsively, when I reached the bottom of Nook Road I climbed one of the fir trees on the edge of the plantation, from where I was able to watch the arrival of the train and, a few minutes later, their unsteady waddles down the rather rough slope (no footpath) towards the beck bridge. When they were directly beneath me I foolishly made some 'monkey noises' which more than startled them and I received a scolding. When we reached Wycoller I received another scolding, this time from my gran (grandpa was at work, in Leeds). I dutifully took their hats, coats and mink fur stoles upstairs to my grandparents' bedroom and laid them neatly on top of the bed. However, I was fascinated by the mink stoles for they had the heads attached and later in the day I discreetly took another peep at them and then (one in each hand) engaged them in a fight. I was caught red-handed and received another scolding, then another from my grandpa when he returned from work. However, after my great-aunts had departed I heard him chuckling to my gran about my misdemeanours. I was only 7 years old.

It was also in 1941 that my grandfather donned his special constable uniform and took me to witness the passage of a 'special train'. There were several policemen along the railway and grandpa had been allocated a spot near the Scholes station bridge. When the train appeared in the distance he told me that it was the Royal Train and to look out for King George VI and Queen Elizabeth. As it passed he saluted and I removed my cap. There were some waves to us from one of the posh carriages. Many years later I learned that the train was taking the King and Queen to the Royal Ordnance Factory at Thorp Arch, where many tons of munitions were made each day and conveyed by munitions trains along our railway. The visit must have been given a high level of security protection, as was this important munitions factory. There were no other spectators in sight, apart from another policeman further up the line.

The approach and passing of the Royal Train was at a very slow speed (c20mph), probably because it was running ahead of schedule. Its subsequent route to the Royal Ordnance Factory (ROF) would have been via Thorner, Bardsey, Collingham Bridge and Wetherby, where it would have taken the branch line to the right to join the Church Fenton-Harrogate line, then to Wetherby Racecourse and Thorp Arch, joining the newly constructed 'ROF Circular Railway'. This railway had internal stations named Walton, Roman Road, Ranges and River, after which it rejoined the Church Fenton-Harrogate line (just to the north of the river Wharfe). I believe that the waves to my grandfather and me must have been from King George VI and Queen Elizabeth as they were close to their destination and would have already received similar salutes from the police further down the line. Also, it would have been most presumptuous for a 'member of staff' to have waved. The purpose of their visit was the official opening of this ultra secret factory. The ROF Thorp Arch covered an area of at least 450 acres [642 acres according to Catford and Jenner] and at its peak employed more than 10,000 workers, operating 24 hours per day, including weekends, in three shifts. As local labour was very limited it was necessary to convey workers, mostly women, by special trains and buses from locations as distant as Leeds, Castleford, Pontefract, Wakefield, Selby, Harrogate, York and even Hull. It was highly dangerous work for their task was the assembly and filling of shells, bombs, land mines and cartridges with highly inflammable explosive and the loading of this ordnance onto freight trains. This necessitated the construction of 25 miles of internal railway, serving dozens of loading points. The locomotives were of a flameproof diesel type which ran on special rails that did not give off sparks whilst shunting. The railway was of a complexity that required the additional support of multiple exchange and carriage sidings. A few light anti-aircraft guns were sited in brick and concrete emplacements to counter any low-level attacks by enemy aircraft, but the primary security for this newly constructed factory was in maintaining the secrecy of its very existence. A comprehensive description of the ROF Thorp Arch is given in 'Thorp Arch, the history of a township, by David Cummings' (pages 146-156), published by the Thorp Arch Village Society in 1999, but without mention of the royal visit. King George VI and Queen Elizabeth had visited several northern locations during 1941 (Sheffield on 6 Jan & 29 Oct, Stoke & Manchester on 20 Feb, Doncaster railway works in Oct and Hull in Aug), but what was the date of their visit to ROF Thorp Arch; the forgotten royal visit? After extensive enquiries and research, helped by the family, I am reasonably sure that it was a Sunday in mid-June 1941. Several internal photographs of the factory at the time of the visit can be found on the internet, including some of the best wartime images of King George VI and Queen Elizabeth that I have ever seen – talking with excited factory workers who had not been given any notice of the visit, but no date!

Food and clothing were in very short supply and became rationed almost immediately after war broke out. The weekly food ration for one person in 1941 was:

Bacon and Ham	4 ozs	Jam	2 ozs
Butter	2 ozs	Meat	value 1 shilling
Cheese	1 oz	Sugar	8 ozs
Cooking fat	8 ozs	Tea	2ozs

One also received 16 points each month for other rationed items.

I remember being quite hungry at times, but not during the autumn, for then we could scavenge the countryside for blackberries, wild strawberries and raspberries growing in the hedgerows and pick mushrooms from the fields. I knew where some old rhubarb roots had been dumped in the corner of a field and these regularly produced delicious fresh shoots. Also, the aged Arthur Chippindale had an overgrown orchard which I and my friends could access from Rake Beck without being seen. There was no need to take fruit from the trees as there were plenty of windfalls. Arthur Chippindale caught sight of us occasionally, and as he waved his stick we scampered away in terror like startled rabbits. Schools were asked to organise the picking of hips for their vitamin C content, and also searches for metal objects in ditches and hedgerows that had been subjected to fly tipping in past years – we willingly obliged. Scavenging, but not stealing, became routine and a way of life. When a farmer's crop of potatoes or turnips had been gathered it was acceptable to look for and take damaged remnants, provided one had the farmer's permission, while spilled coal could sometimes be found on the railway embankment. 'Dig for victory' was a slogan that was taken seriously by everyone with a garden, and my grandfather reluctantly converted the lawn to 'arable', while the school playing field was ploughed. Other Government slogans that I remember were, 'Careless talk costs lives' and 'Coughs and sneezes spread diseases' – one was taught to turn away from people and use a handkerchief. These slogans were to be seen throughout the country. My grandmother took out her knitting needles, as I suspect she had also done during World War I, and knitted pullovers, socks, scarves and gloves for the troops, as well as for her growing grandson.

My mother visited occasionally, usually alone. She was always kind and interested in what I was doing, but it was a rather strained relationship, for my affection was for my grandmother. I once remember my grandfather saying, 'She only comes when she wants something.' Sometimes I was required to return with her to Ivy Mount, Leeds, to the Shipman family home in the lower York Road area, which at that time was one of the city's slum areas. It was an end-of-terrace, two-up-and-two-down-plus-scullery property with a very small yard and outside loo. I suspect that it has long since been demolished. My mother and Herbert had a small dog, which contributed to the fusty smell of dampness, while overhead hung the notorious Leeds smog. The streets were foul with dog faeces. One day, I remember being taken to the home of Herbert's parents in the nearby Marsh Lane slum area and was shocked by the squalor. There was little, if any, household pride in these areas; no 'donkey-stoning'. Herbert's father used a spittoon beneath the table throughout the meal that was served. On other visits I might be taken to the nearby park or to the York Road swimming baths. Leeds was a city blackened by the smoke of dozens of factories, mills and engines and thousands of residential properties for almost two centuries. It was a very different environment to Arthursdale. When my mother suggested to me that I might like to live with her, Herbert and half-brother Frank I burst into tears and pleaded with my grandparents to let me remain with them.

My grandfather worked for Holt & Co. (Leeds) Ltd., manufacturers and wholesale warehousemen, retiring on 30th September 1952 on the completion of exactly fifty years' service. The company's main warehouse and offices were in St. Pauls Street, near City Square, to the rear of the post office building. Sometimes he would leave home early and unshaven, making use of the facility of a very busy barbers near the Leeds city railway station. I witnessed the shaving activity on several occasions, fascinated at the speed and skill of the barbers in the use of hot towels and cut-throat razors which were constantly sharpened on long leather straps. Their clients were mostly comfortably off businessmen or guests of the overlooking Queens Hotel. I never saw a cut or a mark on their smart city suits. Nearby was his Lloyds Bank, but I only got a glimpse inside the bank if it was raining hard; otherwise I had to stand or sit on the outside steps. Children and women were not allowed inside banks at that time.

His normal business attire was a dark three-piece suit with a fine rose in his silver buttonhole insert, with a starched white collar – detachable from the shirt. His grey homburg hat was always raised to passing ladies, some pausing to smell the rose. My attire and manners had to match these standards. As manager of the shirt department and a senior buyer he would sometimes take me with him when he visited mills in West Yorkshire and Lancashire. We always travelled by train, in the maroon-liveried coaches of the London, Midland & Scottish Railway, and as my grandfather was a buyer we were always very welcome. I was privileged to be escorted around those mills at a time when they were working to full capacity, while he conducted his buying. The noise level on the manufacturing floors was so high that normal communication was impossible without speaking directly into the ear of the person being addressed. The machines were all manned by young women with their hair tied above their heads in white scarves so that it could not become entangled in the machinery. Most of them seemed to have learnt to communicate by lip reading. The heat was stifling, and cotton flakes and dust floated around like some tropical snowstorm. I believe they finished work at 5 p.m., but they had started at 7 a.m. There would have been the same distribution of intelligence and other qualities among these young women as there is today, but they had no opportunity to progress to university, no social life and no prospects. Most were destined to live a life of drudgery, with a high chance of lung and other medical problems resulting from their employment in these deplorable conditions. The exhausting labour, grimy industrial backdrop and unbearable conditions that I witnessed on these journeys into the towns of West Yorkshire and East Lancashire left a marked impression on my young mind and later contributed to my resolve to somehow break through the social barrier and move up to something better. The irony was that only a few miles from these lowland mill towns were rolling hills, beautiful countryside and fresh air – while below was a blanket of smog and grime from which the people who lived there were rarely able to escape.

My grandfather's recreational activities were his garden and bowls. As president of the Barkston Ash Bowling Association he took me with him to many of the matches; not only at Thorner, but such venues as Garforth, Allerton Bywater, Crossgates, Swillington and Micklefield. We travelled by train, of course – I do not recollect having ever seen Grandpa on a bus (or tram) until very late in his life, when he lived in Harrogate. The competing teams always seemed to be associated with the pub nearest to the railway station, which was most convenient. As a treat, I was sometimes allowed a sip of cider. It is pleasing to see that the F.G. Pedley Trophy, presented to the Division 2 champions, has been competed for each year since Grandpa presented it in 1947. I hold, and regularly polish, the replica of this trophy with pride, and I am delighted that the association flourishes. It now has four divisions. Grandpa exhibited his chrysanthemums, carnations and roses at the Scholes Horticultural Society's show each summer and was routinely amongst the prize winners. I felt that I had contributed to his achievements for I had collected for him dozens of buckets of Shire horse droppings during the year, which he enthusiastically mixed with water and applied as fertilizer. I can still hear him saying, 'It's good stuff, Hamish' as he stirred the contents.

My grandfather was the epitome of the courteous, kindly, well–mannered gentleman. However, there was one occasion when I witnessed how aggressive he could be if circumstances required. We were walking in the Headrow in Leeds on a busy Saturday morning when we saw a policeman struggling to arrest a man … "Stay there" ordered my grandfather, and he flung himself into physical assistance to the policeman. I watched the scuffle, the application of the handcuffs, and their slow progress along and across the road, eventually reaching the Town Hall, beneath which was a police station and cells. The incident was watched by an increasing number of gawking spectators. Half an hour later my grandfather returned and I proudly handed him his hat. His only words were, "It was my duty, Hamish."

I think it was in early December 1942 that I was advised by my grandfather that we would be spending Christmas with great aunts Peppie and Ada at their home in Harrogate. I disliked Harrogate intensely. It was a smart spa town, with not a factory chimney to be seen, dominated by large and expensive hotels with winding external fire escapes and a population that seemed to be mostly invalids in wheel chairs with attendant nurses, or the wealthy retired, enjoying an unreal social life. I groaned and grandpa gave me a sympathetic, resigned look. I was always amused when a member of staff at the Leeds City station announced in his rough Yorkshire accent the pending departure of a train to this snooty spa town; "The train standing at platform 2 is the ten-fifteen for Marsh Lane, Osmondthorpe, Cross Gates, Penda's Way, Scholes, Thorner, Bardsey, Collingham Bridge, Wetherby, Spofforth and [in the most cultured voice that he could muster, emphasising the **H**] **Ha row gate**". I had to wear my best clothes with tie and cap and we had a taxi to the Scholes station because of my grandmother's leg problem. I always enjoyed the train journey, particularly the stretch between Wetherby and Harrogate which incorporated the 825 yards long Prospect tunnel, followed by the magnificent 624 yards (31 arch) Crimple viaduct which towered up to 110 feet above the valley below. It may still be in use to cross the valley between Pannal Railway Station and Hornbeam Park Railway Station. The transition from the darkness of the tunnel to the dazzling view that the viaduct provided was always a thrilling experience. However, I was surprised to find that WW2 had caught up with Harrogate; many of the smart residential buildings and hotels had been requisitioned for military use, particularly for RAF accommodation and training. Squads of RAF trainees were to be seen being drilled and receiving other instruction in closed side streets just off the centre of the town.

Great aunts Peppie and Ada lived in an apartment overlooking the valley gardens. Except for a solitary electric lamp in the centre of each room, and a radio, it was a time capsule of the late Victorian period. A small coal fire in the sitting room was surrounded by dozens of sepia or black and white portrait photographs mounted in dark wooden frames (mostly of the Christelow and McKenzie families). They all had stern looks on their faces and their eyes seemed to follow me around the room. It was claustrophobic and I wondered when the window was last opened. However, I had been instructed to be on my very best behaviour and I resisted the urge to ask if I might open it. I sat with hands on my knees and with a straight back, speaking when spoken to. There was an acute food shortage at that time and we were fortunate to have a turkey for our Christmas meal, possibly because of my grandpa's business contacts in Londonderry. The roasting of this luxury bird was accordingly rather stressful and high drama, with various heated opinions emanating from the kitchen, much to the amusement of grandpa. However, it was delicious, with the clearing and washing up completed just in time for the King's speech to the nation at 3pm. I had received a small yacht as a present and the following morning I was taken to the immaculate valley gardens to sail it in a concrete boating pool, still dressed in my best clothes with tie and cap, as were many other boys who were sailing their various sized yachts and mechanically driven vessels. I felt rather sorry for them and so fortunate to have my rather wild country life. I was also introduced to the town's 200 acres of immaculate grassland (the Stray) but was not impressed – it was lifeless, but popular with nannies pushing smart perambulators, and with the elderly because of its ultra-smooth footpaths and clean seats. There was much talk about my great uncle (Donald McKenzie Christelow) and his family. He was clearly held in high esteem because of the progress of his career as a teacher and participation in local politics. He became headmaster of Harrogate's Grove Road School, a leading councillor and alderman during the 1950's and early 1960's, and Mayor of the Borough between 1954/55. I believe his wife was called Carrie and that their chorister son sang the York Minster introductory solo one year during a Christmas radio broadcast. It was a relief to return to Athursdale. I quickly changed into old clothes and ran out into the freedom of the countryside that I loved so much, where I defiantly expressed in a loud voice my opinion of the unreal world of **Ha Row Gate**. My opinion was not unlike that of Charles Dickens who, during an 1858 lecture tour described it as *'the queerest place, with the strangest people in it, leading the oddest lives.'*

I would have been about eight and a half years old when Hitler's empire was at its zenith, extending from the Mediterranean to the Arctic, from the English Channel almost to the Caspian, while the only sovereign state between the Pyrenees and the Ukrainian steppes was Switzerland. Hitler had been denied victory only in the sky above London and in the snow outside Moscow. Though they were hard times for our nation, the rescue at Dunkirk, that victory in the sky, the inspiration of Winston Churchill and the sheer bloody-mindedness of our people made one feel very proud to be British. Optimism, pride and patriotism prevailed. I followed the war closely, by listening to the news and adult conversations, reading the daily paper and on occasion watching the continuous hour-long newsreel with my grandfather at the News Theatre at the main entrance to Leeds City station, adjacent to the Queen's Hotel. The Leeds City and Central stations always seemed to be packed with servicemen on draft or on leave, usually carrying their kitbags and rifles. On a few occasions I would return home with my grandfather after dark. This was an eerie experience in wartime Britain, for there was no lighting in the streets and the limited lighting in railway and bus stations was from dimmed blue bulbs. The few vehicles that ran also had dimmed and shielded bulbs. Buses and railway carriages had one or two blue bulbs, and even hand torches had to have coloured paper beneath the glass cover. In later life I found myself discussing these conditions with a friend who attended night school in the city at the time as part of his apprenticeship. He recollected on one occasion groping his way into the 'gents' beneath the railway bridge where there was no lighting, inside or outside. After a while a voice in front of him shouted, 'You dirty bugger!' Ironically, these 'blackout regulations' resulted in crystal clear skies to observe the stars and our universe. In the Spring of 1944 the frequency with which the munitions trains passed our home noticeably increased. Special passenger trains also passed by, packed with servicemen, some from other countries, together with 'goods trains' carrying a variety of armoured and soft– skinned vehicles and artillery. Many were pulled by unfamiliar engines, some belonging to other railway companies, and also numerous ugly American austerity engines. They were all southbound. I was witnessing the build-up to D-Day; the invasion to liberate Europe from the tyranny of nazi Germany. The pending invasion was known worldwide, but the date and detail were top secret, particularly departure and landing zones. I saw very few 'GI's (the noun that was routinely used to describe an American serviceman) for they were mostly based in southern England. However, there was plenty to read about them in the newspapers, where I learned that they were 'over-paid, over-sexed and over-here'. They certainly made a hit with the ladies, who eagerly sought American nylon stockings. The only British item that seemed to be in demand in the USA were leaves of government toilet rolls, each leaf bearing the inscription "WD PROPERTY", to deter theft. They apparently caused much hilarity in the USA. We couldn't see the joke.

I was old enough to understand the events that unfolded. Fifty–nine German Divisions awaited the Allied invasion as it left our shores on D-Day (6 June 1944), with a further 237 Divisions deployed in the remainder of Europe, either occupying conquered sovereign states or facing the Soviet army to the east or the Allied thrust in southern Italy. What a formidable opponent! My understanding of the situation was helped by my grandfather's map of north-west Europe. It was quite a large map, pinned to a sheet of plywood which, together with two identical boards, fitted precisely into our sitting-room windows as part of an exemplary blackout system. Well, as a sergeant of the Special Constabulary, my grandfather must have felt obliged to set an example. A variety of coloured pins, flags and wool showed the Normandy landing beaches and the Allies' subsequent progress to the Rhine and onwards towards the heart of Nazi Germany. A coloured pin was inserted into the city of Paris on 25th August 1944; the day it was retaken by the allies.

With the passage of time, the decline of British influence in the world, and the Supreme Allied Commander being an American (General Eisenhower), it is perhaps not altogether surprising that the allied success in the D-Day landings is becoming increasingly attributed to the USA, with paltry recognition of the enormous British and Canadian contribution. With the exception of military historians few people are aware that the strategy for the landings was the work of a British General (Lieutenant General Sir Frederick Morgan KCB) whilst on the crucial first day British and Canadian forces put 75,215 troops ashore over three separate landing areas, plus

8,500 airborne; compared to the USA's 57,500 troops on two landing areas, plus 13,100 airborne. At sea, Britain's Royal and Merchant navies made the major contribution, whilst almost half of the 11,500 allied aircraft were flown by the RAF, plus 1,800 ground personnel. America's contribution was indeed enormous, but overall it was no greater than that of Britain and Canada; a fact that should not be forgotten.

Two iconic Forces' sweethearts inspired our armed forces and nations at this time, each with huge talent, alluring personalities and beautiful singing voices; both to eventually earn double page obituaries in THE TIMES and other leading newspapers. For the British it was Vera Lynn (née Welch), born in East Ham, Essex (already praised at page 16), who became Dame Vera Margaret Lynn CH DBE OStJ. For the GIs it was Doris Day (née Doris Mary Ann von Kappehof) born in Cincinnati, Ohio on 3rd April 1922 [died 13th May 2019]. THE TIMES obituary of 14th May included the following comments:

"… of German – Catholic stock … blonde, blue-eyed and fair skinned. Starred [after the war] in 'Romance on the High Seas (1948)', 'Tea for Two (1950)', Love Me or Leave Me (1955)', The Man Who Knew too Much (1956)' with its [famous] song 'Que Sera, Sera (Whatever Will Be, Will Be). She suffered much bad luck in her personal life. She was a serial bride, beaten by her first husband, abandoned by her second, swindled and widowed by her third and bored by her fourth. She became America's No.1 box-office attraction, the first woman to hit that spot since Shirley Temple."

Doris Day retired circa 1973, thereafter concentrating on the Doris Day Pet Foundation, at one time sharing her home in Beverly Hills with 17 dogs. So much for the wonder and glitter of Hollywood!

I was not a strong child and recollect having mumps, measles, German measles, chicken pox and jaundice before reaching eleven years. The prevalent diseases that I avoided were diphtheria and whooping cough. At ten I had congestion of the lungs, which almost proved fatal, and I remember the village doctor (Dr. Shires) being with me for most of one crucial night. I was in my grandparents' bed and it was tilted upwards on wooden blocks at the headboard, with me in almost a sitting position. I was too taken up with fighting for breath to be worried about my condition. I recall that when the critical stage had passed I was too weak to walk, and I remained that way for quite a long time. I was given a food supplement called Virol [a barley malt extract] for several months to help build up my strength. I must have lost several weeks of schooling, and my grandparents arranged some private tuition at Wycoller from Miss Spensley. It proved beneficial, for I surprisingly passed the examination that was necessary to proceed to Tadcaster Grammar School. I also saw the kindly side of Miss Spensley, whereas at school I had experienced her discipline and the impact of her ruler on my hand. The most common misdemeanours that resulted in such punishment were lateness, talking, or misbehaviour. I recollect only one, but suspect that there were others; during a lesson I felt a sting on the back of my neck … I foolishly took out my own 'pea shooter' (hollow hedge parsley stem, with hard green elderberries as ammunition) and when Miss Spensley next turned her back and reached for the blackboard I shot back at the culprit. The wimp yelped … Miss Spensley turned … and I was called to the front of the class… There was no difference in how she punished boys and girls, and I remember her inflicting a rather nasty, bloody wound on the hand of one girl. There were no complaints in those days, no one cried and parents supported the teachers.

It was my mother who rushed to tell me of my acceptance to Tadcaster Grammar School, a school formed in 1557, with a catchment area bounded by Leeds, Harrogate, York and Selby. This was to change my life, for it was there that I met my future wife.

EARLY GRAMMAR SCHOOL DAYS

I arrived at Tadcaster Grammar School (TGS) on a wet September morning in 1944 with good intentions, much trepidation and a Rawcliffes of Leeds leather satchel slung over my shoulder, shining like a newly opened chestnut. Within a few minutes the appearance of both the satchel and its naïve carrier were to be radically changed. I was involved in a fight, and lost. A boy named Peter Gill, who I was later to learn had a reputation for prowess in the noble art, picked an argument, and I had the audacity and foolhardiness to respond. He hit me. I returned the compliment, whereupon he floored me. I got up three times from the puddles before being saved by the school assembly bell. My bedraggled appearance was matched by that of my satchel. Fights in the school playground were not uncommon, but that was my only scrap, at least on the school premises. There were three strict, unwritten rules: thou shalt not kick thy opponent, thou shalt not butt him; and thou shalt not hit him on the ground. Prefects stopped any bullying or really vicious fights. Day two turned out to be as bad, though in a different way – I fainted during my first physical education (PE) lesson. The PE [and girls games] teacher was a very athletic, competent and popular Miss Ricketts, perhaps in her mid-30s. She soon brought me round from my faint, further opened a large window, through which I was instructed to take deep breaths of fresh air, whilst she continued with her repertoire of non-stop exercises. I remember the exercises – I hear her voice, and still follow several of them in a daily early morning ritual; 'down, down, down, down … unroll slowly … head up last, … down, down, down, down.' At the end of each exercise I usually say, "and one more for Miss Ricketts; down, down, down, down …

That September morning was also the first day for the new headmaster, Mr W.N. Bicknell MA, who had been selected from 268 applicants. He had been educated at Stratford-upon-Avon Grammar School and then gained a first at Oxford in English. Not surprisingly, he had a specialist knowledge of Shakespeare. He had a very strong personality and presence and a formidable memory of both facts and people. There were 331 pupils in the school when he became headmaster, but this number was to increase rapidly in the next few years. It was not long before 'Billy Bick' could recognise each of them and knew of their family background and progress. He was an easily recognisable figure as he walked the quarter mile to and from the school house each day with gown swirling, intermingling with staff and pupils as they poured from the railway station and bus stops. He was a tall, authoritative man who demanded high standards from his staff and pupils, delegating little and demanding superhuman effort of himself. He was as charming to parents on speech day as he was severe with lazy pupils during term time. My placing was in Form 2B. The academic target was to obtain a good School Certificate five years later. The School Certificate was a defining measure of academic success, issued by regional groups of universities. Failure meant that employment opportunities would be generally limited to manual work. At TGS the following subjects were taught: English language, English literature, French, geography, history, Latin, mathematics, scripture, physics, chemistry, woodwork or domestic science, and art. The minimum requirement was six passes (including English language, mathematics and either physics or chemistry), all of which had to be achieved at the same time. So, if one failed and wished to have a second chance, a complete re-take of all subjects was necessary the following year.

I became quite friendly with my first-day opponent Peter Gill, never fainted again in my life, and settled as best I could to the demanding routine and curriculum of the school. I did not find it easy. It was quite a long day and my satchel was usually bulging with textbooks required for homework – quite a weight to carry to and from the buses. Pupils were rarely parted from their satchels and there was much carrying of them throughout the day between classrooms. They were usually carried on the left shoulder, so it was not surprising that many pupils, particularly girls, developed a distinct and perhaps permanent list to port. By the time homework was completed it was news time, followed by bed time. Progress or otherwise was carefully monitored by fortnightly mark allocations for each subject, which were then totalled. Billy Bick would confront pupils together in their form room with their fortnightly marks on a Friday afternoon, congratulate those who had done well or were improving and scold those whom he felt could do better. Written exams were held at the end of the Christmas and summer terms, with formal reports to parents. I was generally well down the order, keeping a very low profile.

The dismal start to my TGS education coincided with Germany's bombardment of London with 4 ton ballistic missiles. They were made in Germany (Peenemünde), but fired from woodland that provided easy access/exit facilities, plus temporary concealment, along that area of coast opposite London in occupied Holland. These missiles were far more devastating than the familiar V-1 [doodlebug] flying bombs, reaching a velocity of 3,500 mph before dipping from the edge of the earth's atmosphere towards their London target, impacting at 2,000 mph. The first detonated in Staveley Road, Chiswick at 6.41pm on 8th September 1944, demolishing seven houses, but only killing three people. Some 1,300 of these V-2 missiles were subsequently fired at London, killing about 2,700 people and destroying about 20,000 houses and many other buildings. However, because of the quarter– mile reach of their shockwaves, they damaged an estimated 580,000 houses.

I was now old enough to visit Leeds unaccompanied, usually on a Saturday morning, meeting up with my grandfather when he finished work at midday. My walkabout would usually be focussed on the City Square and Boar Lane areas, plus the nearby mainline railway terminals of the LNER (London & North Eastern Railway) and the LMS (London, Midland & Scottish), looking at the merchandise of sport, book and clothing shops, observing the general hustle and bustle; particularly the people. There would usually be half a dozen scruffy men slowly and silently walking around the City Square like zombies, carrying placards over their shoulders which conveyed various religious quotations and messages of doom to sinners, whilst at every corner there would be a pavement newspaper seller shouting the day's headlines. Overlooking these events would be at least one helmeted policeman, directing strangers and traffic if necessary; whistle and trungeon at-the-ready. A few short blasts on his whistle would be likely to summon immediate assistance, for there were always several uniformed policemen in the vicinity. When these very approachable police officers were withdrawn in later years, I suspect that the police lost a most valuable source of information from the public. The noise level was high; trams making the greatest contribution. In the centre of the square there was, and still is, a majestic bronze statue of the Black Prince mounted on his charger. It never crossed my mind to enquire why he had that name, though I wondered why it was necessary to state the colour – everything in Leeds was black at that time, with smoke and the city as inseperably connected as bacon and eggs. Several years were to pass before I became aware that he was Edward Prince of Wales (1330-1376), one of England's greatest military commanders of the Middle Ages, who defeated the French at Crecy (1346) and Poitiers (1356). He was not called the Black Prince until some 200 years after his death, his name tarnished for the alleged massacre of thousands of French civilians in Limoges. However, recent research, incorporating the study of French archives, suggests that this blemish is unjust (*The Black Prince*, by Michael Jones, ISBN 9781784972936). Close to the City Square, at the bottom of Infirmary Street, was a small but intriguing natural history museum with free admission and a magnificent Bengal tiger. It was particularly attractive on cold and wet days. I think it was the only museum in the city. However, it was the people who interested me most; so many were deformed, small and undernourished, perhaps because of rickets.

As the advancing Allied Forces drove deeper into Germany I became increasingly keen to see the latest Pathe News at the News Theatre (located at the side of the Queens Hotel); it was almost entirely war coverage at that time and usually screened only a few days after the event. It was there, accompanied by my grandfather, that I saw the discovery and liberation of Belsen Concentration Camp [15th April 1945] and learned of its horrors. As a special treat, particularly when a good Western was being screened, he would take me to the superb Odeon cinema, located at the junction of Briggate and the Headrow. This cinema, with its Art Deco architecture and spectacular plush interior, provided stalls and circle seating for 2,556 people, and an experience that thrilled its audiences in that war weary city. On a Saturday the queues outside the cinema were sometimes four abreast and fifty yards long, everyone patiently waiting to be ushered in as seats became available. Prior to each performance a magnificent organ could be heard beneath the stage in front of the curtained screen, gradually emerging through the floor – the fourth largest Wurlitzer organ in Europe, with an accomplished organist. At the end of the main film the audience patiently waited for it to rise again and then stood to attention as the National Anthem was played. However, there were few places where smoking was banned in those days and the rear projection highlighted beams of thick tobacco smoke in an otherwise luxurious auditorium.

Germany surrendered on 7th May 1945 and a general election was held on 5th July. However, the counting of votes was delayed by three weeks to allow the votes of thousands of overseas based servicemen to be included. The result was a shock defeat for Winston Churchill, with Clement Attlee's Labour party achieving a majority of 145 seats. Churchill had not lost his popularity, but the people wanted jobs and housing (with indoor loos). It is not generally known outside military circles that Clement Attlee gave distinguished military service in WW1 as an infantry Captain/Major (Gallipoli Campaign, then wounded storming enemy trench during the battle of Hanna in Mesopotania , then the Western Front in France). He and Churchill became close friends as the nation's leaders in WW2: while Churchill led the war effort, Attlee, the nation's first deputy prime minister, looked after the home front. They were a brilliant duet.

I recollect learning of the surrender of Japan and the end of WW2 on 15th August 1945 very clearly. I was walking up Nook Road and when only a few yards from Wycoller an elderly man came running down the road, shouting and punching the air, with tears running down his cheeks, "The war is over … the Japs have surrendered." Others who had heard the radio announcement burst out of their homes, crying and laughing and hugging each other. It was not long before railway locomotives joined in with long blasts on their whistles as they passed by. There was such jubilation and relief. Vast crowds celebrated in London's Trafalgar Square that night and in other cities. I was aged 11 ½ years and very proud to be British.

I was required to visit my mother in Leeds occasionally and she would sometimes take me to see something that she thought would interest me. I recall a stroll along the Leeds–Liverpool canal near Kirkstall Abbey, watching the horse-drawn barges; the woods at Adel; Fewston reservoir; also, the arrival at Leeds Central station from London of a special all sky-blue train, drawn by an LNER streamlined A4 engine of the same colour.

I did not wish to upset my mother, but I had no wish to be part of her urban lifestyle, and an intent to set off on my own when I left school was forming in my mind. I must have said something offensive during one of my visits, for on that occasion the door leading to the stairs burst open and Herbert, who must have been listening behind it, burst into the room, undoing his leather belt with the intention of giving me a good thrashing. My mother pleaded with him not to, and instead I received a clear warning from Herbert of what would happen next time. I was now more intent than ever on setting off on my own when I left TGS, but at twelve years of age I had no idea how I might do so.

Though I had closely followed the war in Europe, I was relatively unaware of the hard fought battles of the British 14th Army in Burma, under the inspiring leadership of one time primary school teacher General Bill Slim [appointed Field Marshal on 4th January 1948], against fanatical and brutal Japanese forces. Conflict was intense and prolonged in dense and rugged malaria-ridden jungle, in which dysentery was rife. The detail and extent of horrific Japanese atrocities [particularly to prisoners] became well known and were shown on cinema newsreels. They should never be forgotten. However, I hasten to add that I now very much admire the Japanese people and their culture; particularly manners, tidiness and lack of obesity.

In the Queen's 2014 Birthday Honours another one time school teacher was appointed to Field Marshal rank; Field Marshal Michael John Dawson Walker, Baron Walker of Aldringham, GCB, CMG, CBE, DL. On leaving school he taught for 18 months at Woodhouse Grove School, a preparatory school near Bradford, before joining the army; commissioned from Sandhurst on 29th July 1966, aged 22.]

The 14th Army became known as "the Forgotten Army" as resources and publicity tended to focus on the war in Europe, but it eventually triumphed; at the decisive battles of Imphal and Kohima, denying Japan the conquest of India. In late 1944 the 14th Army comprised almost a million men; the largest army in the world. The epitaph inscribed on the memorial of those decisive battles is poignant:

"When you go home, tell them of us and say, for your tomorrow, we gave our today."

There are no finer recollections of life at the sharp end in Burma than those of 19 year old private soldier George MacDonald Fraser of the Border Regiment; *"Quartered Safe Out Here"*, ISBN 13: 978 0 00 710593 9, [who in later life created Flashman] and 24 year old Captain Alun Arthur Gwynne Jones of the South Wales Borderers Regiment; *"The Shadow of My Hand"*, ISBN 0 297 813323 [later awarded an MC in the 1948-60 Malayan emergency ... then a prominent journalist, and eventually a peer of the realm – Baron Chalfont OBE, MC,PC]. Read about the leader who inspired them [Wikipedia's: *William Slim, 1st Viscount Slim*] and also about a prisoner of the Japanese [*"The Forgotten Highlander"* by Alistair Urquhart, ISBN 9780349122571.

I did not observe any shame or wringing of hands in Arthursdale when the Hiroshima [6th August 1945] and Nagasaki [9th August] atomic bombs were dropped – memories turned to 7th December 1941 when Japan launched its infamous and unprovoked attack on Pearl Harbour, and also Singapore [from landings at Patani and Singora], whilst cynically and simultaneously declaring war. The words of Winston Churchill to the House of Commons several years later resonated with the opinions of most people: "There are voices which assert that the bomb should never have been used at all. I cannot associate myself with such ideas. … I am surprised that very worthy people – but people who in most cases had no intention of proceeding to the Japanese front themselves – should adopt the position that rather than throw this bomb, we should have sacrificed a million American and a quarter of a million British lives."

My year in the third form was as unremarkable as the previous year, but Mr Bicknell was becoming suspicious of my inconsistency and routinely gave me a hard time when he announced the fortnightly marks. There were so many things to do other than homework – cricket, football, cycling, youth club, boy scouts, hiking, swimming and table tennis. These activities developed me significantly, both mentally and physically. I was never bored.

TEENAGER

My thirteenth birthday on 6 February 1947 was a most memorable day; my grandparents gave me a brand new Raleigh bicycle, incorporating Sturmey-Archer gear change facility. However, because of the harsh winter several weeks were to pass before I could use it. The 1946/47 winter was the harshest since Victorian times, and in the immediate aftermath of World War II it could not have occurred at a worse time. Heavy snowfalls began in late January and continued throughout February, driven by strong easterly winds, resulting in ten-foot snowdrifts. A quarter of the nation's sheep population perished. We were snowed in on several occasions, the longest period being for almost a week. Our railway and all roads became blocked and it was very cold, with minus 21 degrees centigrade recorded in Bedfordshire. The Settle-Carlisle railway line was blocked for two months by deep snow. Coal supplies ceased and it was impossible to scavenge wood from the countryside because of the depth of the snow. We had to rely on the electricity supply, but this was cut off for three hours in the morning and two hours in the afternoon. The ground was frozen so hard that a pickaxe was needed to extract any remaining turnips. It was nice to be away from school for a while, of course, and there was much fun when adults, unable to get to work, joined in snowball fights and helped us to build increasingly sophisticated snow houses. There was no real thaw until early April, and when it came the deeply compressed snow on rooftops and the huge icicles came down in avalanche style, severely damaging guttering and sometimes causing serious accidents, particularly in congested urban areas. The backlog of professional football matches extended the season well into June and I recall going with a group of older boys in May to Elland Road for the first time, to watch Leeds United play a testimonial match against Glasgow Celtic, followed by a league match against Stoke City with Stanley Matthews playing, just prior to his transfer to Blackpool. The stadium was packed to near capacity for each of these matches. Supporters made their presence heard as they converged on the stadium by the whirling of wooden rattle-clackers: a conservative ratio would be about 1/15 [more than 2,000 clackers], creating such noise that hundreds of pigeons fled the city. Only a minority of wealthy supporters could afford a seat in the grandstand; the vast majority stood, with intermittent crash barriers installed to prevent crowd collapse. Spectators allowed boys to squeeze past to the front, but this was not practical when a saturation density was reached and on one later occasion I was fearful that I would go down, never to rise again. In the previous year (9 March 1946) 33 supporters had died at the Bolton Wanderers stadium when two such barriers collapsed, the crowd falling forward on top of each other. The other danger was that of one's foot being pushed beneath a moving tram at the end of the game; the only way to board one as dozens slowly moved forward to a fanciful boarding point. Safety regulations were very weak at that time; one had to make one's own assessments and sometimes just chance your luck. At about the same time I also made the occasional visit to the Odsal Speedway in Bradford.

The summer that followed was exceptionally warm, and I have happy memories of playing junior cricket, watching the Arthursdale teams in the Wetherby league and cycling with my new bike with friends around the countryside on virtually traffic free roads. I would also, usually alone, explore distant woods such as Saw Woods, near Thorner, and Bramham Park. Yes, I was trespassing and had seen the notices on the perimeter that stated quite clearly that 'trespassers will be prosecuted'. However, such a threat added to the excitement and I felt reasonably confident that I could outrun a gamekeeper. I preferred to be alone so that I could move quietly, Red Indian style, and see the gamekeeper and the wildlife before they saw me. I sometimes took my home-made bow and a few arrows with me, to let fly at the occasional rabbit or pigeon. On one occasion I aimed at a cock pheasant perched on a fence at a distance from me of about 70 yards; it dropped like a stone. I was scared stiff. I buried the pheasant in a ditch, covered it with beech leaves and fled.

I was a regular attender at the youth club, which had a weekly evening gathering at the Scholes village school. There would usually be an interesting talk, sometimes by someone with recent war experiences. I found a series of talks by an ex-serviceman who had served with partisans in the Balkans particularly interesting. The club organiser, Mr Leslie McConnell [nicknamed 'Mac'] was a fine man who was to give hundreds of hours of his time over a ten-year period to the village's youth club and its teenage members. He would arrange occasional outings to interesting places, including some very enjoyable coastal walks. Table tennis was very popular and I captained the youth club team that played in one of the lower divisions of the Leeds league. I regularly used and enjoyed my new Raleigh bicycle, with my discovery rides becoming increasingly distant and adventurous. It was a very heavy general purpose bike with mud and chain guards; not a touring bike. However, I was adept at mending punctures and dealing with chain and gear problems and always confided with my grandparents on my plans, leaving with sandwiches and some coins for telephone calls. On one fine summer morning I rode forth for Hornsea; selecting a route via Aberford, Sherburn in Elmet, Cawood, Riccall ... A163, Holme on Spalding Moor, Market Weighton and Beverley ... There was a light westerly wind on my back and my bike and I flew along. However, by the time that Hornsea Mere was sighted in the early afternoon the westerly wind had increased significantly, approaching gale force. I turned round and peddled hard into the gale, keeping grandparents informed of my slow progress. It was a round trip of about 105 miles. I was exhausted, and wiser.

On returning to TGS for the 1947 Christmas term I began to take some interest in the girls, and one girl in particular, who had been in the same form as myself from the day that I started at the school. She was an attractive brunette with short pigtails and a large hockey stick, and her name was Ruth Addy. Ruth must have been aware of my admiration, but she seemed to be far more interested in hockey and athletics than in boys – or perhaps there were more handsome and interesting suitors in Boston Spa, where she lived? There was something special about her, but I was rather a shy boy, particularly with regard to girls. Ruth was always charming and polite, but she gave me no encouragement whatsoever. Her best friend was Nanette Kirk, an exceptionally good hockey centre forward who aspired to be a nurse. They were a lethal combination in the school hockey team, with Ruth playing on the right wing.

I did not make any conscious decision to act more responsibly; tree climbing and cowboy/Red Indian activities gradually became pleasures of the past. There may have been some minor lapses, such as enhancing the performance of fireworks at our Arthursdale bonfire on 5 November, aided and abetted by a bright Leeds Grammar School boy who had been given a very fine chemistry set for his birthday. Fireworks had, of course, been forbidden during the war and there was still an acute shortage of manufactured fireworks. Overall, I was now becoming a reasonably responsible youth.

I never received any teaching of 'the facts of life', but my grandfather had told me at quite a young age that I could read any of the books in his glass fronted bookcase, provided I handled them with great care, and that gave me access to his high quality and well-illustrated medical books. This academic study had been supplemented over the years by my farm observations and listening to the tittle tattle of older boys. However, quite unexpectedly I received a surprise enhancement to my knowledge. I set off on my bike one day without any destination in mind, but on passing close to Bramham Park I decided to stop and explore its attractive woodland. I had not walked far when I came across the derelict Bramham Park prisoner of war (POW) Camp, whose occupants had been mostly Italian and German, but also some from eastern European countries. I decided to look inside some of the buildings, quietly climbing or looking through unsecured windows rather than forcing locked doors. They were empty, but a few had been occupied by talented artists whose explicit graphics remained on the walls, and subsequently in my mind. POWs in the UK must have been reasonably well treated, for at the end of the war 26,000 German POWs alone decided not to return to their home country.

During my return journey I was almost mugged. Cycling along the A64, some three miles from home, I became conscious of a two wheeled cart pulled by a pony closing on me, driven by two rag-and-bone looking characters. Initially, I thought they were enticing me into a friendly race, but their faces were far from friendly. There was hardly any traffic on the road and I felt threatened, realising that my almost new bike and anything of value on me was their target. I gained on the downhill sections and they closed on me on the uphill sections. Eventually, having allowed them to get very close, I turned sharply left down the lane leading to the railway crossing gates at the top of Arthursdale, and they overshot. I knew that the main gates would be closed but there was also a pedestrian gate at the side, through which I could carry my bike.

I had sufficient experience of both town and country life to realise that I was a country mouse, yet my exposure to Leeds and its rough northern character was such that a mild respect for the city was becoming ingrained in me, increasing in later life. Leeds is a unique city, very different to the steel city of Sheffield and the port of Hull, or the 'Red Rose' cities across the Pennines; a city rather lacking in culture, which 'didn't do' quality museums or galleries, lacking even a worthy book on its fascinating history. This did not become available until 1994, having taken two eminent historians more than twenty years to write and publish: *The Illustrated History of Leeds*, by Steven Burt and Kevin Grady, published by Breedon Books, New Edition 2002, ISBN 1 85983 316 0.

On the last day of the 1947 Christmas term we were told to bring a book of our own choosing to school and to quietly read it, without supervision. I was sitting close to Ruth, with only a gangway between us (Nanette, of course, seated on the other side of Ruth). Ruth was reading "Scott's Last Expedition", which had been given to her a few weeks earlier by her parents as her 14th birthday present. It soon became clear that Ruth had read and studied the book in some depth and that she was already a devout fan of Captain Scott. I was allowed to look through the book and shared her opinion of his bravery and leadership, which seemed to please her.

Some inspiring new teachers had now joined the TGS staff. Mr J.L. Heslegrave and Mr M.H. Pocock readily spring to mind. A junior football team had been formed and I proudly wore a TGS dark and light blue shirt for the first time in the under-15s team, playing on the left wing in a game against Knaresborough Grammar School in November. We lost most matches, but not by huge margins. It was a similar pattern during the following cricket season, when I tried hard to emulate Len Hutton as an opening batsman. My performances on Sports Day were modest, but Ruth Addy won the Calcaria House Cup, though aged only fourteen and a half. She won the open hurdles and almost the open high jump, with a jump of four feet, five and three-quarter inches; not a breathtaking height, but facilities were frugal (scissors jumping, landing in a wet sand pit) and she was the smallest and youngest. I occasionally crossed the path of the headmaster during the year and had felt the sting of his cane on my backside, but no more often than was par for the course for a red-blooded Yorkshire youth at 'Taddy Grammar' in those days; as Shakespeare put it, 'Now set the teeth and stretch the nostril wide, hold hard the breath and bend up every spirit to his full height' (*Henry V*). A boy awaiting a disciplinary hearing from Headmaster "Billy Bick" stood outside his study for at least 20 minutes: when his secretary left one knew that the time had come. At least five classrooms were in hearing distance of the cane strokes and a silence descended as they were counted. It was quite a long time before the normal buzz of the school rose again.

However, what hurt most was my headmaster's verbal rebuke and warning to me at the end of term that I would now have to make a massive effort in the next school year to gain a School Certificate.

Shortly before the end of the summer term I came face to face with Ruth and her brother Leslie and their parents and stood by them for a couple of minutes, but not a word was spoken. It was a Saturday, and a friend and I decided that we would go to the Leeds YMCA (Young Men's Christian Association), to play table tennis and receive some quality coaching. We tried to catch a bus at the stop on the A64 that was closest to Arthursdale, but the buses were full and sped past. So, we decided to walk further down the A64 to the junction leading to Thorner, known as Thorner Lane End (opposite Morwick Hall), where an additional bus route converged. We were lucky, for a bus from Thorner soon arrived. The bus stopped, but there was only standing room and we were pushed down the gangway like canned sardines, to a point at which I stood above them. Ruth was sitting next to her father who was puffing on his pipe. She was wearing a green hat and looked even more attractive out of TGS uniform. We exchanged a smile, but not a word was spoken, and very soon my friend and I were pushed further down the gangway. We were amongst the first to alight at the Vicar Lane terminus and my friend and I scampered off towards the YMCA. I glanced back ... but they were not to be seen. It was the only time that I saw the four of them together.

My memories of the summer of 1948 are of a very enjoyable scout camp on the Lune estuary at Sunderland Point, lots of cycling and watching some very good cricket at Headingley. With so little traffic on the roads, cycling was a routine pleasure that we took for granted, exploring unknown areas; the Wharfe at Wetherby and the Nidd at Knaresborough were very popular destinations for rowing and punting. We travelled to the scout camp in the back of an old Army lorry with tarpaulin cover – the exhaust fumes were terrible. Sunderland Point is a tiny village, almost surrounded by marshes, lying on a windswept peninsula between the River Lune and Morecombe Bay, once used as a port for slave and cotton ships. After erecting our tents and setting up camp we had some free time. We were warned that the distant low tide (at least 800 yards from the shore) came in very fast and we ran out to meet it, comfortably keeping up with its drive towards the shore. We then got the shock of our lives as we realised that the tide was racing behind us along the many irregular inlets, thereby cutting us off – we only just made it. My best friend was Barry Appleyard, who lived almost opposite and was in the same form at TGS. We were both cricket mad, but he had real talent and would have reached a very high standard had he lived in the area of the Bradford League and been given the coaching that his natural ball-playing talents deserved. Barry was already making his mark in a very good TGS 1st XI and in the Wetherby League with Arthursdale, and he was to share with me many of the experiences that I describe. He was as avid a supporter of Denis Compton as I was of Len Hutton. I had watched Yorkshire play at Headingley on several occasions in 1947, but 1948 was very special because of the visit of one of Australia's greatest sides, captained by Don Bradman.

The fourth test was to be held at Headingley, beginning on Thursday 22 July, with a rest day on the Sunday. However, the TGS term had not quite ended, so I was only able to attend on the Saturday. The situation at stumps on the Friday evening was that England had scored 496 and Australia were 63 for 1 in reply, with Bradman 31 not out. I caught the first train of the day to Leeds on that Saturday morning to ensure that I got into the ground, relishing the prospect of watching Bradman bat in front of a 40,000-capacity crowd. I was more than disappointed – he was bowled out by a Lancashire bowler called Pollard after scoring just two more runs. I had come to watch Bradman bat, not to watch Pollard bowl. In the second innings Bradman was to produce a match-winning innings of 173 not out, but sadly I was at school. I never had the chance to see the great Don Bradman bat again. However, I saw some excellent cricket that day including a brilliant century from teenager Neil Harvey who had already made history by becoming the youngest Australian to score a Test century (153 against India at Melbourne on 7 Feb 1948). Harvey was also recognised as being one of the finest fielders of the time, reflected in a fine boundary catch in England's second innings off the bowling of Johnston. He then coolly returned the ball by drop– kicking it from the boundary – straight into the wicketkeeper's gloves. I also made some good pocket money. I knew that spectators could hire leather cushions at Headingley to place on the hard, wooden benches, at a cost of about three shillings, plus a £1 deposit that was refunded on return, so I took two large string bags with me. When the day's play ended many spectators were in too much of a hurry to leave to bother returning the cushions and I filled my string bags with them and collected the deposits. I forget how much I made, but it was enough to cover my entry and travel costs, including travel for the Sunday rest day which I spent outside the Queen's

Hotel collecting autographs from the Australian players who were staying there. I was also able to buy some film and other photography items that I needed. It was a frustrating morning for me at TGS on Monday 26 July; wondering what was happening at Headingley. However, one of our masters listened to the lunchtime news and told us not only the score, but that the gates had been closed well before the match started, with 40,000 inside and 20,000 outside. Had I been there, I would inevitably have been one of those on the outside. No crowd trouble!

However, my headmaster's warning at the end of the summer term kept coming back to me. I appreciated that it would be quite wrong and unrealistic to rely on the support of my ageing grandparents when I left school, and on no account would I live with my mother and Herbert in Leeds. So, I did my own research to identify realistic career options that would enable me to leave home and be completely independent. Panic set in as I realised that to have any chance of realising these career options I would need to obtain not only a decent School Certificate next year, but also a Higher School Certificate. I returned to TGS for the start of the 1948 Christmas term determined to pull out all the stops.

I was helped in my efforts by some very good teachers who had not taught me before, while my confidence and morale rose when I was one of only two boys in the form to be selected for the football 1st XI. It was not long before my headmaster noticed the improvement and I no longer feared his announcement of the fortnightly marks. I also avoided any disciplinary visits to his study. Shortly before Christmas the school formed a Combined Cadet Force (CCF), whose activities I threw myself into with much enthusiasm. Initially, it consisted solely of an Army Section which was most appropriate for the school's most famous pupil was a soldier – Thomas Fairfax [3rd Lord Fairfax of Cameron]; the Parliamentary commander-in– chief during the first English Civil War. Lord General Thomas Fairfax led the opposing forces to King Charles I to many victories – most notably at the Battle of Marston Moor (2 July 1644), when Oliver Cromwell was under his command; the crucial Battle of Naseby (14 June 1645) and the siege of Oxford. The ghost of "Black Tom" as he was nicknamed [dark hair, eyes and complexion] may have looked down with some bemusement at the young TGS soldiers of his old school.

Life was good, and it was getting better, for to my delight I received an invitation from Ruth Addy to a party on New Year's Day 1949 at the school house in Boston Spa, where her father was headmaster. I boasted of this to Barry Appleyard, but he also had an invitation and so had some other boys in the form. At least I had made the shortlist. During one of the games that Ruth's parents had arranged, Ruth had to kiss the most handsome boy in the room as a forfeit. Without any hesitation, Ruth walked directly towards me. I was so thrilled, but she kissed Barry Appleyard, who was standing behind me. However, Ruth's invitation had coincided with my invitation to her to attend the CCF Christmas Party on 22 December and Ruth had accepted. Furthermore, the term ended with a quite respectable report that delighted my grandparents.

When the new term began I got down to even harder work and was close to the top in the headmaster's rankings. So, what better reward than a Easter visit to Paris arranged by our French teachers? Ruth Addy was in the group too, but I received no encouragement from her. Our accommodation was in a hotel, with a restaurant; both new experiences to me. We were a conscientious group, recognising that the visit had involved our parents in significant cost; no hanky panky (mouchoir de poche). It was a short visit, but we covered Sacré-Coeur, Notre-Dame, the Madeleine Church, the Panthéon, the Conciergerie, Fontainebleau, the Château de Malmaison, Versailles and, of course, the Eiffel Tower. It was also interesting to see the war damage to Dieppe, where we disembarked. On 4th April 1949 the North Atlantic Treaty Organisation (NATO) was formed; the founding members being Belgium, Canada, Denmark, France, Great Britain, Iceland, Italy, Luxembourg, the Netherlands, Norway, Portugal and the United States – the agreement signed by those nations in Washington D.C.

After Easter it was intensive swotting for the School Certificate examination. At about the same time I began smoking, like most of my friends. It was just the occasional cigarette to begin with, but the number grew as I got older. My plea in mitigation is that a connection with cancer had not yet been recognised, most Hollywood films of the day contained scenes in which the stars were smoking, and it was generally accepted as a sign of approaching manhood. A quarter of a century was to pass before I stopped.

As soon as the exams were over it was back to the active country life that I loved, but in a more adventurous way. My Raleigh bike had been replaced with a far less cumbersome touring bike, enabling quite demanding rides to be made between Scholes and the Lake District (circa 100 miles). They took two days, incorporating overnight stops at youth hostels [of the YHA] located in pleasant en-route locations [Kirby Malzeard and Aysgarth spring to mind]. On the second day of an outward journey to the Lake District we would ride through Wensleydale and Garsdale to Sedbergh, then Kendal – the gateway to the lakes and the fells. The Patterdale Youth Hostel was our favourite in the Eastern Fells, with nearby Helvellyn (3,117 feet) a challenging climb, rewarded with splendid views of the lakes. Return journeys followed a similar pattern. Hitch-hiking was also popular. Having booked accommodation in the YHA hostel in Edinburgh I made a weekend trip with a friend to that fine city via The Great North Road (GNR) – the main highway between England and Scotland from medieval times to the 20th century. We used our bikes to reach the Bramham cross roads at GR432402, where the GNR was crossed by the A64 Leeds-Tadcaster road, leaving them at the crossroads garage; run by the father of a boy in the same form as myself (Rodney Peers). Northbound, the GNR carved its way through the main streets of villages and market towns that had not changed from coaching days; Bramham, Wetherby, Boroughbridge; alongside the home straight of Catterick racecourse and over the Swale river bridge; paralleling the Northumberland coastline to Berwick-upon-Tweed; squeezing past the Lammermuir Hills to enter Edinburgh from the East. We had two nights in the city, no mishaps and thoroughly enjoyed the experience.

I was also enjoying cricket in the Arthursdale 2nd XI (Barry Appleyard was in the first team) and I watched more county matches, at both Headingley and Scarborough. Weather permitting, I would sometimes cycle with my friends on a Sunday morning to Roundhay Park, on the outskirts of Leeds, where there was an outdoor swimming pool with quite a high diving board. None of us could dive from anything higher than the edge of the pool but we enjoyed some jumping. We would then go to the natural steep-sided arena in the park, where there was always an attraction, and at no cost. Usually it would be cycle racing or good–quality cricket, including some county players. I would occasionally spend a complete day of my holidays at the two mainline stations in Leeds watching the activity, soaking up the atmosphere, recording the detail and sometimes getting a lift on the footplate to the engine sheds, most notably on an A4 streamlined Sir Nigel Gresley engine. Watching the engines and their crews under stress never failed to thrill me – the struggle to achieve optimum boiler pressure at the start of a demanding journey, and the smoke, steam, sparks and skidding as the engine slowly gained momentum – two Hunt-class engines in tandem pulling the late-evening Hull Express fighting the steep gradient at Crossgates; the firemen naked from the waist upwards, covered in perspiration and shovelling incessantly.

School Certificate results were received by post at home in my day, instead of at school, but the trepidation on opening the envelope has not changed over the years. I looked up at my anxious grandparents …'I've passed!' I told them, and we hugged each other. I had five credits and three passes.

The past four years (1945 to 1949) became known as the austerity years; the euphoria of WW2 victory had faded. 305,000 British lives had been lost, the country was exhausted and in huge financial debt to the USA. Clement Attlee had achieved a surprise victory over Winston Churchill in the post war general election (held on 5 July 1945) and his Labour government lost no time in formulating the welfare state and the National Health Service. I had watched my grandparents travel in a Conservative car to the polling booth, but I learned that they had voted for the Labour candidate whose party did not provide this facility (my grandmother could only walk short distances). Though some green shoots were appearing in the fight for economic recovery, there was little cheer in 1949. Clothes rationing ended on 15 March, but an attempt to end the rationing of sweets and chocolate a few weeks later failed (because of shortages). A dock strike (7 – 25 June) forced the government to use troops to unload cargoes and on 19 September the pound devalued by 30% against the dollar ($4.03 to $2.80). They were dark days for our country.

SIXTH-FORM YEARS

On returning to TGS in September 1949 I became a lower-sixth-form pupil, studying geography, English and chemistry, but I struggled with the chemistry. The possible careers that were now on my radar were the Army, the Royal Navy, the Merchant Navy or a school teacher, but the school still did not have a careers teacher to whom I could turn for advice. The brightest sixth-form pupils won state or county major scholarships or exhibitions and went to university, while most of those who did not achieve such distinction seemed to aspire to attend a teachers' training college, preferably with grant assistance. There were some notable exceptions, of course – not least the pupil who had recently gained entry to the RAF College at Cranwell (Robert Gamble). I mentioned my interest in Sandhurst to my housemaster, but instead of giving me some help and encouragement he pointed out that unless I became a general I would have to leave when I reached the age of 45, and what would I do then, poor thing? I continued with my own DIY career enquiries. My keen interest in a possible nautical career was inspired further when I read the account of a 1947 balsa wood raft crossing of the Pacific Ocean from Peru to the Polynesian Islands. The crossing of 4,300 miles was made by a Norwegian team, led by Thor Heyerdahl, to prove that South American explorers settled in these islands in pre-Columbian times. The title of the book was 'the Kon-Tiki Expedition'. Whilst an account of the expedition was published in Norwegian in 1948, it was not translated and published in English until 1950. It remains one of the most fascinating and enjoyable adventure stories that I have read.

My activities were very much the same as in the previous year, except that having completed a year wearing khaki in the Army section of the CCF, I now had the option of changing to either the RAF or the Royal Navy section. I chose the Royal Navy section and entered into all its activities with enthusiasm. Shortly after Christmas I plucked up the courage to ask Ruth Addy, who was also in the lower sixth, if she would like to come with me to the Regal cinema in Tadcaster on the following Saturday – and she accepted! It was a particularly popular film and there was almost a full house. Unfortunately, we were spotted by a group of TGS pupils, present and past, who decided to sit immediately behind us, tendering advice. I did not dare to even hold Ruth's hand, for fear of the roar of mirth and further encouragement that such action would have provoked. I forget the name of the film, but it was said to include the longest film kiss of the time, though well below modern achievements. After about three minutes I recollect a rather bored wag calling out, "anyone want a cheese sandwich?"

At the end of the film everyone stood for the national anthem, on the conclusion of which I suggested that a walk along the bank of the river might be rather nice. Ruth agreed, provided that she was still able to catch the next bus, on which her parents expected her to return home to Boston Spa. I think we did hold hands on the walk, but that was all. It was a rather disappointing evening and there was no subsequent date or development of that fragile relationship for another five years. We remained, 'just good friends'. I was nevertheless delighted that in addition to being Calcaria Girls House Captain, Ruth won the school's Victrix Ludorum Cup on Sports Day. My achievements were relatively modest. However, I did get 1st XI mentions in the school magazine: 'A fast and persistent wing-man who makes a lot of ground with the ball, but tends to waste this advantage with poor finishing' and 'A useful left-hand batsman, and a reliable fielder.' I was narrowly second to Barry Appleyard in the batting averages. TGS sport for boys was limited to cricket and football because of its modest size.

Overall, I think we punched above our weight, particularly in my early years at the school when there were two outstanding cricketers (Scott and Atkinson) who, much to the delight of headmaster 'Billy Bick', could stun St Peter's School, York [a leading independent school founded in 627AD] by themselves. Other opponents that spring to mind; The King's School (located in Pontefract) founded in 1139AD, Archbishop Holgate's School (York) founded in 1546AD, Harrogate GS, Knaresbrough GS, Nunthorpe GS (York), Leeds Modern School, Roundhay School (Leeds) and the St John's Teachers Training College York. I also recollect playing in an under 15 years football team against Wennington School (Ingmanthorpe Hall, near Wetherby): it was a Quaker school and they gave us quite a shock by producing a small ultra-hard new ball on a cold and frosty morning and addressing the referee and other teachers with their first names. Had any of us tried it on with our accompanying teacher (Mr J.L. Heslegrave) during the return coach journey to Tadcaster he would have received a very sharp clip of the ear. My summer holiday activities were similar to those of the previous year, except that I do not recall a scout camp. Instead, I went with the Royal Navy section of the CCF for a fortnight-long 'camp', together with contingents from several other schools, on the battleship *HMS King George V* in Portsmouth Harbour. Wonderful! The itinerary included basic seamanship, sailing, rowing, scrubbing of decks, navigation skills, the use of the sextant, flagmanship, steering orders and responses, the meaning of nautical terms, traditions and bosun calls. There were visits to *HMS Victory*, Nelson's flagship, the submarine base and the immaculate gunnery school at Whale Island. *HMS King George V* was built by Vickers-Armstrong in Newcastle-Upon-Tyne. She was the first of her class, launched on 21 February 1939, followed by battleships *HMS Prince of Wales* (1941), *HMS Duke of York* (1941), *HMS Howe* (1942) and *HMS Anson* (1942). They all survived the war except for *HMS Prince of Wales* which was sunk by the Japanese in the South China Sea on 10 December 1941. *HMS King George V's* most notable action was her involvement in the sinking of the German battleship Bismarck on 27 May 1941, but she was constantly involved in escort duties and in 1945 saw action against the Japanese in the Pacific, as well as being present at the Japanese surrender in Tokyo Bay. She also conveyed Prime Minister Winston Churchill on the last leg of his return to the UK from his historic five-day meeting with Stalin and President Roosevelt in Tehran, which began on 28 November 1943. However, Churchill's absence from the UK was longer than anticipated for he decided to meet the President of Turkey (Inonu) in Cairo (seeking Turkish assistance in the war effort) and became seriously ill with pneumonia shortly after the meeting, whilst in Carthage. He convalesced in Marrakesh, but his health precluded any travel until mid-January 1944, when he secretly embarked on *HMS King George V* in Gibralter, arriving in similar secrecy in Plymouth on the evening of 17 January. The following day he strode [unannounced] into the Chamber of the House of Commons ...

'They jumped to their feet and started shouting, waving their papers in the air. We also jumped up and the whole House broke into cheer after cheer while Winston, very pink, rather shy, beaming with mischief, crept along the front bench and flung himself into his accustomed seat. He was flushed with pleasure and emotion, and hardly had he sat down when two huge tears began to trickle down his cheeks. He mopped them clumsily with a huge white handkerchief.'

Sir Harold George Nicholson KCVO CMG

HMS King George V was still in commission at the time of my cadet 'camp' and I scrubbed the quarter-deck on which Winston Churchill had exercised on that epic return to his country with enthusiasm and gusto, as did many other proud cadets. Sadly, this fine ship was eventually sold for scrap and broken up at Dalmuir in 1959.

The visit to HMS Victory left a marked impression on my mind: following an escorted tour of the ship, and at the very spot that Nelson died, a young Royal Navy officer gave a brilliant outline of the battle and the final moments of Nelson's life. Many years later I read "THE LIFE of LORD VISCOUNT NELSON", written by Archibald Duncan, Esq. published by Miner and Sowerby of Paternoster Row, London in December 1805, a few months after Nelson's death at Trafalgar. The final page (327) reads:

The funeral ceremonies of the illustrious hero of these memoirs were of the most splendid character. It would be impossible to convey any adequate idea of the multitude of persons who crowded from all quarters of town and country to witness this interesting spectacle. Every place that offered a possibility of seeing the least part of it was crowded. From the shop windows to the roofs of the houses every space was occupied; the steeples and spires of the churches were filled; and even the top of the opera-house in the Haymarket, was covered; large sums were given for standing in a cart, in a leading street, only for a few moments. The funeral was attended by the seven sons of the Sovereign, by the chief nobility, gentry, and merchants of the empire, and by many thousands of subjects of all classes, with a universal, an unmixed, and a heartfelt sense of grief for his loss ; but at the same time with a glorious exultation in the deeds by which his life had been adorned, and his death consecrated to immortal honours. We trust that this great defender of Britain, this "dear son of memory," and "great heir of fame," has lived for his posterity, and that while the name of Nelson is remembered, we shall never want those who are animated by zeal, and are ardently desirous of imitating his example.

Some way should be found of conveying this moving eye-witness description of the adoration of Lord Viscount Nelson by the British people in 1805 (and unchanged over many generations) to those living at this time.

There were now very dark clouds on the horizon. On 25 June 1950 troops of the North Korean People's Army crossed the 38th parallel that divided it from South Korea. Two days later President Harry S Truman ordered American military forces aid in the defence of South Korea, where horrific atrocities were being conducted by both North and South Korean forces – the start of the Korean War. On 7 July the United Nations Security Council created the United Nations Command (UNC), which was essentially American led. The People's Republic of China (PRC) entered the war (in support of North Korea) on 19 October 1950, shortly followed by support from the Soviet Union. The British and Commonwealth contribution to the UNC was given the title of 'British Commonwealth Forces Korea' (BCFK). The conflict was to last until 27 July 1953 – the most powerful countries in the world engaged in a bitter conflict for supremacy in eastern Asia, escalating to the fringe of WW3, but more of that later.

I returned to TGS in mid-September 1950, aged sixteen and a half, and was now in the upper-sixth form. I had despaired of obtaining a satisfactory result in chemistry and decided to cram the two years of the religious knowledge course into one year in the hope of achieving three satisfactory GCE A-levels, which had replaced the Higher School Certificate. However, there was no Ruth Addy. I learned that on virtually the eve of her returning to TGS as Senior Girl Prefect (head girl), her father had suddenly died on the afternoon of Sunday 9 September, having attended church in the morning with the family. Ruth did not return to TGS and some two weeks later I learned that her education had ended. The tenancy of the Boston Spa school house had to be terminated and both Ruth and her mother needed to earn an income with which to support a new home, and also to enable her older brother, Leslie, to complete his education at Leeds University, where he was reading chemistry. Perhaps I should have jumped on my bike and cycled to Boston Spa to see her, but I lacked the maturity and confidence to do so, and I was not sure that I would have been welcome. Ruth had become very interested in Domestic Science during the previous two years, taught by a Miss Sheila Lewarne and achieving a School Certificate Distinction grade. Ruth admired Miss SL enormously, as did every red blooded teenage boy in the school, for Miss SL was in her early 20s and absolutely gorgeous. Had it not been for the death of her father, I think Ruth would not only have become head girl, but would have achieved a scholarship to university, selecting a course advised by Miss SL.

In late April 1951 our nation and the western world learned of an action in the Korea War that General James Van Fleet (Commander US 8th Army) described as 'the most outstanding example of unit bravery in modern warfare' – the last stand of 1st Battalion the Gloucestershire Regiment on the Imjin, which enabled several American Divisions to escape encirclement. Six months later Queen Elizabeth made her first Victoria Cross investiture; to Private Bill Speakman of the Black Watch (Royal Highland Regiment), though attached to 1st Battalion the Kings

Own Scottish Borderers at the time, for gallantry in the face of the enemy in Korea on 4 November. *[Chinese artillery had pounded the battalion's position with a fifteen-hour barrage, followed by a 'human wave' infantry assault. When the section holding the left shoulder of the company's position had been seriously depleted by casualties and was being overrun by the enemy, Speakman, on his own initiative, collected six men and a pile of grenades and led a series of charges. He broke up several enemy attacks, causing heavy casualties and despite being wounded in the leg continued to lead charge after charge. He kept the enemy at bay long enough to enable his company to withdraw safely].* One felt very proud to be British.

It was only after the brutal Korea War had ended that the contribution and courage of Fusilier Derek Kinne (Royal Northumberland Fusiliers) was revealed and recognised. He was captured in the fighting withdrawal from the Imjin and spent two years and four months as an ultra-rebellious prisoner of the Chinese, defying torture and displaying outstanding leadership and fortitude in maintaining the morale of his comrades; to the extent that he was awarded the George Cross by the Queen on 6 July 1954. He died of cancer on 6 February 2018 (in Arizona); receiving comprehensive obituaries in THE TIMES and other leading newspapers, which did not shield the detail of his ordeal as a prisoner.

Austerity lingered on in Britain and some rationing remained [it ended on 4 July 1954, when meat and bacon ceased to be rationed]. The British people needed something to cheer them up, something to make them laugh. On 28 May 1951 the BBC obliged – with its first broadcast of *the Goon Show*: a crazy mix of ludicrous plots, surreal humour and bizarre sound effects, created by Spike Milligan with brilliant lunatic– support from Peter Sellers and Harry Secombe. No organisation or part of British contemporary life was spared from its satirical intrusion and mockery. It ran continuously, with increasing audiences and export to many Commonwealth countries, until 1960 (238 episodes). Yes, it was daft, but it was sheer genius, and it paved the way for modern comedy. It was loved by people of all ages, who now had an alternative to commenting on the weather in their morning greetings; reciting one of the many catchphrases – 'He's fallen in the wah-taa' perhaps the best remembered by to-day's silver brigade.

The 1950/51 school year followed much the same routine as the lower–sixth year. I applied myself to the best of my ability and was conscious of my responsibilities as prefect, house captain, captain of football and cricket and petty officer in the CCF. However, I was beginning to feel that I was outgrowing school and I was looking forward to leaving and seeing something of the world. I played a lot of sport outside school, particularly during the winter when I sometimes played football matches for TGS on a Saturday morning and the Wetherby Athletic AFC junior side in the afternoon, sometimes followed by table tennis in the evening. There were no showers at TGS, but cold or lukewarm showers were sometimes available at other schools. Matches at Wetherby were played on the Ings, alongside the river, where there were not even changing facilities – we just changed in the open and covered our clothes with our macs (polythene bags were not yet on the market). Later in the season I was invited to transfer to the Tadcaster AFC junior side and readily accepted. Not only were they a better team, but there were changing facilities. I conscientiously revised the year's work, sat the GCE A-level exams in geography, English and religious knowledge, and enjoyed another wonderful summer 'camp' with the Royal Navy, this time at Plymouth aboard HMS *Sluys*, a Battle–class destroyer. We had two days at sea in the English Channel and I had quite lengthy spells at the wheel, responding to the orders of the officer of the watch. I also learned to use the bosun's pipe and make some of the routine calls, the most popular of which was, of course, 'splice the mainbrace'. I loved it. The Royal Navy taught me many useful skills; proficiency in the use of the sextant, learning to read and understand Admiralty nautical maps of various types in different parts of the world, plotting courses with a fair degree of accuracy, recognising obstacles and interpreting tide data etc. Most important of all the Royal Navy instilled in me a well above average national pride and the importance of teamwork.

Sadly, my DIY career research had revealed that Dartmouth was not an option, as I did not have the required standard in physics, but the Merchant Navy, Sandhurst and a teachers' training college remained realistic options if I passed in each of my GCE A-level exams. When I received my results I was able to give my grandparents another hug and thank them for their support – I had passed in each subject.

At about this time I became increasingly conscious of the stigma of illegitimacy, something that today's illegitimate children will find difficult to comprehend. We lived in a semi-detached house and our next-door neighbours on both sides were at best cool and at worst hostile. These were years of ignorance and extreme social snobbery. It was not so much anything that was said as the feeling of being shunned, and occasionally this rankled deeply. For example, I had been attracted to a pleasant girl at the youth club, and one evening I walked home with her and we had a quick kiss and cuddle at the gate as we parted. I had been home only thirty minutes when the telephone rang; I answered it, to be told by her that she did not wish to be further associated with me – I could sense the presence of her mother standing next to her. How I envied my peers, who were able to talk about their parentage openly and fill in application forms giving their father's name, while I had to write 'not known' and be prompted to give further information. How could my mother, who had had the benefit of very caring parents and a private education, have let me down like this, and my father also? I resolved that if I married and had children, they would have a very stable family upbringing of which they could be proud.

It was decided that I should return to TGS for at least a further term, to study at scholarship level. When the term began, I lost no time in revealing my ambitions to Mr Bicknell and he had no hesitation in giving his support. He had become a different headmaster to the one I had previously known – he now talked to me as an adult human being. Nevertheless, on leaving his study a shiver went down my spine as I went past his selection of canes hanging behind the door. He was true to his word, however, and shortly before the end of term I received an offer of a teacher training place (with grant) from a college in London, whilst an application for Sandhurst had been submitted. Merchant Navy application forms were also being perused. It was a sad day when I said goodbye to Mr Bicknell and his staff and walked out of the gates of TGS for the last time, past the enormous John Smith's Brewery with its magnificent chimney and aroma of malt and hops, past the penny bun shop, and to the river Wharfe bridge, where I paused to drop my school cap into the river. I watched it slowly float away, close to the footpath along which Ruth Addy and I had once walked, hand in hand, wondering what she was doing now. Then to the bus stop and whatever lay beyond.

The subject matter taught by secondary schools in my day is well described, and with great humour, in Sunday Times bestseller, "I Used to Know That" by Caroline Taggart (ISBN 978-1-84317-655-8).

1952 AND EARLY 1953

Shortly before leaving TGS I became friendly with a girl from Leeds Girls' High School who lived in Barwick in Elmet. Margaret became the first girl in which the relationship led to her inviting me to her home and me inviting her to my home. Margaret was a very good pianist and hoped to make music her career. The brief romance ended on 6 February 1952, my eighteenth birthday, and the day that King George VI died and Princess Elizabeth became Queen. After a very nice tea with my grandparents I escorted Margaret home – we cycled along Rake Hill Lane, with Margaret in front. It was a narrow cinder track, and at the point where it dropped steeply to Rake Beck, Margaret's bicycle skidded and she had a nasty fall. Worse still, my knee went directly into her eye which, I am told, remained badly bruised and colourful for several days. I was never able to date Margaret again and she was very soon to be seen on a motorbike, sitting behind a far more careful and handsome suitor. Ah well.

While at TGS I had purchased a copy of the *Times Educational Supplement* and had noticed in it an advertisement for supply teachers in Bradford. Mr Bicknell gave me a good reference and I soon obtained employment with the Bradford Education Authority at an inner– city school, close to the Bradford railway station. I travelled by train, changing stations in Leeds, and had little difficulty in arriving at the school by 9 a.m. I taught the lower class of nine-year-old pupils and thoroughly enjoyed the experience. It was a very small school, with only three teachers. My task was to improve their 3Rs ability and general knowledge, including their knowledge of the Bible. There were a few children of low intellect, but the majority were of a fair standard and well behaved. They loved biblical stories, acting out the 'Talitha cumi' miracle of the raising of the dead child in the playground before bemused parents. One parent was heard to boast that her daughter could now not only recite all her tables, but was also learning Jesus's language. I had a rather fine road race bicycle at this time and a friend who regularly competed in time trials, so if the weather was reasonable I would sometimes cycle the fifteen miles to and from Bradford as a training session, and also to save on rail fares.

The school had a qualified teacher for the summer term and I was therefore asked to change to the very much larger Lidgett Green School, teaching slightly older children. Again, it was a most pleasant experience and I made quite a hit with the boys by introducing lunchtime cricket and football practice. However, I began to realise that I would not be happy for teaching to be my career – I needed travel and adventure in my life. Sandhurst or a Merchant Navy college remained as my preferred options, and if neither materialised I would enlist as a private soldier or seaman. A career that anchored me to my home country was not an option.

Scholes was quite an active village for its modest size. The centre of social activity was the village hall, the most popular events being mid-week whist drives and Saturday night dances. I was not, of course, interested in the whist drives but their popularity and competitiveness was such that results were published each week in the local paper. One of my friends suggested to me that we might look in on one of the Saturday dances, as a change from our Odsal Speedway or table tennis routine. I was not keen, for the limit of my experience and ability was the Saint Bernard's Waltz at a TGS Christmas party. Nevertheless, I bought a booklet on ballroom dancing in a second– hand bookshop in Leeds and studied the foot movement illustrations therein for the waltz and the quickstep, whilst my friend's mother gave him some tuition. The next Saturday evening, taking a deep breath, and as well-groomed as we could manage, we ignored the table tennis in the school and walked-on to the village hall … The noise of the band could be heard as soon as we passed the Council Offices. We gritted our teeth – there was no turning back now. We paid our admission at the entrance, and at a nod from the attendant I opened the swing door and we took a couple of steps forward … onto the rectangular shaped dance floor, where we froze, rather like a couple of rabbits caught in car headlamps. To our left was a long row of chairs occupied by females. To our right was a long row of chairs occupied by males. Between them, at the end of the hall, there was a stage and a smart uniformed band. The swing door hit us in the back as we stood there and a couple pushed past us, she turning left and he turning right. We followed him into a male cloakroom and then into a corner of the hall as the music and dancing stopped. After a few minutes the band leader announced, 'the next dance will be a foxtrot' and waved his baton. Males crossed the floor to the female side and invited their selections to dance, and eventually the floor was filled with dancers. Some dances were designated as 'excuse me dances' which permitted a male to tap the shoulder of a dancing male, saying 'excuse me' and, without any argument, take his partner. The next dance was a waltz, but my friend and I 'chickened-out'. The next was a Samba, which we would never have contemplated. The next was a quickstep, but we remained frozen … until two females who were dancing together stopped in front of us, seized us, and introduced us to the joy of ballroom dancing. The origins of ballroom dance can be traced to the 16th century in Bavaria with the ¾ time *waltz*, danced by the lower classes; the upper classes preferring the more stately *minuets*, danced to the music of Mozart and Handel. Following social change, the styles and participation merged. The *tango* was born in Buenos Aires, the *foxtrot* in New York. Then came *swing*, the *charleston* and the *jitterbug*. Led by Hollywood stars Fred Astaire and Ginger Rogers, partner dancing became hugely popular in the mid-1930s. Sadly, it has now been eclipsed by the competitive dance industry; increasingly becoming a professional sport – watched by couch potatoes.

Shortly before the summer holidays began I was more than delighted to receive a letter from the War Office asking me to attend the Army's

Regular Commissions Board at Westbury in Wiltshire in August, giving some date options. I subsequently received my reporting instructions, a railway warrant, and a brief outline of the three-day selection process. I gulped – the moment of truth was now very close. I was not particularly well travelled. Apart from my school trip to Paris in 1949, the RN cadet 'camps' at Portsmouth and Plymouth and hitchhiking with a friend to Edinburgh on one occasion, I had never travelled outside northern England, so a solo journey to Westbury was quite an exciting prospect. I believe that nowadays the Army provides candidates with a two-day preparatory briefing to ensure that everyone is equally prepared for the selection process, but this was not the case in 1952.

I departed on an early train from Scholes station one Monday morning in early August and, together with several other candidates, was met at Westbury station in the late afternoon by two NCOs who were members of the permanent staff of the selection centre. We were given an address that evening by the brigadier in charge. He assured us that there were no hidden cameras or spyholes and urged us to relax and get to bed early. I shared a room with a boy whose school regularly provided candidates for a regular commission and accordingly he had a fair knowledge of the type of tests that we were to be given, but not to an extent that would provide any significant advantage. I pumped him for information until he fell asleep.

The following morning after breakfast we were divided into small syndicates and each given a sleeveless jacket to wear, on which was sewn a large identification number, front and back. Over the next three days we were subjected to a series of virtually non-stop activities, tests and assessments, of which the following readily spring to mind: interviews, IQ and academic tests, practical ability tests, aptitude tests, physical fitness and stress assessments, debates, command tasks, a lecturette, a planning exercise and another medical examination. At the end of each day there would be time for a chat and a drink in the common room, away from our assessors and without our number identifications on display. We would talk about the errors that we felt we had made, as well as about what might be in store for the next day and our experiences of life. Bonds of friendship were beginning to develop – and then it was all over. We gathered on the Friday morning in the common room and were individually called to the brigadier's office in what seemed to be no particular order, though there might have been a link to the distances that we had to travel. He did not waste his time.

'Well, Pedley, we're sending you to Sandhurst, but you must get rid of that strong Yorkshire accent. You must give a good account of yourself while serving in the ranks beforehand and I would advise you to select a quality national newspaper to improve your knowledge of world affairs. Good luck.'

I was, of course, delighted, but rather irritated at the brigadier's reference to my Yorkshire accent. I was very proud of being a Yorkshireman. I never made any conscious effort to dilute or get rid of my accent – it just gradually faded over a period of time – but I did take his advice to improve my knowledge of world affairs. As soon as a telephone became available I telephoned home – 'Gran, I've passed'. I then returned to the common room, seeking in particular my room mate. Sadly, he had not been accepted, but he was encouraged to try again. I believe the pass rate from those selected to attend the Regular Commissions Board at that time was around 45%. The most competitive part of the selection process was getting invited to attend Westbury.

News spreads quickly in a small Yorkshire village, and I was soon receiving congratulations. The body language of many neighbours changed overnight and I now received warm smiles from both the girls and their mothers. I was the first boy to gain admission to Sandhurst not only from TGS but from any of the grammar schools in the area, with the exception of the Leeds grammar schools. Mr Bicknell and his staff and the TGS governors were highly delighted, as were my CCF contingent officers, Captain J.L. Heslegrave and Lieutenant R.D. Swanston RN. The school had already achieved an admission to the Royal Air Force College at Cranwell in 1948, and a year after my admission to Sandhurst the staff would be congratulating the first TGS boy to gain admission to the Royal Naval College at Dartmouth – Christopher Attrill, who lived only half a mile from me.

I immediately started modest training runs and made enquiries about farm work, for my upper-body strength needed improvement. My attention was drawn to an 'agricultural holiday camp' just outside Malton, called Eden Camp. It had been a prisoner of war camp during the war years and now provided Nissen hut shelter and food which one could pay for from one's earnings on the local farms. It seemed to be just what I needed, so I made arrangements to attend, caught the Scarborough bus at my old TGS bus stop on the A64 and got off on the outskirts of Malton. It proved to be ideal for my purposes, but 'agricultural holiday camp' was a misnomer – the facilities consisted of concrete floors with a small bedside mat, straw mattresses, standard WD (War Department) bedding and battered metal wardrobes, a staple diet of beans, stew, porridge and old bread, leaking roofs and a paucity of warm water. Reveille was sounded by a banging of the fire-alarm triangle at about 6 a.m. and at 7 a.m. we were driven to the Malton marketplace in ex-Army 3-ton General Service (GS) vehicles for hiring as cheap labour for the day to the local farmers. The farmers loved the arrangement – you bet they did, it was virtually slave labour. They drove down to the market square with their tractors and trailers and took what they wanted for the day at the going rate of £1 a day. There was a group of Republic of Ireland workers at the camp who had come over to England for a few months, but they rightly demanded a higher rate, for they could work twice as fast as others at the camp. The work that we were given mostly involved harvesting, followed by potato picking and swede or turnip topping. Occasionally, one might get some variation during the eight-hour day by being allowed to lead a horse and cart to and from the farm for a while. Other than that, it was eight hours of back-breaking work in all weathers. The worst task that I got was three days of removing three feet of compressed muck from the byres with a fork. I became quite friendly with the Irish group and later made a point of reading a bit about their history and the potato famine in particular. What a strong, resilient and proud people. I continue to have much respect for them and still wonder if one day we might see a union of the five nations, outside the EEC. I went home each weekend, if only for a good hot bath and my grandmother's traditional Yorkshire Sunday roast, with the Yorkshire pudding served as the first course, in its own right. On returning to Eden Camp one Sunday evening I was asked by one of the Irish lads if I had had a good weekend. I assured him that I had. 'Did you fight?' he asked. I told him that I had not. He looked at me scornfully and told me in no uncertain terms that if I had not had a good fight I could not have had a good weekend, and he meant it. These Irish lads would have been splendid company if one was ever in a threatening situation.

A small group of Belgians arrived at the camp the following week and on the first day I was at the same farm as them, together with some of the Irish group. At the end of the day, the farmer reached for his wallet and gave each male worker £1, plus a bonus for the Irish lads, and 18 shillings to each female worker. A Belgian girl stepped forward and in her best English demanded the same amount as the male workers, as she felt that she had worked just as hard, if not harder. 'No, that's the rate – take it or leave it,' replied the farmer, a Mr Black I believe. 'Je box vous!' replied the irate Belgian girl, and she moved forward, ready to clout Mr Black. The Irish lads loved it and supported her – and she got her £1. It was my first experience of the increasing female demand for sexual equality.

A very important-looking letter awaited me when I returned home on the following weekend. It was from No. 71 Recruiting Centre in Templar House, Lady Lane, Leeds 2, requiring me to report on 26 September for enlistment as an infantry soldier into a regiment of the Yorkshire and Northumberland Brigade, the Green Howards being my preference. I had selected the Green Howards as my preference without any counselling or guidance. At that time, so close to the end of World War II, servicemen travelled and took their leave in uniform (battledress), with the name of their regiment or corps sewn to the top of their sleeves. Most infantry regiments, the Yorkshire regiments included, had their name in white lettering on a red background, with the exception of the Green Howards, whose name was on a green background. They seemed to be a rather elite and popular regiment and they had two battalions, one serving in Germany and the other at Barnard Castle, having just returned from Malaya. On that flimsy knowledge I asked for the Green Howards, the 19th Regiment of Foot, and enlisted for three years' service with the Colours and four years with the Reserve. I was assured that provided my basic training was satisfactory I would proceed to the Royal Military Academy at Sandhurst in March 1953. If my basic training was not satisfactory, and provided it was not my fault, I would be given the option of discharge forthwith, with no further obligation. It seemed a fair deal and I signed the attestation paper, albeit with an embarrassing smudge accompanying my signature.

I continued to work at the 'agricultural holiday camp' until late October, by which time the weather conditions were becoming rather unpleasant and demand for our slave labour had slackened. I also needed to assist my grandparents in their move to their new home in Harrogate. Their move was prompted by my grandmother's sisters who still lived in Harrogate; Rebecca (Peppie) and Ada Christelow, who were unmarried and lived together, and Nell McKenzie (née Christelow). Peppie had had a cleft lip operation as a child, which was not entirely successful. She had a further specialist operation in London at about this time which improved her facial appearance, but with a rather dumpy figure (like sister Ada) she could never be attractive. However, she was kindness itself and talented in embroidery and still life painting. I don't know whether she used her skills professionally, but I treasure three exquisite still life paintings that she gave to my grandparents; perhaps their wedding gift or special anniversary. My grandmother was now virtually an invalid and they pointed out how much more mobile she might be in Harrogate. My grandfather was sceptical and very saddened to leave his beautiful garden. Their new home in King Edwards Drive was a distinct downsize, with a tiny garden.

My Army joining instructions arrived. I was to report to the depot of the Green Howards at Richmond, Yorkshire on 4 December 1952. I received a railway warrant and advice that there would be transport at the Richmond railway station to convey me to the barracks. I was to telephone the guardroom if there was a problem. There was no problem, except that there was no transport at the station when I arrived. I waited about twenty minutes before telephoning the guardroom to explain the situation. Eventually, I found myself listening to the guard commander:

'What Regiment did you say you were joining?' 'The Green Howards.'

'And do you have two feet?' 'Yes, sir.'

'Well use them and report to me within twenty minutes. Do you understand?'

'Yes, sir.'

I learnt that the railway station was at the lowest part of Richmond, the barracks at the highest point, and that it was just possible to carry a heavy leather suitcase between the two in twenty minutes.

The barracks was purpose built in 1877 and had been the depot of the Green Howards since that time, training thousands of soldiers from its North Yorkshire recruiting area. It was built of stone, with high walls and magnificent views of Richmond and Swaledale to the south.

It was a hive of activity at that time, training both national service and regular soldiers for its two battalions. We were blissfully unaware of Britain's Great Smog that was developing in London, and which was to result in 4,000 deaths – almost bringing down Churchill's government. Richmond (Yorkshire) 'didn't do' smogs, specialising in bitterly cold winds from the moors, cold showers, and grouse shooting. I learnt during my ten days at the depot of the Green Howards how privileged I was to be wearing the cap badge of one of the finest infantry regiments in the British Army. Also, that only one Victoria Cross was awarded on D-Day; to a Green Howard (Company Sergeant Major Stanley Elton Hollis from Teeside). His medals are on display at the Green Howards museum, located in the centre of Richmond market square.

I spent about ten days in Richmond before being transferred to the depot of the Yorkshire & Northumberland Brigade at Fulford barracks, York, where there was a course to prepare potential officers for Eaton Hall (national service commission) and Sandhurst (regular commission). It was quite a tough ten-week course, because of the extra high standards demanded of potential officers and some very cold weather. Water pipes were frequently frozen and we had to fill fire buckets from a distant water bowser for our water supply, not forgetting to leave some buckets around the small stove in the centre of the twenty-man barrack room when we retired for the night: for our morning wash and shave. Despite this, I quite enjoyed barrack-room life, the comradeship, the bull and the banter. At the end of the barrack room was the corporal's room, occupied by Corporal Scott, a very competent Green Howards NCO with fine leadership qualities who had just returned from active service in Malaya. He was responsible for much of our training, thoroughly interviewed each of us on arrival and made it clear that he would stand no nonsense. He was an excellent role model and would surely have become a senior warrant officer had he decided to remain in the army for a full career. I believe he later became a policeman in Ripon.

The training at York ended in early March. I held out my pay book (AB 64 Part 2) on Friday pay parade for the last time in my life and received the four shillings per day that was owed to me for the past week. I bade farewell to Corporal Scott and my friends, cast a wistful glance at the gleaming barrack-room floor that I had 'bumpered' on so many occasions, and the cookhouse where I had peeled so many potatoes, and then took a bus to my Harrogate home for a short leave, prior to reporting to the Royal Military Academy.

SANDHURST

My junior intake was required to report two days prior to the return of senior cadets and the start of the summer term. Nevertheless, the number of junior cadets travelling on the train that I took to Camberley from Waterloo station was such that it was packed. It was quite a colourful sight as we were all wearing the uniforms of the corps and regiments in which we had completed our basic training. Buses carried us the short distance from Camberley station, across the A30 and into the academy grounds, stopping at the lower end of the fine and extensive parade ground that lay before Old College, as though fearful to cross. The doors were flung open by immaculately dressed drill sergeants of the Brigade of Guards who called us 'sir', yet screamed at us to get our idle bodies and luggage across that parade ground 'at the double'. As we neared the grand entrance to Old College an impressive figure appeared at the top of the steps. I was soon to learn that he was Academy Sergeant Major J.C. Lord, MBE (later to be awarded the CVO), probably Britain's most famed and feared warrant officer of the time. He too was encouraging us to move quickly, 'at the double'.

When the arrival documentation was completed we were shown to our rooms, given some reading matter on the layout, organisation and history of the academy and instructed to regularly peruse the company noticeboard for instructions. There were three colleges in the academy, named Old College, New College and Victory College. Each of these colleges had four companies of sixty cadets (20 junior cadets, 20 intermediate cadets and 20 senior cadets). It was an eighteen-month course, divided into three terms. I was a junior cadet and had been placed in Inkerman Company, of Old College. If all went well I would progress after six months to becoming an intermediate cadet and after a year to senior cadet. Junior cadets shared a room, and I soon met my room mate, Simon Walford. Simon had attended Harrow and lived in the Republic of Ireland, in County Waterford. I believe Simon had already attended the Mons Officer Cadet Training Unit (OCTU) at Aldershot, where potential National Service and short service commission officers of the Royal Armoured Corps and Royal Artillery were trained. Our room was basic, with a single washbasin, but it had a magnificent view of the Old College parade ground, the lake and Queen Victoria's statue. Simon's experience, awareness and advice proved most helpful to me in my early days there.

For the next two days we were marched around the academy in company squads to learn its layout, with briefings on its traditions and routine. We were issued with new uniforms, sports kit and some mufti items such as blazers and riding coats. Much time was also spent on uniform preparation – polishing leather belts, boots and brasses. We were addressed by the commandant, Major General D. Dawnay CB DSO, and I was interviewed by my company commander, Major D.R. Horsfield Royal Signals, one of the many officers at Sandhurst to have a very impressive World War II record. Though an acting lieutenant colonel during the war, he had to relinquish the rank when it ended, but soon climbed the ranks again and became a major general.

The intermediate and senior cadets had now returned from their leave and the tempo switched to a faster gear overnight. The Sandhurst day began at 0630 with the duty senior cadet shouting the company name along the corridors. That gave 45 minutes in which to wash, shave and get on parade outside the college for roll call and inspection, followed by breakfast at 0730. Training began at 0830 and continued until the lunch break between 1230 and 1330. The afternoon was largely taken up with academic work, immediately followed by sporting activities until about 1830. We assembled for dinner in uniform in our company ante-rooms at 1930 and walked down to the college dining room just before 2000, seated by companies. The time after dinner was our own, but it was a time of much activity as that was when we had to prepare kit for the following day and carry out whatever studies had been set. Lights out was at 2230 for junior cadets. There was usually a parade or some other commitment on a Saturday morning, with academy and college level sport in the afternoon, which one was expected to support if not a participant. A church parade was held each Sunday, with special arrangements for cadets of denominations other than Church of England. It was a very moving occasion, with the Sovereign's Colour marched into the attractive academy church under escort. The church would be packed, with directing staff and their families also present. The weekend was also a time for private study. However, it was not so much the workload, both mental and physical, that was so demanding at Sandhurst, as the culture of pace and excellence. A sense of history and tradition permeated the buildings and the grounds. The greatest sin of a cadet was to be found doing nothing.

I found it both inspiring and demanding, and worrying – how was I doing? Hardly a week passed without news of a cadet or two departing, with a one-way rail ticket. After six weeks we were given individual assessments on the standard of our drill. Few passed first time. I passed at the second attempt a week later and was now allowed out of the academy for prescribed periods at the weekend – rather like the public school exeat system. There were also gymnastic and shooting tests to pass. Surprisingly, there was no swimming pool. Punishments, such as extra drills on Saturday morning, were awarded for trivial things. For example, I found myself in front of my company commander because of a 'fluke' in my tie on one occasion and was awarded an extra Saturday-morning drill. However, the ever-observant drill sergeant who was officiating that day had noticed a flash of white above my boots while I was marking time in front of Major Horsfield. As soon as we were outside he lifted my trouser leg and saw that I had not changed my cricket socks – so it was straight back in and two more Saturday morning parades were awarded. I had had only a few minutes to change from an academy cricket trial into uniform for the company commander's orders parade, but that was no excuse. Worse still, I was not considered good enough for the academy team. However, I did play for the Old College team. A few days later I came close to a further appearance in front of Major Horsfield. Standard military bicycles were provided to reach some distant parts of the extensive training area, and I used this facility one evening to reach the rifle ranges, where I was required for butts duties. I had reached the 400 yards firing point when a loud voice from the butts ordered me to get a move on. I glanced down at my watch, noted that I still had five minutes in hand and carried on peddling at the same decent speed. On arrival at the butts I came face to face with RSM Lord, who gave me one almighty rollicking for not being five minutes early. I still wince at the severity of that rollicking and throughout my life I have always regarded myself as being late if I was not five minutes early. I have such a high regard for RSM Lord and his wartime record that I now consider myself privileged to have had such personal attention.

Each term there was considerable rivalry between Sandhurst's twelve companies for the title of Sovereign's Company and the holding of the Sovereign's Colour. There were three competitions: drill (junior cadets), obstacle course race (intermediate cadets), and shooting (senior cadets), with companies placed in order of 1–12 in each competition and points awarded accordingly. It had been made clear to me and the other nineteen junior cadets of Inkerman Company that we must win our drill competition, particularly because of the pending retirement of our company sergeant major, WO2 Cullen Grenadier Guards, known as 'Daddy' Cullen, to whom a win would have meant so much. The judges were senior warrant officers and officers from the Guards' depot at Pirbright. We gave everything, but sadly only came fourth.

Another keenly contested competition was the juniors boxing. We were all taught the basics of the noble art in a series of tutorials and were matched by the Army Physical Training Corps staff against opponents of other companies of similar physique. It made excellent after-dinner entertainment for the permanent staff of the academy and their ladies. It was brutal. I won my bout (it must have been the Virol), but I decided to retire from the sport there and then – in my prime, and unbeaten.

Stories abound of Sandhurst and the humour and banter that sometimes percolated through its strict discipline. My favourite of these concerns a Brigade of Guards drill instructor and King Hussein of Jordan, who was a cadet in Inkerman Company the term before I arrived. I was therefore not present, so the story is hearsay, but I heard it from several cadets who were on the parade:

'King Hussein, sir, you're idle! What are you?' 'I'm an idle king, sir'.

It was no coincidence that King Hussein had spent his time at Sandhurst in Inkerman Company, with Major Horsfield as his company commander. Both had been carefully selected – Major Horsfield because of his fine personal qualities and record, and Inkerman Company because of its fine first-floor location and views within the oldest of the three colleges. It had been intended that King Hussein would complete the entire eighteen-month course, but important matters of state required an earlier return to his country, and he left a few weeks before I arrived. As a member of the Hashemite dynasty, the royal family of Jordan since 1921, the young King Hussein was a 40th generation direct descendant of Muhammad. He was soon to become one of the most prominent and dynamic rulers in the Eastern Mediterranean Region, terminated only by death from lymph gland cancer on 7 February 1999. He led his country through four turbulent decades of Arab-Israeli conflict, surviving many assassination attempts; skillful combat pilot; married four separate times, fathering eleven children. He was not an idle king!

I found Sandhurst to be tough but fair, and I never experienced or heard of any bullying. Quite the opposite, in fact – the aim was to create an ethos of comradeship and help. There was one occasion when I was given absolute hell by Sergeant F.B. (Blondie) Bedford of the Coldstream Guards during a drill session, watched by Major Horsfield. No matter how hard I tried I could not please him and I received continuous hostile and provocative chastisement. I had seen other cadets receive similar treatment on occasion. Looking back, I believe Sergeant Bedford was acting on Major Horsfield's instructions to put me under a bit of pressure to see how I reacted, for he was relatively pleasant at the next drill session, almost apologetic. He was the epitome of drill excellence and featured as the demonstrator in the Army's drill manual of that time.

The year 1953 was coronation year, and there was much excitement in the academy as Tuesday 2 June approached. The academy was to be represented in London on coronation day by a detachment of fifty from the Sovereign's Company who would take part in the procession and by a street-lining contingent of four hundred and fifty, positioned in the immediate vicinity of Westminster Abbey. Sadly, my junior intake of two hundred and forty cadets could not be included. We were bitterly disappointed, but at least we were to be given leave to attend, and we were determined to enjoy ourselves in London. On the preceding Friday, two hundred and thirty-two Royal Navy cadets from Dartmouth and two hundred and sixteen RAF cadets from Cranwell arrived at Sandhurst for joint street-lining rehearsals on the Old College parade ground and final administrative arrangements. They departed for London on 2 June in two special trains leaving Camberley at 0430 and 0500, reveille having been at 0220. They 'detrained' at Vauxhall Station and marched to Millbank Barracks for a welcome breakfast prior to marching to their allocated street-lining positions, arriving at 0830. By this time I had already been in London for about twelve hours as part of an informal group comprised of myself and twelve other junior cadets of Inkerman Company. We were dressed in 'smart mufti' (blazers, white shirt, academy tie and cavalry twill trousers) and had taken up a good pitch at the roadside in Piccadilly, near the Green Park tube station. While six of us went walkabout, soaking up the electric atmosphere and having a snack and a few beers, the remainder guarded our pitch and then we changed over – again and again. There was so much activity, so much to see. Temporary public washing facilities had been installed in Green Park, so by 0700 we were washed, shaved, bright eyed and bushy tailed. The procession and pageantry was magnificent and I felt very fortunate to have witnessed one of those truly historical British events that no other country in the world can match. There were three million spectators along the procession route, with many miles of grandstands, while 29,200 servicemen and women from Britain and the Commonwealth took part in either the procession or the street lining.

Following a visit by and parade for General Ridgeway (Supreme Commander, Allied Powers in Europe) a few days later, it was soon back to normality at Sandhurst, with exams approaching. Education, both academic and military, never ceases in the British Army and clear standards of attainment are a prerequisite for advancement, for both commissioned and non-commissioned officers. We did not win the Sovereign's Company competition, but fourth out of twelve companies was creditable. I was routinely interviewed by Major Horsfield and was told that I was progressing satisfactorily. We discussed cap badge options on commissioning, and a first choice for a Yorkshire infantry regiment was recorded, with the Royal Corps of Signals as second choice and the Royal Artillery as third choice.

The term ended on 30 July with the Sovereign's Parade – the parade at which cadets of the senior intake pass out and receive their commission. The Queen's representative was HRH The Duke of Gloucester, KG, KT, KP, GCB, GCVO, GBE. There would have been some 710 cadets on that parade, plus the academy band, the academy sergeant major and the other Brigade of Guards warrant officers plus, of course, the adjutant; Major V.F. Erskine Crum, CIE, MC Scots Guards and his horse, Dasteur. In accordance with tradition, the parade ended with the senior intake slow marching up the steps of the grand entrance into Old College, led by the adjutant on Dasteur. The spectacle of so many cadets (plus band) marching from their [out of sight] assembly on the New College parade ground to that of the Old College must have been one of the finest and most poignant sights in British military pageantry; seen only by the parents of those being commissioned and some very distinguished guests. It only took a few minutes; a quick dressing and fixing of bayonets … then silence … the arrival of the Queen [or representative] at Queen Victoria's statue … a short, escorted walk (the King's walk) to the saluting dais …

"Royal Military Academy will advance in review order … by the centre …
quick march [14 steps and halt]".
"General salute … present arms."

The words of command will forever remain in my mind.

Three days earlier, on 27th July 1953 the Korea War had ended. In military analysis it was a victory for the United Nations Command (UNC), but in political assessment both the Soviet Union and the People's Republic of China (PRC) derived satisfaction from the maintenance of their positions and communist ideology in eastern Asia. The cost, in terms of destruction, loss of life and human suffering was enormous; Korea's infrastructure and industry was demolished; four million Korean casualties and five million refugees. British casualties were 1,078 killed, 2,674 wounded and 1,060 missing or taken prisoner. The USA lost 33,600 men killed and 103,000 wounded, whilst the PRC had an estimated one million casualties.

It was lovely to see my grandparents again in their Harrogate home and to describe my first term at Sandhurst. I had written to them occasionally, of course, but the intensity of the training programme provided little time for correspondence. I saw my mother occasionally. I tried hard not to hurt her feelings, but I did not wish to share her lifestyle. I remained completely bonded to my grandparents. I met up with some of my friends from Arthursdale and Scholes, but the numbers were dwindling because of home moves and National Service. Barry Appleyard and his family had moved to Hull. However, I did manage some bicycle tours, staying at youth hostels and watching Yorkshire cricket. It was very pleasant to lead a normal life again for a while – to be able to amble around the shops at a sedentary pace and take a leisurely cup of coffee and cream cake at Bettys if I wished, without a warrant officer of the Brigade of Guards in sight. I went along to the ballroom dancing at the Royal Hall on a couple of Saturday evenings and enjoyed some feminine company for the first time since joining the Army. The ballroom dancing at Harrogate's Royal Hall was a very popular and pleasant social occasion. Jackets and ties had to be worn and the ladies wore nice dresses. Stewarding was discreet and I never saw any serious misbehaviour. Long white silk scarves were popular with the men, draped outside gaberdine coats – mine was of a pale olive-green colour. It was a welcome break, but it was not long before I was yearning to be back at Sandhurst. I returned to find a new company commander, Major D.P.

Carey of the Royal Leicestershire Regiment. As expected, Lord, P.T. de la P. Beresford (Lord PT), the second son of the 7th Marquess of Waterford, was appointed as Inkerman Company Senior Under Officer (SUO). He lived at the historic Curraghmore House near Portlaw, County Waterford (the Beresford family seat), surrounded by some 3,500 acres of formal gardens , woodland and pasture – the largest private demesne in Ireland. Curraghmore was part of a huge grant of more than 100,000 acres made to Sir Roger la Poer by Henry II in 1177 following the Anglo-Norman invasion. Lord PT's father died in an accident in the gun room of their home in 1934 when Lord PT was only a few months old. He was a fine horseman and spent as much time as he could competing in Tweseldown point-to-point steeplechases and polo matches ... ideally followed in the evening by society events in Belgravia. As we were in the same Company, and only a term apart, we shared many conversations in the Company ante-room and at meal times. There could not have been greater contrast in our pedigrees and education [TGS/Eton], but for much of my time at Sandhurst we were humble cadets together.

The pace and demands of the training and study were not reduced in the intermediate term. I was always conscious of the fact that a stream of reports was continuously being passed to the company commanders, recording one's progress or otherwise. Instead of coming home for the five-day mid-term break in late October 1953, I sailed as a crew member on the academy's 25-ton yacht (*Robbie*) in the Channel, with one night in France. Perhaps it was seeing France again and remembering the school trip to Paris in 1949 that prompted me to write a chatty letter to Ruth Addy when I got back, under the pretext of seeking news of some old school friends. I had never forgotten her, but my confidence had grown considerably during my time at Sandhurst so that now I felt no qualms about getting in touch with her again. I described my experiences and asked for her news. She replied a few days later – she was engaged! I was flabbergasted. With a tear in my eye, I wrote again to Ruth, wishing her and her fiancé, Connell, all the best for the future.

The winter term ended on a very high note for Inkerman Company, for we won the Sovereign's Company competition. We accordingly changed our Old College red lanyards to the multicoloured lanyards of the Sovereign's Company and provided the bearer and escorts of the Sovereign's Colour before Field-Marshall Earl Alexander of Tunis, KG, GCB, GCMG, CSI, DSO, MC, DCL, LLD, the Queen's representative at the Sovereign's Parade held on 11 February 1954. Lord, P.T. de la P. Beresford was presented with the Sword of Honour though four other cadets were higher in the order of merit. He was commissioned into the Royal Horse Guards (The Blues). In 1957 he was headline news because of his increasing friendship with senior members of the royal family, particularly Princess Margaret (no longer attached to Group Captain Peter Townsend) and the Duke of Edinburgh (shared polo interest). The relationship with Princess Margaret appeared to be at its highest at Royal Ascot that year when they were together in the royal procession. However, he declared that the army was his career and that talk of a royal romance was "ridiculous … utter rot". He ended a distinguished though not outstanding military career as a major in a squadron of 22 Special Air Service (SAS) in 1965. Sadly, he died of cancer on 18th March 2020, aged 85. Obituaries confirm that he remained close to the royal family throughout his life, inviting the Queen and Prince Philip to his dinner parties. Also, the winner of 50 point-to-points and National Hunt races and some of polo's biggest titles. THE TIMES refers to a gilded life and an admission of losing money at Lloyds, whilst the Daily Telegraph headlined his active service in Cyprus, playing polo with Prince Philip and leading Britain to equestrian glory.

During the ensuing leave break I met a very nice girl called Dorothy at Harrogate's Royal Hall ballroom, and she was soon invited to meet my grandparents.

My final term at Sandhurst began in April 1954.

It was no less demanding than the two preceding terms, but it was more enjoyable because, as a senior cadet, one was given more responsibility and freedom and a degree of respect. Provided I did not slacken off or do anything stupid, my commission was assured. I was not appointed an under officer, nor did I ever anticipate such rank, but I did captain the Old College cricket team on a couple of occasions. A popular under officer selection was that of my friend Azhar Khan Afif [AKA] of our company to be a JUO (junior under officer); the first overseas cadet to achieve under officer rank at Sandhurst. He was commissioned into the Guides Cavalry, one of the most renowned military units in the British Commonwealth (Wikipedia says 'the World'); formed in British India in 1846. I believe AKA may have been killed in the India-Pakistan frontier war of 1965.

We won the Sovereign's Company competition again – a rare achievement. I was pleased to make a more than useful contribution to this in the senior cadets' shooting competition. I was a decent enough shot, but excelled at the right time, producing one of the best scores of the day, which enabled us to take maximum points. My reward was to be an escort to the Sovereign's Colour on one occasion. However, it was to be a one off, possibly because of my slightly bow legs (childhood rickets?). Every dog has its day.

The end of my time at Sandhurst was now approaching. I had had an interview with Major Carey regarding my choice of regiment or corps, and finally opted for the Royal Corps of Signals. My choice was influenced by an interest in the military communications of the time and in the deployment of young Royal Signals officers and soldiers well forward on the battlefield, together with the opportunity it would provide to serve in many different parts of the world. My second choice became the Royal Artillery, which I could have comfortably achieved. I was to have a good career with Royal Signals, but in my later years I sometimes struggled with the rapidly evolving technical advancements. The Sovereign's Parade at which I was to receive my commission was held on 5 August 1954, with Field-Marshal The Viscount Montgomery of Alamein, KG, GCB, DSO representing Her Majesty the Queen. He gave a very stirring address on leadership, ending as follows:

> There is one more point. When the battle is fierce and hard, and conditions are almost unendurable, the British soldier fights on bravely. How is this? Not so much at that time for abstract reasons, of course. It is, rather, because he knows he can rely on his leaders

to dominate the events that surround him, and it is because he gains strength and courage from the presence of his comrades. Those two things, linked closely to his discipline, keep him firm in the battle, and I would recommend all of you to study leadership and comradeship in our Army. These two essentials are nourished by our regimental system. You must always defend this regimental system and must oppose all attempts to tamper with it, or to break it down. It is, in fact, the backbone of the British Army.

Now I would like to wish happiness and success to those of you who leave the Royal Military Academy today, and if some of you should have thought your qualities have not received due recognition here, and that you have not received the promotion you would have liked, I can tell you that I felt the same when I left Sandhurst. I was reduced to the ranks in my last term. I suppose I must have deserved such a shattering blow – I didn't think so myself at the time. But there is hope for everyone, and there is no hurry, and your time will come.

You can all be proud that you are going to command British soldiers – they are the finest all-round soldiers in the world; and if ever you have to lead them in battle you will find that they are staunch and tenacious when times are bad, that they are kind and gentle in victory, and that they are loyal to their leaders and their comrades at all times. And I would say this, that the British soldier is second to none in the annals of fighting men. See to it that you will prove worthy to command such men.

The Sword of Honour was presented by Field Marshal Montgomery to SUO B.L.G. Kenny of Dettingen Company of Old College, who was commissioned into the 4th Queen's Own Hussars. It was a historic moment, captured in the photograph facing page 59 of RMAS Journal "The Wish Stream Vol. 8 No. 2": Field Marshal Montgomery was NATO's Deputy Supreme Allied Commander Europe; the same appointment to which destiny would guide SUO B.L.G. Kenny [Brian Kenny] in later years. He was a hugely talented and popular recipient of the Sword. An Old Canfordian, he had excelled throughout his time at Sandhurst in both military and academic disciplines, whilst also being captain of 1st

X1 cricket, member of 1ˢᵗ X1 hockey, near fluent in German and French and enjoying skiing, golf and racing. We never served together, but were to meet again in Camberley eleven years later.

The parade ended with the senior intake slow marching behind the academy adjutant and his horse up the steps of the grand entrance of Old College to receive their commissions, and face whatever fate had in store for them.

I had invited my mother to attend my commissioning parade and I am glad that I did. She was obviously very proud, and I think it helped her to understand why I was so intent on making my own way in life.

I made many friends at Sandhurst, and no matter where I served thereafter, I invariably found myself meeting up again with at least one old friend from those wonderful Sandhurst days.

COMMUNICATIONS TRAINING

Following some leave, the young subalterns of Sandhurst intake 13 began their 'Special to Arm' training. I was one of twenty-four Royal Signals second lieutenants who reported to Catterick for their training in military communications skills and the use of the equipment of that period. While status might increase significantly with the Queen's Commission, pay did not. When I enlisted in December 1952 I was paid 7 shillings per day (7/– = 35p); on becoming an officer cadet it rose to 8/– and then to 9/6d in my senior term. Now, as a second lieutenant, I received 17/6d per day (88p), less than I had received for picking potatoes and other farm work two years earlier. Had I been able to buy a car (a new A30 Austin 7 cost £355), a gallon of petrol would have cost 4/6d, with a road tax of £12-10-0, while a pint of beer cost 1/3d. Of course, I received free accommodation and meals, but there were numerous mess bill overheads. I record these monetary statistics to make the point that young officers were attracted to the military career because of the lifestyle, travel, adventure and early responsibility, rather than for financial reward. The cost of mess bills and lifestyle in most cavalry and infantry regiments was such that a supplementary private income was necessary, and this was one of the factors that had prompted me to change my first choice of arm from Infantry to Royal Signals while at the academy.

"Part 1 Course" communications training at Catterick lasted about five months. Briefly, by the end of it we needed to be competent in the use of the radio, line and terminal equipment and their power supplies found within a division, have a very good standard of voice procedure and develop a morse code operating speed of at least 12 words per minute. We were taught sufficient electronics theory to be able to sensibly discuss circuit diagrams and faults with radio and line technicians. The theory of radio transmission and frequency allocation was also taught, as well as field cable laying, and we learnt to operate field telephone exchanges and became proficient in message-handling procedures, including low-level encryption/decryption for classified messages. We also had to learn to ride. After about two years in a regiment, gaining practical experience, Royal Signals officers returned to Catterick for a longer and more demanding "Part 2 course." Catterick was the home of the Royal Corps of Signals in those days, with three very large training regiments plus the School of Signals. National Service was at its peak, and the roads were dominated by squads of trainees rather than by traffic. The training was not all work and no play, however, and I enjoyed some good games of football, as well as ballroom dancing with Dorothy on Saturday evenings at the Royal Hall in Harrogate. She was a lovely girl, but she did not quite have that inspirational attraction that I sought. When I tried to break the relationship she was very distressed. On completion of the Catterick training there was a crash course at Ripon of about three weeks' duration to learn to drive up to 3-ton vehicles and ride a motorbike, followed by postings to our first regiments. My posting was to 18 Army Group Signal Regiment in Germany, reporting on 5 April 1955.

I constantly thought about Ruth Addy during my embarkation leave, an additional leave that was granted to a serviceman posted overseas, whether to Europe, the Middle East, the Far East or Africa. On 20 March I could contain myself no longer and wrote an appealing letter to her to ask if I might see her before I departed. We met in early April in Leeds at the junction of Briggate and Boar Lane during her lunch break from E.J. Arnold & Sons, a well-known schools supplier in Butterley

Street, Hunslet. I was, of course, five minutes early and caught sight of her first. It was the first time that I had seen Ruth since July 1950. I was overwhelmed at the sight of the beautiful, elegant, mature young woman walking towards me, dressed in a smart charcoal grey suit. We only had time for a quick coffee, for Ruth had just a short time away from work. However, it was sufficient for both of us to realise that something special had happened and that we could not just walk away from each other. I escorted Ruth back to Hunslet. We parted with a light hug, not knowing what the future might hold, but enthusiastically agreeing to write to each other. The following day I said goodbye to Dorothy, promising to write to her regularly, but thinking of someone else.

18 ARMY GROUP
SIGNAL REGIMENT

April 1955 - October 1955

My route to Germany was by rail to Harwich and then by the military ferry to the Hook of Holland. There were two military trains awaiting the ferry at the Hook of Holland quayside, one for military bases in north-west Germany, and the other for Austria. This was the regular route for British occupation forces. It was run by the Royal Engineers, using chartered vessels and trains. As I relaxed in my seat, passing over the Neder Rijn at Arnhem and into North Rhine-Westphalia I reflected not only on my meeting with Ruth, but also on the bitter fighting that had occurred in the area I was passing through only a decade earlier. Much evidence of the war remained, particularly when the train entered the Ruhr valley and stopped at Essen, the location of the Krupp steel works and the focal point of German industrial might prior to 'carpet bombing' by the Allied air forces. The Krupp arms plant spread over 800 acres at that time and in the spring of 1943 Essen became the hardest hit town in the world. A *Daily Telegraph* front-page headline reported a particularly savage raid on 29 May 1943 as follows:

ESSEN SWAMPED BY 10 WAVES OF ATTACKERS

...

KRUPP CITY'S BIGGEST RAID OF YEAR

...

FIRES WELDED INTO SOLID MASS

...

4,000 and 8,000 POUNDERS IN
50-MINUTE BATTERING

...

FOR 50 MINUTES early yesterday morning, 10 consecutive waves of RAF bombers swamped Essen, the hardest hit town in the world, in the heaviest raid it has had this year.

Many of our crews reported explosions too big to have been caused by the bursts of the 4,000 lb bombs – which were dropped in large numbers – or even of the 8,000 pounders which were also in the load, said the Air Ministry last night....

Of the large number of planes employed , 23 failed to return. These losses are appreciably lower than was expected. The machines which pounded Essen yesterday were slightly fewer than those used in the 2,000-ton raids on Dortmund and Dusseldorf earlier this week. On this basis at least 50 bombers could have been employed in each wave. About 1,000 tons of bombs were dropped.

Meeanee Barracks, in the Kray District of Essen, was to be my home for the next two years. It was directly opposite a large and very dirty coal mine.

The role of the regiment was essentially to complement Bundespost communications circuits linking 18 Army Group Headquarters with the 1st British Corps and 1st Netherlands Corps in the event of hostilities between NATO and the Soviet Union, in an assumed nuclear environment. These communications would be provided by high-frequency radio, multi pair armoured cable (stecker) patching and radio relay, together with associated terminal equipment. The officers' mess was pleasant but not particularly large, so some room sharing was necessary. I found myself sharing a room with Peter Bullard, who had been on the same courses as myself at Catterick and Ripon. We had arrived at the start of the Easter weekend, so there was ample time to settle in. I soon met the other living-in members of the mess, all of them very friendly, but established an early friendship with Geoffrey Newton, who was one year my senior. He told me that a consignment of brand new US Army AN/TRC radio relay equipment had arrived some three weeks previously to enable two radio relay troops to be formed, already numbered 4 and 5 Light Radio Relay Troops. He had been given one, but it was not known who would be given the second. However, rumour had it that it might be myself. These two troops would be the first in the British Army, the equipment hardly heard of in Catterick. Geoffrey loaned me a user's manual and introduced me to duty-free gin and orange as we sat talking well into the night about the equipment and its possibilities and life in the regiment. I wrote to Ruth the day after I arrived, describing my first impressions, and asked her to write to me soon.

When the Easter break ended I reported to the adjutant prior to being interviewed by the commanding officer; Lieutenant Colonel J.D. Elliott. He asked me all the routine questions that COs ask newly joined subalterns, then whether I enjoyed Scottish dancing. He seemed rather disappointed with my negative response, and then asked what I knew about radio relay. I told him what I had learned from Geoffrey Newton and the user manual over the Easter holiday and he said, 'Well, that's as much as anyone else knows in my regiment, so you had better take command of 5 Light Radio Relay Troop.'

I reported to my squadron commander, Major R.E.D. Matthews. He told me that at the moment 5 Light Radio Relay Troop only consisted of myself, a sergeant, three soldiers and a lot of equipment in the quartermaster's stores. However, it was intended that it should be brought up to its full establishment within the next four weeks, with the vehicles and some German civilian drivers arriving the following week. The challenge was to have it fully operational in time for an important exercise in the early autumn. I then went to see the quartermaster, Captain Nick Carter, and we started to work out a plan for the handover/ takeover of the equipment and vehicles.

On 20 April I received a letter from Ruth, which I opened with much trepidation, wondering if it was a 'Dear John' letter. To my relief, it was not, and I replied by return of post as follows:

Dear Ruth,

Thank you so much for your letter, which I received this lunchtime. I am delighted to hear from you. I'm afraid I'm going to 'talk shop' a great deal in this letter, but seeing I've done almost nothing but <u>work</u> since Easter I think you'll understand.

I've been placed in charge of a radio relay troop which, when we're at full strength will consist of 50 men and 20 vehicles. I've already got the vehicles; brand new Austin 1 tonners, plus jeeps for myself and my two Sergeants. The (radio relay) equipment is also brand new and as it's American Army stuff you can guess that it is pretty good. By the time we get everything I'll have signed for about thirty thousand pounds worth of equipment. Though it's extremely hard work and I rarely get to bed before midnight, I'm enjoying every minute of it – I suppose that's only natural really, for this is the first really responsible job I've had after 2¼ years training. I only hope it stays that way and that my keenness won't wear off as soon as the novelty of my job disappears.

Last Saturday night I was invited to supper by the wife of a Major Warner who is second in command of my Squadron. All the officers' married quarters that I've seen are very nice, but his house was undoubtedly the best. The Army even provides a couple of German maids, though he has to share them with some of the other officers (don't take that the wrong way). Also there were the Colonel and his wife and three more officers and their wives. Major Warner's wife was an ideal hostess and a very charming person altogether. The Colonel's wife was rather highbrow and too fond of her own conversation, but I suppose most Colonels' wives are like that. It was a most enjoyable evening and I shall remember the meal with watering lips for a long time to come.

On Thursday I was given the job of going to Mulheim to draw officers' cash requirements, petrol coupons, change currencies etc. It was a tricky task dealing with British Armed Forces Sterling Vouchers and Deutsche Marks (DM12 = £1-00-6d). On Monday I found myself as Orderly Officer, which entails doing a lot of boring random checks and turning the guard out at least once in the middle of the night. The only 'event' was dealing with a soldier, who had been absent without leave, giving himself up. Of course, he would have to give himself up just as I was getting into bed. I had to dress again and place him in close arrest. I'd just got off to sleep when a driver woke me up to get his work ticket signed as he needed to take a recovery vehicle out to bring in a truck that had been involved in a smash. Two hours later the alarm clock woke me to turn out the guard.

I've seen a few pretty girls in Essen but, as I believe I told you, I'm staying on the straight and narrow. Bold words after being here for only a fortnight. One thing I can quite honestly say, I haven't seen a girl over here who is a patch on the beautiful young lady I had lunch with on the fifth day of this month. We should get on well together with all this flattery passing between us across the Channel.

There isn't really much to tell you about Dorothy, except that I think a great deal of her, though I don't love her. I hate doing it but I shall have to ask her to pack it up before I come on leave. The reason that I won't do it immediately is that I don't want her to think that I was using her as a convenience whilst I was on my embarkation leave, which is what she would think as we saw each other frequently during that period. I've told you what happened when I told her that I wanted to pack it up. I feel angry with myself now for giving in to her argument that I might change my mind in the next couple of years.

I'm glad that I have got so much work over here to keep my mind occupied, otherwise I would find living over here twice as hard, in that the girl I love is 400 miles away and engaged to another man. Even so, I often find myself thinking of you before I drop off to sleep and thinking how wonderful life would be if I was in Connell's place as your fiancé. I know you have had a tough time Ruth and I think you know me sufficiently well to believe me when I say that every word that I write is the truth. I feel so helpless over here and there's nothing I can do about it except tell you how much you mean to me. I've always looked upon engagements as very sacred things and always have a guilty feeling when I write to you – that's what stops me from pouring out my thoughts. I'm glad you wrote that little bit about 'playing the game' and I quite agree with you that because you've been shabbily treated is no excuse for treating someone else the same way. However, Ruth, the stumps have not been drawn yet and I shall endeavour to play the right stroke to the right ball.

Cheerio for now

Hamish

We exchanged letters at approximately weekly intervals, describing what we were doing. I confirmed my feelings for Ruth in each letter, but I did not increase the pressure on her – the ball was in her court. Early in May, I bit the bullet and wrote to Dorothy, advising her as gently as I could that

I wished to end our relationship and I wished her well for the future. I really meant it and it hurt me enormously. I told Ruth in my next letter to her.

Developing my radio relay troop was very hard work and very exciting. Gradually, the strength of the troop was brought up to its full complement and I was delighted to receive some high-calibre National Service radio and terminal equipment technicians who had been employed and trained by the telecommunications section of the General Post Office (GPO); Corporals Haslam, Shipperbottom and Pollard springing to mind. At that time the GPO was not only responsible for the state postal system, but also for all forms of electronic communication; telegraph, telephone and radio. However, they eventually chose to return to the GPO on the completion of their two years of National Service. Had they elected to transfer to the regular army they would have been likely to progress to becoming Foremen of Signals and then Technical Officers Telecommunications (TOT's), with opportunity to progress to Major and Lieutenant Colonel rank.

I worked very closely with Geoffrey Newton. There was much rivalry between our two troops, but we shared both our successes and our failures, and the two of us became very good friends. We were fortunate to have superiors who gave us support when needed, but who trusted us to get on with the task. Nevertheless, the importance of a demonstration exercise in which we were to be involved in July, together with 1 Heavy Radio Relay Troop, was made quite clear to us.

Briefly, my troop and that of Geoffrey Newton each had a theoretical capability of providing a 100 to 150-mile radio relay link with a bandwidth that enabled a quality engineering channel plus four other (carrier) channels to be utilised. Each of these carrier channels could carry an additional voice and four teleprinter channels. While the radio relay equipment was brand new, the carrier equipment was old GPO equipment that had been designed for static use, not the mobile use that was now required of it. It was well past its 'best before date'. The AN/TRC radio equipment was crystal-controlled VHF (very high frequency) in the 70 to 105 megacycles range. The Heavy Radio Relay Troop, commanded by another good friend, John Atkinson, had brand new German equipment and operated on much higher frequencies. This Pintsch equipment had just been received from the manufacturers in Lindau, adjacent to Lake Constance on the Austrian border, and it was designed to provide no less than 60 channels. It was pioneering military communications work at that time.

Geoffrey, John and I spent many hours with 1:50,000 maps spread across the officers' mess billiards table, drawing cross sections between different high points in Westphalia on graph paper that incorporated the earth's curvature. Then we would recce the locations for access feasibility. The Pintsch equipment required absolute line of sight between stations, aided by 50-foot masts, but some liberty could be taken with the AN/TRC equipment because of its lower frequency. We had numerous vehicles with winches and became adept at anchoring onto strong trees and then winching ourselves into position when necessary. The Allied forces were still an occupying power at that time [though this was soon to end] and we were able to go virtually wherever we wanted. Nevertheless, we acted responsibly, liaising sensibly with the local farmers and foresters whenever possible. In turn they would sometimes help us with a tractor if we became stuck in soft ground. Geoffrey and I set our troops a target of having the engineering channel of a radio relay chain established within an hour of the last vehicle being in position. We worked all hours, and most weekends.

Responsibilities of the officers of the regiment to their soldiers were continuous – 24 hours per day. We ensured that there was plenty of sport and social activity to occupy their spare time. I regularly played at troop, squadron and regimental level at both football and cricket. As the majority of our soldiers were National Servicemen there were usually a few professionals in the regiment. The standard and the competitiveness were high. We also provided a very competent social service, helped by the wives. I had not been long in the regiment when [as orderly officer] I received a phone call one evening from the adjutant; Captain E.J. Hellier (later Major-General E.J. Hellier, CBE). He told me that there was a savage row going on in a married quarter, and that I was to sort it out. My orderly sergeant suggested that he accompanied me, but as it was a Saturday evening I felt that he would have plenty of work to deal with in barracks. It was not that there was a lack of discipline in the regiment – far from it. However, at that time the majority of our soldiers were National Servicemen, and we therefore received a cross section of British manhood – the good, the bad and the indifferent. There would usually be several demob parties going on at the weekend, and the demon drink was duty free. I was driven to the married-quarters area by the duty driver, who gave me a sympathetic look as I got out. It was quiet, but the number of faces peering around neighbouring curtains indicated to me that more drama was anticipated. The husband, a dishevelled-looking senior corporal, answered the door and showed me to the sitting room, which was in a similar mess to him. I asked if his wife might join us, and he returned with her.

I got a glimmer of a smile when I said, 'You know, I haven't got much experience of this sort of thing.' I asked them what advice their parents would be giving if they were here. By the time they had completed their replies there were tears in their eyes. She got up to make a cup of tea and he said, 'No, I'll do that.' When he returned, she went out to the kitchen and returned with a rather nice sponge cake. They agreed that their quarrel had started two hours ago. I suggested that they wound the hands of their clock back two hours and instead of quarrelling pondered over their parents' advice, and left. My report would be routinely studied by the adjutant and CO and immediately passed to the corporal's squadron commander, whose wife, or the troop commander's wife, would visit the couple. Every effort would be made to help. The CO's wife would be aware of what was going on and would discuss any very difficult cases with her husband. It was a brilliant, unpaid social service run by the officers' wives. I met the corporal and his wife at a social function in the Corporals' Club a few weeks later. They had not only taken my advice and turned the clock back two hours, but now whenever discord seemed to be developing one of them would say, 'Stop. Let's put the clock back five minutes.'

The duty driver car in which I was driven to the married quarter was a Volkswagen Beetle, virtually unchanged from the pre WW2 model that Hitler had commissioned Ferdinand Porsche to design for the working class of his country. They were produced in vast numbers in the late 1930s at Wolfsburg, 45 miles east of Hanover. During WW2 the factory switched to the manufacture of military equipment and was subjected to Allied bombing. At the end of the war the badly damaged factory was deemed surplus to the post-war level of industry by the Allied forces and was scheduled for dismantling. However, in June 1945 a unit of the Royal Electrical and Mechanical Engineers (REME) was operating in the bombed-out factory, repairing military vehicles, and within a few months two REME officers [Major I Hurst and Colonel MA McEvoy] recognised how beneficial VW Beetles could be to the occupying forces. They found and restored an old dilapidated Beetle, sprayed it in military green, and displayed it at the nearby Headquarters 21 Army Group in Bad Oeynhausen (subsequently Headquarters British Army of the Rhine, located in Rheindalen). It was not long before an order was placed for 20,000 and half of that number had been produced by October 1946. Significant numbers of these brilliantly designed little cars with their rear air-cooled engines were still in British military use in 1955, including several in the regiment.

Ruth continued to give no hint as to how her mind was working in regard to our relationship, except that she did mention that her mother had quarrelled with Connell, and she began to ask about other members of my family. I used my grandfather's favourite collective description of my Victorian great aunts in Harrogate – 'the antiques' – and told her of Herbert, as well as of my half-brother (Frank) and half-sister (Jennifer), who would have been aged 14 and 4 respectively at that time, but I did not mention my 'pedigree' because I thought that she was already well aware of it. Ruth had assumed that I was brought up by my grandparents because my father had died. When she did learn the true situation, it was of no consequence to her whatsoever. We continued to write very correct letters to each other, but I made sure that she was in no doubt that there was no wavering in my deep affection for her. On about 10 June I received a surprise package in the post, bearing a Leeds postmark.

It contained a small book; 'A Background Anthology of English Poetry' by D Prothero and JW Roche, published by EJ Arnold & Son Ltd. Written inside the cover: *'Kindest Regards from Ruth – June 6th 1955'*. I was delighted.

How romantic if I had responded with the 1666 lyric of English playwright Ben Jonson:

> *Drink to me only with thine eyes,*
> *And I will pledge with mine;*
> *Or leave a kiss within the cup,*
> *And I'll not ask for wine.*
> *The thirst that from the soul doth rise*
> *Doth ask a drink divine;*
> *But might I of Jove's nectar sup,*
> *I would not change for thine.*

However, though I was familiar with the lyric, the precise words were neither in my memory or kit bag, and Ruth was still engaged!

The anteroom is usually the social focal point of an officers' mess. Ours was typical; it was comfortable and reasonably spacious, with a small enclosed bar in one corner, attended by a German waitress, whose stock included such necessities as stamps, laces, razor blades, toothpaste etc. There were no cash payments; one signed a payment chit, the total of which appeared on a monthly mess bill. In a prominent position in the anteroom was a quality German 78 rpm record player cabinet which was generally in use in the evening, most selections being classical. We were spoilt for choice in Essen's music shops and I soon became an enthusiast. My favourites were Beethhoven's fifth symphony [dit– dit– dit-dah], his fifth piano concerto [The Emperor] and Dvorak's ninth symphony [From the New World]. For a change I would turn to Doris Day, but I did not catch up with Elvis Presley until much later.

The very important July exercise grew closer. We learned that it was intended to demonstrate the capabilities of trunk radio relay communications to Commander Northern Army Group (General Sir

Richard Gale) and his staff and senior officers of the Netherlands and Belgium armies. It was rumoured that if it proved successful a further exercise would be held in the autumn, to which prospective British contractors would be invited. If that was also successful, a trunk radio relay regiment was likely to be formed and the Ministry of Defence would issue a 'staff requirement' to the communications industry for a future area communications system.

We must have deployed to our exercise locations on about 21 July, and we soon had numerous problems. The most serious was interference, not only between the frequencies that we had been allocated but also from some very powerful German and Dutch commercial stations. As our frequencies were crystal controlled and we only had a limited number of crystals to choose from, these problems were serious. The problems were overcome with less than an hour to spare before Commander Northern Army Group and his senior staff officers arrived. The quality of the circuits, on which a few dozen voice and teleprinter circuits were now operating over long distances, was superb. We were all very tired by our efforts, not least from the lack of sleep, but everyone was elated and there was much back slapping and celebration. The timely delivery of the vital crystals was largely attributable to a "gelber Engel/yellow angel"; the nickname for a patrolman of the ADAC (Germany's equivalent of a British AA patrolman with motorbike-sidecar combination). I was travelling at speed in my jeep with the crystals box in my pocket when we broke down, 15 miles short of my destination and on a quiet country lane. I left my driver with the jeep, intent on completing the journey by speed walking and hitch-hiking. I was lucky; after about half an hour, an English speaking "gelber Engel" stopped and told me to sit on top of his sidecar tool box and to "hold-on tight". We bounced into Headquarters Northern Army Group in a cloud of dust and a bemused Technical Officer Telecommunications (TOT) Captain Douggie Crookes whisked me into the communications centre. A very pleased patrolman, with a few bottles of 'duty-free' and many cigarettes in his sidecar, returned to my kaputtes jeep and its patient driver, together with a REME mechanic. They soon had it repaired.

We returned to Essen late on 28 July and I was delighted to find several letters from Ruth awaiting me. One letter advised me that she had broken off her engagement to Connell, while the others reflected her concern that I had not replied. I wrote to Ruth by return of post, explaining the circumstances and confirming my continued adoration of her.

Our subsequent correspondence grew increasingly amorous, but it was probably no different to that of other couples who were head over heels in love with each other. We looked forward to my first leave, which would not be sanctioned until that important autumn exercise was completed. It was decided that following a few days in Yorkshire we would spend some time in London together, seeing the sights and a show, getting to know each other better and enjoying a well-earned rest. Suffice it to say that the autumn exercise was a huge success and a delighted BAOR Chief Signals Officer, Major General R.J. Moberly, OBE, authorised a troop insignia, which we proudly displayed on our vehicles. Despite some complications, due to the RHQ movements clerk making a nonsense of my travel dates on the strictly controlled military route, I was able to meet Ruth at Harrogate station on the evening of 7 October. It was exactly six months since I last saw her. I could not have wished for a better start to my military career, nor could I have wished for a more beautiful and charming young lady to introduce to my grandparents. It was not long before they absolutely adored her.

We covered most of London's attractions, but at a gentle pace, happy to let the stresses of life slowly ebb away. I particularly remember our seeing *The King and I* at the Theatre Royal, Drury Lane, as well as Regents Park Zoo and the Tower, and sitting on the Embankment watching the world and the Thames go by – so happy in each other's company.

When I arrived back in Essen on 30 October, a letter from Ruth awaited me. The enjoyment and happiness of that leave is reflected in my reply:

18 Army Group Signal Regiment
BAOR 4
Sunday 30th October 1955

Dear Ruth,

I've just got time to write you a few lines before I start unpacking and getting ready for Monday morning. First of all, darling, let me tell you that I love you just as much as I knew I would before I came on leave; you're the girl with whom I want to spend the rest of my life. It would be unbearable without you. You've made me so wonderfully happy and I feel like crying with delight, knowing that I've made you happy too. It was absolute hell leaving you. Yes, you can certainly rely on me to remain absolutely faithful and to write regularly – I'm head over heels in love with you and no other girl will interest me now.

Thank you for a wonderful leave, Ruth. Thank you for always looking so beautiful for me, for being so sweet and charming – in fact thank you for everything.

I'll write you a longer letter to-morrow night, but right now I must start to get myself organised.

All my love,
Hamish
XXXXXXXXXX

18 ARMY GROUP SIGNAL REGIMENT

November 1955 - July 1956

We now routinely wrote at least five letters a week to each other, describing what we were doing and reassuring each other of our affection. It was not long before we had decided on an approximate engagement date to look forward to – July 1956 – and at my request, Ruth opened a deposit account for our wedding costs at her Midland Bank, to which I sent at least £5 each month.

It was a very happy time, though very frustrating knowing that it would be January at best before I could obtain any further leave and see Ruth again. The Soviet threat was very real and NATO units had to maintain strict minimum strength levels throughout the year, including over Christmas. I had a wonderful girlfriend and a splendid, efficient troop of 50 soldiers of very high morale, which included a quite outstanding Troop Sergeant Long. He was on the final selection list to be a radio operator member of the 1955–58 Commonwealth Trans– Antarctic Expedition (CTAE), headed by Dr Vivian Fuchs.

Though no further exercises were scheduled, we would occasionally receive a scramble-type test named Exercise Quick Train. The regiment would receive an unexpected Northern Army Group (NORTHAG) message and its response would be monitored by NORTHAG observers. However, the greater part of the late autumn was taken up with individual training and upgrading, and also preparing for a formal administrative inspection by a senior officer and specialist inspection teams. In addition, Lieutenant Colonel Elliott would sharpen us up with his own unannounced inspections. These could be quite brutal, with negligent soldiers placed under immediate arrest. He descended on 5 Light Radio Relay Troop without notice on one bitterly cold morning in his overalls for an inspection of our vehicles and generators and left at the end of two hours with one word: 'Excellent'. The following week, seven drivers of another troop were arrested and charged with negligence following the negative conclusion of a similar unsolicited inspection, with the troop commander on the mat.

Christmas approached and Sergeant Long and I decided on who could be spared for Christmas leave. We also decided that in addition to the festivities that were being arranged at regimental and squadron level, our troop would have an additional party of its own in recognition of its fine work and winning the inter-troop football competition. It was at about the same time that Sergeant Long learned that he had not been selected for the Trans-Antarctic Expedition, but was runner-up. Nevertheless, it was a great tribute to an outstanding sergeant to have been so close to selection.

It was a very enjoyable Christmas, with many social events, plus generous invitations to join married officers and their wives in their homes. A particularly memorable event was a large officers' mess party at which the duty-free champagne and cocktails were liberally consumed. Several civic and other German dignitaries residing in the area of the Ruhr were invited, and I was one of two officers detailed to look after a German dignitary who had held high rank during World War II. I believe it was General Hans-Jurgen von Arnim, the commander of the 5th Panzer Army in North Africa. As the drink loosened our tongues we enjoyed a fascinating and most pleasant discussion on a variety of military matters, particularly desert warfare, and of course on the quality of our respective national football teams. I suspect that other military units had been directed to invite German dignitaries to similar functions, as part of a coordinated policy.

As soon as my Christmas commitments were over, my mind became focused on my imminent fortnight-long leave with Ruth in Yorkshire which began early in the new year, and on the pleasure of seeing my grandparents again.

It was lovely to see Ruth again. She was as beautiful and charming as ever. While we attended a few social events, we were happy just to be in each other's company. Ruth was not able to take any holiday from work as these days were being saved for our planned summer engagement holiday in Germany. Nevertheless, I would meet her from her workplace in Hunslet, so that we could be together for the maximum amount of time. Arrangements for the announcement of our engagement in July or August were confirmed, and we looked at rings in jewellery shops, particularly those displayed by Dysons in Leeds. I was delighted, and immediately accepted, when Ruth offered to give me a signet ring in return. The stage was set. All that was needed was for Ruth to select the ring, at about the price of my monthly pay, and for us to make the announcement.

I returned to the regiment to find everything in good order and my troop straining at the leash to get out into the countryside again. We needed to hone our skills, check that there were no encroachments onto our frequencies, check potential high-point radio sites for access, and train newcomers to the troop to our standards. One of the newcomers was a National Service driver with a notorious civil and military criminal record who was posted to the regiment from the Military Detention Centre at Colchester. I must have upset the adjutant on some matter, for he was directed to my troop. It took him a little time to settle, but not much longer than the norm. He became one of my best soldiers and one of the most popular and reliable members of the troop – a natural comedian and an excellent footballer. He caused no trouble and used his aggression to good effect in the regiment's and BAOR (British Army of the Rhine) boxing team.

Our first exercise of the year was to evaluate the suitability of my US Army VHF radio relay for communication between an RAF control centre and the Northern Army Group's anti-aircraft system, largely the responsibility of the Royal Artillery. I described it to Ruth as follows:

The exercise is going extremely well – everyone is surprised at the clarity of our circuits. Briefly, what we're doing is providing a 100 mile voice radio relay link (with additional teleprinter carrier channels superimposed) from the operations room at RAF Sundern to a Royal Artillery 'ack ack' control room near Ahlhorn. The RAF give a continuous commentary on aircraft positions which they plot by radar, whilst the operations room at this end (which also has radar) gives a running commentary to the 'ack ack' gun positions. It is most interesting to wander around the operations room – they have a huge map, covering the whole of Western Germany, and all aircraft in the vicinity are shown as little red lights.

My troop was later to receive the personal congratulations of a senior Royal Artillery officer.

The savings targets that I had set myself were proving to be realistic and I was able to conclude a letter to Ruth in early April as follows:

I'm proud of my saving last month, darling:

Income: £34-11-9
Expenditure:

£10-8-5	Mess Bill
£1-10-9	Spending Money
10-0	Book
£5-00-0	to sweetie pie (for our wedding ac.)
13-2	Royal Signals Association (mandatory)
£3-3-5	Monthly Life Insurance Premium
7-6	New Birth Certificate
£21-13-3	

i.e. a saving of £12-18-6, and considering my £5 to our joint account and my life insurance premium is also saving, I've really saved £21–1-11. I'm highly chuffed. xxx. The mess bill looks high, but it isn't really because I had to pay 12 shillings for mess maintenance, 1/6d for guests, £2-14-3 for food, 11/11d for laundry, 7/6d for batman, 5/6d towards an officer's wedding present, 1/– theatre, 4/– sports, 1/– barber, 5/– guest night and 1/– for a Scottish dancing evening – a total of £5-4-8. The remaining £5-3-9 was spent in the bar, but it includes not only drink and cigarettes, but sweets, razor blades, shaving cream, toothpaste, stamps, envelopes and writing paper, ink, laces etc. I'm trying to convince you that I'm not being extravagant!

I love you my angel and you've made me so happy.

All my love,

Hamish

xxxxxxxxx

PS. I have to take the Squadron out on a 9 mile run at 7-30 to–morrow morning.

I forgot to mention that it was in full battle order and that I had a football match in the afternoon.

The spring of 1956 was so vibrant and exciting for me, with a 'Darling Buds of May' atmosphere. My exultation and sheer zest for life were enhanced by my receiving a splendid top-grade annual report from my commanding officer. It began, 'A young officer who has made a most excellent start in the Army …' When Lieutenant Colonel Elliott handed it to me for my signature my confidence rose and I spontaneously took the opportunity of discussing my marital plans with him, seeking his approval. He readily gave it, with a twinkle in his eye, for I think he knew that I knew that he had married a brigadier's daughter at an age that was considered most inadvisable at the time – only 23 years. Tut tut! I learnt later that Major General R.J. Moberly OBE (CSO NORTHAG) had strongly endorsed the report, and I felt that my rather inconsistent Part 1 course performance had been more than neutralised.

We were out of barracks on a variety of exercises almost continuously during May and June and in many different areas of Westphalia and southern Holland. During one break I returned to Essen to find a letter from my grandfather telling me that my mother and her husband (Herbert) had split up. It was not a surprise, for she had told me that things were not going well in her marriage when I saw her during my last leave. I felt very angry that she was once again causing anguish to my grandparents and I shared my grandfather's sentiments and my own in my next letter to

Ruth:

> *They gave my mother every possible chance in life; a good education at a first rate boarding school, they spoilt her with large parties and in fact gave her everything she asked for. All her life she has 'sponged' on my Grandparents, continuously borrowing money when they could not afford it and never returning it – they sympathised with her when I was born and allowed her a fresh start in life by unofficially adopting me. Now she's rewarded them with more trouble in their old age and again they're helping her out at great inconvenience to themselves.*

The school that my mother attended was a Harrogate *private school* with boarding facilities. However, I think my mother travelled daily by train from the family home in Thorner. I omitted mentioning that in addition my mother would routinely sponge on her aunts. I felt very sorry for my half-brother Frank and my half-sister Jennifer, who I was to later learn was temporarily staying with my grandparents.

Our engagement and associated holiday was now fast approaching, with all the arrangements being discussed and decided by mail. It was impractical and too expensive to use the international telephone network – calls had to be booked in advance, were limited in duration, and could only be made from a rather distant building. I still have many of these letters and have not the heart to destroy them.

Ruth was more than happy with my holiday suggestions. She would travel overnight on Monday 16 July on the non-military Harwich to Hook of Holland ferry, and then by train to Essen, where I would meet her on the following afternoon. Following some sightseeing and a brief walk round the shopping centre, we would then drive to the extremely pleasant requisitioned house of my squadron commander and his wife for two nights. On 19 July we would set off in my borrowed car for a ten-day tour – Cologne, down the Rhine valley to Koblenz, then turning westwards along the Mosel valley to Trier and Luxembourg, through the Saar and back into the Rhine valley, on to the Black Forest, up the Necker valley to Heidelberg, returning on the autobahn via Frankfurt and Dusseldorf. The final night or two would be spent at another fine hiring – that of recently married good friend, Captain Godfrey Curl, and his wife, Valerie. Ruth would return to England by the same rail and ferry route.

We would set off on our holiday tour with an opal engagement ring, an engraved signet ring and sufficient Deutschmarks, tentage and army composite rations to enable us to either camp or stay in reasonable hotels according to taste and weather conditions.

There was one late change to these plans. I learned that my very good friend Lieutenant Geoffrey Newton was considering selling his 1937 Riley Adelphi, which had been laid up during World War II and only had 60,000 miles on the clock. We eventually shook hands on £90, paid over a five-month period. It proved to be a wonderful car. It was the top of the Riley range in 1937 and far superior to the post–World War II Rileys. I found that if I changed down to third gear at reasonably high revs it would give an ear-splitting backfire, due to a small exhaust hole. I became quite adept at producing this backfire to good effect in crowded German city centres.

Shortly before the holiday began I was delighted to learn from Ruth that she had again won the women's half-mile sprint walking race at the annual sports gala held at Roundhay Park, Leeds; this was the major athletics competition in the county at that time. I was also delighted to learn from Lieutenant Colonel Elliott that he wanted me to form the regiment's second Heavy Radio Relay Troop in the autumn – the equipment was currently being manufactured in Lindau, on Lake Constance, by the German Pintsch Electronics Company.

It was a truly magical time in my life. Ruth arrived at the Essen Hauptbahnhof exactly on time and, of course, looking as radiant and beautiful as ever.

18 ARMY GROUP SIGNAL REGIMENT

August 1956 - April 1957

We had a marvellous holiday and I selected a romantic moment to slip my fiancée's opal engagement ring on her finger and receive my signet ring. We saw some stunning countryside; the weather was perfect and our Riley gave us no problems. Ruth was particularly delighted with the warm reception that she was given by everyone she met. It seemed as though everyone wanted to meet her. There had only been one tiny upset; during a drive in the Black Forest, Ruth tried to bluff her way out of a map-reading error that she had made and this resulted in a very long and tiring journey, and she cried. However, kissing her better was delicious, and Ruth's map reading limitations eventually became a family joke.

On the last day of our engagement holiday, 26 July 1956, the President of Egypt (Colonel Nasser) nationalised the Suez Canal, and it was only a few days after I had returned to work that various highly classified warning orders were received in the regiment. One of these was that either Geoffrey Newton's 4 Light Radio Relay Troop or my 5 Light Radio Relay Troop would be required as part of a large British and French military force to seize the canal. Initially, Geoffrey's troop were the clear favourites because although I was now the same rank as Geoffrey as a full lieutenant, he and his troop were the senior. However, it became a close call and for several days the colonel kept us in suspense. We were both as keen as mustard to go, notwithstanding the fact that I was recently engaged, while, if Geoffrey went, his engagement arrangements would have to be cancelled. I advised Ruth on 4 August that I could be involved if there were any hostilities, and three days later I wrote to her:

> *My Darling Ruth,*
>
> *Please excuse this short note, I've been working non stop because of the Egyptian flap. Don't worry darling, for as things are at the moment I'm not going. However, for the past couple of days the Colonel has been deciding between Geoff and myself and he's got it, lucky devil. I would have loved to go, but at the same time I would have found it unbearable being away from you for so long xxx. It's a funny thing but both Geoff and I were as keen as mustard to go, even though it meant leaving so much behind. Geoffrey's leave is cancelled (i.e. no engagement) and he won't know when he's likely to see his prospective fiancée again. Yet, the chance of a bit of action takes first place. You'll never fully understand darling why this should be so – it must seem so unreasonable and inexplicable to you. When Geoff and I joined the Army this was what we joined for – sheer excitement and the chance (and privilege) of leading soldiers in action. It's something we've looked forward to ever since we joined up and is why I'm so envious of him and why he is so chuffed, despite a cancelled leave (his last was eight months ago). I'm head over heels in love with you darling and I can't describe how very much you mean to me, but do please try to understand me. However, I'm not going.*
>
> *All my love,*
> *Hamish*
> *xxxxxxxxxxxx*

By the end of August, Geoffrey and his 4 Light Radio Relay Troop were in Aldershot, where he was granted a 36-hour 'engagement leave'.

The outcome of the Suez crisis is now history. At first light on 5 November, better remembered for Guy Fawkes than for Prime Minister Anthony Eden, the 3rd Parachute Regiment made a parachute landing on El Gamil airfield on the west side of Port Said, where there was strong resistance, with French parachute landings covering their flank. On the following day the Royal Navy unleashed 40 and 42 Commando Royal Marines onto nearby beaches, in conjunction with a 45 Commando helicopter assault, and severely damaged Egyptian defences with their ships' guns. By the end of that day Port Said had been taken and it was estimated that the entire canal could be secured within another twenty–four hours. Brilliant. However, the political and associated financial pressure on Britain and France from the USA, and in particular from its president (World War II friend and allied commander, General Dwight D. Eisenhower*), was such that a ceasefire was ordered at midnight. Britain and France were humiliated and shortly before Christmas began to withdraw their troops. I still cannot help thinking of Suez whenever I read or hear of our special relationship with the United States of America. It ended Britain's position as a super power.

*A letter to THE TIMES on 8 May 2019 describes Field Marshal Montgomery's opinion of President Eisenhower; an opinion that I shared at the time:

Monty's Manoeuvre

Sir, George Perry had a better reception than I did when I knocked on Field Marshal Montgomery's front door in 1969 (letter, May 7). I asked if he'd like to record a tribute to his wartime colleague General Eisenhower, who had just died.

"I loathed the man," he shouted and slammed the door. Sadly, our TV camera wasn't running at the time.

Bruce Parker
BBC South 1967-2003
Appleshaw, Hants.

The demands of the Suez conflict had necessitated the withdrawal of many units and soldiers from Germany, resulting in the cancellation of several of the exercises planned for that autumn. However, a very interesting and demanding exercise in Belgium survived, with much of the time spent at a 1,700-feet-high location near Rotgen on the Siegfried Line. We were within the clouds – not good for hanging out the washing, as aspired by British troops in 1914.

Without any prompting from me, Ruth was regularly visiting my grandparents and was invited by my Victorian great aunts (the antiques) to visit them. She became very popular and my grandfather told me what I already knew – that I had 'a girl in a million'. My grandmother was admitted to hospital at this time for an operation on her troublesome varicose veins and Ruth visited her with my grandfather on a number of occasions. I became increasingly amazed at her vitality, stamina and diverse abilities – full-time employment in Leeds, regular hockey at a good level, amateur dramatics, riding, theatre-going, home decorating, cookery, dressmaking, knitting and sock darning – the latter a skill that few possess nowadays. The Army provided very high-quality grey socks that lasted well, but holes would appear eventually. Ruth had the skill and patience to repair them to traditional standards, and one could hardly see the darn. As the Army also provided its soldiers with clothing repair kits [called 'housewives'] I was able to provide Ruth with matching wool. She would precisely align the wool threads and pulled the darn so that it remained flat and unpuckered. She enthusiastically encouraged me to post socks requiring attention to her. Now that's love, isn't it?

I discussed with Ruth the feasibility of a wedding in the autumn of 1957. However, our ideas were dashed when I learnt that the start of my nine-month Part 2 course at Catterick had been delayed until September 1959 and that I was to be posted to 4th Infantry Division Signal Regiment in Herford, North Rhine-Westphalia, in four months' time. A wedding in the spring of 1958 now seemed the earliest option. Ruth was very disappointed. I told her that after my Part 2 course I would like an overseas posting, ideally to the Far East or Africa, and I was delighted that she shared my enthusiasm to see a bit of the world. I was pleased to be nominated for a two-week course at the School of Infantry at Warminster in early December, and this enabled me to meet Ruth in Harrogate on her birthday, followed by a fortnight's leave. We had a lovely first Christmas together.

I returned to Essen for a hectic three months in which to build up my new 2 Heavy Radio Relay Troop to operational standard, to be tested on a 14-day exercise beginning on 14 March. There were manufacturer delays, and it was not until the end of February that I was able to set off by train with a party of twenty of my troop for Lindau, on Lake Constance. It was a scenic journey, through the Rhine gorge, across the Swabian Alps and down to the lake, with the majestic Swiss Alps in the background.

The acceptance of the Pintsch radio relay equipment from the manufacturers was hard work, for the inventory was in German, and the clutch plates of most of our vehicles, into which the equipment had been fitted, had seized. However, it was not long before we were routinely referring to technical items in German. For example, 'grundgruppensetzers' and 'zweidrahtsetzers' instead of 'basic group modulators' and 'two-wire modulators'. I made sure that we had some time for sightseeing and I went with some of the Pintsch technicians into Austria and up a cable railway to about 3,000 feet, where we had lunch at a ski lodge. I had a very pleasant time at the Lindau casino in the evening, enjoying special hospitality in the manager's office. This came about because I knocked the scab off a hand injury at the roulette table, and the amount of blood that erupted was out of all proportion to the trivial wound. Once it was bandaged, I had a few drinks and some pleasant chat with the manager, who gave me some complimentary chips. I made a useful profit and used it to buy a nearly top-of-the-range alpine sleeping bag in Lindau the following day. This was a real luxury, for sleeping bags were not provided by the Army at that time and they were rather expensive. I put it to immediate use in the back of one of the vehicles for the one-night stop that we made during our 460-mile return journey to Essen.

I was very keen that my last exercise with 18 Army Group Signal Regiment should go well, and it did. I was dined out at a regimental dinner night, with my future commanding officer, Lieutenant Colonel T.H.C. Grigg, in attendance as a guest. He had not yet decided on my appointment within his regiment, but he told me that I was required to run a drill and duties course for potential NCOs and to give a current affairs talk at an officers' training day soon after I arrived. It was not difficult to pack my entire belongings, including two budgerigars, into the Riley. Subsequent moves would become increasingly difficult, for one begets oneself a wife and household things and the wife begets children and the children beget toys and things.

On Monday 1st April 1957 the BBC (Panorama) achieved the most popular and widely acclaimed April Fools' Day hoax ever; fooling thousands of its viewers with a dead-pan news announcement that thanks to a very mild winter and the virtual elimination of the dreaded spaghetti weevil, Swiss farmers were enjoying a bumper spaghetti crop. It accompanied the announcement with footage of Swiss peasants pulling strands of spaghetti down from the trees.

Two days later I waved goodbye to the smoky Ruhr and many good friends and headed north-east along the autobahn to 4 Infantry Division Signal Regiment at Herford.

11th INFANTRY BRIGADE

The first 15 weeks

I only spent three weeks at Herford before being sent on my way again, to what was regarded as a plum, but very demanding job – at a Brigade Signal Squadron. My destination was Minden on the river Weser, the headquarters of 11th Infantry Brigade. On arrival my squadron commander, Major Tom Foster, lost no time in making our role and my position crystal clear: our brigadier [Brigadier R.A. Fyffe OBE DSO MC (later Lieutenant-General Sir Richard Alan Fyffe KBE CB DSO MC)] commanded two infantry battalions and an armoured regiment, together with the command or support of sub-units of the Royal Artillery, the Royal Engineers, the Army Air Corps and various administrative units. In the event of hostilities breaking out between NATO and the Warsaw Pact countries, our brigade would be deployed in one of the foremost locations. Its task would be to briefly hold an element of the anticipated Soviet blitzkrieg-type advance on our front on a water obstacle (such as the Weser), thereby causing a bottleneck and presenting NATO with a potential tactical nuclear target. Our squadron's task is to provide Brigadier Fyffe with the communications that are needed to accomplish that containment task and to enable him to notify higher command of the nuclear or conventional strike option at precisely the correct moment. If we lose either his confidence, or that of his staff, we will be replaced in a couple of days – get it? … I hear that you are engaged to be married and that you play cricket …'

The brigade headquarters was based in the premises of a very inadequate old factory that had been hit by at least one bomb during the war, and never repaired. However, a new purpose-built barracks of very high quality was being built on the outskirts of the town, nearing completion. The officer's mess was a requisitioned millionaire's house in a pleasant area, while the town centre was particularly attractive, with the East–West Mittelland Canal spectacularly crossing the north bound river Weser.

The officer from whom I took over as Major Tom Foster's deputy was Lieutenant Frank Edwards, who was returning to the UK for his Part 2 course at Catterick. Frank had done very well in the appointment and was most popular – clearly a hard act to follow. Within a couple of days I was out on a three-day exercise, and although it was hard work I enjoyed it. I particularly liked the close, relatively informal working relationship with the brigadier and his staff. I was encouraged to be in his armoured command vehicle whenever I wished so that I could anticipate requirements without the need for instructions. No sooner had we tidied up at the end of the exercise than we were out on another – this time for a week, in the hills above Hamelin to which the Pied Piper had lured the children of the town. A few days back in barracks were followed by a nine-day exercise, part of the time close to Belsen concentration camp, but with no time to visit.

When I got back to Minden I was delighted to find a pile of mail from Ruth awaiting me, although the later letters expressed increasing concern that she had not had any mail from me. I realised that I had not made it clear to her that these 'sharp end' exercises were intended to simulate, as far as possible, actual combat conditions. One was on the go continuously, snatching the occasional nap in one's combat kit beneath a vehicle or trailer, or in a barn if possible, while 36–48 hours without even a nap was not abnormal. There was no mail facility and no time to write letters, even to the most wonderful girl in the world. The few days between exercises were also quite hectic.

The brigadier had decided that his headquarters would provide a team in the Nijmegen Marches Festival in July and selected his intelligence officer, Captain John Speller of the Dorset Regiment, to lead it, with myself as his deputy. These marches were an international event of some stature – the largest in the world. Captain John Speller was one of those characters who responded to any challenge in life with the expression, "Jolly good; what fun!", no matter whether it was to take a fighting patrol deep into enemy territory or an 11th Infantry Brigade team to the Nijmegan international marches. He worked us hard, very hard; a tricycle refreshment contraption was designed by our REME detachment and a craftsman-rider appointed to join in the fun. There were four marches on consecutive days, each of twenty-five miles. Military teams were required to participate in battle order, with each team member carrying at least 40lbs and their personal weapon. As an officer's pistol is much lighter than a Lee-Enfield rifle, John decided that we would all carry rifles. Whenever we were not on an exercise we needed to train early each morning, prior to the normal day's work, for failure or inability to march in on the last day in style before thousands of spectators would be a disgrace. There were a few blisters during the early training, but it was not long before we were able to cover twelve miles at a good, non-stop pace before breakfast, and without any blisters. Most of our training was along the busy Mittelland Canal, where there was also an abundance of interesting wildlife.

I told Ruth that there would be no difficulty in my getting ten days' leave from 14 August, and we agreed that it would be nice to spend it together in modest hotels and Gastattes in the Harz Mountains, with me meeting her at Hannover Airport. The lead-up to that leave was rather daunting, however, with every day between 15 July and 10 August taken up with either an exercise or the actual Nijmegen marches.

Much as I was enjoying the hectic routine of serving in the 11th Infantry Brigade, it was very frustrating being so close to a wedding and yet not being able to make even tentative plans because the date depended on the availability of military accommodation and the vagaries of military commitments. I regularly talked to the helpful station staff officer who controlled the allocation of married quarters (according to a strict military points system), keeping Ruth informed as best I could. However, it must have been so exasperating to her at times because of our inability to communicate for lengthy periods, even by letter. The best that we could hope for was a wedding in January or March 1958.

I had command of the squadron for a brief period in June and was part of a group that attended a briefing and demonstration on the capabilities of the Corporal missile, including its live firing. I was very thoughtful and subdued as I left the firing range, for during exercises I had listened to our brigadier reporting the identification of a suitable target for the firing of the missile, which could be fitted with a 'small', but devastating, nuclear warhead, referred to as a tactical nuclear weapon. It was a heavy responsibility of our squadron to provide the all– important communications that would be required in a war situation. They were very uncertain times. The numerical superiority of the Soviet and Warsaw Pact forces had reached such a level that a very concerned Supreme Allied Commander Europe was calling for thirty additional divisions to augment NATO's Central European Front. I was to learn later that NATO had some 7,000 tactical nuclear weapons deployed in Europe. The brigade now had a new commander; Brigadier R.E.T. St John MC (later Major-General Roger Ellis Tudor St John CB MC). He was commissioned from Sandhurst into the Royal Northumberland Fusiliers.

The 11th Infantry Brigade worked hard, but when there was some respite, it also played hard. There were several dinner and cocktail parties and other social occasions, sometimes in conjunction with a parade or ceremony such as a Beating Retreat by one of the regiments, to which civic dignitaries and high-ranking officers were invited. Sporting events were held and I played some cricket, but there was no respite from the Nijmegen marches training. My first cricket match was against the 7th Armoured Division Signal Regiment. We scored 284 and got them out for 133. My contribution was only 22 but I helped in a stand of 90 for the second wicket, so was not displeased. Five days later I was run out for 2 in a cup game against a superior team, but we managed to win by a few runs. A couple of days later I played for the 4th Infantry Division Signal Regiment in a cup match that we won, scoring 68 not out.

I was not able to take part in subsequent matches because of another exercise commitment, immediately followed by the Nijmegen marches. We were fit and well trained, and we enjoyed them. Not surprisingly, the British teams were very popular in the city and we received generous applause as we came in each day, very well placed in the pack. Our timings for the first three days were 6 hours 10 minutes, 6 hours 20 minutes and 6 hours 30 minutes. Brief refreshment stops were akin to motor racing pit stops and it became a challenge to take on elite teams, including Israeli special forces. We found ourselves arriving at the finish so early that most spectators had not arrived. It was accordingly decided that on the last day we would slow down, with longer refreshment stops. "Jolly good; what fun!".

There was no time to stay for the festivities, however – it was straight back to Minden for a nine-day exercise and then – sheer bliss – I met my beloved fiancée at Hannover Airport.

11th INFANTRY BRIGADE

It all turns sour

Ruth was as lovely as ever and we were overjoyed at being together again, while the countryside, though not the weather, was magnificent. It had been a long wait. However, towards the end of the holiday a rather serious tiff developed. It began shortly after our hotel breakfast as we prepared for a tour in the Riley. I was checking tyre pressures, oil, etc., with Ruth standing at my side, when she realised that she had left something in the hotel. I assumed that she would return to the hotel and collect it and continued with my checks. She did not, making it clear that she expected me to collect whatever it was, in a tone of voice that I had not experienced before. Perhaps this was the flashpoint of a series of matters that had occurred and irritated her. Without a word I went back into the hotel and collected the item. But Ruth's stance troubled me, and we did not have the enjoyable day to which we had looked forward. There were no harsh words, but neither of us made any attempt at the time to put the clock back, and the magic of our relationship had been tarnished. With only a few days of the holiday remaining we did our utmost to restore that magic, but with only partial success.

Ay me! for ought that I could ever read,
Could ever hear by tale or history,
The course of true love never did run smooth …
(Lysander to Hermia, *A Midsummer Night's Dream*, Act 1, Scene 1)

With the benefit of hindsight, I can see now that there were several contributory problems. First, the holiday began with us both exhausted by the intensity and pace of our lives during the preceding months; it had been a long wait and there were such high expectations. Second, Ruth was becoming concerned at Army requirements always having absolute priority and at the apparent long periods of separation that wives were expected to endure. Third, we were both strong– willed and independent. For example, Ruth made it clear that she supported topical and radical trends such as the word 'obey' being excluded from a bride's marriage vows, and she also stipulated that there should be no divorced guests (except for my mother). I was not really concerned whether 'obey' was in or out, as I would never expect my wife to obey, but I was rather surprised at Ruth's determination on such matters. Fourth, there may have been an element of selfishness in me that I needed to correct, but I wonder if Ruth was perhaps confusing selfishness with the fact that it was my duty to put my soldiers and military commitments first and that if I did not continue to do so, I would soon be out on my neck, with no civilian employment qualifications, no pension and no future. Last, but not least, was my belated full appreciation of the heavy responsibility of marriage – for from the moment that I said 'I will', I expected to be solely and totally responsible for providing for my wife and any children she bore, and responsibility was a personal quality that I did not lack.

I had a problem that will be familiar to many young officers who enlisted directly from school. At the time of enlistment one has school achievements and perceived abilities that are acceptable to a variety of potential employers and academic institutions, but after only a few years, one's 'civvy street' employability decreases exponentially. A U-turn for an engaged or married officer whose fiancée or wife develops misgivings about the military lifestyle becomes highly impractical unless there are parents or other relatives in a position to provide significant help, and we were clearly not in that category. The turmoil running through my mind was over whether Ruth was becoming disenchanted with me, with the Army, or with both. Was it merely a lovers' tiff, soon to be blown away in the autumn winds, or was it a warning of serious problems that we needed to address?

There were tears in our eyes as we hugged and kissed each other goodbye at Hannover Airport. I watched her plane take off and followed it until it was lost in the clouds. I returned to Minden and the demands of 11th Infantry Brigade with a very heavy heart and a lump in my throat. Things got worse before they got better, not helped by numerous exercises and some letters to Ruth being lost in the post. The crisis point was reached on Thursday 19 September:

My Darling Ruth,

First of all let me tell you why I didn't ring you to-night. You can only get through to England from either the Red Shield Club or a civilian extension on the army exchange, like that of Major Foster. I tried the Red Shield Club which was booked up, and requires five hours notice. I wasn't prepared to ask Major Foster or any of the other staff officers with this facility because they all have their phones in the living room and whilst no doubt they would have moved out they couldn't have failed to hear the 'shooting match'. You said quite sufficient in your letter, Ruth, and I'm quite sure that had I rung you I'd have said something that would have aggravated the position.

Let me make myself clear, I'm still in love with you Ruth, but I'm fed up to the teeth at the moment, as I know you are. All this is 70% my fault I know, and I'm sorry. I tried as best I could to explain myself in my last letter and I honestly can't add anything to that. Please be patient and let me straighten myself out, and don't write any [more] letters like that last one.

I've got so much work at the moment that I don't know what to do with myself. On Sunday we go on a weeks exercise into the American zone – the day after I get back I've got this Court Martial (as the Defending Officer of a Corporal in Dusseldorf) and as soon as that finishes I go straight out to join the Brigade for another exercise at Soltau. At the moment I'm working every night on Military Law, preparing our defence etc., whilst during the day I've got not only my own job but that of two Sargeants who are on leave as well. Imagine the administrative complexities of moving around some 70 soldiers and 20 vehicles for six weeks (we only have two days in barracks between now and the end of October) and maintaining the vital radio networks at the same time – I just cannot describe how much there is to do. I like the job but it's getting me down a shade at the moment. I love you darling, but to be quite honest I'm frightened of marriage after this upset. You see, I saw some of my mother's upsets and I know what hell a marriage can turn out to be. We're unfortunate in that we've spent so little time together and probably I've expected too much during those short leaves.

Are you still in love with me after all this, or have you had enough? All my love,

Hamish

xxxxxxxxxxxx

I STILL LOVE YOU

It was some time before I got a letter from Ruth, partly because of my being away from barracks on exercise. However, I did not take part in the training at Soltau as I became another victim of a flu epidemic, and was sent to bed for a couple of days with a high temperature. Eventually the virus infected such a high number in one of our battalions, the Sherwood Foresters Regiment, that the Soltau training had to be prematurely ended.

Slowly but surely, fences were mended, though several weeks passed before there was complete harmony and we returned to serious planning for our wedding. In late November I discussed the feasibility of an early March wedding with Major Tom Foster and he gave me every encouragement, including an assurance of four weeks' leave from late February 1958. On 29 November I had an interview at Herford with my commanding officer and wrote to Ruth the same evening:

My Darling Ruth,

The Colonel has given us his 'blessing', so to speak, and hopes we'll be very happy.

I've just written a letter to your mother, hoping that she will understand me a bit better, for I'm quite sure that she's been depressed because of our 'row'. I had already thought that in her anxiety she may have 'peeped' at one of my letters darling, but of course I would not have mentioned it had you not done so first. Even were I sure that she had, I would not bear her any malice, for she must feel very responsible for you and couldn't think of any other way of finding out what the hell was going on.

Darling, are you absolutely positive that you want to marry me? I suppose that I'm getting the last minute jitters, but for goodness sake do say so now, before it is too late. I haven't the slightest doubt of my love for you, bless you xxx.

I've written to my bank, asking if they will allow an overdraft up to £70 between 1st March and 1st July. We'll be able to pay it off once the initial expenditure is over.

All my love darling,

Hamish

xxxxxxxxxxxxx

Ruth replied without any hesitation and in welcome words. The stage was set for an early March 1958 wedding – the 8th of March, provided that the Church of All Saints at Thorp Arch was available. We both realised that we would not see each other until shortly before that date, not even at Christmas. It was now full steam ahead to make the arrangements.

11th INFANTRY BRIGADE

Wedding arrangements

Finance is an important consideration for most engaged couples. We had both assumed that we would have to pay all the wedding expenses ourselves, and we had been saving accordingly for more than two years. It was therefore a pleasant surprise to learn from Ruth's mother that she planned to pay for the reception at the Pax Inn, only half a mile from the church. Nevertheless, that very kind gesture would not change our modest wedding plans. Another pleasant surprise was to learn that the church's very good choir would be present.

I worked out that my monthly income after we were married would be a modest £58, after income tax and national insurance contributions had been deducted. If we had a married quarter (MQ) we would have to pay £11 per month for fuel and light and we estimated that we would need about £21 for food. I had monthly commitments for life insurance (£3) and a standing order to my tailor (£2), leaving us about £21 per month for everything else. Not a lot. If a married quarter was not immediately available there was a Plan B chance of us having some space in the cellar of the Minden Garrison officers' mess (a requisitioned casino with lovely grounds) for a few weeks. This was very basic accommodation that young officers and their wives were allowed to use on an unofficial basis while waiting for an

MQ to become available. It was sometimes referred to as 'the love nest'. Couples using it had in turn contributed some DIY work to improve it over the years. We would have the full use and benefit of the excellent mess facilities above us, on payment of course. If 'the love nest' did not become available, Plan C was for Ruth to return home at the end of the honeymoon for a short time until an MQ became available.

We agreed that Ruth's mother and my grandparents would take first place at the wedding. Ruth invited her uncle Charles MacKeith, a very prominent architect in Blackpool, to give her away, and I invited fellow officer Captain Frank Edwards to be my best man. I hoped to be able to arrive in Harrogate on 2 or 3 March. It was agreed that the wedding service would begin at 11 a.m., with arrival at the Pax Inn at 12.15 p.m., luncheon at 1 p.m. and bride and groom departure for Leeds Central Station at 2.15 p.m. in order to catch the *White Rose* that departed at 3.25 p.m., arriving at King's Cross at 7.42 p.m. We would spend two days in London, in the Craven Hotel, only 150 yards from Trafalgar Square, and then fly to Dusseldorf for the start of the honeymoon proper. I considered that it would be prudent to use a hired or borrowed car rather than the old Riley, for the itinerary included the High Alps. After a couple of days in Dusseldorf we planned to motor to Stuttgart for another two days, followed by three days in Lindau on Lake Constance and then the Alps, making the route up as we went along.

Ruth and I were in complete harmony again and I think we both enjoyed the coordination of the wedding arrangements and overcoming the various problems, despite the limitations of correspondence and military commitments. However, one of these 'commitments' was very pleasant. In early December I was required to take a group of about twenty soldiers to the Army's leave centre at Winterberg in Hochsauerland for a week's skiing instruction. Winterberg is a major German winter sports resort at a height of 2,100 feet, and our arrival coincided with the first major snowfall of the season. The accommodation was in a quality requisitioned hotel and the food and facilities were excellent, with a band playing at lunchtime. Ruth's mail was re-directed to Winterberg, so our wedding-arrangements correspondence was not interrupted. On 13 December 1957 I wrote as follows:

... I got a very nice letter from your mother this morning. She told me what a fine young lady you are etc. I'm head over heels in love with you darling and the more I think of you the more I realise how lucky I am. You really are the most wonderful girl in the world. Please don't stop being so sweet, patient, understanding and loving. I'll do anything for you Ruth, my angel, for I love you with all my heart. I can't wait to be with you again to show you how much I do love you and how sorry I am for our quarrel. Don't doubt my love for you. I think that row has done me a lot of good, certainly it made me realise that I just couldn't do without you. I feel such a cad now and I feel so frustrated because I can't take you in my arms and love you and tell you how sorry I am.

All my love darling,

Hamish

xxxxxxxxxxxxx

On 15 December 1957 I wrote:

My Darling Ruth,

I still haven't managed to break my neck, though I have had some uncomfortable falls. I've now got to the stage where I can do a mile run without falling off, though it's not too steep a descent. We have had a series of races and my best time for the mile is 2 mins 20 secs, so you can see we're just getting past the beginner's stage — it really is good fun. There's a bob sleigh run here, but the snow is not yet deep enough for it to be used.

How are the wedding preparations going? I suppose something is bound to go wrong. For example, if the plane to Dusseldorf is delayed a couple of days because of fog, or Aunt Peppy's taxi has a puncture etc. As soon as I get back to Minden I'll see Peter Whitehead about the car, for honeymoon arrangements hinge around it and I can't book the plane etc. until I get a definite 'yes' from him. If we couldn't get a car, we'd still go down to Austria by rail, same as Taffy and his wife did. Is there anything in particular you want me to do in arranging the honeymoon — any particular place that you want to go to? It should be really exciting at St. Anton at 4,500 feet (it's only 2,000 feet here at Winterberg. If it is like it was at Bregenz when

I was there it will be most impressive – you could see peaks up to 10,000 feet, stretching for miles …

All my love darling, Hamish xxxxxxxxxxxxxx

I don't think anyone in the headquarters was disappointed when an exercise just before Christmas had to be cancelled due to atrocious weather conditions, particularly as another was scheduled to begin very early in the new year. Though my mind was on our wedding, I used my initiative to arrange an interesting programme for our soldiers – skiffle group concert, film shows, six-a-side soccer, barrack-room decoration competition, etc. We had a very good skiffle group and it was selected to broadcast on the British Forces Network (BFN) on Boxing Day. Tom Foster and other married officers kindly invited me to their homes over the Christmas period, so I was never lonely. Wedding arrangements were progressing well and I respected and supported Ruth's firm stance over divorcees, even though it meant excluding my mother's new husband; Harry, a bus driver who, like my mother, was an employee of Leeds City Corporation.

Despite a rather uncomfortable and tiring three-day exercise in the slush and snow during the second week, January 1958 was one of the happiest months of my life as Ruth and I shared the excitement and challenges of planning our wedding, honeymoon and married life together, by courtesy of the Royal Mail.

On 25 January 1958 I wrote:

… I love you so very much Ruth, a much deeper feeling than I've ever felt before. I feel as though I've matured a lot since we planned a wedding date and the thought of you in my complete care, so to speak, has made a lot of difference to me mentally. It's difficult to explain, I've never felt like it before – the fairy tale dreams have been replaced by a feeling of fusion with you that I have never felt before and over all lies so much love that I'm confident that we're going to be so very happy …

The costs of our wedding and honeymoon were rising at an alarming rate and I wrote to Ruth:

I've sold my budgerigar and cage for 30/-, I'm doing my own washing (invested in large packet of Tide which washes whitest of all at 2/-), using Army writing paper, am smoking Players at 1/– instead of Benson and Hedges at 1/2d, have cut down drinking, stopped photography, have given up my 6d egg for tea, sit in cheaper seats at cinema and have got my lighter going to save cost of matches, all because I love thee, thou precious jewel … xxxxx

We had complete confidence in each other and no problem was too difficult for us to resolve. There was time for humour in our correspondence, despite the difficulties, and there was always the unexpected in Army life, including a bit of scandal:

The NAAFI manageress, who is not married, gave birth to a baby this morning in her office. She came in to her work as normal and then it happened, before she could call a doctor. She told the doctor that she didn't even know that she was pregnant.

Early in February our euphoric mood changed abruptly. My grandmother had not been well for some time, but on 5 February I received letters from both Ruth and my grandfather telling me that she was terminally ill (lung cancer). I was shattered and promptly confided in Major Tom Foster. The Armed Forces had a very efficient, fair and strict compassionate-leave procedure of which I was well aware, having helped many soldiers to return speedily to the UK. It was based on a police confirmation of the circumstances to the War Office, where there was a 24-hour duty staff. The War Office was the sole authority. My next of kin at that time was my grandfather, so I immediately changed it to my grandmother, to make me eligible for compassionate leave when her death was imminent. The family agreed without hesitation that the wedding arrangements were not to be changed, if only because my grandmother would have been devastated if any changes were made because of her condition. However, I advised Ruth to be prepared for changed honeymoon arrangements, possibly with little notice. We tried as best we could in our planning to cover every contingency.

On the following day (my birthday) the nucleus of what promised to be one of the greatest club teams in English football history was destroyed in the infamous crash of British European Airways flight 609 at Munich-Riem Airport: Manchester United's "Busby Babes". However, my thoughts were elsewhere.

On 16 February I received a letter from my grandfather advising me that he had been informed by the doctor that my grandmother had a week to two months to live and that she would pass away at the end within an hour. Everyone at Headquarters 11th Infantry Brigade was now aware of the situation and they were all very helpful, particularly Captain Cliff Frater and his wife, who offered to put us up at the end of our honeymoon for a while. This was a most helpful offer, for it now seemed likely that the so-called 'love nest' in the garrison officers' mess would become available at the beginning of April, thereby enabling Ruth to give notice to her employer.

My dear grandmother died suddenly on 26 February of bronchial carcinoma. I had not seen her for over a year and had been warned by Ruth to prepare for a shock when I did. Nevertheless, I was looking forward so very much to seeing her again. If only she could have lived for another four days I would have been able to do so. I was very upset. She was a mother to me and I recollect her motherly kindnesses and love. She was the person to whom I ran as a toddler when I had a nasty fall, the person who sat at my bedside when I was very seriously ill, the person who I teased by pulling her apron strings loose when she was baking, the person whose cigarettes I would sometimes hide and the person who I would like to be remembered by the motto *Tendo, tendo quod tendo iterum.* God bless her.

I returned to England on the military ferry route, arriving in Harrogate on Sunday 2 March 58. During the next five days I helped my Grandfather with the funeral arrangements for my Grandmother, which was to be held on 5 March, and Ruth in finalising the arrangements for our wedding on 8 March. I felt so sorry for Ruth – it was almost exactly three years since we had met again in Leeds, and during that time she had been with me for only three leave periods, amounting to a total of just seven weeks, patiently waiting for our wedding day. My grandfather was, of course, distraught, but maintained his dignity, and he made it clear that it would have been my grandmother's wish that our wedding should be one of enjoyment and celebration. Our guests responded tactfully, with best man Frank Edwards handling a difficult task superbly. I joined my guard of honour and other male friends for a traditional stag party in a Harrogate hotel on the eve of my wedding. Despite the circumstances, it was a very enjoyable evening. We knew each other so well and had shared so many experiences together, yet we had not seen each other for quite a long time.

Ruth looked so beautiful when I turned to see her walking down the aisle towards me on the arm of her uncle Charles, and so did her wedding dress, which she had made herself. The ring that I slipped on her finger was last worn by my grandfather's mother – a poignant moment for him, and I resisted the temptation of showing it to him on Ruth's hand until later, for I thought it might be too much for him. It was a wonderful wedding, as was the honeymoon that followed. Despite the numerous problems with which we had been presented, both went without a hitch. I felt that no matter what the future threw at us, we would 'overcome.'

After the ceremony, the luncheon and the speeches, we departed by taxi for the London-bound *White Rose* train from Leeds Central Station. It was a timeless, breathtaking journey in the taxi – I think I must have kissed Ruth virtually without pause. I had just married the most wonderful girl in the world. Several other newly married couples were on the train. When many more joined at Doncaster and subsequent stations the reason clicked – the Inland Revenue allowed newly-weds to retrospectively claim the married-couple rate of income tax from the start of the financial year. This tax allowance was very helpful to young couples.

As the *White Rose*, pulled by a streamlined (Sir Nigel Gresley designed) A4 engine, steamed towards King's Cross, Ruth told me that her uncle Charles McKeith had paid for the Pax Inn reception, a generous gesture by a wonderful gentleman and an outstanding architect. Among his many achievements he had designed the magnificent Blackpool Opera House

Theatre, one of the largest theatres in the country, with three thousand seats. Sadly, because of our subsequent overseas postings, I never got to know him, his wife Elsie, their son Gordon and his wife Margaret or their family as well as I would have wished. He was born in Crieff in 1898 and left school at the age of fourteen when the local architect asked his headmaster if he had a bright boy with a good hand. However, there was little or no work for the practice when World War I began and he enlisted at seventeen, subsequently serving with the Royal Garrison Artillery in Southern Ireland. After World War I he helped develop the practice into one of the most respected and proficient in the county.

This prompts me to record, as best I can, details of Ruth's younger days and of other members of her family.

RUTH'S PEDIGREE
& CHILDHOOD

Ruth was born on 15 December 1933 at The Close in the small village of Bewerley, which lies three-quarters of a mile to the south of Pateley Bridge in Nidderdale. Her father was Albert Leslie Addy, born 11 September 1901, who became headmaster of Pateley Bridge School in 1927 at the very young age of twenty-six. Her mother was Sarah Elizabeth Addy (née Bramham), usually called Bessie, who was born on 4 February 1900. She also became a school teacher. They met at Sheffield Teachers Training College, which formed part of the University of Sheffield, and married on 31 October 1925. Ruth's brother, Leslie, was born nine months later, on 2 August 1926. It is apparent from the attendance and tributes paid at Ruth's father's funeral that he was a man who had commanded huge respect in the communities of Pateley Bridge and Boston Spa, not only as the headteacher of their village schools, but also for his general service to those communities, particularly during World War II in the Royal Observer Corps and as a church warden.

Ruth's father was one of eleven children, though Dora only survived for 18 months. The family lived in Nab Lane, Mirfield, Calderdale and comprised her grandfather Frederick (Jan 1860 –10 Apr 1915, born in Mirfield), a master shoe and boot maker with his own business, and his wife Grace (née Hall), who was born in Dacre in 1863. Frederick and Grace were married at Christ Church in the parish of Battyeford on 6 May 1882. Their children were:

Oswald (1883)	Lillian (1885)
Dora (10 May 1888-11 Nov 1889)	Nellie (1891)
Gilbert (1893)	Rosella [Rosy] (1895)
Gracie (1897)	Darcy (1899-1984)
Albert Leslie (Sep 1901-Sep 1950)	Reginald (1904)
Frederick Basil (1906)	

Ruth told me that all the children were of well above average intelligence, and all were educated at Mirfield Grammar School. Nine went to university, six becoming school teachers. These were times when it was not easy for women to have a career, but two of the girls became headteachers. Ruth also told me that despite there being so many children, her grandparents were never poor; they owned their own property and ran a sound family business, Oswald eventually taking over the business. Ruth well remembered staying at Nab Lane with Nellie during part of the school summer holidays of one year in the early 1940s. Nellie, spent her life there, helping Grace in bringing up the family.

Frederick Addy's parents were Abel Addy, a farm labourer, who was born in Cumberworth (between Holmfirth and Denby Dale) in 1830, the eldest of seven siblings, and Ann (née Naylor) born in 1839. Abel Addy's father (Ruth's paternal gt.gt. grandfather) was John Addy (21 Dec 1804-Sep 1878), whose wife was also named Ann (née Shaw), born in 1806. They were married on 5 Aug 1827, living in Cumberworth. John Addy had a sister (Mary Addy) and her baptism on 25 Nov 1788 [West Yorkshire, Non-Conformist Records] provides the clue to identifying Ruth's paternal gt.gt.gt. grandparents; Abel Addy and Machell Addy, residing at 'Hoymorehaus' [High Moor House], Shepley (close to Cumberworth). Abel and Machell would have been likely to have been born circa 1765.

Coincidentally, Ruth's maternal ancestors (the Bramham family) can also be traced to Calderdale. They lived at Bankside, Southowram, near Halifax. It was here that Ruth's maternal great-grandfather, Robert Gregory Bramham, was born on 27 June 1841 to Mary Ann Bramham, wife of Benjamin Bramham. As an adult, Robert traded in Halifax as a grainer (creating desirable wood and marble effects), signwriter and general house decorator. His skills were passed on to his son, Walter Justin Bramham, who at the turn of the century moved from Halifax to Blackpool, where there was more demand for his specialist work. It was in Blackpool that he met and married Annie Elizabeth Jones who was born in Plowden in Shropshire. They progressed well in Blackpool, moving home several times and raising five children – Blanche (1897), Ernest Justin (1898), Ruth's mother, Sarah Elizabeth (1900), Olive (1901) and Elsie (1904). Twins, named Donald and Charles, died in infancy in 1912. Walter Justin Bramham must have joined the Army (Royal Horse Artillery) in the early years of World War I as he was awarded the 1914–15 Star in addition to the Victory and British War Medals. His Army number was 55923. He fought at the battles of the Somme, Passchendale and Hill 60 and survived the war.

Annie Elizabeth was apparently very conscious and proud of the family's improving position in the town. When times were hard, as they must have been during the war, it was her children who had to conduct the unwelcome and shameful visits to the pawn shop.

Though Ruth was born in Bewerley, the family soon moved to nearby Pateley Bridge, where Ruth had an idyllic childhood. Nidderdale is one of the most spectacular, unspoilt dales of Yorkshire and there were no boundaries in terms of where she and her brother Leslie and their many friends could roam, safe in a hard-working farming community. One of her closest friends was a farmer's daughter called Ann Summersgill, who attended our wedding. Ruth spent many happy days at the Summersgills' mixed farm on the bank of the river, exploring the farm buildings and observing the livestock, learning to understand the seasons, the weather, the natural dangers, the close traditional relationships between man and beast and how to prepare and cook good food, freshly harvested or slaughtered. Presumably, Ruth made good use of the village sweetshop (the oldest in the country), still selling the traditional sweets of early Victorian days, whilst her childhood love of books is apparent from four small and well-worn 1940 books still in my possession which accompanied her throughout her life: Ameliaranne and the Green Umbrella, Epaminondas And His Mammy's Umbrella, Epaminondas And The Eggs, Worzel Gummidge or The Scarecrow of Scatterbrook.

One needs to sit atop Guise Cliff crags, overlooking the Summersgills' farm and the river, especially in the spring, listening to the wind, the lambs, the curlews, lapwings and skylarks, to understand why Ruth was so passionate about her birthplace. The name of the farm was [and remains] Bewerley Hall Farm [GR 163645, postcode HG3 5JA]. It is no longer an active farm, but the grade 2 listed buildings are protected against change. It became, and may still be, a Bed and Breakfast business.

Ruth was very proud of being a Nidderdale girl.

OUR HONEYMOON

After the snow flurries of our wedding day it was beautiful springtime weather in London. We went to the popular tourist attractions, including the Regent's Park Zoo, and we briefly listened to a well-made argument at Hyde Park's Speaker's Corner, where free speech was guaranteed by act of parliament in 1872; a space where anyone can give vent to their thoughts, provided that they are within the constraints of the law. We kissed and cuddled and speculated on our future life and ambitions. It was wonderful. On the third day we flew to Dusseldorf, collected Peter Whitehead's Vedette and headed south for Stuttgart, then through the Swabian Jura for a restful three days on Lake Constance at Lindau, which I knew so well. On seeing its lighthouse, I was reminded of one of the telegrams from a fellow officer in Germany that was read out at our reception: 'Wait for the light to flash at Lindau.'

During the next fortnight we toured some of the most spectacular regions of the Alps, making up the tour on a day-to-day basis. These were the blissful days that preceded package tours and mass tourist incursion into these delightful areas. We would talk to our hotel or Gästehaus hosts on the options for the following day and they made some brilliant suggestions and gave us very sensible advice. Language was no problem, for there was usually someone at hand with a good knowledge of English, and if there was not, we had a reasonable usage of French. When we had made up our minds as to what we would like to do the next day, the proprietor would pick up the telephone and book our accommodation. I liked to show off my slight knowledge of German to Ruth, for her French was very much better than mine. On one occasion this spectacularly misfired when I ordered a particular schnitzel dish for her. Everyone within hearing distance howled with laughter, which continued for the next five minutes as the joke was relayed on to the more distant tables – I had asked for a Caesarean birth for my obvious new bride.

Our honeymoon ended in late March. As planned, we were accommodated by Captain Cliff Frater and his wife for a few days prior to moving into 'the love nest' in the Minden Garrison officers' mess. The Baby Belling cooker that Ruth had ordered had arrived and we took up residence. This accommodation was not ideal, but it suited us adequately. Ruth was made very welcome and it was not long before she was joining the coffee mornings and other social activities arranged by the wives of the garrison and exploring the town centre. If she did not feel like cooking we could take a meal in the mess upstairs, and we could make use of the bar and anteroom as we wished. The couple we took over from were Lieutenant Colin Shortis and his wife of the Dorset Regiment. They had enjoyed it so much that they had remained there for almost a year. Colin became a major general and director of infantry. Shortly after the end of our honeymoon we worked out our financial situation, virtually to the last penny, and it became a habit to do so at the end of each month throughout our life. Including the value of the Riley (£55) and the surrender value of my life insurance policy (say £60), we were at that point worth £168. This was a good habit for us as it meant there were no secrets and it helped us to plan sensibly, avoiding extravagance.

11th INFANTRY BRIGADE TO 2nd INFANTRY DIVISION SIGNAL REGIMENT

The pace and pressures of serving in Headquarters 11th Infantry Brigade had not changed and it was quite painful getting back into the swing of things. Ruth began to understand the complete military commitment of both soldiers and their wives and was always willing to contribute whenever she could. She soon realised why it had not been possible for me to send letters to her during brigade exercises and sometimes had some difficulty in recognising her camouflaged, very tired, dirty and smelly husband on his return. However, between the military commitments we enjoyed some wonderful social occasions as well as touring the attractive German countryside. An early outing had to be to Hamelin to see the weekly re-enactment of the Pied Piper story, followed by the spa towns of Bad Pyrmont and Bad Driburg and the attractive Weser valley. We also visited Hanover, whose city centre had been virtually erased during World War II by some eighty Allied bombing raids, resulting in more than 6,000 fatalities. Though much war damage was still to be seen, the Germans' reconstruction of their city was truly amazing.

One evening Ruth and I went upstairs from our 'love nest' into the anteroom of the garrison mess to have a drink, to find the famous comedienne and singer Gracie Fields there, sitting alone. She was on a tour of HM Forces in Germany and was staying in the mess for a couple of nights.

Members of any military mess are expected to immediately act as host in such a situation, so we introduced ourselves, bought her a drink, sat down with her and entered into conversation on her career and early life in Rochdale. I told her of my excursions to the mills with my grandfather and my sympathies for those who were trapped in such terrible conditions, and we were soon engaged in quite a long and interesting discussion. She had experienced the conditions that I had seen and was soon freely talking about her personal experiences. She recognised how fortunate she was to have escaped from the life of a mill girl, solely because of an exquisite voice.

Gracie Fields was a star of both cinema and music hall – the top box-office draw and highest paid actress in Britain in the 1930s, for which she was awarded a CBE in 1938. In WW2 she travelled to France [then onwards into Germany] entertaining the troops close to ongoing hostilities, performing in the back of trucks (or whatever was available) and she was the first artist to play behind enemy lines in Berlin. She became Dame Gracie Fields, DBE shortly before her death on 27th September 1979. Songs to be remembered; Sally … the pride of our alley, The Biggest Aspidistra in the World and Wish Me Luck as You Wave Me Goodbye.

Ruth and I considered it a great privilege to have had Gracie Fields as personal company for at least 40 minutes. Eventually, a staff car and escort arrived and she was whisked away to dine with the Garrison Commander and the officers of one of our battalions, together with their ladies. It was a memorable evening.

We spent about two months in the 'love nest' before a married quarter became available in the small, attractive town of Bückeburg, some eight miles south-east of Minden. The quarter was modest, but very pleasant. It was one of a clutch of officers' married quarters, which were largely occupied by the families of one of our infantry regiments; the Dorset Regiment. Bückeburg is a town steeped in history, its palace (schloss) having been the residence of the Princes of Schaumburg– Lippe for many centuries. It is a major tourist attraction and on special occasions some inhabitants, particularly the women, dress in traditional costumes for the festivities.

This was a most enjoyable period of our life, which increased further when Ruth told me in August that she was pregnant. That joy was short-lived, turning to deep sorrow on 2 September when she was admitted to the British Military Hospital in nearby Rinteln, where she had an early miscarriage. The pregnancy was not an accident – we had decided to start a family. I had expected Ruth to share her grief with her mother, but she was adamant that no one should be told, and it remained that way. The medical advice was to live life as normal and not to worry.

We decided to invite Ruth's mother and my grandfather to stay with us for Christmas, and it gave us much pleasure to show them around the countryside and the towns with their magnificent Christmas markets, decorations and festivities. It was a huge success – the first time that either had been abroad, apart from my grandfather's wartime service in France. It was our 'thank you' to them for all the support that they had given to us during some very difficult times.

I soon had a new commanding officer; none other than my first–term company commander at Sandhurst, Lieutenant Colonel David Horsfield. The 11th Infantry Brigade now formed part of the 2nd Infantry Division which, including our brigade, had three brigades under command. Colonel David told me that in order to give me more experience he would be moving me to 2 Signal Regiment at Bünde in the New Year to take charge of the cable troop (C Troop) for a few months, prior to my leaving in the early summer for my Part 2 course at Catterick. As Bünde was only 25 miles away, there would be no need for Ruth and me to leave our current accommodation. I was happy enough with the change and quite fancied the command of the tough, hairy–arsed linemen. However, I had 'heard tell' (a splendid rural Yorkshire expression) that Colonel David was shuffling his pack of junior officers to enable him to form a quality regimental langlauf (cross-country skiing) team in Austria. He was an enthusiastic and ambitious member of the Army Ski Association and one of the Army's best skiers. It was said that he needed the fittest of his unmarried subalterns in Austria for at least two months to achieve his aim, and he was only occasionally seen by the regiment during that period.

We were dined out from Headquarters 11th Infantry Brigade shortly after Christmas and I then took command of my new troop of some fifty linemen. Our role on deployment was to lay cable within the headquarters of 2nd Infantry Division, to flanking formations, our brigades, and to any other units placed under command for special operations. Radio silence would be strictly observed by the division on deployment, so the speedy laying of our cables, mostly quad cable, was vital. When we engaged with the enemy (Redland Forces) on these exercises and a fluid battle began, radio silence would be broken and we would then have to adapt swiftly to the moves of the headquarters and the ever-changing requirements, always trying to think ahead.

I had been told that I would be required to run an upgrading course soon after my arrival, and this gave me an early opportunity to get to know my linemen and to learn of their experiences. They soon became aware that one thing I would not tolerate was untidy, sloppy cable laying. Eventually, we reached a happy compromise. I asked if I could have a trial for their very useful football team and was delighted to secure my favoured position of left wing.

'Charlie Cable Troop' provided me with a touch of the independence that I had enjoyed with my radio relay troops. We left for exercises well before anyone else, in order to get priority lines laid, and we were always the last to return, for we had to recover all the cable. It was a troop of barrow-boy-type characters who tended to take the law into their own hands in much the same way that they were accustomed to doing in their home towns. However, there was rarely any trouble within the troop and, unlike their modern counterparts, they relied on their fists, rather than knives. They were mostly honest rogues and I became very fond of the troop.

A recurrent and irritating problem involved German youths cutting our cables during exercises. The German polizei were always advised at a high level of any military exercises, but I eventually decided on my own initiative to try and improve matters by early liaison at a local level as soon as we deployed. I gave the local polizei clear sketch maps of our intended cable routes and discussed the problem with them. They were most cooperative, and their occasional patrols and presence along the routes significantly reduced the problem. I'm sure they enjoyed the occasional bottle of 'duty free' that we left on their doorstep afterwards. Sadly, the virtual daily travel between Bückeburg and Bünde was taking its toll on the Riley, particularly on its suspension, and it was difficult to obtain spare parts. It was with much regret that we decided to sell the car. Her replacement was a far less interesting, but more practical and economic two years old Borgward Goliath GP700.

As my Part 2 course approached, I began to think about what I would like to do after that course. My wish to see more of the world had not diminished, and Ruth continued to share this sense of adventure with me. I was attracted to a secondment with the Malaya or Ghana Armed Forces, and in April 1959, with Ruth's support, I submitted my applications. If they were unsuccessful, I would state a wish to serve in a Royal Signals unit in either the Far East or the Middle East, provided that married-quarter accommodation was available. In late May we packed our belongings for our return to England for the Part 2 course at Catterick. It was not a difficult move, for we had so few possessions, most of which could be carried in the Goliath. We arrived in England on 2 June.

I had spent four and a quarter years in West Germany and knew the British NW occupation zone better than my own country. When I arrived I had seen the hand plough in the fields pulled by humans, both male and female, and I had experienced the embarrassment of Germans stepping off the pavement when I approached them in uniform. I had observed some German characteristics that I admired and some that I abhorred. I respected their tidiness and the lack of litter in both their cities and their countryside, but I disliked their tendency to use brute strength in situations where the British would form a queue. I admired the German hard graft and skill which enabled them to increase their gross national product (GNP) by some 7% a year while I was there, despite the handicaps and repayments that were imposed. I disliked the German male dominance, typified by the expectation that the wife would bring her husband his slippers when he returned from work. I observed their dilapidated old steam engines departing and arriving at precisely the correct time, with the stationmaster watching the second hand of the platform clock like a hawk, and giving vent to his fury if there was a delay of even half a minute. I liked their traditions and celebrations; their Schützenfests and Bierfests, and the friendly knock of greeting on your table as they entered a restaurant or Gästehaus. The West Germany that Ruth and I were leaving was now firmly entrenched in its miraculous *Wirtschaftswunder* ('economic miracle') recovery from World War II. Thousands of East Germans were currently migrating westwards as West Germany boomed and ran out of labour. With the borders between East and West Germany sealed, they travelled to Berlin, from where they could fly from the Allied Zone into West Germany. This was increasing the tension between the Warsaw Pact countries and NATO and resulted in the Soviet rulers eventually erecting the Berlin Wall to stop the exodus. I have a high regard for Germany and its people and I believe that we have much to offer each other. Yet, I feel that there are significant differences between this hugely talented continental race and my similarly talented island race. Suffice it to say that it is my belief that it would be in the best interests of my island race to stand on its own, outside continental Europe, trading with the world at large, as it has done so successfully for many hundreds of years. In Tennyson's words, 'Though we are not now that strength which, in old days, moved Earth and Heaven, that which we are we are'; still a powerful and respected voice in a turbulent world.

SCHOOL OF
SIGNALS - CATTERICK

My Part 2 Course - September 1959 to March 1960

We returned to England via the Hook of Holland–Harwich route. It was strange to be driving on the left-hand side of the road after so many years in Germany, particularly in a left-hand-drive car. We progressed north at a very slow speed compared with the autobahn travel to which we had been accustomed, for England's first motorway had not yet been built. Hand signals were still in use, to the extent of being quite comical, particularly when we joined the dense traffic of the Great North Road, shunting our way through the busy market towns. Nevertheless, it was good to be back. We spent about ten cramped, but most enjoyable days, with Ruth's mother in her cottage in Boston Spa, met old friends and relatives and visited our favourite locations in Yorkshire. Ruth could not wait to see Nidderdale again, so that lovely dale was top of the list. I was given a grand tour of the places that figured large in her childhood memories and was amazed at how well she was still remembered. I did not wish to see Arthursdale, for a glance at a map revealed that it had already changed beyond all recognition.

An army quarter was not likely to become available for several weeks, so we had arranged to rent an apartment within Frenchgate House, at the bottom of Frenchgate, in Richmond. It had a magnificent view and suited us well. Shortly after we moved in, Ruth coyly advised me, 'I think you're going to be a father – about Christmas.' I was delighted, as was Ruth, who started knitting without delay. Ruth thought it prudent to wait a while before telling her mother, the rest of the family and her friends, but when she did there was so much joy.

When we assembled for the course it was akin to a reunion. We already knew each other well and had shared many experiences together. Most of us had married during the past couple of years, so there were proud introductions to make. There was a good social life in both the Royal Signals Headquarters mess and in our homes to balance the demanding workload.

The Royal Corps of Signals needed its officers to have a sound technical knowledge. This was achieved by attending the Part 1 and 2 courses, along with intervening practical experience and, for the very technically minded, the long telecommunications course. In addition, the corps received a steady inflow of officer graduates from the universities, whilst very talented soldiers who had progressed through the ranks were also commissioned. Every officer and soldier received an annual confidential report which, following an eyeball-to-eyeball interview with the writer of that report, was signed and passed up the line for additional comments from more senior officers. As both the recipients and their reporting officers were routinely posted to other units or establishments every two years, it was unusual to be reported on by the same officer twice in succession. Ministry of Defence Promotion Boards based their selections on these reports, together with course reports, without seeing the names of the candidates. Additionally, there were practical and written promotion examinations to be negotiated that were common to all arms and services, with the exception of the medical, dental and pay services. It was a very competitive but fair system. The route to the rank of lieutenant colonel or higher in the Royal Corps of Signals was usually either a technical one, via a relevant university degree or the long telecommunications course, or via the Army Staff College. My aim was to progress via the Army Staff College, but for the next eight months my mind needed to be focused on fatherhood and obtaining a respectable 'C' grading on my Part 2 course.

The course was quite technical and I found it difficult at times. However, when we progressed to the practical activity of reading circuit diagrams with reasonable understanding, taking measurements to diagnose faults, and constructing basic radio sets, it became more satisfying. Similarly, with line equipment, we became quite adept at diagnosing and repairing faults on the standard ACT 1+4 (Apparatus Carrier Telephone) and on teleprinters. I was disappointed that the AN/TRC and Pintsch Radio Relay, with which I was so familiar, were not included in the syllabus – probably because there were no instructors with any experience of such modern equipment. The fact that much valuable time was allocated to increasing the speed of our morse code communications ability added to my suspicion that in some areas the School of Signals was rather behind the times, whilst the quality of the précis that were issued for revision was very poor.

One area where I felt the school was not behind the times, however, was in its teaching of the theory of transistors. This new technology which enabled cumbersome and power-greedy amplifier vacuum tubes to be replaced with small transistors, was grabbing the headlines with the recent launch of the iconic Bush TR82 transistor radio. In simple terms, the vacuum tubes were voltage amplifiers while the transistors provided current amplification. The significance of this is that as the transistor base drew current, its impedance was very low and accordingly a transistor radio only needed a small 9-volt battery. In comparison, the vacuum tube portable radio of the day needed several relatively heavy batteries to heat the tube elements plus a cumbersome 45-volt battery for the signal circuits – quite a heavy and cumbersome load to carry, while the new Bush TR82 could be carried in the pocket. We were taught the theory behind this new technology (PNP junctions and all that jazz) and speculated how it might change military communications in the future.

A military married quarter soon became available. It was in a circular complex of about fifteen officers' married quarters at Whinny Hill, on the southern side of Catterick Garrison, on the edge of Scotton Moor, and conveniently within walking distance of my place of work. They were all small, very basic semis with coal fires, occupied by students and instructors of lieutenant/captain rank. Some of our neighbours were already our friends, and those who were not soon became our friends. It was a very happy atmosphere, and while the husbands toiled with the intricacies of their Part 2 course the wives held their coffee mornings and outings. Early in November I was informed by the Ministry of Defence that my application to serve with the Federation of Malaya Armed Forces had been accepted and that arrangements were being made for Ruth and myself to travel together by sea in early April 1960. Later in the month we were delighted to attend the wedding of my best man (Frank Edwards) to Marion, in York. Throughout our time in the Army, no matter where we went, we would regularly meet up again with good friends and, of course, make new friends.

It was a very exciting time for us. As is customary, I wrote to my new squadron commander in Kuala Lumpur, Major Freddie Oakes, telling him about myself and Ruth, and her condition. We received a very welcoming and reassuring reply. He told me that I would be in charge of the Malayan Ministry of Defence Communications Centre in Kuala Lumpur, together with some outlying communications posts, and also that I would be required to attend a Malay language course in Singapore. The envelope also contained a very pleasant and helpful letter from his wife (Nan) for Ruth, advising her of what to bring and what not to bring. High on the list of recommendations was a Moses basket in which to carry our baby. There was one other British officer in the Malayan Armed Forces Signal Squadron; Captain Dudley Carnie, who was responsible for the Trade Training School. Dudley also wrote a welcoming letter, as did his wife, Pat, who had recently given birth to her first baby. These letters removed any lingering doubts that we might have had and we looked forward with much anticipation to three years in the mystic East. Later, I was advised that shortly before our departure I would be required to attend a GCHQ (Government Communications Headquarters) briefing at Cheltenham.

Excitement grew in the family, and also amongst our group of friends at Catterick, as Christmas and the anticipated birth of our baby approached. No complications had been experienced during the pregnancy and none were anticipated. Shortly before Christmas, Ruth's mother came to stay, and remain with us until the baby arrived. Was it going to be Amelia or was it going to be Justin, and on what date?

Christmas and the 1960 New Year passed by and fellow students began to return from their leave, telephoning for the news, but there was nothing to report – until late on the evening of the second day of the new year, when Ruth said, 'Now don't panic, but you had better warn the hospital and get the car warmed up.' It was only a mile to the Catterick Military Hospital, where we were met by the gynaecologist, Captain John Bessel. It was unusual at that time for husbands to be present at a birth. Had Ruth asked me to, I would have done so without hesitation, but she did not, and I waited patiently outside. It seemed an eternity. I received cups of coffee, reassuring 'it won't be long now' messages, and then, to my relief, 'Congratulations, Mr Pedley, would you like to come this way and meet your lovely son?' The first sight of your delighted wife as a mother, proudly holding her baby, must be as poignant a moment as turning to see her as your bride, walking down the aisle towards you. I was overcome with emotion; so very relieved that all had gone well, and that Justin was a healthy boy of well above average weight – already expressing a strong vocal opinion on some matter. It was 5 a.m. on Sunday 3 January. I telephoned Ruth's mother immediately, and when I returned to our quarter we informed other members of the family and shared a joyful early-morning celebration together.

It was not difficult to say goodbye to our military friends because we knew that we would be meeting again in future appointments, courses and reunions, but it was not easy for me to say goodbye to my grandfather, now aged almost eighty-six, nor for Ruth to say goodbye to her mother. However, my grandfather had recently established a close friendship with a lady who lived nearby, of the same name as my late grandmother. Elizabeth was a widow, several years younger than he, and she had given him a spring in his step. Shortly before we left for Malaya, Ruth and I called on him and on leaving he accompanied us to the nearby bus shelter. There was no one else in the shelter, and he talked to us about Elizabeth and their relationship. Speaking closely and confidentially to me, he said, 'Of course, there's no sex in it,' in a voice that to him was a whisper, but to those who had quietly entered the shelter and formed a queue behind, it was a tannoy announcement. We all had great difficulty in containing our mirth.

Justin was Christened in March, in the same church that Ruth and I had been married in – All Saints Church, Thorp Arch. The godparents were Valerie and Geoffrey Woodcock and Ruth's cousin, Gordon MacKeith. Valerie was the senior member of staff in the E.J. Arnold showroom in Hunslet when Ruth joined the firm on the death of her father, whilst Geoffrey was the manager of a textile mill. They were to be lifelong friends and lived an enviable hobby-farmer lifestyle at their eight-acre Bunkers Hill Farm at Oakworth, near Keighley, enjoying magnificent views across the Aire and Worth valleys. Sadly, Geoffrey died in September 2014 and Valerie in July 2022.

Gordon MacKeith was an architect with MacKeith Dickinson & Partners, eventually becoming a senior director in the business and President of the Fylde Society of Architects. Between 1958 and 2009 he contributed to thousands of projects within the Blackpool and Fylde area. Sadly, he died on 5 March 2018; 'Beloved husband of Margaret, father of Charlie and James and much loved grandfather of Grace and Iain.'

I was pleased, and relieved, to receive a respectable 'C' grading on my Part 2 course. To achieve my latent ambition of attending the Army Staff College I now needed to ensure that I continued to receive mostly 'excellent' or 'very good' annual reports, obtain an unqualified 'staff candidate' recommendation, pass the requisite practical and written examinations, and then hope that I was able to achieve selection. I had a window of about four years in which to do this. I never had pipe dreams of reaching high rank in the Army, but I was conscious of the fact that the Army would almost certainly be reduced in size, with significant redundancies. I had the foresight to recognise that entry to the Army Staff College at Camberley and the satisfactory completion of that course was my best possible insurance against redundancy, which would have been disastrous. In short, my ambitions were driven more by the need for family survival than by personal ego.

MALAYA BOUND

April 1960

The terms of my secondment provided us with first-class travel facilities. Most of our possessions had been despatched in advance. I carried Justin in his Moses basket and Ruth carried Justin's things and her handbag, while several suitcases were entrusted to a series of porters. The sailing date was Saturday 2 April 1960. It was glorious spring weather and the day of the Oxford vs. Cambridge boat race. I had occasionally seen 'ocean liner' trains indicated on the departure board at Waterloo station and had envied the passengers passing through the barrier for Southampton docks and distant parts of the world, wondering who they were and what adventures lay before them. Now, my family and I were being carefully ushered through by a representative of the Crown Agents and escorted to our reserved seats. We were pleased to have a compartment to ourselves, which eased the matter of feeding Justin. The non-stop train took us into the docks, just 100 yards from the P&O liner SS *Carthage* which was to take us to Malaya. Again, we were met by a representative of the Crown Agents, who escorted us to our first-class cabin, making absolutely sure that everything was in order before leaving.

SS *Carthage* was very familiar with the route that we were to take to Malaya. She was one of the last of the traditional oriental liners, built on the Clyde by A. Stephen & Sons Ltd (Glasgow), a firm whose shipbuilding began on the Moray Firth in 1750. She was launched on 18 August 1931 and was soon given the status of Royal Mail Ship. She had a 14,304 gross tonnage (2018 cruise liner *Symphony of the Seas* is almost sixteen times larger), six steam turbines, twin screws that could propel her to 18 knots (if pushed) and a yellow funnel. In 1940, the RMS *Carthage* became HMS *Carthage*, an armed merchant cruiser, deployed in the Indian and South Atlantic Oceans. From 1944 to the end of the war she was listed as a troopship. Our voyage to the Orient on SS *Carthage* was one of her last, for she was sold for scrap a year later.

We sailed in the late afternoon, with a passenger list that was close to the SS *Carthage's* 391 capacity. It was a traditional send-off, with lots of bunting and streamers and band-playing, a practise still carried out by today's cruise ships. However, there was a significant difference to a modern-day cruise ship departure – several hundred relatives and friends present to say goodbye to passengers whom they did not expect to see again for several years, if ever. Journeys to the Orient, Australia and New Zealand by sea were still the norm, even for England cricket teams, though scheduled flights of the Comet aircraft and its successors were not far away.

Our cabin was of a reasonable size for the three of us, with a standard size porthole and additional overhead ventilation (not air conditioning). We were soon visited by our cabin steward and also by an experienced middle-aged children's nurse, who quickly gained Ruth's confidence. She provided an amplifier and showed us how to position it close to Justin's cot. This was connected to the telephone exchange to enable the operator to regularly monitor our cabin, and any others with young children, on request.

As soon as SS *Carthage* reached the duty-free distance we each had a couple of glasses of champagne, at a genuine duty-free price. We shared a dining table with two rubber plantation managers, returning from leave. They were very helpful, good company, and a mine of information, advice and good stories. I only recollect the name of one of them – a Mr Hook.

The weather was pleasant and we soon became familiar with the very relaxing daily routine; breakfast; read ship's newsletter; walk about; study nautical map; play deck quoits and deck tennis; practise in the cricket net;

have morning coffee; assemble on deck just before noon to place bets on distance covered in the preceding twenty-four hours and listen to our captain's announcements; have lunch; take a siesta; have afternoon tea; go to dinner and enjoy evening entertainment. On the second evening the ship's tannoy disturbed our evening meal by instructing us to return to our cabin immediately due to an extraordinary noise emanating from it – Justin had discovered and seized the amplifier and was alternately sucking and beating it. The evening entertainment was DIY, supervised by the ship's junior officers – horse racing, talent competitions, dancing, quizzes, general knowledge contests and so on. It was rather nice to reflect that I was now receiving the pay of a captain, plus inducement allowance and overseas allowance, for this hardship.

Conditions changed dramatically when we entered the Bay of Biscay and were tossed around for almost three days in a quite severe storm. We were not physically sick, but we could not eat anything other than biscuits and a little fruit. Thankfully, Justin did not mind the conditions. It was a relief to reach Gibraltar, where we spent a day re-fuelling and taking on provisions, and then on to Port Said. The Mediterranean was very calm and I recall a period of total relaxation for four days and the privilege of spending some time with Vice– Admiral Sir David Luce, who was travelling to India to take up the appointment of Commander-in-Chief Far East Fleet. Our meeting came about when we were drawn as partners in a deck quoits knock– out competition. He was as keen as mustard. We won our first round and he invited me to have a celebration drink with him afterwards. Similar invitations followed on subsequent days as we proceeded to win the competition. I cannot recall any detail of our conversations, but I do remember that Ruth and baby Justin joined us on at least one occasion and Ruth endorsed my opinion of him as a most charming and modest gentleman. Three years later he became First Sea Lord – Admiral Sir John David Luce GCB, DSO & bar, OBE. In that capacity he strongly opposed government plans to reduce the carrier capability of the Royal Navy and resigned in protest.

At Port Said I began to sense the history, mystique and excitement of the East. It was there in the penetrating heat, the brightness and the vivid colours, the odours, the noise and the intense activity of vibrant crowds of people made up of so many different nationalities. At that time, the ports and the ships that they served were not shielded, and people surrounded SS *Carthage* en masse with their merchandise, trading initiatives, entertainment and banter. Even young children were determined that we should part with our money, inviting us to throw silver coins from the deck into the water, which they somehow managed to retrieve, displaying amazing agility and underwater swimming skills.

Eventually, at little more than walking pace, our convoy moved south towards the Suez Canal – the highway to India. We had excellent entertainment that evening from a troupe of Egyptian magicians, acrobats and belly dancers, but the heat was very uncomfortable and it was a relief when we eventually reached the Gulf of Suez and the Red Sea, receiving some breeze from the ship's increased speed. The sea was an intense dark blue, as still as a pond, except for occasional splashes caused by shoals of flying fish, which I never tired of watching. I went ashore for a short while by myself at Aden and took a few photographs. I did not realise until later years that a member of the family and ex– TGS pupil, Bill Platt, the elder brother of Ruth's sister-in-law, was there at the time. Bill held the senior financial appointment in the British embassy, with financial responsibilities that extended over the entire Aden Protectorate. Sadly, he died on 26th February 2018, three months short of his 100th birthday. He served in the Colonial Service in the Aden Protectorate and Aden Colony for 13 years, accompanied by his wife (Dorothy), leaving in 1964 during the Aden Emergency. He was a volunteer to serve his country in 1939 at the outset of WW2, serving initially in the ranks of the Royal Artillery in Iceland, and then as a commissioned officer in a Gurkha regiment in India and Burma. I remember him as a very independent, determined and modest gentleman who (despite severe macular degeneration) insisted on looking after himself in Harrogate for two decades, prior to succumbing to a nursing home for the final two years of his life.

As we crossed the Indian Ocean, en route for Bombay, we ran into seas as heavy as those in the Bay of Biscay, but we now had our sea legs and found the rough seas and relatively cooler temperatures quite bracing. Nevertheless, we were pleased when Bombay was sighted. SS *Carthage* docked at the traditional waterfront berth before the Gateway of India monument, where British governors and viceroys had disembarked in past times of Empire. A vast but friendly crowd was held back by the police to allow Vice-Admiral Sir David Luce, in full dress uniform, to disembark first and be welcomed as the British Commander-in-Chief Far East Fleet. Both Ruth and I went ashore for a short time, leaving Justin in the care of the children's nurse. Our taxi driver showed us some fascinating and disturbing sights in this vast, vibrant city – the colourful bazaars, the Taj Mahal Hotel, the hanging gardens at Malabar Hill and the adjacent Zoroastrian Towers of Silence, casually pointing out the preying vultures overhead. The city was inundated with beggars and there was much blood-red spittle on the pavements, which we thought must be from tuberculosis sufferers – indeed, we occasionally saw people with bloody mouths and lips. It was only when we were discussing our experiences at dinner that we learnt that it was not TB spittle that we had seen but the disposed saliva of betel leaf and betel nut chewers, not dissimilar to the disgusting, but less colourful, chewing gum that is spat out on the streets of 'modern' Britain.

It was only another 1,000 miles to our next stop at Colombo, and then a further 1,500 miles to our destination – the port of Georgetown on the eastern side of Penang island, which was regarded as being one of the most beautiful islands in the world. After twenty-three days at sea it looked absolutely stunning. We were taken by a representative of the Crown Agents to the premier hotel, where we were provided with a room in which to spend a day of relaxation, prior to crossing on the ferry to Butterworth, where we would take the night train on the single– track railway to Kuala Lumpur. Ruth enjoyed walking the immaculate grounds, admiring the colourful fauna, and later the magnificent orchids in the restaurant.

As I looked out at this tranquil and colourful island from our hotel window, my mind conjured up the likely scenario there in early December 1941. On the morning of 7 December of that year, without any warning or declaration of war, Japan launched its infamous air assault on the United States Pacific Fleet at Pearl Harbor, utilising 353 fighters, bombers and torpedo planes, demolishing the totally unsuspecting fleet within a few hours and killing 2,402 American servicemen. On the same day and at the same time, only 100 miles from where Ruth and I were now resting, the Japanese 5th Infantry Division was conducting an unopposed amphibious landing on the opposite coast at Patani and Singora, just inside Siam, but with Singapore and the British naval base as the ultimate objective. This invasion, again without any prior declaration of war, was as unexpected to Britain as the attack on Pearl Harbor was to the United States. The 5th Infantry Division was very well trained in jungle warfare and possessed strong armoured support for use when conditions permitted. The British, Australian and Indian forces had no armour whatsoever, for every tank at that time was required to contain Rommel in North Africa. Patani and Singora had valuable airfields, which were soon utilised by the Japanese. Not surprisingly, this well-balanced elite Japanese division was able not only to thrust south along Malaya's eastern coastline, but also to cross the thin neck of Siam to Malaya's west coast, taking Penang shortly before Christmas. Despite some valiant resistance, Allied troops had to withdraw to southern Johore and eventually surrender to the full might of Japan's 25th Army. Some 130,000 British soldiers were taken prisoner in the greatest single defeat in British history.

MALAYA

Japanese Occupation and the Malayan Emergency

The conquering Japanese proceeded to introduce a brutal regime, particularly in Singapore, where all ethnic Chinese males between the ages of eighteen and fifty were assembled and screened. Those considered to be anti-Japanese (many thousands) were executed. Not surprisingly, a predominantly ethnic Chinese resistance movement formed within the security of the Malayan jungle, led by the Malayan Communist Party – namely, the Malayan Peoples' Anti-Japanese Army (MPAJA). A small British-led resistance group, known as Force 136, was also formed. Its members also took refuge in the jungle, conducting sabotage and espionage tasks against the Japanese occupation forces.

Three and a half years were to pass before World War II ended. The British re-occupied Malaya and Singapore in August and September 1945. However, in the eyes of many Malayans, particularly the ethnic Chinese, the ignominious defeat of British forces by the Japanese in 1941 had dispelled the myth of British omnipotence. Times were hard, with high unemployment, food shortages and low wages, resulting in numerous confrontational strikes, which became increasingly political. Japanese prisoners of war were not returned to Japan until 1947 and there was bitter resentment at their use for strike breaking. The attitude of the Malayan workers became more assertive and trade union membership increased sharply, while the ethnic Chinese felt very bitter about not having a vote.

The MPAJA, whose members the British had secretly trained and armed during the later years of World War II, was officially disbanded in December 1946, but the Malayan Communist Party, led by Chin Peng, saw the British as being as great a threat to their objectives as the Japanese had been, and re-formed it as the Malayan National Liberation Army (MNLA). At the time that the Malayan Emergency was declared in 1948 ethnic Chinese comprised about 38% of Malaya's population and ethnic Malays about 50%, with the remainder being largely of Indian, Pakistani or mixed origin. It was estimated that the MNLA Communist guerrillas eventually reached an active strength of between 7,000 and 8,000, the vast majority being ethnic Chinese. The conflict was to last for twelve years and at its peak required a commitment of 40,000 British and Commonwealth troops.

The bases and hideouts of the Communist guerrillas were in the dense and widespread tropical jungle, from which they were able to launch attacks against Malaya's infrastructure and major industries – particularly the rubber plantations and tin mines, which were the major world suppliers of these commodities. The British strategy was essentially to follow the counter-insurgency technique used in the Second Boer War (1899–1902) – the removal of selected population groups that might be sympathetic to the guerrillas. This was done in as humane a manner as possible, for it was recognised that winning the hearts and minds of the people was essential. New villages were constructed for these population groups, located far from terrorist strongholds. The villages were surrounded by floodlit security fencing and police posts, whilst the inhabitants were given money and ownership of the land on which they lived. Concurrently, British and Commonwealth troops were learning the advanced skills of jungle warfare, and confidence grew in launching aggressive patrols deep into enemy territory, inflicting significant casualties against the guerrillas. Other positive action included the enfranchisement of the ethnic Chinese, the formation of a Malayan Army and the bestowing of independence on Malaya, under Prime Minister Tunku Abdul Rahman, on 31 August 1957. Following independence, the insurrection lost its *raison d'être* as a conflict of colonial liberation. The cumulative effect of these measures resulted in reduced support for the Communist guerrillas and in their military defeat, though pockets remained, largely in the area bordering Thailand. The twelve-year (1948–1960) conflict cost 11,052 lives – 6,710 MRLA guerrillas, 1,345 Malayan troops/police, 519 British/Commonwealth troops and 2,478 civilians.

It was against this background that Ruth, baby Justin and I took the evening ferry from Penang to the mainland and caught the night train to Kuala Lumpur (KL), the capital city of the Federation of Malaya, where I was to serve on secondment to that newly formed Malayan Army for the next three years.

MALAYA

Malayan Armed Forces Signal Squadron

The First Eighteen Months

We were met on our early-morning arrival at Kuala Lumpur's stunning Moorish-style railway station by Captain Dudley Carnie and his wife, Pat. They took us to a very pleasant hotel, which was to be our base for about a fortnight while we found rented accommodation.

In addition to Dudley, there were two Malayan officers in the squadron of about my age – Captain Ariffin bin Muda and Captain Bhajan Singh, both of whom had European wives. There were also two unmarried subalterns, Lieutenants Ooi Ah Kiang and Muhammad Yusof. They all spoke fluent English, while most of our soldiers spoke it to a reasonable standard. Communication was therefore no problem, but I took the advice of Squadron Commander Freddie Oakes to use Malay as often as I could. He explained that the gesture of using the language of our employers not only helped in fostering the right relationship, but it would also be very helpful when I went on my language course. As Dudley, Ariffin and Bhajan had all selected very good rented accommodation in Petaling Jaya (PJ), a recent development area on the south-west fringe of KL, and lived quite close to each other, Ruth and

I focused our attention on this area. All three soon invited us to visit them and were most helpful and friendly. It was not long before possible properties were being suggested, and with their help we selected 7 Jalan Lembah as our home. Ariffin kindly bartered on our behalf with the Chinese owner, not only reducing the rent to our maximum allowance, but also arranging the inclusion of some useful additional furniture and electrical equipment. Petaling Jaya is now a city, with a population of well over half a million. 7 Jalan Lembah remains clearly identifiable on popular searches, together with the famous Buddhist Chetawan Temple, both just off Jalan Gasing.

We were soon very comfortably settled in our new home, employing (part time) a Tamil worker (known as a kabun) to look after the garden, a middle-aged amah to do the washing and a young Chinese woman called Seraphim from the convent for general housework. I purchased a new Hillman Minx and, as advised by our friends, we joined the Lake Club and the Selangor Club, both in KL. The Selangor Club was a premier city-centre club frequented by the business fraternity and where we could watch first-class cricket from the balcony, while the Lake Club was on the edge of the city with a swimming pool and facilities that attracted family membership. Both had very good restaurants. Membership was strictly controlled on an invitation/black ball basis.

With the exception of the Minister of Defence (Tun Haji Abdul Razak) and his senior staff, Malaya's Ministry of Defence and the Armed Forces Signal Squadron that served it were located on the outskirts of the city, adjacent to Rifle Range Road. The buildings were single storey, mostly with verandas, set on a gentle slope that backed up to jungle. The slope levelled out at the bottom into our quite extensive and well–kept playing fields. Our neighbours were 656 Squadron Army Air Corps and a very efficient no-nonsense unit of the Malayan riot police, whose training was painful to behold. Walking within the Ministry one day, I recognised a familiar moustached figure ahead of me. It was none other than my previous Sandhurst company commander and commanding officer, now Colonel D.R. Horsfield. He had been on secondment, in the appointment of Principal Army Staff Officer, for almost a year. I caught up with him and we had a brief chat. However, due to subsequent commitments outside Malaya, promotion and his being required for another appointment in the UK, I rarely saw him again during my tour.

My appointment was that of Chief Signalmaster of the Ministry of Defence Communications Centre and Chief Custodian Officer Federation Armed Forces. The work was challenging, not only because much of it was new to me, but also because some aspects required the specialist skills of a traffic officer, and the consequences of error could be high. Though my primary responsibility was the Communications Centre, I also had responsibility for various outstations, the entire cryptographic equipment of the Federation Armed Forces and its proficient use, and the efficiency of the nearby, manually operated, telephone exchange. In addition, there were of course the normal regimental duties. Our communications were mostly teleprinter circuits to military headquarters (Malayan, Commonwealth and British), other governmental departments and the Commonwealth Communications Network (COMCAN). I was also responsible for providing direct radio links to units and ships deployed on operational tasks – for example, to intercept or shadow Indonesian warships that had transgressed into, or were close to, Malayan territorial waters.

We did not experience any significant problems settling in to either our new home or the new environment. The temperature reached some point in the 90s every day, with high humidity, but never seemed to exceed 100 degrees, and we gradually became acclimatised. When it rained, it was torrential, with no half measures, and then the sun burst through again. There were ceiling fans throughout the house and also air-conditioning units in the two bedrooms. Mosquitoes and other insects could be a nuisance at night, so we used nets to cover our beds. We loved sitting outside in deck chairs in the relative cool of the evening, gazing at the brilliant overhead display of planets and stars, for there was no industrial pollution whatsoever, and we also enjoyed listening to the noises of the jungle, which was only a couple of hundred yards distant. If we fancied a snack I would collect some sticks of grilled satay and compressed cold rice from the forecourt of a petrol station about half a mile away – rather like collecting fish and chips in the UK, but without the newspaper. This retailer, like many others, operated from a bicycle-drawn trailer. I now wish that I had taken photographs showing the ingenuity of these bicycle tradesmen. Some of the trailers were quite large and needed two, or even three, bicycle combinations to tow them. Their conveyance of livestock was particularly fascinating, ranging from a single-pillion strapped pig to a few goats, several dozen chickens and even fresh fish and snakes. Whilst the animal conveyance and husbandry was savage and an unpleasant sight, so too was that of seeing aged Chinese women who had been subjected to foot binding; a custom that began in 10th-century China, spreading in that country to almost half the population by the 19th-century. As Chinese families moved to Malaya in the 20th-century, attracted by better business prospects, they would have brought many of these unfortunate Lotus women with their deformed stumps with them. It is unlikely that any are living to-day, in China or elsewhere, but they were to be seen occasionally in Kuala Lumpur whilst we were there. I also wished that I had taken photographs of the scaffolding on buildings, using bamboo poles. They sometimes towered up to several hundred feet.

As we were so close to the jungle we needed to be sensibly alert to the danger of snakes. I had a few encounters with them, but the most alarming was seeing a cobra crossing our lower lawn towards Justin when he was at the crawling age. Both Ruth and I were keeping an eye on our little boy, but it was the kabun who saw the cobra first, killing it with some quick strikes of his chonkel (a large hoe-shaped gardening tool), while I snatched Justin. There were many lizards, colourful moths and butterflies, but not the variety of birds that I had expected. Spiders of almost dinner-plate size could sometimes be seen in webs between telephone wires. When I ventured short distances into the local jungle I was disappointed at both its lack of colour and the absence of wildlife at ground level, only seeing a few birds and an anteater. Most of the noise and activity seemed to be in the tree tops.

We enjoyed a pleasant, but not extravagant social life. On Sundays we would sometimes drive to the coast at Port Dickson and have a swim at a spot that was regarded as being free of sea snakes, whose bite could be fatal within a few minutes. This would be followed by lunch in a

Chinese hotel overlooking the beach. A special treat would be a hotel weekend in the Fraser Hills in Pahang which, because of its height (3,500 feet), maintained a pleasant British-like summer temperature of about 70 degrees. A fire was needed at night and there were interesting nature trails into a more interesting jungle with an abundance of bird life. The approach road was very steep, narrow and dark as it wound through the jungle, and a simple one-way timetable is still used by visitors and tourists.

Because of the different races and their religions, in addition to national and state events, there was much festivity and numerous holidays. Some of the processions were stunning spectacles; vibrant, noisy and very colourful. I particularly recall the Chinese New Year and the Hindu Thaipusam celebrations. On an entirely voluntary basis, I was one of many British in the employ of the Malayan government who fasted during Ramadan, in that we did not eat, drink or smoke during daylight hours during that period. I think this gesture helped to develop respect and friendship. Throughout my life I have never been prejudiced or troubled by race or colour, and Ruth was the same. At Christmas, Ruth invited our Christian, Muslim, Chinese and Sikh friends to join us, cooking with meticulous care to ensure that there was no violation of their religious beliefs. In return, we were welcomed into their homes and felt privileged to be invited to join their celebrations. We also had the privilege of attending the annual Trooping the Colour ceremonies, performed by the infantry battalions of the Federation Army in the Merdeka Stadium on the birthday of His Majesty the Yang di-Pertuan Agong; the five-yearly Tattoo of the Royal Federation of Malaya Police, and many other spectacular events. There were also some fine sporting occasions, of which I particularly remember a football match between Malaya and an English Football Association touring side, with one of my idols, Tom Finney, playing on the left wing. We shared with the Malayan people their grief as well as their joy – I was the only person at the bedside of one of my Indian soldiers as he died from injuries in a motorcycle accident, and I attended his traditional Hindu cremation in monsoon conditions in a remote and distant jungle kampong. Such complete integration nurtured a very good spirit in the squadron.

Malaya was very proud of its recent (1957) independence, its stability and its membership of the United Nations. It was therefore no surprise that when the Secretary General of the United Nations called for a force to be sent to the Congo in July 1960, to restore peace in that country following the granting of its independence, that a Malayan Contingent of 1,947 soldiers was offered, and accepted. My communications centre automatically assumed responsibility for providing the required message-handling facilities between the Malayan Ministry of Defence and its Malayan contingent, which was named the Malayan Special Force to the Congo. This was achieved without any significant problems. After a few weeks the Chief of the Armed Forces Staff (Lieutenant General Sir Rodney Moore) asked if we could also provide a direct radio (morse) link to the Malayan Special Force – a private and faster facility.

This was quite a challenge, for our transmitters had a very modest power output. After a few days of experimenting with different frequencies we heard a very faint morse signal from the Congo and eventually we were able to establish a working link for a period of almost exactly four hours each day on a frequency of 13.705 Mc/s. It was uncanny how the signal came through – very faint at first, at almost exactly the same time each day, gradually fading away four hours later. I briefed General Moore and other senior officers on what we had managed to achieve, emphasising the limitations, and invited them to come and watch our very skilled operators at work. They understood the limitations of the four-hour communication window that we had and gave us their full cooperation, while the operators received the praise and attention that they deserved. After a few months we realised that this communication window was slowly drifting to later and later in the day. Eventually it became stationary, and then slowly returned. I have never heard a satisfactory explanation of this phenomenon. Much to Ruth's consternation, I had one of the bulky Racal receivers brought to our house to enable me to listen to our transmissions when I was at home. Though the morse speed was way above my level of proficiency and encoded, I was able to detect a problem and enquire as to what action was being taken. Coincidentally, this top-of-the-range receiver also enabled me to listen to John Arlott's brilliant cricket commentaries. Such close liaison between communicators and the headquarters staff whom they serve is essential for efficient command and control, and when achieved, it is not only most satisfying, but makes life far more comfortable. I was proud of my communications centre and the trade skills of its multi-racial soldiers – radio and telegraph operators, technicians and crypto specialists. I was also very proud of the telephone exchange, for which I was also responsible. It was entirely manually operated, with about fifteen civilian operators and a supervisor for each shift, all of whom were female. Because of the high level of unemployment there would be about forty applicants for each vacancy that occurred, from which our squadron administrative officer (Captain Ariffin bin Muda) would produce a shortlist of about eight (selected from CVs and references), who would be invited to attend our interview. Eventually, the number would be reduced to three or four very high-grade applicants who met all the mandatory requirements of being intelligent, having an attractive personality, being well-spoken and speaking English fluently. The interior of the telephone exchange and these charming and efficient operators were on open view to its users as they walked to and from and between their offices. We rarely had any complaints. Justin was thriving; very active and strong for his age with a sharp, enquiring mind that drew regular comment from our friends. I recollect the first time that I read a story to him that began, "Once upon a time" – "Why", demanded Justin. Also, if an object, no matter how small, was moved in his absence he would very soon notice it and promptly return it to its previous position. My corner dented silver cigarette case wedding present [from the officers of HQ 11th Infantry Brigade] bears testimony to this toddler's remarkable observation, for he inevitably dropped the case before I could retrieve it. In later years these personal qualities were to enhance his career as a police officer.

For our first leave period, early in 1961, Ruth and I decided to spend about ten days in a hotel at the Tanah Rata hill station in the Cameron Highlands, located about 130 miles north of KL. The peaks of the Cameron Highlands were over 5,000 feet high, but Tanah Rata, at about 4,200 feet, was the end of the road for most vehicles. The road was established in 1931 by hard physical labour – an amazing achievement. It was a rather narrow road through dense, dark jungle, while the gradients were severe, with precipitous drops at the side. Though not dangerous if one drove sensibly, it was nevertheless a relief to reach our destination – I would not have wished to encounter torrential rain on this road.

There was little humidity and the temperature by day was pleasantly warm, while in the evening we experienced the pleasure of a touch of frost and a roaring log fire. The Cameron Highlands has very fertile soil and its commercial potential for tea plantations and for growing vegetables was soon recognised. We enjoyed a very relaxing holiday, mostly spent on short walks along scenic jungle tracks with stunning waterfalls and ravines and an abundance of colourful birds and butterflies.

MALAYA

Malayan Armed Forces Signal Squadron

The Second Eighteen Months

I was now well settled into my employment and decided that it was time to bite the bullet and begin working towards my aim of gaining entry to the Army Staff College. I decided to take a correspondence course in each of the seven written examinations – Tactics A, Tactics B, Tactics C, Military Law, Military History, Current Affairs, and Administration – and wrote to one of the colleges in England that provided this facility. I was soon impressed with the efficiency and guidance that I received. I ordered the textbooks that were required, studied at the recommended pace, completed the test papers that the college sent me, and received in return its tutors' very thorough marking assessments. Ruth gave me every encouragement – we were so happy and entwined in our wonderful marriage, and in the excitement and mystique of the Orient. However, before I could sit the annual written examination as a staff candidate I needed to pass the Army's captain-to-major practical examination and also earn an annual report recommendation that I was of the requisite standard, with the potential to reach the rank of colonel. The practical examination was an assessment of an officer's ability to command an infantry company group in action, irrespective of his cap badge, but with the exemption of officers of the medical, dental and pay corps. The tactical situation would be described and one would have to conduct a reconnaissance and give one's appreciation of the situation to an officer of the directing staff (DS), followed by orders for the attack/defence/withdrawal to the platoon commanders, the tank troop commander, artillery officer and any others involved. The DS would question as necessary and would be particularly interested in whether the orders were delivered in a clear and convincing manner and in the prescribed sequence, as well as whether arcs of fire were coordinated and sensibly linked to artillery and mortar fire plans, timings clear, etc. Voice procedure would also be tested, including a request for immediate artillery support and the directing of the guns onto the target. I had already attended various training days arranged by British and Commonwealth infantry battalions, and I arranged to take the practical examination held by the 28th Commonwealth Infantry Brigade shortly after our Cameron Highlands holiday. I passed, so that was one hurdle out of the way, but there was still a long way to go.

The fitness of officers and soldiers was encouraged by regular morning PT sessions and much evening sport, particularly hockey and football. Captain Dudley Carnie had nurtured an exceptionally strong hockey team that became the Malayan Forces Champions. Their standard was such that they sometimes played the Selangor state team when they wanted a good local workout. I was hardly good enough for a regular place in the squadron football team, but I managed the occasional match. Though matches were played in the early evening, the temperature would still be around 90 degrees. They were well supported, and Ruth, with toddler Justin, and Pat Carnie, with toddler Clive, would often come and watch. Ruth longed to play in a hockey match again, despite there not being any women's or mixed teams. Eventually she got her way and came on as a substitute in two matches, to the delight of spectators and players alike. The spectators were impressed, particularly the Malayan women, while I felt a bit sheepish as I held Justin with one hand and Ruth's handbag with the other. Ruth did not disgrace herself and was soon recognised on the field as not being brittle and a capable player. She loved it! A few months later her gallivanting on the hockey field ceased – when she confided in me that a baby was anticipated in mid-November. I was overjoyed. It was my turn to suggest a name and Ruth readily endorsed that selection – so, it was to be Amelia or Mark. The hospital would be the British Military Hospital Kinrara, close to KL. In late June I attended my five-week Malay language course in Singapore. While waiting on the Kuala Lumpur station platform for the night train to take me there, I noticed a British warrant officer whom I had seen on occasion in the Ministry of Defence. He was carrying an elephant gun. We met in the bar shortly after the train moved off, and I learned that he was on his way to Johore, having been asked by the state authorities to deal with a rogue elephant. He was born in India, of British Army parentage, and had learned his big game hunting skills in that country. I believe his name was Ford and that he was in the Royal Army Ordnance Corps. I had a fascinating conversation with him that lasted well into the night. As more and more beer was consumed, the elephants and tigers became larger and larger and the encounters increasingly fearsome. I remember him telling me that his greatest concern in the jungle was disturbing one of the many deadly varieties of snake as he quietly stalked his prey, as well as the reptile threat in swampy areas.

There were about fifteen of us on the language course, mostly military. Languages were never my forte and I found it quite difficult. Nevertheless, due to some very good and tolerant instructors it became quite enjoyable and I made progress. Singapore was a fascinating, vibrant, duty-free city. As a reward for passing the halfway progress test, we were shown some of the dark areas of the city, which made Hamburg and Dusseldorf almost monastic in comparison. Quality watches were cheap and I could not resist purchases for both myself and Ruth, who also received a nice Mikimoto cultured pearl necklace. I passed the course and was pleased to receive the associated language pay. The smile on my face was soon removed when, on my return to KL, I learned that the annual administrative inspection was imminent, and that I had been selected as parade commander, with commands and communication with the Malay inspecting officer to be in Malay.

Some ten weeks before our second baby was due to arrive, we were having a drink one evening with friends in a hotel lounge in KL and the subject of Ruth's approaching confinement cropped up. During the discussion Ruth mentioned what a wonderful gynaecologist she had had when Justin was born, a Captain Bessel, and how she wished that he was here. A lady who had been sitting nearby walked over and said to Ruth, 'Excuse me, but I think I heard you mention my husband's name.' It was Mrs Bessel. They had just arrived from Catterick and her husband was now the senior gynaecologist at BMH Kinrara. Ruth was, of course, elated. The occasion was probably the departure of Captain Dudley and Pat Carnie and their son, Clive, at the end of their secondment. They had been very good friends and we were very sad to see them leave.

We were able to keep abreast of world news by occasional purchases of whatever lightweight newspapers were available at the airport or in town, though they could be a few days old and with little choice. In August there was worldwide concern of WW3 breaking out: when the Soviet Union sparked the erection of the Berlin Wall. Crisis point was reached in October when 10 American M48 tanks rolled up to Checkpoint Charlie and aimed their guns at the East German frontier police: whereupon the Soviet army sent 10 of their T54s; guns levelled at the Americans. Following frantic high level diplomatic discussion the antagonists slowly withdrew a tank at a time until all were out of sight of each other. If some joker had let off a thunderflash [a military training pyrotechnic], in conjunction with a smoke grenade, who knows what might have happened.

In October I received a confidential report that was of the high standard that I needed in my quest for entry to the Army Staff College. It was a top-of-the-range grading, with unqualified 'staff candidate' recommendation, and it had the all-important support of senior officers. These included Lieutenant-General Sir Rodney Moore, whose next appointment was to be the first Defence Services Secretary and Aide-de-Camp General to The Queen. He retired in 1966 as General Sir James Newton Rodney Moore, GCVO, KCB, CBE, DSO. Throughout one's military service one never saw the confidential report comments on oneself of second or subsequent reporting officers. One only saw the report of the initiating officer, with whom one had an eyeball-to-eyeball discussion on its content. However, the 2000 Freedom of Information Act allowed some relaxation of this regulation, at the discretion of the Ministry of Defence, and that is how I gained not only this information, but copies of all my confidential reports. The comments of senior officers can be very humbling, but I managed to avoid such classic comments as 'I would not breed from this officer' and 'Soldiers follow this officer, if only out of curiosity.'

Mark was born shortly before Christmas 1961 and Ruth and I were thrilled that we had another healthy, strapping son, while Justin displayed emotion that we had not seen before. There were no complications and Ruth was convinced that she had the best gynaecologist in the world.

Telegrams were despatched to England and the family rejoiced. I gulped when I thought of my additional responsibility, particularly as Phase 2 of the 1957 Defence White Paper was about to be implemented. This defence review involved a very significant reduction in Army manpower, including the disbandment of 51 major units and an overall reduction in strength to 165,000 officers and men.

We had a relatively quiet Christmas and early in the new year I stepped up my Staff College work by a couple of notches. The departure of Dudley and Pat Carnie meant that I was now second in command of the squadron. Their replacements were Desmond Lavender and his wife Zoë, who also became close friends. In May I had the privilege of receiving an invitation from the Grand Chamberlain to the Royal Buffet and Sitting in State (Bersanding) Ceremony of the wedding of the daughter of Their Majesties the Yang di-Pertuan Agong and the Raja Permaisuri Agong at the Istana Negara. This is the most colourful and grandest of the various ceremonies, when the bridal couple have the first sight of each other as man and wife, sitting side by side. It was a very moving and enjoyable event. Ruth would have loved to have been there, but such invitations are restricted to men. I asked an aide if I might take some photographs; there was a whisper to the groom, a nod and a smile, and I obtained some fine pictures.

One of the most spectacular sights in Malaya is that of the enormous leatherback sea turtles coming ashore and laying their eggs in May/June on the beach of Rantau Abang in Terengganu, one of the world's few nesting sites. These turtles can reach a length of six feet and a weight in excess of 800lbs. We had hoped to see this spectacle, but it would have involved a long and difficult journey which we considered inadvisable with a very young family; a year later we would be returning to England, so we never visited the east coast. However, I did see quite a bit of the country from the air. I had made friends with our neighbours (656 Squadron Army Air Corps) and in addition to duty trips to outlying units I managed some very memorable flights with pilots needing to test their small Auster reconnaissance aircraft after repair or meet their required number of flying hours. Apart from coming under some small-arms fire from a residue of terrorists in the north on one occasion, I enjoyed some wonderful flights above the mountainous backbone of Malaya; also along the west coast – sometimes at only 50–100 feet above the sea, so that we had to 'jump' the promontories, it was like being in an ultra-fast speedboat. I believe the name of the pilot who gave me this exhilarating low level flight was Captain Ian (?) Horsley-Curry AAC and that he died in an accident in Hong Kong on his next posting. Even the Cuban Missile Crisis (16th-18th October 1962), the closest that planet Earth has come to WW3, could not detract me from my Staff College examination studies.

Justin and Mark were thriving in the tropical climate and I do not recollect a single illness or even a common cold. Many photographs were taken and sent to appreciative members of the family. Seraphim was a wonderful help to Ruth in looking after the boys and became very attached to them. She had her own room with shower beneath the house, which opened onto the lower lawn, but she returned to the convent each evening. There was one amusing incident when Justin peeped beneath her swing door when she was taking a shower and called, '*I can see you Sessin.*' He got a bucket of water in his face the next time he bent down, and 'Sessin' told him she was cross. '*Justin toss too*' was the reply.

Early in July 1962 the squadron was looking forward to the return of Lieutenant Mohammed Yusof from a communications course in

India, when we learned that he was a passenger on the Alitalia Airline's Douglas DC-8-43 that crashed in Junner, Maharashtra on 7 July. We were stunned when the news came through that there were no survivors. I was told to stand by, together with a Malay subaltern, to receive the coffin from Alitalia Airways at Singapore Airport. It arrived about a week later. We flew early in the morning to Singapore in ceremonial uniform in a Twin Pioneer cargo plane of the Royal Malayan Air Force, received the coffin and returned immediately to Kuala Lumpur. We sat next to the coffin in the non-air-conditioned cargo compartment – not a pleasant journey. After more ceremony at Kuala Lumpur airport there was a long journey to the remote kampong of Mohammed Yusof's family, where we attended his funeral. I will never forget the appreciation of his family. It was almost time for breakfast when I returned home, drenched to the skin from the monsoon weather. The crash was eventually attributed to a navigation error.

My annual leave was spent at home engaged in intensive study, with wonderful support and understanding from Ruth. In October I received my annual confidential report and was relieved that it contained the requisite recommendation to the Staff College from my new squadron commander, Major Gordon Cathcart, without which I would not have been able to sit the Staff College examination; I would only have been eligible to sit the captain-to-major promotion examination. However, I was disappointed that the grading was not a top-of-the-range 'A'. When the week of seven examination papers was over I rewarded Ruth with a grand shopping spree for her tolerance and support. We then enjoyed a very pleasant Christmas.

As soon as we were into the new year of 1963 our minds began to focus on our return to the United Kingdom in mid-April. We were very conscious of the fact that there were now four of us, that a wait for Army married accommodation was usually three or four months and that there was no family home to which we could turn, apart from perhaps a few weeks at the modestly sized cottage of Ruth's mother in Boston Spa. Without being stringent in our spending, we had managed to save sufficient for a deposit on an average-priced house. We recognised that we needed to give serious consideration to a house purchase and that we should begin our search in the Boston Spa area.

The Malayan government provided a DIY option for returning to the UK, whereby the cost of first-class travel by ship was added to the final pay and allowances and one made one's own travel arrangements. This enabled the more adventurous to arrange some very interesting and longer return journeys, albeit usually travelling in either second or tourist-class cabins. The most popular route choice was via Hong Kong, the Hawaiian Islands and the Panama Canal. We were only mildly tempted, for it would have been difficult to take Justin and Mark on shore excursions. So, we opted for the same route as that by which we had arrived.

The final weeks were hectic and exciting, involving buying presents and attending or organising farewell parties. We couldn't wait to see our relatives and friends in the UK again, particularly to show off our two sons. In late March I received an interim on-posting report – top grade, with an unqualified recommendation to the Staff College, very well supported by senior officers. I could not have wished for more. On 15 April I was advised that I had comfortably passed the Staff College examination. Three days later the Pedley family caught the morning train to Singapore on the first leg of their return to the UK, again meticulously arranged by the Crown Agents, with accommodation in one of the world's top hotels – the Raffles. It was an important date for Singapore for it was the day of its first live television transmission. We watched it that evening as we had dinner, amused by the sight of dozens of pairs of oriental eyes of the hotel staff peeping from behind pillars in the dimmed lights of the magnificent dining room.

There had been significant changes in Malaya during our three years of secondment. Malaya's independence in August 1957 had incorporated the statutory agreement that Malay would be the national language, that the head of state would be drawn from the Malay sultans and that the Chinese and Indians would have the vote and proportional representation in the Cabinet. These agreements were respected and were working. Aided by the quality of the Armed Forces and the police, a bedrock of confidence had developed that enabled the country to attract significant overseas investment, and now Malaya was on the brink of an economic boom. The rubber plantations were declining in the face of synthetic production, but the increasingly valuable tin mines and palm oil plantations remained, supplemented by a thriving industrial sector. Five months after we left, despite confrontation from Indonesia, Malaya merged with Singapore, British North Borneo and Sarawak to form Malaysia, though Singapore was expelled in August 1965. Malaysia now has a population in excess of 33 million. It is one of the world's largest exporters of semiconductors, electrical goods and information and communications technology products and it also enjoys a thriving tourist industry. I feel privileged to have served that wonderful country during three of its most formative years.

Later Reflections on Malaya

Our Malayan Chinese landlord (Mr Leong) occasionally called on us during our tenancy to check that all was well and we had some very interesting discussions with him, particularly about our western civilisation and culture and that of China. He told me on one occasion that China had an advanced civilisation before my country had even reached the Bronze age (2,000 BC), taunting me with the fact that western men still have hairy chests, whilst the chests of Chinese men are hairless. Whereupon, I poured him another drink and told him that western ladies liked men with hairy chests. However, these good natured discussions prompted me in later life to read more about China's history and develop a deep respect for the people of China, though not its politics. In 2004, China's Ministry of Science and Technology initiated a detailed study on early Chinese civilisation, led by the Chinese Academy of Social Sciences' Institute of Archaeology and Peking University's School of Archaeology and Museology. On 28 May 2018 the results were released, incorporating more than 900 academic papers. Evidence was produced of:

- 5,300 to 4,100 years ago – Hangzhou, Zhejiang province (Liangzhu site). *Remains of a huge city [33ft walls], remnants of large dam [2.2 miles long and over 33 ft thick] and evidence of highly developed agriculture.*

- 4,300 to 4,100 years ago – Xiangfen, Shanxi province (Toosi site). *A capital city, thought to be that of the legendary ruler, Emperor Yao. Remains of an ancient observatory unearthed.*
- 3,750 to 3,550 years ago – Luoyang, Henan province (Erlitou site). *Relics of a capital-level city of a dynasty. [It created] a foundation for a united country with multi-ethnic groups.*

It is interesting to compare these dates with the Great Pyramid of Giza (built 4,600 years ago) and Stonehenge (the stone circle erected in the late Neolithic period about 4,500 years ago). Our Chinese landlord had not had too much to drink – he was just proud of his ancestry. Much later I was to become aware of Malta's prehistoric temples, the building of which began 5,600 years ago.

Shortly before we began our homeword journey Mr Leong and his wife invited Ruth and me to a farewell Chinese supper at a prominent Kuala Lumpur restaurant. Neither of us counted the number of courses, but it was certainly into double figures, each a gastronomic delight, eaten with chopsticks and supported by Chinese music and décor.

Whenever I see images of China's current President (Xi Jinping) with his impeccable smile and courtesy whilst conducting diplomatic negotiations with western heads of state, I suspect that ingrained deep within him lies that sense of history and national superiority that Mr Leong had revealed to me. The personal quality that Mr Leong most admired was 'smartness', in the sense of being keen in business, and I suspect that President Xi Jinping would not disagree. My regard of Xi Jinping became tarnished in 2017 when he described [at the Communist Party Congress] China's intent on world leadership, linked to Marxist-Leninist ideology. I then became dismayed; because of his actions in Hong Kong in 2020 and his ever-increasing territorial claims in the South China Sea.

I also left Malaya with an increased respect for other religions. I always enjoyed religious discussions with 'Haji Barber' as he cut my hair in my office. I forget his real name – he was a devout Muslim who made the pilgrimage to Mecca in 1961, receiving the title of Haji on return.

He spoke good English, and no matter the religious topic that I raised he was able to give sensible and simple comment and opinion. Sadly, extremist hate-preachers in western countries and elsewhere now routinely take religious texts out of context and manipulate the meaning by selective quotation. Haji Barber and I were able to share our thoughts and beliefs; including our having a spirit which survives death – in some manner far beyond human comprehension. He respected Christ as a prophet of similar greatness as Muhammad and I was surprised at the depth of his knowledge of the bible. He was a quietly spoken man, well respected in the Squadron.

Whilst Haji Barber was on his pilgrimage I turned to the local Indian barber, nestled in a row of shops a couple of hundred yards down the slope from where we lived. The customer ahead of me was receiving the traditional Indian barber massage which culminates in a twist and crack of the neck. I did not have the massage, but on the conclusion of my haircut I received that twist and crack of the neck, as did most of his customers – it was routine. When I was sufficiently relaxed in the neck and shoulder area he slowly manoeuvred my head slightly from side to side … and then a sharp twist and crack. I was applauded by others in the shop. I felt magnificent afterwards and received this manipulation on at least two subsequent occasions.

RETURN TO BLIGHTY
AND THE BRITISH ARMY

April 1963

On 19 April 1963 the Pedley family embarked on the relatively new Orient Steam Navigation Company liner SS *Oriana* (not to be confused with the later cruise ship of that name). *Oriana*, the nickname of Queen Elizabeth I, had made her maiden voyage some 28 months earlier, subsequently working the Southampton–Australia route, but this was her maiden call at Singapore. She was one of the fastest (30 knots) and most luxurious ships of the time. She would call at the same ports that the SS *Carthage* had called at three years earlier, excluding Bombay, but with an additional and welcome call at Naples. Again, we travelled first class, enjoying a standard of supreme luxury far in excess of that experienced on modern cruise ships. We were homeward bound and our morale was sky high.

We arrived in Southampton 17 days later, on 6 May – a much quicker journey than our outward journey of 23 days. Ruth's mother had kindly offered to accommodate us, and we had gratefully accepted. The next few weeks were spent visiting friends and relatives and showing off our sons. Our first call was to see my grandfather and his second wife, Elizabeth, in Harrogate. We were delighted to see how well and active they were for their age. They had coped extremely well with the Big Freeze of the past winter which had been the coldest on record in the country; the BBC TV news expressing real concern on one day that the Strait of Dover might freeze over. It began on Boxing Day. On 29/30 December there was a particularly savage blizzard in SW England resulting in drifts of 15 feet. Temperatures plummeted in January; the sea froze for a mile from shore in Kent and four miles from Dunkirk. On 22 January a car was driven across the Thames at Oxford, whilst downstream in London it snowed for three months. This record breaking Big Freeze affected the entire country, lasting until mid-March. Issues of the Railway Magazine provide an insight to the desperate struggle to maintain passenger and freight services. Sheep losses were high but not on the scale of the 1946/47 winter.

Our next stop was to see Nanette Simpson (Ruth's best friend), her husband Ted and their children, at Ivy House Farm, Walton (a 350-acre mixed farm), followed by many other visits. We had kept in regular touch with our friends over the past three years by letter, but such communication is flimsy compared with personal contact.

On Tuesday 4th June, Whit-Tuesday (the third day of the week beginning on Pentecost), we arranged to meet Ted, Nanette and family at the 111th Wetherby Show, held in the Wetherby Grange Park, adjacent to the river – one of the most attractive venues for a one-day agricultural show in the county. The weather was perfect. After looking at the livestock, admiring some of the arena events and listening to the Wetherby silver band, we watched a competitive Wetherby league cricket match (in which Ted was playing), keeping half an eye on Justin (now aged 3 years and 5 months), who had wandered off to join some children who were clambering over the duty fire engine of the Wetherby fire brigade. It was about 50 yards from us, with a member of the crew supervising the children. The other members of the crew were at our side, also watching the cricket. Justin managed to get to the driver's seat and was soon enjoying himself in a fantasy world. This tranquil scene was soon abruptly disturbed by the piercing wail of the fire engine siren. The other members of the crew dashed to their fire engine, whilst I rushed to collect Justin. I learnt that a child had fiddled with the dashboard controls, setting off the siren. I was not particularly surprised to learn that it was Justin. Ruth told me later that she felt sure that it was Justin the instant that she heard the siren. The following day the scandal of the year broke as John Profumo, Secretary of State for War, resigned over an affair with Christine Keeler, amusing the French, who had difficulty in comprehending what the fuss was about.

I paid a farewell visit to my Leeds–Wetherby railway line and Scholes station, standing on the bridge overlooking the track that I knew so well.

The line was to close to passenger service at the end of the year, with total closure scheduled for early 1964. I had followed the Beeching cuts debacle and recognised the need for stringent financial savings within Britain's railway system. However, I could never understand why the lines selected for closure could not have been structurally maintained with periodic review. As it turned out, so many of the lines could have been commercially viable in later years, and others could have helped meet the growing social demand for tourism and recreation tracks by those living in our cities, but the infrastructure was either destroyed or lost. The Leeds city boundary was soon arbitrarily extended to encompass villages such as Scholes, with huge housing developments resulting in thousands of people travelling by car and bus into the city each day. Sadly, the track between Scholes and Leeds, which could have taken commuter trains or high-speed trams, no longer existed, and bridges and stations had been demolished and the land sold. I learnt later that the Crossgates to Wetherby line [Crossgates, Penda's Way, Scholes, Thorner, Bardsey, Collingham Bridge, Wetherby] was the first to be closed under the Beeching Plan.

I had written a formal letter to the War Office (soon to be absorbed into the Ministry of Defence) on my return to England, reporting my arrival and contact details and seeking information on my next appointment. I was told that this was to be with the 2nd Division Signal Regiment in Germany. On contacting my new commanding officer, Lieutenant Colonel N.C. Porter, I learned that I was to be second in command (2IC) of 206 Signal Squadron, which served Headquarters 6th Infantry Brigade Group, located in Münster. I was well pleased with this appointment, and Ruth was happy enough to be going to Germany again, once the immediate provision of a married quarter was confirmed. We had looked at the feasibility of purchasing a house in the Boston Spa area, but when we learned that we might be accommodated within a few weeks in Münster we decided to put house purchase on the back burner for a while.

I realised that being at the sharp end again in an infantry brigade in Germany might be a bit of a culture shock after three years in Malaya, but if I was to have a good chance of Staff College selection I needed a cracking good report from a brigade or division commander of the British Army of the Rhine (BAOR), which was why I was being posted to Münster. Passing the written examination was difficult enough, but selection was even more competitive. There had been organisational changes since I last served in Germany. Brigades had become brigade groups, with an additional infantry battalion under command, plus other extras that gave them additional firepower, manoeuvrability and resilience. Among the many changes, the communications squadron that served the headquarters had an additional officer – the appointment that I was required to fill, in what was now an Army composed virtually entirely of regular soldiers. However, there was no change to the Soviet threat, nor was there any change to the high level of commitment within BAOR units. I was entitled to an 'end-of-secondment' leave of 140 days but accommodating us for that long was far too much to ask of Ruth's mother. When my squadron commander, Major Harry Rothwell, wrote to me and asked if I could reduce it by at least three weeks, because I was urgently needed for an important exercise in France in September, it was a blessing. I agreed to reduce it by several weeks, provided that a quarter and accompanied passage to Germany could be assured. It was assured, and our 'sacrifice' was very much appreciated.

Nevertheless, there was still ample time for us to first enjoy a holiday in Scotland, using the Dollar home of Ruth's brother (Leslie) and wife (Margaret) and their family (John, Pat and Jenny) while they were away on holiday, followed by some time at Filey.

6th INFANTRY BRIGADE GROUP

Münster – September 1963

6th Infantry Brigade Group was commanded by Brigadier C.W. Dunbar (later to be Major-General Charles Whish Dunbar CBE, and honorary colonel of the Royal Highland Fusiliers from 1969 to 1979. The brigade major was Major Roy Birkett, who two years later was to command the 1st Battalion of the Prince of Wales's Own Regiment of Yorkshire (1PWO).

We were provided with a splendid modern married quarter in the quiet outskirts of a most pleasant city. I had no difficulty in settling in as part of a happy and proficient team at the Brigade Group Headquarters. Ruth's British Forces Germany driving licence was quickly renewed and she had already made several friends by the time I departed as part of the advance party for a month's exercise in southern France. I knew that Ruth and the boys would be very well looked after by our military neighbours.

The exercise was to be held on France's 2,400-foot Plateau du Larzac Military Training Area, located between Millau and Béziers in the Cévennes region. In turn, the brigade's three infantry battalions and their supporting sub-units were all to travel the 600-mile road journey from Westphalia to the training area, under German and French police escort, and on arrival would be immediately launched into a testing tactical scenario involving different phases of combat. The length of the journey and the steep climb up to the plateau were in themselves a stern test of both soldier stamina and mechanical maintenance.

There were two night stops en route for our advance party, both in French barracks, one of which was a training unit for the French Foreign Legion. I had a break from this tedious journey on the third day when Major Roy Birkett invited me to accompany him in a helicopter for the next leg. It was a stiflingly hot day. When we were passing through the Burgundy region we flew over a rather fine château where the family were enjoying themselves beside their swimming pool. They waved to us as we flew over, whereupon Roy Birkett scribbled a note – 'If we are welcome to land, please wave again' – and tied it to a spanner. He handed it to the pilot, who turned the helicopter round, hovered, and dropped it beside the pool. The family recovered it and spontaneously waved. We had a very pleasant snack and glass of fine Burgundy, thanked them warmly, and continued our journey. Now that is what I call regimental soldiering at its best!

My task on this series of battalion test exercises was nothing to do with communications – I was an umpire. An enemy force had been formed under the command of an experienced and well-respected infantry officer, while directing staff/umpire (DS) scripts had been written by the very competent and experienced Roy Birkett, who was recognised as being destined for higher rank. I felt flattered to have been selected as one of the small group of umpires, as this showed recognition of my examination successes and of my being a staff candidate. Each evening, Brigadier Dunbar and Major Roy Birkett briefed us and I would then attach myself to the battalion or company headquarters as directed by them, listening to the radio nets and orders that were issued, discreetly moving on foot wherever I wished, without revealing the battalion's tactical deployment to the enemy. I worked to the DS script, but I was allowed some latitude and if I felt the need to change it and impose additional or fewer casualties, for example, I was at liberty to do so, provided that I could justify my decision afterwards. I thoroughly enjoyed the experience.

Arrangements had been made that at the end of an intense and gruelling six-day exercise for each battalion group in turn, there would be forty-eight hours of relaxation on the Mediterranean coast to recuperate, prior to their long return journey. In response to our request for a reserved beach area, so that the soldiers would not be a nuisance to holidaymakers, the French local authority kindly allocated a 400-yard strip in the centre of a nudist camp on the Cap d'Agde. It was an attractive beach with an abundance of large, colourful shells. The military police laid white mine tape along the two boundaries and established military police posts, surveying the area with their binoculars. Soldiers were told that if they crossed the boundary lines they would be in big trouble. No problem, or so it seemed. Never underestimate the ingenuity of the British soldier. On the first day of 'recuperation' I sat with a group of officers wearing our swimming trunks on this reserved slice of beach, eating sandwiches and drinking wine. It was a gloriously hot day, with a gentle breeze. We were not far from the eastern boundary and had noticed that attractive girls and young women, dressed in their birthday suits, were gradually coming closer and closer to the white mine tape as they collected shells. Not surprisingly, there were gasps from the soldiers each time one of them bent down to pick up a shell, and it was necessary for the military police to make their presence felt by patrolling their white line, which stretched about fifty yards into the sea. After a while I felt a nudge in my side from Major Harry Rothwell, who pointed to a drifting log about two hundred yards from the shore. I could not see anything unusual about it, but he pointed out that it was drifting in the opposite direction to the breeze and that the Mediterranean was virtually non-tidal. He passed his binoculars to me. I saw that on the far side of the log there were at least six soldiers gently paddling it towards, and eventually into, the nudist camp. I don't think any serious attempt was made to catch them and I later learned that they had a wonderful day.

Tired of watching attractive nude female bodies, I went on subsequent 'recuperation breaks' with Major Roy Birkett and members of the directing staff/umpires to see other parts of the Languedoc region. We obtained tickets to attend a major bullfighting event one Sunday afternoon in the well-known Béziers arena, leaving with mixed feelings. We visited the Roman triple-tier aqueduct near Nîmes; a truly amazing construction, with the two lower tiers carrying a road across the river and the top tier supporting an aqueduct conduit that carries water into the city. We saw some stunning countryside, with lunar-type terrain on the high plateau, and at one of several small factories in Millau we purchased some of the towns's famous leather gloves for our ladies back home in Münster.

It was a long but uneventful return journey to Münster. The training was most valuable, but the financial cost of moving the greater part of the 6th Infantry Brigade Group such a distance must have been very high and difficult to justify. It did cross my mind that it might have been politically conceived – a demonstration of the capability of a joint Anglo-French military force deploying from France's nearby Marseilles naval base.

It was so very nice to be back with the family. It was not so nice facing the huge amount of work that had built up, with the squadron's many technical and administrative inspections only a few weeks away. Our very enjoyable Christmas and New Year celebrations were preceded and followed by two events that stunned the world – the assassination of John F. Kennedy on 22 November 1963 and the Beatlemania that erupted in January 1964. While I could never understand the mass hysteria for the latter, I was a very strong admirer of the former. Indeed, I looked upon the young President Kennedy with some reverence – he was an inspiration and figure of hope for the future, not matched by any of his successors in the White House. It was little known outside the Kennedy family that President John Fitzgerald Kennedy (JFK/Jack) bore a life of sickness and pain from a young age, now detailed in the 2020 biography "JFK: Coming of Age in the American Century, 1917=1956", by Fredrik Logevall. It describes JFK's courageous fight against Addison's disease (a rare disorder of the two adrenal glands sitting on top of the kidneys), spinal problems, recurrent malaria and near-death hospitalizations; temporarily increasing my high regard of this handsome, charismatic, bright and inspiring man. However, as is so characteristic of men born into great wealth and position, shame and irresponsibility were never far distant. Flirtations and abandonment of some of Hollywood's most glamorous stars were perhaps to be expected, but not revelations of venereal disease as a teenager, priabic extravagance and treating women like taxis. To his credit, JFK was quick to join the United States Navy during WW2, serving in the Solomon Islands campaign as a Lieutenant in Torpedo Boat actions; his six medals including the Purple Heart. Had the bullet fired at him on 22 November 1963 missed, JFK may have become a great President; but with only 1,000 days in office he is low in current rankings, whilst my initial reverence has waned.

Very early in the new year I was called to the office of Lieutenant Colonel N.C. Porter, Commander Royal Signals of the 2nd Division, for interview and to peruse my annual confidential report. I left his office a very happy man. Again, I had a top-of-the-range grading and an unqualified recommendation for the Army Staff College and for promotion to major. Provided that this excellent report was well supported by three additional officers – Commander 6th Infantry Brigade, GOC 2nd Division and Chief Signals Officer BAOR – there was a fair chance that my tour would be cut short and that the Pedley family would be returning to the UK for the next annual Staff College course. The next course began in early January 1965, but it was preceded by a course of almost three months' duration at the Royal Military College of Science (RMCS) at Shrivenham, which was preceded by a three-week Royal Signals preparatory course at Catterick. Ruth was, of course, also delighted at this prospect – though we were very happy in Münster – and once more we began to recognise the importance of house purchase, most likely in the Boston Spa area.

I had been trying for several weeks to get exemption, because of my workload, from entering the corps commander's mandatory (for all captains) 'winter essay' competition. I received a stuffy reply, procrastinated further and eventually, much to Ruth's displeasure, spent a weekend writing it – in a bit of a huff. I cannot even remember the subject that the corps commander had set, but my essay was handed in on the last day for submission to Captain Alex Godsman of the Cameronians, who was one of Brigadier Dunbar's staff officers at HQ 6th Infantry Brigade Group, and I thought no more about it. I received a telephone call from Alex a few days later to tell me that Brigadier Dunbar had selected it as being the best in the brigade and that it had been sent on to

Headquarters 2nd Division. He added that it had to be submitted with a nom de plume, and that as he had been unable to contact me he had chosen one for me. He had not tried very hard and I was horrified at his choice – the name of a woman of such disrepute that I will not mention it. The essay was subsequently selected by GOC 2nd Division (later General Sir Mervyn Andrew Haldane Butler, KCB, CBE, DSO & bar, MC) as one of two essays to be forward to the General Officer Commanding-in-Chief , 1st (British) Corps (later Lieutenant-General Sir Richard Elton Goodwin, KCB, CBE, DSO), who selected it as one of the best three. The top tier of army ranks is not easy to understand. Most people know that a Major is two ranks higher than a Lieutenant, but a Lieutenant-General is senior to a Major-General; both subservient to a General, which is the highest rank in the US Army. However, many countries (including Britain) retain Field Marshal as the highest rank, though this may be discontinued, with Field Marshal Peter Anthony Inge, Baron Inge, KG, GCB, PC, DL perhaps the last of 141 British Field Marshals [a GREEN HOWARD soldier]. The first was a Scottish nobleman; Field Marshal George Hamilton, 1st Earl of Orkney, KT – appointed on 31 Jan 1735. He died two years later (aged 70).

Though the demands of 6th Infantry Brigade Group were as high as those that I had experienced in 11th Infantry Brigade as a subaltern, the workload was eased slightly by our increased manpower 'establishment'. Also, I now had more experience and the benefits of a happy family life. When we were not on the testing, and sometimes exhausting exercises, we had a pleasant social life – formal cocktail parties and dinner nights in the officers' mess and regular private dinner parties. In my early days as a subaltern, virtually all the officers' mess dinner nights were male only and the ladies only attended such functions as the summer and Christmas balls, but now there was an increasing number of 'ladies' nights'. These were also formal occasions with mandatory attendance, usually with a regimental band playing during dinner and the ladies retiring after the toasts, prompted by the senior officer's wife. After consuming more port, we would then join the ladies for dancing and roulette. Out of respect to the hosts, the men would normally wear a lounge suit for private dinner parties, but the hostess would soon invite them to remove their jackets. The table would be attractively laid with the best dinner service and tableware, and each course would be a gastronomic delight. Ruth accumulated some wonderful recipes. One of my favourites was her syllabub, the favourite dessert of Queen Elizabeth I, which made a mockery of Mrs Beeton's recipe and of others. It was most unusual for officers' wives to be employed at that time, and instead they enjoyed a coffee-morning and dinner party style of life that was soon to disappear. However, their contribution to the Army as unpaid social workers should not be overlooked, nor the value of the extra personal attention that they were able to devote to their children. It was a different age, but their lifestyle was probably no different to that led by many middle-class families in civilian life at the time, and for decades before.

I must have received notification of my selection for the next Camberley course in mid-April – several verbal notifications and congratulations arrived at about the same time. However, the first written notification that I received was from Colonel (almost Brigadier) David Horsfield, then Commandant of the School of Signals at Catterick, beating the official Ministry of Defence notification by three days. On reading his kind letter I mentally forgave him for giving me those two extra Saturday-morning-punishment parades at Sandhurst. I thanked Ruth very sincerely and warmly, not only for her support, but for her patience and wonderful, consistent inspiration over such a long period. With redundancy clouds still on the horizon, I now felt far more secure in my career, at least for the time being.

On 12 June 1964 a South African anti-apartheid lawyer named Nelson Rolihlahla Mandela was found guilty in the Pretoria Supreme Court on four counts of sabotage and conspiracy to overthrow the South African government. The prosecution had called for a death sentence, but the judge condemned him (and two others) to life imprisonment. 27 years were to pass before he was released, eventually becoming President of his country.

CATTERICK AND SHRIVENHAM

It would have been mid-to-late August when we returned to the UK. Ruth's mother kindly gave us accommodation, though I stayed in the mess at Catterick for my Royal Signals preparatory course, joining the family at Boston Spa each weekend. It was grand to see friends and relatives again, particularly my grandfather, who seemed so happy and well with second wife, Elizabeth. She was such a jovial person and very active for her age, and they were clearly deriving much pleasure from their regular bus tours around the country. Neither of them had learned to drive. They were of that generation that had enjoyed a very extensive and efficient rail network, with a taxi at their destination, so road excursions were an exciting novelty. Ruth's mother also seemed well, but Ruth told me that she was being treated by the village doctor for depression. We were soon visiting Nanette and Ted Simpson at their farm at Walton and enjoyed showing off to each other our growing families. We advised them of our wish to purchase a home in the area and they gave us some very useful information on what was on the market and for how much. Ruth and I shared the opinion that her mother should be invited to reside with us in the home that we intended to purchase. It would be of mutual benefit, in that she would have a more cosy and pleasant place in which to live, while we could be assured that there was always a reasonable-sized home to return to between overseas postings. She was thrilled with the suggestion and readily agreed.

We became interested in some attractive properties that were being built in stone on the west side of the river Wharfe, close to the road bridge, at a price of about £5,000, which was just affordable. Some splendid stone properties were also being built in Thorp Arch Park on the east side of the river, but they were at a price that we could not afford. However, we were persuaded to look at them, particularly at plot 24, the 'cheapest', but with probably the best river view. We called at the on-site estate office and learned that this could be ours for £6,400. I had already been in touch with the Bradford & Bingley Building Society, where we had a subscription account, and soon obtained a mortgage offer of £4,850 (75%) repaid at 6% over 25 years. I did not quite have the difference of £1,550, which was close to my annual income of £1,640, whereupon Ruth's mother, with whom we had shared our thoughts and calculations, immediately said that she would loan us £1,000. When I hesitated, she told me of some of the sacrifices that Ruth had made when her father died, including giving her the entirety of her father's bequest. Ruth told me that I should accept her mother's offer, with that 'not negotiable' look in her eyes. It was a very happy evening and Ruth was soon planning the garden. During the following week I finalised the arrangements with Crowther Estates and the 'Bradford & Bingley', and on 14 September began my course at the School of Signals at Catterick. The purpose of the course was to make sure that I and the other five Royal Signals students were up to date with the latest military communications developments and changes prior to attending the Army Staff College course. It was well worthwhile.

I went virtually directly from the Catterick course to the General Staff Science course at the RMCS Shrivenham, which began on 12 October, spending the first two weeks in mess. I had been advised several weeks earlier that rented accommodation was likely to become available, and at the end of the first week I took over a most pleasant residence called Vine Cottage, in the delightful village of Stanford in the Vale (the vale being that of the White Horse) and collected the family on the following weekend. At that time Ruth's mother was staying with Leslie and Margaret and family in Dollar. She had written regular chatty letters addressed to Ruth at her cottage in Boston Spa, saying that she had seen the Dollar doctor regarding her bouts of depression and that his tablets were having a positive effect. Nevertheless, she would be seeing her Boston Spa doctor as soon as she returned. Though busy looking after two very active young children, Ruth had done some decorating of the cottage as a surprise for her.

The General Staff Science course was provided in order to ensure that Camberley students, with the exception of some overseas students, had a good understanding of the latest developments in the defence industry and of the ongoing research. There would be stimulating discussions on how these developments might change current tactics and organisations, and one became conscious of the fact that among us were not only the future hierarchy of the British Army but also selected high fliers of the Royal Navy and the Royal Air Force, as well as of the Commonwealth and USA Armed Forces. The tuition gave an indication of what life at Camberley would be like – one really had to get up early each day, with wits well tuned.

On 15th October 1964 there was a general election; won by Harold Wilson with a miniscule majority of four. It did not deter him, and within a week most of the principals of his new government had been announced. It is at this point that the now retired Lieutenant Colonel Alun Arthur Gwynne Jones OBE, MC [The Shadow of My Hand] re-enters my memoirs. He was progressing as a high-flier in the army when in 1961 the editor of *The Times* invited him to lunch, and also to become his defence correspondent. He accepted. Now, on the morning of Friday 23rd October 1964, he found himself inside 10 Downing Street, expecting a discussion on a rather controversial article that he had written on the control of nuclear weapons. To his surprise he was immediately ushered into the Cabinet room, where Harold Wilson asked him to be his 'Minister for Disarmament', with a seat in the House of Lords and membership of the Privy Council. He required an answer within the hour for it needed the approval of the Queen, and Her Majesty was leaving for Balmoral that evening. Following discussion with his wife [Mona] and editor, he agreed. It was the leading news story of the day; it was unheard of! The selection proved to be shrewd and justified. Lord Chalfont had enormous and diverse talent;

outstanding soldier, journalist, politician, historian, first class rugby and cricket player, Chairman of Vickers Shipbuilding. He died on 10th January 2020 (aged 100).

Ruth liked Vine Cottage, while Justin and Mark enjoyed the many pleasant country walks. We were next door to what a long time ago had been a bakery, and sometimes there would be the distinct aroma of bread being baked. A short distance from us lived the poet, comedienne and television presenter Pam Ayres.

Ruth's mother's bouts of depression were still a matter of concern. She did not seem to be responding to the prescribed tablets or taking the advice of her Boston Spa doctor (Dr Lee), and we invited her to spend some time with us in Stanford in the Vale, which she readily accepted. She first spent a few days with her lifelong friend, Mrs Mary Armitage, in Harrogate. We met her at Oxford railway station on 9 November. Apart from insomnia, she seemed very happy to be with us, though sometimes confused, which we attributed to the tablets that she was taking. She loved being with the children. After about a fortnight she stated that it was time for her to return home, particularly to enable her to see Dr Lee again. She was confident about being able to manage her train journey and we waved her goodbye on the platform at Oxford station on 22 November. She was to have telephoned us on her arrival back home, but there was no such call and our calls received no answer. We called one of her neighbours, who went to check. The return call told us to prepare for a shock – she had been found dead in a gas-filled room, a death that was later to be recorded as suicide.

I will not attempt to describe our horror and grief. However, we immediately recognised the need to shield our emotions and the events from Justin and Mark and ensure that their happy childhood days were disturbed as little as possible. I was given compassionate leave and we immediately returned to Yorkshire to face the unpleasant but necessary sequence of events that follows such tragedies, staying in a Harrogate hotel. Leslie and Margaret soon joined us and we planned the funeral. The medical opinion, as well as that of the family, was that Bessie's suicide was the result of side effects caused by an excess of phenobarbitone tablets, prescribed for depression. Indeed, the doctor who treated her in Dollar stated that she had become addicted to them. It was not possible to discuss her tragic death with Dr Lee, for he died of a stroke on the day before her funeral, which was held on 27 November. I was eventually to learn that she had been saved from an attempted suicide in 1942 by her then 16-year-old-son, Leslie.

At one time during WW2 Bessie worked as a "Bomb Girl" at the Royal Ordnance Factory (ROF) Thorp Arch (see p20/21), probably soon after the family move to Boston Spa from Pateley Bridge in 1944. The [nearly two million] Bomb Girls, who toiled in the country's huge munitions factories, were surely our unsung heroines of the war; making the explosives, bullets, shells and bombs that were needed by the armed forces of our nation. It was not only dirty and exhausting shift work, but also highly dangerous. They, their work and the inevitable fatalities were never reported … for obvious security reasons.

The day after the funeral we returned to Vine Cottage and I resumed my General Staff Science course, finding a large batch of précis in my pigeonhole to study. Only two weeks of the course remained, and on 14 December we moved to Camberley for my Army Staff course.

STAFF COLLEGE

Camberley - January 1965

Our allocated residence and home for the next year was 7 Queen Elizabeth Road, Camberley. It was on a small Army estate of officers' married quarters, reserved for Staff College students. Ruth soon met one of our next-door neighbours when the wife of Australian Army Major David Chinn, who I think was called Maureen, knocked on the door and asked if she could beg a fiver. Now £5 was quite a lot of money in those days but Ruth did not hesitate, reached for her handbag and started counting … Maureen burst out laughing, pushing the money aside. 'No, no, no – a *favour*! Can you help me move a table?'

We could not have wished for a better group of neighbours or for a better environment to help us over our bereavement. They were, of course, all of a similar age, some with children of the same age as Justin and Mark. It was the Christmas holiday period and we soon made friends and celebrated Christmas together in a relaxed pre-course atmosphere.

The recommended and popular school for children aged 5–10 years was Yateley Manor Independent Preparatory School, and that is where Justin began his education, shortly after his fifth birthday. Ruth shared the school run with other mothers, while the husbands walked to work. Mark was very happy with the situation – Justin's absence from the house meant that he now had the total attention of his mother and access to his brother's Christmas presents.

It was now time for me to get down to work. There were 168 students on the course (divided into three divisions, A, B and C), of whom 113 were from the British Army, plus three from the Royal Navy, four from the Royal Marines and three from the Royal Air Force. The remaining 45 were largely from countries of the old British Commonwealth, together with (in no particular order) Iraq, Jordan, West Germany, Libya, USA, Spain, Belgium, Iran, Israel, Japan, France, Sweden, Thailand, Finland and Greece. They were all high fliers in their respective countries. They contributed a great deal to the course, not only in terms of their experience, but also through their good humour and vibrant personalities. Sensitive foreign policy matters between nations did not cause a problem – they were outside the scope of the course.

A student from the other side of the pond described his initial confusion as follows:

> Our first big problem was to decide who were the natives and who came from overseas? There were so many uniforms that we never saw more than two in the same outfit on any one day. And man, just look at those costumes and Beatle hair-cuts. Now tell me who are the dolls in the tartan skirts with the purses. Brother, I tell you, they don't even speak English. And their spelling! They leave out all the 'z's and use 's's and then go and complicate things by putting 'u's in all the simple words like armor. And, good heavens, look at that poor fellow who's broken his glasses and is having to stick one of the lenses in his eye – with a string on it, no less. Ah, well, we'll probably be okay once we get down to work. So this is the instructor. Looks like a nice guy – must be real sharp to be Light Colonel. He's a what? He's a Lieutenant Colonel is he? Oh, but a substantive Major, I see. Was temporary? Really? But also p.s.c., M.C., O.B.E. Oh, brother – just what the hell is he?

As anticipated, the course began with the intensive nose-to-the–grindstone study of the fundamentals of military staff work, with staff duties exercises, service writing exercises, service papers, and so on. Not only had the content to be correct, but it was expected to be typed, with precise format and spacing and within a tight time frame. It was a cardinal sin not to leave one space after a comma and three spaces after a full stop. The reference booklet *Staff Duties in the Field* contained hundreds of abbreviations, and one could be sure that any that were overlooked or erroneous would be spotted by the eagle-eyed directing staff (DS). We were, of course, already familiar with much of this work, and had needed to reach a decent standard in our entry examinations, but now our levels of knowledge, precision and speed were ratcheted up, significantly. However, it was not long before we were all singing from the same hymn sheet and able to move on from this 'basics' stage.

Sir Winston Leonard Spencer Churchill, K.G., O.M., C.H. died on 24th January 1965, following a stroke nine days earlier; his eighth since 1949. His funeral, the biggest national event since the Coronation of 1953 (and the world's largest ever state funeral at that time) was held six days later in St Paul's Cathedral. It was a Saturday. The BBC selected Richard Dimbleby as the sole presenter for over four hours of television coverage, watched intently by a grateful nation; the four members of our family included.

My mind drifted back to June 1940 (aged six), listening with my grandparents to a radio news broadcast; his speech to the House of Commons* in defiance of Nazi Germany:

> *"We shall go on to the end. We shall fight in France, we shall fight on the seas and oceans, we shall fight with growing confidence and growing strength in the air, we shall defend our island, whatever the cost may be. We shall fight on the beaches, we shall fight on the landing grounds, we shall fight in the fields and in the streets, we shall fight in the hills; we shall never surrender."*

* Winston Churchill gave this famous speech on 4th June 1940. However, proceedings of the Commons were not broadcast at that time and the speech that we heard would have been read later by a BBC newsreader.

His body lay in state at Westminster Hall for three days from 26th January; the only breaks being a daily one hour closure for the cleaning of the premises. The queue of visitors was usually about a mile long, with a waiting time of upto three hours. The 3,500 gathering of world dignitaries in St Paul's Cathedral was the largest in history. The Queen never attended the funeral of commoners, but Her Majesty made Churchill's funeral an exception. The service incorporated Winston Churchill's favourite hymns; 'Fight the Good Fight', 'He Who Would Valiant Be' and 'Mine Eyes have Seen the Glory of the Coming of the Lord'. The most notable absentee at the funeral service was the President of the United States, represented by the Chief Justice – a snub that later resulted in an apology. Russia was represented by the Soviet Deputy Prime Minister and Marshal Ivan Koniev – one of Russia's most distinguished soldiers. China was the only country not to send representatives.

The pall bearers included four prime ministers; Clement Attlee, Harold Macmillan, Anthony Eden and Robert Menzies (prime minister of Australia).

The funeral procession from St Paul's Cathedral was magnificent. Tears formed in my eyes, but when the cortege passed the huge dockside cranes, and they dipped in salute, I could contain them no longer.

As the sun sank that day this Island Race realised that it had witnessed an astonishing final act of mourning for the imperial past; London would never again be the capital of the world.

There is no better person to appraise Sir Winston Churchill than outstanding military historian and journalist Sir Max Hugh Macdonald Hastings FRSL FRHistS, whose epic book "Finest Years: Churchill as Warlord 1940-1945" was published by Harper Press in 2009. A few months later during an interview he gave the following replies to two interesting questions:

Q1. Your most recent book is about Winston Churchill. What do you think of him?

"I am a huge admirer of Winston Churchill, one of the greatest human beings of all time and certainly Britain's greatest war leader. But many aspects of the story are much more complex than people recognise. To me the story is that of Churchill (himself a hero) always wanting more from the

British people and the British army than they were capable of delivering. Even though I thought I knew quite a lot about Churchill when I started the book, there is always more. I enjoyed writing this book perhaps more than any other I have done, because the man was so irresistible, even when he was wrong."

Q2. Why are we still fascinated by World War 2?

"Because it was by far the greatest event in human history. There is always something more to learn, something more to say. But I don't buy all the nonsense about the people of that era being 'the Greatest Generation'. They were pretty much like any other generation, but when thrust into extraordinary circumstances many of them achieved extraordinary things."

I humbly accept these scholarly thoughts of Sir Max Hastings and consider Sir Winston Churchill to be the greatest Briton, followed by Viscount Horatio Nelson, Isambard Kingdom Brunel, Sir Isaac Newton and Charles Darwin.

Churchill was more than being Britain's greatest war leader. His bravery, charm, rhetoric and wicked wit were unique, whilst his prolific high quality writings won him the Nobel Prize for Literature in 1953. In that same year there was passionate and heated debate concerning our future relationship with Europe; Churchill needed only five poignant sentences on the matter as he addressed the House of Commons on 11th May:

"We have our own dream and our own task. We are with Europe, but not of it. We are linked but not combined. We are interested and associated but not absorbed. If Britain must choose between Europe and the open sea, she must always choose the open sea."

The quality of instruction was so good and the subject matter so interesting that it was easy not to realise how hard we were working. The focal point for briefing and lectures was the impressive Alanbrooke Hall, with its steep theatre-style seating, and invariably included a diorama floor model depicting terrain and other natural features and unit locations. Tactical situations would be described to us, followed by discussion in syndicates and sometimes actual reconnaissance of the ground, followed by written appreciations and plans and, after DS marking and critique, more syndicate discussion.

All phases of war were covered, both tactical and administrative aspects, and at different levels of command. We gradually learned how splendid tactical plans needed to be tempered to take into account administrative practicality. We became competent in the use of planning tables for fuel, ammunition and general stores consumption to determine the requirements of different formations and units in both routine and intensive combat situations. We were taught how to calculate the administrative benefits that might accrue from the allocation of short-range transport helicopters and how such benefits might be used to tactical advantage. We debated the possible tactical changes that might result from the next generation of aircraft, weapons and equipment, and also the increasing threat of international terrorism. Our DS had all excelled as former students as well as subsequently in demanding staff and command appointments, and they had been selected as having the potential to reach at least brigadier rank. With the syndicates being so small (each consisting of a member of the DS and six students), together with the regular visits from my B Division colonel, the commandant and the deputy commandant, there was never an opportunity to keep a low profile and relax.

The ladies were not ignored – there were occasional division coffee parties and numerous impromptu neighbourly gatherings. There were also some most enjoyable division ladies' dinner nights, attended by both husbands and wives. For men only there were occasional Dinner Club functions, with well-known and entertaining guest speakers. The film star David Niven, a Sandhurst graduate, gave a hilarious talk about his military life and Hollywood which received a standing ovation.

There were three terms at Camberley, with leave breaks at Easter and mid-summer. Well before Easter, Ruth had received a copy of her mother's will, and with probate completed we decided to spend most of Easter in

Yorkshire. Ruth's mother had left her entire estate to Ruth in a Will dated 12 July 1952, and explained this in an attachment:

To-day, I signed my Will leaving everything I possess to my daughter, Ruth. This I have done for two reasons.

1. *On the day of my husband's death my daughter was a great comfort to me. Since that time my daughter has helped me financially and in the home.*
2. *During my daughter's School days at Tadcaster Grammar School no fees whatsoever were paid and my daughter left school at the age of sixteen. Fees and travel expenses were paid for my son for eight years at Knaresborough Grammar School; then followed five years at the University. I am equally fond of my two children, and I am quite sure that in years to come my son will appreciate what I am doing for his sister.*

Note: Ruth gave the entirety of the bequest from her father (£686) to her mother. Her brother received the same bequest, but retained it.

The value of the estate was £3,670, being the total of bank savings/shares (£122), building society savings (£1,043), the loan to myself (£1,000), the value of the cottage (£1,400) and the value of household goods/cash (£105).

It was a very sad visit to Yorkshire, and I held Ruth's hand tightly as we entered her late mother's cottage. We prepared it, as well as the contents that we did not need, for sale. We also visited plot 24, the site of our future home at Thorp Arch Park, liaising with the estate agents. The house on plot 24, which was to be called 'Broadacres', was expected to be built and ready for occupation at the end of July. We were delighted to see the continued happiness in the lives of my grandfather and Elizabeth and, of course, we visited Ivy House Farm at Walton on several occasions to see Nanette and Ted Simpson and their family. Justin and Mark enjoyed exploring the farm buildings and going on walks with us through their fields.

I returned to the course at Camberley to find that its intensity had not subsided. A sense of the pressures ahead could be gleaned from the bulky content of our pigeonholes. The very fabric of the buildings was permeated with a cultural ethos of blood, sweat, tears, and much good humour. We were now being encouraged to gel our experience and learning into original thought, and to come up with ideas for the conduct of military operations in the future.

A visit and address from Field Marshal Montgomery was very well received and several students quickly jumped to their feet when questions were invited. However, when his response to the first two questions was, 'Well, what do *you* think?' the numbers trying to catch his eye significantly reduced. I toyed with the idea of asking him why he was reduced in rank as a cadet at Sandhurst, but thought better of it, remembering David Niven's experience in not dissimilar circumstances. He had asked a very distinguished guest lecturer, 'Could you tell me the time, sir? I have to catch a train.' He was placed under arrest for his insubordination, but escaped and fled to Hollywood, where he resigned his commission and made a fortune. I was introduced to military history whilst studying the subject for the staff college entrance examination in Malaya in 1962. Thereafter I became increasingly absorbed, sometimes giving talks at regimental officer training days; the WW2 battles, achievements and personality of Field Marshal Montgomery prominent. I eventually discovered the circumstances of his reduction in rank at Sandhurst in 1908 (named the Royal Military College at that time): in an initiation ceremony he set fire to the clothing of a tied-up junior cadet. For a balanced opinion of Field Marshal Montgomery's complex character one should study his WW1 record; awarded the DSO for extraordinary courage and conspicuous leadership as a platoon commander in an action in which a sniper's bullet penetrated his right lung. When recovered, he returned to the front as a staff officer, taking part in the Passchendaele battle in August 1917; then Chief of Staff of the 47th Division in the rank of Lieutenant Colonel. Some historians have criticised his WW2 battle plans and direction in North Africa as being too cautious, but it is for consideration that they reflected his intense determination to avoid the useless slaughter that he had witnessed in WW1. As the military and political might of the USA escalated during the latter years of WW2 Field Marshal Montgomery experienced much difficulty in adapting to the changing world order, displaying an increasingly egotistical personality of extreme conceit and arrogance. His disastrous and humiliating defeat at the battle of Arnhem [a bridge too far] may have clipped his wings but he showed no repentance, writing in his memoirs (page 267);

> *"In my – prejudiced – view, if the operation had been properly backed from its inception, and given the aircraft, ground forces, and administrative resources necessary for the job – it would have succeeded in spite of my mistakes, or the adverse weather, or the presence of the 2nd SS Panzer Corps in the Arnhem area. I remain MARKET-GARDEN'S unrepentant advocate."*
>
> Field Marshal Sir Bernard Montgomery

I have much admiration for Field Marshal Montgomery of Alamein, but not as much as for Field Marshal Sir William Slim, commander of the 14th Army in Burma. See pages 37/38.

In mid-July we had a welcome break from Camberley – four days in Normandy, to study selected World War II battles. The aim was to give us some feeling of war and of human reaction to its stresses, and also to show the relationship between the planning and execution of tactical operations. The three battles selected for study were:

1. 6 Airborne Division's assault and subsequent employment in the invasion of Normandy – *Operation Overlord*.
2. 11th Armoured Division's part in an armoured battle which took place immediately east and south-east of Caen – *Operation Goodwood*.
3. A typical infantry battle, conducted by 15th Scottish Division immediately west of Caen – *Operation Epsom*.

We were given preparatory reading to do beforehand, as well as presentations on each of these battles at Alanbrooke Hall, together with a presentation on the naval assault on Normandy – *Operation Neptune*. This battlefield tour also formed part of our study of command. So, away we went, travelling by buses and ferry, to the coastal town of Cabourg, where we stayed in a clutch of pleasant hotels. We were in three groups, and a rotation arrangement enabled each group to have a free day during the four-day visit – the 'bottlefield' day.

The detail of each of these battles is well described on the internet and in an abundance of books written by eminent authors, so I will not attempt to describe them. However, *we* had the additional benefit of the presence of several prominent guest speakers, of varying rank, who had participated in these battles. We also had the benefit of having copies of the written orders that preceded the actions, and large-scale, detailed maps that showed unit locations, boundaries, minefields, objectives, etc. We had the further benefit of hindsight.

On 6 June 1944 (D-Day), 160,000 troops crossed the English Channel to liberate Europe – *Operation Overlord.* The vanguard of this huge assault was the airborne drop of two United States divisions (82 and 101 Airborne Divisions) in the west and the British 6 Airborne Division on the opposite flank, to the east of the river Orne estuary. The 6 Airborne Division task was to seize key objectives prior to the arrival of the armada of ships that would appear over the horizon at dawn. The torchbearers of this liberation were 60 men of the 22nd Independent Parachute Company, the pathfinders to 6 Airborne Division. Like all paratroops they were volunteers, but *they* had been handpicked for the task. They had crammed so much ammunition into their pockets and pouches, so many weapons into their webbing, that they had difficulty hitching on their parachute harnesses. They were each carrying about 100lbs and in addition each had strapped to his leg a 60lb kitbag containing lights and radar beacons with which to mark the dropping and landing zones for the rest of 6 Airborne Division. The leading aircraft contained ten men, led by a young lieutenant who, when war began, had been in the chorus of a West End musical comedy. These pathfinders spearheaded the force that had the most vital role in the Allies' plan, its task being to seize and hold the Allies' eastern flank against inevitable Panzer Division counter attacks. If 6 Airborne Division were to fail, the entire bridgehead might be rolled up westwards along this flank before the seaborne armada could become established on land.

It was our privilege to listen to first-hand accounts of the success of these pathfinders and of how 6 Airborne Division achieved its tasks of capturing vital bridges over the river Orne and adjacent Caen Canal, destroying the Merville battery and various bridges over the river Dives and securing the area against the counterattacks that followed. A total of 362 transport aircraft were utilised in this air assault, plus 1,120 gliders. The human cost to 6 Airborne Division was heavy – 1,748 killed or missing and 2,709 wounded. Their brave actions make me feel very humble. I hope that readers will find time in their lives to visit these battlefields and the military cemeteries in order to understand the sacrifices that were made to free Europe of nazi tyranny.

The guest speakers for *Operation Goodwood* included the actual commander of 11th Armoured Division, Major General G.P.B. Roberts CB DSO (2 bars) MC and the opposing commander of 125 Panzer Grenadier Regiment (equivalent to a British armoured brigade) who stubbornly impeded his breakout, Colonel Hans von Luck (Iron Cross 1st and 2nd Class, Deutsches Kreux in Gold, Ritterkreuz), only a major at the time but selected for promotion. He was a Prussian cavalry officer from a family with a very strong military background that could trace its roots back to the thirteenth century. In 1932 he completed his training as a senior officer cadet at the School of Infantry in Dresden, where one of his instructors was Captain Erwin Rommel. He was in the vanguard of the Blitzkrieg invasion of Poland, crossing the frontier at first light on 1 Sep 1939, then in the Russian campaign and later under Field Marshal Rommel in North Africa, commanding the elite 3rd Panzer Reconnaissance Battalion. His memoirs book, "PANZER COMMANDER" is a classic; ISBN 978-0-3043-6401-5 [2002 edition]. It is written in an easy [non-military] style, incorporating detail of the final desperate battle to shield Hitler's Berlin bunker, his capture by the Russians and almost five years of hard labour in a punishment camp in the Caucuasus mountains, mining coal.

To listen to these directly opposing commanders (standing side by side) describing their experiences during this armoured breakout thrust by the Allies through the German-held area south-east of Caen was intriguing. Major von Luck was returning from three days' leave in Paris, where his fiancée (Dagmar) worked, when he reached the area of Caen and saw the carnage inflicted by the unprecedented massive Allied bombing and naval bombardment on his defensive positions. Without emotion, he professionally described the effect of that onslaught and the actions that he took to re-establish cohesion, command and control. These actions included using the four 88mm guns of an anti-aircraft battery that had been sited in his area (but which was not under his command) in an anti-tank role. When the battery commander refused to relinquish the guns to his control, stating that his role was anti-aircraft, Major von Luck drew his pistol and offered the young officer the choice of being a dead man or a hero. He chose the latter, and Colonel von Luck showed us the exact positions where he placed the four guns. These 88mm anti-aircraft guns accounted for 40 of the 126 tanks that 11th Armoured Division lost that day (18 July 1944)! Operation Goodwood played a most important role in the eventual breakout from Normandy, contributing to subsequent success at the Falaise Gap, but at a very heavy cost. Colonel von Luck was taken prisoner by the Russians in 1945 and only released in 1950 following almost five years in the Russian punishment camp. Though they were only engaged, Dagmar had dutifully awaited his release, but within a few days they realised that they had grown apart and they parted amicably. Following initial employment as a night receptionist in a hotel, Colonel von Luck eventually obtained a good business appointment, and then gained popularity as an international speaker on his military experiences. Major-General Roberts became Director Royal Armoured Corps and was awarded the Legion d'Honneur and Croix de Guerre avec Palmes, in addition to his British awards.

Our next topic of study was *Operation Epsom*. At the first stand we were told:

Imagine yourself as a staff officer at brigade or divisional headquarters. You will have begun to realise as the reports come in from battalions that this operation has not gone according to plan and that the start lines, fire plan and objectives, all of which looked so clear and tidy when you wrote the operation order, were meaningless. Already the operation which you saw so distinctly in two phases has gone wrong. But worse is to come, and the battle situation will become still more confused and obscure. As staff officers you exist to serve your commander and the units in the formation, and you must help to create order out of chaos and to retain control …

We listened to vivid descriptions from those who were there of acts of heroism and stupidity, and noted how the actions of individual men, not always of high rank, affected the subsequent course of operations. On the conclusion of the intensive four-day operation, General Montgomery wrote to Commander 15th Scottish Division, 'I would like to congratulate the 15th Division as a whole on the very fine performance put up during the past week's fighting. The Division went into battle for the first time in this war; but it fought with great gallantry and displayed a grand offensive spirit. Scotland can well feel proud of the 15th Scottish Division, and the whole Division can be proud of itself. Please congratulate the Division from me and tell all officers and men that I am delighted at what they have done.' However, it was at a cost – 288 killed, 1,638 wounded and 794 missing.

I have devoted a significant portion of my memoirs to this battlefield tour because the liberation of Europe was the most prominent international event in my lifetime, followed by the equally successful but different Cold War – the western defiance of the very real military threat imposed by Stalin's Russia and the Warsaw Pact countries of eastern Europe shortly after the ending of World War 2.

It was not long before the 'class of 1965' was again in Europe. On 24 July, courtesy of the Royal Air Force, we were flown into Nuremburg Airport, transferred into the awaiting 'whirly birds' of the United States 7th Cavalry Division, and whisked away to their base at Grafenwöhr. Here we were shown the firepower, night-fighting ability, unusual eating and drinking habits, stamina and good humour of an elite United States Army Division.

On our return, the course broke up for the summer vacation. It was a busy time. We immediately went to Yorkshire to take over and occupy Broadacres on 3 August and comply with the completion date for the sale of 2 Spa Lane on 10 August. For the remainder of the month we camped within Broadacres, preparing the garden, purchasing additional essential items and establishing a pleasant, friendly relationship with neighbours of a similar age and ambition. It was a very exciting time, but the days flew by and at the end of the month we returned to Camberley. I recorded our expenditure on items for our new home, which supplemented the items that we had retained from the cottage, as follows (converted to decimal currency):

Hoover (£20.12); carpets for two bedrooms and lounge, including fitting (£107.79); double bed (£24.97); Belling 3/30T cooker, lamp fittings (£21.32); chair covering (£27.86); 210 kitchen tiles (£5.77); four kitchen chairs (£11.50); antique pine chest of drawers (£4); curtain material for main bedroom, lounge and dining room (£48.07); bathroom/toilet fittings (£3.62); and an ironing board (£2).

We tiled the kitchen together and Ruth made the curtains.

Any thoughts that we might have had of a more relaxed final term were soon dispelled by an increasing number of lengthy 'telephone battles' designed to test us in varying staff and command appointments, dissertations to be written on subjects of our own choice (military selection procedures and body armour were my choices), and lectures to be delivered on current affairs matters selected by the DS. However, it was not all work and no play. I was a regular player in a decent Staff College football team, playing as centre forward, and a member of the winning softball competition, coached and cursed at by a ruthless fellow student from the US Army who provided me with a vast store of colourful and invaluable epithets, as well as a shattered finger with which to remember him by for the rest of my life. Our class of 1965 also produced a pantomime, revealing some very rich talent. This was not my forte, but Ruth was selected for a chorus part and I was delighted to see her enjoying herself so much in an excellent production of *Alice in Wonderland*.

The course ended with some memorable social occasions, a respectable grading, the comfort of having made many good friends and a good posting as a staff officer to Major General R.H. Whitworth CBE at Catterick, which would enable me to travel on a daily basis from 'Broadacres', our home at Thorp Arch. Major General Whitworth was a distinguished World War II soldier who had joined up in 1940, shortly after gaining a First in Modern History at Balliol, Oxford. He was commissioned into the Grenadier Guards and served with 24 Guards Brigade in North Africa and Italy. He was in command of the Berlin Infantry Brigade Group at the time that the Berlin Wall was erected, throughout the Cuban missile crisis and during President Kennedy's visit to the city in June 1963.

The Army Staff College class of 1965 included a number of students who would go on to become distinguished senior officers, two in particular springing to mind; Captain Brian Kenny of the Queen's Royal Irish Hussars became General Sir Brian Leslie Graham Kenny GCB CBE, Deputy Supreme Allied Commander Europe, while Captain Julian Thompson Royal Marines became Major General Julian Howard Atherden Thompson CB OBE, Commander of 3 Commando Brigade and the Land Forces during the Falklands War, and subsequently a celebrated military historian.

Justin too had a good year, receiving a very good report from Yateley Manor, which incorporated early recognition of his ability at playing rugby.

My Camberley Staff College Course incorporated a study of British youth and society of that time, with addresses by some eminent people. It was the period of the "Swinging Sixties"; a period of optimism and hedonism as the economy recovered from post WW2 austerity, incorporating the birth of British pop music, Teddy Boy suits and mini-skirts, colour TV, the mini car and Britain's first supermarkets, whilst the beautiful voice and personality of Dunfermline teenage singer Barbara Dickson was making a huge impact on the Clyde … and soon far beyond.

It also incorporated study of the city of London and the nation's finances. I particularly remember a privileged visit to the Bank of England's gold vaults beneath Threadneedle Street; second only in its depository holdings to vaults in the US. That position continues, but it should be appreciated that each of the many thousands of gold bars has a unique serial number etched on it, enabling international and other trades to be conducted without gold bar movement. A sale blunder of UK gold reserves between1999 and 2002 by Chancellor of the Exchequer, Gordon Brown, was to cost our country £2 billion.

Sadly, General Sir Brian Kenny died of Alzheimer's disease on 19th June 2017, aged 83. An almost full-page obituary in THE TIMES was headed, *"Tall, dashing and straight-talking Commander-in-Chief of the British Army of the Rhine during the Cold War"* and continued ... *" He was the Deputy Supreme Allied Commander of NATO at one of the most dramatic moments in history – the collapse of the Soviet Union ... The week following the attempted [but failed] coup against President Mikhail Gorbachev in August 1991 by hard-line Communist elements of the Soviet government and military, General Kenny was required to lead a NATO visit to Moscow to address the general staff of the Soviet Armed Forces, headed by General Vladimir Lobov. It was reported that he received a more than frosty reception but that "Kenny's height, good looks and natural charm won the day – his speech recalling the alliance between the two countries against Nazi Germany and, by the end of it, the generals were smiling and laughing, and the handshakes were firm."*

He was in the same intake and College as me at Sandhurst, winning the Sword of Honour.

YORKSHIRE

1966/67

Occupying our own home in Yorkshire and the prospect of living in it for two years was very exciting. We moved into 'Broadacres' shortly after the Staff College course finished on 9 December 1965, and I was not required to report for duty at Catterick until 17 January. A Christmas tree was soon in place and Broadacres became increasingly homely as the following additional furnishings were purchased:

Two antique chests of drawers (£13); curtaining for children's room, landing, cloakroom and kitchen (£10.30); antique oak bureau (£23.10); hallway parquet floor (£25.13); carpets (including fitting) for sitting room, stairs, landing, childrens' room and bathroom (£175); refrigerator (£36.75); made-to-order oak dining table (£14); dressing table and mirror (£3.10); single bed (£11.25); large antique chest of drawers (£6); two antique wardrobes (£12.50); and an electric Atco 14 grass cutter. Again, Ruth made the curtains and she did the major part of laying the parquet floor.

It was a novel and refreshing experience to live as a family in our own house among civilian friends. The only difference between us and our neighbours was that I drove north in uniform each day to Catterick (42 miles), while they mostly drove much shorter distances to Leeds, York or Harrogate in city suits. Justin [and Mark later in the year] walked a mere two hundred yards with Ruth to the very good Lady Elizabeth Hastings Primary School. Though 'Lady Betty', the unmarried daughter of the 7th Earl of Huntingdon, had died in 1739, her name and her generosity as a benefactor were still well remembered by descendents of some of the families that had lived in the area since that time.

Friendships were made with an increasing number of residents as more houses were built, if only because hedges, bushes, trees and other barricades that are so typical of our possessive human nature had not yet become established. Attractive, unspoilt countryside was an extension to our garden, for when we climbed over the fence we were in it, able to walk through Lady Betty's parkland pasture down to and along the river Wharfe in either direction, virtually as far as we wished. If we walked downstream for a couple of hundred yards we came to the Boston Spa weir and old mill; a little further along was the single-lane road bridge which crossed the river and led into Boston Spa itself, a very attractive stone-built Georgian village, where Ruth had many friends and knew so many people. Half a mile past the school was the church where we were married, and a short distance beyond that was the village of Walton and our longstanding friends, Nanette and Ted Simpson, at Ivy House Farm. We were very happy establishing our home. Ruth would write a list of next-day tasks for herself each evening and would routinely tell me that she had already completed one or two before I left for work, and that was quite early in the day. Her enthusiasm and vigour were most inspiring.

My appointment at Catterick was that of 'GSO2 (Trg & Int)' – that is, a general staff officer, Grade 2, responsible to General Whitworth for military training, training areas and intelligence/security matters. As it was a major's appointment, I was given the acting rank and the pay. To assist me I had a retired brigadier to supervise and look after those who ran the infantry, tank and artillery ranges and other training areas and facilities, and also a GSO3; the very competent Captain David Rothery of the Prince of Wales's Own Regiment of Yorkshire. In addition to overseeing their work, I was personally responsible for arranging and coordinating firepower demonstrations and writing and conducting tactical exercises and practical promotion examinations for the two levels of officer promotion to which I had been subjected as a student and candidate only a few years earlier. These were open to students and candidates not only from Northern Command, but from anywhere in the country, for officers might be unable to attend these events in their own Command (Southern, Eastern or Scottish) for a variety of reasons. There would usually be some 25–40 students/candidates. Planning could not be delayed, for I needed to arrange directing staff who had passed the Camberley course and 'sell' my tactical appreciations and DS solutions/notes to them. Finally, I had to present everything to my GSO1 and General Whitworth for their approval.

I was also responsible for a revision of the extensive Catterick training areas and their approach routes to accommodate the requirements of several units that were soon to be withdrawn from Germany, to help reduce overseas costs. Some of these were units with armoured personnel carriers (APCs) and similar rubber-padded-track armoured fighting vehicles. However, an anxious public, prompted by a mischievous press, regarded them as tanks and were becoming quite hostile. I suggested to General Whitworth that we should take the initiative by giving a demonstration and he readily agreed. I invited the local authority, media and police, and they were soon 'on side', recognising that the manoeuvrability and braking distances of these vehicles were infinitely superior to those of the antiquated agricultural and other heavy vehicles to which they were accustomed. I was ready for the inevitable question of 'how many are coming?', replying that for security reasons the Ministry of Defence had not yet released the details – one of my better 'leg glances'.

Our DIY work on Broadacres and its garden was progressing well. I was a useless gardener, but I was pleasing Ruth by building a wall to interrupt the slope below her extensive rockery. I had purchased some used local stone in nearby Clifford and collected it in a borrowed tractor and trailer. It was the first time that I had ever driven a tractor or mixed cement. It was rather therapeutic and I felt that I was doing something useful. However, there was little progress in our work between 11 and 30 July as we sat in front of the television watching England win the football World

Cup, beating Mexico, France, Argentina and Portugal, and then West Germany (4–2) in the final at Wembley before 98,000 spectators. The event attracted a record 32.3 million viewers on British television, though only 15 million households had a television at the time – a record that may still stand. I include this sporting event in my memoirs not only because of the magnitude of my country's success but to draw attention to the high personal qualities of the English players, each a splendid ambassador of his country. I fear that the likes of Banks, Wilson, Moore, the Charlton brothers, Cohen, Peters, Ball, Hunt, Stiles and Hurst will only rarely be seen again in England colours, let alone together in a World Cup–winning team.

At the other end of the spectrum there occurred at this time an event which grieved me considerably [previously mentioned at page 181] – the closure and destruction of thousands of miles of the British railway system, without achieving the aim of providing a significant financial saving. The zenith of British railways was reached shortly before World War I with a 23,440-mile network, which was to shrink slightly before World War II in the face of increasing road-transport competition. The railways were vital to the nation during the war – not only the trunk lines, but also the tributary lines for food and munitions distribution and troop movements, particularly during the weeks prior to D-Day. Our proud and competitive regional railway companies, with their distinctive livery and magnificent steam locomotives, were as exhausted at the end of that war as the people, and they were in a similarly poor state of repair. It was not long before income fell well below operating costs. The regional companies, including my London & North Eastern Railway (LNER), were nationalised as British Railways. Diesel locomotives replaced the steam locomotives, railway stations no longer competed to have the best floral displays and operating losses steadily increased to £68m in 1960 and £104m in 1962, when the British Transport Corporation could no longer pay the interest on its loans.

The government lost patience, looked for radical reforms, and in desperation appointed a hitherto successful ICI Technical Director, Richard Beeching, as the chairman of the new British Railways Board, with the task of restoring profitability. It was an unenviable task and a gamble that proved to be a disaster. Dr Beeching produced his report in March 1963, recommending the closure of almost a third of the British rail network, mostly rural and industrial, and 2,363 stations. By the time that he was sacked two years later the damage was done – his reports made no stipulation for the handling of land and infrastructure after line closures, with the result that by 1966 significant portions of land had been sold and bridges and stations demolished – indeed, virtually a third of the entire rural infrastructure and vital feeder network to the main lines had been lost to the nation for ever. Towards the end of the decade it became increasingly clear that the closures were not producing the savings that had been forecast and never would. Belatedly, the government began to recognise not only its error, but that many rail services that could not pay their way had had a valuable social role. However, it was too late. If only government had had the *wisdom* to retain and maintain the superstructure of these lines, reviewing them on a triennial basis. We did not immediately dismantle our warships when World War II ended – they were given sensible 'mothball' preservation for several years. Hugely talented and self-opinionated people are not necessarily endowed with vision and common sense. What is *wisdom*? I regard it as a state of mind, developed through deep thought, by those blessed with intellect, knowledge, experience, foresight and common sense. It is a precious personal quality; rarely displayed by politicians, if only because of self or party interest, at the expense of national interest. Successive governments have procrastinated on promises to reverse some of the Beeching cuts and it was gratifying to read in THE TIMES [1st July 2020] that the government had announced on the previous day that the reopening of up to 50 disused railway lines or stations will be considered as part of a reversal of the infamous Beeching cuts. It was also announced that other shortlisted schemes included reopening the Upper Wensleydale railway.

Our home was only six miles from Harewood House, one of the foremost historic homes in the country and residence of the Lascelles family. It was not long before we visited it [as members of the public], enjoying a fascinating and most enjoyable day. At that time there was a sizeable tropical hummingbird enclosure within the bird garden; the visitor area at the same very warm temperature. It subsequently became a regular attraction to us on cold Sunday mornings in the winter!

It was very satisfying to be able to return from work each day to our civilian environment and to help in the development of our own home, though my practical skills were limited. When something needed attention in a military quarter one only needed to make a telephone call and it was attended to by a tradesman – but now I had to learn some basic skills. There were some giggles when I ordered a traditional wooden workbench from the local carpenter, but I remembered some basic woodwork skills from my days at TGS and was rewarded with a new drill for my birthday. There was plenty of fresh air and outdoor freedom for Justin and Mark, both of whom were making good progress at school, while Ruth was positively purring with happiness. I did not find the daily eighty-five-mile return drive to Catterick a problem, except for the persistent and very dense fogs of that time, which then gave way to periods of torrential, monsoon-type rain and flooding. I also encountered some very strong westerly gales on the exposed sections of the A1, and on one occasion counted twenty-two lorries on their side within a fifteen-mile section of the route.

Our 1966 summer holiday consisted of a series of day outings into the countryside and seaside, but the following year we decided on a few days in Cornwall at Sennen Cove, near Land's End. Unfortunately, on 18 March that year the American-owned (Union Oil Co.) supertanker *Torrey Canyon*, carrying its maximum capacity of 120,000 tons of crude oil, was wrecked on Seven Stones Reef, which lies between the tip of Cornwall and the Scilly Isles. At the time it was the largest vessel ever to have been wrecked and the huge oil slick was to kill vast quantities of marine life, not only on the Cornish coast, but also in Normandy. There was no lack of effort to protect the shores, including bombing the wreck to release the oil, burning it with napalm and then spraying the oil slicks with 25 million gallons of detergents. However, the detergents were toxic to many of the marine organisms and caused further damage. An estimated 50,000 sea birds perished. We considered cancelling our holiday, but eventually decided that Cornwall had so much to offer in addition to the beaches that we would continue. We did not regret our decision and we had a most pleasant holiday, sometimes finding tiny coves that had only minor damage. Because the *Torrey Canyon* was registered in Liberia, a Liberian Board of Inquiry investigated the shipwreck, and found Captain Pastrengo Rugiati of Genoa, Italy, guilty of 'a high degree of negligence'.

I was not looking forward to the receipt of my next posting order, as I was so content in what I was doing, and so were my family. It arrived in late September 1967 – I had been selected as the officer commanding the Northern Army Group Air Support Radio Squadron, based in Tongeren, a Roman town and the oldest in Belgium. I was flattered to learn that I had received the command of an independent unit, comprising German, Dutch, Belgian and English soldiers, but neither Ruth nor I were thrilled at the prospect of leaving Broadacres. The anguish of leaving would have been less if Ruth's mother had still been alive, living with us in Broadacres, as had been planned – she would have remained, with appropriate gardener assistance. As it was, Broadacres would need to be left in the hands of an estate agent, to lease at virtually his discretion. We knew him, and we trusted him well – we were in the same class at TGS – but there was sadness in Ruth's eyes. A matter that now occupied our minds was the education of Justin and Mark. The Ministry of Defence, recognising the disruption to the education of children of Services families resulting from frequent moves (some of which were to overseas bases without English schools), provided a scheme to ensure that they were not disadvantaged. In addition to providing primary schools at some overseas bases, it offered a boarding-school allowance and, in conjunction with the schools concerned, an escorted rail/air travel system. The allowance was the same for all, irrespective of the rank of the father, though it was unlikely that a private soldier or a general would have children of boarding-school age (their children would be either too young or would have completed their schooldays). The allowance was based on the education and boarding fees of an average school, less the estimated cost to parents had the child been at a local school. The only alternative for parents was to have their own home in the UK, with the father proceeding unaccompanied on overseas tours, which were usually of two years' duration at that time. One could not jump in and out of this scheme – its purpose was to provide continuity of education for a child.

Not surprisingly, the vast majority of parents chose a boarding-school education for their children.

Ruth and I were keen to provide the best education that we could afford for our children. The schools that we had in mind were the highly regarded northern schools that were not too distant from our Broadacres home – Rossall, Sedbergh and Pocklington. Entry to these public schools was competitive, in that applicants had to pass an entrance examination at the age of about eleven and a half – the Public Schools Common Entrance Examination. Our quandary was whether we could rely on the unknown British Forces primary school in Liège to provide Justin with the level of education that he would need during the next two years to pass that examination. For advice we turned to Ruth's aunt Elsie and uncle Charles MacKeith, and their son Gordon, an old Rossallian, all of whom lived within a few miles of Rossall. They recognised our predicament and gave very sensible advice. Furthermore, they made it clear that whichever school we selected, they would be only too willing to help in any emergency. We eventually selected Rossall and agreed that Justin's chances of passing the Common Entrance Examination would be greatly enhanced if he were to enter Rossall Junior School as a boarder. Education at Rossall Junior School would also ensure that Justin would proceed to the senior school with a group of friends, with Mark eventually following the same route – provided, of course, that they passed the Common Entrance Examination and were selected. We arranged for Justin to be interviewed and tested for Rossall Junior School and he was accepted for entry, starting in January 1969 as a boarder. I have often wondered if we should have opted for Ashville College (Harrogate), or better still, St Peter's School, York (the third oldest school in the UK).

On 8th October 1967 one of our finest Prime Ministers died, aged 84; Clement Richard Attlee, 1st Earl Attlee, KG, OM, CH, FRS. He was a quiet and modest man who practised as a barrister and then lecturer prior to WW1 breaking out in August 1914. Attlee volunteered immediately for military service and was soon in action as an infantry officer, fighting in the Gallipoli Campaign in Turkey; later in Mesopotamia (Iraq), where he was badly wounded when storming an enemy trench during the battle of Hanna; then to the Western Front in France for the final months of the war. The gallantry and self-sacrifice that Attlee displayed in action epitomized his character and enabled him to work easily alongside Churchill in the WW2 coalition government. The social reforms and foreign policies of Clement Attlee's post WW2 cabinet (which included the skills of Ernest Bevin, Hugh Dalton, Herbert Morrison and Hugh Gaitskell) were of supreme help to our nation in its gradual recovery from the ravages and debt of WW2 and the re-shaping of the Commonwealth.

In November 1967 British forces left Aden after 128 years of imperial rule. Most of the 128,000 servicemen and their families returned by air – our largest airlift since that of Berlin in 1948. Two months later, Defence Secretary Denis Healey announced to the House of Commons that in addition British troops were to be withdrawn in 1971 from military bases in Southeast Asia, most of which were in Malaysia and Singapore. This would inevitably involve significant redundancy and it worried me. A few days later the worry was lessened, but not removed, when I received a flattering final report from General Whitworth with the grades that I had sought to achieve. Nevertheless, it was with a heavy heart in early February 1968 that I travelled alone to Belgium to take over my Squadron. Arrangements had been made for me to stay temporarily in the Cygne d'Argent hotel in the steel city of Liège. Thankfully, it was confirmed on arrival that married accommodation would soon be available to enable me to return to Thorp Arch and collect Justin and Mark.

NORTHAG AIR SUPPORT RADIO SQUADRON

Belgium - February 1968.

My studies of European history at school had primarily been of the French Revolution, the Unification of Germany and the Unification of Italy. My knowledge of Belgium and its fascinating history was weak, mainly comprising the Battle of Waterloo outside Brussels, and the gaiety and scandals within the city that both preceded and followed it, largely learned from English literature rather than history reading.

I was not surprised to learn that Liège's strategic location at the confluence of the Meuse and Ourthe rivers and its proximity to the German border had resulted in it being a frequent scene of conflict and insurgency from medieval times, with the seizure of Liège an immediate and successful primary objective of German invasion in both World War I and World War II. I found that the city had a distinct character of its own. It had played a prominent part in the Belgian Revolution of 1830/31, which resulted in the secession of the southern provinces of the United Kingdom of the Netherlands and the forming of the independent kingdom of Belgium. The population of these southern provinces, including that of the Liège municipality, consisted largely of liberal-minded French-speaking Roman Catholics, very different to the Dutch-speaking people of the northern provinces. A conference of the major European powers was held in London in 1831 to discuss the grave situation. The conference recognised the secession and King Leopold I was installed as King of the Belgians. A disgruntled King William of the Netherlands made a belated military attempt to recover his lost provinces, but he was soon beaten when France intervened.

I was immediately attracted to Liège and its people, primarily because of their courtesy and pro-British attitude. Manners, including those of young children, were exemplary. They were a very happy people who lived in the centre of their city as well as on the outskirts, residing above the shops and restaurants that spilled out onto the pavements, so that the city centre was always alive and vibrant, not dissimilar to Paris. It did not take me long to adapt to this relaxed atmosphere and the excellent Belgian lagers.

Liège was to be our home as a family for the next two years, some ten miles distant from my squadron in Tongeren, where it shared a barracks with a Belgian unit. Our role was to provide alternative (radio) communications from the joint war headquarters of Northern Army Group (NORTHAG)/2nd Allied Tactical Airforce (2ATAF) to the British, German, Belgian and Dutch strike aircraft locations. The location of this joint war headquarters was a highly classified NATO secret at that time, but it is now common knowledge that it was deeply within the enormous limestone caves near Maastricht, which already housed a Joint Operations Centre of that name (JOC Maastricht). One could easily drive a small truck along some of the neat, symmetrical avenues that had been mechanically cut into the limestone rock to extract slabs for building. This important military base was the size of a small village, and like all good villages it had its own pub, 'The Flint-Stones'. The war location of my NORTHAG Air Support Radio Squadron was some distance away from these caves in open countryside, but very close to a below-surface communications point to which our radio circuits would be connected – directly into the Joint Operations Centre. Of course, if these caves and the headquarters that they housed had received a direct Soviet nuclear hit we would have all fried together. However, in the event of any of the German/Belgian and Dutch Bundespost circuits, on which this very important NATO Headquarters depended, being interrupted by enemy actions elsewhere, but with Headquarters Northern Army Group/2nd Allied Tactical Airforce surviving, the communications provided by my squadron would have been vital. I was told that these caves were so extensive and complex that during World War II they were occupied by both the German forces and the Belgian resistance movement simultaneously.

I was directly responsible to Colonel Mischke of the German Army, who, in turn, was responsible to Major General H.H. von Hinckeld, the Chief of Staff of Headquarters Northern Army Group. Clearly, this appointment was not going to be an easy ride. I had a Belgian captain (Jacques Willems) as my second in command and also a Dutch subaltern to assist me, both of whom made a very favourable early impression. The handover complete, I returned to England in late February to collect Ruth, Justin and Mark, and I also received with delight Ruth's confirmation that a further addition to the family was expected in mid– July.

I had hoped that we would have accommodation in Liège of a quality that would have eased the pain of leaving Broadacres, which was being leased during our absence, but that was not the case. Our accommodation was a very modest two-bedroom flat, virtually in the centre of Liège, leading directly onto a busy street with a narrow pavement, and with the nearest park half a mile away. On arrival we immediately decided that it was not acceptable for a young family and complained to the RAF administrators. When it was rebuffed we submitted a formal complaint to Headquarters RAF Germany which resulted in the matter being examined by a senior RAF officer. Ruth was never overawed by rank or position, nor by the concierge troll who guarded the entrance to the flats – they took an immediate and intense dislike to each other. I was not able to be present when the air commodore and accompanying officers visited the flat, but I was told that she did not pull her punches – and two weeks later we were told that we could look for our own accommodation, with a prescribed financial ceiling. With the assistance of Captain Jacques Willems we soon had a pleasant house and garden on the outskirts of the city and were the envy of the RAF community, most of whom worked within the Joint Operations Centre at Maastricht.

Typically, Ruth soon made friends with our Belgian neighbours and their friends and joined their coffee mornings, using her French as much as possible. It was not long before she had acquired the vocabulary to discuss pregnancy matters with them, and this proved to be most useful as Amelia or Crispin was to be born in the Liège Civic Hospital. The wife of one of our friendly neighbours was a professional opera singer. The walls were quite thin and we rather enjoyed listening to her arias and voice exercises, occasionally applauding, much to her amusement.

The military exercises were quite demanding. Radio detachments of the 1st British Corps, 1st German Corps, 1st Belgian Corps and 1st Netherlands Corps would arrive, doubling our size overnight. However, my experience with two British infantry brigades was very useful and I made it quite clear to all and sundry that any soldier, irrespective of rank or nationality, would be returned immediately to his country as inadequate if he did not meet those standards. I never had the need to take such action. To Ruth's dismay, however, I would return home as dirty, tired and smelly as ever – it was quite like old times.

Whenever possible we would drive out of Liège into the countryside. Our favourite area was that region of the Ardennes between Eupen and the German town of Monschau called the Naturpark Hohes Venn – Eifel. We found Lake Eupen, just to the east of the small town of the same name, particularly attractive. The forest contained an attractive mix of deciduous and coniferous trees with many clearings and we would regularly come across small herds of deer. The memory of stalking some deer in a clearing and then watching Justin, with Mark not far behind, chase the 'Bambis' into a glorious sunset still remains vivid in my mind.

In Belgium it was abnormal for a father not to be present at the birth of his children, and I attended Crispin's birth. I am glad that I did. It seemed a routine birth to the Belgian gynaecologist and his nurses, but to me it was a very emotional experience that made me feel very humble – and at one point frightened, as Ruth's face turned purple. I feel sure that it helped me become a better husband and father and removed any residual chauvinism that I might have had. We were all very thrilled with Crispin. Within a couple of weeks Ruth had regained her characteristic vitality and wanted a holiday in the sun. So, as I had sufficient leave entitlement remaining, we set off by car for the Costa Brava for a most enjoyable holiday in, or close to, Calella de Palafrugell. I was a little concerned at travelling such a distance with a three-week-old baby, but Ruth was not concerned, pointing out that she had the experience of having raised two young children in Malaya. We stayed in a typical Spanish holiday hotel with a splendid swimming pool and within a short walking distance of the beach. The holiday was a great success, with no problems, and Ruth had a good rest and lots of sunshine, acquiring the deep tan that she desired.

In the summer of 1968 one of Yorkshire's greatest cricketers and characters retired; Fred Trueman – 2,301 first class wickets (307 in Test matches), a record for a fast bowler at that time.

An enjoyable Christmas came and went, and then early in the new year, shortly after his ninth birthday, we took Justin to Rossall Junior School. We travelled together as a family on the Rotterdam-to-Hull night ferry, with the facility of a cabin, reaching the home of Ruth's Uncle Charles and Aunt Elsie at midday, and then on to the school in mid-afternoon. We departed with much sadness while Justin was engrossed in a game of indoor football. There were no tears – it was British stiff-upper-lip behaviour by all. We immediately returned by the same route to Liège, leaving a tuck box filled to the brim with goodies. An early letter from Justin's headmaster advised us that he had settled in well and that he was already making an impression on the games field. There was a weekly exchange of letters between us, while Ruth's Uncle Charles and Aunt Elsie were generous in taking him to their home for exeats and providing us with additional information.

Meanwhile, back in Liège, Mark was progressing very well at his school and Crispin was flourishing. I was enjoying my soldiering and the independence of my multi-national NATO command, while Ruth was very happy in her enormous 'household duties' workload, while still finding morning-coffee time with her Belgian friends. Although we were living in a city, in the evenings we would routinely take Mark and Crispin either into the park or to a small area of particularly attractive copse and scrubland on the outskirts, near Ougrée. The area attracted a variety of birds and butterflies, including swallowtails, but to our dismay the abundant finches were popular with 'netters', who caught them and kept them as cage birds as well as for food. Most Sundays would be spent somewhere in the vast Ardennes forests immediately to the south of the city. We would make up the route as we went along, discovering some stunning countryside for our picnics. There were few formal dinner parties or other officers' mess functions compared with the large number that we had experienced in Germany. However, I recall one of the few formal ladies' dinner nights at the Tongeren officers' mess spectacularly misfiring when the Belgian chef apparently reported late for duty and in a highly intoxicated state. We became increasingly suspicious as to the reason for the delay in the meal being served, gracefully accepting the unconvincing excuses that were given, but eventually it became all too apparent. Senior officers became rather agitated and there were calls for 'fish and chips' to satisfy our hunger. We eventually received a respectable meal and good humour prevailed, but we arrived home rather late.

Excitement was rising among all families with children at boarding schools as July and the summer holidays approached. The military escorted rail/air travel system for children at boarding schools in the UK delivered a happy and very fit Justin to us in early July, at precisely the declared time; at RAF Wildenrath in Germany. There was much jubilation within the family. Our holiday on the Costa Brava in 1968 had been so successful that we repeated it, though in different accommodation. Again, it was most enjoyable – ideal for young children. The return journey for Justin was the reverse of that by which he arrived, and again the combined military and school arrangements went without a hitch.

In late September, Ruth and I were privileged to attend the premiere showing of the *Battle of Britain* film in Liège, only a couple of weeks after its London premiere. It was a formal event, preceded by a civic reception and a Belgian Air Force fly-past, if only because twenty-eight Belgian pilots, having fought in defence of both their own country and France, had then crossed the Channel to England to participate in that epic air battle. The most prominent was a pilot named Donnet who flew 375 missions and became Lieutenant General Baron Mike

Donnet (1 April 1917 – 31 July 2013). Ruth and I felt very proud to be British that evening. It is a wonderful historical film, and I was pleased to note that it incorporated the valuable contribution made by the two very experienced Polish squadrons, comprising 145 pilots – a greater contribution than that of any other country except, of course, the United Kingdom's 2,353 pilots. I clearly remember those Polish pilots and many other Polish servicemen being rightly acknowledged as heroes in the newsreels and on the streets of Britain when I was a boy. It was rather surprising, but nevertheless gratifying, that when the RAF Museum ran a public poll in September 2017 to select 'the people's Spitfire pilot' [in preparation for the centenary of the Royal Air Force in 2018], the winner was a Polish pilot; Franciszek Kornicki, who (with strong support from the Polish community) narrowly beat the much-fancied Sir Douglas Bader. His experiences are well described in his 2008 memoir, *The Struggle: Biography of a Fighter Pilot*. He died in Worthing on 16 November 2017 aged 100 years and received a full-page obituary in THE TIMES. It was a joint funeral, for his wife (Patience) died 10 days later. The last known Polish fighter pilot to fly for the RAF during WW2 (and one of the most distinguished) was Jerzy Glowczewski, who died on 12th April 2020. He flew 100 combat missions and was decorated with the Polish Cross of Valour three times and the Air Medal; author of three volumes of memoirs – *Accidental Soldier* (2003), *Optimist After All* (2004), and *The Last Fighter Pilot* (2017).

Stories of the Battle of Britain abounded at that time. One of my favourites was that of the headmistress of a very posh girls school writing to the Air Ministry, asking if a Battle of Britain pilot might be provided to address the school, describing his experiences. The Air Ministry duly obliged, sending a very experienced and well decorated Flight Sergeant. He did not shield the horrors of mortal combat in the sky … *'Four of us were scrambled and we gained height rapidly. It was quiet and peaceful and we could see the harvest being gathered below. No sign of the enemy, until suddenly about ten f…..s swooped down on us out of some cloud and one of the f…..s got onto my tail and opened fire. I went into a sharp turn that shook him off and got one of the f…..s in my sights …………'*

Some of the girls and members of staff were giggling by this time and the headmistress interrupted, *"Excuse me Flight Sargeant. Girls … girls, I should explain that the German aircraft were Fock-Wulf 190s, commonly called "fockers" …. "No, no, no Ma'am, these f… s were 109 Messerschmitts."*

Shortly before Christmas 1969 I received notice that my next posting was to the Ministry of Defence as GSO2 Signals 33 (Army), reporting on 1 April 1970. I also received the best report of my military career. Although I was responsible to Colonel Mische of the German Army, the report was written by British officers. Not only was it of the highest grade, but it revealed that an additional and special NATO report had been written on me in August, on the insistence of Colonel Mische, in which I was given the highest NATO classification. It also contained a strong recommendation for the Joint Services Staff College – the route for high rank. Strangely, I was more relieved than elated, in that it indicated to me that I was now in the top bracket for my age and rank with virtually no danger whatsoever of redundancy and almost certain to reach at least lieutenant colonel, the rank that became the limit of my ambition. I think it was the first time in my life that I felt secure. I had a wonderful wife and family, and from that time my ambition became increasingly focused on the prospect of a settled family home in rural Yorkshire, rather than on military achievement.

Justin, now quite an experienced air traveller, joined us for another wonderful family Christmas. No matter where we were, Christmas always began for the family on Ruth's birthday [15 December]. On that day Ruth would erect and decorate the Christmas tree, never discarding favoured items that might have lost their glitter and colour, but which invoked memories of happy Christmases past, in different parts of the world.

We waved goodbye to Justin in early January 1970 as he flew back to England and Rossall Junior School, and soon began packing our MFO (Military Forwarding Organisation) boxes, addressing them to our home – Broadacres, Thorp Arch Park, Yorkshire.

MINISTRY OF DEFENCE

Two Years in Whitehall

We were pleased to be back in England. We had been married for twelve years, of which almost eight had been abroad, but we now felt a need to be in our own country again and closer to Rossall School.

I did not relish the prospect of weekly commuting between Yorkshire and London, but I consoled myself and Ruth with the fact that I had an annual leave entitlement of forty-two days plus public holidays, and no requirement to take part in military exercises. I was usually able to leave the Ministry of Defence at about 3.40 p.m. each Friday, catching a train from King's Cross at 4.05 p.m., arriving at York at about 6.20 p.m., where I was met by Ruth, Mark and Crispin. However, I had to return on the Sunday evening in order to be at my desk by 9 a.m. on Monday. The nearest officers' mess accommodation was at Woolwich, but there was a lengthy waiting list and I was able to claim an allowance and find my own accommodation in central London.

Initially, I stayed at the Nuffield Club in Eaton Square, Belgravia, one of the finest residential areas in the city, with Stanley Baldwin, Neville Chamberlain and Vivien Leigh among its famous past residents. This superb accommodation was provided for junior officers of all services during World War II, and the facility continued until 1976. Sadly, it was in such demand that residence was limited to two weeks and rooms had to be shared. I shared a room with a major of the Royal Marines whose snoring was horrendous in terms of both duration and decibels. I lasted a week before finding accommodation in a cheap hotel for a few days, but it was infested with bedbugs. I endured this nomadic life on a five-nightly basis for about three months before comfortable accommodation was provided for me in the Woolwich Garrison officers' mess.

Finances were very tight at this time because of the combination of a hefty mortgage, boarding-school fees and the cost of the weekly rail fare between London and York. However, Ruth and I did not regret any of the decisions that we had taken and it was pleasing to note that the value of Broadacres was rising steadily as properties in Thorp Arch Park grew in popularity.

My appointment in the Ministry of Defence was as a GSO2 to the Signal Officer in Chief (Major General PF Pentreath MBE) with responsibility for Royal Signals manpower and establishments. It was an interesting time to be in the Royal Signals Directorate. New communications equipment and systems were at an advanced stage of development and procurement, and there was high anticipation that they would provide not only much better communications for the Army but also significant manpower savings. A new trade structure had been introduced to reflect the changed skills that would be required, and it was highly desirable that there were equal career opportunities in each of the trade/employment groups. The most prominent change was the introduction of the BRUIN communication system in the British Army of the Rhine which would provide a radical change from conventional combat net radio communications to a mobile area system of far greater durability. Major establishment changes were necessary, not least in the trade training units, which needed instructors in place to train tradesmen in the new skills that would be required. I had a small but very efficient team to help me – a retired officer (Major Frank Pike) and an executive officer (Mr Bill Collins). It was our task to prepare and submit timely proposals and changes to the Army Establishments Committee for its consideration, following close liaison with the units concerned.

There were about six other officers in the Woolwich Garrison officers' mess who worked in the MOD in Whitehall. Identically dressed in dark suits and bowler hats and carrying black briefcases and matching umbrellas, we would routinely congregate at the end of the platform at Woolwich station each morning and share a carriage for the half-hour journey to Charing Cross. One of the group was Colonel Jimmy Hellier, my adjutant in Essen when I was a subaltern, a charismatic and very energetic man who could enliven any group of people and at any time of the day. These journeys, together with the short ensuing walk along the embankment, were all memorable occasions full of mirth and banter as we discussed the political, sporting and military events of the time. Colonel Hellier was never overawed by senior officers or civil servants, always speaking his mind, regardless of tact and diplomacy. His final appointment prior to retirement was as a Major-General at Headquarters United Kingdom Land Forces (HQ UKLF) at Wilton, responsible for the administration and logistics of the UK-based land forces; recognition of an outstanding ability as an administrator as well as being a highly competent Royal Signals communicator. On leaving the army in 1982 he was head-hunted by the government-owned International Military Services (IMS) to oversee its responsibilities for delivery of a complex multimillion-pound British industry defence contract to the Kingdom of Jordan (involving 272 Khalid main battle tanks), plus equipment supplies to Oman and Sri Lanka. His IMS responsibilities continued to 1992, during which time he was Representative Colonel Commandant Royal Signals in 1983. Sadly, Major-General E.G. Hellier, CBE died on 31 October 2011, aged 84. His service to his country as an administrator and communicator was recognised with a full page obituary in THE TIMES on 3 November 2011.

I spent most evenings in the Woolwich officers' mess pursuing my philatelic hobby that had slowly developed over the years, particularly while we were in Liège. My knowledge of British and Belgian stamps was sufficient for me to recognise, to my benefit, some significant disparities between the Stanley Gibbons and Continental (Yvert et Tellier) catalogue valuations. I had occasionally purchased collections at a Liège auction house, retaining those stamps that I needed for my own collection and then, whenever I had the spare time, selling the remnants in booklets through various British philatelic clubs. This initiative enabled me to build up my own collection at minimum cost and make a profit from my hobby. More of my spare time was consumed when I was considered to have sufficient experience of the Ministry of Defence to be included in its duty-officer roster, an interesting but rather unpopular task, particularly at the weekend. The duties largely involved sifting through high-precedence teleprinter messages on a wide variety of military matters from the remaining outposts of the empire on which the sun never set, and then deciding which could wait until the next working day and which needed an immediate telephone call to a senior officer of the appropriate branch for advice, and then following his instructions. Get it wrong and one could anticipate a troublesome interview at best.

On 2 June 1970 I received a telephone call in London from Ruth advising me that my grandfather had died. It was totally unexpected (he had died in his sleep, aged just over 91 years), and I returned to Yorkshire for his funeral service at the crematorium at Harrogate (Stonefall) Cemetery (grave 7120/19). Had it not been for him and my grandmother, I would have been brought up in a slum area of Leeds. I would not have attended Tadcaster Grammar School and would therefore not have met my Nidderdale Girl, and these memoirs would never have been written. Indeed, had I been living in the damp and squalid conditions of the original 1 Ivy Mount, Leeds in 1944, clad in its yellow umbrella of city smog, I might not have survived the critical congestion of the lungs that I experienced as a boy. My grandfather was a Victorian gentleman with outstanding virtues who responded to his country's call during World War I in Flanders Fields and later as a special constable (sergeant), receiving a second bar to his Special Constabulary medal during World War II. His ambition of becoming a doctor was thwarted by his having to leave school at the age of fourteen, but his interest in medicine was apparent from his library of advanced medical books and his regular study of them. I never heard him swear, never observed him lose his temper or detected him telling a lie. He would tell me, and I sometimes heard him say to others, that his word was his bond. I therefore accept as fact his description to me one day of his athletic prowess and of the races that he won, and I remember my grandmother nodding her head with pride when he told me. There was nothing smutty in the household and he set standards of honour, trust and respect by example. Though he would routinely speak his mind, he was not bigoted, but flexible, tolerant and interested in alternative opinion. His dress, speech, manners and deportment were immaculate. As a youth he had taught himself additional skills such as shorthand and improved his education at night school. His shorthand skill was of a sufficiently high standard for him to be presented with a copy of Sir Isaac Pitman & Sons' NEW TESTAMENT IN PHONOGRAPHY on 26 January 1901, when he was aged 21, his handwritten address inside the cover (in both normal script and shorthand), indicating that he was residing at Haworth [20 Mytholme Lane] at the time. He was proud to be a Yorkshireman, and particularly proud of Yorkshire cricket achievements and the Brontë sisters, on whose books and lives he was an authority. He was a Primo of the Royal Antediluvian Order of Buffaloes (Duke of York Lodge 3450). Francis George Pedley was a fine, unselfish man and I feel proud to carry his name forward.

As expected, Elizabeth, his second wife, continued to live in his home rather than live with a member of her family. My grandfather had told me that if he died first, it was his wish that the house was placed in trust, and that Elizabeth continued to live there as long as she wished. In the event of her subsequently deciding to live elsewhere, the house was to be sold and the proceeds invested at the discretion of the trustees, with Elizabeth becoming the beneficiary of the income from the investment. He also told me that I would be the sole beneficiary of the proceeds from the sale of the house when Elizabeth died, but mentioned a very small amount that I might care to pass on to my mother, at my discretion. He made clear his great disappointment with the development of my mother's life following her privileged upbringing.

On 15 August 1971, President Richard Nixon declared that the US dollar would no longer be linked to gold. Until then, the US Treasury was duty bound to exchange an ounce of gold with central banks willing to pay $35. This meant that, *for the first time in history*, the level of the world's currencies depended not on the value of gold, or some other tangible commodity, but on the degree of trust that investors held in that currency; surely one of the most important policy decisions in modern history.

I had saved up as much leave as possible for the summer holidays. The days were mostly spent at Broadacres, with regular drives and walks in the countryside and to the seaside, particularly to Filey, the favourite resort of my grandparents and the Brontë family. These days with the family together were very precious, but things would soon change, for Mark was to join Justin at Rossall Junior School in September. It was not long before Broadacres was the scene of trunks being packed, name tabs being sewn onto every item of clothing, and cakes and other goodies being baked for the tuck boxes. Ruth and I waved goodbye with heavy hearts and the following day I returned to Whitehall, leaving Ruth with Crispin. This routine procedure was repeated each term. We wrote to Justin and Mark on a weekly basis and their housemasters ensured that regular letters were sent in reply. Occasionally, we were able to take them out for exeats, while Ruth's Uncle Charles and Aunt Elsie were generous with their invitations. It was not long before it became apparent that Justin was an outstanding rugby player and Mark an outstanding scholar.

My life in the Ministry of Defence was akin to that of a civil servant, rather than that of a soldier. It was not pleasant being away from home for two years, but I was happy in the knowledge that Ruth and Crispin had a wonderful country home overlooking the Wharfe and close to the villages of Boston Spa and Walton in which Ruth had so many friends, while Justin and Mark were receiving an education far superior to that which I had experienced at TGS, where even biology, the subject in which I was most interested, was not listed. I read my grandfather's medical books instead. However, I had some outings to military units, mostly in the UK, and a particularly pleasant five-day visit to Malta as part of a Ministry of Defence team to draw up new establishments for units continuing to be based there following the British withdrawal from Southeast Asia. There was time to see some of the island and learn something of its intriguing history. I became particularly interested in the long siege by Suleiman the Magnificent against the Knights of St John which began in May 1565. The military engineering, forts, bastions, watch towers, aqueducts, churches and cathedrals constructed by the Knights of St John are truly magnificent. The importance and significance in European history of that very brutal siege is reflected in Voltaire's comment many years later that '*rien est plus connu que la siege de Malte*' [nothing is known better than the siege of Malta]. Sadly, there was insufficient time for me to see Malta's prehistoric temples, the building of which began in 3600 BC. They are recorded as being the oldest free-standing buildings in the world – much older than the Pyramids or Stonehenge. This visit, together with brief en route calls to Naples with Ruth and the traversing of the Suez Canal, were to inspire Ruth and me to return in later years on cruise holidays to the eastern Mediterranean, 'in the wake of Saint Paul', studying and sometimes gasping at the historical treasures of the region.

In September 1971 I was notified that I was to be posted to 21st (Air Support) Signal Regiment at RAF Wildenrath in North Rhine-Westphalia, close to the Netherlands border, as second in command, to report on 10 April 1972. I was delighted, and Ruth shared my pleasure, but I detected her sadness at the prospect of leaving Broadacres, particularly when it subsequently became apparent that there could be a further separation of about three months before a married quarter become available. That apart, it was an exciting posting for me because the regiment provided the ground communications for the clutch airfields of RAF Gütersloh (F2 Lightnings), RAF Brüggen (F4 Phantoms) and RAF Wildenrath (Harriers), as well as an important chunk of the 2 ATAF/Headquarters RAF Germany static radio relay communication system. In addition, an off-base deployment of the Harriers was being developed which would enable the aircraft to quickly move off base and operate from woodland sites as soon as hostilities seemed likely. The communications needed for this unique concept were also to be provided by the regiment.

We were not surprised when, in November, Elizabeth decided to utilise the option provided in my grandfather's will of selling his house, living with her son, Harry, and receiving the interest from the invested proceeds of the sale. When I learned of her decision I wrote to my mother to advise her and to enquire whether she was aware of the content of her father's will:

14ᵗʰ November '71

Dear Doris,

Elizabeth has moved out of 140 King Edward's Drive to live with her son, Harry. She weighed up the pros and cons very carefully before reaching this decision, finally concluding that she could no longer risk being taken ill on her own. The legal situation in respect of Grandpa's house and effects is that the executors of his Will sell all and Elizabeth receives the interest from the invested proceeds. The executors have appreciated that the value of the contents of the house is small and have accordingly suggested that I should take those items which have any sentimental value or other family significance. I removed those items this weekend.

I do not know if Grandpa ever mentioned his Will to you or whether you have learned of its contents from his solicitor or elsewhere. I will be quite honest with you on this subject. When Elizabeth dies the proceeds from the sale of the house pass to myself. Had she continued to live in the house, it would similarly pass to me on her death. Grandpa advised me of this Will a few years before his death, and on a later occasion suggested that I might wish to pass on a small sum to yourself. He mentioned a very small figure. When the time comes I will, of course, honour this suggestion, and that which I shall offer will be in excess of that which he suggested.

Concerning the contents of the house, please let me know if there is anything you would like and, if you will let me have a description of how to get to your flat, I will bring them over.

You will appreciate that this has not been an easy letter to write, and I have deliberately avoided commenting on the Will in the knowledge that to do so would achieve no purpose and only make it more difficult for you to read. For my part, I decided at the age of 16 that I should start a fresh life on my own, at the same time trying to repay to some extent all that I owed to my grandparents. I have subsequently built my own family unit, happy in its independence, but carry no grudges.

Thank you for the autograph album which brought back many memories. I haven't forgotten the photograph of the children that I promised.

Mark continues to be top of the scholarship stream, Justin struggles halfway down the B form but is a splendid rugger player. We are going to Blackpool in December to see him perform in the school's production of Oliver, in which both boys and staff are taking part. Crispin is growing up quickly, very mischievous and running Ruth off her feet.

My next appointment is in Germany in April as second in command of a regiment. Though we don't like leaving our home we do like the prospect of another tour in Germany.

Love from Hamish.

Mrs D Hartland

65 Carlton Gate, Leeds 7

My mother replied a few days later from her new home at 52 Oatland Court, Leeds 7:

Dear Hamish,

Many thanks for your letter received yesterday. No, I did not know the contents of my father's Will, though it turns out to be different to the one which he said he had made after his marriage to Beth. He has evidently altered that Will, but this I did not know.

My father's house and money were his own, and he had a perfect right to leave his property any way he wished. I would not be human if I were not hurt, but, Hamish, he has left things to you, and you are my son, and anything that is to your benefit is alright by me – I do not for a moment begrudge it to you. You have been, I know, a constant source of joy and great pride to my father, and to my dear mother whilst she was living, and for this I thank you, and am always happy to know your life is such a good one – you deserve it, Hamish, you really do.

There are certain things I would like because of their associations – mainly the cut glass vase which I gave mother and daddy on the occasion of their silver wedding – the only worthwhile present I ever gave them – it is the larger of the two cut glass vases. Also, the Queen Anne teapot which mother loved so much. Granddad Pedley gave it to her and she was so proud of it. Also, the teaset with the blue rim and tangerine and gilt decoration – cousin Frank Ward and his wife gave mother that after they had stayed some time with us. There are one or two plates and some small pieces of pottery which are mine and which mother kept in the china cabinet for me, and do you think I might have the silver snuff box which belonged to my grandfather? The only other thing I can think of is the fawn crochet cloth – it's quite a small one, which I did for mother. There are various pieces of needlework which I did too, but that does not matter.

I am delighted at the success of your boys – they are certainly a credit to you, Hamish, and must be a constant source of pleasure and interest to you. I loved seeing Crispin – he is a little darling, and Justin and Mark are both clever in their own particular ways. I wonder which way Crispin will lean towards – knowledge scholastically or sport – maybe both.

When you bring the things, and I shall be pleased to see you, come down Harrogate road …

My love to you, Doris

I delivered the items to my mother and we had a pleasant chat in her eighth-floor apartment. I do not recall there ever being any harsh words between us and I continued to keep her informed of our lives, and of the progress of Justin, Mark and Crispin, as she requested.

Ruth and I thoroughly enjoyed the Rossall Junior School three– day production of *Oliver* in the Museum Theatre in early December, watching Justin perform in Fagin's gang. It was of a remarkably good standard, incorporating seventeen recorded musical numbers. A happy Christmas was too quickly followed by the inevitable packing of trunks and tuck boxes and the start of another term.
 On the afternoon of Sunday 30 January 1972 I was routinely driven by Ruth to York railway station to return to London and my work in the Ministry of Defence. On arrival I learned of the infamous events that afternoon in the Bogside area of Derry, Northern Ireland – later

entitled "Bloody Sunday" or "The Bogside Massacre", when soldiers of the Parachute Regiment fired on a civilian (Catholic) protest march, causing 14 deaths and a similar number of injured. When details emerged, the general opinion of military friends in the mess and office was that it was a tragedy waiting to happen, in that the Paras were the least suited regiment for the Northern Ireland 'Troubles' and should never have been deployed there. Ten years later the Paras gave glorious service to their country when Argentina invaded the Falkland Islands; their Commanding Officer awarded a posthumous Victoria Cross.

My time in Whitehall ended in March. In terms of career enhancement it had been most beneficial and I left with strong recommendations for both promotion and employment as a Grade 1 staff officer. I had learned a lot under the patient guidance of my immediate superiors, Colonel P.H.F. Webb MBE and Brigadier C.E. Tonry OBE. I was particularly indebted to the latter, for he gave me the confidence that I needed, encouraging me to 'change my face' by adopting a more assured manner and to be more relaxed among senior officers. He was a wonderful role model. He was nineteen when he and a small group of comrades broke through the German lines to reach the Dunkirk beaches in June 1940, and only gained his commission in 1944, shortly before serving with 11 Armoured Division Signal Regiment in Normandy and being awarded the Croix de Guerre with Silver Star. After World War II he served in Palestine and soon progressed through Staff College to become Military Attaché in Rangoon, followed by command appointments and Defence Attaché in Sofia, having qualified as an interpreter in Bulgarian. He also excelled at sport – athletics, rugby, soccer, swimming, diving, water polo, tennis, skiing and ice hockey. He was brilliant at delegating, but he always had his finger on the pulse and was most approachable. He made time for a game of squash on most days at a court close to the Ministry and to his delight gained his corps colours while I was there. He was aged fifty-one at the time.

Ruth and I looked forward to our forthcoming tour with the 21st (Air Support) Signal Regiment in Germany , but we dreaded the three months of separation before a married quarter was likely to become available.

21st (AIR SUPPORT) SIGNAL REGIMENT

Wildenrath - April 1972 to July 1974

I was immediately at ease and enraptured by the regiment, partly because of its exciting and vital role, which I have already described, but also because of the very close integration with the Royal Air Force at all levels; the very professional atmosphere; the constant and stimulating noise of jet aircraft; the personalities of both the station commander and my commanding officer; the fine relationship that existed between ace pilots and the minions who supported them, as well as the warm welcome that I received. I immediately knew that this was going to be a very special tour and that Ruth would also be very happy, when she arrived.

My commanding officer was Lieutenant Colonel Roy Phippard, whom I had briefly met on one occasion in the Ministry of Defence. He had a well-balanced technical, staff and regimental background and was highly regarded and very well liked in the corps. He confirmed my role as that of commanding the regiment in his absence, together with having responsibility for military training, officer training, security and whatever additional tasks he might throw at me from time to time. I was delighted when he also asked me to coordinate and develop the regiment's sporting activities, focusing particularly on a very fine athletics team that had won the Army Championship in 1970. From the outset I got on very well with my superiors and also Squadron Commanders Brian Adams, Tony Bushell, Bill Griffiths and Barry Ashcroft, Adjutant Mike Yolland and a quite outstanding RSM (WO1) Vic Prees, who soon accelerated further up the promotion ladder on gaining a commission.

Group Captain George Black AFC was an inspiring, no-nonsense station commander with strong leadership qualities who had earned his AFC flying English Electric Lightnings. His flying abilities were respected by his very talented pilots and he would routinely demonstrate in the air the standards that he required. Post-exercise 'wash ups' would be of several hours' duration as every action and response was analysed in detail, corrective measures identified and orders given for their expeditious implementation. Yet there was much warmth and good humour in his personality, which he readily shared with all on social occasions, and he would always try to briefly attend the Friday 'happy hour' that concluded the week for those not on standby or other essential duties.

The existence of a revolutionary new military aircraft capable of combining the take-off and landing abilities of the helicopter with the conventional performance of a jet fighter plane had been revealed in a Hawker Aircraft press release on 25 November 1960. I was in Malaya at the time and thought little of the announcement, particularly as it was trashed by some very senior officers, including a retired Chief of the Air Staff, who said, 'The press ought to be told that such a machine is a toy, and quite useless …' The prototype was the P.1127, which had had its first tethered 'hover' the previous month. Development and trials were sufficiently successful for Prime Minister Harold Wilson to announce on 2 February 1965, shortly after my Camberley course began, 'We believe that there is an urgent need for an operational version of the P.1127. As soon as it can be negotiated, a contract will be placed for a limited development programme so that the RAF can have, by the time they need it, an aircraft that will in fact be the first in the field, with vertical take-off for close-support of our land forces.' The next development was the Kestrel, followed by the P.1127 (RAF) which, by the summer of 1967, was being called the Harrier.

The first squadron of Harriers (1 Squadron) was established at RAF Wittering in October 1969, followed by 4 Squadron, which moved from RAF Wittering to RAF Wildenrath in June 1970, soon followed by 3 Squadron and 20 Squadron, making a total of 36 aircraft for the RAF Wildenrath Harrier Wing. The wing had been declared operational three months prior to my arrival, with the task of providing battlefield air interdiction, close air support and tactical reconnaissance for the 1st British Corps, and the capability of supporting German and Belgian units on the flanks, if required. The Harriers had caught the imagination of the British public and their exploits were constantly in the news. However, as already mentioned, 21 (Air Support) Signal Regiment was also responsible for the airfield communications of similar numbers of F2 Lightnings and F4 Phantoms at RAF Gütersloh and RAF Brüggen, respectively, as well as providing an important static radio relay communications contribution to the 2ATAF/RAF Germany command and control network. There could not have been a more interesting posting at that time.

Acquiring a thorough understanding of the regiment's diverse communications commitments and the operational requirements of the RAF was challenging and I had to work hard. I missed Ruth enormously and the stress was increased by Ruth not being able to understand that there was absolutely nothing that I could do to shorten the waiting time for a married quarter. It was a situation which virtually all married servicemen and their wives experienced at that time and it is a problem which continues today, exacerbated by an increasingly high percentage of wives also having careers. It was an enormous relief to us both when a married quarter was finally allocated. Speedy arrangements were made for Pickfords to pack and despatch our possessions, while I returned to Thorp Arch in early July to collect Ruth and Crispin in our new car. Arrangements were also made with the estate agent for a furnished Broadacres to be let while we were away.

Ruth settled easily and happily into the regiment and our modest bungalow, which was only a couple of hundred yards from the main runway.

The married quarters were virtually identical; even the furniture and curtains, so there was no envy or jealousy. We were all focused on giving our best in the support of a unique aircraft and its pilots in formative, pioneering days, conscious of the fact that we were playing a most important role in trying to bring the long Cold War to a successful conclusion. Justin and Mark joined us at the end of their Rossall term and we were soon taking them and Crispin on excursions into the attractive Rhineland countryside and re-visiting our favourite spots in the Ardennes. No time was lost in planning a summer holiday. We hired a caravan – our destination a holiday complex on the Lido near Venice. First stop was at the Gästehaus Gutser in Unterjoch on the Austrian border, some twenty miles south of Kempten. This Gästehaus was popular with the regiment's langlauf skiers and was run by Margaret, the wife of an outstanding international skier who helped them in their training. Next day we travelled eastwards through the Bavarian Alps to Garmisch-Partenkirchen, then south via the Brenner Pass to the Lido, where we enjoyed a memorable holiday.

The off-base-dispersal concept for the Harrier force was progressing well. Six top-secret preselected sites had been identified for the thirty– six Harriers. The sites were on the fringes of forest areas through which ran very minor roads, which could be closed to traffic without attracting Soviet attention in the event of hostilities. These minor roads were needed not only to provide important administrative access, but also to provide the Harriers with the choice of either short (STOL) or vertical (VTOL) take-off and landing and adjacent foliage concealment, enhanced by camouflage nets. STOL was preferred to VTOL because it consumed less fuel, so the sites needed to incorporate short stretches of straight road. The Harrier force had a capability of providing a wartime daily rate of about two hundred sorties. Like the Spitfire of World War II, the Harrier had a superior turn to any other aircraft. It achieved this by utilising its nozzles to rapidly decelerate the aircraft in a turn. The communications for this off-base deployment were very efficiently provided by the regiment's 2 Squadron, which was commanded by Major Tony Bushell, with protection provided by the RAF Regiment. Of course, there were the occasional setbacks, and I will never forget Group Captain Black's reaction when one of his pilots forgot to lower the wheels whilst making an otherwise perfect vertical landing.

The regiment was rich in talent. The athletics and cross-country teams, under the dedicated coaching of CSMI Woods of the Army

Physical Training Corps and the leadership of Captain Tom Moncur, went from strength to strength. In 1972 they won the Army Athletics Championships for the second time, while the cross-country team became Army champions for the first time, having been runners-up in 1970 and 1971. Needless to say, the regiment also won the BAOR and Royal Signals athletics and cross-country championships – they were unbeatable. No matter what the sport was, the regiment was always among the favourites and had abundant successes, despite its heavy military commitments. Indeed, without appreciating it at the time, we even had a potential astronaut – Lieutenant Richard Farrimond, who had joined us from the Royal Military College of Science. Twelve years later he was to be selected as the backup crew payload specialist to fly with the Space Shuttle mission STS-61-H which was being prepared to deliver the British Skynet 4A satellite into space. However, the flight was cancelled because of the Challenger catastrophe. He had completed all the spaceflight training and was very disappointed. Richard Farrimond retired early from the Army as a lieutenant colonel, but he continued his very distinguished career working in the space industry, including taking a consultancy appointment at the Kennedy Space Centre.

I was sorry when Lieutenant Colonel Roy Phippard's tour in command came to an end in January 1973. I admired him immensely, while Ruth had enjoyed a very happy relationship with his wife, Gillian. I oversaw the arrangements for his dining out and departure, while Group Captain George Black bestowed on him the unique honour of a flight in one of the two-seater Harriers (most Harriers are single seater), piloted by himself. His next appointment was on promotion, and he soon reached brigadier rank as Director of Telecommunications. It was my good fortune to welcome as his successor, Lieutenant Colonel Alastair de Bretton-Gordon, who was to become another outstanding commanding officer of the regiment.

I had noticed that an RAF freight aircraft flew each week from RAF Wildenrath with supplies to an RAF support unit located at the NATO base at Decimomannu in Sardinia. I asked if I might be a passenger on one of these flights, with a view to arranging a military training exercise on this rugged island for officers and NCOs of the regiment. My request was granted, and over a period of a few days I was able to devise and write a quite interesting and challenging five-day military exercise which would not require any resources other than spare space on this freight aircraft. Furthermore, once established, the exercise could be improved and offered to other units. I made sure, of course, that I also had time to see some interesting parts of the island. Sadly, the exercise had to be cancelled at the nth hour for political reasons, but my initiative was not overlooked and received some complimentary remarks from senior officers of both services.

Caravanning was very popular among families with young children, and there were many superb continental sites to select from. Children loved it, and the reduced cost and duty-free fuel enabled families to travel far and wide. Our summer holiday of 1973 at the Lido near Venice was such a success that we repeated it, though with different overnight locations, including a delightful spot on the bank of the blue Danube. Ruth had some reservations, for such holidays did not give her the total break from cooking that she would have liked. Nevertheless, it was another splendid family holiday. On our return I learned of my selection for promotion to lieutenant colonel and that my first appointment in that rank was likely to be a Royal Signals staff appointment. I was asked if I had any preferences, and following discussion with Ruth, I asked for an appointment in the UK, preferably in northern England, which would enable us to make use of our home in Yorkshire. Broadacres was currently leased to a bachelor who looked after it well enough, but who needed strong persuasion at times from our estate agent to part with his money.

The year 1973 was to become a milestone in our lives, and in the lives of all UK taxpayers – it was the year in which 'financial wizards' introduced a consumption tax, a regressive tax in which the poorest/ least wealthy spend a higher amount of their disposable income than the very rich. It was called 'value added tax', or VAT. Few people can now recall or even comprehend the existence of life without VAT, arguably the greatest scourge since the Black Death.

Holiday travel between Rossall School and our temporary home at RAF Wildenrath was now routine. We found time for a winter skiing holiday at the Gästehaus Gutser in Unterjoch, which was much appreciated by our sons. We had pleasant weather and it provided Ruth with a break from the cooking. We were surprised to find that Mark had exceptionally good balance, and he soon became the best skier. However, there was one spectacular tantrum when he became stuck on his back in a shallow dip in loose snow (rather like a 'rigged' sheep) as a result of showing off his ability. He was at the mercy of our snowballs. Justin and Mark only saw RAF Wildenrath and Germany at holiday time. They never heard the sirens that summoned ACTION STATIONS to repel Warsaw Pact aggression, whilst Crispin was aged only 5 years. They never saw the anxiety of parting parents, who would only learn that it was an exercise several hours later. It required a huge amount of dedicated training, effort, financial commitment and the solid determination of our nation to win that Cold War.

It was not long before I was advised that my next posting, on promotion to lieutenant colonel, was to be on the staff of the United Kingdom Commanders-in-Chief Committee (UKCICC), as the GSO1 Signals, located at Wilton in Wiltshire. It was an appointment that I had never considered, for I was essentially a British Army of the Rhine soldier with very limited experience outside this theatre. I was flattered, but more than concerned as to how I would cope.

Our last six months at RAF Wildenrath passed rapidly. Group Captain George Black AFC handed over to future Air Chief Marshal Sir Patrick Hine GCB GBE in late January. There were umpteen inspections, tactical evaluations (TACEVALS) and rehearsals for the 17 May visit of HRH the Duke of Edinburgh, whom I had the privilege of meeting, followed by a five-day home defence course in the UK in early June. My meeting with HRH the Duke of Edinburgh [HRH] came about because I was temporarily in command of 21st (Air Support) Signal Regiment on that day; Lieutenant Colonel Alastair de Bretton-Gordon being in the UK. Various RAF Wildenrath briefings and demonstrations were followed by a fine luncheon in the officers mess, with several groups of 5-6 officers set apart to meet HRH. I was in one of these groups. The conversation was relaxed and jovial and eventually

I revealed my enjoyment and activities as a schoolboy cadet on HMS King George V and HMS Sluys; whereupon HRH asked me why I hadn't gone to Dartmouth. I confessed that I would have loved to have gone to Dartmouth, but that my low Physics grade prevented me from even applying. HRH replied, "Ah, the dreaded Physics", followed by a sigh and sympathetic smile.

I received a flattering confidential report, incorporating a recommendation from the Chief Signals Officer BAOR that I attend the National Defence College at Latimer. That moment was probably the zenith of my military career.

I was delighted to receive a very nice clock from the athletes of the regiment on my departure. They were not only splendid athletes but young men of fine character and ability who I suspect will have been very successful in life.

On 20 June, Ruth, Crispin and I travelled by car to Wilton.

UNITED KINGDOM COMMANDERS-IN-CHIEF COMMITTEE (UKCICC)

Wilton - September 1974 to September 1976

Our quarter at 21 Bulbridge Road was an unattractive but very acceptable red brick house with a small garden on the south side of Wilton, located within a small estate of military properties. It was a quiet location, close to some attractive woods and the Downs, and only a short drive from my place of work within Headquarters United Kingdom Land Forces at Erskine Barracks in Fugglestone St Peter, a couple of miles north-east of Wilton.

I had four weeks of disembarkation/privilege leave, and we lost no time in exploring a part of England that we had not seen before. We were not disappointed. We began with the nearby Gothic cathedral city of Salisbury, home of the Magna Carta, brimming with historic buildings, quality shops and a market. Then it was on to the stunning West Wiltshire Downs and Cranborne Chase, both areas of outstanding natural beauty and steeped in history with their ancient ox drove and Roman tracks. Next, to the historical sites of Stonehenge, Woodhenge, Old Sarum and the numerous ancient burial sites, some of the barrows dating back to 4000 BC. Ruth, who had a deep interest in history, was more than intrigued with these ancient sites and would be thrilled with our visits, avidly reading about them afterwards. She would have loved to have been able to occupy our Yorkshire home at Thorp Arch, but soon recognised that with these local attractions nearby and the New Forest only twenty-five miles to the south, Wilton was one of the most attractive and interesting parts of England in which a soldier could serve.

Although Ruth and I had had wonderful experiences and a great amount of adventure and enjoyment during our many years of overseas service, we were now beginning to yearn for a future in our own country, and one that incorporated a fresh challenge – particularly Ruth, who had played the traditional wife's role of that time in support of her husband's career. She was a very talented lady who would probably have been more successful than I had she not lost her father when she was seventeen, and consequently also the opportunity of becoming head girl and proceeding to university and her own career. During our relaxing leave, inspired by the stimulating history and attractive countryside of Wiltshire and the New Forest, we shared our thoughts and options for the future. We already had a very pleasant home in Yorkshire, we were both proud children of that county, and our pipe dreams became focused on my seeking military employment in Yorkshire and eventually a home of character within the county with land and outbuildings that offered opportunity for enterprise. My ambitions and effort up to this time had been strongly driven by a fear of redundancy from a continuously shrinking Army, particularly as the family increased. Now that such personal redundancy was highly unlikely I decided that in future, while continuing to give of my best, I would seek appointments within Yorkshire, recognising that eventually such requests would be detrimental to any chance of further promotion. Ruth was so very pleased with this strategy.

The United Kingdom Commanders-in-Chief Committee (UKCICC) consisted of the Commander-in-Chief Naval Home Command, the Commander-in-Chief United Kingdom Land Forces (Chairman) and the Air Commander Home Defence Forces. The committee was responsible to the Chief of the Defence Staff at the Ministry of Defence both for the coordination of joint-service plans for home defence in the United Kingdom and also for the numerous overseas contingency plans to protect British interests and provide the safe evacuation of

British nationals in an emergency. Each of these commanders was represented by a small planning staff in Erskine Barracks, adjacent to Headquarters United Kingdom Land Forces (HQ UKLF). I was responsible for coordinating the communications aspects of these plans, supported by two very competent and helpful officers, Majors Eddie Pickup and Maurice Handsley. In practice, I concentrated on the home defence communications planning while they specialised in the overseas communications planning. Accordingly, much of my work involved close consultation and negotiation with the Cabinet Office, the Home Office and the Central Staffs of the Ministry of Defence. I was also Secretary of the Joint Signals Board chaired by the Chief Signals Officer HQ UKLF. The Commander-in-Chief United Kingdom Land Forces, was General Sir Roland Christopher Gibbs, CBE, DSO, MC. He had distinguished WW2 service as a junior officer of the King's Royal Rifle Corps in North Africa, where he was awarded the Military Cross. He fought in the Second Battle of El Alamein as a rifle company commander in the westward advance through Tunisia. He subsequently participated in the invasion of Italy, the Normandy landings and the fighting that followed until Germany surrendered in May 1945. He was then posted to the South-East Asian theatre, holding various GSO2 and Brigade Major (BM) appointments. Following service in the Palestine Emergency and a series of plum appointments [Sandhurst instructor … Brigade Major 5th Infantry Brigade in Iserlohn … inter-service planning in Whitehall] he was appointed Commanding Officer of 3rd Battalion, Parachute Regiment. By 1963 (aged 42 years) he was a brigadier, commanding the 16th Parachute Brigade in a peace keeping role in Cyprus, then Commander of British Land Forces in the Persian Gulf. On 14th January 1972 he became Commander of 1st (British) Corps with the rank of lieutenant general, then Commander-in-Chief United Kingdom Land Forces (in the rank of full general) on 1 April 1974. General Gibbs subsequently became Field Marshal Sir Roland Christopher Gibbs, GCB, CBE, DSO, MC, KStJ, DL. He was the professional head of the British Army from 1976 to 1979 and Lord Lieutenant of Wiltshire from 1989 to 1996. He died on 31st October 2004 (aged 83).

It was a strange new world for me and rather daunting, not so much because of the higher rank but because of the regular top-secret level of document and verbal security, plus additional caveats imposed by the Cabinet Office. Essentially, I was involved in the detailed planning for a military communications system intended to survive a Soviet nuclear strike to a sufficient extent that it could provide the initial communications that were necessary to facilitate the first green shoots of national recovery. It was necessary for me to be made aware of the outline plans for the survival of royalty, the Cabinet and others who were considered essential to the post-nuclear strike recovery of our nation. I felt rather overawed at the responsibility that I had been given. I also felt rather sad as I recognised the fact that my age and success now meant that I was becoming increasingly distanced from that which had attracted me to my military career in the first place – regimental soldiering and the command of British soldiers, the finest in the world. Thankfully, I was not desk-bound, for in addition to my London visits, I needed to attend regional planning meetings and exercises that took me to many distant and interesting parts of the country. Sometimes this was by helicopter, from which I saw some stunning countryside and on one occasion the RAF's Battle of Britain Memorial Flight flying alongside for several miles, on its way to some demonstration.

These were days when it was still unusual for the wives of senior officers and warrant officers to be employed. Accordingly, our very pleasant social life was virtually unchanged, though it was not on the scale and frequency that we had enjoyed overseas. Dinner parties continued to be a gastronomic delight, an opportunity for the wives to show off their culinary skills, display their silverware and ornate tablecloths and wear their nice dresses. Such events would usually be informal (lounge suit), but sometimes formal (dinner jacket) for a special occasion. There were some splendid formal mess functions, including a Summer Ball, of a standard that one would expect in the mess of our Commander– in-Chief, a four-star general, and also some very popular Sunday family curry lunches. We rarely dined out, if only because there were few restaurants and, as well as being disproportionately expensive, the quality of the food and service of those that did exist was far inferior.

The primary reference document for home defence communications planning was the 'Home Defence Signal Instruction'. There had been many amendments to it and it was in need of a complete re-write. I discussed this with the Chief Signals Officer HQ UKLF (Brigadier F.L. Clarkson MBE) and he agreed that I should make this my primary task. It involved a close liaison with several organisations and headquarters, but the basic structure of the post-nuclear strike communications system to which I have referred was provided by four Royal Signals regiments of the Territorial Army (32, 37, 38 and 71 Signal Regiments). These regiments would provide high-frequency radio teleprinter and message handling detachments at the nation's ten regional war headquarters and numerous government agency survival locations, together with three mobile communications 'gateways'. These 'gateways' would only emerge from their underground survival locations (e.g. disused railway tunnels) when it was deemed sufficiently safe. The most northern gateway was to be located in Scotland, with the other two in Wales and southern England. The four regiments were commanded by Headquarters 2 Signal Group at Aldershot, and I soon established a close liaison with that headquarters. Little did I realise at the time that my next appointment would be the command of one of these regiments.

An intriguing aspect of my task of re-writing the Home Defence Signal Instruction document was incorporating practical measures to be taken to minimise the effect on communications equipment of high-altitude (several hundred miles above the earth's surface) nuclear explosions. While the emission of a pulse of electromagnetic radiation from a nuclear explosion was recognised and well documented, the magnitude of the electromagnetic pulse (EMP) and the effects of detonation height and the interactions with the earth's magnetic field were only just being recognised. This was probably because at or near ground level, EMP was of little significance, with the blast itself, as well as the heat and radiation, being far greater threats to life, structures and equipment. However, the effects at ground level of a nuclear explosion several hundred miles above the earth were very different – there would be no significant blast, heat or radiation, but the intensity of the high-altitude electromagnetic pulse

(HEMP) would be catastrophic on communications equipment, and over an enormous area. Arrangements were accordingly made for me to attend government communications working party briefings on HEMP at the Cabinet Office and seek advice as to how our communications equipment might be shielded from this threat. This advice was incorporated in the new Home Defence Signal Instruction document, together with recommendations for revised spare parts scales and their protection. In these days of email and smart phones I wonder how much thought is being given to the fact that they could be rendered useless in a nuclear environment by HEMP without any structural damage or casualties at ground level.

Due to a spectacular stock market recovery, I had a particularly happy forty-first birthday on 6 February when Ruth and I routinely calculated our monthly financial situation. The FT 30-share index had fallen from an eighteen-year high of 543.6 on 19 May 1972 to 146.0 on 6 January 1975 and had now bounced back in four weeks to 252.3. Our shareholding was modest, but it was nevertheless sufficient to help us to a £333 gain for the month and we had a modest celebration. However, despite this spectacular bounce, the FT 30-share index was no higher than it had been on our honeymoon in 1958. Ruth took a keen interest in our financial situation but tended to leave investment decisions to me, though I always obtained her nod of approval before implementation. I believed in diversification, and the greater part of our investment continued to be in property (Broadacres), with-profit life insurance policies and building society deposit accounts, followed by stocks and shares and philatelic purchases. We never gambled, apart from an occasional modest annual flutter on the Grand National.

Justin and Mark's 1975 Lent term at Rossall ended on 27 March and they travelled by rail to Wilton on what was becoming a familiar timetable – dep Blackpool 0720, arr Preston 0754, dep Preston 0813, arr Crewe 0903, dep Crewe 1006, arr Bristol 1257, dep Bristol 1305 and arr Salisbury 1443, where they were met by Ruth and Crispin. They were very interested in our recently purchased caravan, parked outside the house, and were quite excited when told that we were setting off with it for a holiday early next morning. 'Where to?' they asked. There were some groans when I told them that it was a mystery tour. It was an early night to bed, for reveille next morning (Good Friday) was at 0600, for departure at 0800 – prompt.

The opinion of our sons as we set off was that we were having a long-weekend tour of the Downs. When they recognised that we were travelling south the excitement increased – 'it must be the New Forest'. As we left the New Forest behind and Southampton docks appeared, the excitement increased further – we were sailing somewhere, but where to? When we were settled on the ferry I began to read the *Daily Telegraph* and after a few minutes passed it to Justin. It was a re-print of the Daily Telegraph of 6 June 1944. After an appropriate pause, and recognising Justin's and then Mark's bewilderment, I told them to imagine that they were soldiers on one of the ships or landing craft of the invasion force approaching the Normandy coast on that day, and then went on to reveal that our holiday was going to be of 12 days' duration, exploring the landing beaches and battlefields of the Normandy landings.

I had my Army Staff College Battlefield Tour maps with me and was able to point out precise locations and give an account of what happened, describing the tragic loss of life involved in liberating continental Europe from a brutal Nazi regime. However, it was a family holiday as well as a battlefield tour, and in addition to scouring the beaches for remnants of the invasion that were still being revealed at each tide, we enjoyed the countryside of Normandy and the very warm pro-British welcome wherever we went. Nevertheless, I recollect one quite frightening night when we selected the cliffs near Vierville, overlooking Omaha beach, as our nightly stop. It was quite windy, but during the night the wind intensified to gale force and there was a real danger that we would be blown over the cliffs. We woke the boys, abandoned the caravan, grabbed our sleeping bags and sheltered in the remnants of a nearby German bunker. I crept back and hammered some securing irons deeper into the ground and rejoined the family. We slept well and next morning were relieved to see that our caravan was still there, and that the gale was subsiding. Our last two nights were spent overlooking the beach at Morsalines, two miles south of Quettehou on the northern flank of Utah beach. It was a very memorable holiday, incorporating Paris and the only visit by Ruth or me to the Louvre, viewing the Mona Lisa painting. We had seen a few hundred brilliant paintings before we reached Mona Lisa, several of which equally impressed me. Interestingly, whilst Mona Lisa was painted circa 1506 it attracted very little attention until the early 19th century. Nevertheless, whenever I see the Mona Lisa painting I am reminded of Leonardo da Vinci – the greatest polymath of all time; artist, sculptor, writer, inventor, engineer, astronomer, biologist, geologist, physicist, architect. I so envy people with diverse talents. Bertram Russell is another polymath who springs to mind, whilst Einstein was as gifted on the violin as he was a scientist and humanitarian. Looking to the future I believe that we should encourage the younger generation to explore as many talents and paradigms as they find themselves interested in, whilst in any personal reincarnation appraisal I would plead for the talents of artist, cartoonist, writer, cricketer, and a singing voice that attracted smiles instead of hostile glances in church.

Shortly after our return to Wilton we were delighted to learn that Mark had won the top open scholarship in the Common Entrance Examination for entry to Rossall Senior School, which he had sat in the three-day examination in early March. This meant that we would have to pay virtually nothing for his senior school education. Justin had won one of the lesser scholarships, similar to that which Crispin was to achieve several years later. We were very proud of our sons, and these scholarships were of considerable financial help.

The anticipated Defence Review, following Harold Wilson's narrow overall majority of three in the October 1974 election, was held on 10 April 1975. It is generally referred to as the Mason Review (Roy Mason being the new Labour government's Secretary of State for Defence). I refer to this Defence Review because such periodic reviews are the basis for long-term military planning. I learned of its content at a HQ UKLF Chief of Staff briefing on the same day. It confirmed an anticipated reduction in the defence budget to 4.5% of the gross domestic product (GDP), also that the principal threat to the security of the United

Kingdom remained the Soviet Union. It stated that there were to be further reductions of British forces in the Mediterranean, the Far East and the West Indies and that NATO remained the priority for the nation's defence resources. Areas of particular national importance that were to be given special recognition and support were the UK contribution to NATO front-line forces in Germany, anti-submarine warfare forces in the eastern Atlantic, home defence and the UK nuclear deterrent. The importance of UKCICC's work was apparent, but I was rather disturbed at the continuing UK reduction in defence spending. As a percentage of Gross Domestic Product [GDP] it had fallen from 10% of GDP when I enlisted in 1952 to 4.5%. Now, in 2020, it is 2.2%, compared with Russia 4.3%, US 3.7%, France 2.1% and Germany 1.4%.

We used our caravan for a summer holiday in Cornwall and also, throughout our time in Wilton, for routine weekend outings to the many attractive areas of South West England. It was parked outside the house, and when a fine weekend was forecast we would take a Friday–evening decision and be on the road the following morning. During the 1975 autumn term Justin's rugby ability at Rossall 1st XV level was being noticed by the Lancashire scouts and he was invited to a series of Lancashire trials, followed by a trial for NW Counties. On 20 November at 11 p.m. I smoked my last cigarette. I had tested my resolve a few months earlier, so it was with some confidence that I stubbed it out at the bar at a male gathering of largely fellow smokers and announced that it was the last that I would ever smoke. There was hilarious laughter and I was taunted in a good-natured way with offers of cigarettes for several weeks. I did not tell Ruth and she said nothing, perhaps not wishing to break the spell. After about six weeks she could contain herself no longer and said, 'You've given up smoking, haven't you?' I nodded and received a big hug and kiss. Forty-seven years on, I can honestly say that since that day I have never taken an inhalation of tobacco smoke or nicotine in any form. I soon found that my appetite increased and I started to put on weight. This was corrected by short daily runs through the delightful woods. They gradually became longer and longer and my speed and stamina increased. It was not long before I was feeling as fit as I was in my late twenties, and I am delighted that no member of my family has developed the smoking habit. On 20 December Justin was playing as a centre in an England trial at under-16 years level for the NW Counties against the NE Counties at Penrith. On 2 January 1976 he represented Lancashire schools against Yorkshire schools, followed a few days later by matches against Cumbria schools at Aspatria and Cheshire schools at Sale.

Inflation ran out of control during 1975, the annual consumer price index (CPI) reaching in excess of 24%, a figure normally only associated with third-world countries!

In late January 1976 I was notified of my selection to be the next Commanding Officer of 38th Signal Regiment (Volunteers), based in Sheffield. I was to take over in late September from Lieutenant Colonel Peter Revill TD, whom I knew quite well. Ruth and I were delighted. We would be able to live in our own home at Thorp Arch and would also have the use of a pleasant residence in Sheffield, which was being modernised. We would also be closer to Rossall School. I felt proud to have been selected to command this well-respected regiment with its very important home defence role, particularly as command appointments were becoming increasingly competitive as the Army reduced in size. We promptly gave notice to our American tenants to enable us to occupy Broadacres on 3 July, ahead of the school holidays. I would take a long weekend and then return to live in mess at Wilton. However, I would return to Broadacres each weekend and also take a long leave in August.

There was some gnashing of teeth when we arrived at Thorp Arch and saw the internal condition of Broadacres. The American couple had allowed their young children to scribble with crayon and pencil virtually wherever they could reach, focussing their artistic talents on the very expensive wallpaper in the lounge. Ruth was heartbroken. On learning that they were still in the area and might call, she placed the multi-tipped antlers of a large stag in the centre of the front lawn and spread the word that they would be thrust up the mother's backside if she appeared. She did not appear and the American family soon returned to their own country, unharmed.

The successor to General Sir Roland Christopher Gibbs, CBE, DSO, MC as Commander-in-Chief United Kingdom Land Forces was Lieutenant-General Sir Edwin Bramall, KCB, OBE, MC. He was a popular selection, arguably the most talented senior officer in the British army at that time – destined for the top. My diary records that I met him, together with other members of the UKCICC staff, during his takeover, on the morning of Friday 28th May 1976. On 25th June he was promoted to full general. My farewell interview with General Bramall was on 2nd September 1976. He subsequently became Field Marshal Edwin Noel Westby Bramall, Baron Bramall, KG, GCB, OBE, MC, JP, DL. He was the professional head of the British Army between 1979 and 1982, and as Chief of the Defence Staff, professional head of the British Armed Forces, from 1982 to1985. Field Marshal Bramall later served as Lord Lieutenant of Greater London (1986-1998). He was a talented artist [aged 16 – two paintings hung in the Royal Academy summer exhibition] and cricketer [captain of Eton – President of the MCC and Chairman of the ICC in 1988/89]. Sadly, this most honorable, humble and deeply compassionate man, who was totally devoted to serving his country, both as a soldier and as a public servant, was one of several senior establishment figures targeted in 2015 by Carl Beech, now a convicted perjurer and paedophile. A shameful and naïve investigation by the Metropolitan Police (Operation Midland) eventually resulted in a full apology and substantial compensation. His wife [Avril] died in 2015, before he was exonerated by the police. Field Marshal Bramall died on 12th November 2019. His obituary in the Daily Telegraph of the following day records his feelings; *"I can honestly say I was never as badly wounded in all my time in the military as I have been by the allegations".*

The summer term ended on Friday 9 July. Justin was to join the family later, following a week with the Rossall CCF contingent at the Cultybraggan Training Camp in Perthshire. A week later I received a letter from Jennifer, my half-sister, advising me that our mother, Doris, had died on that day (9 July 1976). It was not a surprise, for she had been in poor health for quite a long time. I was more saddened by my mother's life than by her death. She had been given a privileged start to life, but in tough, uncompromising times had married a carpenter from a slum area of Leeds who, though seemingly hardworking, was never able to earn sufficient to lift his family from a low standard of living. She eventually took employment as a conductress on the Leeds Corporation trams and buses, where she met her second husband, Horace (Harry) Hartland, a bus driver. Doris died of carcinoma of the bladder. In accordance with her wishes, she was cremated without funeral or service.

My time at Wilton ended with a week-long commanding officers' course for some thirty new COs at Winterbourne Gunner, many of whom I knew from Sandhurst days.

38th SIGNAL REGIMENT (VOLUNTEERS)

October 1976 to April 1979

The Regimental Headquarters of 38th Signal Regiment (Volunteers), together with a support squadron and 64 Signal Squadron, was located at Sheffield's Manor Top TAVR Centre, located at the junction of Mansfield Road and Hurlfield Road. Some of the wooden buildings were in a poor state but were to be replaced with a large purpose-built complex in 1978, incorporating drill hall, offices, training rooms, stores, messes, garages and workshops. Three additional squadrons were located outside Sheffield – 46 Signal Squadron at Derby, 87 Signal Squadron at Nottingham and 93 Signal Squadron at Blackburn. In addition to myself there was a nucleus of Regular Army officers, a warrant officer 1 (RSM), senior NCOs and civilian staff to provide training and administrative assistance. Each of the squadrons could boast of a distinguished history, particularly 46 Signal Squadron, which could trace a link back to the North Midland Telegraph Company, formed in 1908. The regiment had an overall establishment of just over 600 soldiers and servicewomen, plus civilian administrative staff, together with 172 vehicles, 82 trailers and 65 generators. Our extensive communications equipment mostly consisted of medium-power D11 transmitters and their associated R234 receivers, which enable teleprinter messages to be transmitted and received over distances of several hundred miles, but we also had radio relay and low-power voice-only equipment.

The regiment was responsible for the recruitment of its own officers, soldiers and servicewomen and for the greater part of their training. However, many enlisted with impressive civilian skills that were ideally fitted for the regiment's requirements; technicians, mechanics, keyboard operators, HGV drivers and electricians being particularly welcome. Some held very high positions in their civilian employment and there were many with valuable experience in the Regular Army who had retired in order to provide a more settled life for their family, but who missed the military camaraderie. My second in command, Major Alan Hawksworth, was on the board of Boots (Chemists), the Squadron Commander of 64 Signal Squadron, Major Toby Seymour, had many years of experience as a commissioned officer in the Royal Signals, while others held advanced technical degrees and qualifications. I was very surprised at the depth of talent, skill and dedication, and also at the high percentage of servicewomen – the highest of any regiment in the Army, regular or volunteer. This was largely because of the many established posts for which young women were well fitted, particularly as data and radio telegraphists.

Like all volunteer units, the regiment trained at weekends plus one evening each week, usually Tuesday. Training schedules had to be precise, with time at a premium, and for important exercise deployments the squadrons would assemble during the Friday afternoon and evening and make ready for very early departure on the Saturday morning, sleeping in vehicles or on the floor of the drill hall. The most intensive period of training was the annual camp, of 14 days' duration. This alternated annually between a full regimental communications exercise covering a wide expanse of the country, and concentrated trade and military training at one of the Army's Special to Arm Training Centres. A good liaison with employers was essential and, when established, it provided mutual benefit, many 'soldier employees' developing personal qualities and trade skills that enhanced their civilian careers. It was not unusual for a volunteer soldier who held a high position in his or her civilian employment to seek only a very modest military employment and refuse promotion, finding the experience rather therapeutic. We were as self- contained as a regular unit, including having our own paymaster, medical officer and padre. I was delighted to find that we had an excellent liaison with the city of Sheffield and with the Master Cutler, and that this was also the case between my squadron commanders at Derby, Nottingham and Blackburn and their civic dignitaries.

I had a military staff car and driver, which enabled me to work en route during the forty-nine-mile journey between Thorp Arch and Sheffield, but the distant locations of the outlying squadrons meant considerable travelling, while I had to adapt to taking time off mid-week to compensate for lost weekends. Ruth was soon meeting and making friends with the wives and supporting me at the many social occasions. She readily invited the seniors of the regiment and their wives to Broadacres for Sunday curry lunches, which were very popular. We gradually adapted to this different lifestyle, our recognition and admiration of the dedication and talent within the regiment steadily increasing. Securing the trust of the hierarchy of the city of Sheffield was essential and I was soon in contact with the Lord Mayor and his secretary [Colin Straw], seeking their advice. I was delighted with their warm response and it was not long before there was complete trust between us, with regular liaison [and refreshment] in the Lord Mayor's parlour. I soon learnt that one of the most powerful voices in the city was that of an inspirational blind man, who I came to increasingly admire as one of Labour's greatest politicians. David Blunkett was born blind into an under-privileged family in Sheffield on 6 June 1947 with improperly developed optic nerves, and he remained blind throughout his life. His father died in a horrific industrial accident when he was aged 12, leaving the family in poverty. Nevertheless, David Blunkett won a place at the University of Sheffield, where he was awarded a BA (Hons) in Political Theory and Institutions. In 1970 he became the youngest-ever councillor on Sheffield City Council and in Britain, and also a Methodist local preacher. The Lord Mayor told me that Councillor David Blunkett was well aware of everything that was happening in the city and that I would soon learn if I or my regiment did anything of which he disapproved!

He became Leader of the Sheffield City Council for 7 years (1980-87), a South Yorkshire County Councillor (1973-97) and then MP for the Sheffield Brightside and Hillsborough constituency for 28 years (holding two Secretary of State appointments and Home Secretary from 8 June 2001 to 15 December 2004). In August 2015 he was awarded a peerage, becoming Baron Blunkett of Brightside and Hillsborough in the City of Sheffield.

The Michaelmas term ended on Friday 10 December. It was nice to have the family together again in our own home, but it was a rather hectic period and I saw little of them. This was due to a succession of pre-Christmas meetings, involving three Territorial Army Volunteer Reserve Associations and two Regional Planning Committees in diverse and distant locations, together with the Sheffield Station Christmas Ball at the Endcliffe Hall. Three days before Christmas I held a conference with my squadron commanders and the holders of the other senior appointments in the regiment. I thanked them for their splendid support and described what I sought from them in 1977, confirmed in a detailed training directive which was then distributed. Ten days of blissful Christmas leave with the family at Broadacres followed. I was ready for a break and so was Ruth, for she had attended many of the functions in Sheffield, including most of the monthly Wives' Club meetings. We would make use of our Sheffield residence for late-night functions and sometimes Ruth would stay for two nights, for she loved the shopping facilities and the friendliness of the Sheffield people, not unlike that of the other steel city that we knew so well – Liège.

The new year kicked off with Justin representing Lancashire schools in the Roses match against Yorkshire schools at under-19 level on 3 January, his seventeenth birthday. The pace of 1977 soon developed, accelerating as the year progressed. It was Her Majesty the Queen's Silver Jubilee year, and I was asked by GOC North East District to coordinate a four-day Sheffield Services Display in Norfolk Park in late July. Everyone hoped for a joyous year, but there were many dark clouds on the horizon, with inflation continuing in double digits for the fourth successive year and many industrial action threats. The mood throughout the country was sombre.

I had my routine annual military medical examination at this time, and was not surprised when the medical officer expressed concern about my hearing. He referred me to an ENT specialist, and I received his examination on 13th January 1977 at the Duchess of Kent's Military Hospital at Catterick Camp. He wrote in his report:

"He has noticed progressive hearing loss for many years, associated with ringing tinnitus. Has always noticed deafness and tinnitus following firing – mostly .303 – in past years. No otalgia or otorrhoea.

OE: Meatus clear. TMs normal – intact and mobile.

Audiogram. Bilateral HF sensori-neural loss, falling to 70-80 dB at 6 KHz.

Diagnosis: NIHL – no treatment is indicated. He should be fully protected from further exposure to acoustic trauma. Review audiogram annually."

I received the annual audiogram checks, and Ruth shouted at me less frequently … fast forward almost 10 years to 23rd October 1986, when I raised the matter of a 'war disablement pension' with the government authority concerned.

The summer term at Rossall School began on 21 April with three Pedley pupils, as Crispin entered the junior school. The option of his education following the route of local schools and then perhaps Tadcaster Grammar School was considered, but Ruth and I felt that he should not be denied the quality of education that Rossall provided. Also, while we hoped that I might continue to obtain military employments in England, accepting that they might be detrimental to further career advancement, we appreciated that a series of such home postings could not be guaranteed. It was not long before Crispin was displaying potential as both a scholar and a rugger player.

There were times when I thought that perhaps too much was being asked of the regiment, but no one ever complained about the workload or the time that they spent away from their families. However, in return they appreciated a sensible balance between social and sporting activities. These included an annual walk. It was a walk that I had never heard of – the Lyke Wake Walk. I was soon to learn that it was no ordinary walk and that it was not for the faint-hearted. Suffice it to record that as the dawn, 'in russet mantle clad', broke on Saturday 7 May, I found myself, along with some ninety enthusiasts from Sheffield, setting off in an easterly direction from Osmotherley towards that colourful sunrise and Ravenscar, forty-three miles distant on the coast. It was a brutal moorland trek rather than a walk, mostly over rough heather, with few worn tracks. It had been a wet spring and the moors were in a super-saturated condition, with dozens of pools of water and small streams, over which one was obliged to leap. It was the biggest test of the strength of my legs that I had experienced, for one tends to habitually use the same leg for every jump, and my 'propulsion leg' was becoming more than tired of propelling me over these countless water obstacles, while the other leg soon began to protest in sympathy. The 'walk' ends with a series of exceptionally steep climbs and descents that are cruel to exhausted leg muscles. At the end I felt that I was within about three miles of my limit, and I was very fit at the time. However, the camaraderie and banter of my Sheffield servicemen and servicewomen, together with several friends of the regiment who accompanied us, was brilliant. My time was a respectable 15.5 hours. A reporter/photographer from the *Sheffield Star* accompanied us, resulting in a page of very welcome free publicity and a surge of applications to join the regiment.

The regiment's fourteen-day annual training period was at Crowborough in East Sussex, adjacent to the Ashdown Forest Training Area. I relished it, for I had my dispersed 38th Signal Regiment (Volunteers) together for the first time. The planning of my 2IC, squadron commanders and training major was faultless and I enjoyed showing the many senior officers who visited us what we had achieved. Nevertheless, all work and no play makes Jack a dull boy, and some most enjoyable social events were incorporated into an intensive training programme, culminating in a challenging and equally successful three–day regimental exercise. Arrangements were made for a reporter from the *South Yorkshire Times* to be with us for a few days, and she gave us splendid publicity, resulting in more applications to join the regiment.

Planning for the four-day Sheffield Services Display in Norfolk Park now intensified. We had been allocated some of the best arena and air displays from the Royal Navy, Army and Royal Air Force, and an abundance of static displays. It was my task to weld it all together and deliver a safe and memorable event worthy of the city of Sheffield. The showground would be opened at noon each day, with the air/ arena displays taking place at 2 p.m. and 6.30 p.m. We had a very close liaison with the police and the city of Sheffield, and they assisted with additional barriers, stands and power supply. Abseiling was uncommon at that time, but the Lord Mayor kindly gave permission for an ace military team to abseil from the city's tallest building during the morning rush hour without prior announcement, providing us with excellent publicity. The weather was kind to us and we provided a quality event with no mishaps, receiving further good publicity for the regiment and the gratitude and congratulations of the Lord Mayor and the Master Cutler. Frequent publicity is very important to volunteer units in order to attract recruits, provided of course that it is not detrimental.

It was now time for a well-deserved Pedley family holiday, though without Justin, who was attending a Rugby Football Union course at the Lilleshall National Sports Centre in Shropshire. We decided on a caravan holiday in Scotland, with the very attractive Caravan Club site at Morvich on the north-west coast as our base. We spent a very enjoyable week there, exploring the north-west Highlands, the coastline and Skye, returning via Loch Ness and the Cairngorms. During our holiday we learned of Mark's brilliant GCE O-level results – 10 A grades. As he had taken two other subjects the previous year, he now had 12 A grades at age 15 years and 7 months! We were very proud of his achievement. With all three sons now attending Rossall School we had to keep very careful watch on our finances, despite the help of boarding-school allowances and Justin and Mark's scholarship awards on entering the senior school. The situation was exacerbated by my no longer being able to use my military staff car between Thorp Arch and Sheffield. This was because work on our Army residence in Sheffield had been completed and the house was now deemed up to standard as a commanding officer's residence. Ruth needed the Chrysler 180 at Thorp Arch and I was obliged to spend more time at the Sheffield residence. It meant that I also needed a small car with very low fuel consumption for travel between Sheffield and Thorp Arch. I selected a year-old DAF 44 variomatic, one of the last of its type prior to DAF being taken over by Volvo. It had an 844cc air-cooled engine and a double-belt continuously variable transmission system. It provided 45 mpg, considered to be very low fuel consumption in those days, and proved to be a little gem.

Ruth and I continued to calculate our financial situation each month. Our assessment on 7 September 1977, the day prior to the start of the Michaelmas term, was:

Lloyds Bank	217.95
Midland Bank	257.00
Cash	19.00
Life Ins. Policies Surrender Value	2,483.00
300 European Ferries @ .90	270.00
Building Society Accounts	1,504.61
Chrysler value	570.00
DAF value	550.00
Caravan value	500.00
Stamp Collection value	1,675.00
Broadacres value	27,200.00
Less Sundry Creditors	5,597.35
(B&B BS 5,495.00)	
	= £29,649.00

The Jubilee celebrations and the summer holidays were over. They had masked the simmering discontent within the country at the continuing high level of inflation and the medicinal 10% maximum wage increase being imposed by James Callaghan's Labour government. As winter approached and the days grew shorter, headlines became increasingly depressing and macabre. Undertakers went on strike in London, resulting in hundreds of bodies without funerals, while young women in West Yorkshire were terrified by the continued murders of the Yorkshire Ripper and dared not leave their homes after dark. There were calls for the reinstatement of the death penalty, which coincided with the last execution by guillotine in France [of a man, for the murder of a young woman]. The nation's firemen were demanding a 30% wage increase and contingency plans were made for 10,000 servicemen to provide emergency cover using a reserve fleet of 'Green Goddess' fire engines, some of which were twenty-five years old. Many were based in drill halls, and our Manor Top TAVR Centre was no exception. It was ideally located, directly opposite a fire station, and as it was on high ground the Green Goddesses had a useful slope in their favour, though hardly a flying start. They did a remarkably good job, but their equipment was very inferior to that of the Fire Brigade and response times were slow, largely because the police first had to check that there was a fire, before leading the Green Goddesses to it. The strike was to last for nine weeks, ending with a 10% wage increase acceptance – the amount that had been offered at the beginning of the strike.

The remainder of the year followed much the same pattern as that of the previous year, but with an increased workload as we trained our many new recruits. The regiment was now in the healthy position of being in excess of its authorised manpower establishment, helped enormously by the contributions of such large public corporations as British Steel at Sheffield and British Rail at Derby, with whom we maintained a very close relationship.

Justin was now holding a secure position as a centre in the Lancashire schools U19 side, playing in a flurry of matches around another very happy family Christmas at Broadacres. When he was selected to represent the North against the Midlands on 11 February 1978 we realised that he could be close to an England cap.

It was to be a very exciting year for the regiment, for the new, purpose-built Manor Top TAVR Centre was nearing completion. When I had taken command of the regiment I was told by Brigadier Webb (Commander 2 Signal Group) to give the regiment an event during my period of command that they would be proud of and would never forget. This was to be it – a grand opening ceremony and parade on

Saturday 15 July involving Her Majesty's Lord Lieutenant for South Yorkshire (Gerard Young Esq. CBE), the GOC North East District (Major General H.G. Woods CB MBE MC DL MA Dlitt (Hon) FRSA FBIM), and the Chairman of the Yorkshire TAVR Association (Colonel L. Turnbull CBE MC TD JP DL), in the presence of the Lord Mayor and Lady Mayoress, the Master Cutler and the Mistress Cutler and many other dignitaries and their ladies of the city of Sheffield who had supported us so well. It was to be followed in the evening by a ball in the Banquet Room of the Cutler's Hall. The regiment's response to this challenge was magnificent, and when it was seen that this was going to be an event of some magnitude, the Signal Officer in Chief allocated the band of the Royal Corps of Signals in support. The stage was set – there was no going back now.

Major-General Henry Gabriel Woods CB, MVO, MBE, MC, DL died on 19th September 2019, aged 95 years. Comprehensive obituaries were published in THE TIMES [9 October] and the Daily Telegraph [10 October]. His MC was an 'Immediate MC', awarded on the battlefield when (aged 20 years) he led a troop of four Sherman tanks of his regiment, the 5th Royal Inniskilling Dragoon Guards (5 RIDG) in late March 1945 as part of the Allied advance from the recently crossed Rhine into Germany's Westphalian Plain…

> "At dusk, his Squadron had advanced to Sudlohn, where it was found that bomb craters had made the town impassable; the only bridge over the river that could be reached was made of wood and would not carry a tank. Woods fought his way into the eastern outskirts of the town and found that the single line railway bridge was intact. With great skill he manoeuvred his troops [tanks] along the line and got them across. When the remainder of the squadron tried to follow they broke their tank tracks, blocked the line and made further movement impossible. In the darkness he made contact with a small patrol from the Rifle Brigade and they advanced to Stadtlohn. They fought their way into the town, where they were engaged by a self-propelled gun and bazookas. Woods knocked out the gun and covered the infantry

while they took up a position in a large house on the main road. The small mixed force was completely surrounded, but for the next three hours, until they were relieved, they hung on and drove off repeated attempts to overrun them."

His Daily Telegraph obituary also refers to his tank being inadvertently strafed by a Spitfire … receiving a German bullet in the leg, and 'for breakfast' taking out a Panzer MK IV at a range of 800 yards. When WW2 ended, Major-General Woods returned to Oxford to complete his Modern History studies at Trinity College, Oxford, gaining a First. He experienced further active service as adjutant of 5RIDG in Korea, and commanded the regiment from 1965 to1967 in Aden and in Libya. He later commanded the Royal Armoured Corps Training Centre at Bovington, followed by military attache at the British Embassy in Washington DC. His final appointment, on promotion to Major-General, was as GOC North East District at York. See photograph of him presenting an award to an ACF cadet at Manor Top, Sheffield on Saturday 15th July 1978.

On Sunday 2 April we took Justin to play rugby at Blackburn, minus Mark, who had more important things to do. On our return Ruth asked Mark if there had been any phone calls. 'Oh, yes,' replied Mark, 'there was a call from a chap in Ireland who wants Justin to play rugby for them at Gloucester next week – he said he'd ring back.' Mark had not appreciated that it was a call from the England U19 team manager in Ireland, requesting Justin's presence at Gloucester the following morning to join the England squad. Justin came close to throttling his dear brother in trying to extract further information. An hour later the phone rang again and Justin learned that the England team had been beaten by Ireland that day and that he had been selected to play for England against Scotland at Gloucester on Tuesday evening. I made sure that Justin was on the first train to Gloucester on Monday morning, excused myself from an important meeting in Liverpool on the Tuesday afternoon and headed for Gloucester instead – there was no way that I was going to miss that match. They take their rugby very seriously in Gloucester, a leading English club that was formed in 1873. There was a lump in my throat as I watched Justin run out in England colours to a roar from a patriotic crowd of about ten thousand in the Kingsholm Stadium. I had a good position at the front of the 'Shed' (Gloucester's equivalent to Liverpool's 'Kop') and enjoyed watching an England win and a good game from Justin. Four days later we were all at Gosforth watching England beat Wales, with another fine performance from Justin.

We had rehearsed thoroughly for our grand opening ceremony and parade on 15 July, resulting in a parade of very high quality, followed by fine lunches and tours of our new premises. The ball in the magnificent Cutler's Hall with our splendid corps band concluded a perfect day. One could sense the pride and happiness in the regiment – it was indeed a day that they would never forget, nor myself and Ruth. However, following another pleasant caravan holiday in Scotland, mostly at sites in Aboyne and Aviemore, it was back to the serious business of training the regiment for its important war role, while finding time for another Lyke Wake Walk. The regiment's fourteen-day annual training period was to be a full deployment to locations not too distant from real pre-strike war locations, and we were required by the DS of HQ 2 Signal Group and HQ United Kingdom Land Forces to respond to the different phases leading to war; Soviet nuclear strike; and then post-strike recovery. Our responses were also under the scrutiny of a series of visiting senior officers. It was a thorough fitness-for-role (FFR) examination, and our performance received much praise, while confirming the need for more modern communications equipment.

Justin's education at Rossall School had ended in July. His examination results had surpassed our expectations and I gave him a big hug when they were received. They had been achieved despite the constant distractions of rugby trials and representation at county, regional and national level in addition to representing his school. He must have experienced prolonged periods of near exhaustion because of the lengthy travel and huge physical effort that was involved, with examination revision nigh impossible. He wanted to be a police officer, and both Ruth and I recognised that he was well fitted to be successful in that career. Not only had he a very good level of intelligence and common sense, but he had remarkably acute powers of observation and he was very, very fit and well motivated. Justin was interviewed for the West Yorkshire Police on 26 October 1978 and began his training on 13 November.

Soon afterwards I learned of my next posting. I was to be the Commander Recruiting and Liaison Staff (CRLS) of the Army's North East District, based in York, beginning in mid-May 1979. I had requested a career interview at the Ministry of Defence Department at Stanmore that dealt with career and selection matters several months previously. I had described my circumstances and asked if I might be run for the appointment, for it was one that was open to all arms and services rather than being tied to Royal Signals. A few weeks later I was interviewed by the Director of Army Recruiting in London and subsequently selected for the appointment. Needless to say, Ruth and I were delighted.

My country was now entering the period known as 'the winter of discontent'. The Christmas lights glittered as usual but the country was in a real mess, with militant trade unions calling widespread strikes for pay increases of a level that could not be justified by a virtually bankrupt nation. Refuse was left uncollected on the streets, and many areas were infested with rats, including Trafalgar Square. An increasing number of gravediggers became involved in strike action, particularly in Liverpool, and there were picket lines outside hospitals, allowing only emergency cases to pass through their barriers. In early January 1979 TGWU lorry drivers began an unofficial and later official strike which resulted in the closure of petrol stations. Oil-tanker drivers appeared to continue to work, but many advised strikers of their destination, enabling so– called flying pickets to reach the destination first and prevent access. The winter became the coldest since that of 1962/63, with blizzards and deep snow. It was against this background that the leader of the Conservative opposition party, Margaret Hilda Thatcher, prepared for the 3 May 1979 general election.

Though Justin sometimes had difficulty in obtaining leave from his police training, he was able to secure a place in both the Yorkshire Colts and the England Colts teams. There were two Rossall School old boys in these teams, both from Pelican House, the other being flanker Pete Winterbottom, who had been injured for much of the previous year, otherwise he too would surely have had an England U19 schools cap. Ruth and I travelled with Pete Winterbottom's parents by car to Paris on Saturday 17 March to watch England beat France on the following day. A fortnight later we were at Hull watching the pair play in an England team that beat Wales, viewing the match again in the evening on BBC TV's *Rugby Special*.

I had enjoyed my time with 38th Signal Regiment (Volunteers). It was a regiment of solid northern character with a core of talented and dedicated officers and soldiers who never let me down. I called on the Lord Mayor of Sheffield and the Master Cutler and thanked them for their support, advice and hospitality; the latter including the privilege of twice being a guest at the historic Annual Feast of the Master Cutler of the Company of Cutlers in Hallamshire (incorporated 1624) and [accompanied by Ruth] the Lord Mayor's Ball. The aim of the 'Hallamshire Cutlers' over the centuries has been to act as an ambassador of industry in Sheffield and is regarded as the most prominent business dinner north of London. In the original Act of Parliament, the company was given jurisdiction over *"all persons using to make Knives, Blades, Scissors, Sheeres, Sickles, Cutlery wares and all other wares and manufacture made or wrought of yron and steele, dwelling or inhabiting within the said Lordship and Liberty of Hallamshire, or within six miles compasse of the same"*. The Cutlers' Hall is located opposite the Cathedral on Church Street; the third to have been built on that original site [in 1832]. Formalities and standards are jealously maintained, and woe betide anyone attempting to remove a jacket or tie at the feast. I feel most privileged to have been a guest at the feast on two occasions; 1977 [341st] and 1978 [342nd]. In the years 2011-12 the distinguished engineer Pamela Edwards Liversidge OBE FREng became the first woman to hold the position of Master Cutler.

I handed over the command of the regiment to my recently promoted and outstanding second in command, Lieutenant Colonel Alan Hawksworth TD, now a senior Director of Boots (Chemists). I was dined out on 28 April at Manor Top and thanked everyone profusely for their support. I knew that I would miss them but realised that my new appointment would enable me to maintain contact. However, I would not miss the considerable travelling, nor their brutal annual Lyke Wake Walk.

COMMANDER RECRUITING & LIAISON STAFF (CRLS) NORTH EAST DISTRICT (NEDIST)

Residing in Broadacres

I began my takeover from Lieutenant Colonel Norman Morley of the Parachute Regiment as CRLS NEDIST on 14 May 1979. NEDIST extended from the Scottish border to the Midlands on the eastern side of the Pennines, covering the counties of Northumberland, Tyne & Wear, Durham, Cleveland and Yorkshire & Humberside. Its headquarters was at Imphal Barracks on York's Fulford Road, where I had received much of my training as a young infantry soldier in the Green Howards. Many of the old brick buildings remained, still serving a useful military purpose, but dwarfed by a fine modern building which was the District Headquarters. The formerly sacred square upon which, back in 1953, there would usually have been half a dozen drill squads, was now the car park.

My staff comprised two retired infantry officers, Lieutenant Colonel Colin Stonor OBE, who had commanded the King's Own Scottish Borderers, and Major Douglas Clarke, while along the corridor was my Schools Liaison Officer for Yorkshire & Humberside, retired Colonel 'Gunner'

Gregg of the Royal Tank Regiment and a small group of serving majors and captains who gave military career presentations in schools to classes of pupils aged about fifteen. 'Gunner' Gregg specialised in giving careers advice to potential officers, focusing his attention on schools that had a tradition of providing a steady stream of officer applicants, such as Ampleforth and Pocklington. I had another schools liaison team at Catterick which was responsible for schools in Northumberland, Tyne & Wear, Durham and Cleveland. To complete my team within Imphal Barracks I had a civilian design consultant [Bill Holden] and his staff who designed and arranged the production of a variety of regularly changing displays for the twenty-two Army Careers Information Offices, our 'kabmobile' mobile display, and any special events. Colonel 'Gunner' Gregg [Tresham] held the appointment that I was now taking over immediately prior to his active list retirement in 1974, subsequently becoming SLO Y&H (a retired officer [RO] appointment). I knew that he had been wounded at Dunkirk and had given further distinguished service throughout WW2, but if discussion on the war cropped up in casual social discussion he would always say that he had had a good war, and change the subject. It was only when I read the national newspaper obituaries that followed his death on 17th March 2014 (aged 94) that I became aware of the extent of his gallantry; culminating in 1944 in the joint leadership of the partisan brigade in northern Italy known as Stella Rossa, with a price on his head. Stella Rossa operated in the mountainous area 35 miles NE of Genoa.

My NEDIST area of responsibility was divided into six recruiting areas, their boundaries consistent with local government areas. Each had a main Army Careers Information Office (ACIO) and a number of outstations:

- Newcastle, with outstations at Ashington, Sunderland and South Shields.
- Middlesbrough, with outstations at Hordon, Bishop Auckland, Darlington and Durham.
- Bradford, with outstation at Halifax.
- Hull, with outstations at Grimsby and Scunthorpe.

- Leeds, with outstations at York, Scarborough, Huddersfield and Wakefield.
- Sheffield, with outstations at Doncaster and Barnsley.

Each ACIO had a warrant officer in charge, together with 2–5 senior NCOs of both sexes, while a retired officer of lieutenant colonel or major rank at each main ACIO was responsible for the overall recruiting effort and efficiency in his/her area. Though they were not under my command, I could also draw on the services of the static and arena displays of corps display teams plus those regimental display teams that had a historical recruiting area within NEDIST, for it was important to maintain the contact and keep their name and cap badge in the public eye.

Recruitment into the Regular Army had been of considerable importance following the ending of National Service in 1963, but in a period of high civilian employment it was difficult to attract sufficient applicants of the high quality that the Army needed. This was a matter of political as well as Army Board concern, resulting in recruiting being given a high priority and generous support. The estimated cost for 1978/79 was £12.32m. Weekly statistics relating to enquiries, applications and enlistments by ACIOs and Districts were sent to the Ministry of Defence for close scrutiny and analysis, and each Friday at 11 a.m. I (or Lt Col Colin Stonor in my absence) was required to routinely brief GOC NEDIST on applications and enlistments during the past week, and on our recruiting efforts and initiatives. Failure rates in training were similarly analysed in the Ministry of Defence, so any reduction in quality in any ACIO or area would soon be detected and investigated. It was recognised that it was essential that the recruiting organisation did not contain any officers, warrant officers or senior NCOs who were not suited to that type of work or sufficiently well motivated, for poor selections would almost certainly have a serious long-term adverse effect. For these reasons, every recruiter, irrespective of rank, was subjected to a personal interview by myself, assisted by the Army Careers Officer (ACO) of the area in which he or she was to be employed. I believe this was also the practice in the other Districts. The system ensured that no blame could be levelled at posting authorities if anything went wrong.

Ruth and I were very content with my new appointment and with our changed lifestyle. We had weekends together again and she no longer had the many social and wives' club obligations of a CO's wife. There was still a great deal of travelling but I usually had free weekends again, and more time for relaxation. I had kept myself fit with perhaps a couple of runs each week whilst at Sheffield, but now it was virtually every evening and I was getting faster, the times carefully recorded in my diary. My favourite route was over the river bridge and along the river path to the viaduct and back along the opposite bank (best time 21.06 minutes).

Our reliable little DAF was sold privately for £290 and replaced with a new Lancia Beta, with the Chrysler demoted to second car.

Each of the armoured, infantry and artillery regiments of the Army (the 'teeth arms') had clearly defined traditional recruiting areas, which they jealously guarded. They recognised the importance of maintaining a close association with these areas, no matter where the regiment might be, helping the recruiting effort by returning a steady stream of satisfied soldiers on two or three week attachments to the ACIOs where they enlisted, and also the occasional special recruiter. However, the major effort was the biennial KAPE (Keeping the Army in the Public Eye) tour which usually included displays, hospitality and a splash of pageantry. Because of my appointment, Ruth and I would regularly receive invitations to these ceremonial and social events, which were always most enjoyable. I particularly remember a cocktail party and Beating of Retreat by the 4th/7th Dragoon Guards in the Piece Hall in Halifax in early July and a Coldstream Guards concert in the City Hall, Sheffield later in the year.

Our summer holiday was spent caravanning in Wiltshire and adjacent counties, re-visiting many favourite and new locations, though now without PC 1222. Shortly after our return, on 18 August, we learned of Mark's brilliant GCE A-level results:

- Mathematics   A1
- Further mathematics   B
- Physics   A1
- Chemistry   A

HAWORTH VILLAGE—MAIN STREET.

Here I was born
April 27th. 1879   *F. G. Pedley*

Left: Birthplace of my grandfather, Francis George Pedley, in Haworth.

Below: Gunner FG Pedley, circa 1916.

" A " SUB-SECTION

Back Row—Brs. SYMONS, TOYE, Sgt. BUCKLER, Gnrs. WILDING, BROOKES, EDMUNDS, HOPE, Br. BAKER, Cpl. MULRENNAN, Br. BEEBE.
Front Row—Gnrs. STANNIER, SUMMERHAYES, PARKER, PEDLEY.   Gnrs. BROCKLEHURST, BRADSHAW, BOTTING.

Above left: My grandparents and mother, circa 1933.

Above right: Ruth's paternal great-grandparents (Addy), circa 1880.

Below: The Addy family at Nab Lane, Mirfield, 1909.

Above left: Ruth's father as student at Sheffield University in 1920.

Above right: Ruth's maternal great-aunt, Sarah Jones, from Plowden.

Below: The Bramham family (circa 1903): father (WJ), Blanche, Ernest, mother, Olive, Elsie Ivy, Sarah Elizabeth (Ruth's mother).

Top: Ruth's maternal grandparents: Walter Justin and Annie Elizabeth Bramham.

Left: The Bramham sisters (from top): Olive, Sarah Elizabeth (Ruth's mother) and Elsie Ivy. Blanche not present.

Top left: Ruth aged 7 years.

Top right: Ruth at Filey, summer 1948.

Middle: Ruth and her brother Leslie.

Left: TGS 1st X1 1950/51 (FHP next to Headmaster WN Bicknell).

Left: Sandhurst
– Cadet FHP.

Below: Sandhurst
– junior term drill
competition (FHP second
in centre rank).

Top: Sandhurst – winners of senior term shooting competition (FHP front row right).

Middle: Sandhurst – Academy parade.

Left: My 1937 Riley Adelphi.

Our wedding day.

Our wedding day.

Top left: Our honeymoon: Ruth at the Lindau Hotel.

Top right: Justin's christening: Gordon MacKeith, Godfather and Ruth's cousin, outside Ruth's mother's cottage with his Rolls-Royce, prior to the ceremony in March 1960.

Below: Carthage – the P&O liner that conveyed Ruth, myself and baby Justin to Malaya.

Top left: Malaya, June 1960 – Ruth and baby Justin outside our new home in Petaling Jaya, near Kuala Lumpur.

Top right: Malaya, 1960: Justin's first Christmas.

Below: Malaya, 1960: squadron officers and families at ceremonial event.

Top: Malaya, 1961: with aborigines in the jungle.

Below right: Our 'Broadacres' home in Thorp Arch Park.

Left: Malaya: Ruth and Justin in November 1961.

Top: Staff College 1965: FHP next to team captain.

Middle: NORTHAG ASRS 1969: Col Mische inspects quarter guard.

Left: Our three sons, summer 1971.

Left: 21 (Air Support) Signal Regiment: Harrier moving into off-base hide.

Middle and below left: Manor Top, Sheffield: *opening ceremony*.

Below Right: Manor Top, Sheffield: opening ceremony ball – with Lord Mayor, Master Cutler, PMC and Ladies.

Top: Old Hall, facing south.
Middle: Old Hall Cottage.
Left: Old Hall fireplace.

Above: Mark's Oxford Degree Presentation.

Below: Crispin's Aberdeen Degree Presentation.

Wedding of Justin and Haley, 12 September 1987.

Above left: Take-off for Ruth's hot-air balloon flight.

Above right: Haley and baby Charlotte.

Below: Nanette and Ruth at the wedding of Geoffrey Simpson, June 1991.

Left: Canberra cruise, November 1993.

Below: Wedding of Crispin and Aileen.

Bottom: Wedding of Crispin and Aileen.

Left: Masham Sheep Fair
Champion, 1991.
Below: Royal Show 1996,
Breed Champion.

Top: Christening of Lois, held by a proud grandmother.

Below: Charlotte, Jessica and Robert, 1996.

Top: Haymaking 1997 – helped by Charlotte, Jessica and Robert.

Below left: Haymaking is fun.

Below right: West Indies Cruise, 1996.

Top: GYS 1997: Ruth's Triple Champion (Breed, Longwool Ewe and Wool on the Hoof).

Below: Ruth and Prince Charles discussing her prize-winning sheep at the 1999 Great Yorkshire Show.

Left: Mark at the 1997 Royal Academy of Arts exhibition.

Below: Foot and mouth disease, 2001.

Top left: Ruth and stud ram prior to changing his raddle colour.

Top right: Hogg in Wool prior to shearing.

Below: Hand-shearing for a championship-winning fleece and a champion ewe.

Top: Ruth's Supreme Fleece at Sheep 2002.

Below: Supreme Fleece Treble – Royal Show, GYS and Sheep 2002, the three major fleece competitions of the year.

Left: Mark in Yosemite, California, 2002.

Below: Aurora Cruise, 2002.

Top: GYS 2002: Ruth receiving the historic Honourable Company of Staplers trophy.

Below: West Yorkshire Police Medal Presentation, 26 April 2004.

Top: Ruth and FHP with champion ram and ewe.

Below left: GYS 2004: Wensleydale Champion, Longwool Ewe Champion and Wool on the Hoof reserve Supreme Champion.

Below right: WLSBA Show and Sale 2004: Supreme Champion

Above: Tidying up the beck.

Left: The wall – another section completed.

Above left: Serving the pudding.

Above right: Charlotte and baby Alex.

Below: Christmas 2006: Marianne playing the accordion, with Crispin holding the music.

Great Yorkshire Show 2007: Ruth presents trophy to Roger Field of Ferrensby, near Knaresborough.

We were all, of course, delighted and very proud of Mark. He had also taken the O level examinations for the newly introduced General Paper and Computer Studies, obtaining two more A grades, making a total of 14 O-level A grades. Mark returned to Rossall the following month for further study and, following an interview at Christ Church, Oxford on 11 December and an additional examination, he was awarded a scholarship at Christ Church beginning in September 1980. As a scholar he would be able to reside in the college for the entirety of his time there, with first choice of room each year. He would also receive a modest but useful grant and a scholar's status symbol long gown. Mark left Rossall School in December 1979, a few days after his eighteenth birthday, and early in the new year obtained temporary employment at the British Library, Boston Spa, located on the nearby Thorp Arch Trading Estate.

Whenever I asked Ruth how she felt about hosting a dinner party for some of my officers and their wives I always got a positive response, provided of course that I was prepared to meet the cost of it being done well. I always readily agreed and Ruth responded magnificently. We would always try to have a mix of military and civilian guests as this seemed to provide a catalyst for more varied topics of conversation and alternative points of view. Ruth was an excellent hostess – she was so genuinely interested in people. She also had an extraordinary memory and many years later could recollect not only who was present and their family details, but where they were seated, what they were wearing, together with the menu and any faux pas that I might have made.

Life was good. I was enjoying my work and Ruth was enjoying her home and garden among her many friends in the Thorp Arch/Boston Spa/Walton/Tadcaster area. Justin had completed his police training, though sadly he was unable to live at home. He was now focused on his police career, to the detriment of his rugby. Mark was over the moon at his Oxford success and Crispin was now settled into the Rossall School way of life, showing well-above-average all-round ability. However, happy as we were, Ruth and I could not contemplate living in Broadacres for the rest of our lives and we were now routinely receiving brochures from estate agents of properties of character with land and outbuildings that offered opportunity for enterprise. Our search was initially for properties in rural areas within twenty miles of Broadacres, but we soon realised that such properties were in high demand in this popular commuting area for Leeds, Harrogate and York and were not only priced out of our range, but also required one to be a cash buyer. We accordingly began looking further afield.

The year 1980 began at a pace at Headquarters North East District with arrangements for the departure of the very popular Major General Henry Woods and the arrival of Major General Ian Helstrip Baker CBE from the Ministry of Defence, where he had been Assistant Chief of the General Staff. He too was an Oxford graduate, the third 'Oxford general' under whom I had served as a staff officer. General Baker had previously commanded the 1st Royal Tank Regiment and the 7th Armoured Brigade. He took a keen interest in the recruiting effort and my 'empire', and within a few weeks had visited it in its entirety. He was a workaholic and a perfectionist, but I sometimes felt that too much of his effort was based on self-promotion. He became very interested in the Sheffield Services Display.

In late June I was required to be in London as a member of an afternoon selection board for the Army Careers Officer post at Newcastle which had become vacant. I wrote to the appropriate adjutant general's office (AG11), advising that I would be in London that day and requested a career interview in the morning, with a view to my two-year tour as CRLS NEDIST being extended. I was reminded at the interview that I had a string of recommendations for promotion to colonel and was told that they had been strongly supported by second and third reporting officers at one-star and two-star level. I was flattered to learn that I was held in such high esteem, but I made it clear that it was my wish to continue in my current employment for as long as possible, and subsequently in lesser appointments if they would enable me to continue and end my military service in Yorkshire. My position was received with understanding.

The next three weeks were hectic, and also rather expensive in terms of millinery purchases for Ruth. The Sheffield Services Display (10–14 July) was a great success and General Baker approved of its quality and enjoyed taking the salute on the final day in the presence of so many civic dignitaries. He was also very pleased with the generous press publicity and photographs, attributable to a contact that I had made with a journalist during a Lyke Wake Walk. Ruth wore a new hat for the occasion, but she needed another for the 38th Signal Regiment (Volunteers) Dinner and Ball on 19 July in the presence of the Colonel in Chief of the Royal Corps of Signals, Her Royal Highness The Princess Anne, held in the Cutler's Hall. Another hat was needed five days later when we had the privilege of attending the Garden Party of Her Majesty The Queen at Buckingham Palace.

That same summer, the 1980 Olympic Games were being held in Moscow, the first to be held in a Communist country, and the only Olympic Games in which the US have not won a medal. This was because of a US-led boycott in protest against the Soviet invasion of Afghanistan which eventually resulted in 62 of 143 countries not attending. We delayed the start of our caravanning holiday so that we could watch the athletics and swimming finals on television and were thrilled with the gold-medal wins of four of our greatest athletes of all time – Daley Thompson (decathlon), Allan Wells (100m), Sebastian Coe (1,500m) and Steve Ovett (800m). A swimmer (Duncan Goodhew) added a fifth gold medal by winning the 100m breaststroke. It might seem a shallow victory winning the 100m track event without US opposition, but Allan Wells accepted a US invitation to run against the American athletes a fortnight later, and beat them.

Our caravan holiday was in Wales, at Ruth's request. She had fallen in love with the countryside and its people in her late teens when she represented E.J. Arnold & Sons at school exhibitions in the valleys. We spent five days in Llandrindod Wells, exploring the Clun and Radnor Forests, and then on to St David's, walking the brilliant coastal paths.

Mark started at Oxford on 8 October. I could not take him by car because of a military commitment, but Ruth and I visited him on Saturday 1 November, together with Crispin, for it was the half-term break at Rossall. The previous day I had learned from AG11 that my request for an extension of tour as CRLS NEDIST had been approved (to

February 1984), so morale was high as we set off to the city of dreaming spires. Ruth and I were overawed by both Christ Church, re-founded by King Henry VIII in 1546 (only 21 years before 'Taddy Grammar'), and the city of Oxford – particularly Ruth, whose interest in and study of history was increasing rapidly. Mark gave us a most interesting and thoughtful tour, for which Ruth and I were very grateful. He had a pleasant, modern room in the Blue Boar Quad, but aspired to have a 'Meadows' room in future years. He was blissfully happy.

Justin completed his probationary service on 13 November. Sadly, we had seen too little of him. We had hoped that after basic training he would have been based within reasonable distance of where we lived so that he could live with us at Broadacres, but this did not seem to be administratively convenient, and perhaps had been discouraged. Instead, he resided as a lodger in the home of a retired policeman in a strange city, working the normal shift system and leading a frugal and rather lonely life, though he never complained. He later stayed with us at Broadacres, travelling to Wakefield on a small motorcycle, but this was too long a journey. The West Yorkshire Police (probably no different to other forces) did not appear to make any differentiation between their school-leaver recruits and adult recruits and did not seem to recognise any off-duty responsibilities. In comparison, young servicemen and women would be provided with good accommodation and excellent food, amenities and recreation facilities, under the close and helpful supervision of both an officer and a petty officer/warrant officer, with their physical condition closely monitored, irrespective of where they might be serving. I feel that if police forces wish to recruit school-leavers they should accept more responsibility for looking after their young constables until they are at least out of their teens. Justin had done well during his probationary service, receiving both a High Court and a Magistrates Court commendation. The former was for the arrest of a drunk, disqualified driver following a car and foot chase, and the latter for keen observation and thorough investigation of a driver whom he stopped and found to have a forged tax disc, forged driving licence and forged insurance. Presumably, the Mayor of Morley also appreciated young PC 1222's zealous work in arresting a burglar on the roof of his town hall.

It was with much sadness that on 21 November 1980 Ruth and I attended the funeral of her uncle, Charles Hamilton MacKeith FRIBA, aged eighty-two years, a very fine gentleman and distinguished architect who gave Ruth away at our wedding. He and his wife, Elsie, had been very generous with exeat hospitality to Justin, Mark and Crispin while they were at Rossall. He was much loved by Ruth, and I always found him very good company. The following week we were back on the Fylde to watch Crispin perform in another quality Rossall Junior School production – *Toad of Toad Hall.*

Ruth erected and decorated the Christmas tree on 15 December and the family gradually converged from their different parts of the country for a very happy Christmas gathering, also shared with our many friends and neighbours; interrupted only by the duty requirements of the West Yorkshire Police. Little did we realise at the time that it was to be our last Christmas at Broadacres. No sooner were the New Year celebrations over than we were celebrating Justin's birthday, but this year was different, it being his twenty-first. We celebrated with a special anniversary dinner, held two days after his birthday because of his police duties. I think Justin was pleased with his cheque, which may have contributed later to the purchase of a splendid Triumph Stag, which remains his pride and joy.

Three weeks later we received a brochure of a very attractive property in the village of Yearsley in the Howardian Hills, some three miles south of Ampleforth College. Bay Tree Cottage was a four– bedroom eighteenth-century (I think) detached property with a very pleasant garden and two acres of land, with the possibility of more land if needed. We visited it on 3 February and were sufficiently interested to make further enquiries about additional land. We also looked at several other properties and I discussed our plans with both my bank manager and the Halifax Building Society (where I had three accounts, spanning many years) to ascertain how they might be able to help. I also asked our estate agent to prepare a sales brochure for Broadacres. I wanted us to be more financially nimble and able to convince owners of desirable properties that we were virtually cash buyers. When it became clear that we would not be able to purchase additional land adjacent to Bay Tree Cottage our discussions regarding that property terminated. However, we were now ready in both mind and financial flexibility to move quite swiftly when the right property came on the market.

I was continuing to enjoy my recruiting and liaison work, and the associated social life. The spring and early summer months were particularly lively with a multitude of events – regimental KAPE tours with their Freedom of the City marches, Beating of Retreat ceremonies and associated cocktail parties, the officers' mess summer ball and dinner nights, and visits to numerous displays, exhibitions, shows and conventions in which we were involved. My regular training runs were keeping me in good shape and I wondered if I might be able to reach half-marathon and even marathon standard. I had been inspired by watching on television the first London Marathon on 29 March, organised and inspired by former Olympic champion Chris Brasher. It was a challenge, particularly at the age of forty-seven and a half, and I gradually increased the length of my runs.

Leeds hit the national headlines in July 1981. Justin, as a policeman, will no doubt remember it for the notorious Chapeltown riots that followed those in Liverpool, but England cricket lovers will remember it for the third Ashes Test match against Australia at Headingley, in which England achieved the greatest reversal ever seen in Test cricket. At about 3 p.m. on the fourth day, England in their second innings (following on) were 135 for 7, still 92 runs in arrears. The bookmakers were offering 500–1 against an England win. Hotel bookings for that final night were being cancelled as it was anticipated that the match would be over within the hour. Botham, with bowler Dilley as his partner, lashed out in carefree manner, and they scored 117 runs between them in 80 minutes. At close of play England were 351 for 9 (Botham 145 not out), with a lead of 124. England scored five more runs the following morning, with Botham 149 not out to add to his first-innings 50. Australia need only 130 runs to win and reduced that to 122 after only two balls. There was no sign of drama until the twenty-one-year-old Willis was switched to the Kirkstall Lane end where, with the benefit of the slope, he became an inspired demon, taking three wickets for no runs in eleven balls.

Australia were suddenly 58 for 4, with 72 runs still needed. Then 75 for 8. Australia hit back – 110 for 8 and then 110 for 9. The yorker with which Willis finished it all will be set apart in cricket history. England had won by 18 runs. Willis had taken 8 for 43, but the man of the match was clearly Ian Botham, and this Test match became known as 'the Botham Test'. It was only the second Test match in history in which a team following on won the match, and it caused thousands of Australians to choke on their cornflakes when they switched on their radios the following morning.

We had enjoyed our 1980 holiday at St Davids so much that we decided to go there again, but we first spent four nights at Charmouth on Dorset's Jurassic coast, staying at the very attractive Wood Farm site in the Char Valley, close to the fossil beach.

I returned from work on or about 3 September to find a very excited Ruth waiting for me on the doorstep. She thrust a large envelope into my hand. It contained a brochure from Smiths Gore (Chartered Surveyors) offering for sale by private treaty The Old Hall, Hunton, in Wensleydale, a Grade 2 listed building with 8.25 acres of land. Offers were invited in the region of £65,000. I didn't go for a run that evening, but my adrenalin was running fast as we pored over the brochure content:

> … The Old Hall lies a few hundred yards to the south-west of Hunton Village, near Captain's Bridge on the Hunton/Finghall road. The house with its service cottage, stone barn and farm buildings has something of the appearance of a grange and may well be the site of the Hall of the De Huntons who held the Manor at the Conquest. The present house is probably mostly 17th Century work with the addition of the arched entranceway and service cottage a Century later, but its south wing seems to show the traditional hall, hearth and screens of an earlier Medieval building.
>
> The grouping of the house, cottage and buildings closely around a small central court with its single arch entranceway gives the property a distinctive appearance and there are some good stone mullioned windows in the west elevation …

OLD HALL

- Ground Floor.
- Rear Entrance Hall with store cupboard. Doors leading to log house and kitchen.
- Kitchen. 13' x 15'2" concrete floor with vinyl tiles. Fireplace with back boiler. Single bowl sink, double drainer (H&C).
- Bathroom (off passage). 11'3" x 10'7". Stone flag floor. Bath, handbasin and WC.
- Dairy. 12' x 10'4". Flag floor, stone shelves and cupboard recess.
- Living Room. 18'2" x 14'10". Flag floor, tile fireplace, recess cupboard with shelves. Steps down to coal store. Door leading to:
- Front Hall. Stairs to first floor and door leading to:
- Sitting Room. 19'4" x 15'2". Fireplace.
- On the First Floor.
- Bedroom 1. 10'9" x 15'. This room is 'L' shaped.
- Bedroom 2. 20" x 12'9". Stone fireplace, hanging cupboard to wall recess.
- Bedroom 3. 11'9" x 11'7". Fireplace.
- Bedroom 4. 19' x 15'11". Fireplace with traditional grate.
- Boxroom. 12'2" x 16'5". With hot and cold water tanks.
- Outbuilding adjoining house.
- Coal Store. With external door to archway.
- Log House. Lean-to building off rear hall, with external door.
- Garden. There is a walled garden before the main house and a stone-walled paddock to the south.

OLD HALL COTTAGE

The cottage is adjacent to the granary. It is built of local stone with a stone slate roof. The cottage is at present under a closing order from the Richmondshire District Council.

- Ground Floor.
- Hall. Leading to:
- Sitting Room. 17' x 15'3". Fireplace with tiled surround.

- Kitchen. 11'3" x 10'9". Belfast sink (H&C).
- Bathroom. Bath, handbasin and WC.
- Larder. With shelves.
- On the First Floor.
- Bedroom 1. 17'1" x 15'7". Fireplace.
- Bedroom 2. 16'11" x 15'. 'L' shaped room. Cylinder cupboard with hot and cold water tank and window overlooking the stairs.

THE FARM BUILDINGS

The farm buildings are accessible through a stone archway adjoining the house and cottage.

- Granary. In loft over archway joining main house and cottage.
- Buildings off Concrete Yard. Range of traditional buildings with stone walls and slate roof. 12' x 53'6" overall. 3 byres consisting of 9 stalls with concrete floor.
- Large Stone Barn. 44' x 22' with part loft over.
- Two Garages. 19'8" x 16'2". These are lean-to buildings of concrete block walls and asbestos sheet roofs.
- Dairy. 17'8" x 10'7".
- Calf Box. 10'7" x 17'8". Lean-to building with pantile roof.
- Cattle Housing. 34' x 17'8". Brick walls with asbestos roof. Lean– to building.
- Byre. Traditional range of stone buildings comprising 9 stalls. 55' x 20' overall. This building has been re-roofed with asbestos sheets.
- Byre. 35' x 20' with stone walls, blue slate roof, comprising 5 stalls.
- Sheep Dip. Adjacent to byre.

I gulped.

'We've got to see it,' said Ruth. I opened the whisky bottle.

'I'll have one too', said Ruth – the first time she had tasted whisky in her life.

COMMANDER RECRUITING & LIAISON STAFF (CRLS) NORTH EAST DISTRICT (NEDIST)

Move to Old Hall, Hunton

During the weekend of 5/6 September 1981 Ruth and I drove up to Hunton, without an appointment, to have a look at the village and to view Old Hall from the outside. We parked about 100 yards distant and walked towards the attractive archway beneath the granary, which divided Old Hall from the cottage. Through the archway we could see a young farmer working with some sheep. When he saw us he walked through the archway and down the drive and introduced himself as Brian Lockey. I asked if he minded us looking at the property from the outside, whereupon he immediately offered to show us around, both outside and inside. He introduced us to his wife, Kathleen, who promptly put the kettle on.

We learned that the Lockey family had lived as tenants at Old Hall Farm for many years, residing in both Old Hall and the cottage. Old Hall Farm formed part of the large Constable Burton Hall Estate, owned by Mr Charles Wyvill. It was Brian and Kathleen Lockey's flock of sheep that grazed the nearby pastures, and in addition they owned land and buildings known as Wild Hill Farm at the top of the hill, some 400 yards distant. Brian Lockey also had quite a large milk round and various other agricultural activities. It was their intention, when Old Hall Farm and its land was sold, to move into a static caravan at Wild Hill Farm and then, when they had sufficient funds, to have a house built there for themselves. They told us that if they had had the funds they would have bought Old Hall Farm – it had been their very happy family home for many years and they loved it. Had they been able to afford it, their first action would have been to renovate the cottage and then let it. They assured us that although a very large amount of restoration work was needed, the structure of Old Hall, the cottage and the farm buildings was sound, apart from the cottage roof. Ruth noted with some relief that none of the interior had been spoilt or damaged by 'modernisation', that there was a wealth of old beams (though covered by plaster), and that the bedrooms had their original seventeenth– century fireplaces. She was intrigued by what might be behind the relatively modern 'boxed-in' open fireplace in the sitting room. We went outside into what the brochure described as a 'stone-walled paddock to the south', which no doubt had once been a delightful garden (centuries ago), to find that it was occupied by three tups (rams) that were resting, their job done for that year. They were contentedly chewing their cud beneath a magnificent copper beech tree which overlooked the lane that led to Wild Hill Farm, then continuing across the A684, and on to Finghall. We walked the fields, noting with pleasure the attractive beck and its abundance of life (including trout), some fine deciduous trees, including a majestic old oak in the centre of the pasture, and a line of splendid mature elms on the western boundary which we were told provided a very useful windbreak. The exterior stone walls were very attractive, but there were several fragile areas needing attention. Ivy covered the greater part of the front wall of Old Hall, giving it a rather forbidding appearance, but otherwise it was a most attractive building of great character. We thanked Brian and Kathleen Lockey for their time and then quickly toured the unspoilt, attractive village of Hunton, with its two working farms and small traditional village school, and then the moors, only three miles away. Here, we got out of the car to stretch our legs and watch the sun sinking over Wensleydale before returning to Broadacres.

Ruth and I talked long into the night. We were both inspired by what we had seen, recognising that Old Hall could be transformed into a stunningly attractive and comfortable home, the likes of which only rarely came on the market, while the land and outbuildings provided an opportunity for enterprise in one of Yorkshire's most beautiful dales – Wensleydale. I don't think we appreciated it at the time, but we were on the verge not only of purchasing an important historic home, but also of becoming part of a wonderful rural community. Somewhere, high on the extensive moors, may have been the lead mines in which my grandfather's family had toiled before moving to Haworth. Wensleydale beckoned Arthursdale Boy and Nidderdale Girl.

We paid a second visit a few days later, incorporating a tour of Lower Wensleydale and Swaledale and the moors between. We estimated that it would take about five years of very hard work before Old Hall was transformed to the dream home that we envisaged. We recognised that it was a high-risk venture, particularly because I could not be assured of spending the remainder of my service in Yorkshire and our good health might not continue. However, we had lived a high-risk life so far and we decided that, provided the survey was positive with regards to the structure of Old Hall, the cottage (roof excepted) and the barn, and the necessary funds became available, we would try to purchase Old Hall Farm.

On 18 September I made the following conditional offer to Mr Charles Wyvill's agent:

Dear Sirs,

I am writing to confirm my telephoned offer of £62,500 (subject to contract) for the Old Hall, Hunton. The offer is made subject to the vendor agreeing to:

a. Not consider any other offers for a period of 5 weeks from the date that the draft contract is issued to me, and that a notice is placed on the Sale Board outside the property stating that it is 'sold, subject to contract', and

b. A delayed completion facility of up to 3 months from the date of exchange of contracts, to allow time for me to find a buyer for my own house.

My house is located in a particularly popular area and has been ready to be placed on the market for some time (agent briefed and brochure printed) whilst I identified the property that I wished to buy. I would therefore be placing my house on the market for the specific purpose of purchasing the Old Hall and for this reason the above assurance and agreement are important to me.

It would be my wish to exchange contracts even if I did not have a buyer for my own house at the end of 5 weeks for I feel confident that I could obtain a bridging facility if necessary. I already have agreement in principle for the requisite mortgage loan.

I look forward to hearing from you …

Six days later Broadacres was placed on the market and we held our breath. There was no immediate acceptance. I took Mark to Oxford on 5 October for the start of his second year. He was delighted to find that he had a Meadows room, albeit on the ground floor. My recruiting and liaison work continued at a brisk pace and so did my half-marathon training, with routine runs of 6 miles in 49 minutes and a 9-mile run in 1 hour 20 minutes on Sunday 1 November. However, that was to be the end of my half-marathon aspirations, for the tempo of purchasing the Old Hall increased significantly the following week, leaving no time for more than the occasional short 'keep-fit' run.

On 2 November I was told by Mr Charles Wyvill's agent that he was prepared to agree to the terms described in my letter, but only at a sale price of £65,000. I tried to get a £500 reduction without success and discussed the situation with Ruth. We agreed to £65,000. Two days later Ruth and I accepted an offer of £58,000 for Broadacres and I wrote to my bank manager as follows:

Dear Mr Atkinson,

HOME MORTGAGE APPLICATION

I am enclosing an application for a mortgage loan of £27,000 to enable me to purchase Old Hall Farmhouse, Hunton, North Yorkshire. My offer for this property has been accepted by the vendor and no other offer will be considered provided that the contracts can be exchanged by 23rd November. I would accordingly be grateful if you would agree in the first instance to providing an advance of £6,500 to cover the 10% deposit which I will need to pay on the exchange of contracts, and subsequently the balance of £20,500 on completion, making a total mortgage loan of £27,000.

I have sold my own house at the above address (subject to contract), and it is my intention to arrange simultaneous exchanges of contracts, so that no bridging loan is necessary. As the purchaser of my house is a 'cash buyer' there should be no problem in this respect.

You will note that I have three Life Insurance Policies to support the desired Endowment Mortgage. They provide a total sum assured of £25,013, which is almost £2,000 short of the £27,000 mortgage loan which I seek. Is it possible for this small difference to be covered by a repayment mortgage arrangement? I would prefer this, but if it is not acceptable I will ask my Insurance Brokers to arrange a new 'low cost' endowment policy with a guaranteed death benefit of £2,000 to cover the difference.

I would be most grateful if this request could be dealt with most expeditiously to enable contracts to be exchanged by 23rd November and completion in late November or very early December (I have in mind 4th December, but I need to discuss this with the purchaser of my house)… .

It was a nerve-racking time for both me and Ruth. It was a huge challenge and we appreciated that there would be many problems ahead, most of which would have to be resolved by our own labour, thrift and ingenuity, together with love and patience.

Lloyds Bank had only recently entered the home mortgage market and its business module was focused on providing mortgages for modern, post–World War II properties, like Broadacres, not seventeenth-century dwellings. We awaited the survey with some trepidation, but we did not have to wait long. We were present during the survey, conducted by a FRICS consultant surveyor. He decided that it would serve no useful purpose to list all the obvious items requiring attention and that he would focus his assessment on structure, roofing, drainage, subsidence and value. At the end of the day he gave us a verbal summary, confirming all that Brian and Kathleen Lockey had told us. He advised us that the roof of Old Hall was sound, apart from two purlins, but would need timber treatment against wood-boring insects. Also, an extensive Chemicure damp-proofing course was needed. There was no evidence of subsidence and the drains and septic tank were satisfactory. He cautioned us that his report would have to incorporate the negative as well as the positive and that my bank manager would need some convincing that we were capable of doing all the work that was necessary. He also told us that the £65,000 price was right, possibly in our favour, and that when the property was modernised and in good repair it would form 'a most valuable unit and magnificent home'. His parting words were 'Go for it – I wish I was able to buy it.'

A few days later I received a message at work to phone my bank manager. I left work early, in order to ensure that our conversation was not overheard or interrupted, returning his call from Broadacres. He had received the surveyor's report and was clearly seeking assurance that we were an acceptable risk. I did my best to convince him, and then in final desperation, with Ruth listening, I told him that I had some experience from my successful military career and that I had a very competent wife. I was to regret those final six words – Ruth almost choked with laughter and mischievously taunted me with them for many years thereafter, particularly at dinner parties. Thankfully, my bank manager gave me the financial support that was needed.

The next problem was to find somewhere in which the family could reside for 4–5 months while some essential work was carried out on Old Hall, for it was not fit for immediate occupation. For example, it needed a complete re-wiring and all the internal walls on the ground floor needed approved Protim rendering prior to external damp– proofing. I talked to the NEDIST quartering staff and asked if they could help. They were most helpful and soon advised me that a married quarter could be provided for us close to the Army Apprentices College in Harrogate.

The week beginning 23 November was hectic. On the Monday I handed in my application for the married quarter at Harrogate and on the Tuesday exchanged contracts on Broadacres and signed the Old Hall contract. On Friday I took over the Harrogate quarter (19 Oak Avenue, Pennypot Lane) and on the Saturday I took Ruth to Rossall to watch Crispin perform the title role in the school's specially commissioned play *The Dream of Chief Crazy Horse*, written by David Pownall FRSL, a Liverpool-born playwright and author, and a graduate of Keele University. I was looking forward to it immensely, not only because of Crispin's leading role, but because so much of my boyhood had been taken up in re-enacting the Cowboy-and-Red Indian scenes that we saw on the Hollywood films of the time, involving making our own quite effective bows and arrows. I was a great fan of the Red Indians. Chief Crazy Horse of the Oglala Sioux was a poet, a mystic, a dreamer and a fighter for the independence of his people. His photograph was never taken, and after his murder by white soldiers in a military prison he was buried in an unmarked grave. No one knows how he looked. David Pownall's play was an attempt to imagine what Chief Crazy Horse felt like, and my son was to be the first to perform the role. He was brilliant. Including the interval, it was a two-and-a-half-hour performance and Crispin was faultless. I will always remember his concluding mourning-song recital as he rode triumphantly on the back of the crawling General Crook:

CRAZY HORSE: Where are the Tainos now?
CHIEFS: Where are the People?
CRAZY HORSE: Where are the Arawaks?
CHIEFS: Where are the People?
CRAZY HORSE: Where are the Aztecs?
CHIEFS: Where are the People?
CRAZY HORSE: Where are the Incas?

As the CHIEFS go down the aisle they involve the audience in the mourning song 'Where are the People?' At the same time the pianist mounts the upper level, finds the white-wash and brush and paints in the remaining portions of the Americas.

CHIEFS: Where are the People?

The refrain is repeated after each tribe.

CRAZY HORSE: Where are the Tainos?
        Where are the Arawaks?
        Where are the Aztecs?
        Where are the Incas?
        Where are the Wampanoags?
        Where are the Pequots?
        Where are the Narragansets?
        Where are the Ottawas?
        Where are the Shawnees?
        Where are the Miamis?
        Where are the Foxes?
        Where are the Chitimichas?
        Where are the Taenzas?
        Where are the Natchez?
        Where are the Karoks?
        Where are the Yazoos?
        Where are the Choctaws?
        Where are the Chickasaws?
        Where are the Bilox?
        Where are the Seminoles?
        Where are the Apalachees?
        Where are the Modocs?
        Where are the Apaches?
        Where are the Mohaves?
        Where are the Paiutes?
        Where are the Shastas?
        Where are the Yuma?
        Where are the Navahoes?
        Where are the Utes?
        Where are the Osages?
        Where are the Pawnees?

Where are the Poncas?
Where are the Santees?
Where are the Cheyennes?
Where are the Teton Sioux?
Where are the Arapahoes?
Where are the Kiowas?
Where are the Comanches?
Where are the Nez Perces?
Where are the Brules?
Where are the Minneconjous?
Where are the Oglala Sioux?
Where are the People?

As the last CHIEF exits, the pianist paints in the last portion of the map. He then exits. By this time the lights have dimmed and only the moon is illuminated. It darkens, goes out.
   The End.

David Pownall (born 19th May 1938) retired as an internationally-renowned playwright for stage, television and radio, with over 60 plays broadcast and 10 novels published. His best known work was probably *'Master Class'* (Faber and Faber 1983); a portrayal of composers Shostakovich and Prokofiev in the grip of Stalin's savage cultural dictatorship.

We moved out of Broadacres and into our temporary Army home near Harrogate on 3 December 1981. The following day was completion day on both the Broadacres sale and the Old Hall purchase. Ruth and I felt very sad as we left Broadacres but we never regretted our decision.

We quickly settled into our temporary new home. It was ideal for our purposes and it did not take Ruth long to make it very comfortable. The weather was quite mild for the time of year, but that was soon to change, for between 8 December and the end of January 1982 the United Kingdom experienced some of the coldest, snowiest and most severe winter weather ever recorded. It was the coldest since 1890 and the snowiest since 1878. It was very cold when Ruth attended the end– of– term evening carol service at Rossall on 10 December and collected Crispin, but as they crossed the Pennines the snow began to fall and they were very relieved to reach our Harrogate home safely (no mobile phones at that time). Two nights later there were several UK readings of −20°C, with −25.2°C recorded at Shawbury in Shropshire. However, although it was bitterly cold, the snow was not particularly deep and we were able to obtain speedy approval from Richmondshire District Council for the ground-floor bathroom to become a breakfast room, bedroom 3 to become the bathroom and the boxroom to become the fourth bedroom. We were also able to meet on site and obtain contractor quotations for damp proofing, timber treatment, re-wiring, central heating and bathroom installation. There was no water supply, for it was turned off at an outside, below-ground meter point some 150 yards distant, and it had become flooded and then frozen. 'No problem,' said the Water Authority, 'we'll replace it with a new meter at the end of your drive, just as soon as the ground thaws' – and they did. On one brief visit a very hungry cat walked out of the barn and rubbed itself against our legs. We had nothing to give it apart from the half carton of milk that Ruth had brought for a cup of tea – but the milk froze before the cat had completed its lapping. Everyone was being so helpful – characteristic of the country folk of Wensleydale. We also received a very pleasant letter from Mr Charles Wyvill, inviting Ruth and me to call on him when we moved in.

The Old Hall dining room had a very old flagged floor, but several flags were broken and the floor was uneven and damp. After taking professional advice we decided to replace the flag floor with concrete, laid within 1000-gauge polythene, and contracted a builder to carry out the work. To reduce the cost it was arranged that he would do the work on a Saturday morning in his own time, with myself as labourer, doing the shovelling and barrowing. Weather conditions caused a postponement, but then on Saturday 16 January, Readymix delivered 3 cubic metres of 421 mix at the archway, the flags already removed and the polythene in position. There is no time to spare in this type of work and I was relieved when it was completed.

Ruth and I were delighted – the renovation of Old Hall was under way. She took an axe and hacked into the base of the ivy, found it harder than she had anticipated and left me to finish it off. Next was a masonry contractor from Ripon to repair a damaged area near the archway, followed by re-wiring completion and electricity connection, Protim damp proofing and Rentokil wood preservation (both with 30-year guarantees), and the re-plastering of the kitchen. Ruth insisted on doing the tiled floor herself, as well as installing the kitchen units and decorating, and she did it to a very good standard. I contributed by scraping the oak beams and cleaning and later grouting her wall tiling.

It was now late February, the harsh winter was behind us and the curlews were diving and soaring in flirtatious manner above our fields, their evocative and high-pitched 'cur-lee' cries penetrating the crisp and chilly air descending from Wensleydale's snow-capped moors. I loved watching and listening to them – 'I take my gladness in the cry of the gannet and the sound of the curlew instead of the laughter of men' (from 'The Seafarer'). Sadly, the UK breeding numbers of the curlew have declined by 62% since 1969 and this iconic wading bird is now 'red– listed'. Bolton Castle hosts an annual Curlew Festival in June, enabling visitors to see first-hand one of the remaining strongholds of curlews in the country and learn about conservation work.

We were encouraged by our progress, but we recognised that much had still to be done before we could leave Harrogate. I would use a military car for my work whenever possible, enabling Ruth to use our Lancia to travel to Old Hall, where she would brief and supervise contractors and do whatever she could. Weather permitting, some of her time would always be spent in shaping the garden. Sometimes, when I had military duties in my northern area I would drop Ruth off at Old Hall and collect her on my return. On one such day in early March I returned to Old Hall and gave my customary 'Hello' call as I entered, but there was no reply. I was rather concerned and went into the sitting room, to see Ruth standing there looking worse than a chimney sweep – she had removed the Victorian fireplace and opened-up the massive original seventeenth-century fireplace that was still in place behind it. Her triumphant grin stretched from one ear of her blackened face to the other. That picture will remain forever in my memory.

Old Hall had impressive original oak beams throughout, but in the nineteenth century it became fashionable to cover them in lath and plaster. Encouraged by Ruth, and inspired by her opening of the original fireplace, I began to remove this covering from the two beams in the room, which was to become our lounge. To our delight they were in excellent condition. It was filthy but rewarding work. Having removed the laths and the plaster, I scraped the wood with a double-handled 8-inch draw knife, which sometimes came close to removing my nose; this was followed by wire-brush work, and then the application of recommended preservative and restoration treatments. We were thrilled with the result.

We could have purchased a further 10 acres of pastureland in addition to our 8.5 acres, but we felt that we did not need it, and neither could we afford it. With the benefit of hindsight we should have asked for a larger mortgage and bought that extra land and then leased it, for quality agricultural land was probably the finest investment of the time. But irrespective of whether we purchased the extra land or not, we were obliged to erect a 210-yard-long, four-rail stock-proof fence along the line of what was to be our southern boundary. Accordingly, rails, posts and a vast quantity of 3-inch nails were delivered, a heavy thumper borrowed, and I made a start, helped by Mark when his Oxford term ended in mid-March. It was while I was doing this work that I met farmers John and Frank Tunstill from Sawmill House Farm, located in the centre of the village. They had just purchased 'ten acres' and were looking over it. I called Ruth and she joined us in a good chat about what we might keep on our land and about the village in general. We took an immediate liking to John and Frank, just as we had done to Brian and Kathleen Lockey. We could not have had better farming neighbours. We soon learned that not only was their livestock farming of the highest standard, but between them and a third brother (a carpenter named Brian) there was nothing involving mechanical or electrical engineering, construction or woodwork that they could not undertake. They were highly respected in the village, as was their aged mother, who told us, 'Now if you need any help, Mr and Mrs Pedley, just let us know – we farmers, we help each other.' The advice of Frank and John was that we kept the same crossbred ewes as they did – Mules and Mashams – which they put to a Suffolk terminal sire to produce fast-growing lambs for the meat trade. They were only too willing to help us as we gained experience.

The Public Schools Entrance Examination had been held over a three-day period in mid-February. On 12 March Crispin was interviewed at Rossall for a Newall Scholarship, and shortly before the end of the month and the end of the term, we learned of his success. Ruth and I were very proud, and his scholarship award was of considerable financial help, though even with the additional benefit of the military boarding-school allowance we would still be paying more than £500 per term 'out of our own pocket.'

Shortly before Easter the Falklands War began. Argentina invaded the islands, which had been held by Britain for 150 years, without warning on 2 April. The United Nations (UN) Security Council condemned the invasion two days later, and under the positive leadership of Prime Minister Margaret Thatcher, Britain responded positively, and at speed. Within hours of the UN condemnation a British nuclear submarine (HMS *Conqueror*) was dispatched from her Faslane base in Scotland, and on 5 April the aircraft carriers HMS *Hermes* and HMS *Invincible* sailed from Portsmouth as part of a task force of more than 100 ships. The nation held its breath for three weeks – the time that it would take the task force to reach the South Atlantic and engage.

I took two days of privilege leave in addition to the Easter holiday, so that between 9 and 13 April, Ruth, myself, Mark and Crispin were able to travel on a daily basis to Old Hall. Our tempo of work was increasing for we hoped to be able to move in by the end of the month, but there was no panic, only excitement. I had hoped that I might be able to take more of my privilege-leave entitlement at this time but found it impractical for I was in the middle of a rather demanding six– month period of being PMC (President of the Mess Committee) of the officers' mess. It is a rather time consuming and irksome appointment, additional of course to normal duties. However, I couldn't grumble, for I had managed to dodge a PMC selection throughout my career. Unfortunately, Major General Ian Baker was to hand over to Major General Patrick Palmer (later to be General Sir Charles Patrick Ralph Palmer, KCVO, KBE, Commander-in-Chief, Allied Forces Northern Europe and then Constable and Governor of Windsor Castle) at the same time that Ruth and I planned to move into

Old Hall. Furthermore, Major General and Mrs Baker were moving into the mess for a while. This GOC changeover significantly increased the number of mess functions, but everyone was very understanding and helpful, and my PMC responsibilities were completed without any significant problems. I was helped enormously by Lieutenant Colonel 'Tank' Nash of the Army Catering Corps, who was responsible for the very high quality of catering throughout NEDIST.

On 25 April the Royal Marines recaptured South Georgia and Margaret Thatcher told the nation to 'rejoice' – but she knew, and the nation knew, that the main conflict had not yet begun.

COMMANDER RECRUITING & LIAISON STAFF (CRLS) NORTH EAST DISTRICT (NEDIST)

Early Days at Old Hall - The Battle for the Falklands

We moved into Old Hall just before the May Bank Holiday, on 29 April 1982. There were no significant problems and no regrets. We aimed at authentic and sympathetic restoration without denying ourselves sensible modern amenities and comforts, and we were prepared for the long haul and for the hard work that would be involved. Brian and Kathleen Lockey had assured us that it was a happy dwelling, and that is how we found it. Our morale was sky high and we took great delight in pleasing each other with our efforts. The day after we moved in we received a letter from the North Yorkshire County Council informing us that under the provisions of the Local Authorities (Historic Buildings) Act 1962 we had been granted £647 towards our renovation and restoration costs. It could not have been more timely.

Three days later, on 2 May, HMS *Conqueror* stalked, torpedoed and sank the Argentinean cruiser *General Belgrano* with the loss of 320 lives. The *Belgrano* was a threat to the approaching British task force and it was a correct, though difficult, Downing Street decision to fire. There was strong protest from a naive nucleus of British anti-war campaigners, but their howls subsided somewhat when the following day the British destroyer HMS *Sheffield* was hit and sunk by an Argentinean Exocet missile. The battle was now truly under way and the outcome could not be predicted. [An enquiry was held afterwards into the circumstances of the loss of HMS *Sheffield*, but the Ministry of Defence did not publish the details until 2006, whilst the findings were censored. It was not until October 2017 that the litany of errors that resulted in the loss of HMS *Sheffield* and 20 sailors were released: at the time of the attack, the anti-air warfare officer had left the operations room for a coffee, while his assistant was having a toilet break; when the approaching warplanes were spotted by HMS *Glasgow*, the principal warfare officer in the *Sheffield's* operations room failed to react, 'partly through inexperience, but more importantly from inadequacy'; the Captain was never called; when the missiles came into view, the officers on the bridge were mesmerised by the sight and did not broadcast a warning to the ship's company …]

We decided not to expend any time or finance on the renovation of the cottage, apart from giving it a new roof as soon as we could afford it, utilising as many of the existing Yorkshire stone slates as possible. It would have been a distraction from our work on Old Hall and we had no desire to have neighbouring holiday-makers or tenants. Another early decision was to sell a 10-yard strip of land adjacent to the elm trees to John and Frank for £1,250, to enable their sheep to reach the beck – much better than a pipe extension to a drinking trough. We also decided to apply some Nitram fertiliser and take a hay crop from the entirety of our grassland. 'You can't have too much hay and you've got plenty of room in your barn', advised Mrs Tunstill (senior); 'It's like money in the bank, Mister Pedley.'

I am now going to transgress into a continued description of the Falklands War, for it involved the biggest air/sea conflict since World War II, incorporating amphibious and land conflicts that were no less remarkable; and which resulted in the deaths of 1,000 men within two months. It was a battle in which the outcome could not be predicted and which required similar British political and military resolve, character and bravery to that of the 1940s. The pomp and ceremony at the departure of the British task force from Portsmouth and other ports and on its return was high theatre, yet the drama that was to unfold emanated from a bizarre 'Act 1, Scene 1' scenario of some scrap merchants being sighted on one of the most barren, distant and dead-end outposts of Britain's former colonial empire. It was a battle that gripped the British people, not least Ruth and I at Old Hall.

On 21 May, British landings began at San Carlos and a beachhead was established by some 3,000 troops, but at a cost. The frigate HMS *Ardent* was sunk by enemy aircraft with the loss of 22 lives, and two other ships were hit by bombs that did not explode, but two more lives were lost. A tremendous battle for air supremacy raged over the Falkland Islands and beyond, involving later types of the Harrier aircraft to that with which I had been familiar whilst serving at RAF Wildenrath; launched from our two carriers. Fifteen Argentinean aircraft were shot down that day and seventeen more over the next 3–4 days, but with the loss of another frigate (HMS *Antelope*) and a destroyer (HMS *Coventry*) and many more lives. Significantly, the Merchant Navy container ship (*Atlantic Conveyor*) was hit by an Exocet missile on 25 May with the loss of 12 crew and vital supplies, including the three much-needed Chinook transport helicopters that it was carrying. Our eyes were glued to the television news each evening and I well remember sitting with Ruth and listening to BBC journalist Brian Hanrahan on HMS *Hermes* circumvent reporting restrictions with his famous description of a Harrier attack on Argentinean positions near Port Stanley – 'I am not allowed to say how many planes joined the raid, but I counted them all out and I counted them all back. Their pilots were unhurt, cheerful and jubilant, giving thumbs-up signs.'

I remember the next few days very well. On 26 May the 2nd Battalion of the Parachute Regiment (2 PARA) advanced south from the bridgehead, tasked with seizing the heavily defended Argentinean positions near Goose Green and Darwin. To the dismay and intense anger of the military, both in the Falklands and at home, the thrust was reported on the BBC World Service. In particular, it was heard by the CO of 2 PARA, Lieutenant Colonel 'H' Jones, as he planned his attack! In my capacity as PMC I attended a GOC's luncheon the following day, followed by cocktails at Major General Palmer's residence with Ruth in the evening. I suspect that everyone present recognised that the Falklands War would be won or lost in the next few days, that the result was in the balance, and that there would be heavy casualties. Most of those attending these social functions had friends who were now fighting for their lives. Not surprisingly, conversation at both functions focused on the battle. The atmosphere was sombre. The BBC was bitterly criticised for its naivety, but I do not recollect anyone ever being held to account. The Argentinean numbers at Goose Green and Darwin were higher than expected (790 Army + 212 Air Force/ Navy) and they were, of course, in well-prepared defensive positions. The 2 PARA strength was 690. Following an intense 14-hour battle the Argentinean force surrendered on 29 May. 2 PARA lost 17 soldiers, with 64 wounded, while the enemy lost 47, with 120 wounded and 1,000 surrendered. The British casualties included Lieutenant Colonel H Jones, who was killed while leading an assault on a forward enemy position when the 2 PARA attack was losing impetus. He was awarded a posthumous Victoria Cross and became a national hero.

On that day Ruth and I were at the Rossall School Prize Day and proudly listened to the confirmation of Crispin's Newall Scholarship. He accompanied us home for the associated Prize Day Weekend cum Spring Bank Holiday. I think he was pleasantly surprised at the progress that we were making at Old Hall. Ruth and I decided that we needed a break, so we downed tools and visited Mark at Oxford. He told us that he was doing well, and he was clearly enjoying himself immensely. We had a most pleasant break.

The Falklands War would only be won when British infantry and Royal Marines forced the surrender of the Argentinean commander at his headquarters in Port Stanley; the capital and only town on the islands. The effort of the task force was accordingly focused on supporting these elite troops not only by preventing enemy air and sea interference, but also by providing close air and naval support to help them close with and defeat the enemy in hand-to-hand combat, bayonets fixed. The vast majority of the British people were shocked by the ferocity and brutality of this close combat action, praying for success, but never wavering in their support. I was more aware of the public mood than most because they called at our recruiting offices on their way to work, expressing personal emotion and advice. Many of them had fought for their country and with that experience were tendering firm advice that we must not take any prisoners; "it slows the rate of advance." Port Stanley was protected by extensive and formidable enemy defensive positions on a cluster of dominant peaks overlooking the town. These peaks – *Mount Longdon, Mount Harriet, Two Sisters, Tumbledown* and *Wireless Ridge* – had protective rocks and extensive views, in front of which were minefields. A multitude of machine-gun posts with interlocking arcs of fire covered the approaches that the British infantry and Royal Marines would have to take. This awesome task was exacerbated by freezing temperatures, rain and strong winds that combined to produce a penetrating dampness and brutal chill. It would be necessary to close with the enemy in silence and engage with grenades and hand-to-hand fighting under cover of darkness – a very difficult skill, particularly when carrying on the back very heavy loads of essential equipment, ammunition, grenades and radio.

The British advance from the bridgehead towards Port Stanley, some 56 miles distant, began in earnest on 31 May. It was preceded by the occupation [by D Squadron of 22 SAS] of the dominant but virtually undefended Mount Kent feature (only 12 miles from Port Stanley) between 25 and 27 May. This happened just in time to repel the enemy's elite 602 Commando Company, which was being deployed to reinforce and secure the feature. Two days of fierce fighting patrol actions between these elite special forces ended on 31 May with the enemy defeated and the arrival of some 600 Royal Marines of 42 Commando. Any jubilation at this success was quelled a week later when two Landing Ship Logistics (LSLs) of the Royal Fleet Auxiliary (*Sir Galahad* and *Sir Tristram*) were hit by 500lb bombs from enemy aircraft as they prepared to disembark soldiers of the Welsh Guards and offload stores in Port Pleasant, off Fitzroy. These hits resulted in 50 dead and 57 wounded. BBC cameras were on site, recording the heroic rescue efforts, with graphic images of the severely burnt casualties.

The conclusive battles to secure the peaks overlooking Port Stanley, upon which victory depended, began on 11 June with night assaults on *Mount Longdon, Mount Harriet* and the *twin peaks of Two Sisters*. The assault by 3 PARA at *Mount Longdon* was to be particularly closely contested and crucial. The silent approach to the very edge of the forward enemy trenches under cover of darkness achieved the desired surprise, but thereafter this close combat battle edged to and fro for about 12 hours before the Paras had secured their objective, well supported by the 105mm light guns of 29 Commando Regiment and the 4.5-inch gun of HMS *Avenger*. British casualties consisted of 23 killed and 47 wounded, while enemy casualties comprised 31 killed, 120 wounded and 50 captured. Sargeant Ian McKay of 3 PARA was awarded a posthumous VC.

The assault on *Mount Harriet* by 42 Commando was preceded by a noisy diversionary attack and an even noisier naval bombardment from HMS *Yarmouth*. There was brave and stubborn resistance from enemy machine gun posts, which were only taken out by some heroic close–quarter actions and the use of MILAN anti-tank missiles. However, this was a particularly well-planned and well-executed assault which resulted in enemy casualties of 18 killed, 50 wounded and 300 captured. British casualties comprised 2 killed and 26 wounded.

The task of defeating the enemy forces occupying *Two Sisters* and their connecting saddle was given to the 600 Royal Marines of 45 Commando Regiment. The leading Company (X Ray Company) made contact at 11.30 p.m. but was pinned down on the mountain slope for several hours by heavy machine gun and mortar fire. A quick appraisal of the situation brought Yankee and Zulu Companies into action on the northern peak and the combined assault, supported by very heavy artillery and naval gunfire from the two 4.5-inch guns of HMS *Glamorgan*, soon overcame the enemy resistance. Enemy casualties consisted of 20 killed, 50 wounded and 54 captured. British casualties comprised 8 killed and 17 wounded.

On the following night (13/14 June) there were similar actions to secure the three remaining peaks shielding Port Stanley; *Mount Tumbledown* was defended by 500 enemy marines, while *Wireless Ridge* and *Mount William* were each defended by 500 enemy infantry soldiers. The battle for *Mount Tumbledown* involved the 2nd Battalion Scots Guards (2SG) and the 1st Battalion 7th Duke of Edinburgh's Own Gurkha Rifles (1/7GR) and a troop of the Blues and Royals (4 light tanks). The attack began at 8.30 p.m. with a diversionary action, followed by the main assault at 9 p.m., with intensive artillery support plus naval bombardment from HMS *Yarmouth* and HMS *Active*. However, the enemy were well entrenched in bunker-type constructions in the rocky terrain and it required several bayonet charges and much hand-to-hand fighting before their resistance crumbled. A lance corporal of the Scots Guards described his experience as follows:

> *... we ran forward in extended line, machine-gunners and riflemen firing from the hip to keep the enemy heads down, enabling us to cover the open ground in the shortest possible time. Halfway across the open ground 2 Platoon went to ground to give covering support, enabling us to gain a foothold on the enemy position. From then on we fought from crag to crag, rock to rock, taking out pockets of enemy and lone riflemen, all of whom resisted fiercely.*

Enemy casualties consisted of 30 killed, more than 100 wounded and 30 captured. British casualties consisted of 10 killed and 53 wounded.

The task of seizing *Wireless Ridge* was given to 2 PARA and a troop of the Blues and Royals (with four light tanks). The battle began during the afternoon of 13 June with several hours of intense artillery support plus naval support from HMS *Ambuscade*, together with direct fire from the light tanks, though they were soon to incur heavy losses (5 killed and 50 wounded). The 2 PARA assault began shortly before dusk against some stubborn resistance, but the enemy (7th Infantry Regiment) had already suffered heavy daytime casualties from the artillery airburst shells and resistance gradually waned. Enemy casualties consisted of 25 killed, 125 wounded and 37 captured. British casualties comprised 3 killed and 11 wounded.

There was no battle for *Mount William*. The Gurkhas were ordered to seize this prominent feature as soon as *Mount Tumbledown* was secured. They lost eight soldiers to artillery fire during the approach, but on reaching their objective they found that the 500-strong Argentine infantry battalion, on learning that they were coming up the hill, had already fled. Such is the Gurkha reputation!

These overwhelming successes resulted in hundreds of beaten and demoralised enemy troops retreating into Port Stanley, paying no heed to the appeal of their President and Commander-in-Chief (General Leopoldo Galtieri) to re-group and fight on. By noon on 14 June British troops had reached the outskirts of Port Stanley. At 2 p.m. it was all over as 9,800 Argentinean troops surrendered and British troops marched into the capital. Three days later Galtieri resigned.

The Falklands War, probably the last of our colonial wars, had been won at a cost of 255 British lives and approximately 300 wounded. In addition, we lost two destroyers, two frigates, a container ship, an LSL, twenty-four helicopters and ten Harriers. One should not ask whether it was worthwhile, but whether it was right, and before answering the question one should reflect on the fact that the Argentinean aggression was denounced by both the United Nations and the inhabitants of those bleak islands, and then read the views of eminent historians. Both Ruth and I believed that it was right, and so did the vast-majority of the British people, who gave the task force a tremendous welcome on its return. However, I had anticipated that our 'special relationship' with the USA would have prompted early political support from the Reagan administration. On the contrary, that administration adopted an early pro–South American stance. Thankfully, the US Defence Secretary, Caspar Weinberger, took a solid stand in Britain's favour in the face of every kind of local opposition. He challenged the pro-Argentina stance, talking the President and the Pentagon into giving some support to the British action – in particular, allowing us to use the Ascension Islands as a forward base and providing recently enhanced American AIM-9L Sidewinder air-to-air missiles, for which our Harrier pilots were extremely grateful. He also gave personal instructions to his military subordinates that 'Britain be given every possible assistance in terms of hardware and intelligence'.

I feel that it would have been disrespectful of me as a soldier not to have halted my recollections of our early days at Old Hall to incorporate this account of the Falklands War, particularly as Ruth and I listened to or viewed virtually every news bulletin to which we had access, despite our heavy workload. Our thoughts were truly with those servicemen and their families. On the evening of the surrender, the southern hemisphere winter arrived in the Falkland Islands, described by Admiral Sandy Woodward, the victorious Battle Group Commander on HMS *Hermes*, as 'a blizzard gusting to 100mph'. Victory was achieved by the narrowest of margins, in terms of both the conflict and the arrival of such savage wintry conditions.

However, at Old Hall it was glorious summer weather. Our restoration work was progressing steadily and we had our first livestock – eight point of lay hens (Rhode Island Red, Light Sussex and Marans, plus a very fine Marans cockerel) which soon gave us a steady stream of eggs both for our own consumption and for sale to neighbours. When I got home from my military work I could not wait to get into my old clothes, working on a wide variety of projects, but with particular enthusiasm for the 'Cheese Room', the first-floor 12'2" x 16'5" room described in the sales brochure as 'Boxroom, with hot and cold water tanks'. This room was in the oldest part of Old Hall, later dated by eminent architectural and local historian Jane Hatcher BA MPhil as circa 1590. The words 'Cheese Room' had been inscribed on the lintel above its south-facing two-light chamfered mullion window (to avoid the window tax) which had probably originally been a doorway, with outside steps. The water tanks were in a corner, resting on some original sixteenth-century oak floorboards, but the remaining original floorboards had been badly damaged over the years by unsympathetic plumbers and electricians. I needed to remove them as best I could and lay new wooden flooring over very uneven oak beams to link up with the oak boards in the corner, having first scraped and treated the beams and boards. When that had been done the plan was for a well-worn oak timber (17'6" x 10' x 10') to be manually lifted through the window as a new ceiling beam for structural reinforcement. While waiting for this stage to be reached, I planned to gently chip away the layers of white paint that covered the attractive stone of the deep niche and the ashlar chamfered windows, whilst also making new window frames and ledges. The room would then be re-plastered, whereupon I would fit new skirting boards, following which a carpenter would be employed to make fitted wardrobes and an airing cupboard to link with the water tanks. Finally, Ruth would do the decorating and it would become our preferred bedroom, nice and snug above the boiler in the kitchen. We recognised that this project, together with our plans to create a study from the coal store, a workshop from the second (exterior) dairy and a garden room from the log store, plus numerous improvement plans for outbuildings, would take many months and much patience. We had never been closer or more happy. Ruth inspired me enormously.

Despite the workload, I made time to have at least two runs each week of about 30–35 minutes duration, thereby maintaining a reasonable level of fitness. The runs would usually be at York during my lunch break, and to and from Old Hall via Constable Burton at the weekend. However, I no longer had any aspiration to run a marathon – the training time that would have been required could not be spared.

It was not all plain sailing, and I particularly remember the problem of a blocked drain leading to the septic tank. The fifteen rods that I had connected to dislodge the blockage became stuck. I could get no movement in either direction, nor any twist (clockwise, of course). After about an hour I called Ruth, and with myself down the inspection pit and Ruth above, we pulled and pushed hard together. We had a rest, Ruth made a coffee and we tried again. It began to rain. We were tired, wet, dirty and rather smelly. Two hours had passed. 'One last time,' said Ruth, so we pulled and pushed again and again and again and … the rods suddenly shot backwards (together with Ruth). Carefully [whilst twisting to the right], we pushed the rods forwards again and at last they responded! Half an hour later the obstruction was clear and the rods cleaned. I was made to strip naked outside in the rain (not a pretty sight) before being hosed-down and allowed entry into Old Hall. We promptly decided that an additional, intermediary inspection pit had to be constructed as a matter of some urgency, but there were other things on the urgent list, and it had to wait its turn.

We could not afford the time or expense of going away for a summer holiday, but I used three weeks of my leave entitlement during July for work on Old Hall and the farm. During this period we took a good hay crop that filled the barn, with sufficient left over for some useful sales. Ten goslings were purchased (£28) for the Christmas trade, together with some rather special Marans hens from a breeder at Silsden whose grandfather had imported fertile eggs from a top breeder in France, their country of origin, in the 1930s [contrary to regulations]. They were alleged to be quicker growing than the British Marans and their eggs were much darker. It was not long before I purchased a very cheap polystyrene incubator and began hatching fertile Marans eggs. None of the hatchings was a disaster and my success rate gradually improved to about 85%. I found that there was a good demand for young Marans hens for breeding purposes, and Ruth was never short of a quality free-range chicken for our supper. Her garden was also beginning to provide delicious vegetables and soft fruit. I had suggested to her that I might be responsible for the vegetable garden, but I received a funny look in response that clearly indicated that she was not in favour. I soon recognised and accepted that I was only welcome in the garden to admire it and when called to lift, empty or move something. I was not concerned – I had plenty to do elsewhere; dividing our eight acres into four smaller fields and a collecting ring to facilitate easier handling of a flock of sheep that was planned for late September. Also, I needed to remove the remnants of the now-shrivelled ivy from the front wall, roof and gutters and brush and re-point. In this respect I was careful to meet the mortar mix requirement of one part cement to two parts lime and nine parts sand (minimum 50% sharp sand), brushing when almost surface dry.

All the interior doors, together with the splat-baluster staircase and beam, had been painted white, much to our irritation. We located a firm in Aberford that undertook such paint removal and I took a door to them to see the quality of their work. We were well pleased, and eventually most of the interior doors were taken to Aberford for their attention. Ruth set about removing the paint from the staircase and beam, using a variety of paint removers and a heat gun, with occasional assistance from myself. It was very time-consuming work, but neither of us was lacking in patience and the end-result was very rewarding. We were well pleased with our overall progress, helped by Crispin, but sadly he had to return to Rossall [Senior School] on 8 September. He therefore missed the purchase of our flock of sheep at the opening sale of gimmer shearlings (young breeding ewes) at Leyburn market on 24 September. Under the guidance of John and Frank Tunstill we purchased fifteen shearling ewes, ten of which were North Country Mules and five Teeswater Mashams. The cost was £1,019; after receiving some 'luck money' from the vendors. The production of the best-quality lamb meat that both the butcher and the customer seek is a two-stage process. The first stage is to produce cross-bred ewes that are noted for being prolific, hardy and good mothers with plenty of milk, like our Mules and Mashams. A Bluefaced Leicester ram crossed with the horned Swaledale ewes that one sees on the Yorkshire moors produces the Mule, while a Wensleydale or Teeswater ram produces the Masham. Stage two is to put the Mule and Masham ewes to a 'terminal sire' such as a Suffolk or Texel; the offspring providing the quick-growing, succulent, lean lamb that we like to eat. We would shortly be buying a Suffolk ram to run with our ewes. Different breeds of sheep, developed over centuries of selective breeding, are used in different parts of the country, but follow a similar two-stage breeding process.

At about this time we purchased a young gander for £10 from a breeder near York. He was a disaster – he would not graze and was not the slightest bit interested in our flock of geese. They would toddle off to the beck each day and graze the surrounding sweet grass and vegetation while 'Charlie' hung around the back door, shouting for kitchen scraps, which he enthusiastically devoured. We telephoned Charlie's breeders for advice and learned that they purchased confectionery waste from a well-known chocolate business in York and fed it to their geese. This was no good – we needed a working gander. I described our predicament to poultry specialists G. Potter & Sons of Baldersby, near Thirsk, when purchasing some more pullets from them. They had a good laugh, whereupon Mrs Potter said she needed a gander and would sort him out, offering the same price that I had paid for 'Cream Bun Charlie'. I readily accepted. Mark's final year at Oxford began in early October. He was delighted to have secured one of the best rooms in Christ Church, on the top floor, overlooking the meadow, with the Isis (the part of the Thames that flows through Oxford) in the distance.

The combination of my military and Old Hall work was very demanding, but I was enjoying both enormously, and so was Ruth, for we continued to support and enjoy the many fine military social events of our HQ NEDIST officers' mess, though I was no longer the PMC. We also enjoyed the tattoos, band concerts, Beating of Retreat ceremonies, cocktail parties and other social events to which we were invited because of my appointment. It was a particularly intensive time with winter approaching, and as quickly as we completed tasks, others would appear. We purchased a rather aged, but still very willing, Suffolk ram from John and Frank Tunstill for £50 and we carefully followed their instructions on changing the coloured crayons on his harness every seventeen days so that we could be sure of his fertility and thus be able to calculate lambing dates. We had given each of the fifteen ewes an identification name, based usually on facial features, but sometimes on character (Dopey, V, Fu Man Chu, Freckles, Grumpy, etc.), so Ruth might come in from an early-morning check while I was shaving and tell me that Fu Man Chu had been marked blue overnight. I would then record the fact that, provided no other colour subsequently appeared, we could anticipate her lambs in about 147 days. John and Frank also taught us how to treat minor hoof problems, which if ignored would quickly become serious problems. Ruth always did this clinical work, while I became the joker responsible for turning and holding the sheep. Also, Ruth was better at paring the hooves; there would be blood all over the place [and not all of it was from the sheep] when I tried to turn and hold a sheep and simultaneously do the paring, as proper shepherds do.

Early one Saturday morning there was a loud knock on our door from John to tell us that they were dipping their sheep that morning and if we could have our sheep ready at half past eleven they would put them through their dip too. We duly gathered our flock in the collecting ring, expecting them to be taken through the village in a vehicle or trailer, but John arrived at the appointed time on his tractor without a trailer and alone, apart from Meg, his beloved collie, who accompanied him everywhere … 'Now then, Mister Pedley, you run down to the bridge and stop them turning left, and Meg and I will do the rest.' Ruth didn't want to miss anything, so jumped onto the back of the tractor behind John. I ran off and took up my position as instructed, deeply concerned that our sheep would scatter all over the village, entering the many fine gardens. Not a bit of it. As soon as the villagers heard John's whistles and calls to Meg they knew exactly what was happening and rushed out to protect their gardens and those of any neighbours who might be out. John drove the sheep from his tractor, with the aid of Meg. Ruth, with a very happy smile on her face, gave me a wave and put her tongue out at me as they passed. It was all very orderly, causing no stress to the sheep. Ruth and I helped with the dipping, learning a lot. Each sheep was carefully examined; dirty or matted wool at the rear end was clipped off (a process called 'dagging'), feet were examined and treated as necessary, and then each sheep was carefully lowered into the dip and held for the requisite time to ensure protection against sheep scab and other parasites. Meg watched and helped when necessary, but when the last sheep was in the dip she was nowhere to be seen. She knew [and John knew that she knew] that traditionally it was her turn next. She was soon found, cowering in her kennel, but obeyed John's call to heel. He picked her up, gave her a pat and gently lowered her into the dip.

On 5th September 1982, ace Battle of Britain pilot Group Captain Sir Douglas Robert Steuart Bader, CBE, DSO & Bar, DFC & Bar, DL, FRAeS died, at the age of 72 years. He had 22 kills of enemy aircraft, four shared kills, six probables, but no legs; a double amputee. To read about Douglas Bader makes one feel very, very humble – even when he became a POW he tried to escape. However, Sir Douglas Bader was not voted as "the People's Spitfire Pilot" in a poll launched by the RAF Museum in September 2017; the honour going to ace Polish pilot Squadron Leader Franciszek Kornicki [18 December 1916 – 16 November 2017].

We did not overlook Mark's twenty-first birthday on 17 November, but such were our commitments that we were unable to visit him. It was now a race against time to prepare for Christmas and the winter.

Our geese had flourished on the fine grazing surrounding the beck and, following some supplementary barley feed, they were now ready for the Christmas market. They were killed, plucked and dressed locally and sold without difficulty for £8 to £9 each (£1.30 per lb), with three retained for home consumption. Our poultry initiative was giving us much interest and pleasure, as well as providing good food for the kitchen, together with additional breeding stock and fertile eggs. By the end of the year, some six hundred hen eggs had been sold at the door for 6p each. However, as many of the local purchasers of these doorstep sales were invited inside by Ruth for a cup of coffee and chat, there could have been little profit margin.

Christmas had a Dickensian touch, with ash logs roaring in our huge seventeenth-century fireplace, an abundance of home-grown fare, plus home-made beer and wine, and Christmas cards hung from the oak beams.

Beechwood fires are bright and clear If the logs are kept a year.
Oaken logs burn steadily If the wood is old and dry.
Chestnut's only good they say If for long it's laid away.
But ash new or ash old
Is fit for a queen with a crown of gold.

Birch and fir logs burn too fast Blazing fast but do not last.
Make a fire of elder tree
Death within your house you'll see. It is by the Irish said
Hawthorn bakes the sweetest bread. But ash green or ash brown
Is fit for a queen with a golden crown.

Elmwood burns like a churchyard mould E'en the very flames are cold.
Poplar makes a bitter smoke
Fills your eyes and makes you choke. Apple wood will scent your room
With an incense like perfume.
But ash wet or dry
For a queen to warm her slippers by.

—Lady Celia Congreve, 'The Firewood Poem'

On Boxing Day we held our first social gathering in Old Hall, inviting some of our new local friends to join us for a lunchtime drink. Ruth made some delightful savouries and a generously strong Christmas punch, which I suspect is still remembered by Crispin.

COMMANDER RECRUITING & LIAISON STAFF (CRLS) NORTH EAST DISTRICT (NEDIST)

Second Year at Old Hall

Excitement mounted as we moved into 1983 and the days began to lengthen. To give us a flying start to the year, we re-valued Old Hall at £80,000, to reflect the rise in property values during the year and all the work that we had done on it. During February we gave our ewes supplementary feed, for the first lambs were expected in early March, as were the first goose eggs. We had been told that the geese would start laying on or about Saint Valentine's Day, but the first egg, a huge double yoker, did not arrive until 23 February. Thereafter we had a steady stream of fertile eggs, for which there was strong demand.

At the beginning of March we began bringing our ewes in each evening into the long byre, to make lambing easier for them, and for ourselves. The byre was well lit, and I had divided it into four sections, with small intervening gates, so that we could easily separate the ewes into small straw pens as they lambed. Beginning on 8 March, our silver wedding anniversary and the day that our first lambs were expected, I took seven days' leave to ease the pressure on Ruth. We had a pleasant meal that evening in the company of some friends at the A66 Motel, with a further celebration cum house-warming party to be held four days later, on the Saturday, when the Oxford term ended. Our first lambs arrived on 10 March. We had checked that all was quiet at about midnight and I checked again at about 3 a.m. – all still quiet. Next check at 6 a.m., while Ruth was making a cup of tea, and I heard for the first time the now-familiar noise of a ewe 'talking' to its lamb. I approached whistling a tune, so that I did not startle the ewes, otherwise they would have been likely to panic, stampeding and treading on the lamb. I found that there were two lambs, both standing and being suckled by their mother; V. No assistance was needed apart from a quick spray of their navels with Terramycin. I then returned to the kitchen to call Ruth, and we shared a wonderful moment sitting on a bale of straw among our ewes as they chewed their cud, watching V and her lambs, and drinking our cups of tea. During the next three weeks a further twenty-three lambs were born, without any mishap. John had told us to contact him immediately if we had any problems, and we took him at his word on two or three occasions. He was magnificent, demonstrating exemplary shepherding techniques and giving us patient tuition. We subsequently kept a bottle of sherry in the long byre and were to spend many happy hours together sitting on a bale of straw with a glass of sherry in one hand and the Terramycin spray in the other.

We were integrating well into the farming community of Wensleydale, making many new friends, while still enjoying the military lifestyle. I particularly remember the Kohima Day celebration and parade in Imphal Barracks, York, on 16 May 1983, in the presence of Her Majesty The Queen, with the 1st Battalion Argyll and Sutherland Highlanders on parade; the barracks now accommodating both Headquarters 2nd Infantry Division as well as Headquarters NEDIST, with dual responsibilities for Major-General Patrick Palmer and his staff officers. I also recall an outstanding formal (mess kit and long dresses) reception and Beating of Retreat by the Light Infantry early in the evening of 17 June at Raby Castle. It began with a sunset call from trumpeters on the roof of the castle, the conclusion of which signalled the emergence of the hitherto unseen drums and bugles, marching towards us from dead ground only two hundred yards to our front, closing on us at their impressive Light Infantry pace, with the now-lighted castle in the background. I was, of course, accompanied by Ruth on both these occasions. We felt so fortunate to be experiencing the pomp and ceremony of military events such as these while simultaneously enjoying the simpler but very demanding pleasures of our farming lifestyle in Wensleydale, with the Old Hall renovation continuing apace.

Mark completed his studies at Oxford in June, achieving a splendid first-class honours degree in physics. It was a time of acute unemployment, with a record high of 3,224,715 registered in early February. Not surprisingly, few representatives of industry and commerce were to be seen on the campuses that year coercing students to join them, not even at Oxford. Mark was attracted to, and obtained employment with, the British Antarctic Survey; and it was not long before white garments and strange-looking footwear arrived at Old Hall, together with reporting instructions for preparatory training. I don't think he ever regretted his decision. He was feeling rather institutionalised at the time and sought and found adventure away from academia, prior to eventually entering the more real and intensely competitive world of high technology.

We had reserved a meadow field for hay, which was cut for us on 5 July. We were fortunate with the weather and were rewarded with 439 bales of good-quality hay six days later; the day before the Great Yorkshire Show, which is always held on the Tuesday, Wednesday and Thursday of the second week of July. We could not afford either the time nor the money to have the usual family summer holiday, and it would have been impossible to find a farmer to look after our livestock at that time of the year. However, I don't think Crispin minded, for there was always something interesting going on and we made time for occasional outings. I don't recollect him ever saying that he was bored. Our best twenty lambs were sold for £740 at the opening store lamb sale at Leyburn Auction Mart on 29 July, with the remaining five realising £169 two weeks later – prices with which we were well satisfied. We were farming on a commercial basis, intent on gaining recognition for producing sound quality stock, while our tiny poultry unit was beginning to make a modest contribution.

Both Ruth and I were delighted when I received notification in August that I had been selected as the next Officer Commanding of the Royal Signals Demonstration Team in late February 1984, based in nearby Catterick Camp. It was a major's appointment, but that did not trouble me, particularly as it would not affect my pay, and for the first time for more than eight years my place of work would be less than an hour's drive from my residence. Indeed, it would be only a five-minute drive away. Furthermore, it was an appointment which I knew I would enjoy, and it offered a degree of independence.

Mark left for the Antarctic on 12 October, not yet twenty-two years old. It was the beginning of an adventurous, very competitive and sometimes lonely lifestyle that I cannot and would not wish to record, in the hope that he will eventually write his own memoirs. Ruth and I were very sad to see him go, and also concerned, for at that time the Antarctic was still a very dangerous environment, without the communications facilities and rescue services that are now available. For the next three years he would routinely spend mid-October to mid-March in the Antarctic, followed by six months in England evaluating the data that had been collected, taking some holiday and preparing for the next trip. We decided that while we could not afford a restoration of the cottage it was now essential that we provided it with a new roof to prevent further deterioration. We accordingly obtained a Lloyds Bank improvement loan to cover the cost of £4,901, and work began on 21 November. New timbers and felting were needed, but where possible, we utilised the original Yorkshire stone slates, supplemented with matching slates from other sources. The work was completed just before Christmas and the cottage was then used as a store for household items. Again, five of our geese were killed and dressed locally, the remainder being required as breeding stock. Two were retained for our own consumption and the others sold. We invited nineteen friends and neighbours for lunchtime drinks on the Sunday before Christmas, all of whom seemed genuinely surprised at the progress that we had made during the year. We then settled down for another typical family Christmas, though it was relatively quiet in the absence of Mark, while Justin's presence was erratic because of police duties. We had purchased two additional very good-quality Mule shearling breeding ewes in the autumn from Mr and Mrs Topham of Kirby Malzeard, making a total of seventeen. They were all satisfactorily marked by our Suffolk tup, and we were now able to relax and make merry before the roaring log fire in our huge fireplace, the lights switched off, the candles lit and the Christmas cards hanging from the exposed beams, looking pretty much as they must have done three centuries past.

1984 began with Major General Patrick Palmer handing over as GOC NEDIST/Commander 2nd Infantry Division to take over as Commandant of the Staff College at Camberley. His replacement was another high-flier; Major General Peter Inge KG, a Green Howard, eighteen months younger than me, whose home was also in Wensleydale. He was later to become Field Marshal the Lord Inge KG, GCB, PC, DL. The Headquarters said goodbye to Major General Palmer on 11 January and welcomed Major General Inge on the following day. It was the day of a savage gale that ripped holes in the roof of the long byre. I well remember hastily making an ad hoc wooden roofing ladder [that was to last for many years] and spent most of the following weekend repairing the damage – tiresome work. Ten days later the snow came – slowly at first and then very heavily. Local news broadcasts urged all but emergency services to cease work early (if possible) on the afternoon of Monday 23 January, and Major General Inge obliged by closing his headquarters, sending everyone home apart from duty officers. I only just made it home from York. Ruth had already brought the sheep in and they were happily chewing their cud in the long byre as the blizzard raged outside. The following day we were snowed in, and although I was able to get into York on the Wednesday, the region was virtually at a standstill for the remainder of the week.

My extended tour as Commander Recruiting and Liaison Staff of North East District was now virtually over. I had no sooner briefed Major General Inge than I was making farewell calls throughout the area and briefing my successor. The snow disappeared as quickly as it came, and it was like spring when Ruth and I attended a fifth-form parents' evening a fortnight later, discussing Crispin's progress with his biology, chemistry and physics teachers and then collecting him the following week for his half-term break. He was doing fine, seemed very fit and well, and was soon eagerly helping Ruth with the garden.

I had a pleasant farewell lunch with my staff in the Yorkshire Club and said goodbye to the Deputy Commander and staff of HQ NEDIST/ Headquarters 2nd Infantry Division, and also the Director of Army Recruiting in London. I then began my final tour, commanding the Royal Signals Demonstration Team in Catterick Camp, with the takeover from the retiring Lieutenant Colonel F.C. (Freddie) Lockwood OBE completed on 2 March 1984.

MY FINAL TOUR

Commanding the Royal Signals Demonstration Team - March 1984 to 20th October 1986

At the time that I joined it, the Royal Signals Demonstration Team (RSDT) was preparing for a short move within Catterick Camp to form part of the very large 8th Signal Regiment, commanded by Colonel B.J. Austin, which, together with the School of Signals at Blandford, was responsible for Royal Signals trade training. The RSDT consisted of two troops, each commanded by a captain who had been carefully selected as an excellent representative of the corps. They were named the *Quicksilver troop*, which demonstrated the skills of Royal Signals soldiers and their equipment throughout the country to schools and at events where the attendance of potential recruits and their parents might be expected; and the well-known *White Helmets* motorcycle display team, which had thrilled audiences at major outdoor and indoor events since its formation from dispatch riders in 1927.

These two troops needed the support of a small, efficient and imaginative administrative team, particularly as they were constantly on the move between events for most of the year. In this respect I was very fortunate that the now-retired Lieutenant Colonel Freddie Lockwood had been selected as a civilian to be my administrative officer, supervising a clerical officer and a typist. He had not only considerable experience, ability and enthusiasm, but also the personality to be able to punch well above his weight when necessary, a valuable asset for a unique and virtually independent sub-unit that had to stand on its own feet, resolving its own problems.

The Quicksilver troop was commanded by a most competent and enterprising Captain Danny Lamerton. As one might expect, it had its own establishment of personnel and vehicles, though much of the display equipment that we needed had to be borrowed through personal contacts with operational units, and from elsewhere.

The White Helmets troop, commanded by a quite outstanding Captain John Terrington, was very different. It had only a minimal establishment and was dependent on Royal Signals regiments and squadrons being prepared to release volunteer soldiers for selection and, if successful, part with them for up to two years without replacement. The troop was also very dependent on the generosity of a few corporate and individual sponsors and on the payments that it was able to negotiate for its performances. It had to be run as an efficient business and faced competition from other arena display teams, both military and civilian. Accordingly, the elderly bus that conveyed the team had been purchased out of income several years previously and was maintained and insured out of income, while the sponsored bikes and their spares were carried in rather unsatisfactory borrowed transport. The smart blue (No.1 dress) uniforms used for public performances were donated by retiring officers and soldiers, while the riders' helmets and many other items were also provided under sponsorship agreements. Non-availability of essential spares for its 750cc Triumph motorcycles was a constant headache.

The premier event for the Royal Signals Demonstration Team (apart from the Royal Tournament) was the 'Opening Show', held at the beginning of May, when both the White Helmets and Quicksilver would give of their best before the Signal Officer in Chief or his representative, the media and a large audience, including families. There would be many White Helmets rookies performing because the display season ended in the autumn, when about half of each team would depart, to be replaced by novices who would be trained over the winter period. I was taking over at a busy time, not eased by the RSDT's move to new premises, as well as some residual responsibilities at York lasting until 20 March (due to my successor not yet having arrived), and lambing was imminent.

I persuaded Ruth to jot down some notes on our activities at that time with a view to her writing an article at a later date. She never wrote the article, but some brief notes have survived, which I have put together as follows:

It is early March in Wensleydale. I am rudely awakened by the piercing pips of my portable alarm radio and the 3 o'clock news of the BBC Overseas Service. I am an avid listener to news broadcasts, devouring every word of both world and local news stories, but this morning I dare not remain in bed for longer than the headlines – it is lambing time and my turn to check that all is well. I slide out of bed, dragging on my Nora Batty stockings, three sweaters and old trainers … into the boot room and I put on my woolly hat and anorak and the first pair of wellies that I stumble across. The cold air hits me as I make my way to the lambing shed to check that there are no problems with my beautiful ewes. They are like children to me and I cannot bear to see them in pain. Each has its own character and name and I have a mental record of its history and any previous complications. The night is bitterly cold and there is not a sound in the village, just the odd light from other farms that are also busy lambing. I sing as I approach, so that they will not be startled – anything from grand opera to the national anthem.

My torch beam flicks from ewe to ewe – damn, a swollen head protrudes from Fu Man Chu's rear, with no sign of the front legs. Speed is vital – husband and Army officer 'Hamish' responds to my alarm call as he would to a military 'stand to' as I lather my hands and arms with soap flakes in a bucket of warm water. With hubby holding the ewe in a standing position I manage to slowly push the head back into the womb between her contractions and then explore the womb and its content. There are two lambs. When I am certain that I have identified a front leg that belongs to the foremost lamb with the swollen head I manoeuvre it into its correct position at the side of the head and slowly pull the one leg and head forward with the contractions (no space for second leg – it will have to follow in folded back position). Fu Man Chu slowly collapses onto her side but we are making progress and have the lamb out. No sign of life – the lamb's cord is broken so if not already dead it will die within about a minute if it does not breathe – clear mouth – massage – mouth-to-mouth resuscitation – swing lamb by rear legs in a pendulum motion – more mouth to mouth, massage, tickle inside of nose with piece of straw … : a heartbeat, a cough, a life! Though almost exhausted, Fu Man Chu, still on her side, begins to lick her lamb as soon as we have dried it, sprayed the navel and moved it to her head. Whilst Fu Man Chu is on the ground I pull the second lamb out to make it easier for my very tired but happy ewe.

I recollect that night well. Dawn was breaking by the time we had finished and the lambs had taken their mother's colostrum. This is vital – if a lamb does not receive a ewe's colostrum within an hour or two of birth it is unlikely to thrive and may die, for at that time artificial substitutes did not seem to provide that magical stimulant and sufficient protection against infection. If natural colostrum is so important for a new born lamb, then surely it is more than advisable that the first food for a human baby should be from its mother? If in doubt, talk to a shepherd's wife or a vet, but not to a pharmaceutical representative.

I showered, donned my uniform and had a normal working day. When I got home I went straight to the lambing shed near the back door, soon joined by Ruth, who had heard me arrive. The two lambs were snuggled up together beneath a warm pig lamp in the corner, while Fu Man Chu was on her feet devouring the best-quality hay that we had. Pride and satisfaction was written all over Ruth's face. When we described the event to John he said to Ruth, '*You did it absolutely right, Mrs Pedley – that was very good shepherding.*' Ruth was over the moon.

Lambing was very tiring, but we were rewarded with a good crop of lambs. It gave us so much pleasure to walk the fields and see them running races along the side of the beck, with the curlews calling and swooping above. There were numerous trout and other fish in the beck. We would often see a heron fishing and sometimes we would catch a glimpse of a kingfisher, both oblivious to the fact that the deeds of Old Hall bestowed fishing rights solely to Ruth and myself.

The RSDT Opening Show was held on Friday 4 May with Brigadier D.H. Baynham GM, Commander Training Brigade Royal Signals, representing the Signal Officer in Chief as inspecting officer. I was very tense, not because of concern about the arrangements, the weather or the quality of the display, but because of potential serious injury, particularly during the 'Irish whip' crossovers. This would be the first public display for many of the riders and there would be the temptation to show off, to the extent of almost clipping wheels, to impress parents, wives and girlfriends. The show began in traditional theatrical manner, with the riders out of sight … 'Ladies and gentlemen … the *White Helmets!*' An Oscar announcement pause followed, and then a roar as the engines of some twenty 750cc Triumph motorcycles simultaneously burst into life. I was glad when it was all over. There were a few dramatic falls, but only sufficient to enhance the show, in that they emphasised the danger, and at times spectators could be seen turning their heads or closing their eyes. Brigadier Baynham was delighted with both the White Helmets and the Quicksilver displays and there was much back slapping, followed in the evening by a party at the White Rose Club.

The following day the White Helmets and Quicksilver were on the road – the show season had begun. The White Helmets headed for two days at the Air Show at Bayley Wells, while Quicksilver headed for three days at the East Midlands Festival near Lincoln. The most prestigious and demanding engagement for the White Helmets was always the Royal Tournament, the largest military tattoo in the world, held each year since 1880, except during World War I and World War II. Since 1950 it had been held at Earls Court, for three weeks during July. However, prior to the Royal Tournament the White Helmets had numerous engagements, with performances at Donnington, York [Kohima Day], Blandford, Addington, Wetherby, Wolverhampton, Bristol, Cheltenham, Scotland tour [several performances], Sutton Coldfield, Codnor, Hillingdon,

Northampton and Redcar. The Quicksilver team had an equally, if not more, demanding programme. I would visit the teams at some of these events, but I had two first-class officers in charge with whom I kept in regular touch and in whom I had complete confidence.

It was John who first noticed the Dutch elm disease; little passed his notice in the countryside. Travelling behind him on his tractor reminded me of the BBC's *Children's Hour* radio programme '*Out With Romany*' that thrilled me as a boy of about eight years. The rambles of 'Romany' (The Rev. George Bramwell Evens) in his vardo, drawn by Comma, with two children (Muriel and Doris) and their spaniel (Raq), describing the animals and plants that they saw, was so authentic that many years passed before I realised that it was all pre-scripted and studio produced. It captured my imagination – I could see what they saw and feel the wind and the rain, and it inspired me into exploring and loving the countryside.

'*I don't like the look of yon elms, Mr Pedley*', shouted John, over the noise of the tractor.

We were about two hundred yards distant from the elms but they looked OK to me, apart from a few branches that seemingly hadn't yet leafed.

'*We'll go across and 'ave a look at em*', said John …

'*Now, Mr Pedley, you see how some of the leaves at the end of those branches are yellowing and wilting – that's not reet in this weather*' …

John jumped down from the tractor and I followed him to one of the trees, where he climbed onto the fence, reached up, pulled down a branch and cut part of it off with his knife. When he had jumped down to the ground he peeled back the bark …

'*See those brown streaks, Mr Pedley – we've got Dutch elm disease.*'

Ruth and I were aware that the disease was gradually spreading north, but there was always the chance that it might pass us by, as had occurred in some areas. We were both devastated by the news – they were beautiful 60-foot trees, and in their prime. Though they formed part of the strip that we had sold to John and Frank we still regarded them as our trees. Our loss, however, was a minute part of a catastrophic epidemic that resulted in a UK loss of virtually the entirety of its 30 million elms. The loss permanently changed the appearance of much of our landscape and I suspect that none of my grandchildren have ever seen and may never see these magnificent trees. However, there may be hope; Hillier Trees (Britain's largest growers of trees) has partnered with specialist elm breeders in the USA and Europe to develop a new disease resistant species, one of which is Ulmus 'New Horizon'. The announcement was made by devotee and famous actress Dame Judi Dench at the 2019 RHS Chelsea Flower Show, standing alongside an impressive 15 foot sapling in full leaf. Hillier Trees stated that it had 2,500 saplings of various sizes in its fields; available for purchase by garden centres. Readers who wish to see pictures of Britain's majestic elms in their prime have only to turn to John Constable's rural paintings; my favourite being "the Cornfield" (1826), which also incorporates a young shepherd snatching a quick drink as he and his dog drive their sheep towards the cornfield. The Wildlife Trust estimates that only 1,000 mature elms are left in the UK, and that this decline of the elm has resulted in a similar decline in both abundance and occurrence of the white-letter hairstreak butterfly, which lives exclusively in elms.

As the Royal Tournament approached my mind became increasingly focused on this event. It was highly dangerous for the White Helmets. Apart from being caught out occasionally by the parched-grass slippery surfaces [caused by the heat wave that we were having] they were having a good season, but I felt that they were getting rather complacent and were lucky not to have had some severe injuries. The relatively narrow indoor Earls Court arena would be so very different from their usual venues, and a huge challenge. I felt that Captain John Terrington was being pushed too strongly by organisers who would not have to pick up the pieces. For example, there was generous JCB sponsorship, and in return the organisers had indicated to the sponsors (perhaps they had even promised) that one of our best jump riders would clear their latest 9'6"-high model, one of which was delivered to us for practice. Our jumpers were briefed to jump slightly to the side of the cab, and their confidence gradually increased. However, it became apparent that cab clearance could not be assured in the Earls Court arena and that there was a very real chance of a jumper clipping the top of the cab and the bike landing on top of him. It was decided that the rider would jump as high as he could but slightly to the side of the cab, and most spectators would be none the wiser. There were also concerns about the state that the arena would be in after it had been churned up by the Musical Drive of the King's Troop Royal Horse Artillery and the Royal Navy's field gun competition.

I travelled down to London on an early-morning train on Monday 9 July intending to be present for the afternoon rehearsal, the dress rehearsal the following day and the opening performance on the Wednesday. As the train slowed on the outskirts of York I noticed a fire in the city centre. It soon became apparent that it was York Minster that was burning; one of the finest medieval buildings in Europe, and the pride of Yorkshire. There was a shocked silence in the carriage and several people were in tears. There had been thunderstorms that night and the subsequent enquiry concluded that lightning had been the cause, striking the thirteenth-century south transept roof. A total of 150 fire fighters were deployed but they could not save the roof, which soon crashed to the floor. Skilful restoration, including a virtually identical oak-beamed roof and painstaking repair of the severely damaged and famous rose window, took four years, funded by generous worldwide donations.

I found the White Helmets in good shape, raring to go, but I was soon to be bloodied to the drama and danger of their lifestyle when there was a crash in one of the crosses that resulted in a badly fractured leg. I sat next to the rider [a Tadcaster soldier] in the ambulance, as the show carried on. He was in intense pain, shouting some colourful language at the driver at the slightest jolt. The language and threats intensified when it became apparent that the ambulance crew had taken a wrong turning and hadn't a clue where they were. The incident stunned but did not unsettle the team and they produced some fine displays, including spectaculars before HRH The Princess Anne, our Colonel in Chief, and a live TV broadcast. Though tired by three weeks of the very demanding pressures of the Royal Tournament and the claustrophobic atmosphere of Earls Court, the White Helmets were on the road again the day after it ended, not yet halfway through their extensive programme. Their dedication was not fully appreciated by some senior officers in the corps, and I had to bite my tongue on several occasions. I then scolded myself for not ensuring that those officers were better briefed.

Mark was now temporarily back in England at the home base of the British Antarctic Survey in Cambridge. Ruth and I attended his degree presentation ceremony at Oxford in the Sheldonian Theatre on 4 August, sadly unable to take any other member of the family because of a strict ticket restriction. We were very moved by the ancient and unique ceremony, conducted entirely in Latin, and felt very proud.

We had taken a smaller but very good-quality crop of hay in early July (257 bales) and at the end of the month we again took our best twenty lambs to the opening store sale at Leyburn Auction Mart, where a few thousand lambs were being sold.

'*Make sure you enter 'em for the judging, Mrs Pedley*', I heard John telling Ruth. '*They give prizes for the best two pens of twenty and it costs nowt to enter.*' We were both surprised, but we took John's advice. Two judges were soon to be seen studying and entering dozens of pens of twenty sheep, examining the sheep and engaged in deep discussion. After about an hour they came back to our pen and then disappeared. A distant shout soon indicated that they had selected the winner. We thought no more about it … until they returned, stopped at our pen, gave Ruth a blue-coloured card and congratulated her on her second prize. We were elated – this was a serious commercial sale with very experienced judges. We wondered if perhaps it was an 'encouragement award' to us as beginners. There was some laughter when we asked if that might be the case. We were assured that any such award would result in the judges losing a reputation built up over many years and never being asked to judge again. Of the many awards that Ruth was to receive over the years none gave greater pleasure than that award at Leyburn Auction Mart on 27 July 1984. In a year in which prices were very low, the award enhanced the price that we received at the auction (£748), followed a fortnight later by £350 for the remaining eleven lambs. Part of the proceeds was used to purchase two more high-quality Mule shearling ewes from Mr and Mrs Topham, together with one of their scarce Tropaeolum speciosum (flame creeper) climbing plants that

Ruth had spotted the previous year. It settled happily near our kitchen window, adjacent to two Campsis radicans (trumpet vine) climbing plants which were already thriving on our south-facing wall.

Ruth's garden was now looking most attractive, while eyesores at the back such as an old railway container van and a breeze-block garage and storehouse were being dismantled and removed, together with the concrete on which the buildings stood. Crispin helped Ruth with much of this work, while Mark gave valuable help whenever he visited, particularly in the re-roofing of the byres between the cottage and the barn – no mean task with such heavy lower slates. I always returned home at the end of my military work with some trepidation, wondering what Ruth and Crispin had been up to in my absence – for example, digging a pond in the middle of the lawn. Eventually, I had to accept that they were totally out of control, but I was pleased that they shared so much interest in the garden, fields and beck, and surprised at the depth of their combined knowledge.

In mid-October, Captain John Terrington's outstanding tour in command of the White Helmets came to an end. I was very sorry to see him go, but soon realised that Captain Roddy Nicholson was a worthy successor – a fine officer with strong leadership qualities. Having taken over the command of the team, he would then train alongside the new batch of volunteers who would arrive on 2 November for the White Helmets selection course. This intensive and very demanding 16-day course would identify which volunteers had the personal characteristics and potential riding skills that the team needed. There was no weekend break during the 16 days, and each day only ended when bikes had been immaculately cleaned and made ready for the next day – rarely before 7 p.m. and sometimes much later. Although the volunteers would ideally have some motorcycling experience, it was not unusual for a volunteer who had previously only ridden a pedal bike to pass the course and eventually become a top rider.

The year at Old Hall ended with customary revelry and much satisfaction, for we were progressing well. Friends who had questioned our judgement and even sanity three years previously were now saying, 'You are so lucky.' Despite our commitments we were still able to accept and return the occasional weekend hospitality of distant friends while the number of new Wensleydale friends and acquaintances continued to increase, for which Ruth must take most of the credit. Such interesting people, from so many different backgrounds. Ruth made friends easily because she was so genuinely interested in and helpful to people, always willing to lend a hand in assisting worthy causes and charities.

Ruth loved stone walling, and there were always some repairs to be done to the lengthy and attractive walls along our boundaries. If I were to suggest that I mix some cement she would say, 'Yes please' before I could complete the sentence, and she would rush upstairs to get into appropriate old clothes. Stones were a precious commodity to us and we had 'grown' a stone pile on an area of concrete close to where the railway wagon had been. The pile began with the remnants of two outside loos and then it became a habit to add to it whenever and wherever we came across useful stones on our land, in the garden or in the beck. As soon as I had mixed the cement and taken it to where Ruth wished to work, I would select a few wheel-barrow loads of mixed stone from the pile and take that to her as well. By this time Ruth would usually be in happy conversation with someone as she worked. I think she already knew everyone in the village. A couple of hours of stone-walling work would inevitably be followed by ice cream and coffee at the recently opened Brymor Ice Cream Parlour at High Jervaulx Farm near Masham, probably the best in the county, with the ice cream produced from the milk of an outstanding Guernsey herd that grazed the adjacent fields. The farm, the Guernsey herd and the ice cream business had been developed by Brian Moore and his wife Brenda, who had previously farmed near Harrogate. As regular customers, we got to know them quite well. On leaving Heckmondwike Grammar School, Brian had bought a cow, leased some pasture, and never looked back; a self-made man.

Early one Saturday morning there was a particularly loud and urgent knock on the door. I rushed downstairs and there was John standing in the doorway.

'Ye've got a bull in yer field, Mister Pedley'. 'Have I John? That's just what I wanted'.

'*Aye, we've been chasing 'im since daybreak. Now you and Missus Pedley keep out of the way – he's a nasty old bugger. Me and the lads will soon 'av 'im now – we'll fix the wall.*'

'*Oh, don't worry about the wall, John*', said Ruth. '*We owe you lots of favours.*'

I gasped when I saw the damage to the wall, and even Ruth winced. It was very late afternoon before we reached the Brymor Ice Cream Parlour. This 'bull saga' was in early February 1985. On 26th February the £/$ exchange rate sank to its lowest ever rate, almost reaching parity (1.042). Five days later the miners' strike ended, almost a year from the date that it began.

We had a very successful lambing (thirty-seven lambs from seventeen ewes), but such prolificacy in a small flock results in much extra work. In a large flock there is likely to be a ewe that has just given birth to a single lamb that can be conned into taking a lamb from a ewe giving birth to triplets, but in a small flock the chances of that happening are slim, so bottle feeding becomes desirable, if only to prevent damage to the ewe's teats.

A very fit and tanned Mark flew into RAF Brize Norton on 6 April and joined us for the remainder of the Easter holiday. He had clearly had some more than exciting experiences in Antarctica and later showed us some stunning photographs.

The RSDT Opening Show on 3 May was another huge success and I felt very proud of both the White Helmets and Quicksilver. They were both fully booked for the season ahead, with the White Helmets particularly excited at having engagements in both Scotland and western Germany in addition to the Royal Tournament, with a second trip to Germany (Kiel and Hamburg) in mid-November.

Neither Ruth nor I had ever seen a badger, so when I heard that one of the civilian employees of 8th Signal Regiment was an enthusiastic observer and protector of badgers, I contacted him and asked if there was any chance of him taking us to watch a sett one evening. Such was his knowledge of and enthusiasm for badgers that he was called 'Badger Clarke'. He agreed to take us on 2 June, together with Crispin, who was with us for half term. We took up our position just before last light in the vicinity of Colburn and were soon watching an upwind fox on his rounds. Then I felt a tap on my shoulder and 'Badger Clarke' pointed to the distinct snout of a badger protruding from one of the burrows. It was a bright moonlit night and we spent more than an hour watching a family of badgers and their cubs at play, only a few feet from us. It was as entertaining and exciting as any West End Show that I have seen.

The Royal Tournament was becoming increasingly spectacular, due to the combination of improving special-effects technology and the flair of event organizer Michael Parker, now Major Sir Michael Parker KCVO CBE. He retired from the Army in 1971 and was appointed producer for the 1974 Royal Tournament and thereafter, until its demise in 1999 for financial reasons, following the 1998 Defence Review. His 1985 production did not disappoint, and I felt proud of the White Helmets' performances, though always relieved when they were over. Michael Parker wrote in his memoirs, *It's All Going Terribly Wrong*:

The motorcycle display teams were always very good value. The speed, skill and courage they displayed were hugely impressive. It always used to amuse me that most of the young men in the teams had not passed their driving tests and were therefore not allowed onto the roads. But they were allowed to do fast triple cross-overs at closing speeds of 50mph in the arena!

One year the White Helmets, the Royal Signals Display Team, had a series of accidents. You could always tell which acts the other participants liked because every nook and cranny would be filled with faces watching from the roof, the lighting gallery or the emergency exits. When the White Helmets came on there was not a space to be seen anywhere. The motorcycle teams were supposed to enter the arena at high speed, jumping over two ramps to do a cross-over in mid air. On this occasion the first two bikes mistimed it, and hit each other with some force. Onto the ground they fell, and all the other bikes following closely behind piled on top of them. The scene looked horrific, a twisted mangled mess of bikes, wheels spinning and men lying everywhere. I lit another cigarette. It looked much worse than it really was and one by one the men got up, dusted themselves down and wheeled their bikes off, until there was just one man left lying there. The stretcher bearers came on and carried him off. Fearing the worst, I asked the Arena Master if the man was badly injured.

'Not at all', he said. 'He just split his trousers up the middle and didn't want to show everything walking off!'

I wanted to reward the White Helmets in some way. I was conscious of their urgent need for a tractor/trailer unit to carry their bikes, spare parts and repair equipment and I renewed my efforts to obtain sponsorship from a manufacturer, for there was no chance of any financial contribution from military funds. I decided to begin with the truck/tractor manufacturers, and if that failed it was my intention to talk to some of the leading advertising companies for advice. I wrote directly to the chairmen of these manufacturing companies, enclosing a folder of information and some brilliant photographs and crossed my fingers.

The remainder of the year followed the same pattern as 1984. Our summer holiday was a working holiday on the farm, taking in the hay crop, going on day trips to the many interesting attractions in the county and preparing and selling our thirty-seven lambs at Leyburn, realising a welcome £1,384. Though there was much routine, every day on the farm was full of interest and activity. In addition to the sheep and geese we now had quite a thriving, though small, Marans poultry unit, with a full order book. Including some Rhode Island Red and Light Sussex birds, our stock sheet at 30 September listed 154 birds (including chicks). In late October I took a telephone call in my office from a director of Iveco, a Mr Fox, advising me that Iveco was prepared to loan one of its new tractor/trailer units with rear lift, and at no cost to ourselves apart from the insurance. The White Helmets were delighted. They deserved it. It was not long before Captain Roddy Nicholson was meeting Mr Fox at their factory in Lancashire to discuss details. I later attended the White Helmets display that we gave at the factory, with some very useful publicity for both the

White Helmets and Iveco. It was a superb tractor/trailer combination, the envy of rival teams on the circuit.

I was now approaching my fifty-second birthday, which would put me within three years of compulsory retirement from the Army. I did not wish to retire. I felt fit and young, well within the required medical standard and still running three miles several days each week at a decent pace. Furthermore, I was very conscious of the fact that I was the sole income earner, that we had hefty mortgage and improvement loans, and that while Rossall School fees would soon be coming to an end, they would be followed by university costs. There were also the continuing improvement costs for our beloved Old Hall.

I decided to apply for a civil service appointment as the Army Careers Officer for West and North Yorkshire, based in Leeds, but with subsidiary offices at York, Wakefield, Huddersfield and Scarborough. The appointment was to become vacant in October 1986. These popular appointments only became vacant occasionally and were never short of applicants, so I was far from being confident of selection. However, if successful, I could look forward to employment until the age of sixty. The downside was the 51 miles between Old Hall and Leeds, though I would not need to be in the office until 9 a.m.

I attended a selection board chaired by the Director of Army Recruiting in the Ministry of Defence on the afternoon of 27 February 1986. The following day, to my relief, I was informed that I had been successful. Ruth and I had not had a proper holiday for several years and I had plenty of leave outstanding, so, prompted by my success, we decided that we would have one that year. We eventually decided that, together with Crispin, we would see the higher Austrian Alps at a time when the skiers had left and the alpine flowers were in bloom. We selected the village of Obergurgl (6,330 feet) in the Ötztal region, quite close to the Italian border, which claimed to be the highest parish in Europe. The selected hotel was the Hotel Josl on the southern fringe of the village. We would travel by car, following some of our favourite routes through Belgium and West Germany. No caravan this time – to Ruth's delight, this was a hotel holiday!

With that decision taken, it was now all go – so much to do in so little time. Lambing was as tiring as ever, but very rewarding, with the same return of thirty-seven lambs from seventeen ewes as in 1985. We reduced the poultry numbers significantly and made arrangements with John, Frank and Brian for the stock to be looked after in our absence.

Perfect hay-making weather enabled us to cut the hay meadow on 26 June and take 235 top-quality bales three days later. Freddie Lockwood was magnificent in taking on many of my military responsibilities while I attended re-settlement courses. Having seen the White Helmets settle into the Royal Tournament in early July, we set off on 14 July for the night ferry from Felixstowe, arriving in Zeebrugge the following morning.

We travelled through Liège and the Ardennes into the Rhine Valley and through Baden Wurttemberg to Lindau on Lake Constance, where Ruth and I had spent some days of our honeymoon. We had a car problem at this point but hired another and drove on through the Bavarian Alps and the Tyrol to our destination. We had selected the right place at the right time, and our week at Obergurgl, walking higher and higher through the alpine flora at its best to the very edge of the glaciers with Ruth and Crispin, remains one of my most memorable holiday experiences. It was in these Ötztal Alps five years later that the almost perfectly preserved 5,300-year-old remains of a Neolithic hunter were discovered, so well described in *The Man in the Ice*. As soon as the discovery was made Ruth ordered the book and would read it in bed late into the night, thrilled by the forensic discoveries. Our car was repaired and ready for us at Lindau and we had an uneventful return journey, arriving at the Old Hall on 25 July to find everything in order. We also learned, to our delight, of Justin's engagement to an attractive young WPC detective called Haley Wood, who had recently become a regular visitor to Old Hall.

Mark at this time was in the process of his first change of employment. He had enjoyed the adventure of the Antarctic but now felt that he needed to be at the hub of electronics and computer research and joined Marconi at the Cambridge Science Park. Here he was able to develop specialist knowledge in the field of digital signal processing. Crispin was patiently awaiting his GCE A-level results that would determine whether he would achieve his preferred choice of reading Forestry at Aberdeen University. Perhaps it was the frustration of the wait that prompted Crispin and Ruth to start hacking through a reasonably tidy area of concrete near the rear gate to reveal an old well. They had noted a circular patch in light snow conditions during the previous winter and were proved correct. I became the 'joker' who cleared most of the rubbish within the well, a tad concerned that it might collapse with me in it, while Ruth and Crispin enthusiastically hacked away more concrete – to create a space in which to plant a Mulberry sapling. However, I have to admit that when the project was completed we had an attractive fresh-water well feature within a walled area that we called 'Mulberry Court'. The sapling flourished; in some years producing a laden and spectacular crop of delicious berries. They were guzzled by greedy birds to an extent that they sometimes became tipsy, flying into windows with fatal result.

Crispin's exam results comfortably exceeded the grades that he needed for his Forestry course at Aberdeen. The family congratulated him, and on 12 September Ruth took Crispin for a long weekend in London, staying at the Union Jack Club. Three weeks later I drove Crispin to the granite (and floral) city of Aberdeen, which, since the discovery of offshore oil in the 1970s, had become the focal point of Europe's petroleum industry. I was particularly impressed with the magnificent architecture. I sensed that Crispin would be very happy there.

I was overwhelmed with the gratitude and the glowing formal reports of my superiors when I relinquished the command of the Royal Signals Demonstration Team. I thanked Freddie Lockwood, the clerical staff, Quicksilver and the White Helmets for their splendid support and handed in my military identity card.

ARMY RECRUITING

A Wedding and a Wensleydale Ram

I started taking over from Lieutenant Colonel Derek Hall as the Army Careers Officer in Leeds responsible for a large chunk of Yorkshire on 6 October, retiring from the Army on 20 October; a total of 34 years and 24 days since my enlistment in that same city. I hardly noticed the change to being a civil servant for apart from my deputy (Captain Sheila Macey WRAC) and a clerical officer, I was in charge of warrant officers and senior NCOs serving in the Regular Army, and I had to regularly wear my uniform – especially when enlisting and on public duties.

I purchased an economical Metro car with 8,040 miles on the clock and found that if I left Old Hall at 7.25 a.m. I could be in the Leeds office at 9 a.m., as required. Captain Sheila Macey lived near Barnsley, so in addition to our primary duties in Leeds it became mutually convenient for her to pay particular attention to the Wakefield and Huddersfield outstations, while I focused on those in York and Scarborough. Despite my experience in recruiting it was necessary for me to attend a two-week training course, which I found most valuable, so it was not until late November that I was really in the chair. It was quite a busy period because the Leeds office, which we shared with the Royal Navy, was soon to be given a major renovation, entailing a complete evacuation.

I was happy in my work. The quite substantial Army Careers organisation was focused on providing the training units with well motivated recruits of the requisite calibre and ability, including the selection of appropriate trade training courses. Prior to my final in–depth interviews with applicants, I would have studied written and physical test results and the assessments and recommendations of a sergeant or staff sergeant, as well as having a verbal brief from the warrant officer in charge of the office. There would also be testimonials, employer and school reports, and any record of crime to be studied. I found it a stimulating challenge, and when we received a report from a training unit that soldier X had failed in his or her training there would be a depressed office discussion to try and identify if possible why it had gone wrong, and to try and learn from our failure. My interview and assessment write-up would take about an hour to complete. In exceptional circumstances I would do five interviews in a day, but two or three was the norm, for these interviews were but one of many of my recruiting activities and responsibilities.

Enlistment, which could be several weeks or even months later, was always a happy event, usually with members of the family present. Even more satisfying, probably several months later, was a knock on the door from a trained soldier to thank us for our help and advice, describing the wonderful time he or she was having.

On 23rd October 1986 I wrote the following letter to The Controller, Central Office (War Pensions), DHSS, Norcross, Blackpool:

Dear Sir or Madam,

DISABLEMENT DUE TO SERVICE IN HM FORCES

Four days ago I retired from the Active List of the Army, having served continuously since December 1952. It has been a very happy career, but regrettably marred by acute damage to my hearing as a result of regular weapon firing and pyrotechnic explosions in training exercises. I have a continuous high frequency note in my ears which makes conversation at best difficult and virtually impossible whenever I have to contend with any background noise. This hearing condition has been monitored on an annual basis by the Army Medical Authorities since 1978 when I was first referred for specialist attention and is, I believe, well documented in my military records. The specialists whom I have seen have all described my condition as "high frequency deafness", due to firing high velocity military weapons.

I wish to apply for a war disablement pension, for the condition I describe is wholly attributable to my military service.

I would be grateful for your advice as to how I should apply for such a disablement pension.

Yours sincerely …

Three and a half years later (April 1990) I received my first monthly disablement payment, following success at an appeal tribunal. As was my right, I was provided with a copy of my entire military medical records shortly before the tribunal; mostly minor sport injuries in my early years and my hearing in later years, plus annual physical data throughout. Were it not for my bow legs I think my height might have just touched 6 feet.

My high frequency disability is permanent. Nevertheless, on 2nd January 2022 I was thrilled by the close-up images and clarity of bird song in Sir David Attenborough's release of *Wonder of Song*. He is a man who I admire immensely; broadcaster, natural historian and author of amazing diverse achievement, respected by our nation [OM GCMG CH CVO CBE FRS FRSA FLS FZS FRSGS FRSB] and worldwide. He was born on 8th May 1926, a few days after the Queen.

There was a special glitter to the traditional family Christmas celebrations that year when we met Haley's parents, Jack and Betty Wood, for the first time on 23 December. Due to family members being so widespread, plus the complications of police shift working, it had not been easy to arrange the gathering, but it was well worth the wait and we all looked forward to a 1987 wedding.

That year was less than three weeks old when a kidnapping occurred that shocked the country, including Ruth and myself, and most of the Christian world – the kidnapping in Beirut of Terry Waite, the

Archbishop of Canterbury's special envoy, while he was negotiating the release of hostages. The son of a Cheshire village policeman, Terry Waite began his working life in the Church Army, after which he took on the dangerous role of adviser to the first African Archbishop in Idi Amin's Uganda, followed by working in Rome as consultant to religious communities. When he became the Archbishop of Canterbury's special envoy he negotiated with heads of state over the plight of hostages in Tehran and Libya and gradually emerged on the world stage as one of the most remarkable figures of his generation. He survived 1,763 days in captivity in Beirut, almost four years of which were in solitary confinement in brutal, medieval conditions. Later in our life, Ruth and I met Terry Waite on a cruise-ship holiday, during which we listened to his talks and read his remarkable autobiography, an amazing account of human endurance. This brave and powerful humanitarian impressed us enormously. He was a huge man with considerable presence.

Ruth and I next met Jack and Betty at their home in Bradford on 11 April, shortly after lambing had ended. It was another memorable day, not solely because of the meeting up again with such delightful new family members, but also because of the news that the wedding of Justin and Haley was likely to be held in the autumn in Bradford Cathedral and the visit that they kindly gave us to nearby Saltaire.

I had never even heard of Saltaire; the creation of Sir Titus Salt, a leading manufacturer in the world's woollen industry, which was focused on Bradford. He was born in nearby Morley on 20 September 1803 into a family already well established in the wool industry and was educated at a local grammar school, followed by practical experience in the trade. When he was aged thirty he took over his father's business and became mayor of Bradford fifteen years later. He was distressed by the smoke, pollution and working conditions that he saw around him and, having decided to expand his business, he selected a new site three miles outside Bradford in open, worker-friendly countryside on the western fringe of the then village of Shipley. Here he built a model textile mill in quality stone, sufficiently large to absorb his entire (3,000-employee) business, alongside the river Aire and the adjacent Leeds–Liverpool canal. It was opened with a magnificent banquet on his fiftieth birthday and was followed by the similar construction in stone of some eight hundred houses, as well as bathhouses, shops, schools, a hospital, almshouses, an institute and churches, but no public houses. It was a unique creation of a model village by a man who was deeply religious, though seemingly rather diffident and inarticulate, whose additional offices included Chief Constable of Bradford, Deputy Lieutenant, President of the Bradford Chamber of Commerce and Liberal Member of Parliament. He was created a baronet in 1869 and died seven years later, at the age of seventy-three. It is recorded that the number of people lining his funeral route exceeded 100,000. I admire the Victorian period, which produced so many distinguished people, and I might never have become familiar with the remarkable achievements of Sir Titus Salt had it not been for Jack and Betty. Saltaire is now designated by UNESCO as a World Heritage Site.

On 16 April, the day before the Easter holiday, Ruth and I attended the funeral of Ruth's aunt Elsie, with whom she had had a very close and loving relationship from the time that she was a small girl, a relationship that had developed further following the tragic death of her mother. Ruth was by now quite hardened to the shock of bereavement, but nevertheless she was extremely distraught. Elsie Ivy MacKeith (née Bramham) was an exceptionally kind lady, and quite a beauty in her younger days. Her generosity and kindness, and that of her husband Charles MacKeith who pre-deceased her, were extended to Justin, Mark and Crispin in the many exeats from Rossall School that they hosted at Duchally, their Blackpool home, particularly when Ruth and I were overseas. We were joined at Old Hall for Easter by Mark from Cambridge and Crispin from Aberdeen.

Shortly after Easter Ruth and I joined the Conservative Party. It was Ruth's suggestion, probably prompted by friends in the area, and I agreed that it was a good idea. She had been a member of the Young Conservatives as a teenager and had never changed from that position, while I was impressed by the leadership of Prime Minister Margaret Thatcher and her philosophy of deregulation and privatisation and reducing the power of trade union barons, as well as her inherent

European scepticism. It was an interesting time to become involved in politics, for on 11 May Margaret Thatcher called a snap general election for 11 June, seeking a third term in office. The following day we attended our first Conservative social event, a local-branch sherry evening, and soon became caught up in the excitement of the election. A week later we were supporting the Conservative candidate for Richmond, Leon Brittan QC, PC, DL (Home Secretary 1983–85) in various ways in the campaign to retain his seat. The election result was a third success for Margaret Thatcher, though with her majority reduced from 144 to 102 seats, while Leon Brittan was returned with a majority of 19,576 votes (18,066 in 1983), one of the largest majorities in the country.

On the afternoon of Friday, 4 September I arrived home early to find Ruth in an excited state. She had just returned from shopping in Leyburn and had seen a huge Wensleydale ram being taken around the market square on a halter by local farmer David Ford in a 'guess its weight' competition, to raise funds for the Round Table, and I had to see it, **now**. One could not reason with Ruth when she reached that level of excitement so I returned with her to Leyburn, explaining en route that we did not have the resources to mix pedigree and commercial sheep breeding, that the Wensleydale was a crossing sire breed, not a terminal sire, and so on, but to no avail. On arriving in Leyburn I was relieved to see no sign of David Ford or his Wensleydale ram and we returned to the car, Ruth bitterly disappointed. I had no sooner started the engine than Ruth shouted, '*There he is!*' I looked out to see David Ford leading his ram down the steps of the Midland Bank. I groaned, followed Ruth to the bank and met David and Joan Ford and their magnificent Wensleydale ram; 'Harmby Moor Snowdrop.' Later that weekend we visited David and Joan at their farm at Harmby, purchased his best Wensleydale ram lamb a few days later, and gradually adjusted our farming to the breeding of pedigree Wensleydale sheep.

The big family event of the year, the wedding of Haley and Justin, was held at 2 p.m. on 12 September 1987 in Bradford Cathedral [the Cathedral Church of St Peter], a beautiful Anglo-Saxon church, though with a turbulent history, having been reduced to rubble first by the Normans and then by marauding Scots three centuries later. The threat and scale of these Scottish raids was such that in 1311 it was necessary for Richmond to build a protective wall around all but the river side of the town, whilst in 1323 the Scots destroyed Yorkshire's Egglestone Abbey, founded by the Premonstratensians (known as the White Canons because of the colour of their habit); a long way south of the border! However, these historical events were far from our minds on Haley and Justins' wedding day; it was an ultra joyous occasion, with meticulous arrangements and the service supported by a fine cathedral choir. A more bonny bride than Haley could not have graced the aisle.

That autumn Ruth and I joined the Wensleydale Longwool Sheep Breeders' Association (WLSBA), one of the oldest sheep breed societies in the world, and we purchased additional breeding stock at the association's annual show and sale. We also founded a new branch of the Richmond Conservative Association at a meeting held at Old Hall, while I became a member of the Executive Committee of the Yorkshire Area of Boys' Clubs and Ruth a committee member of the Wensleydale branch of the Council for the Protection of Rural England, with responsibility for publicity. These voluntary organisations were to introduce us to many new friends and enrich our lives.

The tranquillity and beauty of a glorious autumn was soon to be dramatically disrupted by the worst storm in the United Kingdom for almost three hundred years. The storm caused twenty-two deaths within a three-hour period on the night of 15 October, with 115-mph gusts uprooting 15 million trees. The devastation was widespread, the damage costing £2 billion. It was most severe in southern England, and particularly in Sussex, Suffolk and Kent. It was the storm that the nation would not allow BBC weather forecaster Michael Fish to forget, his lunchtime forecast categorically trashing reports of a severe storm approaching. It turned out to be one which the Home Secretary was to later describe as '*the worst, most widespread night of disaster since the Blitz.*' Four of the twenty-two storm deaths were in France. It was generally accepted at the time that this storm was the worst since 1703, the detail of which was chronicled the following year by Daniel Defoe in his book, *The Storm*; a storm of such severity that it killed approximately 8,000 people on land and sea as it tore across the country, described by Queen Anne as '*a calamity so dreadful and astonishing, that the like hath not been seen or felt*'. However, the most thorough scientific comparison of the severity of Britain's storms is probably that of Hubert Lamb (1913– 1997), the founder of the University of East Anglia's Climatic Research Unit. He created a 'severity index' which incorporated assessment of wind speed, damage to landscape and property and lives lost (human and animal). His conclusion was that this 1987 hurricane was the most severe, followed by the storms of 1792, 1825 and 1694, with the 1703 storm in only fifth place. UK (Met Office) recordings only began in the early 20th century (about 1910), so the expression, "since records began" needs to be borne in mind when used in any discussion on UK weather in past centuries [particularly on climate change]. Parish records describe an abundance of great storms and floods in earlier times. Two Yorkshire examples; in 1673 all but two of the bridges [stone] in upper Wharfedale were swept away; one night in October 1754 the River Rye overflowed above Helmsley, destroying the town bridge and several houses and drowning 13 people, with the same fate for at least three other bridges downstream, plus other extensive loss/damage to livestock and infrastructure in the dale.

While looking around the Leeds Kirkgate market during a lunchtime break, just before Christmas, I noticed some dressed geese for sale. I talked to the stallholder and told him that I could provide him with better birds. He asked me to bring a couple, which I did, and for the remaining five years prior to my final retirement I would supply him with a number of his '*preemyun Wunzlydoyl geez*'. I would have loved to have spent a morning working on his stall, helping him sell his poultry, and told him so. He readily agreed, but I eventually chickened out – how would I explain my presence there if seen by X or Y (and here, many names flashed through my mind)?

Christmas was very special that year because of our enlarged family. We continued to host quite a large Christmas lunch on the Sunday before Christmas for local friends, followed by a relatively quiet Christmas Day, but the Boxing Day gathering was enhanced by the presence of new family members, whose number was to steadily increase as the years passed. No matter how many were there, it was sheer joy, and Ruth had the skill, stamina and enthusiasm to make it all look so easy.

1988

Wensleydale Sheep and Politics

Mark was now the owner of an apartment in Cambridge, but many of his possessions and a variety of items of furniture were still at Old Hall, so Justin arranged the hire of a good-sized van and on the second day of 1988 the Pedley family became removal contractors. Justin drove the van with Mark and Haley sitting alongside, while Ruth, Crispin and myself followed in our Rover. It was rather like a seaside outing, but without the candyfloss.

My daily journeys to work were largely spent listening to the morning news broadcasts and concentrating on my driving, no different to thousands of other commuters. They took rather longer than I would have wished, but I was not unduly concerned and I found the first half hour very relaxing as I cleared my mind to focus on the day ahead. An interesting feature before the weather forecast and the BBC eight o'clock news at that time was the reading out of what the BBC considered to be the best 'mini saga' received from listeners the previous day. The rules were simple – it had to be precisely fifty words in length, excluding the title. There were some brilliant contributions, and when I was at the Scarborough office I would sometimes drive to the edge of the Burneston Barracks cliffs during my lunchtime sandwich break and relax by composing my own. I never submitted any, for they had to be typed and sent by post and I had more important things to do. Email and 'cut and paste' were years away. However, three survived in my diary:

A Matter of Life and Death
The body lay lifeless in the shallow pool into which it had fallen. With only a flickering light and with lips smarting from the storm she dropped to her knees, massaging the heart and breathing warm air into the deflated lungs. A twitch, a cough. Life. The lamb was born.

Foul Murder
He selected the arrow carefully, feeling its point and preening the feathered flight as he took it from the quiver. The bow bent and his aim steadied on the victim's heart. Twang! The body dropped to the ground as a stone, blood spilling over the chest. So died Cock Robin.

Politics
The crowd silenced as the swarthy miner turned, sleeves rolled and lips pursed. He accelerated towards a short, defiant figure. A gasp as the stone hard object that he unleashed reared abruptly, sinking into the man's chest. Silence. 'Well bowled Harold,' said Jardine. Bradman rolled in agony. An Empire shuddered.

It was proving rather difficult to keep up with my fitness runs, but I enjoyed them so much that I was determined that they should not be abandoned. There were no changing or shower facilities at Leeds, but I made time between interviews and other work at York each week to drive from the office in Micklegate to the Imphal Barracks gymnasium and run with the soldiers at lunchtime on a quite attractive route near the golf course, the times meticulously recorded in my diary. I was also able to find time for at least one run at the weekend. Ruth did not take any specific exercise apart from badminton, but her day overflowed with continuous hyperactivity of one kind or another, and she was rarely off her feet – she was pretty fit for her age.

The Late May Bank Holiday was held on 30 May and Ruth suggested that we visited the Finghall barrel push, an event that had apparently been instigated two years earlier by the inhabitants of that village to raise funds for charities. It was the fiendish idea of the landlord of the village pub, the Queen's Head. It involved pushing, huffing, kicking and cursing an 18-gallon beer barrel up a steep half-mile hill, against the clock. Anyone could enter, and in addition to the men's class there were classes for ladies and strong lads. Ruth had heard that there were many supporting attractions, including afternoon tea and cream cakes in the very fine gardens of the post office. It sounded like a good idea and I readily agreed. We found that the starting point was at the bridge near Akebar, and that it finished at the Methodist chapel in the centre of the village, with individual performances meticulously timed throughout the day.

We had a most pleasant afternoon and admired the ingenuity of the villagers' supporting stalls, particularly farmer Richard Bradley's chicken races. We were later delighted to learn that Brian Lockey had won the men's barrel push event. Brian was to win that race for 11 consecutive years, retiring unbeaten in 1999 at the age of 47 years, by which time he had also successfully competed in the Great North Run and the London Marathon, raising hundreds of pounds for charities.

The Finghall barrel push raised more than £3,000 for charities that year and was to continue to do so year on year, another example of the community spirit and generosity evident in Yorkshire Dales villages. Other villages held annual events to raise funds for their local charities, each uniquely different. The major fundraising event in the area was the Masham Sheep Fair, held in the centre of the delightful market town of Masham, and which Ruth and I were to support in later years with sheep entries. Held in late September, it attracted hundreds of visitors and raised more than £10,000 each year to distribute to such worthy causes as Marie Curie, the Alzheimer's Society, the Yorkshire Air Ambulance, Jennyruth Workshops, and various schools and hospitals.

Although we only had a few Wensleydale sheep, Ruth and I decided to enter a couple at the Great Yorkshire Show (GYS) in July to gain experience and to get to know more of the breeders. I needed to be at the show for at least one of the three days as I was responsible for the coordination of a quite large military static display, so I was able to mix a bit of business with pleasure. The GYS was the most competitive agricultural show in the country for Wensleydale sheep breeders, largely because the Wensleydale was a Yorkshire breed that had had classes at the show for more than 100 years. There were 10–15 entries in each class at that time, with exhibitors from as far afield as Wales, Scotland and Somerset. We did not expect any rosettes, nor did we receive any. However, we learnt a lot and made many new friends, not only in the sheep lines but also at the very fine barbecue that fellow exhibitors arranged in one of the show rings when the public had left and the gates were shut.

In the eighteenth century, large longwool sheep called '*Muggs*' were being bred around the river Tees and in some lower areas of North Yorkshire, Durham and Northumberland. They may have been descendants of sheep kept by the monks of nearby abbeys prior to their dissolution in 1538. These *Muggs* were improved by further crossing with Dishley Leicester rams in the early nineteenth century and became known as 'Teeswaters', though a further half century was to pass before the world's first sheep-breed societies were formed and descriptive characteristics and breed names formally recorded. The Wensleydale type of longwool sheep developed from a well-documented cross between a Dishley Leicester ram and a Teeswater ewe that produced an outstanding bluefaced ram that was called Bluecap, born in 1839. Bluecap became the founder sire of the Wensleydale breed, without the infusion of any further Dishley Leicester blood. No other sheep breed can trace its history so positively. The new breed type evolved at the right time to take advantage of the demand for rams to cross with the smaller hill breeds in a revolutionary double-crossing system that was needed to provide good carcasses of mutton to feed the growing populations of the wool and cotton towns of Yorkshire and Lancashire (Manchester in particular) during the Industrial Revolution. 'Wensleydale breed' as a title was first recorded in 1876 when a group of enthusiasts asked the GYS authorities to provide classes at the show. Two rival breed societies were formed in 1889, eventually amalgamating in

1920. The breed was to reach the zenith of its popularity at the beginning of the twentieth century as a dual-purpose commercial sheep: (1) it was used as a crossing sire to be put to northern hill-breed ewes, particularly the Dalesbred, to produce the strong, milky and prolific Masham ewes, which were then put to a terminal sire such as a Suffolk – the product being the ideal mutton or lamb meat sought by the discerning housewife of that time; and (2) it was a quality wool provider, producing the finest– lustre longwool in the world.

Sadly, wool value had gradually diminished from the Middle Ages 'golden fleece' period when such fortunes were made from its production that a famous ransom was able to be paid. I refer to the ransom paid to the Holy Roman Emperor (Henry VI) for the release of King Richard the Lionheart when he was captured during his return journey from the Third Crusade. The exorbitant ransom demanded of Richard's kingdom was for more than 2,000 tons of silver and three years' income of the English Crown. A huge chunk of that sum was met by the English Cistercian Monasteries' donation of their annual wool clip. Even at the end of King Henry V's reign almost two thirds of the Crown's income was derived from the wool industry!

Both Ruth and I were strongly attracted to the Wensleydale sheep not only because it was our local breed, carrying the name of the dale that we loved, but also because of its characteristics and fascinating history.

Our 1986 holiday in Obergurgl had been so enjoyable that we repeated the holiday, though a month later, in August. Again, accompanied by Crispin, Ruth and I travelled on the Felixstowe–Zeebrugge night ferry crossing but varied the route thereafter. It was as enjoyable as before and we found new treks into the mountains, where the alpine plants were even more stunning and I took a lot of photographs for Ruth to pore over in later years. It was hay-making time in the upper regions of the Alps, with the grass cut by scythe in tiny meadow pastures containing a vast variety of flowers and grasses. The weather was perfect and the hay, of the highest quality that I have ever seen, was raked, gathered and bundled by hand. These bundles were then attached to pulleys on high wires of permanent construction and despatched down steep slopes to the nearest point from which they could be led by horse and cart to barns in the lower villages. Our sheep would have loved that hay.

On one day of the holiday we drove from Obergurgl past Hochgurgl to traverse the 8,117-feet-high Timmelsjoch pass into Merano and Bolzano in Italy, a breathtaking journey with magnificent views that could only be undertaken by slow-moving cars and motorcycles; the road closed for most of the year. On our homeward journey we made time to visit the attractive city of Bruges, sometimes referred to as the *Venice of the North*, with its maze of winding cobbled alleys and picturesque canals – one of the most popular resorts in the world in the late nineteenth century.

At the end of September Ruth and I were assisted by one of Yorkshire's best-known livestock farmers in the selection of further Wensleydale breeding stock. Jack Ripley farmed in the adjacent village of Hauxwell and was renowned as a breeder and outstanding exhibitor of shorthorn cattle and Charollais and Teeswater sheep. He was a quietly spoken and modest self-made farmer who, if he needed to criticise, would always express his opinion in a gentle and diplomatic manner, choosing his words with care. For example, if you asked his opinion of a ram that you quite fancied, he might say, '*He's fine enough and tall enough – pity about his pasterns*' – which meant that the staples of his fleece were far too tightly purled (curled), that he was a lanky bugger without substance, and that he was well down on his pasterns [the sloping part of the foot just above the hoof], and should be sent directly to the butcher. Jack kindly agreed to accompany Ruth and me to the WLSBA annual show and sale at Skipton on 30 September to help us select six good ewes/ewe lambs from at least four top flocks. He selected a good, strong ewe and five ewe lambs. It was quite a costly purchase, but we wanted the best and never regretted going along with his selections.

Ruth was now a member of the Executive Committee of the Richmond Conservative Association. A by-election was on the horizon, for Leon Brittan had indicated that he would be resigning at the end of the year. There were well over 300 applications to replace him, from which a shortlist of six potential candidates was selected by the chairman of the association and a small team to attend a final selection board in mid-November. Ruth was involved in that selection as one of two 'minders' who met the six candidates, served them with coffee and chatted to them while they waited for their interview. When the interviews were concluded, and before a decision was reached, the chairman of the selection board asked the 'minders' for their opinions. Ruth's 'champion' was a 27-year-old management consultant employee of McKinsey & Company, a London-based global management consulting firm. William Hague was born in Rotherham and had been educated at Wath Comprehensive School and Oxford, where he became President of the Oxford Union and obtained a first in PPE (Philosophy, Politics and Economics), followed by an MBA at the renowned INSEAD Business School in Fontainebleau.

1989

Exhibiting Wensleydale Sheep and Serving the Community

Ruth was delighted when William Hague [now The Rt Hon The Lord Hague of Richmond] was selected, and it was our pleasure to give him active support in the by-election that was held on 23 February 1989, and for many years thereafter. Richmond was one of the safest Conservative seats in the country, but this time it was a contest that became too close for comfort. This was because William Hague was virtually unknown at the time and because of the popularity of a local farmer (the Social Democrat candidate) and the influx of a multitude of well-organised Liberal and Social Democrat canvassers from other parts of the country. The result was declared as:

- William Hague (Conservative) 19,543
- Mike Potter (Social Democrat) 16,909
- Barbara Pearce (Social & Liberal Democrat) 11,589

Three of our aged Mule and Masham ewes had now died and the remaining fifteen would be '7 or 8 shear' when sheared in the summer. This would have to be the last year for most of them. We gave them very special care in their late pregnancy and at lambing time, but six produced triplets and there were inevitably some weaklings that did not survive. Nevertheless, we were still able to raise twenty-seven lambs, though a few were bottle fed. The record of *Freckles* was quite spectacular – nineteen lambs in seven years – though in each of the five years that she had triplets one lamb was bottle fed. *Wellington* was a close second. When the time came for them to go, they were not sent to market but received the same individual attention from a veterinary surgeon as a well-loved household pet would have received. They were well used to injections and some of them died chewing their cud.

No matter how busy we might be, Ruth and I rarely missed daily news broadcasts. One event in particular gripped us from mid-April until its brutal climax on 4 June: the huge student-led uprising in Beijing [Peking], capital of the People's Republic of China, demanding democracy, freedom of the press and speech, and a more western lifestyle. It was characterised by the typical passion, vigour, disorganisation, naïvety and optimism that we elders love to see in young people when unleashed from the parental home; all sharing their diverse liberal thoughts. Enormous numbers of students and other young people of the city (population 6,626,000 at the time) converged on Tiananmen [the Gate of Heavenly Peace] and on 21 April more than 100,000 had occupied its great square – the symbolic heart of Communist China. Numbers were to reduce as they became besieged by the military and pounded by foul weather, becoming increasingly weak with hunger and illness. Then, during the night of 3/4 June the People's Liberation Army moved forward, launching an unforgivable assault at first light with tanks and bullets. An iconic image that illustrates the brave defiance of the students remains entrenched in my mind; an unknown man in a white shirt blocking the path of the lead tank … as the tank commander tried to move round him he danced in its path, again and again … then scrambled onto the turret, shouting at the crew to turn back. He remains an unknown hero; the image now as famed as that of the naked little girl screaming in terror as she ran down a street in Vietnam in June 1972 following a napalm attack by the US airforce.

Ruth and I were intent on exhibiting our Wensleydales again at the GYS. We were grateful for the valuable advice and help from Jack Ripley, and also for that from Stanley Bainbridge, the head of the Bainbridge family who were third-generation sheep farmers at Marrick Abbey (at the side of the river Swale) and his son Andrew. The Swale is known in Yorkshire as the *holy river*, gaining this title in the seventh century when St Paulinus carried out mass baptisms along the river; authenticity confirmed by St Bede a century later. The Bainbridges' pasture farm extended along the *holy river* and northwards and upwards to the moors – in all, about 750 acres. What they didn't know about sheep wasn't worth knowing, so when they invited Ruth and me to bring our hoggs (unclipped yearlings) to Marrick Abbey on 8 May for some preparatory work and for washing in the *holy river*, we readily accepted. When this preparatory work was completed the sheep were returned to our trailer and I was instructed to back it up to one of their large open trailers, into which the sheep were transferred. With ourselves and Stanley Bainbridge in the trailer [with the sheep], we were towed by a tractor down to a select spot on the river where there was a rocky shelf, a deep pool, and no mud. Andrew backed the trailer into the water; we lowered the tail gate, whereupon Andrew backed a few more feet … until the water was just entering the trailer and we were overlooking a six-foot-deep crystal-clear pool. All we had to do was push the sheep out. By the time they had swum to the bank they were wonderfully clean and soon glistening in the warm sunshine. The process was repeated three weeks later, when decisions were taken as to which should be clipped for GYS entry as shearlings and which should remain unclipped as hogg in wool entries. In taking these decisions we would also consider whether any of the fleece taken from the shearlings might be of GYS fleece class quality. It was important that this preparation was conducted at the right time and in the right conditions to ensure that the fleece had recovered its lustre, while sheep that were to be entered as shearlings had time to grow sufficient new fleece. Ruth and I were soaking-in all this information, and it was not long before Ruth was showing a real talent with the [hand] shears. However, our clever *holy river* washing procedure was to go spectacularly wrong a year later when one sheep set off for the far bank and the others followed. Two collies were already positioned on the far bank and tried to turn them, but to no avail for our Wensleydales had never been disciplined by a collie. They climbed up the steep bank into a thicket, and it began to rain. An hour later we had them back – but you have never seen such a mess.

There was a lump in my throat when Ruth received her first rosette in the show ring at the GYS on 11 July. It was only for Reserve (fifth place), but it was a very competitive class of some twelve entries. Soon afterwards she received a green rosette for fourth place in another large class and £9 prize money. We were both delighted, and again we enjoyed the camaraderie that we had with fellow exhibitors, as well as the evening barbecue and banter. Our modest success at the GYS encouraged us to enter at other northern shows, and by the end of the year we had won two Breed Championships, two Reserve Championships, nine first prizes, five second prizes and four third prizes. I would pay the entry fees and Ruth would take the prize money, an arrangement that she loved, but she rarely spent any of it on herself.

It was in the autumn of 1989 that the Communist Soviet empire, which had threatened Western Europe since the end of World War II, began to noticeably crumble. There was widespread unrest, including two million indigenous inhabitants of Estonia, Latvia and Lithuania joining hands on 23 August in an uninterrupted 600-kilometre-long chain (the Baltic Way) to demand freedom and independence from the Soviet Union. On the following day a non-Communist became head of government in Poland. Two months later Hungary abolished the Hungarian People's Republic. The West held its breath.

On 15 October Ruth and I were deeply shocked to learn of the sudden death that day of James Edward Simpson (Ted), the husband of Nanette, Ruth's best friend from early TGS schooldays. Nanette, Ruth and I were together in the same form for five years, and Ruth and I were godparents to their second daughter (Carole). Ted Simpson was only 65 years old, a strong and active man of good physique who, in conjunction with Nanette and their two sons, Edward and Geoffrey, ran the family's mixed farm of 350 acres in Walton. Their eldest daughter was Sheila. Ted died from a vicious heart attack, without any forewarning. We were devastated. He and Nanette were regular visitors to Old Hall and to our delight would spontaneously drive up the A1 to see us whenever their busy farming programme permitted. We attended Ted's funeral at a packed St Peter's Church, Walton, four days later.

The late-evening news of 9 November 1989 will remain in my mind for ever, as Ruth and I sat together listening to the first reports of the Eastern Bloc crossing points at the Berlin Wall being thrown open by the border guards following a dramatic, unpredictable and rapid escalation of events during the day. To view live images of the joy of East and West Berliners embracing and celebrating on top of the wall and within the 'death strip' where so many freedom-seeking people had been shot as they tried to escape to the West was very emotional. The building of the wall began in August 1961, while we were in Malaya, an enormous and cruel obstacle intended to prevent thousands of disillusioned citizens each year from circumventing Communist emigration restrictions and border patrols and defecting in their quest for a new life of liberty and opportunity in the West. The wall was built to plug one of the most popular escape routes, for once entry was achieved to West Berlin it was possible to fly from there to freedom. Some 5,000 East Germans had braved the watchtowers, the machine guns, the razor wire and other obstacles in dashes for freedom. Few succeeded. The best known of the 12 strictly controlled crossing points was Checkpoint C, but the phonetic alphabet Charlie was naturally adopted, so it became Checkpoint Charlie. Arguably, the most daring and ingenious escape through Checkpoint Charlie was that made on 5 May 1963 by Austrian Hans Meixner who wished to take his East German sweetheart (Thurau) and her mother to a new life in his homeland. The problem was how to drive the three of them at speed beneath a 37½ inch high obstructing steel barrier manned by armed guards? It was resolved by purchasing an Austin-Healey Sprite, removing the windscreen, deflating the tyres slightly, lying an out of sight Thurau behind himself, with potential mother-in-law in the boot (behind a few bricks to absorb likely hail of bullets). **Action**: hit accelerator; whiz round vertical bars; duck at last moment [2 inches to spare] … and **"welcome to West Berlin"**. Perhaps this lyric springs to mind:

Blossom of snow, may you grow and grow
Bloom and grow forever
Edelweiss, Edelweiss
Bless my homeland forever …

The Berlin Wall was a symbol of the Cold War and the Soviet Iron Curtain that NATO had defied since its inception on 4 April 1949. Having served with or alongside NATO forces for so many years, Ruth and I were able to understand and share the exultation and sheer delight of the East and West German people as they danced together on the wall that night, for NATO's military wives and their children had faced the same Soviet threat and danger as their husbands. In their jubilation, some of those who climbed on the wall just before midnight wielded sledge hammers, fracturing the concrete. The destruction of the wall began with their first strikes, seen by Ruth and me, tucked up in bed – observers of an event which may prove to be of similar magnitude as the storming of the Bastille in Paris on 14 July 1789.

Revolutions and changes of government in Czechoslovakia and Romania followed. The end of the Cold War was determined on 3 December 1989, when Soviet leader Mikhail Gorbachev met with US president George Bush aboard a Soviet ship in Malta's Marsaxlokk Bay. However, two years of political "unshackling action" were needed before the Soviet flag was symbolically lowered from Moscow's Kremlin, on Christmas Day 1991.

There seemed to be no limit to Ruth's stamina and willingness to serve the community and the organisations in which she believed. She was now a governor of Hunton School and I enjoyed escorting her to the open day and the annual carol service. We both believed that an abundance of voluntary help was an essential ingredient to a happy community, though I must admit that my contribution was mostly to help Ruth in her commitments. However, I was continuing to support the Yorkshire Area of Boys' Clubs as a member of the Executive Committee, and rarely arrived home before 10 p.m. following their monthly evening meetings in the Bradford/Leeds area.

Christmas was as active and enjoyable as ever. In addition to the school carol service there was a quite large village carol-singing group which would always sing two or three carols at Old Hall, while early in the new year there was an annual three-day village pantomime, which always revealed unexpected talent. Hunton was a vibrant, unspoilt farming village.

Ruth and I enjoyed the traditional family gathering at Old Hall and also the exchange of hospitality with our increasing number of friends in the dale. The family also learned with delight from Justin and Haley that a baby could be expected in early May!

1990

IRA Attacks, a Granddaughter and Crispin's Degree Presentation

1990 began with Poland withdrawing from the Warsaw Pact, the US invading Panama, Glasgow heralding its year as European Capital of Culture and the tower of Pisa almost falling. However, these diverse events soon paled to the unexpected release from prison of Nelson Mandela on 11 February after serving 27 years of his life sentence. The release was on the order of South Africa's President F.W. de Klerk, who realised that to procrastinate further would plunge his country into racial civil war. The leaders of the anti-apartheid movement, the African National Congress (ANC), were in exile in Lusaka (capital of Zambia) where there was much jubilation when the news was verified. However, many wondered how effective Mandela might be after so many years behind bars. Their concerns soon evaporated as Mandela eloquently described his vision and objectives; the dismantling of apartheid and fostering racial reconciliation throughout the country. He became President of the ANC in 1991 and led his party to victory in the 1994 election. Mandela was South Africa's President for five years, receiving more than 250 honours, including the Nobel Peace Prize. He died on 5th December 2013, aged 95, one of the greatest national leaders of his generation.

There had been numerous IRA attacks on the British mainland against both civilian and military targets for the past two decades, but in early 1990 there was strong intelligence that Army recruiting offices and recruiting staff were to be singled out. We had been in close liaison with the appropriate security services for several years and protective actions and plans were reviewed for the umpteenth time. The first action of the day was always a thorough examination of one's own car, including the boot and the engine compartment, as well as beneath with a long-handled mirror torch, though the geese would always tell us during the night if there were any prowlers. Routes to work were varied, as well as where we parked our cars, and I and my staff would try to be in civilian clothes as much as possible, regularly checking whether we were being followed. The security of each recruiting office was regularly reviewed and tested by the security services and their recommendations promptly implemented. Nevertheless, we all felt rather vulnerable. The first office to be targeted was the Combined Services Recruitment Centre in Leicester on 20 February, when a device was attached to a vehicle, injuring two people. This was followed five days later by a device being detonated at the Halifax Recruiting Office, but there were no injuries. Devices exploded at other recruiting offices later in the year and on 17 September an Army colour sergeant was shot and injured as he sat in a car outside the Finchley Recruiting Office. But apart from following the recommendations of the security services and being vigilant, there was not much else that could be done by recruiting staff.

There was intense excitement and some concern within the family on the evening of Sunday 8 April when we learned of Haley's early admission to the Clarendon (maternity) wing of Leeds General Infirmary. The telephone rang at Old Hall at 1 a.m. on the following day and a jubilant Justin announced the arrival at 12.17 a.m. of a daughter weighing 8lb 3ozs, later to be called Charlotte, confirming that mother and baby were both doing well.

Further pride soon followed when Ruth and I learned from Crispin that he had obtained a very creditable 2/1 degree in Forestry at Aberdeen. The degree ceremony was held on the afternoon of 5 July and we travelled up by car, spending two nights in Aberdeen so that we might have plenty of time to see the city as well as the ceremony. We thoroughly enjoyed the occasion and returned with Crispin to Old Hall for a weekend of intensive shepherding and preparation for the three-day GYS, penning our exhibits at the showground on the Monday afternoon. We gained more experience, but only one rosette (pink) for a fifth place, such was the level of competition. However, we did enjoy the 8th Signal Regiment Summer Ball on the Saturday evening. John had kindly cut our grass while we were at the show and the hot weather conditions were perfect, enabling us to lead in 199 high-quality bales of hay from our top meadow on the Sunday afternoon.

We were more fortunate with our entries at the Royal Lancashire Show on 28 July, winning three second prizes, but sadly we lost the very good company of Crispin the next day, as we had to take him to Dunoon, the primary resort on the beautiful Cowal peninsula, for his first employment. This was with Tilhill Forestry, where he was involved in commercial forest management, from design and approval to site preparation, supervision of fencing, draining, planting, weeding, fertilising, thinning and harvesting. Dunoon was close to Holy Loch, where the USA Polaris nuclear submarine base was installed in 1961, but with the gradual evaporation of the Cold War its importance was in decline, and there were now plans for its closure. This was causing much consternation in the local area because of the inevitable reduction in employment and local business. We visited Crispin again in early October and he seemed well settled and happy in his work. Mark was now living in Woking, working for Smith Associates, a high-powered technical consultancy firm in Guildford. Much of his time was spent on classified work for the Ministry of Defence, so he did not say much about it, preferring to talk instead about the crazy kayaking escapades that he and his friends enjoyed in such diverse locations as the Thames weirs, Dartmoor, Scotland, Wales, France and the Himalayas.

The spell of hot weather continued, peaking in early August. It was a particularly uncomfortable day in Leeds on 2 August (93.9°F/34°C), while on the following day it reached 98.8°F/37.1°F in Cheltenham. We continued to exhibit our Wensleydales at a series of agricultural shows that hot summer, considering these activities to be our annual holiday; the Lancaster & Morecambe Show, the Wensleydale Show at Leyburn, the Reeth Show in Swaledale, the Westmorland County Show at Crooklands near Kendal, the Nidderdale Show at Pateley Bridge and the unique Masham Sheep Fair. We were quite successful, taking the Breed Championship and Reserve Supreme Championship at Masham, the Breed Championships at both the Westmorland County Show and the Nidderdale Show, and the Reserve Breed Championship at Leyburn, together with several first prizes. Most of the shows would forward the prize money by post a few weeks later, but at some shows it was the practice for the judge's steward to hand out the prize money in a sealed envelope at the same time as the rosettes, as each class was judged. Ruth and I would stuff the envelopes into the large pockets of our white coats as we hurriedly returned sheep to their pens, bringing out others for the next class. As soon as the judging was over, Ruth routinely disappeared. I would eventually find her in some quiet corner counting all her money. When she saw me, Ruth would beckon me over, turn out my pockets, and continue her counting. These events gave us so many happy memories, irrespective of our success. We enjoyed the atmosphere and the competition; the woolly smell of the sheep within an aroma of newly cut grass; the banter and socialising amongst wonderful country folk; and talking to visitors – describing the history and attributes of the breed, and our amusing experiences with them on the farm. As we won more prizes an increasing number of people became interested in purchasing our Hunton bloodline, and we began to recover the cost of purchasing quality foundation stock.

The dramatic dismantling of the Berlin Wall obstacle on 9 November 1989 and the subsequent resignation of the East German politburo had been followed in March 1990 by free multi-party elections. By October, East and West Germany were reunited and all trace of Communist control was evaporating. Furthermore, during 1990 Yugoslavia staged a series of elections that saw the Communists rejected in favour of nationalist parties in each of the federation's six republics. Four of the republics soon declared independence from what was left of the Yugoslav state, which by

1991 comprised just Serbia and Montenegro. Bulgaria and Albania soon followed suit, discarding Communist rule during 1990 and 1991.

In a rural community the autumn is a relatively quiet period that falls between harvesting and Christmas. It is therefore a period that attracts a multitude of social events, particularly fundraising events. Ruth had now been invited to be a member of the Constituency Women's Committee, which raised thousands of pounds each year for the Richmond Conservative Association by organising and running formal events in the many grand houses and castles in the constituency, and she had been pleased to accept. The ladies on this committee were very talented, hands-on and sleeves-rolled-up people, not lacking in social position and contacts. Their leader was called Sheilah; the lady who had chaired the committee that had selected William Hague to be our MP. I recall being an usher cum dogsbody at one such event and having to advise a very important gentleman that he was in a no-smoking area. 'Who says so?' he snapped. 'Sheilah Pitman,' I replied. He put the cigarette out immediately. No one trifled with Sheilah, but a more kindly lady you would never find, and Ruth and I were to eventually regard her as a good friend. Never a week passed during the autumn without there being a good selection of either constituency or branch fundraising events, and it mattered not whether we were involved in the behind– the-scenes work or were attending without any obligations. Indeed, the kitchen or bar-work banter and chat often enhanced the evening, while everything stopped for William Hague's witty after-dinner oratory, which was second to none in the country. In addition to these political events there were also CPRE (Council for the Protection of Rural England) and charity fundraising events plus, of course, private functions with local friends. And to think that when Ruth and I purchased Old Hall some of our friends living at a distance were concerned that we might find Wensleydale rather lonely and isolated when the clocks were put back, with nothing to do on those dark evenings.

In early August 1990 there was shock, anger and widespread international condemnation when Iraq's President Saddam Hussein invaded and annexed Kuwait, prompting an immediate build-up of United States–led coalition forces to regain the illegally seized territory and protect Saudi Arabia against similar conquest – Operation Desert Shield (2 August 1990 – 16 January 1991), the first phase of the Gulf War.

On 28 November, Margaret Thatcher, the longest serving British prime minister of the 20th century, and one of the greatest, was removed from office. I never tire of reading about her life (avoiding her tragic death): from humble grocer's daughter to **The Baroness Thatcher LG OM DStJ PC FRS Hon FRSC**. Of the many opinions that I have read on the 'Iron Lady' I have selected that of biographer John Campbell;

Margaret Thatcher was not merely the first woman and the longest-serving Prime Minister of modern times, but the most admired, most hated, most idolised and most vilified public figure of the second half of the twentieth century. To some she was the saviour of her country who [...] created a vigorous enterprise economy which twenty years later was still outperforming the more regulated economies of the Continent. To others she was a narrow ideologue whose hard-faced policies legitimised greed, deliberately increased inequality [...] and destroyed the nation's sense of solidarity and civic pride. There is no reconciling these views: yet both are true.

Margaret Thatcher died on 8th April 2013, aged 87.

1991

Ruth's Wensleydale Flock, a Holiday and Another Granddaughter

The traditional Old Hall Christmas was as enjoyable as ever, but there were more dark clouds on the horizon as the recession deepened and we moved into 1991. On 5 January gales across Britain caused 27 deaths and twelve days later the second phase of the Gulf War began – Operation Desert Storm (17 January – 28 February 1991). Unemployment passed 2 million, rising sharply. The IRA launched a mortar attack on Downing Street on 7 February which blew in the windows of the Cabinet room during a meeting of the War Cabinet, followed by bomb attacks on Paddington and Victoria stations on 18 February. A vicious cold snap did not help with our early lambing and the village was cut off due to heavy snow for a couple of days; minus 16.0°C recorded at Cawood (near York) on 14th February. A depressing start to the year.

Operation Desert Storm involved coalition forces from thirty-four nations, led by the United States. It was an efficient military operation that began with a devastating 38-day air campaign against Iraq's political hierarchy, military command and communications structure, to ensure air superiority. The subsequent ground assault began on 24 February and required only four days to achieve the mandated aim of liberating Kuwait

– a decisive victory for the coalition forces. British forces made the second-largest contribution, behind that of the United States.

The Joint Commander of the British Force was Air Chief Marshall Sir Patrick 'Paddy' Hine GCB GBE, under whom I had served while at RAF Wildenrath. United Nations Security Council Resolution 687, passed on the cessation of hostilities, required Iraq to relinquish any weapons of mass destruction and also any related materials or development programmes. It placed Saddam Hussein in a quandary, in that if he were to fully and transparently comply, Iraq's vulnerability would be apparent to neighbouring states (notably, Iran), while defiance of the UN resolution could result in serious consequences. Subsequent resolutions and political disputes were to eventually lead to further hostilities twelve years later in the Second Iraq War.

Commenting on this first Gulf War many years later, former SAS commanding officer, Colonel Richard Williams MBE MC wrote in an article for THE TIMES: … *But ultimately, success and failure on the battlefield comes down to the leadership and operator skills at the sharp end, where the metal meets the meat. For all the technical advances in warfare we have seen since 1991, it remains the case that wars are not won by equipment, plans or information alone. In the final analysis, it comes down to fighting men and women who simply refuse to be defeated by circumstances, fear, loss of comrades or the unexpected. As an old boss of mine – and one of the greatest combat leaders of the Falklands war – told me once, 'Battles are won by the side that can absorb the cock-ups better than the other side'. Or to put it another way, as the great historian of the Roman empire Edward Gibbon did when describing the characteristics of Alaric the Goth, 'an invincible temper of mind that rises superior to all adversity'.*

Two of my enterprising sergeants approached me in early April for permission to arrange an abseiling event in Wakefield at the end of the month to raise funds for the Gulf Trust. I checked that the team was authorised by the Ministry of Defence and told them that they had my full support. I gave them some sponsorship money and congratulated them on their initiative. By the time that I arrived at the tallest building in Wakefield that Saturday morning there was quite a crowd of spectators cheering on the abseilers, together with a media presence. I was very pleased and relieved to see how well the event had been organised by

Sergeants Hawes and Holt and joined in the applause, dipping further into my wallet to sponsor the volunteers. 'Will you have a go, sir?' asked Sergeant Hawes. I could hardly chicken out, so I replied, 'Only if you can get a minimum of £50 sponsorship,' hoping that everyone had run out of money. He came back in about ten minutes with a grin on his face and I climbed the stairs to the top. I changed my trilby for a helmet, though I could not understand how it might help me in an emergency, and started to descend with some trepidation, in my best tweed suit. I had not gone far when I was joined on an adjacent rope by a charming young lady with a camera; an enthusiastic and ambitious correspondent called Coral Kovac. I just wanted to get to the bottom slowly and safely, but Coral insisted on teaching me how to bounce off the wall and all that jazz – for her camera shots.

It was at about that time that Ruth and I showed some potential buyers around our Wensleydale flock. As usual, I probably did most of the talking. When they had departed I found Ruth rather quiet. Eventually, she said, '*My* Wensleydale flock,' and went on to tell me that she had supported me in my military career from the day that we were married and that in terms of Wensleydale sheep activities it was time for the roles to be reversed. I was rather taken aback, but the more I thought about it the more I realised that she was right. A couple of hours later I said to Ruth, '*Your* Wensleydale flock,' and received a very nice kiss of appreciation. It was a symbolic moment – from the time of the suffragette movement and during two world wars the role and freedom of women in British society rapidly changed, but during the time that I served in the Army, the wives of British officers were still expected to more or less continue the traditional subservient role of supporting husband and regiment, almost as it had been in Victorian times. Ruth had given me tremendous support in my military career and I had no problem in repaying that support, Wensleydale sheep included. The appropriate change was made to the breed society (WLSBA), and show entries were subsequently submitted excluding my name.

Despite our best efforts, Ruth was only awarded a fourth prize at the GYS, but it was in the particularly competitive Hogg in Wool class. We were both disappointed that her shearling ram had not been in the prizes, but we were told that he was at '11 o'clock' and needed at least another month of maturity. This proved to be the case, for *Hunton Cavalier* went on to take the Breed Championship at both the Westmorland and Nidderdale shows later in the year. Ruth was now a member of the WLSBA Council and overall had a good year, taking a total of three Breed Championships and three Reserve Championship awards. She also won the gimmer lamb class at the WLSBA annual show and sale at Skipton, the lamb selling for 270 guineas.

It had been a particularly hectic summer, for in addition to the farming and sheep activities and the Summer Ball, we had been involved in several charity and political fundraising events, including participating in the new Hunton open gardens event to raise funds for a new scanner at the Friarage Hospital in Northallerton. However, this year we had a holiday to which we could look forward – an 'autumn getaway' cruise on P&O's *Canberra*. Also, another grandchild, due at Christmas.

Our journey to Southampton docks on 24 October to board *Canberra* reminded us of our departure for Malaya in 1960, though it was at a different time of the year. We travelled by train to King's Cross, hailed a porter and took a taxi to Waterloo, where we parted with our luggage, not to see it again until we were in our cabin; then by a boat train which stopped alongside *Canberra*. However, there was no responsibility for a Moses basket and baby this time – only ourselves to think about. *Canberra* was a very popular ship because of her contribution to the Falklands War as a troop carrier, anchoring in San Carlos Water on 21 May 1982 with a passenger list of Paras and Royal Marines. She was known as the Great White Whale and was launched at the Harland & Wolff yard in Belfast a fortnight before we sailed for Malaya, built as a liner for the UK–Australia route, but refitted as a cruise ship in 1974. *Canberra* had a displacement of 45,000 tons and authorisation to carry 1,641 passengers, which placed her among the largest cruise ships at that time, but rather puny compared with some of the monsters of today which are many times that size.

We departed in traditional manner with band playing, much ticker tape and a glass of champagne as the sun was setting. As *Canberra* eased from her berth and the music of the band faded in the distance Ruth and I had a second glass of champers and relaxed. It was total relaxation, for everything that we needed for the next thirteen days and 3,811 nautical miles would be provided for us as we sailed to and from the South Atlantic, calling at La Coruña, Gran Canaria, Tenerife, Madeira, Gibraltar and Lisbon. We had fine weather, pleasant company of similar age at our table, magnificent food and theatre entertainment of West End standard, and a nice balance of the informal and formal.

The ports were sufficiently interesting that we only made two hinterland bus tours. The first was a full-day tour on 30 October in Tenerife, incorporating the Teide National Park, the volcanic crater of Las Cañadas, the Orotava Valley and lunch at a good restaurant in the popular resort of Puerto de la Cruz. We thought the overall tour cost of £64 for both of us, including lunch and wine, very reasonable. The following day we were fast alongside at Funchal, Madeira at 9 a.m. and only thirty minutes later we were sauntering towards the town centre and the colourful fish and flower markets. We had heard so much about the world-famous Belmond Reid's Palace Hotel from Ruth's uncle Charles and aunt Elsie that we decided to walk up the gentle slope to the hotel and chance our luck at being able to have morning coffee on its well–known terrace. Having explained our mission, we were well received and guided to a virtually empty terrace for a memorable morning coffee at a modest price, looking down on the bay used by the Sunderland flying boats that carried Charles and Elsie to and from Madeira for their winter holidays many years previously. I made use of the famous gents' marble toilet in the basement and described it to Ruth on my return. She was rather envious, and appropriate arrangements were made for her to have a discreet private viewing. In the afternoon we went on our second bus tour – to the interior of the island, incorporating a most pleasant Levada (mini-canal) walk.

We had thoroughly enjoyed our 'autumn getaway', and on the boat train to Waterloo we decided that we should aim to have a similar holiday in a couple of years' time. It was virtually impossible for us to take a holiday at any other time of the year because of our farming commitments, and the climate of the South Atlantic isles in late October/early November was ideal. Ruth told me that as far as she was concerned the ship need not stop at a port – it would be just as enjoyable if it cruised slowly round and round the islands for ten days, allowing her to swim, sunbathe and read while enjoying the good food and entertainment.

1991 was a historic year for democracy and freedom in Europe. With the Eastern Bloc free of the Soviet Union, the Soviet empire itself began to crumble. In April, Georgia voted to secede from the USSR and Russia eventually recognised the independence of Latvia, Lithuania and Estonia, its Baltic republics. Following a failed coup against Soviet leader Mikhail Gorbachev in August, the Soviet Union began to disintegrate – the Ukraine declared independence, followed by the Soviet Union's Central Asian republics. On 8 December the Soviet Union ceased to exist.

The Cold War ended on 24th/25th December 1991 with Gorbachev resigning as Soviet President and the post abolished … the Soviet flag was lowered from the Moscow Kremlin.

A key insider at crucial events in the Cold War was British diplomat and ambassador Sir Christopher Leslie George Mallaby GCMG GCVO. I recommend his memoirs, "Living the Cold War [ISBN 978 1 4456 6961 8]". His chapter 18 [SUMMING UP THE COLD WAR] is the most scholarly that I have read. This biography is also very interesting in the description of his formative years and the value of outstanding linguistic ability.

Christmas excitement at Old Hall was more intense than ever that year as we awaited the arrival of the new baby. Then, precisely as forecast, the telephone rang at midday on 27 December 1991 and Justin proudly announced the arrival at 11.15 a.m. of a second granddaughter (Jessica), weighing 7lbs 13 ozs. We were delighted and the champagne flowed.

1992

Political and Show Successes, but Annus Horribilis for Her Majesty

Although the United Kingdom was still in recession and almost 10% of the workforce unemployed, 1992 began with a degree of optimism, and also some glitter as the Queen celebrated her Ruby Jubilee on 6 February. However, Ruth and I were very unhappy on the following day as our country's signature was given to the Treaty on European Union (the Maastricht Treaty), while by the end of the year Her Majesty was describing 1992 as her 'annus horribilis'. This was because of the break-up of the marriages of her second son (the Duke of York) and her daughter (the Princess Royal), together with the publication of the Princess of Wales' more-than-embarrassing book, *Diana, Her True Story*, and a serious fire at her beloved Windsor Castle.

The Conservative Party, to which we continued to give much active support, won a fourth term of office at the general election held on 9 April 1992. It was a surprise victory, for as late as 1 April opinion polls were forecasting a Labour victory. On the eve of election day Ruth was canvassing in Garforth, near Leeds, with a group of fellow Conservative activists and returned with morale sky high, confidently predicting a Conservative win. Labour leader Neil Kinnock had delivered an arrogant, over-confident speech at a rally in Sheffield a few hours earlier, but Ruth was adamant that he was in for a shock and that the tide had turned at the nth hour. On election day the front– page headline of the *Sun* newspaper, which had strongly supported the Conservative Party throughout the campaign, urged the last person leaving Britain to 'turn out the lights' if Labour won. We stayed up late that night and had very little sleep, enjoying the succession of surprise results in favour of the Conservative Party in a high (77%) turnout. The outcome defied all predictions – the Conservative Party had received the largest number of votes in British history, breaking the record set by Labour in 1951, though with an overall majority reduced to 21 seats. The euphoria did not last long, for on 16 September, due to market pressure, the government was forced to withdraw the pound sterling from the European Exchange Rate Mechanism (ERM) that it had joined in October 1990. The day came to be known as 'Black Wednesday', but as the years passed it became apparent that this 'catastrophe' was a blessing in disguise, and as I write these memoirs the pound sterling remains one of the world's strongest currencies.

Our farming activities were now following a regular pattern. We had adopted the practice of 'sponging' a few of our Wensleydale ewes in August to bring them into season early, with a view to their lambing in late January or February, some six weeks earlier than normal. This was the practice of several of our competitors, and we followed suit to ensure that our lambs could compete with theirs without handicap in the show and sale rings. However, it was not always successful, and it extended the lambing period and made the grass management very difficult in prolonged wintry conditions. We hosted a WLSBA Workshop at Old Hall in early May 1992, which proved very popular, followed in early July by participation in the now regular Hunton Open Gardens Day – to raise funds for the Friarage Hospital scanner. A week later it was the GYS at Harrogate, followed by a clutch of other shows, and haymaking. The GYS was as enjoyable (and competitive) as ever, but a third place in the Shearling Ewe class and Reserve in the Hogg in Wool class was very modest progression. I felt rather sorry for Ruth, particularly as she was always such a good loser. However, during the remaining weeks of the show season she won the Breed Championship at the Royal Lancashire Show, the Wensleydale Show (Leyburn) and the Masham Sheep Fair, followed by presentations to her of three very fine silver trophies at the WLSBA show and sale at Skipton, plus lots of pocket money, so there was no need for any further sympathy. Ruth was also doing rather well with her stock and wool sales. We treated ourselves to a long weekend in London in early November, seeing *The Phantom of the Opera*, soon followed by a tenth brilliant family Christmas gathering at Old Hall; the family getting larger year on year.

1993

Retirement, More Show Successes and a Grandson

The year 1993 was to be my final full year of employment, as I was obliged to retire on reaching my sixtieth birthday. My work as an Army Careers Officer based in Leeds was as intense as ever and my ability to give so much time to our farming life and other activities at Old Hall was due to very careful planning and utilisation of my annual leave allocation, plus evening, weekend and public holiday time. However, I was now beginning to look forward to retirement day, especially to no longer having to drive such long distances to and from Leeds and its sub-offices each day. Although the workload continued to be quite heavy it was no less interesting and inspiring, while the social occasions were as enjoyable as ever. I no longer record these activities in my memoirs because they were routine and no different to previous years. The 1993 GYS was even more interesting and enjoyable than usual, which was attributable not to significant successes in the show ring, but to some balloon flights. Weather permitting, early each morning and sometimes in the evening, about two dozen colourful hot-air balloons of various shapes and sizes would lift off from the showground, each with a crew of 2–3 enthusiasts. They made a magnificent spectacle. On the second morning of the show, when we were not involved in any judging, I chatted to one of the teams, and on learning that they were only making a short flight, arranged a place in their basket. It was an exhilarating experience and we landed about half an hour later with only a few bumps on the Stray, not far from Bettys, where we had morning coffee – very civilised. Ruth was quite jealous and implored me to arrange for her to have a flight, which I did, for that evening. I also arranged an evening flight for myself, in a different balloon. Our cluster of balloons ascended at about 6 p.m. in a moderate breeze, travelling in a south-westerly direction. Again, I found it most exhilarating, though of a rather longer distance than I had anticipated, with landings in and around the gardens of Harewood House. I had no idea where Ruth's balloon had landed, but when we met again she told me that her balloon and that next to her had clipped some trees and crash-landed in front of Harewood House, much to the annoyance of Lord Harewood, who immediately descended the steps and remonstrated with the nearest group of 'hooligan intruders' in a threatening manner, waving a stick. He then recognised one of the hooligans – none other than the 17th Viscount Mountgarret, who was of national fame, not least for having shot at a hot-air balloon that had flown too low over his grouse moor in 1982, spattering the occupants with lead shot, and also for advocating in the House of Lords for the return of the birch, execution by lethal injection and the castration of rapists.

'... and you, Richard, the very last person that I would expect to find amongst these hooligans!'

Ruth and the other 'hooligans' resisted the temptation of contacting the Yorkshire Post with a stop-press story – Viscount Mountgarret was a rather lovable eccentric, not only descended from King Henry VII but also a keen supporter and past president of their Yorkshire County Cricket Club. They had persuaded Viscount Mountgarret to take a flight with them with much difficulty, and they were not now going to tell tales.

The next few months were a most memorable time. Ruth took both the Breed Championship and the Reserve Championship at the

Royal Lancashire Show in its centenary year, followed by the Breed Championship at the Wensleydale (Leyburn) Show and then the Supreme Championship at the annual WLSBA show and sale, collecting an armful of silver trophies. Then, on Saturday 9 October at 8.50 a.m., Justin telephoned to tell us that 25 minutes earlier Haley had given birth to our first grandson (Robert), weighing 9lbs 7ozs. We were thrilled. Life was good, especially as a fortnight later we were able to reflect on our good fortune on a relaxing twelve-day P&O cruise, again on *Canberra*, calling at Madeira, Tenerife, Gran Canaria, Lisbon and Vigo.

Another merry Christmas family gathering at Old Hall (tables sparkling with silver trophies) was followed by my army 'dining-out', in conjunction with that of my opposite number in Sheffield; Lieutenant Colonel W.J. Holbrook MBE Coldstream Guards. We had the rare privilege of the drums of the Coldstream Guards playing before us after dinner. On 6 February 1994 I retired.

During the 40+ uniformed years that I served the Army, civilian standards of personal conduct and self-discipline in my country changed enormously: noticeably following the end of National Service [1962/63] and then the very liberal ethos of the "Swinging Sixties", so strongly opposed by Mary Whitehouse CBE. The gap between military and civilian standards continued to increase, and to such an extent that **in late October 1993 the Ministry of Defence [Adjutant General] felt obliged to issue a directive paper**, "for the attention of all ranks" [of both the Regular and Territorial Army]. It was entitled, "**The Military Ethos**", and its aim was to explain the requirement for high standards of personal conduct and respect for the law demanded of those in military Service. Debate on the Military Ethos will never cease in democratic countries. However, for the record**, the following extracts describe the standards that the British Army sought in October 1993:**

TRENDS IN SOCIETY
5. Within society the formative influences in promoting positive attitudes towards authority have been in steady decline: religion, education and

the family no longer always provide the framework of behaviour, social structure, and responsibility they have in the past. More liberal attitudes prevail, leading many parts of society to reject or reduce in importance those values which the Armed Forces seek to maintain and regard so highly: sense of duty, loyalty, self-discipline, self-sacrifice, respect and concern for others.

6. The rights of the individual are enshrined increasingly in legislation which has been enacted to eliminate discrimination on the grounds of race, colour, creed and gender. Similarly other minority groups have sought to legitimise what they believe to be their rights where these are perceived to be distinguished not by physical characteristics, place of birth, or creed, but by individual behaviour. The rights and freedoms of the individual tend to be promoted over the attitudes of society generally, and where individuals fail in their responsibilities to society there is an increasing propensity to attribute this to some broader social cause or failure of government. The increase in individual freedom now available to the citizen has in many cases led to decline in both individual and corporate responsibility. This in turn has led to an erosion in respect for the law, with increases, for example, in violent street crime, burglary, and drug misuse. The promotion of individual rights has contributed to an ambivalent attitude towards an individual's responsibilities to society.

7. The Army cannot remain wholly immune from the changes in the society it serves, and from which it recruits, but neither must it allow itself to follow trends which tend to undermine the traditional values essential to its unique responsibilities and operational role. The Army recognises that its adherence to its standards must be defended on pragmatic rather than emotional and traditional grounds. It also recognises that where reform is appropriate, this must be addressed as a matter of timely policy rather than a damage limitation exercise in the face of events. Society expects a high standard of behaviour from those in public positions, including the Army. When those standards are relaxed, the trust and confidence of society risk being lost.

THE SERVICE ENVIRONMENT

8. The terms and conditions of military service differ markedly from those of civilian life. The Service aims to foster group cohesion within a structured chain of command, which is such a decisive factor in battle; but by its very nature, such cohesion can be destroyed quickly where there is a loss of trust or confidence. The majority of the military community comprises young, robust, heterosexual people. They are required to live in close proximity with others often in single-sex accommodation, to work at times under great stress and physically in close contact with one another. Servicemen and women do not have the right to choose the company with whom they work or share accommodation which often has only limited privacy. Unlike civilians they do not have the opportunity to leave their employment if the conduct of their colleagues causes offence. The effectiveness of the Army depends upon the efficient and contented service of these individuals, who make up the overwhelming majority. To allow any element to affect adversely the morale, cohesion, and hence the operational efficiency of any unit would be detrimental to its role.

THE OPERATIONAL IMPERATIVE

9. Society requires those serving in the Armed Forces to place the interests of the nation before self. It is the soldier's obligation to follow orders in the face of an enemy and to do his duty despite the risk of death or injury. It is that operational liability, with the possibility of self-sacrifice (accepted by every soldier on enlistment), that marks the Armed Services out as being essentially different from the rest of society. In order to meet these demands, the Army insists on a more exacting code of conduct.

10. A high standard of discipline is essential for operational effectiveness and the most effective discipline is that which is self-imposed. Self-discipline is the core of all discipline, and the foundation on which leadership, motivation, courage, morale and corporate discipline, are built. Without these qualities no Army could be deployed on operations with any degree of success.

11. The operational imperative of the Army stresses the importance of the group over self-interest. Armed conflict is, by its very nature, a group rather than an individual endeavor. A sense of unity, cohesion and loyalty are decisive factors in any armed conflict. Nothing must be allowed to detract from the forging of close bonds, based upon mutual trust and respect, between members of the group, and between the group and its leaders, be it section or brigade. This applies equally to low-intensity conflict where stress upon the individual can be considerable.

12. All ranks must have trust and confidence in their comrades, and in their superiors. Without this trust and confidence, sound personal relationships will not withstand the severe pressure imposed by the battlefield. In November 1944 Montgomery noted that high morale was based upon discipline, self-respect, and confidence of the soldier in his commanders ["High Command in War", Montgomery, June 1945]. The officer corps, in particular, is required to maintain the highest standards, in order that they may set an example and impose disciplinary measures when necessary. Anything less than total honesty and a high standard of personal behaviour would reflect a lack of integrity on the part of the individual, and may lose him the respect and trust of those he commands. In the military environment, leaders at all levels will, when necessary, expect their orders to be obeyed without question. Such obedience is only given by subordinates if they trust and respect their leaders.

THE LAW

13. On joining the Army, servicemen and women remain subject to the criminal law applicable to civilians. They also become subject to military law, which in a number of respects makes certain conduct a criminal offence, where in civilian life it would be lawful. The law thus imposes further obligations and demands on Service personnel.

14. Following a military or civil conviction for an offence, administrative action may be taken against an individual. Such action may also be taken for misconduct even if the individual has not been convicted of an offence. Administrative action may result, in the case of an officer, in being called upon to resign or retire, or, in the case of a soldier, in being discharged.

A Section on *Standards of Conduct* follows, under the following headings: ALCOHOL, DRUGS, DISHONESTY, INDEBTEDNESS, BULLYING and INITIATION CEREMONIES, RACIAL and SEXUAL

DISCRIMINATION and HARASSMENT, HOMOSEXUALITY, SOCIAL MISCONDUCT, SINGLE PARENTS each setting out an unambiguous military stance, summarized as follows;

> *49. Operational effectiveness requires sound discipline within the Army at all times. Discipline cannot be switched on for war and off for peace, and therefore the standards demanded of soldiers tend to be more strict than those of society as a whole. It is axiomatic therefore that all members of the Army must respect the law. For commanders, and those in positions of responsibility, where integrity is a vital ingredient of leadership, standards of conduct must be beyond reproach. Those who fail to meet these standards are failing in their duty to themselves, their superiors and their subordinates. In extreme cases this may prejudice the reputation of the Service. The standards of conduct set out above are those required to support our military ethos and maintain operational effectiveness.*

Mary Whitehouse CBE was still active when The Military Ethos was distributed to the British Army, publishing at age 83 her autobiography "Quite Contrary" the following month [ISBN 0-283-06202-9].

1994

Scottish Wedding, Royal Show Success, Kayaking and Another Granddaughter

I had been invited by the Chairman of the WLSBA, Peter Titley – later to become a very good friend and President of the Rare Breeds Survival Trust (RBST) – to provisionally be the Honorary Secretary of the WLSBA from 1 January for a few months until the AGM. I readily accepted, for I had developed a deep interest in the breed. I was accepted at the AGM on a more permanent basis and I soon found that there was no danger of my becoming idle in my retirement – membership was increasing steadily towards two hundred, the Articles of Association required an urgent rewrite, and a website and database were needed. My secretarial responsibilities extended to press and publicity, registrations and the publishing of an annual flock book. I also learned that as WLSBA Secretary, I became an ex-officio council member of the National Sheep Association.

The prospect of a second daughter-in-law was now confirmed – a delightful young lady, and of royal descent, for Aileen was a MacGregor. I was soon reading the history of the clan and the exploits of Rob Roy MacGregor. All weddings are wonderful joyous occasions, and the Church of Scotland (St John's Church) wedding of Aileen and Crispin in the seaside town of Largs, not far from the historical Highlands home of the clan, was no exception. It was a pleasure to join with Aileen's parents, Allister and Kate, and other members of the clan in the celebration of marriage and the bond between our families.

Crispin had switched from forestry to finance, and was currrently employed by Tilney & Co., founded in 1836 as R.J. Tilney and now one of the largest fund managers and stockbrokers in the country. Head Office was in Liverpool's Royal Liver Building, but with an additional office in Glasgow, where Crispin now worked. It was not a big surprise, for he had followed the stock market as a hobby for many years.

On 13 June I attended an enjoyable 40th anniversary reunion commemorating the commissioning of Sandhurst's intake 13. It was a lunchtime event, held at the Royal Hospital, Chelsea, and it was well attended. We were seated by colleges and companies, so it was not difficult to meet up with old friends, though now of very different shapes and sizes. Sadly, there was insufficient space for wives to attend, but Ruth did accompany me to the 40th anniversary reunion of those commissioned into the Royal Corps of Signals over the weekend of 6–7 August, held in the Royal Signals headquarters officers' mess, now at Blandford – an even more enjoyable event, subsequently repeated at five-yearly intervals.

As Secretary of the WLSBA I felt that I should attend the Royal Show, which was always held during the week before the GYS, together with Ruth. We then considered the feasibility of entering some of Ruth's sheep at both events and decided to go for it, without missing the 8th Signal Regiment Summer Ball. Ruth won not only two classes at the Royal Show but also the Breed Championship and consequently a place in the line-up of Breed Champions along with thirty-eight others, from which another judge would select the Supreme Champion. The judge gradually reduced the numbers until only eight champions remained, one of which was Ruth's Wensleydale champion, a hogg in wool later to be called Honeysuckle, the ewe that featured in a children's book that I was to write, *Baa Baa – the Story of a Wensleydale Sheep*. The following week Ruth won the Shearling Ewe class at the GYS and several third and fourth places, followed by Breed Championship successes at the Wensleydale

(Leyburn) Show and the RBST National Show and Sale. She was now well past the novice stage and was delighted when invitations began to arrive for her to judge at some local shows the following year.

Later in 1994, Mark was in the Himalayas with a group of kayaking friends, seeking increasingly stimulating descents. The group included a young lady whom Ruth and I never met, called Sally, whose company Mark clearly enjoyed. Not satisfied with merely dangerous descents, they ran Nepal's swift-flowing and deep Kali Gandaki Gorge, which is flanked by stunning 26,000-feet peaks; the area noted for Shaligram fossils, revered as one of five non-living forms of Lord Vishnu, the Supreme God of Vaishnavism and the second god in the Hindu triumvirate of Brahman. Mark was to describe his 'holiday' as follows:

We flew into Kathmandu and then took a local flight to the village of Pokhara which lies underneath the Annapurna Massif and next to the lake of Phewa Tal. Whilst kayaking on the lake we met some young Nepalese lads who wanted to become Gurkhas. Then we split into two groups. Six of the crazy guys including myself hired some porters to carry the kayaks (one kayak to each porter, with a head band carrying the weight), and we headed up the trail towards Annapurna base camp alongside the Modi Khola river. We had to travel light since there was little room in the kayaks, so I had just a sweater and plimsolls. We spent the night in a village under Annapurna (26,545 feet) and watched the mountain glow red in the evening sun. I was frozen since I was sleeping on the floor with a thin flea covered blanket over me. Then for the next two days we kayaked through the steep gorges of the treacherous Modi Khola, a psychotic, icy and very demanding mountain river, not for faint hearts. Each night we would find some shelter in a local village and try to warm up in our damp clothes, reflecting on the exhilaration of the run and the scares that we had experienced.

Meanwhile, the rest of the group, including Sally, were hiking down the Kali Gandaki gorge between Annapurna and Dalhaguri. Perhaps one day in my retirement I'll do that hike. We met up on a stormy day on the Kali Gandaki and then kayaked that river for the next week. It was a very, very strange trip, sort of hallucinogenic in its weirdness. The river never went anywhere near a road and all we saw were remote villages where the local children would run out of school and dive into the river for a ride on the kayaks. At night we would camp on the sandy river beaches. It became stranger and stranger as we went down the river … a bit like Conrad's story of going up the Congo in 1880 in his book 'Heart of Darkness'. I saw funeral rites with two or three family members gathered around a small bonfire, always at the junction with a third river since a fourth spiritual river went straight to heaven. I remember exploring an old abandoned Hindu Temple at night by torchlight. And then we found a bus to take us to the Himalayan 'White Water Rodeo,' where western kayakers arranged to meet up under the full moon for a few days of drinking and extreme kayaking …

Hinduism is the third largest religion in the world (after Christianity and Islam), but it is additionally, and significantly, far broader; *a way of life*, incorporating philosophies, concepts and traditions that have withstood the test of time over many thousands of years, prescribing virtues of honesty, non-violence, patience, self-restraint and compassion. One of its tenets is reincarnation, with personal actions leading to reward (or punishment) in a higher (or lower) form of life; followers striving to attain the pinnacle caste of Brahman (akin to priesthood). Without diluting my Christian beliefs, my respect for other religions and particularly Hinduism has progressively increased over the years. When Ruth did kind or goodly deeds [frequent occurrences] she would routinely comment to me that they were good for her Karma.

The year ended on a very high note with the birth to Crispin and Aileen of a baby daughter weighing 7lbs 12ozs (later to be named Lois Catherine), our fourth grandchild. The Pedley and MacGregor families were delighted!

1995

Wensleydale Sheep Activities and a Scottish Christening

No sooner was the traditional and enjoyable family Christmas at Old Hall over and the New Year of 1995 let in (by myself with lump of coal) than Ruth and I would be crossing the Pennines with some of our sheep, a WLSBA banner and a multitude of large photographs, notices and other association publicity items – to establish a display at a large 'sheep fair' within Penrith Auction Mart. We had volunteered our services a few years previously and now seemed to be saddled with the event. Livestock markets are cold, draughty places in the winter, but none colder than Cumbria's Penrith in the second week of January. However, it was always a very well-attended event and we would usually record a good number of potential members, while the wintry views from the A66 were often stunning. For Ruth there was an additional attraction, for she was a great admirer of Lady Anne Clifford (1590– 1676) who, after a legal battle lasting many years (including those of the Civil War, in which she was loyal to the King) finally inherited in 1643 the greater part of the Cumberland estates of her father, the 3rd Earl of Cumberland. At the age of almost sixty, with no remaining family responsibilities, she abandoned a comfortable life in London and travelled north to Cumbria, dedicating the remainder of her aged years to the restoration of five inherited castles that still survived, all in ruins or in poor condition. One of them was Brough Castle, which, to Ruth's delight, we passed on our journey to and from the sheep fair each year. Lady Anne Clifford refers to it in her 1659 diary as follows:

> … and this Aprill after I had first bin there my selfe to direct the Building of it, did I cause my Old Decayed Castle of Brough to be repaired, and also the old Tower called the Roman Tower in the sayd Castle and a Courthouse for keeping of my Courtes in some 12 or 14 roomes to be built in it upon the old foundacion.

Ruth was an avid reader, particularly of historical books, and of all periods. Each was studiously read by her [some many times over]. Aided by her wonderful memory, she was becoming quite a knowledgeable self-taught historian. Finding the above reference to Brough Castle in Lady Anne Clifford's diary gave her so much pleasure.

Lois was baptised in the church in which Crispin and Aileen were married (St John's Church, Largs) on 28 May, before a large Sunday–morning congregation. Ruth and I were very touched by the Church of Scotland custom of passing the newly baptised baby along the aisles, which Lois seemed to enjoy. It was a most enjoyable day and we had time to explore more of this delightful seaside town.

I had arranged a rather unusual workshop for WLSBA members a fortnight later at Sprotbrough, near Doncaster. One of our members, Alan Oliver, earned his living on the river and adjacent canal and was the owner of Sprotbrough Riverboat Company, which had a variety of freight-carrying boats and also a passenger boat named *Wyre Lady*, built on the Clyde at Dumbarton in 1938. Adjacent to *Wyre Lady*'s berth were a few acres of lush grassland – an ideal setting for our workshop. Alan not only agreed to our use of his facilities but also provided lunch and a most interesting cruise on the canal and river Don in his *Wyre Lady*, a boat with a fascinating history. At her launch she was named the *Ashton* and was first used for trips on the Clyde, where the partially built RMS *Queen Elizabeth* was a particular attraction.

Throughout World War II she served as a tender for the Royal Navy, returning to the Clyde in 1945 for a brief period as the new Gourock–Dunoon ferry, soon followed by the Largs–Millport run, which lasted until 1962. She was later used for the summer ferry service between Gourock and Helensburgh and re-named the *Gourockian*. She was given her current name in 1971 when she became the Fleetwood–Knott End ferry across the mouth of the river Wyre. Alan bought her in 1977 and brought her by sea, river and canal to Sprotbrough, where she became a popular passenger vessel on the river and canal. The workshop was a huge success.

A few days later Ruth and I were in Scotland again, this time exhibiting at the Royal Highland Show (RHS) at Ingliston, near Edinburgh Airport. It had been many years since Wensleydales had had classes at the RHS (Scotland's premier agricultural event) and shortly after becoming WLSBA Secretary I drummed up the necessary exhibitor support and applied to the Royal Highland and Agricultural Society of Scotland for classes to be re-introduced – with success. It was a four-day show and the Wensleydale classes attracted three exhibitors from Scotland and five from England. It was tremendous fun, and not only because Ruth won the Breed Championship. I particularly recollect the hospitality of one of the Scottish exhibitors, Lady Hilary Menzies, and her husband, Lord Duncan Menzies (one of Scotland's most senior judges). They kindly invited all the Wensleydale sheep exhibitors to their splendid country home one tranquil evening for strawberries and cream and other refreshment on their extensive lawns. We learnt that Lord Menzies habitually cut the lawns himself on a small tractor at high speed and in aggressive manner. Perhaps this was his way of winding down after difficult days in court. Hilary was a member of the WLSBA Council and would regularly spend the night at Old Hall prior to meetings. She and Ruth became good friends. I also recollect, albeit with some pain, the generosity of Scotland's whisky producers in the Food and Drink Exhibition Area of the RHS …

We returned to Old Hall on Sunday 25 June with a busy week ahead:

- Monday – lambs speyned (separated from their mothers).
- Tuesday – 18 ewes sheared.
- Wednesday – dental, drench rams and prepare for council meeting.
- Thursday – drench ewes and prepare for Hunton Cottage Gardens Open Day.

- Friday – WLSBA council meeting at Langho.
- Saturday – Write minutes and submit WLSBA annual return to Companies House.
- Sunday – Hunton Cottage Gardens Open Day.
- Monday – Depart for Royal Show (Ruth judging Wensleydale classes).

On our return from the Royal Show we had four days in which to complete the preparation of Ruth's entries for the Great Yorkshire Show. She did quite well, winning one of the ram classes; second in the Hogg in Wool class and several other placings. Ruth was also doing rather well with her fleece exhibits. She had now won fifteen Breed Championships; including the Royal Show, the Royal Highland Show and the WLSBA Supreme Champion award – but it was the Breed Championship at the GYS that she sought most.

I remember the summer of 1995 as being exceptionally hot and dusty, with high pollen counts. It was, in fact, the second driest since records began, with August entering the record books as the sunniest and hottest month ever recorded. These conditions made it extremely uncomfortable for Ruth, who suffered from hay fever, particularly in the dusty sheep lines at the GYS. The efficient show organisers arranged an almost continuous sprinkling of water from large bowsers but it was of little help. In some parts of the country that year, the hay crop was being used in September and then when the rains eventually came second silage crops were being taken in late October.

It was also a time of dispute in the WLSBA concerning the breeding and registration of black Wensleydales, and accordingly it was not the most comfortable time to be its secretary. Coloured fibres severely downgrade commercial white wool and the breeders of white Wensleydales were concerned that the increasing numbers of breeders of black Wensleydales and careless flock management might result in a significant increase in the hitherto small percentage of white Wensleydales carrying the black gene. This might disadvantage them in their sales of white Wensleydale rams as crossing sires on hill-breed ewes; their traditional role for more than a century. The matter was eventually overcome by the adoption of sensible recommendations by a working party, but not before the dispute had made the front page of the *Daily Telegraph*.

The combination of our many activities [notably Old Hall restoration, sheep farming/showing, WLSBA support, political activity, charity work, Hunton school and CPRE] sometimes prevented us from seeing as much of the family as we would have wished, but we made time to visit Crispin, Aileen and Lois in early August and hosted Charlotte and Jessica at Old Hall for three days in October – and of course, to our delight, everyone converged on us for Christmas, with Old Hall absorbing the increasing numbers with ease.

1996

Genetics, the BSE Crisis and a West Indies Cruise

The year began with me being extremely busy with WLSBA secretarial work, particularly in getting the annual flock book out in good time, while Ruth, in addition to her many other commitments, had volunteered to be editor of the association's occasional journal; *Wensleydale World*. Very soon our attention, and that of all sheep and cattle breeders, was focused on genetics.

Early in March 1996 two lambs seized the front pages of Britain's leading national newspapers. Two cloned lambs were experimentally bred by the Roslin Institute near Edinburgh. The institute's research showed that cells taken from a donor embryo could be extensively cultivated in a laboratory and then used with eggs taken from other female sheep from which all genetic information had been removed. These eggs would then develop into new embryos which would only have the characteristics of the donor cell, resulting in cloned lambs. Though the ram would be needed to help create the first embryo, it was suggested that he might become virtually redundant for, unlike nature's method of reproduction, where an animal inherits half its chromosomes from each parent, the cloned sheep acquires all its chromosomes from the laboratory-grown cells. The significance of this research was that it now seemed to be technically feasible to create [by genetic engineering] flocks of identical sheep, with such attractive in-bred characteristics as increased disease resistance and low-fat content. At one of the National Sheep Association (NSA) committee meetings that I attended I learnt that the NSA was as sceptical about this news, and the birth of Dolly on 5 July 1996, as it was concerned about serious proposals to re-introduce wolves to the Highlands of Scotland.

Then, on 20 March 1996 the 'Mad Cow'/BSE (bovine spongiform encephalopathy) crisis erupted, when the government finally admitted that 'BSE was likely to have been transmitted to people' – recognition that that there might be a link between BSE-contaminated beef and a variant of Creutzfeldt Jakob Disease (vCJD) in humans. Beef sales and prices plunged. On 22 March the European Union prohibited the import of British beef, resulting in crisis in the beef farming industry. Other meat products, including lamb (which was already enjoying a vintage year) were to benefit from the consequent change in consumer demand, but in the case of lamb [and mutton] there was growing concern later in the year that this might be short-lived. The reason for this concern was that, like CJD and BSE, a sheep disease called 'scrapie', which had been endemic in the national sheep flock for some 250 years, was also a transmissible spongiform encephalopathy (TSE). It had been known for several years that sheep could succumb to BSE, though only when fed BSE-infected brain material. However, this led to speculation that it might be possible for BSE not only to become established naturally in the national sheep flock but also to be undetected, because of a similar animal behaviour pattern to that of scrapie-infected sheep. Not surprisingly, there was soon a strong demand for sheep of the R/R genotype that was resistant to scrapie. As a member of the Council of the National Sheep Association, I was privileged to attend some of the association's meetings at which this crisis received lengthy discussion. On learning that the Wensleydale breed had the highest percentage of the R/R genotype of all British sheep breeds, Ruth had her flock tested for this genotype – it was 100% R/R, and this significantly increased the demand for her sheep.

The Hunton flock produced some very good lambs that year and Ruth and I prepared for the show season with our customary zest, optimism and attention to detail. We attended another most enjoyable Royal Highland Show in late June, though without notable success, but this was followed by Breed Champion success again at the Royal Show. Three days later we were on our way to the GYS, with some very competitive entries.

I would always visit the showground on the Sunday before the show and prepare our pens. This would involve deciding which of our allocated pens should be changed to doubles, lining them with hessian, spreading the straw and placing hay racks in position. It was always time well spent for it enabled us on the Monday afternoon to drive directly to the most convenient point, reverse the trailer into a gap adjacent to our pens and offload and settle the sheep quickly, and without any stress. Having fed them in the late evening we would return to Old Hall, while friends who were staying on the showground would keep an eye on them. Judging would begin promptly at 10 a.m. on the Tuesday and we would routinely set our alarm clock for 5 a.m. with a view to arriving at the showground not later than 7 a.m., for the sheep needed to be fed, and this would be followed by meticulous final preparation for the judging ring.

Ruth and I always enjoyed that early-morning drive from Old Hall to the GYS showground at Harrogate. The roads were so quiet and the countryside looked so enchanting as the sun percolated through the early-morning mist, and there would always be an abundance of wildlife. We would listen to the first news broadcast of the day on the radio, which was always preceded by a medley of traditional music, with each piece merging into the next – *Sailor's Hornpipe … Greensleeves … Blow the Wind Southerly … Drunken Sailor … The British Grenadiers … Dashing Away with the Smoothing Iron … Early One Morning … John Peel*, etc.

Ruth did well, winning the Ram Lamb class (with a lamb that went on to become Reserve Male Champion), coming second in the Shearling Ram and Shearling Ewe classes, and being awarded three other rosettes. We were delighted.

On 3 August Mark's friend Sally died, aged twenty-seven. We had never met her, nor had any other member of the family. However, we had seen photographs of a very attractive young woman and had been eagerly looking forward to an introduction. We learned later that her death was attributable to medical incompetence – failure by a London specialist two weeks before she died to recognise that her asthma was causing her heart to fail.

The origin of the Wensleydale type of longwool sheep from a famous ram called Bluecap has been described earlier in these memoirs. However, Ruth needed some proof of the location of his birthplace and the residence of his owner, a Mr Richard Outhwaite, to support an article that she was writing for the *Wensleydale World* journal. She succeeded in obtaining this proof, and presented her findings to the WLSBA membership and the media as follows:

Society records are that Mr Richard Outhwaite came to Appleton in 1834 and that his 'Bluecap' was the foundation ram of the breed, but which Appleton? There are several places bearing that name! Appleton–le-Moor, near Kirby Moorside, has been a favoured speculation, probably because it is the nearest Appleton to the farm of Mr Sonley (who supplied the Dishley Leicester sire). I was not convinced and decided to do some research, which included examination of the 1841 census. The census shows that no-one by the name of Outhwaite resided at Appleton-le-Moor. However, the census lists 'Richard Outhwaite – Farmer, aged 40 years' as residing in the township of Appleton, two miles from Catterick village and five miles NNW of Bedale, together with his wife Elizabeth of the same age and their five children, subsequently increased to seven children. The 1851 census contains additional information on Mr Richard Outhwaite; that he farmed 634 acres and employed 28 labourers, plus three farm servants and two house servants to assist Elizabeth. He was born in the nearby hamlet of Hornby and was buried in the graveyard of Hornby Church in 1854. Elizabeth Outhwaite was born in Masham, the township that was to give its name to the Wensleydale x Dalesbred sheep. The headstone of Mr Richard Outhwaite's grave records that he lived in the East Appleton hamlet, where the only substantial property at that time was that currently known as the Manor House, but previously called East Appleton Farm and East Appleton Hall. As the other dwellings were labourers cottages it is reasonable to assume that Mr Richard Outhwaite lived at the Manor House and that 'Bluecap' was born in one of the adjacent fields or farm buildings in 1839.

Ruth and I felt very close to the origins of the breed, for the Manor House and Old Hall were only 3.6 miles apart.

The show season finished with a flourish, with Breed Championship wins at the Wensleydale (Leyburn) Show and the Ryedale Show, while at the WLSBA annual show and sale one of Ruth's rams was awarded Male Champion and Reserve Supreme. Each show involved much preparatory work and early departures, especially the two-day annual show and sale of the RBST, held at Stoneleigh on the site of the Royal Show. My diary records that for this event we set our noisy old-fashioned alarm clock for 3 a.m., departing at 4 a.m. and arriving at 8 a.m., having had a 10-minute break en route. This event was important to us for the sale of our sheep, but it was also a chance to meet with breeders from the south, which we always enjoyed.

We had visited Crispin, Aileen and Lois in Paisley in mid-September, and it was probably during that visit that we learned to our delight that identical twins were expected at about the turn of the year, though the sex would not be known until they were born. The Pedley family was now expanding rapidly. Crispin, Aileen and Lois then visited us at Old Hall for a weekend in mid-November, shortly before we flew to Malaga to join P&O's MV *Victoria* for a holiday in the West Indies, calling very briefly at Madeira en route.

Victoria was the smallest of P&O's cruise ships at that time; a mere 27,670 tons and carrying only a maximum of 730 passengers. She was built on the Clyde in 1966 as a dual-purpose cruise ship/liner for the Swedish American Line as MV *Kungsholm*, and was to hold six different names before retiring as a floating hotel in the Oman many years later. There was still a touch of the traditional liner about her, and the uninterrupted five-day crossing of the Atlantic developed a pleasant relationship between crew and passengers. In addition to entertainment from *Victoria*'s Theatre Company, we were fortunate to have vocalist Stuart Gillies, also from the Clyde. He had not only a splendid voice, but a personality and wit to match, which Ruth and I discovered during several deck-quoits games with him – a great character. He was an *Opportunity Knocks* winner; his albums included '*Introducing Stuart Gillies*', '*Amanda*' and '*All My Love*'. There was also the well-known ventriloquist Ray Alan with his puppet *Lord Charles*; between them, they unmercifully teased the ship's officers from the Captain downwards, to the point that our Captain became wary of making any announcements over the ship's tannoy system. Our first sighting of the West Indies was of Barbados on 12 December where we spent a full day, followed by Grenada and Dominica, arriving at St Thomas on Ruth's birthday. We arrived early at San Juan (Puerto Rica) the following day, from where we flew to Manchester, arriving at about 4 a.m. on 17 December to a well-below– zero temperature – it was *brrrrrrrr*!

We were soon to learn that Aileen, who had been admitted to the maternity hospital a couple of days prior to our holiday for observation and tests, was still in the hospital and likely to remain there until her babies arrived. The family numbers at Old Hall were accordingly depleted that Christmas and an atmosphere of concern mingled with the festive celebrations, for we appreciated that premature births were more than a possibility.

1997

Twin Granddaughters and a GYS Triple Champion

Ruth and I were thrilled in the new year when we learned of the arrival into this wonderful world of Cara Ruth (3lbs 10ozs) and Marianne Elizabeth (3lbs 15ozs). They were still very premature (Aileen was just under 33 weeks' pregnant when they were born), but they were not lacking in vitality, broadcasting their arrival in no uncertain manner. There was some concern a week later when the respective weights fell to 3lbs 2ozs and 3lbs 5ozs, and then relief as slowly but surely they steadily increased. Ruth travelled by rail to see them and their very proud parents and sister on 6 February, returning the following day. I was unable to accompany Ruth as it was lambing time.

Because of the BSE crisis, 1997 was one of the worst years in living memory for British beef farmers, as their livelihood was under threat. TV images of stricken cattle, shaking uncontrollably, and staggering across their farmyards, shocked consumers and led to an international boycott of British beef; hitherto regarded as the finest in the world. The situation deteriorated further as the year progressed, and several years were to pass before British beef regained consumer confidence and international acclaim. I continue to regard it as the highest quality and safest in the world.

In mid-March Ruth and I collected from the printers the third edition of *Wensleydale World*, of which she was editor. It was a splendid publication that had involved her in considerable work, and I was very proud of her. It incorporated some good technical and historical articles, including, of course, her '*Bluecap's Birthplace*', together with some splendid cartoons drawn by rival competitor and good friend Graham Steventon. Furthermore, Ruth had cleverly balanced the cost of production with the income from members' flock advertisements and commercial advertisements. No mean achievement, for which the association was very grateful.

On 22 April I had a nasty fall. One of the asbestos-covered byre roofs was being replaced, and to reduce the cost I had arranged that I would creosote the old timbers prior to the workmen nailing the laths and covering everything with pantiles. The old timbers seemed strong enough, but as I leaned back on one of them the joint broke and I lost my balance and dropped backwards from about fifteen feet. Fortunately, my back hit a traditional concrete partition between two milking bays before hitting the edge of the concrete drainage channel, otherwise I think my head would have hit the floor. It was very painful and I only managed to slowly crawl as far as the sheep dip, fighting to remain conscious. I was not capable of shouting and there was no one around. Coincidentally, at that moment Ruth came out of the house and ran towards me – '*Are you all right?*' – '*No ... get an ambulance ... quickly.*'

The response of the ambulance team from Richmond was brilliant and it was a relief to hear their approach over the hill and receive some morphine and oxygen. The journey to the Friarage Hospital in Northallerton was very slow, with a halt for further attention in Bedale market place. I had broken five ribs, with significant internal haemorrhage and a collapsed lung. I remained in the Friarage for nine days. I was very concerned as to whether Ruth would be able to manage the livestock by herself, but she did; magnificently, helped by our local farmer friends. When I was discharged I was only just able to walk, and it was several weeks before I could make any useful contribution on the farm. The nursing and medical attention that I received at the Friarage Hospital was magnificent.

The 1997 general election was held on 1 May, the day after my discharge. As expected, it was a landslide victory for Tony Blair (a politician whom I had disliked intensely from the time that he became the Labour Party leader) and his 'New Labour'. Labour had a record 418 seats, the Conservative Party (John Major) had 165 seats, while the Liberal Democrat Party (Paddy Ashdown) had 46 seats. Following the general election, William Hague became leader of the Conservative Party, aged thirty-six. Tony Blair's leadership of the Labour Party followed the untimely death of the much-respected John Smith from a heart attack in 1994. I felt that John Smith, had he lived, would have been a fine Prime Minister, taking decisions and formulating policies that he felt were in the interests of his country, while I suspected that Tony Blair would be more focused on promoting himself, if necessary at the expense of the interests of his country. Ruth shared my view, and she had a similarly low opinion of most of his 101 'babes'. Our low opinion of our country's new Prime Minister and his government deepened year on year.

Ruth had completed a useful Wensleydale ram semen sale while I was in hospital, selling 200 straws @ £7 per straw to a buyer in the US. There were no Wensleydale sheep in the US, but a keen interest was developing in breeding-up, using Wensleydale ram sperm within similar Longwool breeds. On 8 May we duly took three of our rams to Edinburgh Genetics to complete our part of the contract, collecting them about three weeks later. They had performed well, and it was rather nice to think that we were involved in the introduction of the Wensleydale to North America. However, one of the internal airline carriers did not handle the semen correctly and it was wasted. We were as disappointed as the purchaser (though we had adequate insurance cover), but semen from some other British breeders was successfully received and used; and now, many generations later, there are virtually 100% pure Wensleydales in the US, carefully nurtured by a thriving and responsible breed society.

Except for Mark, who was working in California, the Pedley family converged on Largs on Sunday 1 June for the Christening of the now-flourishing Cara Ruth and Marianne Elizabeth, in the same church in which Lois had been baptised. Again, it was a traditional Church of

Scotland ceremony; integrated into the well-attended morning service. I found it very emotional as the two small bundles were slowly and gently passed along the aisles, happily gurgling to the elders of their faith. Later in the month we were in Scotland again, for another very enjoyable Royal Highland Show. Ruth was delighted to win the Hogg in Wool class and Reserve Champion, especially as she had not brought her best sheep. They were being withheld for the GYS.

I prepared our GYS pens on the Sunday afternoon and Ruth and I took our entries to the showground on the Monday afternoon, as required by the stewards. Unfortunately, there was a long delay on the A1 motorway and when we arrived at the showground we found that our best sheep, a hogg in wool, had lain down and been trampled on by the other ewes in the trailer. She was in a right mess. Ruth calmly asked me to find a hosepipe and then I led her hogg to a quiet spot on a halter and held her while Ruth carefully hosed her down. Ruth then instructed her soaked husband to walk her soaked hogg up and down on a grass area for an hour and a half in the warm evening sunshine while she fed and watered her other sheep. When this was completed, Ruth joined me in sitting on a bench and calmly read *Harry Potter and the Philosopher's Stone*, which had been published the previous week, occasionally getting up to check the drying of her hogg. We returned to Old Hall late in the evening, but set the alarm very early to provide time for further drying the next morning, for judging began at 9 a.m.

The medley of traditional music had ceased by the time we turned off the A1, and we were listening to the 6 a.m. news when Ruth saw her first solitary magpie, prompting her to silently recite the words, '*Good morning Mr Magpie, I do hope that you, Mrs Robinson and all the children are well.*' I could see her lips moving slightly out of the corner of my eye and was well used to this element of Nidderdale witchcraft, which she had learned as a young girl. If two magpies were seen together she would make no response, for it could be assumed that they were happily wed. To not acknowledge a single magpie would bring bad luck. There were dozens of magpies on that section of the A59 as we approached the showground and Ruth's lips were in constant motion, while I was almost in hysterics. I learned later in life that similar salutations to solitary magpies are followed in many different parts of the country, but I never traced any others that specifically named 'Mrs Robinson'. I also read that ideally one should simultaneously flap one's arms like a bird, but thankfully it would seem that this was not practised in Nidderdale.

We worked quickly and skilfully on the sheep that morning, but surprisingly, Ruth's hogg required no more than a short walk and a brush with the hand to remove straw. Her fleece looked magnificent and she had the poise of a model, immediately capturing attention. She won her class, then Best Female, then Breed Champion. Next day she beat the breed champions of the other Longwool breeds (Leicester, Bluefaced Leicester, Cotswold, Teeswater) to become Female Longwool Champion. But there was more to come – on the final day of the show she won the Longwool Wool on the Hoof Championship, followed by the Wool on the Hoof Champion of All Breeds (Supreme Champion), a unique triple championship success that had never before been achieved by any breed. Several different judges had been involved. Ruth also had good placings in other classes: Shearling Ram – second and fourth; Shearling Ewe – third and fourth; Ewe Lamb – third; and Group – first. The magpies were certainly with her that day.

It was a memorable month, not least because on 19 July the IRA announced a ceasefire after twenty-eight years of bloodshed. This led to the Belfast 'Good Friday Agreement' of 1998, whereby it was acknowledged that Northern Ireland would remain part of the United Kingdom until a majority of the people of Northern Ireland and the Republic of Ireland wished otherwise. On the same day as that ceasefire we cut our hayfield; the continuing hot spell enabling us to lead-in 193 bales of high-quality hay just four days later.

Show successes continued later in the year with championship awards at the Ryedale and Wensleydale (Leyburn) shows and very satisfactory sales at the WLSBA annual show and sale at Skipton Auction Mart, including 300 guineas for one of Ruth's rams.

Justin, Haley and family spent the last weekend of August with us and we had a most pleasant visit to the Beamish Museum, while Crispin brought Lois to us for a week in November. Cara and Marianne were now steadily putting on weight, but several years were to pass before they really took-off; representing their school and county in swimming and cross country running, as did elder sister Lois. Because of the distances and our many commitments, we did not see as much of the family as we would have liked, but we helped whenever possible. Christmas was another joyous family affair, with a full house (including six grandchildren), while Mark introduced a new friend to us – Claire, an executive with Pfizer.

1998

Agricultural Recession and Ruby Wedding Anniversary Cruise

I will also remember 1998 as a year of conflict and natural disaster. In early February an earthquake [measuring 6.1 on the Richter scale] killed more than 5,000 people in Afghanistan. This catastrophe was followed sixteen weeks later with a 6.6-strength quake, which killed a similar number. On 17 July a tsunami destroyed ten villages in Papua New Guinea, killing an estimated 1,500 people, plus 2,000 unaccounted for – thousands more made homeless. On 4 August the second Congo War began; it was to end in 2003, by which time 3,900,000 had been killed in the bloodiest conflict since World War II. On 29 October Hurricane Mitch killed an estimated 18,000 people in Central America. Horrific as they were, these disasters seemed as distant to me as the *Lunar Prospector* spacecraft orbiting our moon and the *Galileo* probe exploring Jupiter's moon [Europa]. Like most people, I was enshrined in my own world, which I (again like most people) regarded as being the *real world*. To British farmers at that time, the *real world* of 1998 was one of deep recession, the worst year in living memory, sparing no sector of the agricultural industry and threatening disaster to the rural economy as a whole. Little sympathy or understanding emanated from a predominantly urban population, which had itself experienced decline and redundancy in coal mines, steel plants and shipyards in the past, but which now enjoyed an abundance of cheap food in the supermarkets.

Beef farmers continued to suffer the crippling effect of the BSE crisis, though the export ban was lifted at the year's end. By the autumn pig farmers were losing £20–£25 a pig. Cereals carrying £80 to £90 in production costs were trading down to £60 a ton. In the sheep sector prices slumped, with good-quality store lambs and even finished lambs realising little more than might have been anticipated for pet lambs a few years previously. Incessant rain in the summer and early autumn ruined much of the hay crop and harvest, adding to the gloom and despair felt by those living in rural Britain.

The reasons for this acute agricultural recession varied between the different sectors of the industry, but all sectors were adversely affected by the exceptional strength of sterling. In addition, the sheep sector had to cope with the virtual cessation of livestock services by the major ferry operators (as a result of protests by animal-welfare activists); an ill-considered British rule came into effect banning spinal cord in the carcasses of sheep over 12 months old; there was no longer a market for sheep pelt; and there was a sharp drop in wool prices, aggravated by the crisis in the economies of countries in Southeast Asia. The cumulative result was an almost total stoppage of the export of sheep meat (dead or alive) to the Continent, and a non-competitive home market that benefited the supermarkets and other wholesale buyers.

The frustration and despair experienced by the rural community (farmers in particular) was reflected in a number of demonstrations and protest marches, not all of which were peaceful. The largest and most memorable was that of 280,000 grim country folk in London in March, the largest to be held there for over a decade. Other positive actions included the launch of a self-help 'farmers-ferry' (Dover–Dunkirk) to convey lambs to mainland Europe again; an attempt to recover trade worth in excess of £70 million which had been lost during the past 12 months.

Although Ruth and I were only small-scale sheep breeders, we were nevertheless producers, and so entwined and active in the agricultural world that we shared the grief and despair of the farming community at that time.

Our ruby wedding anniversary was on 8 March 1998, but because of lambing commitments we delayed our celebration, taking a long weekend break in Paris in early June. We travelled by Eurostar, which had been opened by the Queen in conjunction with French President François Mitterrand in May 1994. The London terminal was at Waterloo station in those days, so it was still quite a long journey:

- Dep Leeds 1005
- Arr King's Cross 1228
- Dep Waterloo 1357
- Arr Paris 1756

It was a splendid anniversary break, with perfect weather and Paris in the spring looking at its best.

Ruth's achievements at the GYS were modest compared with those of 1997, but she nevertheless had a good year, with Breed Championship wins at the Royal Lancashire Show and the Wensleydale (Leyburn) Show, Reserve Champion at the Royal Show and Supreme Champion at the Rare Breed Survival Trust Show at Stoneleigh. The major Wensleydale show successes of 1998 were quite exceptional; achieved by friends and rivals J.A. & F. Elliott from Knaresborough and J. Watkinson from Constable Burton. The J.A. & F. Elliott 'Providence' flock had been established in 1945 and was now largely in the hands of Mark Elliott, whose hogg in wool at the Royal Show won the Breed Championship followed by second Reserve Supreme Champion in the inter-breed line-up of 39 breed champions (2,055 sheep entries). Jack Watkinson's achievement was that of winning a newly introduced 'Exhibitor of the Year' competition, taking six Breed Championship and six Reserve Breed Championship awards.

I do not mention the many other activities in which Ruth and I continued to be involved during the year for they have already been described in previous chapters and were now routine and I cannot recollect any being discarded over the years. On the contrary, we seemed to be adding to them, giving our time and enthusiasm on a voluntary basis to activities and organisations in which we believed. However, by the time autumn arrived we were rather tired, and as it was our ruby anniversary year we went on another P&O Cruises 'autumn getaway' break. Again, Ruth told me that she didn't care where the ship went and that she did not mind if she never saw land, providing she could sunbathe each day, have a liberal supply of ice cream cornets, and enjoy exquisite food and quality entertainment – and without air flights. Ruth was not frightened of flying – she just considered the repetitive recirculation of disease laden coughs, sneezes and fumes within the aircraft to be a health risk, exacerbated by close-seatng and the lack of hygienic manners; describing it as '*nauseating ... ugh*'. So, we opted for another Atlantic Isles cruise, incorporating a stop at the Moroccan port of Casablanca, followed by the now-familiar Gran Canaria, Lanzarote, Tenerife and Madeira; with Vigo on the homeward leg. Our ship was the ten-year-old French-built ship *Arcadia*, whose name had only recently changed from *Star Princess*. She was an unremarkable but very pleasant average-sized cruise ship of that period (63,500 tons) and she and her crew gave us the relaxing holiday that we needed. Sadly, the days of boat trains from Waterloo to the side of the ship at Southampton were now over and we travelled in a chartered bus from Leeds, having left our car at the home of Justin and Haley. Again, we had another most enjoyable P&O cruise holiday.

The family gradually converged on Old Hall for another very merry Christmas, with Mark arriving from California on 20 December, looking very fit and well.

1999

End of the Second Millennium and the Old Hall Oak

The final year of the second millennium began with the introduction of the euro currency, but thankfully Britain had wisely chosen to remain with the pound sterling. Both Ruth and I were very sceptical about Europe, wishing the United Kingdom to be a good trading partner with Europe but not shackled to it. We were at ease at that time with the position of the leader of the Conservative Party (William Hague), who was to fight the 2001 general election with a policy of 'In Europe – Not Run by Europe'. We accordingly became increasingly angry as more of our sovereignty was surrendered to Brussels.

There was a strong gale in North Yorkshire on 3 February which overturned twenty lorries on the A1, resulting in the closure of a particularly exposed twenty-mile stretch close to where we lived. It continued throughout the night and was no less severe the following morning, when Ruth and I heard a crash. It was our beloved old oak tree – torn completely out of the ground with its roots in the air. We dashed across the field to check that none of our sheep were beneath it, for it was one of their favoured 'chewing of cud' resting places. They were unharmed, cowering in a corner of the field near the beck, possibly as distraught as ourselves. English oaks sometimes live for more than 1,000 years, so it would not be too fanciful to reflect on our tree being a sapling during the Wars of the Roses and the Tudor period. In addition to it being the national tree of England and many other countries, the oak has been a revered tree on our planet and its gods from time immemorial – the sacred tree to Zeus (king of the gods) and to Thor (Norse thunder god), and the most exalted tree to the Druids. The Oak of Old Hall and its faeries were special not only to the Pedley family but also to the Lockey and Tunstill families and many of the elders of the village, and as such, it deserves this eulogy – the telephone never stopped ringing that morning. The Oak of Old Hall must have withstood hundreds of gales in its long life, but this savage gale was one too many.

Charlotte, now aged 8 years and 10 months, was showing a well–above-average ability as a swimmer and my diary proudly records on 11 February a best 100-metre medley (butterfly/backstroke/breaststroke/ crawl) of 1 min 58 secs. However, although talented, Charlotte never developed any real enthusiasm for the sport.

Our show season began at the Royal Show on 5 July. Ruth won both the Ram and the Shearling Ewe classes, with the latter receiving the Reserve Champion award. It was a good start, but it got better, for the same ewe won the Breed Championship at the GYS eight days later and two Reserve Breed Championships at other shows later in the year. Ruth was also making her name with numerous Supreme Fleece awards. Whenever we could find the time Ruth and I delighted in day or half-day outings to different parts of our county, usually incorporating a walk. To get off to a good start in the year we made a habit of driving to the coast and along it on New Year's Day, taking in a section of the moors. The roads were usually quiet and the sea often spectacular as it beat against the cliffs and harbour walls. Ruth's favourite outing was to Pateley Bridge, with a walk on the moors that she knew so well. Other favourites were Stump Cross Caverns and the castles, priories and abbeys. However, if time was short we could be on our adjacent moors in fifteen minutes, walking in the heather among the lead mines and listening to the curlews and grouse. Sadly, I could no longer hear the skylarks, because of high frequency deafness and tinnitus. Occasionally we would go further afield, and I recall that a couple of days after the GYS we went to the Holy Island of Lindisfarne close to the Scottish border. We left early in order to drive across at low tide, and we had a wonderful day studying the history of the monastery founded by Irish monk Saint Aidan in AD 634. We found the visit very humbling, and it continues to trouble me that both practising and non– practising Christians in England are sometimes reluctant to speak openly of their beliefs, or even to wear a cross, for fear of offending atheists and those of other faiths.

As the new millennium approached there was an air of confidence and optimism in the United Kingdom, for the past decade had provided a degree of national prosperity that had not been seen since 1914. The exception was a bewildered and depressed agricultural industry, with most sectors in financial crisis and disarray, not least the sheep sector. The reasons were complex and varied between sectors, but common factors were the continuing strength of sterling and over-zealous government interpretation of a raft of European Union (EU) regulations, resulting in excessive overhead costs. There was some relief and celebration in August when at last the EU officially lifted the three-year embargo on British beef exports, but this quickly turned to anger and frustration at French and German defiance and the prospect of a trade war developing. This would have been devastating to the British sheep industry, which was already in crisis, with many hill farmers destitute and relying on social benefits. Ironically, it was against this background that a record price of 1,220 guineas was paid for a Wensleydale ewe at the WLSBA annual show and sale on 1 October.

Christmas was as enjoyable as ever, and Ruth and I shared the new millennium celebrations with Justin and Haley and family at their Tingley home, watching a spectacular fireworks-display in the distance. As we drove home to Old Hall shortly after midnight I reflected on the now-past twentieth century, in which Britain had bade farewell to its Empire, fought two world wars, endured economic hardship and industrial strife and adapted to social change, nuclear power and the internet. The words of an Anglo-Irish satirist written three centuries previously came to mind – they were food for thought for the new millennium, and they seem just as pertinent as I write these third edition memoirs:

> … and he gave it for his opinion, that whoever could make two ears of corn or two blades of grass, to grow upon a spot of ground where only one grew before, would deserve better of mankind, and do more essential service to his country, than the whole race of politicians put together.
>
> —Jonathan Swift (1667–1745)

I was disturbed at much that I saw or gleaned as the 20th Century departed. An alarming gross ignorance of history and associated tradition had permeated into my country and much of the western world: manifest in selfishness; rootlessness; inability to recognise communal rights, and an abandonment of personal pride, courtesy and honesty. The days of chivalry had ended.

2000

Reflections on Sheep
and Our First Aurora Cruise

I think it was the combination of advancing years and the beginning of a new millennium that prompted me to consider the future, sharing my thoughts with Ruth. We were now sixty-six and beginning to realise that the zenith of our energy and aspiration was now past and that a more moderate pace would soon be necessary. Ruth did not like to discuss the subject but made it clear that she would spend the rest of her life in our beloved Old Hall, into which we had spilled blood, sweat and tears for the past eighteen years. Also, we felt 'hefted' to Wensleydale and bonded to the breed of sheep that carries its name. I shared Ruth's passion, but recognised that sooner or later a sensible change of farming practice and lifestyle would be necessary. Ruth was becoming one of the leading exhibitors of longwool sheep and fleece in the country and had already realised her ambitions, but we decided that perhaps another couple of years of procrastination would do no harm and I applied for entry forms for another raft of our favourite and most competitive shows.

The beauty of Wensleydale and adjacent Swaledale is reflected in the vast number of visitors at weekends and during public holidays, but one needs to be linked to the sheep-farming community to fully appreciate these alluring dales. Furthermore, no one will understand an addiction to sheep, and Wensleydale sheep in particular, without keeping them.

A few personal observations and experiences, together with those of other shepherds, past and present, might help.

Sheep, like horses, have a pleasant smell and I feel comfortable when handling them in close proximity, while I find the smell of dogs and pigs and their faeces rather unpleasant, particularly when trodden on. I cringe when I see doting dog owners allowing their dogs to lick their faces, for I am reminded of some of the distasteful places where that mouth may have been previously. Yet I much enjoy brief meetings with my friends' dogs, particularly as the character and behaviour of the pet seems often to reflect that of the owner, while I have considerable admiration and liking for working collies, whose importance was well described by James Hogg in 1809:

A single shepherd and his dog will accomplish more in gathering a stock of sheep from a Highland farm than twenty shepherds could without dogs, and it is a fact that without this docile animal the pastoral life would be a blank. Without the shepherd's dog the whole of the open mountainous land in Scotland would not be worth a six-pence. It would require more hands to manage a stock of sheep, gather them from the hills, force them into houses and folds, and drive them to markets, than the profits of the whole stock were capable of maintaining.

Ruth and I found the oily smell and handle (i.e. feel) of a sheep's fleece to be distinctively attractive, and the sheep will only eat the cleanest herbage and hay. With our relatively small flock and acreage it was easier to manage the sheep to do as we wished than to train and feed a collie.

To many people, not least George Orwell, the sheep is a stupid animal of low intelligence, but not to a shepherd. Perhaps this reputation is partly because [like deer] it seemingly panics when startled; fleeing in an irrational manner at any sudden sight or sound with which it is unfamiliar and, if in an enclosed space, throwing itself against the obstacle in a frantic and reckless manner; the instinctive survival reactions of their ancestors in their endeavour to outpace the wolf and the leopard. However, the ewe will attack a threatening dog to protect its lambs and the ram will engage with a bull, often winning the contest, while stories abound of sheep ingenuity in overcoming fencing, gate and grid obstacles – the latter by rolling over them. Our beck field sometimes resembled a children's playground, with groups of lambs running races along the side of the beck, and I have seen mothers join in, while a muck heap in our collecting ring attracted some very serious 'king of the castle' contests. Ruth and I would delight in watching these activities, for it showed that the sheep and their lambs were happy and fit. Whichever of us saw them first would rush to tell the other. The beck races would usually be on fine spring evenings when the lambs were only a few weeks old.

There have been some scientific tests and measurements carried out on sheep intelligence, but none that I regard as thorough. Neuroscientists of the University of Cambridge considered sheep to have brainpower equal to rodents and monkeys, and in some tests equal to humans, while the University of Illinois found that they were on a par with cattle, but just below pigs. These scientists were generally surprised at the high level of sheep intelligence, but had their tests incorporated a week on a hill farm working with shepherds they would have learned how extremely smart the sheep can be and also that it has many endearing human characteristics, not least guile, and I believe their conclusions would have been significantly enhanced in favour of the sheep. If sheep were any more intelligent and smart they would be unmanageable.

Sheep can recognise individual members of their flock and will habitually graze with their friends, but they can also recognise human faces, taking a liking to some and developing a hatred for others. For example, at the 1999 Royal Lancashire Show the judge, as is customary, asked the exhibitors to take off the halters and let the sheep run free in the ring, while the exhibitors stood back in distant parts of the ring. It was the class for ewes that have suckled a lamb, and all the exhibitors were wearing white coats. The ewe that I was exhibiting broke away from the group and ran to me. I returned it to the group and then hid among some exhibitors in a different area – but she soon found me. She was returned a second time to the group. This time I took my white coat off and remained still in a corner, almost surrounded by spectators. Again, she soon found me, much to the amusement of the spectators.

When a sheep needed some medical or lambing attention I would hold and console it while Ruth did whatever was necessary. We were therefore not too surprised when it became apparent that some of the older ewes regarded me with more favour than they did Ruth, and one old ewe in particular. I could do anything with her, but if Ruth were to just place her hand on the ewe's pen at lambing-time she would charge it with a ferocity that one associates with an ill-tempered ram. I would then tease Ruth by going into the pen, where the ewe would respond to my presence like a doting spaniel. On another occasion I sat on the bank of the beck on a fine day listening to the sounds of the countryside and watching for a sighting of a kingfisher, when I felt a nudge from behind. I stroked the nose of the ewe that had nudged me for a few minutes until this touching scene was interrupted by the ewe being bundled down the bank by another ewe, which then pushed its nose forward for similar treatment – sheer jealousy!

I now turn to the experiences and writings of William Youatt (1776– 1847), a leading veterinary surgeon two hundred years ago and the author of *Sheep – their Breeds, Management and Diseases*, with particular reference to his chapter on the intelligence of the sheep:

The domesticated flock of sheep, whatever show of resistance they may occasionally make, are usually put to speedy flight by a determined individual – all except the ewe, who remains with her lamb and braves all danger in its defence; but in proportion as the sheep are withdrawn from the control and protection of man they become (increasingly) courageous. In some of the northern parts of the kingdom they range on extensive mountains, and are scarcely seen during many successive weeks. A ram will then boldly attack a single dog, and generally be victorious. Should several foxes or strange dogs come in sight, the sheep adapt their defence to the degree of danger. They form themselves into a compact body, placing the females and the young behind, while the males take the foremost ranks, keeping closely by each other, and presenting an armed front to their enemy. In this order they advance upon their assailants, and when they have come within a certain distance, the rams rush forward, and generally destroy their foe ….

A gentleman of Inverness, while passing through a lonely and unfrequented district, observed a sheep bleating most piteously, and hurrying along the road to meet him; on his approaching nearer, the animal redoubled its cries, and, looking earnestly in the face of the traveller, seemed to implore some favour or assistance. Touched with a sight so unusual, he alighted; and, leaving his gig, he followed the sheep to a field in the direction whence it had come. There in a solitary cairn, the ewe stopped: and the traveller found a lamb, completely wedged between two large stones of the cairn, almost exhausted, but still continuing to struggle feebly. He instantly extricated the little sufferer, and placed it safely on the neighbouring greensward, while the mother poured out her thanks in a long-continued and grateful, if not musical, strain. (Quoted by Youatt from Thomas Brown's *Biographical Sketches and Authentic Anecdotes of Quadrupeds*, p. 569)

When a sheep becomes blind, it is rarely abandoned to itself in this hapless and helpless state: some one of the flock attaches himself to it, and, by bleating, calls it back from the precipice, and the lake, and the pool, and every kind of danger. (From *The Shepherd's Calendar*, vol. II, p. 188)

An interesting provision of nature, with regard to these animals, is, that the more inhospitable the land is on which they feed, the greater will be their kindness and attention to their young. I once herded two years on a wild and bare farm, called Willenslee, on the border of Mid Lothian; and of all the sheep I ever saw, these were the kindest and most affectionate to their young. We had one very bad winter, so that our sheep grew lean in the spring, and the thwarter-ill came among them, and carried off many. Often have I seen these poor victims, when fallen down to rise no more, and even when unable to lift their heads from the ground, holding up the leg to invite the starving lamb to the miserable pittance that the udder could still supply … .

One peculiarity, and most strikingly evident in the comparatively wild and aboriginal breeds, should perhaps be noticed – their attachment to the place in which they were bred. It is more evident in the wilder sheep of the black-faced and Highland breeds; it seems to be always a powerful principle with them, but it prevails most at the time of yeaning. There is something very interesting and consistent with natural feeling in this. A black ewe that had lately lambed was missed from the farm of Harehope in Tweeddale. A shepherd was dispatched in pursuit of her, who traced her many a mile, and then abandoned the chase. He was told that she had been several times stopped, but that she absolutely persisted in travelling on, regarding neither sheep nor shepherd by the way. Her lamb was often far behind, and she had constantly to urge it on by impatient bleating. She unfortunately came to Stirling on the morning of a great annual fair, about the end of May, and judging it imprudent to venture through the crowd with her lamb, she halted on the north side of the town, lying close by the roadside during the whole of the day: but, next morning, when all became quiet, a little after the break of day, she was observed stealing quietly through the town, in apparent terror of the dogs that were prowling about the streets. The last time that she was seen on the road was at a toll-bar near St. Ninian's. The man stopped her, thinking that she was a strayed animal, and that some one would claim her: she, however, found some means of eluding him, for home she came at last having been no less than nine days on the road. Her former master paid the price of her, and she remained on her native farm until she died of old age in her seventeenth year. (From *The Shepherd's Calendar*, vol. II, p. 186)

Another example of a ewe imploring human help in similar circumstances to that experienced by the *gentleman of Inverness* two centuries ago occurred in Gloucestershire in 1858. The incident is recorded in *The British Workman* edition of 1st August of that year, as told by two visitors taking a country walk: '… *we were about half way across [the field] when a ewe came up to me and bleated very loudly, looking up in my face, and then ran off towards a brook. I could not help re-marking this extraordinary behaviour; but my attention was particularly roused when she repeated it, and bleating louder, seemed to wish to signify something in particular; she then ran off in the same direction, repeatedly looking behind her, till she reached the brook, where she stood still. After standing to look at her for some time, we continued our walk, and had nearly reached the gate that led into the net meadow, when she came running after us the third time, and seemed, if possible, more earnest than before. I then determined to discover the cause of this singular procedure; I followed the ewe towards the brook; she peeped over the edge of a hillock into the water, looked up in my face, and bleated with the most significant voice I ever heard uttered by a quadruped. Judge of my surprise, when, on looking into the stream, I saw her lamb just under the hillock, nearl immersed in water, and unable to extricate itself. I at once drew it out; it was still alive. The fond mother instantly began to lick and suckle it, and looking up to me, uttered several sounds very different from those that I had heard before, and evidently expressing satisfaction and pleasure'.* Impressive sagacity!

The description of the travels of the ewe and lamb from *the farm of Harehope in Tweeddale* reminds me of the Metro-Goldwyn-Mayer film *Lassie Come Home*, which I watched at the age of ten at the Regal Cinema, Crossgates, near Leeds. It was an outstanding Technicolor film of the time, not least because it included the gorgeous rising child star, Elizabeth Taylor.

Sadly, in late February, Mrs Elizabeth Tunstill of Hunton's Sawmill House Farm died. She was the epitome of the dedicated, hard-working and talented Dales farmer's wife of the twentieth century who gave everything to the well-being of her livestock farm and family, setting the highest standards. And she was a lady. Ruth used the word 'lady' sparingly. It was nothing to do with class or wealth; it embraced a woman who showed high standards of behaviour, modesty, refined manners and generosity to others, in terms of time, sympathy and encouragement. Although they held high positions, the Duchess of York and the Prime Minister's wife, Cherie Blair, were not ladies. Ruth's friends were all ladies, otherwise they would not have been her friends, though some standards might have temporarily fallen at election time. Mrs Elizabeth Tunstill was a true lady, whom Ruth and I respected enormously.

Although it did not significantly affect Ruth and me, 10 March 2000 was a historic date in the financial world. It was the day that the 'dot-com' bubble [also referred to as the internet bubble or IT bubble] reached its zenith, as measured by the NASDAQ index peak; followed by a spectacular fall in value of companies that specialised in the internet sector – the 'dot-coms'. There was such feverish demand for shares in these companies during the 1990s that virtually any company could inflate its share price by adding an 'e-' prefix to its name or a '.com' to the end. Crispin, now in a senior financial appointment and a 'dot-com' sceptic, was to receive much gratitude from his clients for his level-headed management of their portfolios during this roller-coaster period.

Ruth and I made an early start to the show season by competing for the first time at the then two-day Shropshire and West Midlands Show, near Shrewsbury, in mid-May. It gave Ruth a flying start, for she took both the Breed Championship and Reserve. Further Breed Championship awards followed at the Westmorland Show and the Rare Breeds Survival Trust National Show and Sale, but her achievements at the prestigious Royal Show and GYS (which had a record 85 entries) were modest compared with other years, and she was the judge at the Royal Highland Show that year. We travelled to Edinburgh by train and enjoyed some sightseeing in the city as well as our time at the show.

We had a pleasant surprise visit from Mark in mid-August, following on from a business trip to Paris and Germany. He was now at about the halfway point of six years' employment in Silicon Valley in northern California, near San Francisco. He had initially been employed by Philips Electronics in the development of the company's mobile phones, and he was now with the German company Infineon, developing semiconductors. It was a particularly happy time of his life, which he described to me as follows:

The working life was very tough, but I loved the freedom to explore a completely new continent. To the west, just ten miles away, was the icy Pacific Ocean and the coastal redwood forests shrouded in fog. Ten miles to the east were the dry scrub oak woodlands of the eastern bay area, with a totally different micro climate, and a further 150 miles eastwards across the central valley were the stunningly beautiful Sierra Nevada mountains and Yosemite. Beyond the Sierra Nevada lay the high dry plains of Nevada.

I continued with my white water kayaking passion, but it was difficult without my UK friends. I would run the rivers 'solo' without anyone else, which is one of the most dangerous things one can do, and then hitch my way back to the top of the river. My kayaking came to an end after a near death experience on the California Salmon river on the California-Oregon border when I became trapped under a huge boulder pourover.

It was a time when high technology had plenty of money. I must have made 20 or 30 trips to Japan, Taiwan, Singapore and Hong Kong. There were times when I felt that I'd died and was in purgatory – doomed to continuous flight across the Pacific, like the crew of the Flying Dutchman.

The hiking was good, the skiing was good and there was a good looking Californian girl called Robin. However, I guess I'm not the marrying type.

A photograph of Mark and Robin together on a snowmobile at Zephyr Cove, near Lake Tahoe in California, was never replaced from its prominent position in his room at Old Hall.

The 'Mad Cow'/BSE crisis continued to be a cloud hanging over the British sheep industry, for if found (in sheep), the implications would be even more serious than they would be for BSE in cattle, if only because BSE in cattle infects only limited parts of the body, while laboratory tests had indicated that in sheep it affects the whole animal. In November the industry shuddered when the national press reported contingency plan options that were being considered by the Food Standards Agency – options which included the destruction of the entirety of Britain's 40 million sheep. The eradication of scrapie from the national flock was accordingly recognised as essential. Wensleydale sheep breeders were able to derive some comfort from the fact that 90% of the breed was of a genotype resistant to scrapie, but there was little trust in the competency of the government and its agencies, as indicated in the WLSBA flock book for the year:

> Whilst the 'BSE cloud' was the most disturbing matter threatening British sheep farmers in 2000 there were others that gave much concern. The most significant were an over zealous enforcement of EU (European Union) red tape, revealed in a report commissioned by the Prime Minister, and the increasing numbers and influence of conservationists, welfareists, environmentalists and consultants, all deriving an income on the back of an industry on the brink of disaster. However, it was rain clouds that provided the final agony of the year, particularly in April and the Autumn which were the wettest since records began in 1766. The incessant Autumn rain saturated fields, resulting in roads becoming water courses and causing disastrous flooding which competed with the great floods of 1947. Barely a region was spared and many crops were ruined.

On 2 November the rainfall and flooding in Wensleydale and Swaledale were the most severe within the memories of the farming communities. The land was at super-saturation point, and the accumulated waters from these dales together with the water from the other tributaries of York's river Ouse descended on the city forty-eight hours later, resulting in the highest river level ever recorded – 17'9" above normal, flooding 5,000 properties and thousands of acres of land.

It was a relief to board P&O's new flagship *Aurora* on 1 December for another most enjoyable cruise in the South Atlantic. P&O would have liked her to be built on the Clyde, but sadly there was no yard of sufficient size incorporating the requisite construction facilities, so she was built by Meyer Werft in a modern German shipyard, to exacting standards. *Aurora* had a 76,152 gross tonnage and a crew of 850 to serve some 1,900 passengers. She had been christened by HRH Princess Anne on 27 April, so was in sparkling condition. Unfortunately, the champagne bottle did not break on hitting the ship's side and fell intact into the sea, something regarded as a bad omen by seafarers. However, Ruth and I were immediately attracted to her and she became our favourite cruise ship, in that whenever we were planning subsequent cruises we would always look to see if it was feasible to holiday on *Aurora*, and if so, we would immediately select not only her, but also cabin E103. She was, and still is, a beautiful ship, with a stunning atrium.

It had not been an easy year, but our wonderful cruise on *Aurora* was followed by a delightful Christmas with the family.

2001

Foot and Mouth Epidemic: Our Longest Year

The year 2001 began well at Old Hall. I had a new pair of reading spectacles, which made a significant improvement, and a new computer. They could not have been more timely, for in conjunction with Mark, I was establishing a WLSBA web site, one of the few sheep breed societies to have the facility at that time, as well as preparing the annual flock book. Ruth and I were also chuffed at getting the manure from our muck heap spread onto frozen land in the nick of time before it thawed. On the night of 9 January we had a very clear sighting of a total lunar eclipse, a bad omen in both Chinese and Japanese mythology, requiring great noise to be made (including the use of cannon in later years) to fend off the dragon that was intent on devouring the moon.

As was our custom, Ruth and I provided a WLSBA stand at the North West and Borders Sheep Fair at Penrith Auction Mart, held that year on 17 January, taking one of our best rams and a hogg. It was a popular and important event for the commercial sheep farmers of Cumbria and Lancashire and we were kept constantly busy. Other WLSBA members helped us man the stand so we had ample time in which to wander around and meet friends and acquaintances representing other breeds. Despite the severe and prolonged agricultural depression there was an atmosphere of hope – surely this was going to be the year in which British farming began to claw its way back to some degree of recovery from the agricultural recession and the associated BSE crisis? Apart from the lunar eclipse, the omens were favourable, for the low market prices were generally slightly better than the disastrous prices of the previous year, and the super-saturated land was finally beginning to dry.

But it was a false dawn. On 20 February a pig at an abattoir in Essex was found to have foot and mouth disease, which was traced to a farm in Northumberland. It was identified as the virulent pan-Asiatic O-type virus. By the end of the week the number of confirmed cases had risen to six and 2,000 animals had been culled. By the time the disease was eradicated at the end of September there were to be a further 2,024 outbreaks, with more than four million animals slaughtered, including 595,884 cattle, 3,297,385 sheep and 144,931 pigs, on 9,804 premises. The experiences of myself and Ruth are described in the following emails (mostly to Mark, for he was in California, while Justin and Crispin received regular telephone calls). This is our story:

15 February (Me to Mark):
Is your overseas trip reasonably certain, hopefully followed by a call on us? Election fever now building up and at last a high pressure belt has settled over the country for a few days. Mum's opinion of e-mails and the web is improving, boosted by my being able to find the source of a plant that she seeks. I am becoming more familiar with the new system, but am proceeding very carefully in uncharted waters. Have a good day.

19 February (Ruth to Mark, on learning that Charlotte had passed exam and been admitted to Heckmondwike Grammar School):
She's done well. She learned of her success whilst on a weekend school trip to London, visiting various attractions including the Eye and an evening show. What a weekend for her! No school fees, but there will be uniform/kit overheads.

23 February (Me to Mark somewhere outside USA):
Foot and Mouth disease outbreak is national news headlines. Could be devastating to British farmers if not quickly contained. No movement of any animals permitted throughout UK for at least the next seven days. Race meetings and rural events cancelled and public requested to keep clear of the countryside. Outbreak has been traced to a pig farm about 10 miles west of Newcastle. However, it also affects sheep, goats, deer and cattle. Last outbreak was some 20 years ago, but this is a more dangerous virus. Meat exports halted. Only remedy seems to be the mass slaughter of all livestock in the area and burn on site.

There is speculation that Blair could go for a 5th April election. He is 20 points ahead in the polls. We are having supper with William Hague and Ffion at a local pub function at Finghall to-morrow. How he manages to be so cheerful I don't know.

Mum says you have an idea to resolve my First Choice printing problem by using two printers and a magic box. Please elaborate.

The ground has dried up very quickly this week. Snowdrops are out and crocuses and daffodils are pushing themselves up. We have a cold snap forecast for the weekend. I don't mind the cold, but hope the rain/snow keeps away – it would just turn the fields into a quagmire again. Have a good weekend.

26 February (Me to Mark):
Wet weather and mud again. Foot and Mouth virus spreading at an alarming rate. We have a notice requesting no entry into the yard and use a footbath ourselves. Not much else one can do apart from monitoring outbreak locations. Thousands of animals now being burned on site. Bradman dead, aged 92 years – best batsman ever – my idol as a schoolboy.

28 February (Me to Mark):
Six inches of fine snow overnight and clear blue sky. Major rail crash near Selby. Caused by vehicle skidding off M62 motorway, down

embankment and into path of a 125 at full speed, which in turn collided head on with oncoming freight train. At least 13 dead. Many seriously injured. Several more F&M outbreaks, but none any closer.

3 March (Me to Mark):

F&M outbreaks continuing and have now passed 50. Still no outbreaks in Yorkshire thank goodness. Very cold weather. Leyburn was mentioned on the news as being −10C last night, with −18C somewhere in Scotland. The ground is covered with about 6 inches of fine powdery snow and we have clear skies and sunshine with daytime temperatures hovering about zero. Warmer weather and heavy snow forecast. Hope you enjoy the ski-ing.

7 March (Ruth to Mark):

To-day I went for lunch with friends from the Royal Signals and we had a great gossip. Very bad news – a F&M outbreak has been confirmed at Hawes and there is a ten mile exclusion zone. It really is dreadful as my beautiful ewes are heavy in lamb and yesterday the first lambed, producing twin gimmers. The snow has begun to melt at last; the yard has been lethal. Nobody but nobody is allowed in the yard and all deliveries are made to the front door. It is like the children's programme that used to be on television where Mr Benn used to go in one door in a bowler hat and come out at the other end in a fez. I go in the front door in best clothes and out of the back door in wellies and moleskins. Everywhere you go is so desolate without the farmers buzzing about.

11 March (Ruth to Mark):

As we are now advised not to go anywhere because of the F&M epidemic* I decided to start the decorating and cleaning of the sitting room. It has been a mammoth furniture removing exercise and so far I have decorated part of the ceiling and part of the walls and the whole place is in turmoil and I've decided that I have done enough for one day, so we are sitting in the middle of a big mess. We decided to get to grips with disinfecting everything thoroughly now that we've been able to get some anti F&M disinfectant – contains sulphuric acid so God help our shoes and car tyres. Lois is now having swimming lessons and to-day is her ice skating lesson. Evidently she is doing very well.

* The correct term is 'enzootic' but MAFF's [MAFF = *Ministry of Agriculture, Fisheries and Food]* own forms and most farmers use 'epidemic'.

13 March (Me to Mark):
Middle of the night lambing. All went well – two nice lambs. Bush telegraph informs that there could be a F&M outbreak near Thirsk. Too close for comfort. The outbreak is now getting out of control. Due to overstretched resources there is now a gap of about 2 days between reporting and confirmation plus 2–3 days between confirmation and slaughter and a further 3–4 days before disposal is completed. During this period the virus continues to spread.

16 March (Me to Mark):
The ewes seem to be selecting the middle of the night this year as the best time to produce their lambs. It is now 2am and we have just moved a ewe that has lambed to her own accommodation with a very good ram lamb. A second is likely to follow. Hope she does not keep us waiting too long. F&M is now at epidemic proportion in Cumbria and Devon, resulting in some quite draconian measures being introduced. Still only one case in North Yorkshire. Bush telegraph reports that there could be a case near Driffield (awaiting blood test results). Have a good trip to Singapore.

17 March (Me to WLSBA member in the Netherlands):
Many thanks for your phone call and best wishes at this most difficult and stressful time and also for the copy of the e-mail that your VSS has sent to our Ministry of Agriculture, Fisheries and Food. The option of vaccination has been discarded following comprehensive debate, with

support from UN Food and Agriculture Organisation and EEC partners. Countries that cannot demonstrate a completely clean bill of health (including absence of both F&M vaccination and carriers) cannot export live animals or animal products to countries that are free of the disease. UK has approximately 40 million sheep and is the primary producer of sheep meat in Europe (33%). The export of sheep and sheep meat is as important to UK farmers as is the export of wine to French farmers.

However, the Government's recently announced intention to cull all sheep in the counties of Cumbria, Dumfries & Galloway that are within 3 kilometres of an outbreak (and which are not themselves infected) is not supported by our National Sheep Association or Rare Breeds Survival Trust, with whom WLSBA is co-operating. If our Government does not modify such intention there is likely to be trouble in these counties.

Again, many thanks for your concern. I fear that it will be several months before the disease is eradicated.

18 March (Ruth to Mark, in Singapore):
We have had snow overnight and flurries all day. It is wet, miserable and damned freezing cold. There are more F&M cases at Hawes and Burtersett and we dare not go out in case we meet someone carrying the virus. The whole countryside really is in crisis with many of our friends closer than we are to the outbreaks. My fridge has never been so low on provisions but I went out on Saturday and stocked up. Shops are suffering badly, as are guest houses and pubs. There are now over three hundred cases. I feel so sad about the slaughter of so many animals, also sheep with lambs at foot and ewes in lamb on high ground that cannot be moved to shelter because of the restrictions. They will be lambing in freezing, exposed conditions. All very depressing. By the way what is an adobe photoshop? Should I have one?

20 March (Ruth to Justin, Mark and Crispin):
Quads born in early hours and we are just about to go to bed at 4-30am. These are the first quads that we have ever had. It is a rare

occurrence. The dam was Great Yorkshire Show Breed Champion and Royal Show class winner in 1999. Justin – tell Jessica that they are three little girls and a little boy.

21 March (Ruth to Mark in Singapore):
F&M continues to spiral out of control. Now four cases in Hawes area. 272,824 animals have been slaughtered and there are 130,636 awaiting slaughter. Much depression in rural areas. Tourist favourites like Coniston and Windermere are ghost towns. Glad you are enjoying Singapore. You must visit your Kuala Lumpur birthplace sometime.

Quads are progressing well, but have not yet got them trained to take milk from a bucket contraption with teats on the side. The ewe will only have sufficient milk for two. However, we are making progress. Weather has turned wintry again.

23 March (Ruth to Mark):
Another day 'confined to barracks'. It really is quite desperate with cases creeping closer all the time. Life goes on and I have been painting the large window in the sitting room and intend to put the gloss paint on tomorrow. Everything is cancelled, even church services. Did you cash in on the crash on the New York Stock Market?

At last the snow has melted and temperatures are a little higher. It really has been bitterly cold. I'm now going to mix some milk for the quads. They are all piled in a heap under the heat lamp with a very proud mother watching over them. I wish she'd only had two.

My personal feelings and recollections at this time are reflected in the following note that I drafted for the Preface of the 2001 WLSBA flock book:

There is much anger amongst farmers at the incompetent and high handed manner in which the epidemic is being handled by government officials and probably many years will elapse before trust is restored. In particular there is anger that extensive pastoral, environmental and ecologically friendly sheep farming may again have been the victim of greed and cheap product procurement.

The cost to the taxpayer, the rural economy and the environment is phenomenal, but it is personal experiences that will linger in the mind rather than financial data – the smoke and acrid smell of the pyres, the empty market towns, farmers in tearful rage at the futility of official actions and the silence of the moors. The media is bringing the tragedy into every home, none better than this front page report of the Daily Mail on 27th March:

A Squadron of bulldozers is clearing the topsoil in immaculate lines while the diggers carve a trench the size of a canal. From a distance, they could be building a motorway through the Cumbrian countryside. But this road is going nowhere. It is the end of the line for hundreds of thousands of sheep and the first arrivals are just appearing out of the back of a huge red tipper truck. I expect them to come tumbling out as big balls of fluff. Instead, they slide out in one big glob. From my helicopter seat, they hardly resemble sheep at all. They look like huge grey maggots. The lorry moves off for a rigorous shower of disinfectant and another rumbles up to repeat the process. Once this grisly machine has settled into its rhythm, it is expected that 20,000 sheep will be buried here every day.

28 March (Me to Justin, Mark and Crispin):
F&M outbreak confirmed at Danby Wiske, near Northallerton yesterday (9 miles distant) and two outbreaks confirmed to-day at Bellerby (4 miles distant). Very depressing situation. These locations (and ourselves) are in the path of the prevailing westerly wind which could well have carried the virus from the Hawes area outbreaks along the dale. We are just crossing our fingers that we escape the devil's wand.

28 March (Ruth to Mark):
Thank you so much for the beautiful bouquet – a lovely variety of flowers. It couldn't have been delivered at a more poignant moment, with the disease only four miles away. What can we do? I feel so sad for my beautiful sheep, but we must sweat it out and just hope that

we are spared. I can't smile and it should be such a happy time with all the new lambs.

My personal thoughts at this time were that it was highly unlikely that Ruth's flock would escape the disease. However, I was determined to do everything that I could not only to save her flock but also, as Secretary of the WLSBA, to help save the flocks of other members and indeed any shepherd seeking help or advice. I began with the following letter:

The Wensleydale Longwool Sheep Breeders' Association (A COMPANY LIMITED BY GUARANTEE)
Honorary Secretary: Frank Pedley
Old Hall, Hunton, Bedale, North Yorkshire, DL8 1QJ.
Bedale (01677) 450579
www.wensleydale-sheep.com

PRESS RELEASE – 29th MARCH 2001
Unique Rare Breed Threatened

The spread of the foot and mouth epidemic into Wensleydale is a grave threat to the rare and unique sheep that has carried the name of the dale for 125 years – the Wensleydale longwool. The leading flocks and bloodlines are concentrated in North Yorkshire, and Wensleydale in particular, where breeders who have dedicated much of their life to the promotion of the breed are praying that the devil's wand does not descend upon their flocks.

The breed is unique in that it is the largest of our indigenous breeds, has the finest lustre wool in the world and, ironically, the highest genetic resistance to what the sheep industry had hitherto regarded as the most threatening disease of the new millennium – scrapie.

The Wensleydale is a dual purpose sheep, having been developed by astute Wensleydale shepherds for both wool quality and for rams of a type ideally suited for crossing with hill breed ewes to produce desirable crossbred ewes. These crossbred ewes are then put to terminal sires of the Suffolk, Texel and Charollais breeds to provide the housewife with the highest quality lamb.

Wensleydale wool is entirely kemp free as a result of the unique characteristics of the wool-producing follicles. It is used for top quality hand knitted garments and is noted for its silky softness and handle. The Wensleydale Longwool Sheepshop near Leyburn has twice won the British Wool Marketing Board International Quality Award. The epidemic could affect not only its flock of Wensleydale sheep but also shop sales which rely to a large extent on tourist purchases. The wool quality is particularly appreciated in North America, where breeders are engaged in a breeding-up programme using imported Wensleydale ram semen which attracts prices up to £95 per straw.

Further information on the breed can be obtained from the Association's web site – www.wensleydale-sheep.com

Honorary Secretary.

Distribution: Daily Telegraph, Daily Mail, Independent, Sunday Times, Times, The Guardian, Daily Express, Yorkshire Post, Darlington & Stockton Times, Northern Echo.
Copied to: Rare Breeds Survival Trust.

One could now smell the burning of the pyres of cattle in upper Wensleydale and debris could be seen in the air and on the land, carried by the prevailing westerly wind. Ruth and I were concerned that these on– site pyres were instrumental in spreading the disease further; down the dale and onwards to the Yorkshire Moors. It was not just a hunch – one of the conclusions of the 1967 F&M outbreak was that 'there is little doubt that infected debris from fires contributes significantly to the spread of the disease'. I telephoned a number of farmer friends about this and found that they shared our thoughts, whereupon I sent further WLSBA press releases to all and sundry, including the Rt. Hon. William Hague, whom Ruth and I knew quite well, describing this local concern and urging the cessation of on-site cremation in Wensleydale, and instead the removal of carcasses for burial.

31 March (Secretary Wensleydale Longwool Sheep Breeders' Association to Daily Telegraph, Yorkshire Post etc.)

Restrict Burning of Cattle Carcases.

Very strong feeling amongst farming community that selective exemptions must be made to the current inflexible policy of only burning F&M infected cattle. An example is Wensleydale, where the prevailing westerly wind is carrying infected F&M debris from burning sites along the dale towards the Yorkshire Moors. Probably too late now to save Wensleydale, but not too late to save Yorkshire Moors and Vale of York. Farmers believe that burning is significantly contributing to the spread of the disease.

The argument for burning cattle is entirely environmental, an important consideration, but it should be weighed against other factors in making a rational appreciation for different parts of the country.

Yours sincerely,

Frank Pedley

Can you exert pressure to change current inflexible policy?

There was encouraging media support and the *Daily Telegraph* published my letter on 3 April. The burning eventually ceased, at least in Wensleydale. Whether or not my efforts had helped in this change of policy matters not – I had spoken up and made a contribution.

1 April (Ruth to Mark):

I've done a bit of gardening and tidying up as Spring shoots are now coming through. The pond is full of frog spawn and despite being frozen for so long it is coming to life. I then went for a walk along the stream. I haven't done that for some time because I don't want people to think that they can do likewise. I couldn't believe how deep the stream pools are, because of the bottoms being scoured out. Many trout – darting all over. There are now MAFF signs at the road ends stating entry into a F&M zone. Blair and Brown continuing to say everything is under control. Under control my ...!

What a lying group of control freaks. I've got everything planned of what I shall say if the TV cameras come to our farm, provided daddy doesn't stand on my foot too hard.

3 April (Me to Justin, Mark and Crispin):
Text of letter sent to Daily Telegraph and published to-day attached. I have no intention of becoming a regular armchair scribe, but I have never been so incensed in my life at the incompetence and arrogance of MAFF and this British Prime Minister who puts himself first, the Labour Party second and the Nation that he represents last. If he is indeed in overall charge of the crisis he needs to get a grip and take decisions.

I had a chat with a vet from Northumberland this lunchtime. He is now well used to telephone conversations with farmers in tears. Many are so broken that a member of the family has to make the call advising of a feared outbreak. Little veterinary work as some clients no longer have any stock, whilst those with stock do not want a vet on their land in case of infection and are resorting to DIY veterinary work.

9 April (Me to Justin, Mark, Crispin):
Another case at Bellerby, slightly closer (3.9 miles). Strong rumour that large burial pit being dug on the Catterick Training Area to receive carcases from Cumbria, Whitby and Wensleydale. Nobody wants these pits near them, but carcases have to go somewhere. 40 Wensleydales culled in Durham a few days ago. Steady trickle of phone calls from distressed WLSBA members whose flocks have been culled or anticipated. Very sad – they are such nice people.

14 April (Me to Mark returning from Taiwan):
There has been an outbreak at Tunstall, 4.5 kms to the NE. However, the affected farm has sheep in a field only 2.5 kms from our flock. The cull distance is 3 kms! A further outbreak is suspected to the south of Richmond. The MAFF assessment is that the whole of Wensleydale is now threatened. We have brought all our animals inside, into the byres

and barn, and have assurances from the National Sheep Association, Rare Breeds Survival Trust and others that they will support the appeal that we will make for exemption. A knock on the door from a MAFF official would be no surprise. If we get the disease we accept that all must be culled, but we will fight hard against culling just because we are in a contiguous location. The outbreak at Tunstall has resulted in all cattle and sheep on 12 neighbouring farms being culled, whilst the outbreak at Aysgarth resulted in 14 farms losing their livestock. These are typical 'knock on' figures that are concealed in MAFF statistics. Five WLSBA flocks have now been culled because of this policy of culling livestock on neighbouring farms.

The legality of this precautionary culling policy, whereby livestock within 3 kilometeres of a confirmed outbreak would also be culled, was now being questioned in legal circles, and Ruth and I were particularly encouraged by the following article by Christopher Booker in the *Sunday Telegraph* of 1 April, which we had kept close to hand:

KILLING OF STOCK CANNOT BE ENFORCED
No feature of MAFF's handling of the foot and mouth crisis has been more bizarre than the way the ministry has been acting outside the law in its attempt to kill off all animals in 'three kilometre protective zones' round infected farms even when these animals show no sign of infection.

Even Downing Street was last week forced to admit that MAFF has no powers, either under EU or British law, to order the destruction of animals on any holding not directly infected. Yet a key part of MAFF's strategy has been to suggest that it does have such powers, and to persuade farmers that, unless they sign a paper agreeing to the slaughter of their animals they will forfeit the right to compensation. This has particular relevance to the owners of rare breeds who, if they lose their stock, will in many cases never be able to replace them.

Leonora Parsons of Chaddesley Corbett in Worcestershire, one of a handful of owners of Britain's 400 surviving Leicester Longwool ewes, has been told that all her sheep must be slaughtered, because her farm is surrounded by three [outbreak zones] to which the now well-known west Midlands sheep dealer Kevin Feakins delivered infected sheep in February.

However, since her lovingly protected Leicesters show no sign of infection, ministry officials have no power to insist on their destruction, any more than they did to order the killing last week of an array of rare animals on a farm-park at Berkeley in Gloucestershire, which sent a wave of shock across the West Country. This issue will feature heavily in arguments to be heard in the Kindersley case in the High Court tomorrow. But in the meantime, as even Downing Street concedes, the law is clear. MAFF's officials are in no position to order such slaughter and it is outrageous for them to pretend that they are.

It became apparent to us that MAFF vets were justifying their actions in culling healthy animals (without owner permission) which had not been in any contact with infected animals, within their arbitrary 'three kilometre protective zones', on the basis that the animals therein 'had been exposed to infection', which accordingly could only have been airborne. We learned that the expression 'in any way exposed' had not been defined in law and read with interest the opinion of a barrister-at– law representing the Green Party Agricultural Working Group that, if tested in law, it would be unlikely to incorporate long-distance airborne exposure. The barrister-at-law concluded his commentary with the following opinion: 'In the event that an owner of animals is of the opinion that [the animals] have not been "exposed" it is anticipated the police would support his refusal to allow MAFF officials on his land to carry out a slaughter until a court order had been obtained by MAFF.'

So, we were not ill prepared if a man in a white coat knocked on the door!

15 April (Ruth to Mark):
We have just heard that they are doing a contiguous culling almost in Hunton, so the men in white coats are getting nearer. What an Easter Sunday! I woke up ready to tackle the world but now I feel thoroughly

dejected. Everything is now inside the byres and barn but it's a real squeeze for them and not easy feeding and watering them. I should really be giving the house a good clean but I can't be bothered. It can wait. The new village hall is well under way – if it is marked out for badminton I may take it up again because I did enjoy it.

17 April a.m. (Ruth to Mark in France – explaining to him that it will not be feasible for him to visit):
I'm getting worried about your proposed visit. Now there is culling on the outskirts of Hunton. We visited Charlotte on her birthday but have not been anywhere since and nobody but nobody has been on our property since February. We have a complete decontamination system where nothing that we have worn outside our land comes in contact with anything that goes out onto the farm. For example, we wouldn't sit on anything in the Old Hall wearing our 'shopping clothes' in case we picked the virus up on our farm clothes. Quite simply, you would be confined inside all the time. Should our flock become infected you would not under any circumstances be allowed to leave Old Hall – MAFF rules. There is another greater issue – I wouldn't want the USA to get F&M from your clothes. I never thought I would ever be discouraging you from visiting. We had a very good paper sent to us last night explaining our legal rights. We won't go under without an almighty fight.

17 April p.m. (Ruth to Mark in France):
Thanks for a bit of humour – we need it. Three new cases in the area to-day: one at Bainbridge and two at East Cowton, near Northallerton. Half a million carcases awaiting disposal, rotting on farms. Everything under control says the Government. I wonder how George Orwell would have portrayed the blatant lies and political cover up. Have you noticed that on the MAFF web site you now have to look under the heading 'Topic of the Week' to find F&M data? Phone has never stopped ringing to-day with enquiries and good wishes from Wensleydale breeders and other farmers.

The following morning (18 April) we were woken to the sound of nearby gunshots from the direction of the nearest farm to Old Hall – bang … bang … bang … bang … bang …

'They're culling at Scrogg Farm,' cried Ruth. I dashed downstairs to investigate, returning a few minutes later with a smile on my face. 'What are you laughing at?' cried Ruth, tears rolling down her cheeks. 'It's OK,' I replied, 'it's a bird scarer!' We hugged each other, laughing and crying at the same time.

That evening, following an unofficial report of an outbreak at nearby Patrick Brompton, I sent the following email to our veterinary surgeon and good friend, Brian Linscott:

Dear Brian,

With reference to our telephone discussion this morning, attached is the Application for Exemption from Slaughter for Ruth's flock of Wensleydale sheep in the event of an outbreak occurring within 3 kms of our flock. Ruth and I would be grateful if you would insert the name and location of the farm at which the outbreak has occurred on the Application for Exemption form and then forward it soonest to the Divisional Veterinary Manager at Leeds, with a supportive cover note.

I telephoned the Leeds MAFF office this morning and was given the following communication advice …

Of course, should the flock become infected with the disease we are resigned to the fact that it must be culled.

Yours sincerely,

Ruth and Frank Pedley

Two days later the reported outbreak at Patrick Brompton was confirmed and the following exemption application was duly signed by Ruth and dispatched:

APPLICATION FOR EXAMPTION FROM SLAUGHTER
Wensleydale Sheep Flock at Old Hall Farm, Hunton, Bedale, North Yorkshire DL8 1QJ

Telephone: 01677 450579
GR 186924 (Sheet 99)

Divisional Veterinary Manager, Leeds
Mr JM Williams BVMS MSc MRCVS

Dear Mr Williams,

   My flock of pedigree Wensleydale sheep (Herd Mark 128294) is under threat of slaughter as a consequence of the recent outbreak of Foot and Mouth disease at:

   Patrick Brompton, near Bedale, for my flock is 2.9 kms from that location. I request your authority for exemption from slaughter on the following grounds:

- *The sheep are not infected and have not been in contact with any infected animals. They are housed indoors and only 100m inside the 3 kms zone.*
- *The Wensleydale breed of sheep is not only a rare breed, but a valuable genetic resource, in that it has the highest genetic resistance to scrapie of all British sheep breeds (92% ARR/ARR). It is also unique in having the finest lustre wool in the world.*
- *My flock is recognised as being one of the three leading Wensleydale flocks in the United Kingdom. During the past decade the flock has won 24 Breed Championships, including the Royal Show (twice), the Great Yorkshire Show (twice) and the Royal Highland Show. In 1997 my Great Yorkshire Show champion (still with the flock) achieved the unique distinction of additionally winning the Supreme Female and Supreme Fleece trophies.*
- *As a result of only infrequently using rams from other flocks my flock has a much sought after and distinct bloodline which could not be replaced.*

The Hunton flock of Wensleydale sheep comprises a shearling ram, seven yearling rams, eleven ewes with lambs, three ewes in lamb, and fifteen yearling ewes. No other sheep or animals are kept on this small farm which specialises in the breeding of high quality pedigree stock. It is vitally important to the Wensleydale breed that the few remaining flocks in the dale from which the breed acquired its name in 1876 remain intact if at all possible.

Yours sincerely, Mrs Ruth Pedley.

18 April (Ruth to Mark, Justin, Crispin):
A busy day getting all the paper work in place in case the men in white coats come knocking on the door. Many farmer friends ringing us for advice, not realising that we ourselves are in a desperate situation. Need to do a mammoth shop. As Scarlett O'Hara said, 'Tomorrow is another day'.

21 April (Me to family):
Have just been advised of an outbreak at a farm just to the west of Patrick Brompton. That places us in the culling zone. A copy of our appeal to the Divisional Veterinary Manager at Leeds is attached. The appeal is with our Local Veterinary Officer who will Fax or e-mail to Leeds as soon as we have a formal approach from MAFF officials concerning a cull. We will keep you informed.

For the next two days the silence was deafening. Our tending of the flock continued as normal and we took many 'final photographs' of our sheep. On the morning of 24 May a MAFF inspector arrived and formally served the anticipated 'D Notice', a restrictive notice which advised us that our sheep had been exposed to infection and imposing several pages of restrictive measures that we were now required to implement. These included the placement of a notice in block letters of at least 10 cms height at the entrance to Old Hall: FOOT AND MOUTH DISEASE – KEEP OUT.

24 April (Ruth to family):
'D' Notice served to-day, so we have a big notice at our entrance. We are not only contiguous but contagious and flipping fed up. However,

we are bearing up reasonably well and are expecting the men in white coats to visit anytime to examine our stock or whatever. I was speaking to someone up the dale this morning and they said the smell up there is dreadful. A not very happy mummy – I just have the most terrible nightmares about animals being slaughtered.

25 April (Ruth to family):
The swallows have arrived and are doing a recce. We have had a hail storm with hail the size of marbles, followed by thunder and lightning and the beck is flooded. There are rumours of a case at Bedale and at Masham, but we think they are unconfirmed.

28 April (Me to family):
Regrettably, another Wensleydale flock has been culled. The owners are commercial farmers who have lost 1,500 sheep plus a large dairy herd. They only kept a few Wensleydales. They are from the Castle Douglas area and are in a contiguous situation, the same distance from an outbreak as ourselves. The compensation will enable them to re-stock, but they have been advised that this will not be permitted until this time next year. No income in the meantime – in fact not until the replacement stock have 'produced a harvest'. The postman delivered the mail in tears a few days ago. He had just delivered the mail to the farmer at Patrick Brompton whose cattle were in the process of being culled. The farmer had just given an apple and a pat on the rump to each animal before the slaughtermen were allowed in. Another local farmer had insisted on the recently born lambs being given a short outing in the meadow prior to slaughter. I am sure that there are many similar stories. There is so much bitterness at the incompetency and inconsistency of MAFF and the brutality of their hired hatchetmen – the ministry will have much difficulty in obtaining the co-operation of farmers in formulating a plan for the future.

The sheep will have to be let out on Tuesday or Wednesday as we are running out of hay and the byres are becoming rather unhealthy. We still have a small amount of straw but Robin has exacerbated the problem by building a nest on the top bale, on which his wife has laid four eggs, plus another, rather carelessly, outside the nest.

Mum is very excited at having seen a newt this afternoon. The lambs that are being bottle fed are very tame. We sit on a bale of straw with two bottles each and are overwhelmed by them. They jump on our knees in their excitement, whilst the ewes have become attracted to your Mum's hair and the smell of the aniseed ball that is usually in her mouth. If the flock gets F&M I think we will also succumb.

Hope Crispin, Aileen and the children have had a nice holiday in Spain.

Two days later I went into Bedale to do some urgent shopping for Ruth, having first thoroughly washed the car, sprayed it with the requisite disinfectant and changed into 'clean' clothing and footwear. Driving home along the A684 I saw three white-coated persons ahead in a group at the junction to our lane. They were in discussion with our farmer friend Colin Ellwood. 'This is it,' I thought, for if the disease had reached that point, only half a kilometre from Old Hall, they would surely demand the inclusion of our flock in the cull, and I braced myself accordingly. As I drew level I realised that they were re-painting the metal railings at the front of his house.

1 May (Me to family):
May Day, and heard first cuckoo this morning. Spent most of the morning drenching [i.e. worming] 15 ewe hoggs, clipping their faces and trimming feet etc. Then sat on garden bench and listened to the Curlews. Clear blue sky and warm. I still haven't seen a newt in the pond but your Mum reports several sightings. MAFF veterinary inspector visits to-morrow. It is the first F&M visit that she has made, so unlikely to be carrying the virus. Sheep are in very good health.

2 May (Ruth to family):
Today the 'clean' MAFF vet came to look at our animals and pronounced them healthy. She will be coming again in 10 days. It was

a great relief to us both. We then decided that as it was a very still day and sunny we would let three ewes out with their lambs and watched them race and race until they were quite breathless – a wonderful sight. The cuckoo arrived yesterday morning, robins continue to sit on their five eggs and the swallows are in every building because byre doors are partly open to let air circulate. It is just the wretched F&M that puts a damper on everything. Mark – I love the cat carrier, we are going to send it up to John Prescott, our vet friend in Northumberland. He may be able to sell a few!

5 May (Ruth to family):
We still have all these blessed restrictions on us and can see no end to it. We know that the government are not giving a true figure of actual F&M cases. However, all the sheep are out now as we no longer had the hay and straw to feed and bed them. The joy of the lambs was a sight to be seen. They raced until they were totally out of breath, to the delight of onlookers. I cleared out the beck this morning – so much plastic and corrugated iron. The kingcups are out and more trout than I've seen for years – some at least 12 inches. Gosh, when all this is ended I'm going on the biggest spending spree I've ever done.

6 May (Me to family):
I always read the letters to the editors of the Times and Daily Telegraph each morning, usually whilst making your Mum's cup of tea. My favourite last week was from well known author Frederick Forsyth to the Daily Telegraph:

Landscape Farmers
Sir, – I see Mr Blair has come up with another wizard wheeze (report, 28 Apr). In future, farmers will become custodians of the rural landscape, i.e. the countryside.

We will plough and sow, reap and mow; clip and crop, prune and lop; weed and strim, hedge and trim.

We will clear the ditches, unclog the culverts and haul away the winter's fallen deadwood. We will control nettle and dock, bramble and briar, ragwort and thistle. In betwixt, we will mend the barns, string the fences, hang the gates and erect the stiles.

In short, we will maintain the countryside as the most beautiful rural landscape in Europe.

So what does the twit think we have been doing for the past 500 years?
Frederick Forsyth, Hertford.

Robin's first egg hatched yesterday and when I peeped this morning there were three small robins and one unhatched egg. The parent birds are rarely off the nest and we are very careful not to disturb. Whenever we walk along the stream someone crosses the road to tell us how nice it is to see the sheep and lambs out and to wish us well. There is no doubt that they are very popular.

7 May (Me to Mark):
Many thanks for speedy update of WLSBA website. One never knows but the sight of the insert could be the salvation of a flock and save someone much distress. I understand that a legal advice download that I sent to a member in Durham was handed to a neighbour and saved a large dairy herd. Another beautiful morning. It would be nice to go off for a drive and walk in the countryside, but we dare not risk bringing in infection. Footpaths remain closed.

15 May (Ruth to Mark):
On Friday night Justin brought up Charlotte, Jessica and Robert to stay, as both of them had to work and Betty and Jack were on a QE2 cruise. It was a sweltering weekend and, of course, we were rather restricted. However, we set off with high hopes to visit Middleham Castle, but a local farmer is grazing his sheep on the land and cannot get permission to move the animals. So, the castle must remain closed. Thankfully, a long string of racehorses came by and the children were thrilled to bits. We then set off for some Brymor ice cream, knowing

that the farm and parlour was closed but that purchases could be made at Masham town hall, where we had drinks and ice cream (Charlotte managed two). We then headed for Bolton Castle, which was open, and we had the most wonderful day, with afternoon tea in their café. They went everywhere, including high up on the leads. Jessica has come on leaps and bounds and I find her the easiest to manage. She did her ten spellings without a mistake and she read The Wind in the Willows. She really is a lovely girl.

The MAFF veterinary inspector comes again on Thursday and from what I can gather from other farmers it could be a long time before the restrictions are lifted. There are now cases at Malham Tarn, which is a real worry for Wharfedale and the moors. We are now more relaxed about the whole thing, probably because we have lived with it for so long. Unfortunately, they are not allowing itinerant shearers to clip so I may have to shear forty sheep, which will be a challenge. Life goes on. Hope you enjoyed Texas.

17 May (Me to family):
Your Mum tripped over and fell awkwardly on an upturned metal feeding trough about three weeks ago, incurring a nasty gash on her leg just above the ankle. She refused to see a doctor and would not let me tell you. Though the swelling has gone down, the wound has turned septic and I took her to the Friarage Hospital at Northallerton this morning where she got prompt attention in the casualty department. Further visit on Saturday morning. In the meantime lots of tablets to be taken, but not penicillin because of allergy. Could need some plastic surgery.

She can be very strong willed and stubborn, but there was no way that she was going to avoid treatment this morning. Will keep you informed.

24 May (Ruth to family):
Went to the hospital again yesterday (following daily visits for changes of dressing) and they are much happier with the leg. They have got

to grips with the infection but having taken seventy seven antibiotic tablets in seven days it should be looking better. Today was the last day of tablets so I can get back to Carlsberg Special Brew – only joking. I hope to be fit to start shearing soon. The garden looks lovely and that will keep me occupied if the restrictions continue, but hopefully this area will soon be declared free of F&M, though we will need to have blood tests taken to make sure the sheep don't have antibodies. General Election fever continues here with fly posters everywhere. I hope the SATS tests went well for Charlotte and that she gets the grades she needs. Looking forward to your visit Mark but am still worried about the F&M getting in the way.

31 May (Me to Mark):
Your Mum's leg continues to respond satisfactorily, but she still needs to visit the Friarage hospital every two days for attention and change of dressing in the casualty department. They are brilliant, and we are rarely kept waiting more than a few minutes. We have Charlotte, Jessica and Robert for a few days. Not sure where to take them to-day as countryside walks still closed. Looks as though the Conservatives are going to get thrashed next Thursday. Look forward to seeing you on the Friday.

The Conservatives were indeed well beaten in the general election on Thursday 7 June, but no worse than they had been in the previous election in 1997. In fact, they gained a seat, making a total of 165, but Labour had a massive 413 and the Liberal Democrats 52. Ruth and I felt very sorry for William Hague, who promptly resigned as leader of the Conservative Party. With the strong economy that Labour had inherited in 1997 continuing, falling unemployment and Tony Blair at the height of his popularity, it was an inevitable result, particularly with the Conservatives divided on Europe. Ruth and I still entirely agreed with William Hague's slogan 'In Europe, but not run by Europe' and, indeed, a large poster board bearing the words was erected on our land.

However, in December 2015 I was very disappointed when he abandoned his "In Europe but not run by Europe" stance: the central pillar of his political career up to that time. He became an advocate for remaining permanently in the European Union, accepting the inevitable loss of British Sovereignty. I continue to resolutely believe that now free of the shackles of Brussels my very talented country will soon prosper significantly; as when it broke with Rome some 500 years ago – the Reformation [1517-1648]. Nevertheless, I admire William Hague [Baron Hague of Richmond, PC, FRSL] as one of the most talented British Statesmen of his generation; world class orator, writer, debater, raconteur and very good company. I still chuckle when I recall his witticisms at Conservative Party functions that I attended with Ruth; particularly gems at the expense of Tony Blair. I respect him as a self-made man of great wisdom and principle.

By mid-June the F&M epidemic was seemingly beginning to wane in our area, but surprise outbreaks ensured that there was no complacency, and we continued our vigilance. In Yorkshire the disease was particularly rife in the Upper Dales and Yorkshire Moors, where there were no barriers to arrest its spread. Ruth's leg was almost healed and she was now allowed to do her own dressings at home, though with strict instructions to return to the hospital if there was any problem.

24 June (Me to family):
Up at 6am to a haze that clearly indicated a vintage summer day. If the cuckoo has changed its tune I have not heard it and as the kettle was boiling for your Mum's early morning cuppa it was the Curlew's cries that dominated the still countryside. Checked, fed and watered the sheep. Shearing of a ewe began at 9am and as she was reasonably docile the job was completed in 35 minutes, including the 'manicuring' of her feet. Extra attention needed for an old ewe (10 shear) that is to be 'put down' by the vet to-morrow. She has been one of our best ewes but is now having difficulty walking.

Decided to remove rubbish that has accumulated during the time that we have been on a 'D' notice to the tip and in case of infection put the old Volvo through an automatic wash on the return journey, followed by spraying of tyres with Deosan. Trimmed the lank Garth grass with my little red tractor cutter and it now looks like a miniature golf course, whilst your Mum cut the lawns. Evening relaxation gazing at the garden, which has never been better. The copper beech is magnificent. Birds everywhere, including a number of goldfinches. Watched the last few overs of Yorkshire's defeat of Northamptonshire and poured glasses of a rather nice Californian Chardonnay as the temperature fell from about 24 to 18 degrees. A couple of hours of secretarial work, followed by arrangements to receive 150 bales of top quality Nidderdale hay to-morrow, with a similar load later in the week.

30 June (Me to Mark in Japan):
F&M now well established in both Yorkshire Dales and Yorkshire Moors and now approaching Leyburn along Bishopdale. Very worrying.

On 1 July Ruth and I reflected that were it not for this damned F&M epidemic we would have been travelling on that day to the Royal Show, where she had been selected to judge. No new hat for Ruth this year.

10 July (Ruth to Mark):
Crispin and Aileen and the three girls stopped over at Old Hall en route for a seaside holiday in the Scarborough area. It was a very happy time. Cara and Marianne are making good progress and Lois is just a little poppet, but shy. We went to Middleham Castle, which had a group of people there re-enacting how they wove the wool and cooked and made leather goods. I thought it was beautifully done and could have stayed much longer. We had hoped that Justin and family would be able to come up as well but both Haley and Justin were called in to work because of the riots in Bradford. Justin involved in riot control

and Haley having to cover for other officers. They sounded shattered when I spoke to them. Been cleaning to-day and mowed the lawns but am fed up to the teeth with F&M crisis. It just gets worse in North Yorkshire.

23 July (Me to Mark):
Mum has won £100 in a Conservative draw. Ministry vets are now taking blood tests in our area and are likely to visit us shortly. If all are negative there is a chance that the 'D Notice' might be lifted. However, it has just been announced that special intensive bio-security measures are to be enforced in an area centred on Thirsk, affecting 2,700 farms. There is a rumour that movements of farmers and their families are to be restricted and that vehicles can only visit the farms on licence. I do hope that we are outside the boundary!

24 July (Ruth to family):
Thirty of our sheep had blood taken to-day to see if there is any trace of F&M. We just hope that no antibodies are found. If every farm in the area is clear then the 'D notice' can be lifted, but it could take three to four weeks to get the results through.

The brightness of the morning burst into Old Hall on 25 July – it was clearly going to be a gorgeous summer's day. When I brought Ruth's early-morning cup of tea to her I asked her, 'Would it be daft to go to Headingley and watch Yorkshire play in a one day match?' Ruth's response was short, positive and immediate, 'Yes, please!' So was the response of her best friend, Nanette, whom we picked up at Walton. We needed a break and thoroughly enjoyed the day, though Yorkshire lost a tight match against Warwickshire. I recollect that Ruth and Nanette were fascinated by the content of the lunch boxes of nearby spectators. A very popular 'ice cream man' would sell his wares from a shoulder tray, announcing his location after each replenishment with a shout of "Yummy, yummy ice cream", to which potential buyers loudly replied, "Yummy, yummy, yummy". I provided Ruth and Nanette with a generous supply of his wares. They chatted virtually non-stop, but nevertheless in the evening, when we were all back home, they had a telephone natter of at least another hour's duration.

The number of F&M outbreaks each day was anxiously monitored by the farming community, rather like the number of enemy aircraft incursions during the Battle of Britain in World War II. An encouraging decline in the number of outbreaks was now apparent and on two consecutive days in early August there were no new outbreaks. As the month progressed it became clear that the wretched disease was nearing its end.

September began with jubilation. We beat Germany 5–1 at football in Munich in a World Cup qualifying round, while Yorkshire became cricket champions again after a lapse of 33 years – though still having won the championship on more occasions than any other county.

The eleventh day of that month is likely to be remembered for as long as mankind remains on this planet. Ruth and I watched the attacks by the Islamic terrorist group al-Qaeda on the twin towers on our television screen as they occurred. Crispin telephoned, as shocked and dumbfounded as ourselves and the commentators on both sides of the Atlantic. Gradually, the horrific picture began to unfold of four hijacked passenger planes being targeted at the twin towers of the World Trade Center, the Pentagon and Washington, DC. Including the 19 hijackers and 227 passengers aboard the planes, 343 firefighters and 72 law enforcement officers, almost 3,000 people died as a result of the attacks. The numbers would have been significantly higher but for the preventive actions of passengers on the plane heading for Washington, DC, which crashed instead into a field, and the fact that the Pentagon plane only glanced its target. These terrorist attacks were attributed to al-Qaeda and resulted in a US-led invasion of Afghanistan in October, supported by the UK, Australia and other close allies. Their aim was to depose the Taliban organisation that was concealing al-Qaeda and possibly its leader, Osama bin Laden (eventually killed by US Navy SEAL Team 6 on 2 May 2011 in a special operation launched from Afghanistan). The 9/11 atrocity was carried out by 19 hijackers, of the following nationalities: Saudi Arabia (15), United Arab Emirates (2), Egypt (1) and Lebanon (1).

As the foot and mouth epidemic further declined in late September, horrific news began to percolate through to an already demoralised farming community that interim research results from the Institute of Animal Health laboratory in Edinburgh indicated that BSE had crossed the species barrier into the national sheep flock. As a draft government contingency plan was known to be in place to slaughter the entire national flock of 40 million sheep should this occur, the sheep industry was in despair and on the verge of panic. However, on 18 October the Laboratory of the Government Scientist reported that the Institute of Animal Health's four-year research was seriously flawed.

An unbelievable scandal was then revealed – cow brain material had inadvertently been used in the four-year research programme instead of sheep brain material. Shepherds did not know whether to laugh or cry. The excuse – that a junior had made a labelling error – could have been predicted.

We felt sufficiently relaxed about the decline of the F&M epidemic for Crispin and family to spend a few days with us in late September, incorporating a visit to the Forbidden Corner, near Leyburn. Lois described the visit in an email to Mark in the following words: *'Bedtime. I have had a lovely day. The Forbidden Garden was a bit scarey but I enjoyed it. We got wet with water squirts. There were lots of nasty things. We have just got back from a nice supper at the Wyvill Arms. Lots of stars and a bright moon when we came out.'*

29 September (Ruth and me to family):
Supper at a Conservative function at Bolton Castle yesterday. Nice food and company. Mum won a bottle of Chardonnay in the raffle, whilst Dad won an antiques book of £18 value in a competition in which you had to answer 20 questions on value, date etc. of a variety of antiques on display. Actually, it was the booby prize – I only got four correct answers. Mum says it is a very good book and is reading it from cover to cover. There was a roaring fire in the huge fireplace. Lady

Bolton acted as a waitress, whilst Lord Bolton was stoker and odd job man. The castle was floodlit and with an almost full moon one could see much of Wensleydale in the background – a lovely sight. Spent this morning clearing muck from the byres and then to Masham Sheep Fair. Of course, no sheep allowed this year because of F&M disease, but this had not daunted the organisers. The main competition was for the best 'scarecrow shepherd and sheep in a pen', with a first prize of £500 (donated by local brewery). There must have been 35 entries, the majority of a very good standard. Each pen had a secure collecting box fastened to it, in which members of the public donated a sum of their choice to what they assessed to be the best entries. The winner will be the exhibit that collected most money from the public. All donations to charity. Other activities included a children's fancy dress parade, fair, harvest display, band, hand bell ringing, stalls, glass blowing, spinning, weaving, brewery trips, longsword dancers etc. The grandchildren would have loved the ferret stall, where you placed the ferret in a circular arena and had to guess which of ten holes it would disappear into. A simple life but we are never bored.

In mid-October we had the fourth F&M inspection of our flock and premises, this time conducted by an inspector from the Department for Environment, Food and Rural Affairs (DEFRA), that had come into existence as a result of MAFF merging with another government department. The inspection was satisfactory and Ruth was told that our 'D Notice' might be lifted in two to four weeks. However, in the meantime we had to continue to implicitly follow the imposed restrictions. I spent much time cleaning and disinfecting the outbuildings and repairing and painting doors and windows, while Ruth was putting the garden to bed ready for the winter. She began swimming at the Bedale pool for more exercise and couldn't wait for the opening of the village hall on 27 October, to enable her to play badminton again.

To our delight, on 6 November we received an 'E Notice' – signifying the withdrawal of our 'D Notice'. We had been subjected to its restrictions for six and a half months. It was like having a heavy load lifted from our shoulders, and the year drew to a close in a relaxed atmosphere:

7 November (Ruth to Mark, who was in South Korea, about to leave for Japan): Yesterday the D notice was lifted. It really is a relief and we have had a delivery of gravel for the front drive to make it look a bit tidier. Look forward to seeing you soon.

11 November (Ruth to family, including Mark in Singapore):
To-day has been a beautiful Autumn day and Rat Bag has been busy in the garden, which is full of colour. There are still blue and pink delphiniums, nerines, schistolylus, phlox, pyrethrums, pansies, antirrhinums, roses and other flowers which really should have gone to bed a month ago. I've had a lovely day. We then went to Brymor and had a quick ice cream, giving the 'new' (207,000 miles) Jeep an outing, and I drove it back. It's automatic and apart from a rattle, which daddy seems to have cured, it went well.

I envy you in Singapore, Mark, particularly eating satay. It always used to be served with cold solidified rice wrapped up in plaited banana leaves. Very, very nice indeed. Daddy and I are both reading Harry Potter in bed at night and I can't wait to go and see the film. We'll certainly be able to keep up with the grandchildren.

4 December (Me to Mark, now back in California):
You must be feeling rather drained after long flight and reception! We have been on a Christmas present buying trip to Northallerton and Darlington. It went better than I had anticipated for your Mum had done some useful research regarding possible presents which saved a lot of time.

She is in the early stages of a good Yak Yak with Nanette on the telephone, so supper is likely to be delayed for at least 45 minutes. She adopts a trance like posture looking out of the breakfast room window for 'Nan conversations', even when it is pitch black outside – seems to help her concentration, and stamina.

Hope you have a good meeting. Computer seems to be behaving itself and the virus does not seem to have caused any problems.

The Christmas tree and decorations were installed as usual on Ruth's birthday and we were delighted to receive Mark and girlfriend Claire three days before Christmas, followed by the traditional family gathering, celebration and gaiety.

How blessed is he who leads a country life, unvexed with anxious cares and void of strife!

—John Dryden (1631–1700)

2002

Exceptional Exhibitor Success and a Memorable Cruise

The last cull of the 2001 foot and mouth disease epidemic was performed on New Year's Day 2002 on some 2,000 sheep at Donkley Woods Farm, Bellingham, Northumberland, and I regard this as the date on which the epidemic ended, though the official date was 14 January and restrictions on livestock movement continued well into 2002. It was estimated that the epidemic had cost the country £8 billion.

The epidemic was at its height in late March 2001, when the daily number of new cases was of the order of 50 per day. At this time there was much pressure on the government to use vaccination as a method of control and eradication. This came from both within the UK and from abroad; particularly from the Netherlands, which adopted vaccination when the disease reached the country. The National Farmers' Union stance was to strongly oppose vaccination in Britain because export rules would have prevented the future export of Brititish livestock; an industry worth £600 million per annum. The decision *not to vaccinate* subsequently proved to have been wise, for the Dutch were eventually obliged to slaughter all vaccinated animals, which resulted in significantly more cattle from infected premises being slaughtered in the Netherlands than in the UK.

Ruth and I were determined to make up for the lost year of 2001. We made an early decision to have a cruise holiday, which was only feasible in the late autumn. When we found that our favourite ship, *Aurora*, was cruising in the eastern Mediterranean at that time we immediately made a booking (securing cabin E103). We also decided to reduce the number of shows at which we would exhibit, as well as stepping down from some other commitments, in order that we might see more of the family. Furthermore, I gave nine months' notice of my wish to retire from my WLSBA responsibilities of Secretary and Press & Publicity/Registration Officer, after a period in office of nine years. I had intended to retire earlier, but I abandoned such thought when the foot and mouth epidemic broke out.

A large luncheon at Old Hall was planned by Ruth for people who had helped us during the epidemic. Despite a busy Christmas, she was bursting with energy and was enjoying ten-length training swims as well as her badminton.

Lambing began for us at 2 a.m. on 27 February in a vicious gale. I remember it well, not only because of the weather, but because one of our ewes had prolapsed six days previously, requiring Ruth's best shepherding skills to re-position the uterus, place an insert and tightly bind. The ewe, which had provided our quads of the previous year, needed to be under close surveillance thereafter. We had to be present at the right time, and we were – Ruth delivering two fine ewe lambs. Tiring work, but the subsequent pleasure of watching two healthy lambs suckling on a happy mother made it well worth the effort. We knew our sheep so well that sometimes when a championship trophy was being presented, the mind flashed back to the moment when that champion took its first breath. A fortnight later I sent a routine email to Mark (in California) shortly before midnight, an extract of which reflects the satisfaction [and reward] that we derived from good shepherding practice:

> Late lambing. Another ewe has had twin gimmer lambs. All went well in the end, but early complication due to exit blocked by an atrophic lamb. We are now relaxing with Bailey's Irish Cream. Enjoy yourself in Paris …

The once sturdy garden wall on the eastern side of Old Hall had been in need of repair from the time of our purchase, but there had always been more important tasks requiring our attention. However, its repair was now a matter of some urgency, for our grandchildren loved to climb it and run along the huge capping stones, and we were frightened that it might collapse on them. Ruth still loved stone walling. Indeed, after she had watched the dry-stone-walling contests at several agricultural shows it took all my powers of persuasion, and a few threats, to stop her entering the Nidderdale Show contest. On closer examination of the wall it was apparent that a complete re-build was necessary. We decided to do it ourselves, and it became a labour of love. I was responsible for mixing the cement, heavy stone lifting, pointing and tidying up, whilst Ruth selected each stone, instructed me on its precise placement and then cemented it in, together with loose stone infill. Every stone selection and placement involved an element of disagreement and banter. It was a slow process, particularly as every passer by stopped for a chat. My email to Mark of 29 March (Good Friday) reflects the pleasure of our lifestyle:

> High pressure zone that has been over the UK for the past few days continues. Blossom out, grass beginning to grow and have not seen a cloud in the sky all day. Countryside at its best. Mum very happy because I mixed a large barrow load of cement for her to do some walling, then took her for a drive in the jeep (extra height gives better view) along very minor roads to avoid the Easter tourists. She has just finished a strong lager and is positively purring.

The following day became one of deep sorrow when the death of the much-loved Queen Elizabeth The Queen Mother, wife of King George VI and mother of Queen Elizabeth II was announced, at the age of 101. She had been active in public life until very recently and had outlived her younger daughter, Princess Margaret, Countess of Snowdon. She was the last Empress of India. As a small boy I remember my grandparents commenting on the wonderful support she was giving to King George VI during World War II, particularly during the Blitz, when they remained in London and shared the grief of Londoners on the streets, surveying and stumbling through the damage caused by German bombing. Hitler described her as 'the most dangerous woman in Europe'. To Ruth and me she was the epitome of a Royal Lady.

Lambing finished on Easter Monday and on the following Sunday we hosted eighteen guests at Old Hall to thank them for their support and encouragement during the F&M epidemic. Ruth was a magnificent hostess and cook, serving venison, beef, chicken breasts and five vegetables. I remember that on Haley's sound advice she cooked each of the chicken breasts individually wrapped in foil prior to putting them into the sauce. I also remember that the selection of puddings included syllabub – my favourite, and also the favourite of Queen Elizabeth I. Everything was cooked to perfection. No outside help, no hassle, lots of laughter and enjoyment and much washing up (by hand).

Although we had much work to do, we had a day out on 10 April to one of Ruth's favourite locations. Extract from her family email:

After we had done our chores, we set off fairly early for the Lake District. It was bright sunlight but an icy wind. We headed up to Windermere and had a light lunch at the Langdale Chase Hotel, watching the boats sail by, then headed up to Grasmere and visited the Dove Cottage Museum (Wordsworth's first family home) which I think is wonderful. Then we went over the Kirkstone Pass, which was quite nerve racking, and through to Patterdale, where we believe the artist painted my water colour. Then a drive along Ullswater which was looking really superb, returning home along the A66. It was a most lovely day out …

Local elections were held in early May, but I could no longer muster the enthusiasm of years past for them, conserving my passions and stamina for the general elections. Not so Ruth, whose enthusiasm I described in an email to Mark on 2 May:

Local election results will be announced from 11pm onwards. Your Mum is intent on watching the drama, using bedroom TV. Unfortunately, every success will be followed by a harsh cackle and an irritating bouncing up and down on the bed. It could be a sleepless night. I will enter into the spirit of things when Blair and his cronies fall in four years, but cannot get excited at local results …

It was hardly 'Darling Buds of May' weather:

8 May (Ruth to family):
Almost winter again. Got soaked and very cold washing mucky sheep. However, went to Friar's Head at lunchtime and had a drink and a snack which was most enjoyable. The wall is now almost half done and looks good but it is very hard dirty work and we still have a long way to go. Have started to plant my flower pots and mangers but it has been so cold – I wonder if we may even get a frost. It is the AGM of the WLSBA on Saturday, so daddy is up to his eyes with work. Will be glad when he packs it in …

However, the scenario was rather different a week later:

16 May (Me to family):
Have just been relaxing in a comfortable chair in the garden on a glorious evening with a bottle of Arniston Bay Chenin Blanc Chardonnay (shared with Mum of course). Not a cloud in the sky, nor a breath of wind, so just threw my head back and gazed at the heavens. Quite surprised at the number and variety of birds and insects that appeared: Swifts, House Martins and Swallows were criss crossing with Jackdaws and Rooks at the higher altitudes, but leaving space on the lower flight paths for eager Thrushes, Blackbirds, Pied Wagtails, Robins, House Sparrows and Dunnocks, whilst Goldfinches, Blue Tits and some Wrens darted between bushes and plants at ground level. I have never seen so many birds in the garden. We have not made any deliberate attempt to look for nests, but cannot help stumbling across

them – Robins and Swallows in pigsty, Wren in wall, b … Starlings everywhere, and to cap it all a Pied Wagtail nest with eggs beneath the gas tank cover. Nice to see the 'Tingley clan' yesterday. Look forward to seeing the 'Scottish clan' soon and hope it will not be long before we see Mark again …

The dotcom crash had smashed much of the high-technology business. However, Mark was still in California, with German company Infineon, which relied for much of its income upon DRAMS (Dynamic Random Access Memory) chips for personal computers. Times were tough, but he had the vision to recognise that it was probably time to pack his kit bag and return to the UK. He was planning accordingly, but not before he had enjoyed some wonderful holidays in the Sierra Nevada, Yosemite and Hawaii.

The Queen's Golden Jubilee holiday and the customary Spring Bank Holiday immediately followed the first weekend of June, providing the UK with an extended four-day holiday period from 1 to 4 June for which, to our delight, we were joined by the 'Scottish clan'. The wee girls were extraordinarily active, and on detecting my fear of crocodiles, tore my nerves to shreds. The weather was perfect and we had a wonderful time. I remember our visit to the annual Finghall barrel push, where we enjoyed the customary afternoon tea and cakes in the post office garden overlooking Lower Wensleydale, and the many stalls. Lois, Cara and Marianne were intrigued by the chicken races [incorporating an obstacle course in later years]. It was the year in which Brian Lockey made a comeback to the barrel-push competition at the age of fifty, having retired in 1999, undefeated for eleven consecutive years, for health reasons. He was two minutes slower than his personal best record of 1992 but still able to achieve second place.

Ruth and I were very pleased when the Royal Show authorities decided to invite the judges of the 2001 show, which had had to be cancelled because of the F&M epidemic, to judge at the 2002 show. Within a few days of receiving the invitation, Ruth was prowling the posh millinery shops of Harrogate. She also decided to enter the fleece competition, which would be judged by an expert wool assessor from the British Wool Marketing Board.

Although Ruth had judged previously at the Royal Show, the 2002 event was particularly memorable, for Her Majesty The Queen was present, and Ruth's fleece won not only the Longwool section, but also the Best of All Breeds. She had clipped the fleece a week previously, with me holding the sheep. Some shepherds would give anything for such an achievement at the world's largest and most prestigious agricultural show, but Ruth and I – together with most Yorkshire people – considered the Royal to be rather tatty on the fringes, and the GYS to be the best. We added a particularly pleasant day at Stratford-upon– Avon to our trip to the Royal Show, incorporating, of course, William Shakespeare's birthplace and most of the tourist sights, not forgetting Sheep Street, the restaurant area.

Our commitment at the Royal Show left us only three days in which to prepare our entries for the GYS, including my preparation of the pens at Harrogate on the Sunday. Ruth had some good entries, particularly males, but we knew that so would our competitors. The rams were named after Harry Potter characters (Hagrid, Dumbledore, etc.). Sadly, our grandchildren were never able to attend the GYS, or other shows. We would have loved to have been able to share our experiences with them. Instead – and as they had recently visited us and seen some of the preparation – I sent them a briefing 'owl' two days before the show, but it was not quite the same thing.

We followed the normal GYS routine of rise and shine at 4 a.m. on the morning of the show, listening to the traditional music on the radio as we travelled down the A1, with Ruth paying her customary respects to the magpies. Morale was high, not because of high expectations, but because that dreadful epidemic of the previous year had gone and we were meeting up again with our country friends and experiencing the atmosphere of the finest agricultural show in the world.

Judging began at 9 a.m. and ended some three hours later, by which time we and our competitors were approaching exhaustion point and longing for the customary lunchtime assembly in the shepherd's beer marquee, with drinks paid for by the exhibitor(s) of the Breed Champion. It was not Ruth, but our shearling ram (Hunton Hagrid) was selected as Best Male and Reserve Champion. Furthermore, Ruth had won the Ram Lamb class and achieved second place in both the Shearling Ewe and Hogg in Wool classes. We were over the moon, not least myself, for while Ruth's overall achievements were exceptional, the fact that she hadn't won the Breed Champion title meant that another joker would be paying for the drinks.

There was a tap on Ruth's shoulder from one of our friends. 'Have you seen the fleece results?' 'No,' replied Ruth, whereupon she was told that she had repeated her Royal Show success by winning not only the Wensleydale and Longwool sections but also the Best of All Breeds award. It was with a different fleece to that which had won at the Royal Show, which had been rather mauled by admirers. I reached for my wallet, paid for the next round of drinks, and that evening sent another 'owl' to the family. On the following day Hunton Hagrid became Reserve Longwool Champion, only beaten by the Bluefaced Leicester Champion. On the final day of the show Ruth was presented with the bronze trophy of the Company of Merchants of the Staple of England, founded in 1314, for her fleece success. Because of its weight the trophy needed two people to hold it, and because of its value (approximately £10,000 at the time) it had to be immediately returned to its owners. Such a pity – it would have looked nice on our long oak dining table at Old Hall.

Jack and Betty were at the show and shared our jubilation.

On the last day of this most memorable month of July I attended the National Sheep Association's SHEEP 2002 event, held on the permanent Three Counties Showground at Malvern, where the WLSBA had a display. It was an important biennial commercial sheep event, probably the largest in Europe, and attracted several thousand visitors. Ruth was not providing any livestock and therefore decided that she would spend the two days that I was away in catching up with household chores and gardening. She had entered the fleece competition, so I was entrusted to take her GYS winning fleece. Again, it won the Supreme Fleece award.

I was asked to be present at the awards presentation at 2 p.m. and duly arrived in good time, enjoying a five-minute chat with the Chairman of the National Sheep Association. I told him that Ruth had not only bred the donor sheep, but had sheared it and entirely prepared the fleece herself, suggesting, 'Now that's not bad for a pensioner, is it?' I was to regret those words – I had not realised that the press had arrived and were taking notes behind me. I eagerly purchased the *Farmers Weekly*, *Farmers Guardian*, *Yorkshire Post*, etc. when they were published and was delighted to see that Ruth's achievement had indeed been included, but I groaned when I saw their headlines: 'Not Bad for a Pensioner!', 'Pensioner wins top award' etc. Ruth, like most of her sex, kept her age a closely guarded secret, and I hastily hid the papers. However, it eventually leaked out and I was in big trouble.

Ruth's triple achievement of winning the Supreme Fleece award at the three premier fleece competitions of the year – the Royal Show, the Great Yorkshire Show and SHEEP 2002 – was, and remains, unequalled. On Sunday 22nd September 2002, London staged the largest protest march ever held in the UK; a Countryside march of 404,000. Its purpose was to highlight the needs of rural communities, incorporating strong opposition against a ban on hunting with dogs in England and Wales. It had been planned for 2001, but it was postponed because of the foot-and-mouth disease epidemic.

We had some very satisfactory sales at the WLSBA annual show and sale in early October, a reflection of Ruth's show successes. One of our ewes was selected as Female Champion and overall Reserve Champion and realised the second-highest price of the day (320 guineas), while we also won the Ram Lamb class. On 2 November I handed over my WLSBA responsibilities of Secretary and Press & Publicity/Registration Officer to a very good friend of ours of many years; Doctor Lynn Clouder, now Professor L. Steventon.

Eight days later Ruth and I were boarding *Aurora* in Southampton, sailing in the late afternoon on a cruise entitled 'Pyramids and Palaces', focusing on the eastern Mediterranean. We needed a good holiday and the opportunity to forget the stresses of life, particularly the 2001 F&M

epidemic and its after-effects. We were well acquainted with the route to our first stop in Gibraltar, beginning with various southeasterly courses through the Solent towards the Nab Tower, where the pilot disembarked, and then, as we entered the restaurant for the second sitting, a southerly course into the English Channel. By the time that we retired for the night *Aurora* was sailing in the busy east–west shipping lane at a speed of about 19 knots, prior to altering course to the southwest for the northwestern shores of France and the Bay of Biscay. As I switched off the lights of cabin E103 I was totally relaxed, both physically and mentally, in the knowledge that for the next eighteen days and nights I had no responsibilities and need not worry about anything. All my needs would be provided for by Captain Hamish Reid and his very professional crew – superb food, brilliant entertainment in the theatre, good company, wonderful tours to some of the most historical regions of the ancient world. I had calculated that the daily cost for each of us was £108, but this excluded tours, drinks and tips. We thought this was very reasonable.

We arrived at Gibraltar after a gentle crossing of the Bay of Biscay at first light on 13 November. We knew Gibraltar well, and as *Aurora* would only be staying there for half a day, to take on fuel and provisions, we just had a leisurely morning strolling around the shopping area. In the afternoon we sat in our favourite spot on one of the upper decks as *Aurora* set an easterly course into the Alboran Sea, paralleling the Algerian coast. There would now be three days at sea before we reached Port Said. Each day was tranquil and calm with scattered cloud and consistent daily temperatures of 23 degrees. It was sunbathing and swimming weather, perfect for Ruth, but I preferred the shade.

We woke early on 17 November to the sound of the mooring lines being secured to the buoys within Port Said harbour and the rigging of her pontoon onto the snake; a wooden, floating construction that meandered between ship and shore, enabling one to walk to the quayside. After an early breakfast we joined one of about six coaches that formed part of a military convoy (armed police on each bus) which took us on the two-and-a-half-hour journey across the now well-irrigated desert strip to Cairo. At that time Egypt was doing its utmost to protect its very valuable tourist industry in a turbulent and dangerous region. A short coach tour of the city was followed by lunch in a luxury hotel and then on to the Sphinx and the pyramids. When Ruth detected an opportunity to join a small group that was set to shuffle with hunched backs to the centre of the Pyramid of Cheops she thrust her handbag at me, grabbed my money, and joined them. I was more than relieved when she eventually reappeared with a broad grin on her face, but I winced when she then seemingly inspected the armed military security guard. The Pyramid of Cheops is better known as the Great Pyramid of Giza, the oldest of the Seven Wonders of the Ancient World. Built in the 26th century BC and standing at 481 feet it was the tallest man-made structure on our planet for more than 3,800 years. It was covered with the highest quality white limestone from a quarry at Tura, located about 10 miles South of Cairo on the Eastern shore of the Nile. Whenever possible stones were broken in the quarry and then laid adjacent to each other on the pyramid, thereby ensuring identical height. However, a massive earthquake in 1303 AD loosened many of them and they slid down the pyramid, exposing the drab [inner] structure that we see to-day. They were subsequently used elsewhere, reducing the height of the Great Pyramid of Giza by about 26 feet. Ruth was very lucky (and brave) to be able to join the small group that groped and crawled into the most sacred area of this magnificent pyramid – only a month short of her 70th birthday. The quarry at Tura was partly underground and used by British forces in WW2 to store shells, bombs, small arms ammunition and other explosives.

The following day we were in Cyprus (Limassol), where we had selected a tour that included Kolossi Castle, a former Crusader stronghold built by the Hospitallers in 1454, and the magnificent ancient open-air theatre of Curium, which is located on high ground with a stunning coastal view. We had not realised that it was still in regular use for a variety of theatrical productions, including dance and opera. Although much of the time was spent on the coach, we saw some brilliant countryside and we not only enjoyed conversation with fellow passengers but also had a fascinating chat with a member of the theatre group. This was possible because of company policy that each coach had a crew-member escort in addition to a local guide, and over the years we had enjoyed some very interesting conversations with musicians, dancers, vocalists, celebrity speakers, etc. The coach tours were also enhanced by a sensible dispersion policy, whereby the several hundred passengers on the cruise were provided with an attractive and widespread choice of tours.

We left Limassol as the first-sitting passengers were taking their seats for dinner. It was only 270 nautical miles to our next port of call, the medieval town of Rhodes, famous for one of the seven wonders of the ancient world – the bronze-plated Colossus, sadly destroyed by earthquake in 226 BC. We watched the mooring of *Aurora* while taking breakfast on deck and then toured the town, followed by a most interesting visit to the picturesque and ancient village of Lindos. The village is a maze of narrow cobbled streets and charming old buildings, overlooked by a towering acropolis which we reached via a steep track, puffing somewhat in a pleasant temperature of 24 degrees. In addition to selling souvenirs, the villagers provided stunning displays of flowers around their properties and in window boxes. Ruth seemed to know the Latin name for all of them, which immediately established a rapport with the owners. We only just reached our coach in time.

Rhodes to Kuşadasi on the west coast of Turkey was an even shorter distance (186 nautical miles), so Captain Reid was able to reduce *Aurora's* cruising speed to a mere 15.5 knots as we dodged between the many islands en route. Kuşadasi is only nine miles from the pearl of our holiday – the ancient city of Ephesus. It was another glorious sunny day and again we had breakfast on deck, watching the interesting mooring proceedings. The local pilot had embarked at about 7.15 a.m., with the first mooring line secured half an hour later. At 8.30 a.m. Ruth and I boarded our coach for the short drive to a dropping-off point in the upper city. Tourists are then able to amble through the marble-lined streets and buildings in the same general direction, boarding their coach at the lower end of the city, without the hassle of people walking in the opposite direction. This is an important consideration, for the fame of Ephesus is such that it is one of the most visited archaeological sites in the world, receiving almost two million visitors a year.

There are in fact three Ephesus cities. The oldest was founded in the sixth century BC on the Ionian coastline of that time, surrounding the huge temple of Artemis, which became another of the seven wonders of the ancient world. However, earlier ancient remains have been found dating back to the eighth century BC. Due to year-on-year silt deposits at the estuary of the nearby river (Menderes), the groundwater level steadily rose, resulting in the city becoming not only waterlogged but so infested with mosquitoes and malaria that in 300 BC a new city was founded, on the slopes of Mount Coressus (1.2 miles away). The Romans made this new city the capital of Asia Minor and it grew to become the fourth– largest city of the eastern Roman Empire, after Alexandria, Antioch and Athens. However, by the seventh century AD its inhabitants had moved to the area around the Basilica of St John, eventually creating the modern city of Selçuk. Therefore, the Ephesus that we were visiting was an essentially Roman city (population arguably 200,000), unencumbered by earlier Greek or later medieval habitation. The streets that Ruth and I walked, and many of the adjacent buildings, would have been familiar to Alexander the Great, to gospel writer St John and the Virgin Mary (both of whom died there), to Cleopatra and Mark Antony, and also, of course, to St Paul, who came close to being slain there (see Acts 19 – the riot in Ephesus). They would all have seen and possibly contributed to the same worn steps and chariot ruts, and presumably they would all also have admired some of the splendid wall and floor mosaics and the still-colourful wall paintings. Most of the buildings and facilities that one would expect of an important Roman city were identifiable –temple, baths, marketplace, latrines and a brothel, plus the stunning library of Celsus at the foot of the Curettes Street and the huge open-air theatre that could seat 25,000 spectators, initially used for drama but later for gladiatorial combat. The city also had a magnificent aqueduct system and water-powered machinery that could slice through marble columns. If only I could have visited Ephesus in my formative years at TGS, how enlivened my studies might have been. The incredible parting statistic that our coach guide gave us was that only 16% of the city had been uncovered.

That night we slowly cruised westwards in direction and backwards in time, waking up in Piraeus, the nearest port to Athens and the gateway to another historical feast. It was in Athens that St Paul delivered his Areopagus sermon (Acts 17: 16–34), famously painted by Raphael in 1515. St Paul had been distressed on his arrival in Athens to find it full of idols, and bravely went to both marketplace and synagogue to preach about the resurrection. Many did not like what they heard and he was 'summoned' to Areopagus, which was both cultural centre and high court, to explain himself. St Paul did not mince his words and began, 'As I walked around and looked carefully at your objects of worship, I even found an alter with this description: "To an unknown God". So you are ignorant of the very thing you worship – and this is what I am going to proclaim to you.' He then explained the concepts in which he believed, making both friends and bitter enemies. However, the focus for myself and Ruth while we were in Athens was on the period long before Christ and St Paul – the period when Athens, under Pericles, reached her zenith and the heights of intellectual and poetic creativity. We went to the Acropolis and to Plaka on its northern and eastern slopes – the old historical neighbourhood of the city, built on top of the ancient city and known as the 'neighbourhood of the Gods'. We were reminded of the great thinkers, writers and artists who flourished in the city during that golden age of the fifth century BC: Herodotus (the father of history), Socrates (the father of philosophy), Hippocrates (the father of medicine), Phidias (creator of the Parthenon on the Acropolis and the Temple of Zeus at Olympia), Democritus, Euripides, Aristophanes, Sophocles, Pindar, Plato, Aristotles and many more. It was another unforgettable day – one for thought and deep reflection.

One matter rather tarnished this wonderful cruise. Ruth and I witnessed for the first time in our lives a dark and ugly side of the Indian caste system; a burly and vociferous Hindu woman (travelling alone), who clearly considered herself to be of the highest level, repetitively and loudly chastising the lower caste Hindu waiters at our table. Her degree of insolence and lateness was such that we, and other diners at our table of eight, were obliged to demand alternative seating arrangements. This bombastic, pompous and repulsive woman was eventually seated elsewhere, out of sight.

On the return journey we had half-day calls at Malta and Malaga, both of which made pleasant breaks, but we were now looking forward to getting home. The weather had been ideal throughout our time in the Mediterranean, and even in the Bay of Biscay it was fine, with sunny spells and a mere force 4 wind. We arrived at Southampton at 7 a.m. on 28 November. It had been a wonderful cruise, enhanced by good weather, by ideal temperatures, and also by being at an off-peak tourist period. I would not have been quite so ecstatic about it had it been during hot weather among a suffocation of families and children in the summer holidays. Each meal had been a gastronomic delight, and I was rather shocked on returning to Old Hall to find that I weighed 14.7 stones. Having given myself a severe reprimand, I gradually ran it down by 8 pounds before Christmas. It must have then increased again, for the weight recordings in my diary ceased at that time. Though I continued to occasionally sneak up on Ruth as she stood on the scales in the bathroom, I was never sufficiently quick to catch her weight.

There had been no dramas while we were away. John Tunstill had looked after our sheep well, and tupping was satisfactorily completed. There was some very good news – Justin was to be promoted to the rank of inspector early in the new year, based at Weetwood. Ruth and I were very proud of him. We were not so happy on 13 December when the European Union announced that Cyprus, the Czech Republic, Estonia, Hungary, Latvia, Lithuania, Malta, Poland, Slovakia and Slovena were to become members, from 1 May 2004. The British people had not been consulted and both Ruth and I felt that we were losing our country to bureaucrats, supported by Europhile politicians of all parties who may have relished the prospect of being rewarded with future lucrative appointments within the Union.

Our contempt for and distrust of Prime Minister Tony Blair was not subsiding. His political actions and ambition seemed to be focused on attaining high international recognition and becoming Europe's leading politician, even if this required giving virtually total support to the foreign policies of George Walker Bush, 43rd President of the United States, with little regard to the best interests of his own country. However,

I had not been as sceptical as other members of the family regarding the government's 'Assessment of Iraq's Weapons of Mass Destruction', a document that had prompted the recall of Parliament on 24 September 2002 (and subsequently referred to as the 'September Dossier'). Perhaps this was because of my high respect for Joint Intelligence Committee (JIC) documents while serving on the staff of the United Kingdom Commander in Chief's Committee. I was to later realise that the JIC's sparse and inconclusive intelligence had been 'jazzed up' in Downing Street, with the sole intent of producing a dossier that made a convincing case for war.

Ruth and I were contemptuous of the lifestyle and antics of Prime Minister Blair's wife, Cherie Blair CBE, QC, whose health and well-being consultant, or 'style adviser' if you like (Carole Caplin), was involved with Peter Foster, an Australian conman with criminal convictions. It was alleged that Peter Foster had helped Cherie Blair purchase two flats at a discount. Also, at least one British newspaper had credited Carole Caplin with introducing Cherie Blair to various 'New Age' symbols and beliefs and a 're–birthing' procedure while on holiday in Mexico, also attended by the Prime Minister. Taken together, these matters and the ensuing denials, apologies and tears became known as the 'Cheriegate Scandal'. When a furious Prime Minister Blair stated on 12 December, 'Everyone has had their pound of flesh. Now it is time to move on,' even the *Daily Mirror*, that loyal bastion of Labour Party support and propaganda, lost patience and exploded on the following day (Friday 13 December 2002) with the following front-page headline and columns inside by the paper's editor and political editor:

MOVE ON?

HOW CAN WE, MR BLAIR, AFTER NEW COURT PAPERS BOMBSHELL?

Spinning a Web of Lies and Deceit ...

Politics is a dirty business. It always has been and always will be. It is fuelled by rumour, deceit and ruthless personal ambition which all too often overshadow its grander aims.

All governments routinely distort the truth, most will tell the odd lie to get themselves out of a corner. But never has lying been institutionalised the way it has under Labour.

Never has there been such a cynically manipulative, loathsome misinformation machine at the heart of national political life.

Its venal tentacles stretch out from Downing Street into virtually every corner of Whitehall – corrupting the Government's legitimate right to spread its message by twisting facts and evading accountability.

For the best part of 15 years, I have been on the touchline for all the big games at Westminster, cheering, jeering and mocking.

I watched as Margaret Thatcher rose to the height of her awesome power and was then brutally betrayed by her own party.

I shared the incredulity at the way John Major and his sleazy, bickering, corrupt MPs contrived to bring the country to its knees.

Like millions of others I yearned for a breath of the fresh air promised by Tony Blair as he swept into office on May 1, 1997.

Our new Prime Minister, the first Labour leader in 10 Downing Street for 18 years, pledged to banish sleaze and to head a government that was 'whiter than white'.

The hollow nature of those promises was exposed within a few weeks of that historic election victory.

The Bernie Ecclestone affair, although few of us realised it at the time, was to set the pattern of the years ahead. First a fact emerged, in this case that New Labour had trousered £1 million from the Formula 1 boss at the same time as it was threatening to wreck his sport with a tobacco advertising ban.

A Messianic Mr Blair was eventually forced to apologise and ask people to trust in him.

He got away with it. The country and the media were not yet ready to admit he was as bad as the last lot. But it didn't end there.

Over the intervening five years we have watched the departure of Peter Mandelson (twice), Stephen Byers, Jo Moore, Geoffrey Robinson, Keith Vaz.

Some resigned, some were forced out. All lied their heads off before falling on their swords. Interwoven in this web of deceit, behind every Government announcement, was the corrosive influence of spin.

Blizzards of meaningless initiatives spewed forth from Whitehall, billions of pounds of taxpayers' money were spent and respent – to give an entirely deliberate false impression of New Labour's achievements… .

VOICE OF THE DAILY MIRROR

All we want is honesty from No 10

Tony Blair demands that the media 'move on' from the Cheriegate.

That's a familiar New Labour rally cry when caught with their backs nailed to the Downing Street walls.

The Prime Minister understandably wants everyone off his wife's case. He thinks we've had our 'pound of flesh' – an appropriate phrase given that the first to say it was Shylock, the dodgy money-lender in The Merchant of Venice.

Mr Blair says there are many more important things to worry about. But why should we down our inquisitive tools and move on when very serious questions remain unanswered.

Only yesterday, new revelations emerged alleging Mrs Blair read conman Peter Foster's deportation papers after her mate – and his lover – Carole Caplin, had them faxed to Cherie's private flat.

It is further alleged that she then called Foster to talk to him about his case.

Cherie denies all this. But then, at the start of this farrago, she denied having any relationship with Foster at all – only coming clean when their extraordinarily cosy emails were disclosed.

DAMAGING

What is clear from recent polls is that the majority of the public no longer believes what she says, an incredibly damaging situation for a top QC and the wife of a Prime Minister.

What is also clear is that a lot of that distrust is now extending to Mr Blair himself.

The Blairs and their PR team, led by the increasingly demented Alastair Campbell, can lambaste newspapers as much as they like. It's what they do when they get into trouble, and it has usually worked.

But this story is running and running because the media, and the public, feel a distinct unease about where the truth lies.

It may seem a trivial story at a time when we are about to go to war with Iraq. But it is not.

This country must have absolute trust in its Prime Minister and his Downing Street officials before such enormous decisions are taken.

The Daily Mirror is totally opposed to a futile scrap with Saddam Hussein. But if the country does go to war, at the very least we want to feel utterly certain that we can believe what this country tells us.

How can we have that certainty when we can't even trust the Blairs to tell the truth about a conman acting as their financial adviser?

That is why this is a serious matter. And that is why we won't be 'moving on' just yet.

We are not after any pound of flesh, Tony. We are just after the truth, however many more tears have to be spilled.

In their extreme frustration, and with war clouds on the horizon, the editor of the *Daily Mirror* and his political editor thus finally admitted the scale of deception and sleaze of Tony Blair and New Labour, both so eagerly supported by the paper for more than five years.

The Old Hall Christmas was as enjoyable and vibrant as ever, with a more than full house. We were pleased to see Mark's friend Claire again, while Nanette was picked up from Walton en route by the Tingley Pedleys on Boxing Day. Justin was in good form with recently acquired card-trick and conjuring skills.

2003

Blair Takes the United Kingdom to War

With the Christmas and New Year festivities over, the British people became increasingly concerned at the prospect of a USA-led war against Iraq, justified by intelligence reports that President Saddam Hussein intended to reconstitute nuclear weapons programmes, and that he was holding weapons of mass destruction in defiance of UN Resolution 687. I too was now more than suspicious that Blair and the Bush administration were manipulating or exaggerating intelligence reports in order to justify military intervention in Iraq with a view to achieving a regime change. On 3 February, Prime Minister Blair's Director of Communications and Strategy (Alastair Campbell) released a government briefing document to the media entitled 'Iraq – Its Infrastructure of Concealment, Deception and Intimidation', to clarify and justify government policy. When it was found that much of its content had been plagiarised from unattributed sources and that the most notable source was an article by a Muslim graduate student, it lost all credibility and became known as 'The February Dossier' or, more appropriately, 'The Dodgy Dossier'.

There was little or no support in the UK for Iraq's President Saddam Hussein, whose atrocities within his own country against the Marsh Arabs and Shias had been horrific, but the UK was tired of conflict and needed more positive and convincing evidence before participating in further hostilities. On 15 February, two million people demonstrated in London against British aggression in Iraq, the largest demonstration in British history, while worldwide protests numbered more than 10 million people in 600 cities.

Prime Minister Blair would need to convince Parliament and the British people that a war with Iraq was a just war. It was not long before the words of Psalm 55:21 were ringing in some people's ears: 'His talk is as smooth as butter, yet war is in his heart; his words are more soothing than oil, yet they are drawn swords.' [Or, as they say in rural Yorkshire, 'He's got the gift of the gab and wants a scrap'].

The United States initially sought a UN Security Council resolution to authorise the use of military force against Iraq but withdrew it in the face of vigorous opposition from several countries. UN Inspectors were pressed hard to find evidence that would justify war but were unable to find any such evidence – the *casus belli* for invasion. Blair was not deterred. He quoted 'just war statements' by ancient writers such as Augustine, Grotius, Vattel and Aquinas. He turned to moral justification and creatively blended very weak legal support with samples of traditionally acceptable moral argument – helping a friend in need, bringing relief to the oppressed, preventing future threats, etc., creating an illusion of morality that was infused into the minds of a sceptical Parliament and nation by masterful linguistic sleight of hand, supported by the professional skills and spin of his communications department, led by Alastair Campbell.

On 18 March the House of Commons gave Blair the authority that he needed, though without enthusiasm, and many MPs wondered afterwards how they could have succumbed to Blair's seductive oratory. Though sceptical, I too was deceived by that oratory at the time. On 20 March the United Kingdom and twenty other nations joined the United States in the invasion of Iraq, whose military forces were quickly defeated. Baghdad fell within three weeks and on 1 May President Bush declared the end of major combat operations. Amazingly, there was no plan as to what to do next, apart from continuing the futile search for the non-existent weapons of mass destruction. If only the United States and its allies had installed a new government with a fair mix of Shia, Sunni and Kurds and had retained the Iraqi Army to enforce its governance, the ensuing conflicts, involving the loss of thousands of lives, might have been avoided.

Mark had returned to the UK in March and soon secured employment with a venture-capital-backed start-up company, Global Silicon, in Cambridge, conveniently enabling him to reside in his own flat. He was to work for Global Silicon for three years, spending at least a quarter of that time in the southern China industrial cities, particularly Shenzhen, and also in Hong Kong. He was dismayed at the continuous 'pea soup' smogs – probably as bad as those in Britain's cities during the Industrial Revolution. They had transformed a hitherto pleasant oriental countryside into an ecological disaster area in which trees and birds were no longer to be seen. About his work there, Mark told us: 'Business with the Chinese regularly continued late into the night … in Karaoke bars with customer representatives, a bottle of whisky and a bevy of girls … me trying to sing Cantonese pop songs and not look embarrassed.' Ruth and I had assumed that his early-morning commuter-boat crossing of Kowloon's Pearl River estuary would be stunning, with the sun percolating through the oriental mist, until he told us that the sun rarely penetrated that intensive and unrelenting barrier of smog.

Ruth and I maintained contact with our widely dispersed sons by regular email communication, and I now turn to a random selection of them to illustrate our simple country lifestyle and Ruth's vitality, inspiration and selfless character as she approached three score years and ten:

1 April 2003 (Me to family):
Intruder – by the name of J Daw broke into Old Hall this lunchtime, despite recent security improvements. He was caught following a brief scuffle in the sitting room, trying to exit via the east window. His intentions had been apparent for some time and security experts had capped the chimney with a wire mesh top only the previous evening. However, Mr Jack Daw was intent on building a nest in the chimney and found a gap. Regrettably, he was unable to exit vertically and

descended with much noise, soot and defiance which was only matched by your Mum's colourful rhetoric. After capture and my reprimand he was allowed to fly off from the front door and following two victory rolls was seen no more.

Love from Dad

13 April 2003 (Ruth to family):
A Beautiful Day – Had our first day out for ages. We did the animals and then set off for the North Yorkshire moors, ending up in Robin Hoods Bay which looked as lovely as ever. Walked along the beach and enjoyed the sea air and watched children making sand castles. Couldn't believe that the little field that we used to park in is now a proper car park surrounded by bungalows. I just love the fishermen's cottages all huddled together. To-morrow we are going to do another mix of cement for the front wall. With a bit of luck we may just get it finished by the end of the year. Hope Charlotte had a nice birthday and that Haley is feeling much better. If it's the same bug that we've had then I feel very sorry for her. If we'd been to Singapore then I would have suspected that we had SARS. Remember, we are not available on Sunday because of our hosting a political fund raising day with Euro MP (Timothy Kirkhope MEP) at Old Hall. Shall be glad when it's over. Have a good weekend.

Love you all lots. MUM XXX

4 May 2003 (Me to family):
We had a quiet holiday weekend, in a state of siege, for the roads are severely congested with tourist traffic, most of which is heading for the festival of food and drink at Leyburn. The town centre is filled with huge circus sized marquees within which all the drink and food of Wensleydale are displayed, sold and consumed. Visitors use a very efficient park and ride system.

Mum's garden is looking superb. The Swallows and House Martins arrived three days ago. The Pied Wagtails have again laid five eggs in a nest beneath the gas tank filler cover and there are several Robins' nests. The lamb that broke its upper leg bone is now walking and running normally – a nice success story.

We are, of course, delighted with the local election results, but dismayed at the BBC's biased reporting. The appropriate headline of 'Tory Landslide Gains' was carefully avoided.

Love from Dad

13 May 2003 (Ruth to family):
Shepherding this morning, including shearing, then I'm going to plant some pots of petunias. The blossom in the garden has been beautiful this year but sadly it is now falling. It would be so nice if Jessica could start riding lessons. She would love it – I remember her face when she got on a horse at Colin Ellwood's stables. I looked out my hacking jacket last night. I wore it until I was 24 years (only weighing about seven stone). It was the best that I could get and I notice that the lining is hand stitched into the sleeves and the button holes hand made. Jessica is welcome to it if it fits her and I will buy her riding hat if she shows enough interest.

Love Mum XXX

On 29 May a major political row broke out when BBC journalist Andrew Gilligan reported on BBC Radio 4, and three days later in the *Mail on Sunday*, that Blair's government had knowingly 'sexed up' the 'September Dossier' with misleading statements about Iraq's weapons of mass destruction and capability of launching such attacks within 45 minutes. Gilligan named Blair's press secretary Alastair Campbell as the driving force behind the alteration of the dossier. The government denounced the reports and accused the BBC and Gilligan of poor journalism. During the next few weeks the BBC and Gilligan stood their ground, saying that they had a reliable source …

24 June 2003 (Me to family):
An uneventful day, but every day has something interesting if one digs deep enough. When an excited ex Victrix Ludorum Mum came dashing across the field to where I was grass cutting in mid morning

I feared a calamity, but it was to drag me to the pond to see some dragonflies emerging from the water. The speed of change to precision flying is remarkable. The afternoon was dominated by Mr Henman's routine annual torturing of your Mum as he lurched into the second round at Wimbledon, and in the evening I had my first sighting of a humming bird moth. It was taking nectar from the blue Anchusa flowers as we sipped a glass of Chardonnay in the garden. At a distance of three feet its long proboscis was very clear.

In between these highlights there were preparations for the forthcoming Great Yorkshire Show, which will increase in intensity over the next fortnight, together with routine shepherding tasks, with particular lookout for fly strike and maggots in these sultry weather conditions.

Various important looking e-mails arrived for your Mum a short while ago, but the school governor is too absorbed in her reading of the latest Harry Potter book to give them any attention. I have been given instructions to print off copies for her attention at the breakfast table to-morrow.

Love to you all from Dad

By Ruth's standards, her achievements at the 2003 GYS were modest – no lack of rosettes, but no first prizes. Neither of us was dismayed; the primary attraction of the GYS was the opportunity to meet up with so many friends, the banter and the camaraderie, and we respected the judge's opinions, just as we expected exhibitors to respect our opinions when we were judging, which was generally the case. However, the Hunton flock was not out of the limelight, for one of the rams that Ruth had bred and sold the previous year (Hunton Dumbledore) took the Breed Championship at the Royal Show. As Ruth was now only exhibiting at the GYS and shows that had an associated sale, there were no silver trophies to adorn our large oak table that year – until early October, when one of her ewes was adjudged Female Champion and Reserve Supreme Champion at the WLSBA annual show and sale.

While we were at the GYS we learned that, following much speculation and pressure, the BBC and the press had named Dr David Kelly, a biological warfare expert and former United Nations weapons inspector employed by the Ministry of Defence, as the source of the allegations that Blair's government had knowingly 'sexed up' the 'September Dossier' …

14 July 2003 (Ruth to family):

A big tidy up has been done, but a lot more to do. Saw more dragon flies today and heard a cricket. I have also seen the spotted woodpecker again in the garden. Fancy, twenty young ducklings on the stream!

Hope Jessica's riding went well this evening. Is Haley's hand recovering well?

Yesterday evening we set off at 7.30pm up to Grinton lead mine and didn't leave until about 9pm. We were the only people up there and it was a glorious walk and so tranquil. Saw so much wildlife.

*So hot – going to have a cold bath.

Love you all lots. MUM XXX

*The UK summer of 2003 was one of the warmest of the last three centuries and cold baths became a regular feature of our lifestyle at Old Hall. A new record for Scotland of 32.9°C was established on 9 August at Greycrook [Scottish Borders], beating the previous record of 32.8°C at Dumfries on 2 July 1908, whilst on 10 August the UK record of 37.1°C on 3 August 1990 was replaced by 38.5°C at Brogdale [near Faversham].

On 18 July, Dr David Kelly was found dead in a field near his home with slashed wrists … An enquiry was announced by the government the following day and hearings began on 11 August, chaired by Lord Brian Hutton PC, QC a former Lord Chief Justice of Northern Ireland and British Lord of Appeal in Ordinary – the Hutton Enquiry was under way …

24 July 2003 (Ruth to family):

Went a walk yesterday down by the beck. Senior Mrs Mallard was on the bank with her brood of eleven but soon told them all to plop into the water. Further up was Junior Mrs Mallard with her nine still intact. What on earth will we have next year if they all decide that Old Hall is a safe haven?

Have done the lawns and all the edges and planted out the leeks AND picked the peas and broad beans and put them in the freezer. The place is looking more tidy. Got behind because of the GYS.

Hope you are enjoying the TV Mark, particularly Mrs Blair singing 'When you're 61'. Isn't she a Pratt?

Love you all lots. MUM. XXX

21 August 2003 (Ruth to family):
I'm certain that the dragon flies in the pond are Anax Imperator or Emperor Dragon flies. The description of the nymph and how they emerge fit exactly with how I observed them in the pond. It says they lay their eggs in pond weed and also that the nymph feed on tadpoles! Can't win can I?

It was lovely to see you all yesterday. Sorry about the chaos. Put two more capping stones on to-day. Tired. Hope you enjoy your trip to France, Mark.

Love you all lots. MUM XXX

7 September 2003 (Ruth to family):
I went for a walk this morning and picked masses of blackberries ready for the winter. I have never seen the hedgerows looking so beautiful with bryony and honeysuckle (berries and flowers) and so many hips and haws. My mother would have forecast a hard winter – more likely the result of a good summer.

Daddy has been busy this week making two new stable doors, and a very good job he has done.

I'm trying to do a good winter clean up in the garden and to–morrow, if the wind is in the right direction, I'll have a good burn. Justin – do you want some cooking apples? We've had a lovely apple pie this evening.

Leslie and Margaret are around and called in, and are coming for supper on Tuesday. They both look very well.

Love from MUM XXX

8 September 2003 (Me to family):
Within 48 hours – England won a Soccer International, a Rugby Union International and a Cricket Test match. All major tournaments. It could be a long wait for a repeat of this achievement.

Dad

The Soccer International was a European Cup qualifying match against Macedonia (won 2–1); the Rugby Union International was against France (won 45–14); and the Cricket Test match was against South Africa (won by 9 wickets). A rare treat.

17 September 2003 (Ruth to family):
Had a wonderful clear up of the garden to-day. Yesterday in the shade it was 80 degrees and to-day not much less. Burned all the rubbish this evening. Went blackberry picking early this morning and there were masses. Lots of nice pies this winter.

The butterflies on the mint along the beck are quite spectacular. Six different species plus whites which I can't recognise. Red Admirals, Peacocks, Commas, Tortoiseshells (Greater & Small) and White Admirals all on the same plant at the same time. Really quite beautiful.

Daddy is continuing his job restoring the stable doors and the back barn door. He's doing a great job.

Apples galore. I will store them in the dairy and when anyone wants some, please ask. They really are in very good condition. Haven't seen the Kingfisher again, but I'm told he's around.

Love to you all. Love you lots. MUM XXX

Readers may have noticed butterflies being mentioned from time to time throughout these memoirs, starting in my childhood. Ruth and I shared a fascination of them, particularly in Malaya, Belgium and Austria, but also in our own country; on the Downs, buddleia bushes wherever, and at Old Hall. Is there a more refreshing sight for a weary soul than that of a shimmering of butterflies in the warm sunshine; randomly opening and closing their wings in cascades of pastel variation? Aristotle called the butterfly Psyche, equating it with the soul, an association that has been made by so many diverse cultures worldwide. I often reflect on the metamorphosis from the obese caterpillar to mysterious, inert chrysalis and the eventual emergence of these beautiful, fairy-like creatures as one of our world's wonders.

13 November 2003 (Ruth to family):
Went up to Dentdale for an outing to-day, but Dent was closed because the tiny little village alleyway was being re-cobbled. Managed to get a drink and a cup of soup at the one pub still open.

As you know, I'm coming up to three score years and ten. No, I'm not asking for presents but wondering whether we could arrange a party here. It would be too much for me to have a birthday party here and then everyone at Christmas but I could put my birthday back a week and have my birthday at Christmas. What are your thoughts boys? I don't want to pressure you because I know that you all have busy lives. We had thought of a trip to London but we have booked Brian in for June when we go to Norway. Also, John Tunstill is in such a bad way with back trouble that daddy is doing his shepherding each day until he is fit, so we have ruled out London and I really would prefer to be with the family. I did purchase 15lbs of competition quality Aberdeen Angus beef recently at the 'Northern Smithfield' event at the Great Yorkshire Showground.

Love you all stacks and stacks. MUM XXX

25 November 2003 (Ruth to family):
Delighted everyone can come on Boxing Day. Please check what perfume Haley wants. Aileen – please, what would you like? I've got to get cracking on this present buying.

Daddy still working on the end building. It really is quite amazing. You have just got to admire it. I've had a baking day and have quite enjoyed it. A large chocolate cake is now in the freezer plus other goodies.

Love you all lots and lots. MUM XXX

16 December 2003 (Ruth to family):

My Birthday – Had a lovely day yesterday. Daddy took a day's holiday and we had a nice meal at the Black Bull at Moulton. I received some beautiful flowers so Old Hall is looking very colourful. I'm saving the chocolates because once opened I would just guzzle them.

I don't like being seventy, so from now on I'm going back a year. Next year I'm sixty nine, so in fifteen years I shall only be as old as you lot.

Very cold. I've been doing a lot of baking so there is plenty to eat, but I have no doubt whatsoever that it will be chaos on the day.

Daddy has been working on the pig sty to-day. He looks rather like Saddam Hussein when he packs up for the day. I'm delighted they've caught the old beggar.

I love the whole lot of you to bits and thank you for a lovely day. Looking forward to seeing you all so very much.

Love MUM XXX

21 December 2003 a.m. (Ruth to family):

Looking forward to Matthew and family coming on Boxing Day. The more the merrier. I'm doing a final final shop to-morrow and if we haven't got it – tough. We certainly won't starve, but we may have to sit on our thumbs.

Had some old ladies from the village in for a Christmas tea, which they enjoyed. Of course, they were a lot older than me! No snow yet.

Love you all lots and lots. MUM XXX

21 December 2003 p.m. (Ruth to family):

Christmas Festivities – Blowing a freezing gale up here and I guess snow is not far away. Just been out in the garden digging up beautiful organic parsnips in case I can't get to them if we have a heavy snowfall. I am going to cook a new vegetable this year, maybe even two new vegetables if I get my act together. I always have the best of plans but things do catch up on me on the day. I'll keep off the special brew!

Feel happier now I have written my cooking plan down.

Love you all. MUM XXX

23 December 2003 (Ruth to family):
Had the village brass band playing last night accompanying the carol singers. Very nice too. Looking forward to seeing you all.
    Love. MUM XXX

It was a wonderful Christmas cum seventieth birthday party and a remarkable achievement by Ruth, as vibrant a hostess as ever, to cook such a brilliant meal for twenty members of the family. She loved it, and the family loved her, for her selfless and awesome effort and infectious gaiety. A choice of several puddings were always offered, each a gastronomic delight. My favourites were her syllabub and her pears in tarragon cream dressing. Here are her recipes, hopefully to be enjoyed by our descendants for many generations to come:

Syllabub
Juice and rind of two large lemons 7oz caster sugar
2 glasses (4 fluid ounces) sherry
2 small glasses (2 fluid ounces) brandy 1 pint double cream
4 ounces macaroons

Place grated rind and lemon juice in a bowl. Stir in sugar till dissolved, then add sherry and brandy. Gradually stir in cream. Cover the base of a serving dish with half crushed macaroons. Whisk the cream mixture until it gains in bulk until thick and creamy, then spoon over the macaroons. Place in refrigerator to chill. Decorate with remaining macaroons and sprinkle lightly with nutmeg before serving. Serves 10 to 12 (it is very rich).

Pears in Tarragon Cream Dressing
3 Pears (ripe and juicy) Lettuce leaves
Paprika pepper.

For Tarragon Cream Dressing:
Egg

Rounded Tablespoons Caster Sugar. 3 Tablespoons Tarragon Vinegar
Salt and Pepper
Quarter Pint Double Cream

Break egg into a bowl and beat with a fork. Add sugar and gradually
add the vinegar. Stand in a pan of boiling water. Stir the mixture until
beginning to thicken (takes some time), then draw off the heat and
continue to stir. When mixture has the consistency of thick cream
take basin out of the pan. Stir for a few seconds longer. Season lightly
and leave to go cold. Partially whip cream and fold into the dressing.
Peel pears, cut in half and remove core and place on lettuce leaves and
spoon over the dressing. Shake a little paprika over. I only put the
dressing on immediately before serving, otherwise the dressing slides
off the ripe pears. You can make the dressing the day before, up until
adding the cream and that is what I did.

Ruth collected recipes over the years from friends from all parts of the
world – a collection that is a gastronomic treasure trove.

31 December 2003 (Ruth to family):
New Year's Eve – I hope you all have a wonderful 2004. I did enjoy
Christmas and being with you all. Something to remember always.

Simply bitter to-night and we really have the fire half way up the
chimney. I don't think we shall have the energy to stay up to see the
New Year in but will get into a nice warm bed. Will phone to-morrow.

Love to all of you. MUM XXX

2004

Hutton Report, Many Silver Trophies, 'Crusher Pedley' and a Horrific Tsunami

1 January 2004 (Ruth to family):
Snow – It was snowing heavily as we went to bed last night and this morning the depth is about six inches. I haven't heard a single car on the road, nor the snow plough or gritter. Thankfully, we still have plenty of food in, so won't starve. Rather like the weather in Catterick when Justin was born. Going to get the pregnant ewes in if it continues. All is well and I do like snow.

Love you all lots. MUM XXX. A HAPPY NEW YEAR

Ruth and I were denied our routine New Year's Day drive to the east coast because of the inclement weather conditions. However, I remember the day clearly, first because I was shocked at the amount of weight that I had put on over the festive season, and second, because Mark had sent us an email download of an enchanting song that thrilled Ruth and even amused me. He also sent some depressing predictions about our planet running out of oil, but we will forget that because of the enjoyment that the song provided. It was a short animated film clip by Pierre Coffin – the Hippo Jungle Song:

The Lion Sleeps Tonight; https://www.youtube.com/watch?v=399 syDv0bBm Whilst "Wimoweh – The Lion Sleeps Tonight" was animated by Pierre Coffin, the credit for this lyric must be given to a tall Zulu farmer born in Msinga in 1909, then moving to Johannesburg, where he worked in a furniture shop – Solomon Linda. At night Linda sang in a choir as a soprano with an impressive falsetto [The Evening Birds]. He was very successful in Friday and Saturday night competitions, for which a cow or a goat was usually top prize. The Evening Birds impressed a Gallo Records talent scout and in 1939 made history with *Mbube* (Zulu for 'lion'). Music historian Rob Allingham, who at one time was archivist for Gallo Records, subsequently described what happened; "On the second take, above the last repeated chorus, Linda improvised a unique soprano melody line against the mid-range and bass voices of other singers in the group". This, together with the main refrain of *Mbube* gave the lyric a strange and enchanting mystical quality.

Mbube sold around 100,000 copies over the next few years, making Linda a star, and later a legend, particularly in his Zulu tribe. However, Linda was no businessman and could neither read or write. He was paid ten shillings for the recording and there were no royalties for popular music at that time. In 1952, while sweeping floors for a living at the Gallo packaging plant, Linda assigned copyright of the lyric to the company. He died on 8 October 1962, aged 53, virtually penniless, his family too poor to erect a headstone on his grave. Many years later, each of his three daughters received around $250,000, far less than that which had been anticipated. I wonder what the reaction of the isithunzi [spirit] of Solomon Linda might have been in 2019 on 'viewing' the premiere of *Lion King*, a seemingly real warthog and meerkat, in a seemingly real jungle, singing the lyric he improvised in 1939.

2 January 2004 (Ruth to family):
In the Jungle – I just loved it – so much so that I came in to-day and switched on the computer and had another titter at it. The reactions

of the hippo's eyes, knees and hands are lovely. It didn't half take some downloading! We did think that the Pedley grandchildren could do an amusing imitation of it ...

3 January 2004 (Ruth to family):
Hippo – Sneaked in to have another look at the Hippo. I really do love it. It is a great smiler if you know what I mean. Had a little more snow to-night. Daddy has been working all day on his workshop project. I've had a quiet day looking through all my cookery books – Boeuf Wellington and baked chocolate pudding, and other such delicacies.

Love you all lots and lots. MUM XXX

We decided that in the spring the 'Soup House', which we had been told was where the poor of the village had been fed in earlier centuries, should be upgraded to 'Garden Room', with two large oak glass-paned doors that opened into the garden, together with other improvements and exterior re-pointing. I was to convert my rather basic tool shed cum paint store into a workshop and Ruth was to re-decorate the entrance hall, staircase and landing, with labourer assistance from myself when required. In the meantime there were the basic shepherding tasks in preparation for lambing and the rather unpleasant task of sending 2003-born lambs that were not up to our high pedigree-registration standards to slaughter, some of which would finish up in our deep freezes.

In January there is usually a brief surge in social and other events in the dale prior to the commitment of lambing, other farming tasks and the influx of tourists. This year I particularly recollect a very interesting and amusing talk by William Hague on 9 January to the Richmond Civic Society in the old Zetland cinema in Richmond – on the younger Pitt. It was a prelude to talks to far more distinguished audiences around the country prior to the publication of his book *William Pitt, the Younger* in September. I also recall the always interesting and enjoyable Wensleydale CPRE AGM and supper, held on 27 January at the Friar's Head.

27 January 2004 (Me to family):
Lovely, bright and sunny day, though rather chilly in the NW breeze. It was so nice that your Mum had two consecutive walks round the 'estate', with myself joining for the second. The largest flock of geese that I have ever seen flew over at noon in a WNW direction. There were at least 200 birds, flying in two large V formations. Very colourful red sky this evening, but the forecasters do not predict a shepherd's delight. However, the pregnant ewes are in the long byre looking very smug and cosy, chewing their cud.

Take care. Love from Mum and Dad. xxx

The following day the 'Hutton Report' was released. The evidence presented to Lord Hutton had indicated that: (1) dossier wording had been changed to present the strongest case for war with Iraq and that some of these changes had been suggested by Alastair Campbell; (2) reservations had been expressed by intelligence experts on dossier content and that Dr Kelly had direct contact with dissenters within the defence intelligence staff and both he and they had advised several journalists of their reservations; (3) following Dr Kelly's admission of being one of BBC journalist Gilligan's contacts, Alastair Campbell wanted his name to be made public, while Prime Minister Blair had personally chaired a meeting at which it was decided that Dr Kelly's name would be confirmed by the Ministry of Defence (MOD) if put to them by journalists. This led to Dr Kelly's name being subsequently confirmed after journalists made multiple suggestions to the MOD press office.

There was therefore much incredulity and anger when Lord Hutton's report virtually cleared the government of any wrongdoing and ruled that any failure in the intelligence assessment fell outside his remit. This delicate 'leg glance' ensured that the intelligence services also escaped censure, and the bulk of the criticism was accordingly directed at Gilligan and the BBC, most of which had been accepted during the enquiry.

Prime Minister Blair was delighted with the report, but most of the media and the BBC were dismayed, though for differing reasons. Half of the front page of the *Independent* contained one word in small type:

'Whitewash'. The headline of the *Daily Express* was 'Hutton's whitewash leaves questions unanswered'. The *Daily Mail* wrote in its editorial: 'We're faced with the wretched spectacle of the BBC chairman resigning while Alastair Campbell crows from the summit of his dunghill.' The *Daily Telegraph* and the Conservative Party had hoped that the report would find that Prime Minister Blair had misled the House of Commons and must have dreamed of an 'O wise and upright judge!' headline. Instead, they were only able to console themselves by adding to the criticism levelled at a Labour-biased BBC. The *Sunday Times* delighted in depicting Lord Hutton as the Three Wise Monkeys who would 'see no evil, hear no evil and speak no evil'. Left-wing newspapers (the *Guardian* and the *Daily Mirror*) were in a quandary, for they had been opposed to British participation in the war against Iraq, yet needed the continued support of the BBC – so they both moved on with indecent haste to other matters that might appeal to their readers.

Ruth and I were not lacking in opinion:

28 January 2004 (Ruth to family):
Hutton Report – What a whitewash! The report is so biased that I believe it will rebound on the Blair government. Even Labour MPs are saying it is a whitewash. Can't wait for tomorrow's papers. Had blizzard conditions overnight and to-day but Varleys have delivered a ton of feed for the sheep so they will be all right. We are cosy and I have a good book, so it will be an early night.
      Love you all lots. MUM XXX

29 January 2004 (Ruth to family):
Hutton – Hutton is a silly old fool in his dotage who should be put out to grass or better still call a vet and have him humanely shot. I do think though that the [report] is so over the top that even Blair must be embarrassed and really wouldn't have wanted his two Labour allies at the BBC to resign. He would have been hoping that [the BBC] would sack Gilligan and apologise. I suspect that if Gilligan is forced to resign there will be a walk out at the BBC.
      Love MUM XXX

31 January 2004 (Me to Editor of Daily Telegraph):
Hutton Report – Sir, My sympathy for the BBC, the victim of the Hutton Report, becomes diluted when I recollect the savage, biased mauling that it gave the Conservative Party during the last general Election campaign. Hopefully, the Corporation will learn to do as it would be done by.

Frank Pedley, Bedale, North Yorkshire

Mark drew our attention to a joint letter to the *Guardian* from specialists in the field of vascular surgery, pathology, radiology, trauma, anaesthesiology and public health. They all agreed that it was highly improbable that the primary cause of Dr Kelly's death was haemorrhage from transection of a single ulnar artery, as stated by Lord Hutton in his report, and that the verdict of 'suicide' was an inappropriate finding. They gave the following opinion:

> To bleed to death from a transected artery goes against classical medical teaching, which is that a transected artery retracts, narrows, clots and stops bleeding within minutes. Even if a person continues to bleed, the body compensates for the loss of blood through vasoconstriction (closing down of non-essential arteries). This allows a partially exsanguinated individual to live for many hours, even days.

They also provided specialist opinions that the alternative causes of death that had been considered (toxicology and ischaemic heart disease) were similarly not credible and stated their belief that 'the verdict given (of suicide) is in contradiction to medical teaching; is at variance with documented cases of wrist-slash suicides; and does not align itself with the evidence presented at the inquiry'. They called for the reopening of the inquest by the coroner, to which a jury could be called and evidence taken on oath. Their call fell on deaf ears. A reopening never materialised.

Most people seemed to have very sceptical opinions on the Hutton Report, and I continue to believe that it represented a spectacular failure of accountability.

After much procrastination an inquiry into the nation's role in the Iraq War was announced in 2009 by Prime Minister Gordon Brown, who selected Sir John Chilcot (career diplomat and senior civil servant) as chairman of a small committee. It became generally known as the Chilcot Inquiry, which seven years later (on 6 July 2016) published a report of 2.6 million words in 12 volumes [Wikipedia provides a useful, and less time consuming-precis].

I heard and read nothing in the ensuing media debate to change my contempt of Tony Blair, particularly for his misleading of the Commons on 18 March 2003.

On 9 February the attention of the family was drawn to an exclusive full-page report in the *Daily Express* that featured Justin …

Uninsured drivers are being stopped in their tracks by a senior policeman who has pioneered a zero-tolerance policy in which illegal cars are seized and crushed. The crusade has led to 350 cars – or 70 a month – being destroyed in the first five months of its operation. Now the scheme, which is being piloted in Leeds, is set to be adopted nationally, after impressing the Home Office.

The man behind it is Inspector Justin Pedley of West Yorkshire police, who says it has already led to a drastic reduction in the number of drivers being stopped without insurance.

There has also been a dramatic fall in other crimes such as burglaries, which have gone down by 40 per cent in the areas where the scheme is being operated.

Inspector Pedley agreed that the measure was draconian, but asked that it be judged on results. 'It's a constant battle we're fighting against this underclass of drivers,' he said. 'We think this is the most effective way of stopping them.'

He said there has been a massive reduction in the number of crimes on his Leeds city and Holbeck beat – some smashed by more than half. Besides the drop in burglaries there has been a:

- Sixty-eight per cent fall in the number of motorists making off without paying for petrol.
- Sixteen per cent drop in thefts of motor vehicles.
- Forty per cent drop in thefts from motor vehicles.

The initiative comes as the Association of British Insurers told ministers to 'get tough' by confiscating cars of illegal motorists – whose accidents cost £500 million a year.

There are more than two million uninsured drivers on Britain's roads. Even if caught they often escape prosecution or are fined between

£150 and £200 – much less than it costs to insure a car.

Since last September, officers in Leeds have stopped and questioned motorists they believe may be dodging insurance. If a driver is caught without cover, officers immediately remove the offender's vehicle from the road. It is towed to a massive 'car pound' in the city where the driver can pay £105 plus VAT – along with a £12 per day charge to release the car once they have produced valid insurance cover. Alternatively, the drivers can disclaim the car completely – condemning the car to be crushed.

Inspector Pedley said success of the project was due to a wider clampdown in Leeds.

'We are targeting criminal use of vehicles,' he said. 'Without a car they cannot move around and commit these crimes.'

A Home Office spokeswoman said, 'West Yorkshire police are to be congratulated on an excellent operation, with impressive results.'

The *Daily Express* report incorporated a double-column 17-cm-long picture of Justin, with the newspaper's daily cartoon depicting a police officer and culprit gazing down at a 3' x 3' compressed car, with the caption 'Just think of it as part of the trend towards smaller cars, sir.' The report was also favourably commented upon by the editor. Thereafter, Justin became known in police circles as 'Crusher Pedley'.

Seventeen days later, on 26 April, Ruth and I proudly attended the Long Service and Good Conduct medal presentations to both Justin and Haley, together with several other worthy recipients, by the Chief Constable of West Yorkshire. Charlotte, Jessica and Robert were also present, as were Jack and Betty. Those medals had been very well earned in a particularly tough inner-city area and I remain full of admiration for Justin's and Haley's achievements. It is a lifestyle for which few people are fitted and it requires personal and social sacrifices that can only be appreciated, seen and understood by family members, particularly their children.

Ruth and I were now working hard and fast on our respective decorating and workshop projects, with builders at work on the Garden Room creation, re-pointing, etc. We were also into what we called the 'show preparation period' (10–11 weeks prior to the GYS), when we would select our GYS entries, first discussing which of the yearling ewes were likely to be the 'hogg in wool' entries. Preparation would begin with basic shepherding tasks and injections, particularly against fly strike, followed by trimming of excess wool on heads and tails, opening up of the fleece and then washing in clear water. Due to movement restrictions following the foot and mouth epidemic, we were no longer able to take our sheep to Marrick for washing in the Swale, so had to make do with immersion in clean water in our rather antiquated 1911 concrete dip, together with cunning use of a variable– jet hosepipe. When the fleece had regained its natural lustre after several days, Ruth would hand clip those destined to be shearling entries (both male and female), plus some reserves, with myself holding the sheep. Ruth's meticulous clipping would take about forty minutes, so 2–3 was the daily norm, followed by a return to the decorating. I was responsible for the progressive halter training of all show sheep, and by the time the GYS arrived, each would respond to a halter like a well-trained pony. The first lesson would involve the tying of three haltered sheep to a farm gate, allowing them to pull and fling themselves all over the place in a tantrum for about 20 minutes and then, as they calmed down, taking them individually on a succession of short walks. This preparatory work and attention to detail became increasingly refined as the GYS neared.

Because of our farming commitments, Ruth and I had routinely taken holidays in the late autumn. However, we both wanted to see the Norwegian fjords and the midnight sun, so an exception was made. Following a judging appointment for Ruth at the Royal Bath & West of England show on 2 June, we departed from Southampton eight days later on P&O's *Adonia* (77,000 tons), built in 1998. She was the latest addition to the fleet, not to be confused with a later and much smaller P&O ship of that name. We revelled at the prospect of 13 days of total relaxation in cool temperatures. The pensioners had worked hard and planned well for this cruise, which was to incorporate Stavanger, Hardangerfjord, Gcirangerfjord, Trondheim, Trondheimsfjord, Hollandsfjord, Honningsvåg, a midnight cruise off North Cape, Tromsø, Åndalsnes, Romsdalsfjord and Bergen.

We had a cabin with unobstructed picture window, so could look out at stunning fjords, mountains, glaciers and the occasional picturesque village from dawn to dusk. However, I was a tad disappointed at not seeing any wildlife – the fjords seemed dead. When the officer of the watch announced (probably out of boredom) that an elk could be seen swimming on the starboard side, the ship lurched in that direction as a few hundred passengers dashed for the glimpse of a pinprick-sized elk head in the far distance. Ruth had dashed for the library as soon as we boarded the ship and had a good stock of books to hand which she read with enthusiasm, while still able to digest the conversations of all around her – a rare talent. I too used the library, but my selections would largely be biographies, while Ruth's were far more varied.

We had very interesting tours of Stavanger and the charming old city of Trondheim, but the highlights of the cruise were the call at Honningsvåg and the tour of the high-plateau wilderness above, together with the midnight passing of the North Cape, at 11 p.m. on 17 June at our highest latitude (71°11.3'N). The silence of the high plateau between Honningsvåg and the North Cape and the ominous chill were awesome – we were humbly conscious of the fact that we were overlooking the end of the Nordic landmass, beyond which there were only icy and frozen waters to the North Pole. As we passed the North Cape the temperature was a not unpleasant 5 degrees and it was sufficiently bright and calm at midnight for me to play a serious game of table tennis on the open, unlit deck. Because of haze we did not see the midnight sun that night, but we did see it on the following night.

It was a cruise that we had to include in our itinerary, but it could not compare with our eastern Mediterranean experiences.

We found that there was no need to live extravagantly on our biennial cruises, and with detailed expenditure records of our Norway cruise still retained, I include a summary as an example:

Tariff for 'Outside Twin Shower' cabin (two sharing), less a 45% discount, but including £20 insurance was £3,482, plus £465 for tours and on board drinks/shop, plus £93 car parking at Southampton = £4,040 (£155 pp per day).

Considering the wonderful food, service, facilities and theatre entertainment, we considered our P&O cruises to be good value for money. Eastern Mediterranean cruises tended to be more expensive because of the greater distance/duration and more costly shore excursions.

We arrived home to find that there were no problems and thanked Brian Lockey profusely for looking after our sheep so well. We had a fortnight to prepare for the GYS. Nine sheep had been entered (which would entail two delivery journeys) plus two fleeces. The preparation of a fleece sometimes took as much time as preparing a sheep. After clipping and being left in the sun for a while, it would be spread out on the tiled kitchen floor and Ruth would meticulously pick and shake out any bits of dirt, hay, straw and stained wool, prior to rolling – sometimes repeating the process several times until she was entirely satisfied. The garden was running wild and the soft fruit needed picking. There was much work to be done.

There was a record entry of 1,581 sheep at the GYS that year, 85 of which were of the Wensleydale breed, the third-highest breed entry. The competition was intense, yet it was to be one of Ruth's highest GYS achievement years. Her hogg in wool was selected by different judges as Breed Champion, Longwool Ewe Champion, Longwool Wool on the Hoof Champion and Reserve Wool on the Hoof Supreme Champion, and achieved fourth place in the overall Supreme Championship of all sheep in the show. She also won the Wensleydale Shearling Ram and Group classes and the Best Wensleydale Fleece. Her other sheep were also well placed. It was a vintage year and an expensive bar bill!

On 6 August Ruth and I drove to the Royal Signals Headquarters officers' mess at Blandford in Dorset to attend the anniversary dinner of 21 fellow officers commissioned into the corps on precisely that day fifty years earlier. Sadly, three were deceased and two were unable to attend, and there was one lost contact. Nevertheless, a most enjoyable occasion was shared by fourteen 'old soldiers', ten wives and a widow. Accommodation was provided in the mess for those who needed it, so most of us assembled for afternoon tea and also enjoyed breakfast together on the following day, providing just sufficient time to share family news and worldwide experiences. I wonder how many non–military organisations retain such contacts.

Ruth's success at the GYS was followed by the Breed Championship (plus Reserve Champion) at the Rare Breeds Survival Trust annual show and sale at Melton Mowbray in early September and then Supreme Champion at the WLSBA annual show and sale at Skipton, where she won six beautiful antique silverware items with which to adorn our Christmas dining tables. She also had some good sales, a reflection of her outstanding show successes. On examining the P&O Cruises brochure for the following year we noted that *Aurora* was cruising the western Mediterranean for fourteen nights from 20 October 2005. We booked without delay, securing an early-booking discount of 45%, and our cabin E103.

The approach of Christmas and the assembly of the family was always an exciting time, with the lead-up period as usual beginning on Ruth's birthday. The exchange of Christmas gifts that year was quite hilarious as Mark emptied a bag of 'valuable' watches from the Orient in the kitchen and invited everyone to take their pick.

However, no sooner had our Christmas Day enjoyment ended than (on Sunday 26 December) one of the deadliest natural disasters in human history occurred, killing more than 230,000 people in fourteen countries. A huge earthquake beneath the Indian Ocean, caused when the Indian Plate was subducted by the Burma Plate, produced a series of devastating tsunamis along the coasts of most landmasses bordering the Indian Ocean, with waves reaching a coastline height of up to 100 feet. The epicentre was off the west coast of Sumatra, Indonesia. Across the world, people were horrified as they viewed the graphic images of disaster on their television sets, but they soon responded magnificently.

2005

Thrilling Sporting Achievements, Fox Hunting Ban, More GYS Success and Another Aurora Cruise

The 2005 New Year celebrations throughout the United Kingdom fell silent for two minutes as a mark of respect for those who died in the tsunamis.

A week later North West England, and Cumbria in particular, experienced a severe overnight gale, with torrential rain on the night of 7/8 January. The Environment Agency issued 100 flood warnings. We caught it quite badly at Old Hall, with 87-mph gusts recorded at Leeming. At 7.30 a.m. on Saturday 8 January the electricity supply in our area failed, which was later found to be due to a fallen tree about a mile away. We were without power until 9.30 p.m. on the Sunday, by which time the gale was subsiding, so we had to improvise ...

10 January 2005 (Ruth to family):
Old Hall – Power came on at about 9.30pm last night after we had gone to bed. In fact we were both asleep, but the light and television woke us up. It was a pleasant surprise. Daddy created a stand for me to put a pan on the log fire and I stewed steak and vegetables and we did enjoy it because we were so hungry. So, if the 'crunch' comes

I now have some experience. I also found that if I washed potatoes and wrapped them well in foil and put them in the ashes of the fire underneath, that in two hours we had delicious jacket potatoes. This morning, daddy replaced the six tiles that had come off the byre roof, but the Old Hall roof is without a ridge tile, which is worrying if we are to get more gales. Sadly, we have lost two trees. Mark – we used so many candles, so it was good advice of yours to stock up.

Love you all lots. MUM XXX

12 January 2005 (Ruth and me to family):
Old Hall – A generator would have been useful if the power failure had been more prolonged, if only to save the freezer contents, which would have been unlikely to remain frozen for more than a further day. However, we are far better off than most people because of our open fires facility, with two years of firewood on site. Had we felt the need, we could have brought into use our calor gas fire, small calor gas cooking ring and calor gas lamp. How far does one go in contingency planning?

We are delighted at Robert's success [selection for Heckmondwike Grammar School].

I have a semi-tame cock pheasant that is now almost eating sheep nuts out of my hand. He follows me around the fields at feeding time and shelters in the lamb creeps or behind the hay racks. He nearly came to an end when your Mum suggested that he should be ringed. I was getting quite attached to him and was not happy with the suggestion but didn't say anything. I thought she was referring to his neck.

Love from Mum and Dad. Xxx

A few weeks before Christmas an Englishwoman had set sail from Ushant (an island off the northwest coast of Brittany) in a 75-foot yacht in an attempt to break the world-record time for a solo circumnavigation of the globe (72 days, 22 hours and 54 minutes), held by Frenchman Francis Joyon. My attention and admiration had been drawn to Ellen MacArthur when she obtained second overall place in the 2000/2001 Vendée Globe race, simultaneously setting the world record for a single- handed monohull circumnavigation by a woman. For this achievement she was voted runner-up BBC Sports Personality of the Year, beaten by footballer David Beckham. The Christmas festivities and the horrific tsunami disaster had distracted me from the race, but when I returned to it, aided by Ellen MacArthur's video-diary postings on the web and television coverage, I realised that we were witnessing another feat of supreme human courage and endurance at sea. Ellen MacArthur had extraordinary determination as well as stamina. As a schoolgirl in Derbyshire she had been inspired by Arthur Ransome's *Swallows and Amazons* books and wanted a small sailing boat of her own – so she saved her dinner money for three years and bought one. Where there's a will, there's a way! In mid-January 2005 she was fighting for her life in a 75-foot trimaran in atrocious South Atlantic seas, her despair, tears, exhaustion and injuries recorded on camera for all to see, her snatched sleep periods of no more than 20 minutes' duration.

15 January 2005 (Myself to family):
Ellen MacA having a rough time – see www.teamellen.com. Cumulative exhaustion setting in, but she's a tough nut. Could be Dame Ellen and Sports Personality of the Year if she succeeds.

16 January 2005 (Ruth to family):
A beautiful day just like Spring and I'm going to give the dairy a once over and then see what is coming through in the garden. We may even go up the dale. I watched with horror the TV pictures of old Babylon being destroyed by the USA forces. They have built a heli-pad and dug ditches everywhere and it showed all the artefacts that had been chucked aside. It then showed earlier footage of a US Colonel saying that they would take good care of the site! If any of you want a visit then please come and see us.
Love you all lots MUM XXX

On 7 February at 10.29 p.m. an exhausted but jubilant Ellen MacArthur crossed the finishing line at Ushant, beating Francis Joyon's record by

1 day 8 hours and 35 minutes, watched by mass European television audiences, myself and Ruth included. Her immediate award of Dame Commander of the British Empire (DBE) when she returned to England was reminiscent of the awards by the sovereign to Francis Drake in 1580 and Francis Chichester in 1967 for their circumnavigations. She was also awarded the French Chevalier de la Légion d'honneur. In October 2009 Dame Ellen MacArthur announced retirement from competitive racing to concentrate on resource and energy use in the global economy. On 2 September 2010 she launched the Ellen MacArthur Foundation; a charity focusing on accelerating the transition to a regenerative circular economy.

12 February 2005 (Ruth to family):
Old Hall – Cold to-night. Got up early and headed off to near Colne for a Wensleydale Sheep meeting. Tired, and I think it will be an early night with a hot water bottle. Hard to believe that I cut all the lawns two days ago. Mark, I hope the helicopter flying went well, but I would have thought that it would have been too windy. Lovely to see the Yorkshire Pedleys yesterday. Crispin – has Aileen got her new oven yet? It would make a beautiful Valentine present!

Love you all lots MUM XXX

20 February 2005 (Ruth to family):
Old Hall – Got our first lamb. He is snuggled up under the heat lamp in the pig sty with his mother – a very 'ancient' (9 shear) ewe. This morning I have been fettling up around the big mullion window in the dining room, where David [Hughes] put in a new window. It has been a long job as I had to re-plaster and then paper and this morning I have put on the emulsion paint, so a very good winter job finished.

Then, as my kitchen cupboards are now so shabby I decided to re-varnish them in a slightly darker colour and so far this morning I have done the set of cupboards and drawers as you come in at the back door. To-morrow I shall do another lot. Daddy has been hard at work getting to grips with lambing sheds etc. so we are ready when the other ewes lamb. It is so damned cold that there are icicles along the beck.

We are having a Sunday lunch to-day for a change and then it is going to be a quiet afternoon in front of the log fire. Mark – when do you go to China again?

Tell me all your news. Love MUM XXX

28 February 2005 (Ruth to family):

Old Hall – Most of the snow has gone but it is so damn cold. Been down at the school with one thing and another, so intend to go to bed with a book. To-morrow, the Conservative Women's Committee are doing a lunch for over 70 guests, so another fairly active day. We don't have much time to sit around. My kitchen cupboards look quite good – a bit darker than before but the cupboard doors under the sink look particularly nice. It certainly looks more tidy. Hope the Chinese are being nice to you Mark. Justin, don't forget to let us know about Robert please.

Love to you all. MUM XXX

4 March 2005 (Ruth to family):

Old Hall – Thank you for the Mothers Day card – very nice indeed. I liked it a lot.

Tremendous news about Robert [entry to Heckmondwike GS].

We are truly thrilled.

Had a very tiring (lambing) day. Been up since five and not everything has gone according to plan, but now settled and intend to go to bed soon.

You are welcome to come whenever you want but I do know you are always busy with one thing and another. However, there is always a meal waiting for you.

Bitterly cold but Spring must be around the corner.

Love you all. MUM XXX

5 March 2005 (Ruth to family):

Old Hall – Well, one thing it isn't is lambing weather. Whenever we go out we get a blast of sleet or rain. It is none stop. We are going to bed early as we have a ewe that will surely lamb to-night and we have a not very well lamb that needs a lot of attention. Daddy is getting the brunt of the bad weather.

Love you. MUM XXX

13 March 2005 (Ruth to family):
Old Hall – Been busy on the farm with the odd lambing problem. Hopefully, things will be quiet to-day. The weather really has been against us with a bitterly cold wind and showers. As we are 'confined to barracks' with the lambing we have emptied the small bedroom and daddy is making good the very badly laid floorboards which were never put back properly after the central heating was installed. Then we are having a new carpet laid. The room looks better already and this morning I am going to paint the skirting boards.

Have a good day. Love you all lots. MUM XXX

21 April 2005 (Ruth to family):
Old Hall – Hello again! We are back in business thank goodness. Daddy hasn't done anything – machine [computer] just started working again. I now have to catch up with all the news.

I have been sticking hundreds of labels on envelopes for the election and then stuffing them with leaflets, so I have kept myself busy, with the garden in good order despite awful weather. The garth is flooded with ducks enjoying themselves. Please send us lots of news. We are still feeding three lambs but all the stock seem OK. However, fields puddled, with very little grass. Will send more news this evening IF this darned machine is still working. Love you all lots.

MUM XXX

The following day I appreciated how well Crispin was doing in the financial world when his opinion on a hostile bid for Securities Trust of Scotland was quoted in the *Daily Telegraph* … and proved to be correct.

4 May 2005 (Ruth to family):

Old Hall – I'm back! Mark fixed it [the computer] when he came up this weekend – said it was the 'fire wall'. We had a nice May Bank Holiday, but wet. Mark cooked a Thai meal on Saturday night which was very tasty. We have been washing sheep and I have got three sheared ready for the GYS. We have also been doing a lot of envelope filling and leaflet delivering for the Party. I shall be up waiting for the first results to come in to-night. The garden looks well and very lush, but a blessed rabbit has been visiting the garden and has dug a very large burrow under my border. We have barricaded all the entrances and wait to see whether we can keep it out. What news from the family? Anyone want a Wensleydale hare?

Love you all lots and lots. MUM XXX

The Wensleydale hare was accidently hit by our car near Patrick Brompton but not run over. He was a magnificent animal in his prime and at first we thought he was just stunned. He provided Ruth and me with three delicious meals. If it was safe to stop, Ruth would routinely pick up the occasional pheasant in like manner on quiet country roads. Waste not – want not.

The election results were very disappointing for the Conservative Party, led by Michael Howard, though William Hague increased his Richmond constituency majority slightly to 17,867, making it still one of the safest Tory seats in the country. Tony Blair's Labour Party won its third consecutive victory, though with a popular vote of only 35.2%, the lowest of any majority government in British history. The need for urgent electoral boundaries reform in England was again obvious when statistics revealed that despite the Conservatives winning the popular vote in England they finished up with 91 fewer MPs [in England] than Labour.

12 May 2005 (Ruth to family):

Old Hall – Another glorious day. The sun is shining and all the trees are heavy with blossom. Yesterday, Daddy shot one of the rabbits [with Crispin's air rifle] and nearly got another this morning. They are devastating the veg patch and flower border. I think that when I blocked the entrances last week I may have locked the rabbits inside the garden. We shall see. We sheared another GYS sheep this morning and I am attempting to paint the new garden room windows, but it ain't easy. Going to try and relax this afternoon and pretend I'm in the south of France. Mark – I'll also be doing the crossword, ensuring all the words fit (somehow).

Love you all lots. MUM XXX

16 May 2005 (Ruth to family):
Old Hall – A young rabbit is still giving us the run around and we don't know how to catch it. I have blocked up all the holes in the wall but it still runs off and hides. When we got up this morning it was devouring the runner beans, then I looked at the pond and two mallards were paddling around in it. Half an hour later a squirrel was doing a dance on the lawn.

Yesterday, we drove up to Chester le Street to the Riverside stadium to see Yorkshire beaten by Durham. It was a beautiful day and the cricket field is excellent with beautiful trees planted all round.

Remember, you are welcome to visit. We always look forward to seeing you.

Love from MUM XXX

23 May 2005 (Ruth to family):
Old Hall – I think the last rabbit has been dealt with and with a bit of luck we are now rabbit proof. Crispin – I have found another small clump of meadow saxifrage (along the beck), a great find. Garden looks great and tidier than it has been for many a year. Shearing underway for GYS entries. Please give us all your news.

Love you all lots. MUM XXX

12 June 2005 (Ruth to family):
Old Hall – It is not cold … It is absolutely freezing. It is raining and grey like a November day. I have had to soak in a bath to warm up and

am now in winter clothes. I didn't get my hanging baskets done, but the vegetable patch did need some rain. It was nice to see the Tingley Pedleys. To-morrow I'm getting some wool off by courier to a London shop and then buy some new shoes. Keep in touch.

Love MUM XXX

22 June 2005 (Ruth to family):
Old Hall – Have been very busy painting the front windows in the dining room and sitting room. It has been a very tiring job but they look very much better. I am trying to do as many as possible before the bad weather sets in. It is like painting the Forth bridge. This evening, Daddy is stacking a load of hay in the barn that's just arrived – a very hot and tiring job. Mark – if you want to come up, you are always welcome.

Love you all lots. MUM XXX

6 July 2005 (Ruth to family):
Old Hall – Busy again to-day getting stock ready for the GYS. Wet and cold – not at all nice. We are getting there but it hasn't been easy. I shall be glad when it is all over and I can get back to my plants and painting the windows. The weather has been like November and the roads have been flooded quite badly. I'm glad that we beat France for the staging of the Olympics in London in 2012 but I suspect that we will make a total horlicks of the whole thing. I am going to have an early night and watch the Roman dig snuggled up in bed.

Love MUM

Ruth had another highly successful Great Yorkshire Show, with the following placings, in class order:

- Aged Ram – 2nd
- Shearling Ram – 1st (Reserve Male Champion) and 3rd
- Ram Lamb – 6th

- Hogg in Wool – 1st (Breed Champion) and 4th
- Shearling Ewe – 1st
- Ewe Lamb – unplaced
- Group – 1st

The show was as enjoyable as ever – a gathering of an increasing number of friends, with a splendid WLSBA barbecue in one of the sheep judging rings on the first evening. To most of the livestock exhibitors at the show, this was their annual holiday and they were intent on enjoying themselves. Weather permitting, they would have taken most of their hay crop before the show, the remainder as soon as possible afterwards, then the harvest festival thanksgiving (often called the 'harvest home' in Yorkshire), followed by the autumn livestock sales. It is not unusual to meet livestock farmers who have never been able to take a conventional holiday, with perhaps the exception of a honeymoon of a few days. Their bronzed, healthy faces and physique, with not a spare ounce of flesh on their bodies, are the result of an outdoor life shared with the elements every day of the year, come what may. It is a tough life, particularly on the high fells, requiring a sense of humour and neighbourly cooperation and trust, which they have in abundance. They never retire.

Most were very, very angry that year. This was because of the government's act banning fox hunting which had been imposed on them and their families five months earlier. Notwithstanding the fact that the hunt was part of their rural culture (and in many cases had been so for several generations), they felt that the imposition of the ban reflected ignorance of a hunt's vital role in the livestock farming industry, also an element of political spite from those who did not live in or understand the world of food production. The ban was also hurtful to them because they had been portrayed by their adversaries in the preceding debate as people who were uncaring, even callous towards animals, while in fact their care for their livestock and the creatures of the countryside that they manage, and the sacrifices they make for them, are second to none. Initially, Ruth was 'anti-hunt', despite best friend Nanette and her family being supporters of the Bramham Moor hunt, while many of the hierarchy of the Bedale hunt were also good friends. However, she gradually changed her position and eventually gave vigorous waves to a bemused scarlet-coated gentleman with four brass buttons whenever we passed 'the Bedale' on the country lanes.

When 522 MPs of the House of Commons voted on the hunting issue I wondered how many of them had taken the trouble to visit the kennels of a hunt to observe the service that the kennels provided to livestock farmers and the community. If they had, they would have seen the overnight casualties being brought in – perhaps a newly born dead calf and its dead mother, perhaps a road casualty (a badger, dog or deer). The good meat would be cut up for the hounds, the remainder would be flung into one of the skips. They might then have appreciated that these self-supporting kennels, like abattoirs, are essential cogs in a vibrant livestock industry, and that some 6–8,000 full-time jobs depend on hunting in the United Kingdom. Had they made such visits and talked to the kennels staff and the livestock farming community they might have belatedly recognised that, on balance, they should support that hard-working community with their vote.

Following the ban on fox hunting, hunts follow artificially laid trails, or make use of exemptions laid out in the Hunting Act. I am delighted to record that the hunts are thriving, with 174 packs of foxhounds in England and Wales, and a further 10 in Scotland; record membership and very strong support from a more understanding younger generation.

21 July 2005 (Ruth to family):
Old Hall – Back again after a very tiring time at the GYS. Daddy went down with an awful cold and then I got it and we have been a couple of sad old things – very tired with no energy at all. The garden is full of wildlife. A squirrel amuses us doing acrobats in the bay tree trying to reach a bag of nuts. The varieties of birds that use the garden is quite amazing, including a woodpecker. Justin – please let us know if we can help out during the holiday – I mentioned it when I spoke to Haley.

Love you all lots. MUM XXX

27 July 2005 (Ruth to family):
Old Hall – Had a wonderful day out in the Lake District on Monday, visiting the museum in Grasmere. Returned via Patterdale and verified that the pub in the watercolour that I bought is indeed of the White Lion, dated 1913, so am pleased. Squirrel Nutter is now taking not only the nuts but the containers as well. He is such a persistent little beggar. Justin – if we can help with the children here or at Tingley then let us know, or if you want to bring them for a meal then you are very welcome. We do want to see them. I have been busy picking blackcurrants for winter. If anyone wants some for the freezer then say so and I'll pick some more. Keep in touch.

    Love. MUM XXX

11 August 2005 (Ruth to family):
Old Hall – Restful day watching cricket and doing bits of gardening. Edward, Nanette's eldest son has had a nasty accident. He was combining and the engine overheated, so he climbed up, unscrewed the cap, leant back to avoid getting scalded and fell backwards, breaking his arm and hitting his head on the ground and causing spinal concern. Now out of hospital but laid up for some time, having to be careful with his movements. We are continuing with our exterior painting – looks good.

    Love. MUM XXX

In order to introduce some fresh bloodlines into the Hunton flock we decided to purchase five ewe lambs from the very discerning owners of a flock in Powys; Jim and Sandra Thompson, who were also close friends. Ruth and I spent several hours studying the pedigrees of their lambs and were delighted with their quality when they brought them to us for examination on 26 August – the price was right, the lambs seemed happy with their new home and we enjoyed a most pleasant social afternoon with Jim and Sandra. Such small private sales among friends, where there was time to compare facilities and sheep husbandry practices and to meet other members of the family, were most enjoyable; together with the shows and workshops, they cumulatively added to the quality of our lives and the inherent strength of our breed society. We had a reasonable show and sale at Melton Mowbray in early September, but there were fewer buyers than normal.

It had been a jubilant summer for red-blooded Englishmen (and women), for England's cricketers beat Australia in what was probably the most thrilling Ashes series ever. Australia were firm favourites and won the first five-day test match comfortably. However, the second was won by England by 2 runs and the third ended in a nail-biting draw, with England only one wicket away from a win. The fourth provided a 3-wicket win for England, while an exciting draw in the final match secured a 2–1 overall win for England and the return of the Ashes after 18 years of biennial contest. Andrew Flintoff of Lancashire was the England player of the series, scoring 402 runs and taking 24 wickets, with Shane Warne the Australian star (40 wickets).

13 September 2005 (Ruth to family):
Old Hall – Been catching up on everything – sleep, cleaning, washing and sheep work, but found time to watch our wonderful cricket team. What a win! Hope that Lois does well at the swimming championships next weekend. We are going to rebuild the broken down wall by the pinfold – sick of waiting for it to be rebuilt by the people who chopped down the trees. Off to a Conservative meeting this morning.
    Love. MUM XXX

17 September 2005 (Ruth to family):
Old Hall wall building – We started early this morning with the pinfold wall and stopped at 4 o'clock, but haven't finished. A truly amazing thing happened. There was one stone just under the triangular capping stone that was out of alignment with the rest of the wall but was totally cemented in so I hacked and hacked and finally lifted the stone out and there, spreadeagled on the mortar, was a very black toad, which I was sure was dead but I could see that its eye was bright. I lifted it out and put it by the stream and after a while it walked into the water. I

reckon it had waited fifteen years for me to let it out. The round cobble fitted perfectly into the mortar. I have read about toads being walled up but this was cemented in. It made my day. Isn't that a nice story?

Love from MUM

I can verify Ruth's description of the release of the imprisoned toad – I was working alongside her and she drew my attention to it immediately.

20 September 2005 (Ruth to family):
Old Hall – Well done Robert with the music exam. Crispin – the toad was TOTALLY locked in. I just wish that I had kept the cobble and the surrounding cement.

Love to you all. MUM XXX

23 September 2005 (Mark to family):
Cannot have the peasants being rude to their masters, can we? …

Girl arrested over Bollocks to Blair shirt

H&H staff writer 22 September 2005

Police arrested a 20-year-old gamekeeper for wearing a 'Bollocks to Blair' T-shirt at a game fair last weekend

A girl was arrested for wearing her 'Bollocks to Blair' T-shirt at the Midlands Game Fair last weekend. Charlotte Denis, 20, a gamekeeper from Gloucestershire, was stopped by police as she left the Countryside Alliance stand because of the 'offensive' slogan.

Shocked and dismayed to be made a public spectacle, Denis tried to reason with the officers: 'What do you want me to do? Take my top off and wear my bra?'

At this point, two officers marched Denis towards a police car. 'They grabbed me as if I was a football hooligan,' she says.

Although the 'Bollocks to Blair' slogan was in evidence all round the Game Fair police maintained it was the first time that they had seen it.

'They had to walk past a huge banner in order to get to me and there were lots of people wearing the T-shirts,' explained Denis.

A tearful Denis was driven to a mobile police unit. 'I asked the officers how they could arrest someone for wearing a T-shirt and they told me it was because it could offend a 70-80 year old woman,' she said.

After agreeing to wear a friend's coat, Denis was released without charge. But the incident ruined her day: 'You don't expect to be treated like that at a country fair,' she said.

Denis bought her T-shirt at the Badminton Horse Trials last year, as well as a matching badge she wears on her coat. 'Bollocks to Blair' merchandise is manufactured by Splash and first appeared last year.

'The demand has been crazy,' said Splash director Toby Rhodes. 'The slogan is an expression of anger in the countryside – which we are not trying to incite. We originally thought it a bit too direct for us but it has been popular with all ages. I've been told that some police officers wear the T-shirts under their uniforms'. 'It's complete nonsense,' said the Countryside Alliance. 'The police surely have better things to do with their time than protect the Prime Minister's modesty.'

23 Sepember 2005 (Ruth to family):
Re: Girl arrested over Bollocks to Blair shirt – Perhaps it might be more acceptable if the slogan was changed to 'bullocks to Blair', launched with a delivery of the beasts to 10 Downing Street. He is loathed in the country areas.

Love to you all. MUM XXX

The WLSBA annual show and sale at Skipton Auction Mart at the end of the month was a disaster and we brought several of our sheep back home. Ruth did well enough in the show, winning three items of silverware, but there was a paucity of buyers and very low prices. Minds now focused on our fortnight's cruise in the western Mediterranean. We were ready for a break. I had been annoyed with myself on previous cruises at the amount of weight that I had put on and was determined that on this cruise I would apply more self-discipline. So, before leaving on 20 October, I wrote in my diary in large font, '12st 4lbs'. 'I hope you're not going to be an old bore,' said Ruth.

Instead of driving to Southampton, we made use of one of P&O's chartered coaches, departing Darlington at 6.45 a.m. Our luggage was loaded for us into the bus hold and we would next see it outside our cabin. The bus stopped on the quay, adjacent to *Aurora* – short walk into passenger lounge for documentation check and embark early afternoon. Easy. At 5 p.m. *Aurora* let go her mooring lines and thrusted clear of her berth. Band played, ticker tape thrown and we were on our way, with not a care in the world for the next fourteen days. As soon as an introductory glass of champagne had been consumed we headed for cabin E103 and then to the library to ensure first choice of a fine selection of books. Ruth was already purring.

We woke the following day to showers and a force 6 wind and saw the Union flag flying, a most unusual sight on a merchant ship. This was because it was the 200th anniversary of the Battle of Trafalgar and the government had given special dispensation. I also met a Royal Signals friend whom I had not seen since my young officer days – Alan Yeoman, with his wife, Barbara. Ruth and I were waiting for the lift – the doors opened and there they were. Recognition was immediate and we enjoyed several hours of military reminiscences and social chat during the cruise. Alan had been one of the most successful Royal Signals officers of my age group, retiring as a major-general. He was awarded Companion of the Order of the Bath (CB) in the Queen's Birthday Honours in 1987. Sadly, Barbara was now confined to a wheelchair.

Our first port of call was Barcelona, Spain's second city. We were torn between visiting the city centre, particularly the historic Gothic Quarter, or travelling some forty miles by coach and rack railway to the famous 1,000-year-old Benedictine monastery of Montserrat. We selected the latter and did not regret the choice. The rack railway lifted us to the top of the mountain (2,400 feet), where there are spectacular views of the monastery, nestled into the mountain crags, and of the river Llobregat below. We returned to *Aurora* at 5 p.m. and an hour later we were sailing overnight to Villefranche, in the Principality of Monaco (269 nautical miles).

We woke at 7 a.m., after excellent late-night theatre entertainment, as *Aurora* entered the scenic natural harbour of Villefranche. She was to be anchored, and we delayed our breakfast to watch nine shackles (270 yards to landlubbers) of cable paid out under power and *Aurora* brought up to the cable. We had been spoilt with a choice of eight attractive tours. The most expensive was an eight-hour (£56 per person) tour of Monaco, including lunch and the glitz and glamour of Monte Carlo – the expensive designer boutiques, restaurants and gardens, the lobby of the Grand Casino (supplementary charge to enter the gaming rooms), Café de Paris, Hotel de Paris, etc. We were tempted, but we decided upon a less strenuous four-and-a-half-hour (£28pp) coach tour along the tier roads known as the Corniches, from which we had spectacular views of Nice, Beaulieu-sur-Mer, Cap Ferrat and Villefranche. On the Upper Corniche we passed the Vista Palace, from which we had a marvellous view extending over the border, with the Principality of Monaco below. Shortly after 6 p.m. we watched the anchor appear and we were on our way to Livorno, only 156 nautical miles to the east, which *Aurora* could have comfortably reached in seven hours. However, good cruise ships do not disturb their passengers' sleep by arriving at ports in the middle of the night, and *Aurora* loitered at 12.5 knots, to be nursed through the narrow harbour breakwater by two tugs at 7 a.m. The tugs then gently swung *Aurora* around and eased her into a tight berth position.

Livorno is an attractive gateway port for visits to Florence and Pisa, but our choice was to take a full-day coach excursion into the attractive countryside of Tuscany. Heading east from Livorno, we passed several medieval hill towns surrounded by beautiful valleys, the landscape adorned with cypresses, olive groves, vineyards, small churches and farms. Thankfully, in addition to a splendid traditional Tuscan lunch (with good Vernaccia wine) at a farm, we had plenty of time to explore two enchanting medieval hillside towns; San Gimignano and Volterra. We were very surprised at the preservation of San Gimignano, almost unchanged since the Middle Ages, with cobbled streets, impressive 'noble' towers and strong medieval walls surrounding the old centre. The Etruscan town of Volterra is on a high plateau with splendid long-distance views. It is well known for its locally mined and carved alabaster statues.

The talk at dinner that evening not only covered the tours that we had experienced, world news and the evening's entertainment, but also included speculation as to how long the perfect weather would continue – clear skies, light airs and daytime temperatures of 19–22 degrees from the time that we entered the Med.

An onboard event that we always looked forward to was the Captain's cocktail party. Not only because of the generous supply of cocktails and canapés and meeting more interesting people, but listening to the amusing addresses of the Captains. One in particular lingers in my mind: describing a famous millionaire's entry for dinner on his first cruise; *George Dawson* (GD), accompanied by his wife. No, not the famous GD preacher, nor the GD grandson of a slave who championed literacy for the remaining five years of his life after learning to read at 98 years, but a GD who lived a life at the opposite end of the saintly spectrum: his early years were typical of the two fisted lifestyle of a Bermondsey kid born in 1910, but by the age of 15 years our GD had started his own scrap metal business, soon specialising in dodgy deals involving Army surplus scrap metal. He had been a millionaire for many years when he took his first cruise …

> *"Good evening Mr Dawson, Mrs Dawson", greeted the Maître D, "please follow me … you will be dining at the Captain's table".*
>
> *"Hey lad, cum ere … ave paid good money for this ere ollidy and am not etting wit crew …"*

George Dawson was made bankrupt on 24th September 1957 and on 26 March 1959 he was sentenced at the Old Bailey to six years in jail for fraud (guilty on 10 charges).

Again, it was a short, loitering overnight journey to our next port of call; Civitavecchia – the gateway to Rome, the destination to which Ruth was most looking forward. Apart from using the P&O coach facility to travel to and from Rome, we explored the city as we wished, beginning with the Colosseum, which was Ruth's primary 'must see' attraction. I too became so entranced with this magnificent building, which could hold up to 55,000 spectators in its prime, and with the horrific events that it hosted, that we must have spent at least two hours there. At Ruth's request I took many photographs, which she was to repeatedly pore over later. Next was a pavement glass of wine, coffee and a snack, watching the pretty girls go by, followed by a lengthy open-roof bus tour that enabled us to see so many historical parts of the city, followed by the stunning Pantheon and St Peter's Square.

A truly inspiring and memorable day, and again the weather was kind; 20 degrees and a clear sky. I recommend Rome as a city that must be visited during one's life, but not during the summer heat; which, unfortunately, is also the peak tourist season.

A similar overnight journey took us to Naples, and again we visited the ever-intriguing ruins of Pompeii ... The baths and the theatres, the wrestling ground and the luxurious villas stand empty, yet there are many echoes of Pompeii's daily life; the wine jars are still set on the counter of the wine shop, the stepping stones are there to help you cross the street in the rainy season, and the mosaic floors and brilliant frescoes remain, a wonder to this present day. The plaster casts of Vesuvius's victims in the precise positions in which they died in August of AD 79 are particularly poignant, and a reminder of our mortality.

Ruth and I were always thrilled with our visits to Italy. We liked the people, the countryside and its history; Roman ghosts never far distant. Whilst being proud of the achievements of our own nation, we should not forget that we received from this boot shaped peninsular an advanced way of life and the foundation of our language in AD43, and then the Renaissance.

We were now more than halfway through our cruise and had visited what to us were the major attractions. *Aurora* now turned homewards, but there were still visits to Cagliari (Sardinia), Palma (Majorca) and Gibraltar to come. We decided to remain on board at Cagliari, resting and reading, but the opportunity of a glimpse of Majorca could not be missed. Of the numerous tour options, we shortlisted two – a visit to the Caves of Drach, with their cathedral-sized halls, stalactites and stalagmites and the largest underground lake in the world, or a tour into the mountains. We selected the latter. The coach took us along the seafront, passing the cathedral, Almudaina Palace and other splendid buildings, then climbed through spectacular landscapes of almond and olive groves and into forest and rugged mountains, halting at the blonde stone village of Valldemossa, renowned for its outstanding beauty and favoured by hikers and nature lovers. Yet, we realised that we had seen but a small part of this beautiful island, which we had not previously visited. It was a brief visit, for *Aurora* sailed in the early and hot afternoon for Gibraltar, the temperature reaching 28 degrees – a sunbathing afternoon for Ruth, while I took a shady siesta. Majorca had been a very pleasant surprise, the day ending with *Aurora* sailing into a stunning sunset.

Half a day in Gibraltar was quite sufficient, for we knew it well. The wonderful Mediterranean weather continued into the Atlantic, and as we followed the Portuguese coastline on 1 November the temperature was still a pleasant 21 degrees, with a warm south-westerly wind, and we hadn't seen a spot of rain since leaving Southampton. Surely our good fortune couldn't continue through the Bay of Biscay? But it did, and as *Aurora* rounded the island of Ushant off the northwest tip of Brittany (where Ellen MacArthur had finished her epic journey) in the early evening of our last day at sea, Ruth and I were still able to relax on an open deck in a moderate breeze, with the temperature a cool but comfortable 17 degrees. Amazing weather for the time of year.

6 November 2005 (Ruth to family):
Old Hall – It is wonderful to be home. We have had a really good holiday with marvellous weather but I do love Old Hall. A bit sad isn't it. I've done ten loads of washing and have just finished ironing. The leaves are still holding and the sweet gum will soon be looking fantastic. Please send me some funnies. We have been having so many late nights. The (second) theatre performances didn't start until 1030pm so you can imagine what time we have been getting to bed.

Love to you all. MUM XXX

16 November 2005 (Ruth to family):

Old Hall – Hope that you had a restful journey to China, Mark, and that the flu has improved, otherwise the Chinese authorities will put you in quarantine. Not going to be easy for you with all the meetings. A cold morning and I'm glad that I have got my geraniums into the cottage. I have been redecorating the kitchen, a wall a day, otherwise I would get too tired. It is now finished and looks better. Working in the dairy now and then I'm going to tackle the sitting room and give the spiders the run around. We are going into Northallerton to look for an outside Christmas tree.

Love MUM XXX

20 November 2005 (Ruth to family):

Old Hall – Daddy has been strimming the far side of the beck to tidy it up and I've been helping a bit with picking up tins, bottles and other refuse. It looks a great deal better already. Very cold, but sunny. Hope you can get your computer to work, Justin. Take care. Love you all. MUM XXX

5 December 2005 (Ruth to family):

Old Hall – Joy of joys. I have finished decorating the sitting room. It has taken five days and looks much fresher, but it was a tiring job. All spruce for Christmas. Going shopping in Northallerton to-morrow, before the rush really begins. I'm enjoying these long, dark evenings with a good book or a bad book, just as long as I have something to read. We love to hear about the [grandchildren] skating in Scotland. They are obviously pretty tough to fall heavily and continue. Daddy has done a wonderful job of clearing up the far side of the beck, so we should have some wonderful Spring flowers.

Love you all lots. MUM. XXX

It was about this time that the BBC Sports Personality of the Year was announced. Ellen MacArthur and Andrew Flintoff were the deserving and clear favourites, and the winner was ... Andrew Flintoff. I admired both, but my choice was Ellen MacArthur, for her achievement involved breathtaking bravery, and she was one of the so-called weaker sex in a minority sport pitted against both man and the brutal elements. She was a heroine of her age. Twice runner-up.

The run-up to Christmas was as exciting, enjoyable and intensive as ever – a multitude of social events, stocking up on good food for both family and sheep, decorations and glitter everywhere, with cards hanging from the oak beams. First to arrive was Mark, but the festive period really began a day later with the visit of the very talented village carol singers. Then, on Christmas Day, with a roaring fire in our huge seventeenth-century fireplace to welcome them, the arrival of Crispin and Aileen and family from Scotland and the celebration, wit, banter, good food and drink that followed, all repeated on Boxing Day when we converged on Justin and Haley and family at Tingley. Like all Christmases it was over too quickly, but it was very good while it lasted. The family dispersed in good heart, none more than Mark, who was looking forward to an imminent visit to Vegas with the chairman of his company, followed by some hiking.

31 December 2005 (Ruth to family):
Old Hall – The snow has just about gone, but it is damp and miserable and we decided not to go out on our usual New Year drive. We are still 'eating up'. Goodness knows how long I thought you'd stay. There are steaks, fish, pork and beef and fruit of every sort which we never seemed to get a chance to eat, and so much chocolate. I doubt that we will ever get through it. We shall be celebrating New Year on our own, but will have a drink of something nice and we shall be warm and snug. Daddy is enjoying the new television and spends a lot of time fiddling with the controls. Whenever I touch it something goes wrong!

Love you all lots. MUM. XXX

2006

Winding Down

4 January 2006 (Ruth to family):
Old Hall – Christmas decorations are down and Old Hall looks very bare and sad. I'm going to have a good clean this morning and then to a Royal Signals wives luncheon. Bitterly cold with a white over. Hope the trip to the USA is going well Mark and that it can be a bit of a holiday for you. It is a long time since you had a break, and just be careful driving through Death Valley. Take plenty of water with you. Looking forward to our friends David and Rita Newton from Tadcaster coming for lunch next week – it is some time since we saw them. Hope that you can come and see us soon Justin.
    Love MUM

It was early in the new year of 2006 that I shared my thoughts with Ruth on the future, and in particular on the continued breeding and exhibiting of Wensleydale sheep. We both recognised that we could not maintain our current pace of life indefinitely and Ruth eventually agreed that it was best to dispose of our flock while it was in its prime, and in a controlled manner. I had raised the matter previously, but got a funny look and a stuffy answer. This time Ruth nodded her head in sad agreement and I drafted the following dispersal sale notification for release later in the year, with which she agreed:

DRAFT
Old Hall
Hunton, Bedale, North Yorkshire DL8 1QJ 01677 450579
June 2006
Section A Breeders
Wensleydale Longwool Sheep Breeders' Association

Dear Wensleydale Breeder,

Dispersal Sale of the Hunton Wensleydale Flock (743)

It is with much sadness that Ruth and I write to you to describe the arrangements for the dispersal sale of the Hunton Wensleydale flock, due to advancing years. Adult sheep are offered for sale this year by private arrangement from mid July and at the Association's official shows and sales at Melton Mowbray (9th September) and Skipton (29th September). This year's lambs will be offered for sale in 2007.

The Hunton flock was founded in 1987 from carefully selected stock of North Yorkshire breeders, with the Harmby Moor flock (636) of JD & J Ford providing the major bloodline infusion. Subsequently, all stock have been home bred, apart from three rams from the Providence Flock (468) of JA & F Elliott.

The flock has been recognised for many years as one of the leading Wensleydale flocks in the country. Its quality is reflected in numerous Breed Championship awards at the most competitive level, including the Association's Annual Show and Sale at Skipton (twice, plus 3 x male champion & 3 x female champion), the Royal Show (twice) and the Royal Highland Show. However, it is the Great Yorkshire Show that offers the highest Wensleydale competition and it is at the GYS that the Hunton flock has excelled, with Breed Championship awards in 1997, 1999, 2004 and 2005. The flock has also had interbreed success at the GYS, the most memorable in 1997 when the Hunton flock Breed Champion also took the Longwool Championship and the Wool on the Hoof Supreme Championship, an achievement that has yet to be equalled by any longwool breed.

Wool and fleece quality have received very high commendation from the wool trade and British Wool Marketing Board judges. The Hunton flock had particular success in 2002 when its fleeces took the Interbreed Supreme Award at the Royal Show, the Great Yorkshire Show and at the NSA's Sheep 2002 event.

The Hunton flock is MV accredited and all sheep are ARR/ARR. The sale includes five shearling ewes purchased as lambs from the Maesafon flock of J & S Thompson (flock 890) in August 2005, with a view to absorbing new bloodlines. They are the only females brought into the flock since 1991.

The list of sheep for sale is attached. There have been no recent private sales and none will be conducted before mid July. Whilst all the sheep are of high quality, it will be seen from the list that some have been pre-selected for the Melton Mowbray and Skipton Sales to ensure a balanced and equal opportunity to potential buyers residing in distant parts of the country. We will, of course, continue to support the breed for as long as we are able.

Yours sincerely,

Ruth and Frank Pedley

We considered entering both the GYS and the Royal Show that summer, but with only four days between the two shows this would have been too demanding. We opted for the Royal Show, thereby ensuring that Ruth retired from the Great Yorkshire Show on a championship high. We both adored Old Hall and I had no problem in recognising and appreciating Ruth's stated intent that she would never leave it. Indeed, I couldn't visualise living anywhere else either. Old Hall had some eight acres of good pasture, a barn, stables, numerous other buildings and two entrances, so it was not stretching the imagination too much to visualise these being leased, the income more than providing for gardening and household assistance. The prospect was not daunting, and we would have far more free time and leisure.

The 2006 Winter Olympics were being held in Turin in mid-February, but with no serious British contention apart from curling (essentially Scottish teams), Ruth focused her attention on this event, and with strong vocal support that matched the loudness of election-result declarations. I was also intrigued, particularly with the tactics and character of the sensible 'skip' of the women's team, Rhona Martin – her cautious 'Yeah, but …' observations to her team still resound in my ears.

14/15 February 2006 (Ruth to family):
Enjoying watching the skills and progress of the Scottish Curling teams. We have watched each of the four matches and are beginning to understand the tactics. I think we can describe ourselves as dedicated supporters …

Have been enjoying the curling again though baffled to-night why the last Scottish player didn't just knock off the Norwegian stone, because as I saw it Norway could only have scored one point and so lost the match. Crispin – please explain.

Mark – hope business is good in China and that Madam Lei is taking good care of you.

Love MUM XXX

8 March 2006 (Ruth to family):
Old Hall – Lambing started a week ago and at last I'm catching up on E mails. We've had a tiring few days but the sheep and lambs are thriving. To-day is our 48th wedding anniversary and we are going to pop down to the Friar's Head for a bite of lunch. It has been so very cold (−8 one night) and we have certainly felt it, being up in the night and not getting much sleep. Crispin – the girls did well with their swimming but it is a long day for Lois. Look forward to hearing from you.

MUM XXX

4 April 2006 (Ruth to family):
Old Hall – It has been bitter to-day with snow on the hills above Leyburn. To-morrow is set to be even colder. Wonderful pashmina weather! Justin – we would love you to come up for a meal but understand all your commitments. Do give us a ring when you can get up. Can't wait to get out in the garden. Leslie had lunch with us yesterday and I put a block of butter on the table for the cheese and biscuits and a butter knife, and he spent the rest of the meal stabbing it with the knife. What a mess it is! I wonder who takes after him?

Love you all lots MUM XXX

13 April 2006 (Ruth to family):
Old Hall – I do hope that you all have a great Easter. We have no plans. The weather is so cold but we may go off in the car somewhere and have a break, though things have eased up quite a bit on the sheep side now that lambing is over. I am painting the landing and staircase prior to the new carpet being laid, but am making heavy weather of it. Hope that the Paisley Pedleys are having a good rest at Duchally. Mark [in China] – sorry about the tough time you seem to be having, are they beginning to see the problems of dealing with the Chinese? You will be ready for the holiday in the States.

Love to you all. MUM XXX

7 May 2006 (Mark to family):
I've arrived in Phoenix – Staying the first night at a hotel near the airport. Weather hot with blue skies. I don't think they've had any rain for two years or so. I love the Arizona deserts. My friend Sean is flying in from Boston and should arrive in an hour or so. The flight was excellent – first class is the only way to go. Off to-morrow northwards into Utah to stay with some Navajo friends and partake in the Peyote ceremony.

TTFN Mark xxx

7 May 2006 (Me to Mark):

Re: I've arrived in Phoenix – Hope you have an enjoyable holiday. You have earned it. A rainy day in most of the UK, but warm – just what the ground needs to give us some good grass growth. Mum is thoroughly enjoying the discomfort of the Labour Party. The pressure on Blair to go is now mounting and after the dismal performance of Labour in the local elections (lost 319 Councillors and control of 17 Councils) his successor is unlikely to call a snap election.

TTFN? – I thought that abominable short lived phrase became extinct half a century ago. Is it now back in fashion, replacing 'see ye later'?

Love from Mum and Dad XXX

Wensleydale and neighbouring Swaledale are at their brilliant best in May. The countryside bursts into life, prompted by the cries of the curlews and the excitement of the ewes and lambs as they are moved to fresh, lush pastures outside the vicinity of their home farms. I always looked upon the day that John and Frank Tunstill moved their flock into 'Ten Acre Field' (above Old Hall) as the day that winter ended and the real spring began, so accurate was their judgement. The markets would be a blaze of colour and there was time for an evening drive or walk, while on Sunday mornings we still regularly drove to Cogden Heugh (Grid Reference 054968) on Grinton Moor to read the papers; our view extending over Swaledale, with the Lake District just visible on the horizon on a good day. Our Wensleydale branch of the CPRE, on whose committee Ruth continued to serve, would usually hold a carefully selected spring walk in May, guided by a knowledgeable person. This year we met on 10 May at Aysgarth Falls for an enjoyable and most interesting tour of the ancient Freeholders' Wood and adjacent, recently planted St Joseph's Wood on the north side of the river Swale, conducted by Dr Robert Hall. It was the same day that John and Frank moved their flock through the village to 'Ten Acres'. Freeholders' Wood, now a nature reserve, derives its name from a group of local families in the nearby village of Carperby who have ancient estover rights, permitting them to coppice the trees and gather firewood. In addition to the hazel trees there are holly, wych, rowan, elm, oak and ash, together with 120 species of flowers, including the early purple orchid, the rare burnt-tip orchid and a fine carpet of bluebells.

1 June 2006 (Ruth to family):
Old Hall – It was wonderful to see you all [Spring Bank Holiday] and I did enjoy everything. Yesterday was a glorious day and the washing machine never stopped. I also coped much better with the new lawn mower. Daddy lowered the handles and I set it at tortoise instead of hare. No wonder that I couldn't control the darned thing. I was almost having to run to keep up with it. To-day I've been cleaning and then I'm going to finish my flower containers.

Mark – hope you had a good run back and thank you for everything. Aileen – thank you for the photographs. They are such beautifully behaved girls. By the way I forgot that I had a chocolate cake in the freezer, but I don't think they starved.

Love you all MUM/Grandma Sheep XXX

Most of flaming June's emails concerned preparations for a visit to Old Hall by a party from the CPRE to see our listed building, garden, trees and rare-breed sheep, with afternoon tea etc.; also a visit by a very large toad. It was boiling hot weather and Ruth decided to get out a watering can that had not been used for some time and give her plants a bit of a drink with some liquid fertilizer. She found toad wallowing in the can in an inch of water and was baffled as to how he had got in and how long he had been there. No matter where she placed him in the garden, he kept reappearing ...

6 June 2006 (Ruth to family):
Toad of Old Hall – Because the CPRE are visiting us soon I decided that I would sweep up outside the soup house and so moved pots etc. and got to the flag that covers the drain in front of the breakfast room window (not the kitchen drain), lifted it and there, looking at me was

toad. Yuks – you've found me again. I'm still baffled how a toad can crawl up a plastic watering can. He really was enjoying his jacuzzi.

Love MUM XXX

15 June 2006 (Ruth to family):
Old Hall – We had quite a crowd for the CPRE visit yesterday and some VERY knowledgeable tree people and botanists among them. They really did appreciate the trees and the garden looked better than it has ever done, whilst the sheep also looked great. However, this morning we both feel pretty tired as it did involve quite a bit of work. I hope the exams are going well for Charlotte. We think about her in this hot weather, toiling away. Keep in touch.

Love MUM XXX

On 22 June I posted the Hunton flock dispersal sale letter that I had drafted for Ruth in late January to WLSBA members. We knew that it was the right decision, and once the Royal Show was over our minds would need to be focused on its implementation.

28 June 2006 (Ruth to family):
Toad of Old Hall – This morning the water wasn't running out of the sink so I went outside and pulled away the flag that stops leaves getting into the drain and there was toad, and guess what … he climbed up the small waste pipe till only his back legs could be seen, so I went inside and ran water. Daddy said he backed down the pipe and crouched there enjoying a shower. He must like Fairy Liquid, but what about the bleach that I pour down? What funnies from you?

Love you all MUM

30 June 2006 (Me to family):
Royal Show – We will be leaving at 3.30am to-morrow (to ensure quick and cool journey for sheep) and will be back at Old Hall at around 1030pm next Wednesday. Should be able to see England v Portugal match at the Royal Show, but if England win it will be frustrating

travelling back whilst the semi-final is being played. We are taking five sheep and a fleece. Looks as though there will be temperatures of 30–34 degrees in the Midlands next week.

Dad

6 July 2006 (Me to family):
Royal Show – We're back. Won two of the three classes, but the winner of the third class (in which we were third) took the championship. Our ewe was awarded 'Reserve Champion'. Nice to be home – it was very hot at the show.

Dad

9 July 2006 (Ruth to family):
Old Hall – It is just so wonderful to be home in a spotless bed and clean surroundings. Thank goodness that we are finished with showing and are not taking any sheep to the GYS, only a couple of fleeces. We are both tired but have stood up well considering our age, but we take longer to recover. It is very sad to be giving up on our wonderful Wensleydales but it is right to go out at the top.

What a surprise to see Tilneys name plastered everywhere in the flower marquee at the Royal Show. Please keep in touch everyone because I love to hear from you all. Am now going to watch the world cup.

Love mum xxx. I LOVE YOU ALL LOTS

We were getting an encouraging number of enquiries and visits regarding our dispersal sale, and with Ruth judging at both the Royal Lancashire Show and the Ryedale Show in July and myself at Ripley in mid-August, together with our success at the Royal Show, the Hunton flock was attracting the attention that we needed.

29 July 2006 (Ruth to family):
Old Hall – At last it may be a bit cooler. We have been busy with odd jobs. Daddy is installing a new farm gate which entails digging out an old post

set in concrete. I went to the Tennants sale and bought a nice side table. I think it will be our last major purchase as I am very happy with everything that we have, even if a lot of our things were bought for very little.

Mark – life does seem exciting. I do hope you get the job that you seek, but I wouldn't be sucked into something that involves you chasing around the world so much.

Justin – Looking forward to seeing you all to-morrow.

Crispin – Mark told us some lovely stories about the girls. He was very impressed and he liked your paintings.

Love to you all. MUM XXX

On Sunday 6 August Ruth and I drove to Leslie's eightieth birthday celebration in Scotland. We could have stayed the night in a hotel, but that would have entailed asking Brian Lockey or John Tunstill if they would yet again look after our sheep during our absence. They had been so helpful to us that we felt it would be wrong to ask again, particularly as we had only recently returned from five days at the Royal Show. I therefore decided to drive there and back in the same day.

7 August 2006 (Ruth to family):
Old Hall – Had a very good journey to Scotland and it was great to see all the Scottish Addys. It was a very happy time there. We stayed four and a half hours then motored back. Leslie and Margaret have six grandsons and one granddaughter. I'm glad we went. Back to normal duties today.

Love you all MUM XXX

11 August 2006 (Ruth to Mark):
Old Hall – We are delighted with the news of the new job [with Freescale] and hope that it will not be quite as stressful as you think. Be optimistic and give it your best and buy some new casual clothes. I don't want to see you in scruffy old T shirts and those awful bags. Mum has spoken. You can be casual, comfortable and smart. Go and give M&S a bit of trade. When do you start?

Love MUM XXX

17 August 2006 (Ruth to family):

New Flat – Mark, the flat sounds beautiful from what Crispin has said. Two bathrooms to mess up and two bedrooms to fill with all your clutter. I bet you only use one room. We are delighted for you and hope the job is up to your expectations.

This really is a new start and surely you will be able to get some serious walking in and see new parts of the British Isles. There is so much to see in Scotland but the midges don't half bite.

Love you all MUM XXX

Ruth and I were thrilled to learn just before the Summer Bank Holiday weekend of Charlotte's O-level results – 5 As (including maths, physics and English), 7 Bs and a C. The Saturday of this weekend was the traditional annual show day of what Ruth and I regarded as our local show; the Wensleydale Show at Leyburn. It is one of the oldest agricultural shows in the country, for records indicate that it was previously held further up the dale at Hawes at least as early as 1845. Though Ruth had not exhibited at the show for several years, I had supported it both as a sheep steward and in helping to erect and dismantle the pens. This year the Wensleydale classes were being judged by our very good friend Peter Titley, accompanied by his partner Stella Lambert. Ruth and I had the pleasure of accommodating them at Old Hall the night before the show, in addition, of course, to looking after them at the show. Virtually every village in North Yorkshire has its special annual summer event; a show, fête, feast, steam rally, gala or fair, each rich in history and as varied and colourful as the villages themselves – the only common feature being that they are run by volunteers, for all to enjoy, with thousands of pounds donated to charity.

29 August 2006 (Ruth to family):

Old Hall – Saw an interesting thing this morning. Just got up and the bedroom window was wide open and I heard such a screeching and twitter of birds. I looked out to see a really large group of an assortment of small birds simply swamping a Sparrow Hawk, which dived beneath the rhubarb and stayed there until these small birds dispersed. Then it walked out … under the red currant bush, through the runner beans and onto the compost heap. It only flew off when I called to daddy. The sheer bravery and ganging together of those little birds was amazing.

Love you all MUM XXX

9/10 September 2006 (Ruth to family):
Had an excellent show and sale at Melton Mowbray – Champion and Reserve Champion and sold all our sheep for decent prices. We are so exhausted and must try and have a quiet time if that is possible. Do hope that Lois is enjoying big school. The Campsis Radicans have been and still are magnificent and we are overwhelmed with apples. Look forward to seeing you all again. Skipton sale in three weeks.

Love you all lots MUM XXX

In addition to our stock being in demand, Ruth had no difficulty in selling her fleeces. The Wensleydale Longwool Sheep Shop at Barden, only three miles from Old Hall, always had first choice, but all of Ruth's fleeces were of high quality and immaculately prepared. A particularly interesting demand came from Janice Jordan from West Wycombe, whose business sought exemplary, well-purled (curled) and very long staples (strands) to make quality modern-style doll wigs.

13 September 2006 (Ruth to family):
Old Hall – Lovely Autumn day so am intending to paint the new window in the dairy. Will be free this weekend but the next two weeks will be involved with getting sheep ready for our big sale at Skipton. Then we should be left with only a couple of old ewes and twenty six lambs. Very sad but necessary.

Love MUM XXX

The five shearling ewes that we had purchased in 2005 as lambs from Jim and Sandra Thompson were sold back to their Maesafon flock. Sandra could not bear the thought of them being sold at auction and split up. Jim collected them the week before Skipton. We learned later from Sandra that they immediately recognised their birthplace, responding with obvious delight as they explored familiar pastures, nooks and crannies.

It was a very tiring day at Skipton on 29 September, leaving Old Hall at 5.30 a.m. and not getting home until 7 p.m. However, we sold all our stock, and at reasonable prices. Not surprisingly, no silver trophies were won, for the best of the Hunton flock had already been sold privately. While Ruth and I were busy preparing our own sheep for judging, Ruth still found time to help a friend win his first trophy. John McHardy from Cupar, Fife had been a member and breeder for several years but had never exhibited a sheep at any show. Shortly before the judging began Ruth had a quick word with him:

'That's a nice ram lamb you have there, John.'

'Aye, but he's just for the sale, am noo showing im.'

'Oh yes you are,' replied Ruth.

Whereupon, she took out her shears and slowly but carefully transformed a rather scruffy-looking lamb into one that really caught the eye, then pointed John in the direction of the show ring, where his lamb not only won its class and Reserve Male Champion, but sold for 480 guineas, the highest price of the day. Ruth and I watched a gleeful John slip away to a quiet corner of the market to call his wife (Sylvia) in Scotland, his smile stretching from ear to ear. Their achievement gave us so much pleasure.

3 October 2006 (Ruth to family):

Old Hall – Where are you all? Surely you have some news.

We have been cleaning up our ram lambs to-day and are exhausted but worse still our main farm drain became blocked so we have been having a delightful time unblocking. We are trying to slow down a bit but I don't think we can for another couple of weeks. Send some funnies. MUM XXX. Love you all lots

Ruth had a horrid time for the next few weeks as she grappled with the responsibility of chairing a tribunal at the village school (Hunton &

Arrathorne CP School) involving unpleasant, but not sexual, allegations against the headmaster and another teacher. She had been invited to chair the tribunal and felt that it was her duty to accept. Newspaper reports soon placed the matter in the public domain, generating increasing interest, speculation and pressure. The tribunal found the allegations mostly 'unfounded', but recognised some fault in the actions of the teachers. I suspect that most teachers in the county who followed the proceedings would have thought, 'That could so easily have been me.' I felt that Ruth, whose service as a school governor was entirely voluntary, was unfortunate to find herself involved in such an unenviable task, particularly at her age, but she loved Hunton school and its pupils, and supported it and its many functions to the hilt.

Ruth's voluntary commitments were typical of her nature. Her first commitment was always to her family, but throughout our married life she always found time to help and to give – doing social work within the military units in which I served, being involved in the organisations mentioned in these memoirs, fundraising for charities and other worthy causes and just helping individuals with their problems and loneliness, and she always had a few coins for charity collection cans, occasionally holding one herself. She was one of those who instinctively give their time and whatever abilities or talents they possess, without any expectation of reward or recognition. Sadly, there are others who, though not lacking in intellect, ability or time, give nothing. There are also those who seem to delight in complaint and obstruction, tending to focus their attention on the soft target voluntary organisations and individuals that provide the very supportive fabric and events that enrich our communities and the environments that we cherish. The precious voluntary element of our country, already handicapped by over-zealous health and safety issues and high insurance demands, needs more support, not hindrance.

I was very conscious of the approach of our golden wedding anniversary on 8 March 2008 and wanted to please Ruth with something special. I shared my thoughts with Justin, Mark and Crispin in the following self-explanatory letter:

Old Hall
Hunton, Bedale
North Yorkshire DL8 1QJ
27th October 2006

Dear Justin, Mark and Crispin,

Golden Wedding Anniversary Celebration

As you know, Saturday 8th March 2008 is our Golden Wedding
Anniversary and Justin has described to you in outline the two
alternative celebration options that we have in mind:

Option 1.
A semi formal (lounge suit) luncheon at the Friars Head, Akebar on
Saturday 8th March 2008, to which we would invite about 60 friends/
family. It would be held in the banqueting suite which was added a few
years ago. I doubt that any of you will have seen it. It is very nice and
quite separate from the pub and its dining area. We would, of course,
meet the entire cost.

Option 2.
A family cruise, hopefully including Jack and Betty and Allister and
Kate. This would need to be during the school holidays. However,
Scottish/English school holiday date variations and their relatively
short duration at Christmas will probably rule out the Christmas/New
Year period. We suggest, therefore, that the feasibility of a summer
holiday cruise is examined. We would be pleased to contribute
£3,600 towards the fares of our six Grandchildren (£600 each). We
would prefer that the cruise was on either P&O's Aurora or Oriana,
particularly the Aurora, the P&O flagship, which we know so well.

I have made telephone calls to both P&O and the Cumbria Cruise
Club (www.cumbriacruise.co.uk), which not only gives excellent agent
service but also gives the best discounts (52% reduction on brochure

tariff for our last cruise). However, this large discount incorporates a significant early booking discount and is one of the reasons why we are writing to you now. I am advised by P&O that the 2008 cruise brochure should be available in April or May 2007 and that the early booking discount applies to only a limited number of cabins in each category. Once this quota is reached the discount ceases. Both P&O and Cumbria Cruises confirmed that they give additional discounts to 'passenger groups', over and above the early booking and family saver discounts mentioned in P&O brochures. However, they would not be drawn on giving hypothetical quotations, advising that it depended on the cruise and size of party (16 seemed to be the minimum). Apparently, this group discount is sometimes given in the form of 'on board credit' or by charging a reduced fare for an elder child who technically should be charged at the adult rate. It might be possible to obtain a 'passenger group' discount (or benefit in kind) from both P&O and Cumbria Cruises.

Of the two options we prefer the second, for instead of having a wonderful half day with the family we would have 12–16 days, sharing with you the excitement of your first cruise. It would probably be a 'one off' opportunity for the entire family to get together and share an event that six children would be likely to remember for the rest of their lives. The downside would be that we would not be sharing the occasion with our many friends, but they nearly all live in the County and we see many of them regularly. Both the Aurora and Oriana are very large, modern ships, of a size and design that would allow each of us to disappear and do our own thing during the day, only meeting for dinner (followed by the evening entertainment), yet bumping into each other from time to time during the day.

We will not be offended if after due consideration you opt for Option 1, but it would be a shame if it became the only option due to time slipping by and it becoming too late to get our act together. If it is to be Option 1 we would like to be able to book the Friars Head banqueting suite in February next year (only three months away). May I suggest that you each obtain and peruse a copy of the P&O 2007 brochure (the one that incorporates the Mediterranean and South Atlantic cruises). The 2008 itinerary will, of course be different, but we would be surprised if it was significantly different. We feel that the 2007 brochure gives sufficient information on P&O cruises and costs for serious discussion at Christmas, leading to a decision early next year.

As for cost assessments, you should not be far out if you base calculations on 50% of 2007 brochure tariff (then anything extra would be a bonus), perhaps adding a little for inflation. Bear in mind that you spend very little time in the cabin apart from sleeping and that inside cabins are of equal quality to outside cabins. We used inside cabins on our earlier cruises – we left the cabin at about 7-30am and hardly visited it again until it was almost dark, to change for dinner. There are not many holidays where the cost per adult can be only just over £100 per day, including accommodation, all meals, quality entertainment and facilities and also be able to watch the world go by.

Our love to you all.

Mum and Dad

At about the same time, conscious of the fact that it had not been possible for Ruth and myself to take a holiday in 2006, I made a booking with P&O Cruises for a 12-night cruise in the South Atlantic isles from 25 November to 7 December 2007.

13 November 2006 (Ruth to family):
Old Hall – Having an early start in the garden to get it tidied up before winter. Must do all the edges. Accolade has died which is sad. I don't know what got it but cherries do get lurgies. I think all the village will miss it.

Love you MUM XXX. I feel fit enough to have a house full this Christmas. We are already finding it easier with less sheep.

Early in December Ruth and I received an exciting and more than interesting invitation to judge a variety of sheep classes at the three-day Hatfield Country Show in mid-August 2007, involving Longwool, Hill and Heath, Downland/Closewool, Manx Loghtan and Hebridean – a total of twenty-four classes. In addition, Ruth was invited to judge on the third day the fleece competition and two Wool on the Hoof classes, plus Best Veteran Sheep, Best Ewe and Lamb, and Best Sire and Lamb. We were advised that Lord and Lady Salisbury usually hold a reception in Hatfield House, which also provides an opportunity to look round the house. We were delighted to accept.

Christmas began early that year with three particularly enjoyable events – Christmas lunch at Bolton Hall on Sunday 3 December and supper with Colin and Joyce Ellwood within the ambience of their 'Friar's Head' at Akebar a few days later, soon followed by the Richmond Conservative Association's 'Christmas in the Dales' supper at the splendid Tennants auction house premises at Leyburn on Ruth's birthday, when, of course, the Christmas tree was erected and decorated at Old Hall. The village carol singers were in good voice and were growing in numbers, Mark joined us on the 22nd, the Paisley Pedleys came on Christmas Day, the Tingley Pedleys, Jack and Betty and Nanette on Boxing Day, and a very good time was had by one and all, with the customary jollity, good food, drink and banter before roaring wood fires.

This is the last mention of Nanette in my book; lifelong best friend of Ruth and good friend of myself from September 1944 when the three of us started our secondary school education together at 'Taddy Grammar' in form 2B. Ruth and Nanette always sat together in class and were never far apart – if you caught sight of one of them, the other was nearby. This close relationship between them became a bit of a nuisance when I became more than enchanted with Ruth as a teenager, for I found it virtually impossible to have a personal boy-girl chat with Ruth outside the hearing of Nanette. I need not have worried, for in later years I learnt from Nanette that when Ruth told her that she was engaged [to Connell] she replied, 'I wish it was Hamish'. Nanette died on 3rd February 2018, following a long and courageous battle against cancer. We kept in regular contact after Ruth's death, enjoying birthday outings together; to Haworth, Whitby (via the Yorkshire Moors railway), a day trip to London, cricket at Headingley, and numerous Conservative Christmas functions in Leyburn.

2007

The Last Chapter

Our 2006 sheep disposal sales had gone well, but we still had nineteen 2006-born lambs (now referred to as hoggs) to sell during 2007. Two ewes that had not been sold were put to the ram, together with a favourite ten-year-old ewe (743/97/157) that had been a prizewinner at the 1998 Royal Show, so there would be little lambing commitment. By the time that we went on our autumn cruise there would be no sheep at Old Hall, and having rested the land over the winter, we planned to lease it in the spring of 2008 for grazing, and then lead a more leisurely life.

The intended autumn 2007 cruise was consistent with our habit of only taking a holiday at 2-3 year intervals. We had not been able to afford more frequent holidays and considered P&O cruising to be the best value for money. Our cruises were:

1991: South Atlantic   1996: West Indies   1998: South Atlantic
2000: South Atlantic   2002: Mediterranean   2004: Norway/Cape
2005: Mediterranean   2007 -

5 January 2007 (Ruth to family):
Old Hall – Have taken down all the Christmas decorations to-day and everywhere looks bare and rather sad, but at least I've been able to dust. This house loves to be filled with children …
Love you all lots. MUM XXX

On 17/18 January 2007 the UK and continental Europe were hit by hurricane-strength winds from an extratropical cyclone, called '*Kyrill*', which had crossed the Atlantic from Newfoundland. It struck the Needles and Dublin with recordings of 99 and 93 mph respectively, causing torrential rain and gale-force winds throughout the UK and heavy snowfall in Scotland. Huge areas experienced prolonged loss of electricity as power cables were torn down, and there was enormous damage to buildings. However, it was continental Europe that received the full force of *Kyrill*, the cold front spawning several tornadoes in Germany, wind speeds of 120 mph in the Harz Mountains and a gust of 150 mph in *Śnieżka* in Poland.

20 January 2007 (Ruth to family):
Old Hall – Well, we have survived the storms and had a quiet day, but it looks as though the gales could be building up again. I don't like wind. There has been a lot of rain and flooding on the roads but we are warm and cosy and have a good stock of food. Look after yourselves.
Love MUM XXX

Mark advised us that he had read an article and correspondence concerning animals being entombed for several years and surviving. It reminded him of the experience that Ruth and I had described to the family in September 2005 when repairing the pinfold wall in the corner of Old Hall beck field. He sent the following interesting email:

20 January 2007 (Mark to family):
Toads in Concrete – an experience by a Mr Dave Stacey – This account comes to mind after reading your section on 'Animals Sealed in Stone'.

I'm a landscape gardener and a few years ago we were demolishing a shed and breaking up its old foundations. As one lump of concrete came up I found three or four fully grown toads underneath, all pushed against and on top of each other, as if they were in a little nest. I called my mate and the lady we were working for and all agreed that they must have somehow crawled up inside the concrete from beneath the foundations. But on a closer look, I saw that this couldn't be the case because the hollow they lay in took their shape completely like a jelly mould, as if the concrete had set around them. Also, there was concrete beneath, meaning that they were fully encased. Judging on the state of the old shed the base was at least 20 years old, so I suppose the toads had been there that long as well. Yet within a couple of minutes of being freed they became very lively and hopped off into the undergrowth. Concrete is slightly porous, but surely not enough to provide enough air or moisture to survive for decades. So do they go into suspended animation, like an extended hibernation? Mark

Having witnessed this phenomenon with Ruth I cannot be dismissive. Internet searches reveal many similar accounts and the phenomenon is mentioned by John Wesley and Charles Dickens in their writings, while the *Fortean Times* refers to more than two hundred recorded cases.

3 February 2007 (Ruth to family):
Old Hall – Well, will Blair stick it out or will the police get him for something? Hope Aileen is keeping fit and well. Crispin – Do you have an expected date yet as you seemed a little unsure at Christmas? We will be rugby viewing to-day and to-morrow so I intend to spread some manure around the garden this morning so that I don't feel guilty sitting around this afternoon. Everything is coming through in the garden and we have a lovely display of snowdrops. Take care all of you.

Love you. Mum XXX

Mark was now well settled and happy in his new employment with Freescale Semiconductor in East Kilbride, one of Scotland's largest employers with some 1,200 employees at the time. The plant had been created in 1969 by Motorola, out of which Freescale was spun in 2004. Mark was responsible for consumer marketing in the European, Middle Eastern and African (EMEA) territories, with the specific task of expanding the market for Freescale's communications processors into consumer electronics applications. In an interview for Scottish Enterprise, Mark was quoted as saying, 'I am one of those people who likes to spend their spare time putting on a rucksack and heading for the hills, so Scotland is wonderful for me! I am loving it here, there are plenty of places to go, we have a good transport infrastructure which is nothing like as congested as in the south. In many respects coming to Scotland is the perfect combination of working "abroad" but being at home, it is a different country from England but very similar too. It was an easy decision. I was offered the job on a Friday, found a great apartment in East Kilbride that weekend, and started work soon afterwards.'

Ruth and I were interested to learn that our previous home, *Broadacres*, at Thorp Arch Park, had been placed on the market (at £650,000) for the first time since we sold it in 1981 (for £58,000) – an increase in value of 1,020% over the 26 years. Old Hall and its land, for which we had paid £65,000, was probably now worth £1 million, an increase of 1,438%. Not that we would ever dream of selling it.

4 March 2007 (Ruth to family):
Old Hall – Had a rabbit search this morning in the garden and dug out a nest with three little ones in it. They are a damned nuisance and cause so much damage. We have one clump of frog spawn but this morning a drake and his wife were bathing in the pond and I don't know if it has survived. Do ducks eat frog spawn? The daffodils are nearly out and should look lovely in a few days. I would like to visit Farndale to see the wild daffodils. Hope the girls do well with their swimming.
Love MUM XXX

14 March 2007 (Ruth to family):
Old Hall – Cut all the lawns yesterday. The daffodils are out and look lovely. A total white over this morning but it is melting fast and I intend to have another crack at the garden to-day. The Scottish Pedleys have done so well with their swimming – the new baby will have to get used to watching! The school is having an OFSTED inspection to-day and to-morrow so I am keeping my fingers crossed that all goes well.
Love MUM XXX

The family were ecstatic when the new baby arrived – Alex MacGregor Pedley, weighing 8lbs 3ozs. He was to be the last of our seven grandchildren and Ruth and I could not wait to see him.

24 March 2007 (Ruth to family):
Old Hall – I am catching up on all my E mails as I have been involved with other things such as forthcoming District Council Elections [Ruth was agent to local farmer and very good friend, Keith Loadman].
Interesting that Mark saw two adders as only the previous day it was said on TV how rare they have become. The garden is very Springlike with the blossom just about to come out. Justin – thank you for lunch the other day; I tried to ring but got no reply. The house looked very nice. I hope that Haley enjoys her new job and that the hours are easier for all of you. I really don't know how she has carried on so long. Take care the Scottish Pedleys.
Love you all MUM XXX

1 April 2007 (Ruth to family):
Old Hall – Yesterday, we decided to visit the vale of the wild daffodils in Farndale. We walked along the little river Dove and the banks were covered in flowers. It was bitterly cold but simply beautiful and it was a lovely walk.
What an April Fool surprise we had this morning … an old ten shear ewe that we decided was not in lamb gave us two lovely little

gimmer lambs. We were thinking of having her put to sleep this coming week! Well, cold or not, I'm going to do some work in the garden.

Love you all MUM XXX

11 April 2007 (Ruth to family):

Ovens – Horror of horrors! This morning I thought that I would pull out my oven and clean the floor behind it. Guess what, I yanked off the whole of the top oven door which ended up on the floor. It just can't be fixed! What shall I do? Such a pity isn't it. Daddy had a bit of a scowl! Watch this space!

Love you all lots MUM XXX

19 April 2007 (Ruth to family):

Old Hall – We have been out delivering leaflets for the forthcoming District Council elections. We have them everywhere. It will be an interesting experience at the count.

We are looking forward to seeing the new baby, but will make our stay short so we don't tire Aileen. I hope she is feeling better now that the antibiotics are kicking in.

Mark – looking forward to seeing the flat; has the vacuum cleaner been flying around?

Love you all MUM XXX

29 April 2007 (Ruth to family):

Old Hall – Yesterday morning we washed and wormed 11 mucked up sheep – a good start to the day. Then I decorated the back entrance with orchid white and it now looks very clean and bright. We then had coffee and ice cream at Jervaulx (naughty but nice), with a political planning meeting at Old Hall in the evening.

Interesting report in to-day's Sunday Times News Review, 'Dancers at the Royal Ballet are causing a sensation with their latest costumes; they're hardly wearing any. The ballerinas wear skimpy underwear to dance a version of Kurt Weill's Seven deadly Sins. The male dancers have been excused tight-fitting trousers after a nasty moment in the Nutcracker.'

Love to you all MUM XXX

2 May 2007 (Ruth to family):

Old Hall – Decorated the laundry room yesterday, then we went for a lovely drive up the dale, then along the start of the Wharfe and Hubberholme, returning via Buckden. It was a super day. To-day, I have a finance meeting in the school in the morning, then lunch with Royal Signals wives, but will watch Yorkshire cricket with Daddy this afternoon.

Hope the new boy is behaving well and that the twins are enjoying 'boot camp'.

Love you all lots MUM XXX

4 May 2007 (Me to family):

Specialists Opinion – The growth that was removed from my neck close to a gland on 25th April is 'Squamous Cell Carcinoma' which I understand is neither the worst nor the least significant of the skin cancers (somewhere in the middle). He says that arrangements will be made with the James Cook University Hospital in Middlesbrough to open the area up again in about three weeks to make sure that nothing nasty has been left behind. If any remnants are found they will remove. It will only be a local anaesthetic job and I will be home the same day. He says the only danger is if it gets to the gland [lymph*] and I shouldn't worry too much. We feel more relaxed with the situation. Thanks for your interest and support.

Brilliant day at the polls, followed by a champagne lunch. We virtually swept the board (Mum ecstatic).

Love from Dad xxx

* cause of death of King Hussein of Jordan on 7 Feb 1999.

7 May 2007 (Ruth to family):

New Oven – I think I am going to get an Indesit 100CX which is stainless steel and has two ovens, a warming area and six hobs …

Daddy has ordered on the internet at a very good price. Hope it fits.

Love MUM XXX

11 May 2007 (Ruth to family):
I've been busy planting petunias and then out to lunch with jubilant Councillor Keith Loadman and Judy Loadman. To-morrow we are in Lancashire for the WLSBA AGM. I shall be glad when we can relax.

Love MUM XXX

13 May 2007 (Ruth to family):
Old Hall – Cara did do well. Sorry about Alex. Do you think if you sat him more upright when you feed it may help. He may be a bit cramped in that little relaxer chair and may be better lying flat after he has got his wind up. I really don't know as things have changed so much. There can't be much wrong if he is putting on weight as you say he is and he seems to be thriving.

A chilly day after yesterday's glorious weather. Washed 18 mucky sheep and planted up the mangers at the front with petunias. Resting this afternoon.

Love MUM XXX

21 May 2007 (Ruth to family):
Daddy – Just got back from the James Cooke Hospital. Been there all day. Daddy has had another piece of his neck removed to be on the safe side. It will go away for biopsy and we hope it will be clear of anything nasty. You can hardly see any scar and daddy does heal very quickly. Daddy drove back so I didn't have to worry about finding my way through the traffic. Take care all of you.

Love MUM XXX

23 May 2007 (Ruth to family):
Old Hall – The garden looks glorious and if anyone wants to visit us we are open all hours! Daddy's neck seems to have healed very well

and he has the stitches out in ten days. I am trying to make sure that he keeps out of the dirt but it is very difficult as you can guess. We are away to-day catching up on odd things but remember if you want to come then please do. It is the Finghall barrel push this Bank Holiday weekend.

Love to you all MUM XXX

28 May 2007 (Ruth to family):
Old Hall – It was great seeing you all on Saturday and we were lucky with the weather. Having a good clean up to-day and then if the weather is good this afternoon intend to go over to Finghall for the barrel push and have tea in the Queen's Head gardens, but it doesn't look too promising.

Love MUM XXX

3 June 2007 (Ruth to family):
Old Hall – Washed the hoggs in wool yesterday and clipped one, and this morning have clipped a second – only twenty to do! The garden looks lovely with lots of colour. A beautiful day.

Crispin – Have you got your new vehicle yet [Mercedes Viano]? Have you any pictures of the wedding? Had no idea he [Scott] was getting married. You don't tell us much. Is Alex doing better on the new milk and is he sleeping better at night?

Justin – Tell Charlotte I like her hair long and the natural colour. She looks lovely that way.

The gypsies were on the village green on the way to Appleby Fair. Some people don't like it but it was very picturesque.

Well, I'm going to clean the windows and then rest up for the day.

Love MUM XXX. Please send some news

It was a busy week ahead. First, it was the National Sheep Association's 'North Sheep' event in Co. Durham on Wednesday 6 June, though we didn't have any commitments apart from helping to man the WLSBA stand. It was a big event and we enjoyed meeting up with many friends and acquaintances in the sheep world from all over the country. The remainder of the week was spent preparing for a Conservative fundraising cum social event at Old Hall three days later – a curry lunch, with Edward McMillan-Scott MEP (Vice President of the European Parliament) as guest speaker. Attendance was by invitation, ticket only, and limited to 45 (£18.50 including wine). A very good contract caterer had been arranged, while members of our Hunton Moor branch committee served the food and drink. The garden, pastures and sheep were immaculate, the rain kept away and the event was a huge success, in terms of both funds raised and social enjoyment. Ruth received warm thanks and appreciation for staging and coordinating the event. We were lucky, for June 2007 was one of the wettest months on record in Britain with an average rainfall across the country of 5.5 inches (140 mm), more than double the June average. The May to July period of 2007 was to be subsequently recorded as Britain's wettest for those months since records began in 1776.

We were not so lucky the following week. We had been invited by the British Wool Marketing Board to contribute to its display at the two-day 'Countryside Live' event that had been arranged for mostly urban schools by the Yorkshire Agricultural Society on its Harrogate showground. The aim was to make children from these schools better aware of farming and the countryside and help them to understand the food processes from farm to supermarket shelves by learning the facts directly from the farmers. Much of the commentary was given by Yorkshire's ace agricultural commentator Mike Keeble, who had the skill to adapt to any audience. When a very well-endowed Limousin bull was led into the small ring and the children burst into giggles they got a brilliant country-style facts-of-life talk that received smiles and nods of approval from escorting teachers. It was most enjoyable talking to the children, describing the purposes of our sheep, the care and attention that was given, and allowing them to handle them. Virtually none of the children knew that sheep had no upper-jaw teeth, and Ruth and I would show them the difference, and explain the reason, and also how one could tell the age of a sheep from its teeth. One little girl commented that the teeth were just like those of her granny. Sadly, Mike Keeble died on 27 September 2015 after a long and brave fight against prostate cancer. He was known as the "voice of the shows", commentating at more than 40 agricultural shows each summer, including 40 years in the beef ring at the GYS. He was also a vociferous correspondent on all farming matters. His outstanding career in agriculture began at the Harper Adams agricultural college, where he met his future wife (Peta) but he seemingly did not impress in his early years as a farm manager: rather accident prone, with six employments in five years! Peta was to recall later, "I never knew whether it was worth unpacking." I attended Mike's funeral on 7 October at East Witton. The church was packed and I stood at the back, near the porch. When the coffin bearers had retired I half turned to see a solitary figure standing in the porch: a Hindu and our Richmond MP; Rishi Sunak. We had met five days earlier at a Conservative function and exchanged sad smiles of recognition.

14 June 2007 (Ruth to family):
Old Hall – What weather. We have the central heating on. It is like winter! We have had a hectic eight days with 47 attending the Conservative function at Old Hall last Saturday, then two days of bitter wind and driving rain at the GYS showground, displaying some of our sheep to thousands of schoolchildren. I need a week to recover. The children were all very well behaved.

How are Charlotte's exams going?

Look forward to seeing you to-morrow evening, Mark. I will have a meal ready – rice or baked beans?

Love to you all MUM XXX

15 June 2007 (Me to family):
Flooding – Very heavy rain and flooding in our area. The beck is above the level of Captain's Bridge and is well up the garth and endangering the village hall. Local news reports that two soldiers on the Catterick Training Area were washed away by the Hipswell beck and perished. I will unhitch the Jeep and try to get up to Tesco when the current torrential rain lets up a bit.

Mark – exercise some care this evening, it really is nasty. Look out for landslides – there was a fatality in the Blubberhouses area this morning, and also for sudden braking by vehicle in front when driver encounters unexpected small lake.

Dad

20 June 2007 (Ruth to family):
Old Hall – My new oven is beautiful and fitted perfectly. The instructions on cleaning it are so complex I doubt that I will ever cook in it. Wiping over with a damp cloth is never an option after cooking pork, more like get the paint scraper! The wire in the loft above the laundry room had melted so thank goodness I pulled the handle off my old oven. The rain last night was torrential with thunder, so can't do much at base and am having a morning break in Northallerton. Just hope the fields are not flooded again.

Take care all of you. Love MUM XXX

22 June 2007 (Ruth to family):
Old Hall – Been clipping another hogg in wool but now the rain has started so it is back to inside jobs. Hope that the girls do well in their swimming.

What news of Charlotte's exams? Do hope that they have gone well for her.

Crispin – Will look forward to seeing you with the new Mercedes.

Any date for the Christening yet?

Take care all of you. Love MUM XXX

The wretched weather may have made our outdoor lives and shepherding very uncomfortable and quite exasperating at times, but it could not interfere with our social events. On 23 June we attended the launch of William Hague's second book, *William Wilberforce*, about the life of the great anti-slave trade campaigner, held in the stunning Thorp Perrow Hall, home of Sir John and Lady Ropner. Six days later we attended a Constituency Women's Committee fund raising function at Constable

Burton Hall, the Georgian mansion owned by Charles Wyvill, from whom we had purchased Old Hall. Both events were packed with our friends and an abundance of fine food and wine as we caught up with local and family news and perhaps some political chat and gossip.

We were very thankful that we were not exhibiting our sheep that summer, and hoped that the weather would improve by the time of the autumn sales.

2 July 2007 (Ruth to family):
Old Hall – More flipping rain. We even lit the fire on Saturday. Intending clipping a ram this morning. Had them under cover overnight. The piccis of our Paisley grandchildren are lovely. Want to hear how Charlotte's visit to Nottingham went. Hope Jessie's first day with work experience goes well. She will be tired and miss TV!
Love from MUM XXX

The four-day Royal Show, in which we were not involved, began on 1 July, but the weather forced its cancellation of the final day. Ruth had been excited at her selection as the judge for the GYS, but as the event drew near she understandably became rather nervous at the responsibility. I kept telling her that she was one of the best three Wensleydale judges in the country and I meant it! After eighteen years of competing at the GYS we had no regrets at retiring as exhibitors, particularly in a year of such atrocious weather conditions. Instead of the hustle and bustle of the sheep lines we looked forward to receiving the pampering and hospitality that the Yorkshire Agricultural Society provides for its judges and their guests, with ample time to wander around and see other attractions. We also looked forward to a three-night visit from Crispin, Aileen and baby Alex that was planned for the following week.

8 July 2007 (Ruth to family):
Old Hall – It has been a glorious day and lovely evening and I have just come in after cutting the edges of the lawns and watching Jamie Murray win in the mixed doubles.

Mark – How does the major laying-off of people affect yourself?

It is an awful time for everyone with the company.

Judging at the Great Yorkshire Show on Tuesday. I shall be a nervous wreck.

Hope Jessie has a good week at her work.

Love MUM XXX

We set off from Old Hall for the GYS judging on Tuesday 10 July at 6 a.m. to ensure that we did not get caught up in traffic, and Ruth paid her customary respects to the magpies. She was relaxed and looking forward to the judging, which was scheduled for 2 p.m. We were well received in the judges' and officials' pavilion and, following a light breakfast and short walkabout, rested up there for the remainder of the morning, for judging is tiring work and would take about two and a half hours. At precisely ten minutes before judging an ever-attentive bowler-hatted steward collected Ruth and escorted her to the ring. She gave me her handbag, and confidently began her judging. There was no indecision – she was brilliant. Very correctly, she did not talk to anyone between the classes, apart from her steward, though I caught her eye on a few occasions and gave her a smile, nodding my approval. Her judgement was vindicated on subsequent days of the show when both her male and her female champions won Longwool Section Champion awards. The weather had been perfect. Following the customary post-judging refreshment at the bar, we returned home very happy with the day.

We had intended to be at the GYS on the following day, but this was not practical as Ruth had an important school governors' meeting at 4 p.m. which lasted about an hour. Shortly after a steak and mushrooms supper Ruth had stomach pain and diarrhoea. We wondered whether this might have been due to something that she had eaten at the GYS on the previous day, or perhaps it was caused by the supper that she had just eaten. Another possibility that occurred to us was that she had picked up some bug while handling the sheep at the GYS. Her condition did not improve overnight, so on the morning of 12 July I arranged a home visit from a doctor of the Leyburn Medical Practice, and he came round promptly. I was present during his examination. He prescribed Buccastem and codeine tablets, which Ruth took in accordance with his instructions, but there was no improvement in her condition. She remained in bed on Friday 13 July, feeling very tired.

14 July 2007, 9.55 a.m. (Me to family):
Mum – No change to yesterday's condition. Dry retching on two occasions during the night, but no bile brought up and no diarrhoea. Will keep you informed.
    Dad

Ruth expressed some concern that there might be a liver problem. At about noon I advised her that I was going to call the Leyburn Medical Practice again – but she didn't want to bother them and wanted to wait and see if things improved.

15 July 2007, 8.17 a.m. (Me to family):
Mum – Sleepless night due to further retching and tummy ache. She is rather weak and needs assistance in and out of bath. When she is better and descends the stairs I will insist that it is backwards, with myself steadying her from below. I am trying to get her to take more liquid and tried apple juice with some success earlier this morning. She is now sleeping, having had a bath, but ignored the Sunday papers. Will continue to keep you informed.
    Dad

At about 11 a.m. my concern was such that I telephoned the medical out-of-hours service and described her condition to the doctor on duty. She asked me to take Ruth to the Duchess of Kent's Military Hospital for an examination at 1.30 p.m. No sooner had I put the phone down than Justin arrived, from Tingley. After seeing Ruth he telephoned the on-duty doctor to whom I had spoken, expressing a view that Ruth needed to be admitted to hospital immediately as an emergency, by ambulance. On learning that Justin was an experienced police officer she readily agreed and telephoned for an ambulance, which arrived without delay. Justin and I followed the ambulance and were present while Ruth was being examined in the emergency section and a drip inserted. On the conclusion of that examination we accompanied Ruth to the Medical Assessment Unit, where she was admitted to an isolation room. After half an hour we left, hoping that she would sleep, and I told Ruth that I would be back during the 6–8 p.m. visiting period …

15 July 2007, 9.12 p.m. (Me to family):
Mum – I have just returned from the Friarage Hospital, Northallerton (9pm). Mum is in the Medical Assessment Unit in a very nice room to herself and is receiving very good attention. She has had a blood sample taken but though the result is known in the Unit, the nurses say that they cannot comment until the specialist has seen it, except to confirm that there is an infection. She has had an injection in the tummy as a thrombosis preventive measure and three X-rays. She has been on a drip since she arrived in the hospital and this has enabled her to have her first good pee since the problem began on Wednesday evening. She retched whilst I was there, bringing up about a half cup of bile which was needed for analysis. Mum is quite exhausted, not having had any decent sleep or any food for four days, exacerbated by the retching. She expressed concern that she might have a liver problem because of the prolonged retching and bile. I will be visiting her at the next opportunity which is 3pm to-morrow, but will telephone the Unit before that for the latest news.
    Dad

On Monday 16 July I telephoned the Medical Assessment Unit just after 10 a.m. and was delighted to learn that there had been significant overnight recovery. I was told that she had eaten some porridge and had drunk some fruit juice and that there was a possibility that she might be discharged that evening. I was elated.

I arrived at the Friarage Hospital at 3 p.m., the earliest visiting time. Ruth had been advised that she could return home after the evening meal, but she asked if she might be discharged slightly earlier in view of my arrival and the fact that I had brought the clothes that she would need. This request was agreed. Ruth told me that she had been told that her liver and kidneys were OK and said that the specialist had told her that it would take two weeks for her to make a full recovery.

Ruth was too weak to attempt to walk to the hospital entrance, so was taken down by the nurse and transferred to our car at the ambulance point. It would have been about 4.15 p.m. I had handed in my camera's digital card for one-hour printing at the photographer's at the bottom of Northallerton High Street before I collected Ruth. The card contained the photographs of her judging at the Great Yorkshire Show. I asked Ruth if she minded if I collected them, provided that I could find a parking place nearby. She nodded her approval. I was away for only five minutes as the photographs had been paid for and there was no other customer in the shop. However, as I approached the car I was concerned to see that she had opened the door, and had her legs outside the car – I thought she was about to be sick. She told me that she had opened the door because it was humid and she wanted some fresh air. The journey home was uneventful – Ruth wanted the windows fully down, rested her head on the headrest, said little, but wanted me to talk to her.

Shortly after we arrived home at about 5 p.m. the telephone rang – it was Ruth's nurse at the Friarage Hospital. She told me not to worry, but said that the specialist had been looking again at the X-rays and had said that if Ruth's bowels didn't start to work and she started to feel more bloated and had tummy ache she was to be brought to A&E without delay. I told Ruth – she did not comment. With my assistance she went upstairs to bed and I left her in the hope that she would sleep. I crept upstairs after about fifteen minutes but she was still awake. At the next check, some ten minutes later, I felt sure that she was sleeping, but ten minutes later I heard movement and found Ruth on the landing, wanting to come downstairs. I helped her down. She walked with my assistance to the back door, seeking the cool air of the thunderstorm that was in the area, then rested in the sitting room. While she was resting I sent an email to Justin, Mark and Crispin, describing Ruth's discharge and the current situation:

16 July 2007, 5:52 p.m. (Me to family):
Mum is Home – When I visited this afternoon Mum was out of bed and off the drip, nibbling at a bar of chocolate. Nice to have her back.
　Dad

An hour later Ruth collapsed and died.

EPILOGUE

You can shed tears…

You can shed tears because she is gone
or you can smile because she has lived.
You can close your eyes and pray that she'll come back
or you can open your eyes and see all that she's left.
Your heart can be empty because you can't see her
or you can be full of the love you shared.
You can turn your back on tomorrow and live yesterday
or you can be happy for tomorrow
because of yesterday.
You can remember her and only that she's gone
or you can cherish her memory and let it live on.
You can cry and close your mind,
be empty and turn your back
or you can do what she'd want;
smile, open your eyes,
love the living and go on.

David Harkins

The Service of Thanksgiving for the life of Ruth and her interment took place at St Patrick's Church, Patrick Brompton on Wednesday 25 July 2007. It was a warm day, with haymaking at its peak and the smell of newly cut grass hanging in the still air. Afterwards, several people were to describe it to me as a beautiful funeral. At first I thought it was rather odd to use an adjective that is usually associated with a wedding. However, I soon realised that they were referring to rather more than the cloudless summer day and Wensleydale looking at its very best. It was beautiful because of an accumulation of sentiment; the adjacent images on the Order of Service card depicting the little girl in the garden with her wicker basket and the mature, vibrant lady of later years; the hymns 'The Lord is My Shepherd', 'All Things Bright and Beautiful' and 'Jerusalem'; the gusto of the singing; the vicar's address; and in particular, the eye-watering sight and sound of Charlotte, aged just seventeen, playing 'Amazing Grace' on her flute over her grandmother's coffin before a congregation of nearly two hundred people.

Ruth's commitment to and successes at the Great Yorkshire Show over the years were recognised and honoured by the Yorkshire Agricultural Society with the presence in traditional bowler hats of two senior stewards, Henry Watson and Colin Ellwood. The WLSBA was represented by council members from diverse parts of England and also from Wales and Scotland. The Rt. Hon. William Hague, the Richmond Conservative Association, the Wensleydale CPRE, Hunton & Arrathorne CP School, the Wensleydale Agricultural Society and other agricultural and charitable organisations were also represented, while cards and letters indicated that the attendance would have been even higher had it been outside the summer holiday period. After the interment there were many joyous recollections of shared experiences in life with Ruth in the ambience of the Friar's Head at nearby Akebar, where Colin and Joyce Ellwood had provided a magnificent floral display. It was indeed a beautiful funeral.

The post mortem had identified the cause of Ruth's death as:

Ia. Infarcted loop of small bowel

Ib. Small bowel obstruction

Ic. Internal hernia

The consultant histopathologist commented: 'An internal hernia is a rare cause of small bowel obstruction. It occurs when a portion of bowel becomes entrapped after passing out of its normal lining. In this woman's case a portion of small bowel passed through a defect in the omentum and then became entrapped. The omentum is a prominent fold that hangs down from the stomach and beneath which are positioned the normal small bowel loops. It is most likely that the defect in the omentum was congenital in origin.'

Having discussed the sequence of events, the family was unanimous in the opinion that there had been gross negligence at Northallerton's Friarage Hospital in not identifying the infarcted loop on an x-ray and proceeding with the appropriate surgery. The coroner was notified, and in early August instructions were given to my solicitor to proceed with a potential negligence action against South Tees Hospitals NHS Trust. My solicitor obtained Specialist opinions and briefed Counsel accordingly. Matters came to a head with my solicitor's 'letter before action' being sent to the NHS Trust in late February 2008, a prerequisite to the matter being taken to a High Court for judgement. This letter prompted an admission of negligence from the South Tees Hospitals NHS Trust and subsequent letters of apology from both the Chief Executive Officer and the physician concerned.

I only learned quite recently that Ruth was often fondly referred to by residents in Hunton and nearby villages as 'Bo-Peep'.

Arthursdale Boy continued to live at Old Hall, Hunton for two years following the tragic death of his Nidderdale Girl, before downsizing to an apartment in Swaledale. He continues to support, as best he can, the Wensleydale Longwool Sheep Breeders' Association as a Council Member and past President, whilst an unchanged political belief is reflected in a letter that appeared in the Daily Telegraph a few years ago:

Sir,

    I am concerned that the EU flag could replace the Royal arms on all official documents within three years under new Brussels regulations, including death certificates (report Aug 10). If this comes about I will not die.
    Yours sincerely, Frank Pedley

Arthursdale Boy regularly reflects on the high octane life that he had the privilege of sharing with his Nidderdale Girl: particularly the very enjoyable secondment years in Malaya and with 21st Signal Regiment at RAF Wildenrath; cruising and travel with P&O, and Christmases wherever. Family reflections are endless; an adult grandchild writes (14 years-on), *"I always have such fond memories of her at Old Hall. Her big kisses and hugs as soon as you walked through the door into the kitchen. Usually the smell of food being cooked in the background."* Ruth will never be forgotten.

APPENDIX

THE PEDLEYS

Who were they?

Ancestry research identifies PEDLEY as an interesting name of Norman origin: the nickname for a stealthy person, from Old French 'pie de leu' (wolf's foot), but neither the Normans nor the PEDLEYS were French. They were Norsemen and Danes from Scandinavia and northern Europe who, amongst many conquests, seized the territory that is now known as Normandy from the vast Frankiss Empire in AD911. Britain had experienced their vicious raids and conquests since at least the ninth century and it is recorded that before he died in AD735, Benedictine monk Saint Bede had worried a great deal as to whether the roots of Christianity were sufficiently strong to survive the threats of both these Norsemen and Islam. Invading from the east, by AD850 the Vikings had control of Canterbury and London ... AD867 York ... AD876 Northumbria. The PEDLEYS were not peddlers.

Britain was ultimately saved from the Vikings by Alfred, king of Wessex (the appellation of 'the Great' was given many years later by the Tudors), who became the first king of all England. Alfred is also, of course, well remembered in England for having carelessly burnt some cakes, just as Scotland's hero, Robert the Bruce, is well remembered for having been inspired by a very persistent spider four centuries later.

The first image in this book records, in the handwriting of my grandfather Francis George Pedley (FGP), the precise house and room in which he was born in Haworth (Main Street) on 27th April 1879. Two years later the 1881 census (taken on 3rd April) records the family residing at 88, Low Street, Keighley (Eastwood, p58, entry 291), the household consisting of his father John Pedley (23 years, a book seller, born in Healaugh), his mother Harriet E Pedley (24 years, born in Haworth), FGP (1 year [but only 3 weeks short of his second birthday], born in Haworth) and a sister (Mary Anna, aged 10 months) born in Keighley. The 1891 census records them as having returned to Haworth (20, Mytholme Lane), where a second sister (Elsie) had been born two years earlier.

My grandfather had told me on several occasions that his ancestors were lead miners in Swaledale, but I never knew exactly where in Swaledale until I learnt from the Keighley 1881 census of his father's birth in Healaugh, near Reeth. With some excitement, I reached for my OS Explorer Map (OL30) and soon found this small and historic village, named as 'Healy' on Saxton's famous 1577 map of Yorkshire, one mile west of 'Reth' (Reeth). The name of the village is derived from the old English (heah+leah), meaning high clearing or wood.

When I examined the 19th century censuses of the *civil parishes* of Melbecks and Healaugh (north of the river Swale) I discovered an abundance of PEDLEY lead mining households, the men, youths and boys employed by agents of the 'Lead Barons' in the mines of the Melbecks and Reeth moors, an area that included the well-known *Old Gang* and *Surrender* mines. I subsequently found that they had toiled on these moors for many generations. I also traced some Pedleys who had a very different lifestyle to my lead miner ancestors; the wealthy Sir Nicholas Pedley MP (17 Sep 1615 – 6 Jul 1685), the member for Huntingdonshire variously between 1656 and 1679. He was a leading lawyer of his day and became an acquaintance of Samuel Pepys whom he first met in 1669. Pepys subsequently entrusted him with his family legal business. Sir Nicholas's eldest son (John) also became a politician, elected as MP for Huntingdon in 1706 – gentlemen unlikely to have had peddler ancestry!

I learned from the Melbecks church of Holy Trinity that the Norse invasion into Upper Swaledale was from the west, following the collapse of the Norse Kingdom of Dublin around AD915, though this was not the case in Wensleydale which, like York, was conquered from the east. My reading of the translations of 'The Normans' by Francois Neveux gives credence to this western invasion and provides further evidence that the history of the Normans in our isle began a long time before 1066. Supportive evidence of Norse penetration into Upper Swaledale is also provided by the name of Melbecks, its largest civil parish, and by the names of some of the small lead mining villages close to Reeth; Feetham, Gunnerside and Low Row (Low Wra [nook] and written as Lawrawe in 1561), names that became increasingly familiar to me as I pursued my ancestry research.

On examining the 1871 census of Healaugh, (pronounced 'he' [as opposed to she] and then 'lore', like folklore), I was astonished to learn that eleven households (serials 37-47, in close proximity) held a total of 39 Pedleys, all associated with the lead mining industry.

Turning to the 1861 census (entry 21) I found the household that included FGP's father (John), who was aged 3 years at that time. The household was headed by John's father (Francis Gill Pedley) a lead ore miner aged 29 years (born in Healaugh in 1832), together with John's mother (Mary Ann) aged 28 years (born in Co. Durham) and siblings Robert (1854), James (1855), Margaret (1856) and Jane Ann (1860).

I then turned the clock back a further 20 years, looking for Francis's father in the 1841 census. I soon found him, for Healaugh was a very small village, and remains so to-day:

PEDLEY Robert/40 years/lead miner PEDLEY Alice/30 years PEDLEY Isabella/12 years [born 11Dec 1828 to **Jane Gill**, daughter of Francis Gill]
PEDLEY Francis Gill/9 years [born 25 Feb 1832 to **Jane Gill**, daughter of Francis Gill]
PEDLEY Jane/6 years

PEDLEY John/3 years

[ie. Robert Pedley had fathered two children by Jane Gill during a previous marriage, prior to marrying Alice, a widow with two children. Perhaps Jane died during a third childbirth?]

My gt.gt.gt. grandfather was therefore Robert Pedley, born in Low Row (3 miles further up the dale from Healaugh) in 1800; a lead miner throughout his life, who died in April 1859. I later learned that he had been baptised at the Smarber Chapel (only one wall now remaining – GR approx. 972977) on 16th November 1800. He was buried at the former Low Row Methodist Chapel, the remains of which [I have read] may lie beneath the Old Dairy Cottage garage. Robert's second wife (Alice, née Hunt) was born in the adjacent village of Feetham. Eventually, Alice was to have a total of ten children – two by her first husband (Anthony Demain) and eight by Robert Pedley [all born in Healaugh]; Jane (1835), John (1838), Mary (1842), Robert (1843), Adam (1845), Margaret (1847), William (1850) and Elizabeth (1852); an overall family of twelve. Desperate for income when her husband died, Alice founded and taught in a small school in Healaugh, perhaps initially utilising part of the family home.

My gt.gt.gt. grandmother was therefore Jane Gill, daughter of Francis and Jeane Gill (née Winnington). I learnt that Jane was from a staunch Congregational family connected with the chapels at Low Row and Reeth, but they baptised most of their children including Francis Gill (8th April 1832) at the Methodist chapel in Healaugh, now a private house. So, who were my maternal **gt.gt.gt.gt.** grandparents? Helped by welcome and enthusiastic assistance from the Upper Dales Family History Group (UDFHG) I learnt that they were John Pedley (born 1776 and baptised at Smarber chapel) and Isabella (née Metcalfe), who were married at Grinton [St. Andrews] church on 18th October 1796. They were both buried at this church.

Patient and very time-consuming research by UDFHG (Tracy Little), to whom I am most grateful, eventually established my **5xgt. grandparents** as William Pedley, baptised at Grinton [St. Andrews] on

5th May 1754 and Mary (née Brown), who were married at St. Andrews church in 1773. They lived at Blades, a tiny hamlet just above Low Row (GR 981986), where John Pedley (their only child) was born. The church register (page 360) records the burial of William Pedley of Blades on 13th March 1784. Three years later, at the same church, widow Mary married Emanual Nicholson, a widower who had lost his wife in childbirth a couple of years earlier; a marriage of only four years duration, for Emanual died in 1791. Such harsh times. Poor Mary.

The 'Grinton' baptism entry of William Pedley (page 200) records his father as 'Thomas Pedley of Blades' – my **6xgt grandfather**. Subsequent perusal of these 'Grinton Registers' identified my **7xgt grandfather**, for page 196 records the burial on 26th June 1751 of 'Thomas, son of **John Pedley of Blades**'. I suspect that my maternal ancestral search ends at this point with John Pedley, for I have now completed my sifting of the 'Grinton Registers', whilst the County Records Office in Northallerton advise that they do not hold any other documents or registers that might be helpful.

Unable to pursue my ancestral search further, I turned to a more thorough study of the early history of lead mining in Swaledale, and Upper Swaledale in particular.

It is generally accepted that the Romans extracted lead from Swaledale, presumably by the basic opencast system of identifying a vein at ground level and hacking it away until it became too dangerous to follow. However, the Romans were not lacking in ingenuity and may have followed some particularly rewarding veins to very risky depths or lengths. There would have been no lack of these outcropped veins, nor wood fuel for the smelting of the lead ore, as the moors would still have been well forested.

It was not until Henry II took over the Honour of Richmond in 1171 that the dale began to develop as an important source of the mineral. He recognised its importance for roofing, particularly of castles, royal houses, monasteries and other religious buildings, and provided incentive for expansion – enticing the struggling hill farmers to join the existing small groups of lead miners and smelters. The lead ore was smelted in wood or peat fires close to the point of extraction and was carried by packhorses or mules to Richmond, which provided a marketing point. When the woodland fuel supply had been burnt, peat became as important a commodity to the lead ore smelters as hay to the farmers at the lower levels (both needed to be harvested in June). The fledgling industry developed steadily during the late middle ages when marketing became controlled by professional agents and their merchants, and it is recorded that in 1536 the *Merchant Adventurers of York* chartered some 18 ships to carry Swaledale and Nidderdale lead to Antwerp and other European ports. This was a remarkable logistics achievement, involving packhorse transportation to Boroughbridge and then by barges to the Humber. Packhorses/mules could routinely carry 280 lbs (127 kgs). A pig of lead weighed 144 lbs, so there would be a pig on each side of the animal. There was a well-established network of packhorse routes in the country at that time, just as there were drovers routes for livestock. Usually, the packhorses carried their loads in a 'train' of at least a dozen (12) animals. By the end of the 18th century the Swaledale packhorse loads of lead were being transferred in Richmond to waggons and carts drawn by oxen for their onward journey. The combination of a new road from Reeth to Richmond in 1836 and the construction of a railhead in the town in 1846 heralded the end of the packhorse era in the dale, also contributing to the demise of the stagecoaches.

Lead mining in Upper Swaledale in the 18th Century became a booming and potentially prosperous industry, but the miners had no ownership of the mines in which they toiled, and they lived as tenants in small cottages provided by the agents of the mine-owners, who had total responsibility for the management of the mines. The lead miner's average life expectancy was about 48 years, though wives and daughters usually lived significantly longer (provided that they survived childbirths) producing large families and contributing to family income in a variety of employments, such as knitters, carriers, dressmakers, shop assistants and servants. They did not work underground, as did the wives and daughters of coal miners at that time. An interesting and rare example of longevity in a lead mining family is recorded in the Registers of Grinton parish church (p189); 'the burial [in 1748] of Mary, mother of Thomas Peacock of Harkeyside, aged 104 years or upwards.'

Ownership of successful mines provided considerable wealth, but not without high risk and fierce competition. In 1738 the *manors* of Healaugh and Muker came on the market [following the death of the Duke of Wharton], incorporating ownership of the mines and the mineral rights within the extensive *manorial boundaries*, which contained the most valuable lead ore veins and mines in upper Swaledale at that time. The successful bidder was a powerful, ambitious and wealthy lawyer in London named Thomas Smith, who paid £10,500. Interestingly, he was educated at Richmond (Yorkshire) Grammar School. Thirty years later he became embroiled in a fierce boundary dispute with Lord Pomfret, the owner of adjacent land, regarding mineral rights to a particularly rich vein of lead ore at Beldi Hill, near the western boundary of the Old Gang mines. The dispute became known as the 'Beldi Hill Dispute', one of the most extraordinary court cases of the 18th Century because of its duration and gravity. Legal action began in 1769, with early success for Thomas Smith at a jury trial at the 1770 York assizes. However, Lord Pomfret successfully appealed to the House of Lords which resulted in a second jury trial in 1772, this time at the King's Bench in Westminster, involving two of the most senior judges in the land; the Attorney General and the Solicitor General. Lord Pomfret lost and the financial costs were such that he was financially ruined. Thomas Smith's success was short-lived for he died the following year in his chambers in Gray's Inn, aged 80. The years of dispute saw riotous confrontation between the mining families of the opposing sides, sparked by early instructions from their employers to start work within the disputed area without delay. It is unlikely that the Pedley miners and their families were not involved to some extent in this saga and the rioting. Thomas Smith had a nephew (Layton Smith) who lost his inherited fortune through a combination of extravagance and poor financial judgement. To the disgust of his uncle he became bankrupt and a prisoner in the notorious Fleet debtors prison, to which Dickens and Shakespeare respectively sent Samuel Pickwick [The Pickwick Papers] and Sir John Falstaff [Henry IV Part 2]. Thomas Smith, who never married, bequeathed a trivial amount to his nephew compared to that bequeathed to his three illegitimate children.

The mines that the Pedleys worked (men, youths and boys) included the valuable *Old Gang* and *Surrender* mines, the word 'gang' derived from the Old English word meaning a road, and the name 'surrender' probably derived from the legal surrender of mineral rights in a lengthy boundary dispute, decided in early 1798. To reach this mining area and view the remains of the various mining activities, go to the 17th Century *Punch Bowl Inn* at Low Row [www.pbinn.co.uk) (DL11 6PF). A prior perusal of Explorers Map OL30 1:25,000 scale is recommended to understand the detail and magnitude of the lead mining activity; the Old Gang complex alone produced almost 2,400 tons of lead in 1840. Well refreshed, take the Langthwaite road from the Inn, and at Surrender Bridge turn right, parking at the viewpoint overlooking the bridge and the remnants of the Surrender smelting mill, and try to imagine the activity on and beneath the moors in front of you – two hundred years ago. I imagined the lead miners of Healaugh (plus those living in the adjacent hamlets of Daggerstones and Thirns) *walking* the 3 – 4 miles to and from their work on these high and barren moors. However, when I learned of their extensive use of horse and pony power the image changed. These lead miners not only used ponies in some of the near horizontal access mines in the same way as coal miners (eg. Brandy Bottle Incline – two parallel 10 foot high tunnels), they also used them in horse "gins" (short for engines), whereby the horse walked in a circle around a capstan, which wound a rope over a wheel and down the vertical shaft; they would also have used them to pull cart loads of stones to dam streams and create reservoirs which, when broken, would release a torrent of water to scour the banks at the side of the gill, revealing the lead ore seams (hushing); the horses would have pulled carts loaded with the lead ore to the smelting mills and the dried peat that was needed as fuel. There must have been many hard-working horses and ponies on those high moors and it is unlikely that they would have been left there overnight; more likely that they were led back to their stables for fodder, rest and attention, carrying many of the equally tired miners in their carts or on their backs.

I had now researched my maternal PEDLEY ancestry as far as possible and I had learned that the PEDLEYS were largely employed in the *Old Gang* and *Surrender* mines area, within the Civil parishes of Melbecks and Healaugh. However, I could not find any summarized data on household and family numbers and their employments within these Civil parishes. I therefore decided to analyse the 1841 census returns of each of the 48 parishes of Swaledale and Wensleydale. I selected the 1841 census because that census was the first to record names, ages and occupation by household, together with the head of the household, who was responsible for its accuracy [the four earlier censuses of 1801 – 1831 were merely head-counts]. Also, it was taken very shortly after the 1840 record output of the Old Gang mine, at a time of near peak production in the lead ore mining industry in England, and prior to its erratic decline from about 1870; a decline that resulted in the exodus of the lead miners and smelters of Swaledale and Wensleydale to better employments and prospects elsewhere, some abroad. Censuses taken during the period of decline would have been likely to record the stragglers and the elderly of that once vibrant industry, who gradually adjusted to other employments. Outside the civil parishes of Melbecks and Healaugh I found two small Pedley households in Muker and two children of the Pedley name (aged 8 and 15 years) within two Grinton households. Those apart, the Pedleys were to be found solely in the civil parishes of Melbecks and Healaugh, but in quite large numbers, as given below:

In 1841 there were 314 households in Melbecks and 54 in Healaugh, a total of 368 households, of which **262** were lead mining or lead ore smelter/dresser households, followed by 20 mixed, 18 farming, 17 not known, 13 craft [blacksmith, joiner/carpenter, stonemason], 12 retail [footwear, tailor, dress or hat maker, grocer, butcher, tobacconist], 12 wool industry, 14 remainder [gamekeeper, groom, domestic service, land agent, publican, clergy, miller/meal dealer]. *Analysis of the **262** lead mining or lead ore smelter/dresser households* revealed that the most recurrent family name was that of HARKER (95 persons), followed in descending order by RAW (86), BELL (77), PRATT (69), PEDLEY (68), METCALFE

(66), SUNTER (49), PEACOCK (48), SIMPSON (43), WHITE (40), a further twenty-two (39>20 category), and twenty-four of the (19>10 category).

However, when the civil parish of Healaugh [which incorporates the hamlets of Thirns, Dear/Birk Park, Dagger Stones and Riddings] is analysed separately, the most recurrent family name was that of PEDLEY (32 persons), followed by DOLPHINS (23), ROBINSONS (22) and METCALFES (20). Because of their numbers the Pedleys must have been involved in most of the lead mining activities within those bleak moors and certainly in the construction of the now inaccessible '*Pedley's Crosscut*', located approximately 500 feet beneath GR 967024 [400 yards SW of the peak of Great Pinseat], referred to in the authoritive 'Swaledale, it's Mines and Smelt Mills', by Mike Gill (p100).

By 1881, only twenty Pedleys remained in Healaugh, of which only one was a lead miner; Adam (aged 36), living with his elder sister Mary as housekeeper. The lead miners of Swaledale had left for better paid work, particularly in the cotton and woollen mills of Lancashire and West Yorkshire; others had emigrated or became farmers and carriers. The demise of the industry was largely because of the severity of the competition of cheap lead imports and the lead fields becoming exhausted, and it resulted in the population of Swaledale declining by 50 per cent between 1871 and 1891. In one of her essays, researcher and historian Marion Hearfield wrote, "Of the 51 Heads of Household who left Swaledale for the West Riding [of Yorkshire] between 1881 and 1891, forty-four households – 323 people – went to Haworth. In 1881, the average age of those 323 people was just 16 – an awful lot of young children accompanied by their parents and most of them were working in the mills by 1891. Of the forty-four heads of household, thirty-one had been [lead] miners."

KELLY'S DIRECTORY 1897 (page 259) recorded the end; "Here are lead mines, which have been worked for many generations, but are now not worked."

However, due to the work of the museums at Reeth, Richmond and Hawes the lead mining industry of Swaledale and Wensleydale is not forgotten, nor the miners and smelters and their families – ghosts of the past. I am reminded of my lead mining ancestors whenever I pass Healaugh village and see the tiny village square and the old school that Alice founded. Park at the traditional red telephone box, which is at the side of the tiny square, with the old school at the other side.

THE CHRISTELOWS

Who were they?

If you look at Hartlepool (Headland) images of its old lighthouse (built in 1846/47) you will see a detached house with two south-facing chimneys and four first floor windows; numbers 1 and 2 Bath Terrace. On 16th December 1914, number 2 was the home of John Christelow (1850 – 1927), who was census recorded three years earlier as a 'Coal Merchant; clerk & manager' and his wife Rebekah, née McKenzie (1853 – 1925), when [without warning] Hartlepool's headland, Whitby and Scarborough were shelled by German cruisers (see page 16). They had eleven children (two died at an early age) – the other nine were:

Thomas (1873 – 1943)	born Ferryhill
[married Catherine L Davies]	
Margaret Helena (1875 – 1947)	born West Cornforth
John George (1877 – 1966)	born West Cornforth
[died in Lambeth, Surrey]	
Elizabeth [Lizzie] (3 Aug 1880 – 26 Feb 1958)	born West Cornforth
[my gran]	
Rebekah [Peppie] (1883 – 1963)	born Castletown
Nellie (1886 – 6 Jul 1965)	born Hartlepool
Ada Mary (1887 – 1964)	born Hartlepool
James Thornton McKenzie (1890 – 19 Jan 1934)	born West Hartlepool
Donald McKenzie (17 Nov 1893 – 1978)	born Hartlepool

It is not recorded who was within the house during the bombardment, but my grandmother was certainly not present – she was married and living with my grandfather in Leeds.

The old lighthouse was demolished in 1915, presumably because it clearly indicated to the German navy the precise location of the adjacent Heugh Battery and its guns, also to provide more military space. A comparison of the OS (Ordnance Survey) Six Inch 1888-1913 and the OS 1.1 million – 1:10K 1900s maps against a current map of the Headland indicates that at the time of the German bombardment in December 1914 the northern end of Bath Terrace was further to the east, within a few yards of the old lighthouse. It then gradually converges to the junction with Cliff Terrace on a different (SSW) alignment. I therefore suspect that concurrent with the demolishment of the old lighthouse and the strategic enlargement of the military area, numbers 1 and 2 Bath Terrace were requisitioned and demolished, and the alignment of Bath Terrace to Cliff Terrace altered accordingly.

The Christelow family were well settled in 2 Bath Crescent prior to the bombardment and would have been one of the first families in the country to become homeless because of enemy action. Nellie and sibling James were elementary school teachers, whilst sibling Donald was a student teacher. They were now, of course, obliged to seek new homes. Most of them decided that the popular spa town of Harrogate was a safer and more attractive place in which to live, and it was here that Donald McKenzie Christelow became a Headmaster and Mayor. His mother and father selected the adjacent and equally attractive town of Knaresborough.

Census records show that in 1891 the family resided in the Borough Hotel in Hartlepool's High Street, where John Christelow was the hotel manager. Ten years earlier, John and his family were residing in Sunderland, where he was a clerk in the ironworks (my grandmother aged about 8 months). They must have recently moved from West Cornforth (Co. Durham), for that was where my grandmother and siblings Margaret Helena and John George were born. My grandmother was pleased to have been born in Durham, the same county as her father.

I recollect regular visits to Harrogate with my grandparents as a boy, usually meeting in the town centre, where great aunt Ada worked in a tiny but very busy tobacconists, but sometimes at 12, Arncliffe Road (just off the Knaresborough road), the home of great aunt Nellie and her husband James Thornton McKenzie (JTM) [not to be confused with sibling James Thornton McKenzie Christelow (JTMC). They were cousins, who had married in Hartlepool in the last quarter of 1912 (Vol. 10a, p329), JTM describing himself as a Tobacco Traveller. JTM (1882 – Dec 1958) was known as Jim McKenzie. He did not serve in WW1, which seemed to be an irritation to my grandfather. Jim and Nellie McKenzie did not, of course, have any children. JTMC, a bachelor school teacher in Harrogate, enlisted on 4th September 1918 (317855) into the Royal Tank Corps.

Who were the Christelows? Only 14 male Christelows in the country in 1841. When I was aged about 10 years I recollect my grandparents discussing this question on one occasion, my grandmother saying that she had heard that they might have come from Spain. Spanish Huguenots?

DNA Results and More Census Discoveries

FHP DNA Test Results [December 2021]:

99.9% European	
British & Irish	85.6
French & German	7.3
Scandinavian	2.1
Broadly NW European	4.0
Italian	.9
	99.9

My mother had told me (page 1) that my father's name was Wood and that he lived at Thorner [a small village, one mile from Arthursdale]. A search of the **1911 census** records only one person with that name in Thorner or its environments:

Henry Wood, born in 1896 in Nun Appleton [near Appleton Roebuck]
(5 miles East of Tadcaster)

Aged 15, Farm Labourer and Servant residing at Intake Farm Thorner, together with Thomas Mapplebeck (Head, aged 63), Grace Mapplebeck (Wife, aged 63) and Ada Kilburn (Granddaughter, aged 16).

Unlikely that Henry Wood was my father. He was 15 years older than my mother (born 29th February 1911). When I was conceived (in 1933) my mother was aged 22 and Henry Wood would have been 37 years. No trace of him in the 1921 census.

When the **1921** census [taken on 19th June 1921] was released on 6th January 2022 I lost no time in contacting the help desk of *Findmypast,* asking for details of anyone with the surname of Wood residing in or close to Thorner on 19th June 1921. Their reply provided the details of the family headed by Hilda Madelene Wood, residing at Claremont, Thorner [the same building as that in which my grandparents and mother were residing at the time that I was conceived in May 1933]:

Hilda Madelene Wood	Head	Born 1889 [31yrs]	Born Huddersfield
Ronald Irving Wood	**Son**	**Born 1915 [5yrs]**	**Born in Thorner-**
Ruth Barbara Wood	Daughter	Born 1917 [4yrs]	Born in Thorner-
Lillie Brooke	Mother	Born 1859 [62yrs]	Born Huddersfield
Dorothy Irene Taylor	Governess	Born 1900 [20yrs]	Born in Leeds

This is convincing evidence that her son **Ronald Irving Wood [RIW]** was my father; there is no credible alternative, not even when similar surname spellings are searched. Claremont is a large <u>semi-detached</u>

property, built in 1901. It is on the northern side of the village, just into the Bramham Road from its junction with Church Hill and close to the site of the old Thorner railway station.

> The census also records that RIW's father was dead. I wondered if he might have been a WW1 casualty, but nobody with the Wood surname is included in the memorial plaque on the west wall of St Peter's Church, which lists the 38 fallen of Thorner and Scarcroft. A Victory Hall, intended as a village institute, was built after the war and opened on 26th April 1924, the names of the 112 survivors also recorded [as Life Members]. The list includes my grandfather; Francis George Pedley.

The 1921 census is the most revealing record set up to that time; the first census to recognise divorce and to capture people's employment details. Sadly, the 1931 census was destroyed in a fire, whilst the 1941 census was cancelled due to WW2. So, the 1921 census is of extraordinary importance.

In May 1933 (when I was conceived) RIW was aged 17½ years [he was born in Sep 1915] and my mother aged 22 years. He married Florence M Hartley in Leeds in 1940. The Claro Registration District of the West Riding of Yorkshire records (page 963) that he died [age 61] in the second quarter of 1976. My mother died shortly afterwards on 9th July 1976.

I have a photograph of my dear grandmother sitting in a deck chair with her terrier doggie (Rack) outside Claremont in August 1930. She looks so content; blissfully oblivious to forthcoming world, national and family events that she and my grandfather were soon to face.

For exclusive discounts on Matador titles,
sign up to our occasional newsletter at
troubador.co.uk/bookshop